FINDING A BALANCE IN THE EXCLUSIVE ECONOMIC ZONE

Zhen Sun analyses the important and understudied subject of jurisdiction in the exclusive economic zone (EEZ) over five groups of activities. She explores whether the basic premises and essential compromises of the EEZ regime established by the United Nations Convention on the Law of the Sea still hold true or whether there has been evolution in the regime in terms of accommodating the EEZ regulatory scheme to meet new needs and challenges. Significantly, the analysis of State practice indicates that coastal States have progressively asserted greater authority in defending their rights and jurisdiction in the EEZ, which have been broadly tolerated by the legal regime and other user States. The stability of the EEZ regime is maintained by two legal doctrines that guide the attribution and exercise of the rights and freedoms of different States. This title is also available as Open Access on Cambridge Core.

ZHEN SUN is an associate professor (Research/Ocean Sustainability, Governance & Management) at WMU-Sasakawa Global Ocean Institute, World Maritime University. She obtained her degrees in both China and the United Kingdom, including a PhD from the University of Cambridge. Before joining WMU, Zhen was a research fellow at the Centre for International Law, National University of Singapore. She is actively engaged in teaching, supervision, multidisciplinary research and capacity development programmes. Zhen has worked on a wide range of subjects in the law of the sea and ocean governance, and collaborated with academics, practitioners, officials from government agencies and international organisations.

FINDING A BALANCE IN THE EXCLUSIVE ECONOMIC ZONE

Conflict and Stability in the Law of the Sea

ZHEN SUN

World Maritime University

CAMBRIDGE
UNIVERSITY PRESS

CAMBRIDGE
UNIVERSITY PRESS

Shaftesbury Road, Cambridge CB2 8EA, United Kingdom

One Liberty Plaza, 20th Floor, New York, NY 10006, USA

477 Williamstown Road, Port Melbourne, VIC 3207, Australia

314–321, 3rd Floor, Plot 3, Splendor Forum, Jasola District Centre, New Delhi – 110025, India

103 Penang Road, #05-06/07, Visioncrest Commercial, Singapore 238467

Cambridge University Press is part of Cambridge University Press & Assessment, a department of the University of Cambridge.

We share the University's mission to contribute to society through the pursuit of education, learning and research at the highest international levels of excellence.

www.cambridge.org
Information on this title: www.cambridge.org/9781009471305

DOI: 10.1017/9781009471329

When citing this work, please include a reference to the DOI 10.1017/9781009471329
First published 2025

A catalogue record for this publication is available from the British Library

Library of Congress Cataloging-in-Publication Data
Names: Sun, Zhen (Legal scholar), author.
Title: Finding a balance in the exclusive economic zone : conflict and stability in the law of the sea / Zhen Sun, World Maritime University.
Description: Cambridge, United Kingdom; New York, NY : Cambridge University Press, 2024. | Includes bibliographical references and index.
Identifiers: LCCN 2024019493 (print) | LCCN 2024019494 (ebook) | ISBN 9781009471305 (hardback) | ISBN 9781009471312 (paperback) | ISBN 9781009471329 (epub)
Subjects: LCSH: Economic zones (Law of the sea) | United Nations Convention on the Law of the Sea (1982 December 10) | Territorial waters | Continental shelf–Law and legislation. | Conflict of laws–Maritime law.
Classification: LCC KZA1560 .S86 2024 (print) | LCC KZA1560 (ebook) | DDC 341.4/48–dc23/eng/20240509
LC record available at https://lccn.loc.gov/2024019493
LC ebook record available at https://lccn.loc.gov/2024019494

ISBN 978-1-009-47130-5 Hardback

To James Richard Crawford

Judge, Professor, AC, SC, FBA (14 November 1948–31 May 2021)

In loving memory of the mentor who illuminated my path and profoundly influenced my journey. Your enduring wisdom, unwavering guidance and boundless support continue to inspire me every day.

CONTENTS

Foreword x
TOMMY KOH

Preface xiii
Acknowledgements xv
Table of International Cases xvii
Table of International Treaties xxi
List of Abbreviations xxiv

1 **Introduction** 1

PART I **The Development and Status of the Exclusive Economic Zone** 11

2 **Origins and Evolution of the Exclusive Economic Zone** 13

2.1 Early Claims to Marine Living Resources 13
2.2 The 1930 Hague Codification Conference 17
2.3 Early Initiatives for a 200-Mile Maritime Zone 22
2.4 Development of the Exclusive Economic Zone Concept 27
2.5 Conclusion 35

3 **The Exclusive Economic Zone in the United Nations Convention on the Law of the Sea** 37

3.1 The Exclusive Economic Zone as a New Legal Regime 38
3.2 The Jurisdictional Framework of the Exclusive Economic Zone 45
3.3 The Status of the Exclusive Economic Zone 64
3.4 Conclusion 71

PART II **Competing Uses of the Exclusive Economic Zone** 75

4 **The Impact of Coastal State's Rights on the Navigational Freedoms** 77

4.1 The Scope of the Navigational Freedoms 78

4.2 Sovereign Rights over Natural Resources and Other Economic Activities 82
4.3 Jurisdiction to Protect and Preserve the Marine Environment 103
4.4 Rights and Jurisdiction with Regard to Artificial Islands, Installations and Structures 124
4.5 Resolving Disputes Concerning the Navigational Freedoms 134
4.6 Modified Freedoms in the Exclusive Economic Zone 139

5 Coastal State Rights and the Freedom of the Laying of Submarine Cables and Pipelines 142

5.1 Basic Facts about Submarine Cables and Pipelines 143
5.2 The Legal Framework of Submarine Cables and Pipelines 148
5.3 Limitations on the Freedom to Lay Submarine Cables and Pipelines 156
5.4 Protecting Submarine Cables and Pipelines 177
5.5 Resolving Disputes Concerning the Laying of Submarine Cables and Pipelines 193
5.6 Conclusion 196

PART III **Resolving Conflicts Regarding Unattributed Rights and Jurisdiction in the Exclusive Economic Zone 199**

6 Military Activities 201

6.1 Military Uses of the Sea in Peacetime 202
6.2 Military Security in the Exclusive Economic Zone 221
6.3 Conflicts Regarding Military Activities in the Exclusive Economic Zone 233
6.4 International Efforts to Reconcile Conflicts over Military Activities 260
6.5 The Way Forward 267

7 Maritime Security 271

7.1 The Concept of Maritime Security 272
7.2 Legal Framework to Address Maritime Security Threats 278
7.3 Coastal State Implementation under the Current Legal Framework 285
7.4 International Efforts to Enhance Maritime Security 300
7.5 The Way Forward 313

8 Underwater Archaeological and Historical Objects 322

8.1 Introduction 322
8.2 Overview of the Legal Framework 325

8.3 Rights and Jurisdiction over Activities Affecting Archaeological and Historical Objects 345

8.4 Settlement of Disputes 357

8.5 Conclusion 359

9 **General Conclusions** 362

Select Bibliography 369

Index 377

FOREWORD

I thank my friend and former colleague, Dr Sun Zhen, for inviting me to contribute the foreword for her important book. Dr Sun is a member of a new generation of brilliant young Asian international lawyers. The future is bright for international law in Asia.

The book is important because it discusses one of the most important inventions of the Third United Nations Conference on the Law of the Sea (Third Conference). The concept of the Exclusive Economic Zone (EEZ) is new to international law. The objective of the EEZ is to put an end to the decades-old dispute over fishing rights between the Coastal States and other States. It will be remembered that such a dispute between Iceland and the United Kingdom ended in a shooting war between them.

The EEZ gives Coastal States sovereign rights to the resources in the EEZ. It does not give the Coastal States sovereign rights to the water column.

One of the most difficult issues at the Third Conference was the status of the EEZ. The issue was finally resolved by a small negotiating group, convened and chaired by the leader of the Mexican delegation, Ambassador Castaneda. It came to be known as the Castaneda Group. What did the group agreed upon?

The group agreed on the following:

1. The EEZ is a *sui generis* zone. It is neither the Territorial Sea nor the High Seas.
2. No State can subject the EEZ to its sovereignty.
3. The international community enjoys the freedoms of navigation, overflight and the laying of submarine cables and pipelines in the EEZs of Coastal States.
4. A second group of rights and freedoms of the international community in the EEZ is qualified and is subject to the compatibility test. Article 58(2) makes Articles 88–115, the basic articles of the High Seas regime, applicable to the EEZ, in so far as they are not incompatible

with Part V of the Convention. Part V contains the EEZ. This means that a right of the High Seas – for example, to conduct military exercises – can be carried out in the EEZ if it is not incompatible with the resource rights of the Coastal States. The test is imprecise and has given rise to disagreements. Many Coastal States reject the right of other States to carry out such exercises in their EEZs. The maritime powers insist that the two rights are not incompatible.

Professor Tommy Koh
President
Third UN Conference on the Law of the Sea

PREFACE

The history of the law of the sea has been dominated by the competition between *mare liberum* and *mare clausum*. Throughout history, coastal States have sought to expand their rights and jurisdiction beyond the coastline by establishing various jurisdictional zones, while other States, notably States concerned with maritime transit, trade and distant-water fisheries, have sought to safeguard high seas freedoms. This tension is still evident today, just as it was when the text of the United Nations Convention on the Law of the Sea (UNCLOS or the Convention) was negotiated in the 1970s and adopted in 1982. At the very heart of this tension and crucial to the success of UNCLOS is the exclusive economic zone (EEZ), a *sui generis* legal regime officially codified by UNCLOS in which the rights and duties are attributed to the coastal State and other States according to its provisions. The EEZ represented a mini-package deal within UNCLOS in which States made various compromises at all levels. The consequence of these compromises and the necessarily ambiguous language contained in the relevant provisions of UNCLOS is that many States have adopted different interpretations of their rights and duties in the EEZ. This, in turn, has led to conflicts, frequently between the coastal State and other user States in the same maritime space.

This book examines the conflict and stability in the EEZ in light of State practice since the adoption of UNCLOS. It explores whether the basic premises and essential compromises of the EEZ legal regime still hold true or whether there has been evolution in the regime in terms of, for example, accommodating the EEZ regulatory scheme to meet new needs and challenges. Significantly, the survey of State practice indicates that coastal States have progressively asserted greater authority in defending their rights and jurisdiction in the EEZ, which have been broadly tolerated by the legal regime and other user States.

In exploring the theoretical basis for the stability of the EEZ legal regime, a core argument is made that the delicate balance is sustained by a body of flexible prescriptions for dynamic adjustment to prevent and resolve conflicts, which ultimately has the potential to strengthen the *sui generis* legal regime. Two key legal doctrines formed the body of flexible prescriptions. The first is the formula of attributing rights and freedoms between the coastal State and the other States that runs through Part V of UNCLOS and is further highlighted in Article 59. As such, rights and duties attributed to coastal States must be adequately associated with their sovereign rights over natural resources and explicitly recognised jurisdiction. The second legal doctrine is the reciprocal due regard obligation relating to the exercise of rights and freedoms that applies to both the coastal State and other user States in Articles 56(2) and 58(3) towards each other's rights and duties. This means that neither parties' rights nor freedoms are absolute and must be exercised in recognition of the legitimacy of their counterpart's freedoms or rights.

The book applies these two legal doctrines to analyse State practice in five thematic issues since the adoption of the Convention. The five thematic issues have been grouped into two categories. First, competing uses between rights and freedoms that have been explicitly attributed by provisions of UNCLOS Part V are examined, in particular whether and to what extent coastal State's rights and jurisdiction may affect the exercise of the freedoms of navigation and overflight and the laying of submarine cables and pipelines. Second, un-explicitly attributed rights and jurisdiction that have attracted conflicting interpretations and applications are analysed, specifically how States, both coastal and other States, can assert and exercise their rights over the conduct of military activities, the combat of threats to maritime security, and the protection of archaeological and historical objects found in the EEZ.

The evaluation of State practice presented in this book demonstrates conclusively that through the application of this body of flexible prescriptions under UNCLOS and related instruments, States have predominantly been operating within rather than significantly diverging from the *sui generis* legal regime. This feature of the EEZ has the potential to maintain the stability and balance of rights and duties of States in the contemporary law of the sea. This, in turn, contributes to good order at sea and thus international peace and security.

This work reflects the law and State practice as they stood, to the best of the author's knowledge, on 26 July 2024, unless otherwise indicated. All website addresses were accurate as at 26 July 2024, unless otherwise indicated.

ACKNOWLEDGEMENTS

Much of the research contained in this book began as part of my PhD at the University of Cambridge, where I was enormously fortunate in the support I received from the Faculty of Law, Wolfson College, Squire Law Library and the Lauterpacht Centre for International Law. First and particular thanks are due to my supervisor, the late Professor James Richard Crawford. I am indebted to his critical and constructive comments on drafts, which had significantly improved this work. The topic of my PhD originated in the course of writing a master's thesis under the supervision of the late Professor Alan Boyle at the University of Edinburgh, and I was lucky to have the benefit of his early influence. My research work at Cambridge was enriched by the discussions with many scholars and colleagues. In this regard, I would like to thank Dr Naomi Burke, Dr Thomas D Grant, Professor Christine D Gray, Professor Martti Koskenniemi, Dr Federica Paddeu, Dr Kate Purcell, Dr Rumiana Yotova, Professor Malcolm Nathan Shaw and Professor Surabhi Ranganathan. I was fortunate to have had Professor Andrew Serdy and Professor Douglas Guilfoyle as my doctoral examiners who furnished comprehensive, demanding and beneficial comments for me to finalise the dissertation.

Since the completion of the PhD, I had the opportunity to discuss the topic of my research with a number of scholars who have contributed to sharpen my intellectual thinking about the development and implementation of the law of the sea. I wish to express my gratitude for the advice, guidance and support received from numerous mentors and colleagues with whom I crossed paths during my tenure at the Centre for International Law, National University of Singapore. I had the privilege to engage with and learn from the pioneers who had negotiated the United Nations Convention on the Law of the Sea: Professor Tommy Koh Thong Bee, Professor Shunmugam Jayakumar, Ambassador Hasjim Djalal and the late Ambassador Satya N. Nandan. I have had many opportunities to discuss my thoughts on various ocean law and policy topics with Emeritus Professor Robert Charles Beckman, Dr Leonardo

Bernard, Professor Aldo Chircop, Sze-Wei Chan, Denise Cheong, Assistant Professor Tara Maria Davenport, Associate Professor Michael Ewing-Chow, Dr Lynn Kuok, Junianto James Losari, Dr Youna Le Berre Lemaire Lyons, Millicent McCreath, Ambassador Arif Havas Oegroseno, Dr Nilüfer Oral, Dr Hao Duy Phan, Captain J Ashley Roach and Ranyta Yusran.

The transformation from dissertation to book was completed during my time at the World Maritime University–Sasakawa Global Ocean Institute, and I am grateful for the guidance and support of Professor Ronán Long and Professor Clive Schofield. Many other scholars and colleagues have provided me with insightful advices and comments, and I wish to express my gratitude especially to Professor Mariano Javier Aznar Gómez, Dr Rián Derrig, the late Professor Meinhard Doelle, Professor David Freestone, Professor James Harrison and Assistant Professor Aleke Stöfen-O'Brien. I have benefitted from a supportive environment at the Insitute where I was surrounded by an energetic and motivated international multidisciplinary team. I would like to acknowledge the generous funding of the Institute by The Nippon Foundation. My thanks also to my colleagues at the Secretariat, the Procurement Office, the Finance Office and Office of the President for their assistance during the delivery of the manuscript.

I would like to express my gratitude to Joe Ng for accepting the book proposal and supporting me through the publication process. I thank the anonymous reviewers and the editorial team at Cambridge University Press for all their assistance in producing this book. I also thank Susan Rolston for proofreading the manuscript, Rosie Wood for preparing the index and Dr Robin Cleverly for providing me with a map.

Essential to me throughout this undertaking are those who provided indispensable moral support. I thank my families and friends for their unconditional love and affection which I have relied on at all stages of my life.

Last, I want to thank the Nippon Foundation and the World Maritime University for the financial support of the Gold Open Access.

TABLE OF INTERNATIONAL CASES

Arbitrations

Award between the United States and the United Kingdom relating to the Rights of Jurisdiction of United States in the Bering's Sea and the Preservation of Fur Seals, 15 August 1893, Reports of International Arbitral Awards, Volume XXVIII, 263–276 (United Nations, 2007) https://legal.un.org/riaa/cases/vol_XXVIII/263-276.pdf

Bering Sea Fur-Seals Case (Great Britain/United States of America), (1999) 1 International Environmental Law Reports 44–52

Dispute Concerning Filleting Within The Gulf of St Lawrence ("la Bretagne") (Canada v. France) (1990) 82 International Law Reports 590-670. doi:10.1017/CBO9781316152102.045

Permanent Court of Arbitration

Arbitral Tribunal Constituted Pursuant to Article 287, and in Accordance with Annex VII, of the United Nations Convention on the Law of the Sea in the Matter of an Arbitration between Barbados and the Republic of Trinidad and Tobago, Award, 11 April 2006, PCA Case No. 2004-02

Arbitral Tribunal Constituted Pursuant to Article 287, and in Accordance with Annex VII, of the United Nations Convention on the Law of the Sea in the Matter of an Arbitration between Guyana and Suriname (Guyana v. Suriname), Award, 17 September 2007, PCA Case No. 2004-04

In the Matter of an Arbitration before an Arbitral Tribunal Constituted under Annex VII to the 1982 United Nations Convention on the Law of the Sea the Italian Republic and the Republic of India concerning the 'Enrica Lexie' Incident, Award, 21 May 2020, PCA Case No. 2015-28

In the Matter of an Arbitration Pursuat to an Agreement to Arbitrate Dated 3 October 1996 between the Government of the State of Eritrea and the Government of the Republic of Yemen, Award (Maritime Delimitation), 17 December 1999, PCA Case No. 1996-04

In the Matter of the Arctic Sunrise Arbitration before an Arbitral Tribunal Constituted under Annex VII to the 1982 United Nations Convention on the Law of the Sea between the Kingdom of the Netherlands and the Russian Federation, Award on Jurisdiction, 26 November 2014, PCA Case No. 2014-02

In the Matter of the Arctic Sunrise Arbitration before an Arbitral Tribunal Constituted under Annex VII to the 1982 United Nations Convention on the Law of the Sea between the Kingdom of the Netherlands and the Russian Federation, Award on the Merits, 14 August 2015, PCA Case No. 2014-02

In the Matter of the Chagos Marine Protected Area Arbitration before an Arbitral Tribunal Constituted under Annex VII to the United Nations Convention on the Law of the Sea between the Republic of Mauritius and the United Kingdom of Great Britain and Northern Ireland, Award, 18 March 2015, PCA Case No. 2011-03

In the Matter of the South China Sea Arbitration before an Arbitral Tribunal Constituted under Annex VII to the 1982 United Nations Convention on the Law of the Sea between the Republic of the Philippines and the People's Republic of China, Award, 12 July 2016, PCA Case No 2013-19

International Court of Justice

Alleged Violations of Sovereign Rights and Maritime Spaces in the Caribbean Sea (Nicaragua v. Colombia), Judgment of 21 April 2022, ICJ Reports 2022, p. 266

Case Concerning the Continental Shelf (Libyan Arab Jamahiriya/Malta), Judgment of 3 June 1985, ICJ Reports 1985, p. 13

Case Concerning the Continental Shelf (Tunisia v. Libyan Arab Jamahiriya), Judgment of 24 February 1982, ICJ Reports 1982, p. 18

Case Concerning Delimitation of the Maritime Boundary in the Gulf of Maine Area (Canada/United States of America), Judgment of 12 October 1984, ICJ Reports 1984, p. 246

Case Concerning Maritime Delimitation and Territorial Questions between Qatar and Bahrain (Qatar v. Bahrain), Merits, Judgment of 16 March 2001, ICJ Reports 2001, p. 40

Case Concerning Maritime Dispute (Peru v. Chile), Judgment of 27 January 2014, ICJ Reports 2014, p. 3

Case Concerning Military and Paramilitary Activities in and Against Nicaragua (Nicaragua v. United States of America), Merits, Judgement of 27 July 1986, ICJ Reports 1986, p. 14

Case Concerning Pulp Mills on the River Uruguay (Argentina v. Uruguay), Judgment of 20 April 2010, ICJ Reports 2010, p. 14

Case Concerning Territorial and Maritime Dispute between Nicaragua and Honduras in the Caribbean Sea (Nicaragua v. Honduras), Judgment of 8 October 2007, ICJ Reports 2007, p. 659

Fisheries Jurisdiction Case (United Kingdom of Great Britain and Northern Ireland v. Iceland), Merits, Judgment of 25 July 1974, ICJ Reports 1974, p. 3

Fisheries Jurisdiction Case (Federal Republic of Germany v. Iceland), Merits, Judgment of 25 July 1974, ICJ Reports 1974, p. 175

Land, Island and Maritime Frontier Dispute (El Salvador/Honduras: Nicaragua intervening), Judgment of 11 September 1992, ICJ Reports 1992, p. 351

Legality of the Threat or Use of Nuclear Weapons, Advisory Opinion of 8 July 1996, ICJ Reports 1996, p. 226

North Sea Continental Shelf Cases (Federal Republic of German v. Netherlands; Federal Republic of Germany v. Denmark), Judgment of 20 February 1969, ICJ Reports 1969, p. 3

The Corfu Channel Case, Merits, Judgement of 9 April 1949, ICJ Reports 1949, p. 4

International Tribunal for the Law of the Sea

Case concerning Land Reclamation by Singapore in and around the Straits of Johor (Malaysia v. Singapore), Provisional Measures, Order of 8 October 2003, ITLOS Reports 2003, p. 10

Delimitation of the Maritime Boundary in the Atlantic Ocean (Ghana/Côte d'Ivoire), Judgment of 23 September 2017, ITLOS Reports 2017, p. 4

Detention of Three Ukrainian Naval Vessels (Ukraine v. Russian Federation), Provisional Measures, Order of 25 May 2019, ITLOS Reports 2018–2019, p. 283

M/T 'San Padre Pio' Case (Switzerland v. Nigeria), Provisional Measures, Order of 6 July 2019, ITLOS Reports 2018–2019, p. 375

M/V 'Norstar' Case (Panama v. Italy), Judgment of 10 April 2019, ITLOS Reports 2018–2019, p. 10

M/V 'Saiga' Case (Saint Vincent and the Grenadines v. Guinea), Prompt Release, Judgment of 4 December 1997, ITLOS Reports 1997, p. 16

M/V 'Saiga' (No. 2) (Saint Vincent and the Grenadines v. Guinea), Provisional Measures, Order of 11 March 1998, ITLOS Reports 1998, p. 24

M/V 'Saiga' (No. 2) (Saint Vincent and the Grenadines v. Guinea), Judgment of 1 July 1999, ITLOS Reports 1999, p. 10

M/V 'Virginia G' Case (Panama/Guinea-Bissau), Judgment of 14 April 2014, ITLOS Reports 2014, p. 4

Request for an Advisory Opinion submitted by the Commission of Small Island States on Climate Change and International Law, Advisory Opinion of 21 May 2024, ITLOS List of cases: No. 31

Request for an Advisory Opinion submitted by the Sub-regional Fisheries Commission (SRFC), Advisory Opinion of 2 April 2015, ITLOS Reports 2015, p. 4

Southern Bluefin Tuna Cases (New Zealand v. Japan; Australia v. Japan), Provisional Measures, Order of 27 August 1999, ITLOS Reports 1999, p. 280

The 'ARA Libertad' Case (Argentina v. Ghana), Provisional Measures, Order of 15 December 2012, ITLOS Reports 2012, p. 332

The 'Camouco' Case (Panama v. France), Prompt Release, Judgment of 7 February 2000, ITLOS Reports 2000, p. 10

The 'Hoshinmaru' Case (Japan v. Russian Federation), Prompt Release, Judgment of 6 August 2007, ITLOS Reports 2005–2007, p. 18

The 'Juno Trader' Case (Saint Vincent and the Grenadines v. Guinea-Bissau), Prompt Release, Judgment of 18 December 2004, ITLOS Reports 2004, p. 17

The 'Monte Confurco' Case (Seychelles v. France), Prompt Release, Judgment of 18 December 2000, ITLOS Reports 2000, p. 86

The M/V 'Louisa' Case (Saint Vincent and the Grenadines v. Kingdom of Spain), Provisional Measures, Order of 23 December 2010, ITLOS Reports 2008–2010, p. 58

The M/V 'Louisa' Case (Saint Vincent and the Grenadines v. Kingdom of Spain), Judgment of 28 May 2013, ITLOS Reports 2013, p. 4

The 'Tomimaru' Case (Japan v. Russian Federation), Prompt Release, Judgment of 6 August 2007, ITLOS Reports 2005–2007, p. 74

The 'Volga' Case (Russian Federation v. Australia), Prompt Release, Judgment of 23 December 2002, ITLOS Reports 2002, p. 10

TABLE OF INTERNATIONAL TREATIES

Agreement between the Department of Defense of the United States of America and the Ministry of National Defense of the People's Republic of China on Establishing a Consultation Mechanism to Strengthen Military Maritime Safety, Treaties and Other International Acts Series 12924 (in force 19 January 1998), www.state.gov/12924

Agreement between the Republic of Finland, the Republic of Estonia and the Kingdom of Sweden Regarding the M/S *Estonia* (23 February 1995, in force 26 August 1995) 1890 UNTS 176

Agreement Concerning the Shipwrecked Vessel RMS *Titanic* (6 November 2003, in force 18 November 2019) UKTS No 8 (2019) www.state.gov/multilateral-19-1118

Agreement for the Implementation of the Provisions of the United Nations Convention on the Law of the Sea of 10 December 1982 Relating to the Conservation and Management of Straddling Fish Stocks and Highly Migratory Fish Stocks (4 August 1995, in force 11 December 2001) (Fish Stocks Agreement) 2167 UNTS 3

Agreement to Promote Compliance with International Conservation and Management Measures by Fishing Vessels on the High Seas (24 November 1995, in force 24 April 2003) 2221 UNTS 91

Antarctic Treaty (1 December 1959, in force 23 June 1961) 402 UNTS 71

Basel Convention on the Control of Transboundary Movements of Hazardous Wastes and their Disposal (22 March 1989, in force 5 May 1992) 1673 UNTS 57

Convention for the Protection of Submarine Telegraph Cables (14 March 1884) (1884 Paris Convention) https://cil.nus.edu.sg/wp-content/uploads/2019/02/1884-Convention-for-the-Protection-of-Submarine-Telegraph-Cables-1.pdf

Convention for the Protection of the Marine Environment of the North-East Atlantic (OSPAR Convention) (22 September 1992, in force 25 March 1998) 2354 UNTS 67

Convention for the Protection of the World Cultural and Natural Heritage (16 November 1972, in force 17 December 1975) 1037 UNTS 151

Convention for the Suppression of Unlawful Acts against the Safety of Maritime Navigation (SUA Convention) (1678 UNTS 221) and Protocol for the Suppression of Unlawful Acts against the Safety of Fixed Platforms Located on the Continental Shelf (SUA Platforms Protocol) (10 March 1988, in force 1 March 1992) (1678 UNTS 304); Protocol to SUA Convention and Protocol to

SUA Platforms Protocol (14 October 2005, in force 28 July 2010) (3432 UNTS A-29004)

Charter of the Association of Southeast Asian Nations (20 November 2007, in force 15 December 2008) 2624 UNTS 223

Charter of the United Nations (26 June 1945, in force 24 October 1945) 1 UNTS XVI

Convention on Fishing and Conservation of the Living Resources of the High Seas (29 April 1958, in force 20 March 1966) 559 UNTS 285

Convention on International Civil Aviation (7 December 1944, in force 4 April 1947) 15 UNTS 295

Convention on the Continental Shelf (29 April 1958, in force 10 June 1964) 499 UNTS 311

Convention on the High Seas (29 April 1958, in force 30 September 1962) 450 UNTS 11

Convention on the International Maritime Organization (6 March 1948, in force 17 March 1958) 289 UNTS 3

Convention on the International Regulations for Preventing Collisions at Sea, 1972 (20 October 1972, in force 15 July 1977) 1050 UNTS 16 (COLREG)

Convention on the Prevention of Marine Pollution by Dumping of Wastes and Other Matter (29 December 1972, in force 30 August 1975) 1046 UNTS 120 (London Convention); 1996 Protocol to the London Convention (7 November 1996, in force 24 March 2006) (London Protocol)

Convention on the Protection of the Underwater Cultural Heritage (2 November 2001, in force 2 January 2009) 2562 UNTS 3 (CPUCH)

Convention on the Territorial Sea and the Contiguous Zone (29 April 1958, in force 10 September 1964) 516 UNTS 205

Convention to Ban the Importation in Forum Islands Countries of Hazardous Wastes and Radioactive Wastes and to Control the Transboundary Movement and Management of Hazardous Wastes within the South Pacific Region (16 September 1995, in force 21 October 2001) (Waigani Convention) www.sprep.org/convention-secretariat/waigani-convention

Fisheries Convention (London, 9 March 1964) https://assets.publishing.service.gov.uk/media/5a7c6f4bed915d696ccfcc12/Fisheries_Conv_March-April_1964.pdf

International Convention for the Control and Management of Ship's Ballast Water and Sediments (13 February 2004, in force 8 September 2017) 3282 UNTS I-55544 (BWM Convention)

International Convention for the Safety of Life at Sea, as amended (1 November 1974, in force 25 May 1980) 1184 UNTS 2 (SOLAS)

International Convention on Salvage (28 April 1989, in force, 14 July 1996) 1954 UNTS 165

International Convention relating to Intervention on the High Seas in cases of Oil Pollution Casualties (29 November 1969, in force 6 May 1975) 970 UNTS 211 (Intervention Convention).

Nairobi International Convention on the Removal of Wrecks (18 May 2007, in force 14 April 2015) 3283 UNTS I-55565 (RWC)

Protocol of 1978 relating to the International Convention for the Prevention of Pollution from Ships, 1973 (17 February 1978, in force 2 October 1983) 1340 UNTS 61 (MARPOL)

Statute of the International Court of Justice (26 June 1945, in force 24 October 1945) 1 UNTS 21

Treaty for the Prohibition of Nuclear Weapons in Latin America (14 February 1967, in force 22 April 1968) 634 UNTS 281 (Treaty of Tlatelolco)

Treat of Amity and Cooperation in Southeast Asia (24 February 1976, in force 15 July 1976) 1025 UNTS 297

Treaty on the Prohibition of the Emplacement of Nuclear Weapons and Other Weapons of Mass Destruction on the Sea-bed and Ocean Floor and in the Subsoil Thereof (11 February 1971, in force 18 May 1972) 955 UNTS 115 (Seabed Treaty)

United Nations Convention against Transnational Organized Crime and the Protocols Thereto, UNGA A/RES/55/25, 15 November 2000 (in force 29 September 2003)

United Nations Convention on the Law of the Sea (10 December 1982, in force 16 November 1994) 1833 UNTS 3 (UNCLOS)

Vienna Convention on the Law of Treaties (23 May 1969, in force 27 January 1980) 1155 UNTS 331

ABBREVIATIONS

ADIZ	air defence identification zone
AIS	automatic identification system
ASEAN	Association of Southeast Asian Nations
CDEM	construction, design, equipment and manning
COC	Code of Conduct
COLREG	Convention on the International Regulations for Preventing Collisions at Sea
CPUCH	Convention on the Protection of Underwater Cultural Heritage
EEZ	exclusive economic zone
EUMSS	European Union Maritime Security Strategy
FAO	Food and Agriculture Organization of the United Nations
IAEA	International Atomic Energy Agency
ICAO	International Civil Aviation Organization
ICJ	International Court of Justice
ICNT	Informal Composite Negotiating Text
ICPC	International Cable Protection Committee
ILA	International Law Association
ILC	International Law Commission
IMO	International Maritime Organization
ISNT	Informal Single Negotiating Text
ITLOS	International Tribunal for the Law of the Sea
IUU	illegal, unreported and unregulated (fishing)
LL/GDS	land-locked and geographically disadvantaged States
LRIT	Long-Range Identification and Tracking (System)
MARPOL	International Convention for the Prevention of Pollution from Ships
MASTREP	Modernised Australian Ship Tracking and Reporting System
MDA	maritime domain awareness
MOU	memoranda of understanding
NM	nautical mile
PCA	Permanent Court of Arbitration
PSSA	Particularly Sensitive Sea Area

RSNT	Revised Single Negotiating Text
RWC	Convention on the Removal of Wrecks
SAR	search and rescue
SOLAS	International Convention for the Safety of Life at Sea
SUA Convention	Convention for the Suppression of Unlawful Acts against the Safety of Maritime Navigation
SUA Platforms Protocol	Protocol for the Suppression of Unlawful Acts against the Safety of Fixed Platforms Located on the Continental Shelf
UCH	underwater cultural heritage
UN	United Nations
UNCLOS	United Nations Convention on the Law of the Sea
UN DOALOS	United Nations Division for Ocean Affairs and the Law of the Sea
UNESCO	United Nations Organization for Education, Science and Culture
UNGA	United Nations General Assembly
UNODC	United Nations Office on Drugs and Crime
UNSC	United Nations Security Council
UNSG	United Nations Secretary-General
UNTS	United Nations Treaty Series
VHF	very high frequency
WMD	weapons of mass destruction

1

Introduction

The doctrine of the 'freedom of the seas' came to be accepted as a general principle of maritime law in the eighteenth century when the coastal State was recognised as having sovereignty, or at least exclusive authority, over a limited band of territorial waters (although there was no consensus on its precise breadth).[1] Since then, the history of the law of the sea has been dominated by the competition between two opposing yet complementary principles, *mare liberum* and *mare clausum*.[2] While coastal States seek to expand their rights and jurisdiction beyond the limit of territorial waters by establishing various jurisdictional zones, other States, notably States concerned with maritime transit, trade and distant-water fisheries, vie for the maximum of high seas freedoms within these zones. This competition is predominantly illustrated in the exclusive economic zone (EEZ) as established in the 1982 United Nations Convention on the Law of the Sea (UNCLOS).[3]

The EEZ is a multifunctional maritime zone where rights and duties of the coastal State and other States co-exist.[4] The EEZ, when claimed, may extend up to 200 nautical miles (NM) from the baseline and overlap to

[1] James B. Morell, *The Law of the Sea: An Historical Analysis of the 1982 Treaty and Its Rejection by the United States* (McFarland 1992) 2; Thomas Baty, 'The Three-Mile Limit' (1928) 22 Am J Int'l L 503, 503; James R. Crawford, *Brownlie's Principles of Public International Law* (9th ed., Oxford University Press 2019) 242, 281.

[2] Daniel P. O'Connell, *The International Law of the Sea*, Vol. I (Oxford University Press 1982) 1; Edward Duncan Brown, 'The Exclusive Economic Zone: Criteria and Machinery for the Resolution of International Conflicts between Different Users of the EEZ' (1977) 4 Marit Pol Mgmt 325, 328.

[3] United Nations Convention on the Law of the Sea (10 December 1982, in force 16 November 1994) 1833 UNTS 3, Part V (UNCLOS).

[4] Maria Gavouneli, *Functional Jurisdiction in the Law of the Sea* (Martinus Nijhoff 2007) 62–69; Alexander Proelss, 'The Law on the Exclusive Economic Zone in Perspective: Legal Status and Resolution of User Conflicts Revisited' (2012) 26 Ocean YB 87, 89.

some degree with the contiguous zone and the continental shelf.[5] The importance of the EEZ both as a component of the modern law of the sea and in political and material terms should be acknowledged. It has been estimated that the claims of the EEZ worldwide cover the ocean surface that is mostly used for navigation and the extraction of natural resources.[6] The seabed and the water column of the EEZ will continue to provide the major focus of human activities both in the short and long terms.

The legal status of the EEZ was one of the most complex issues negotiated at the Third United Nations Conference on the Law of the Sea (Third Conference), and the provisions adopted thereafter fully reflect this tension.[7] The codification of the EEZ was achieved in a broader context of the balance that was reached by the Third Conference on UNCLOS.[8] It is one of the components in the overall package deal that included the establishment of a 12 NM maximum breadth for the territorial sea, the creation of passage rights through straits used for international navigation and archipelagic waters, the recognition of rights over the extended continental shelf, guaranteed access to and from the sea for landlocked States, the establishment of the Area and a compulsory dispute settlement mechanism.

The EEZ was adopted as a *sui generis* legal regime where 'the rights and jurisdiction of the coastal State and the rights and freedoms of other States' are provided by the relevant provisions of UNCLOS.[9] In general, the provisions relating to the EEZ reflect a heavily negotiated package of delicately balanced compromises, with substantive rules protecting the respective rights and freedoms of different States, general obligations of exercising their respective rights and freedoms, and procedural and

[5] UNCLOS, Articles 33(2), 57, 76; Robin Churchill, Vaughan Lowe and Amy Sander, *The Law of the Sea* (4th ed., Manchester University Press 2022) 253.

[6] IILSS-International Institute for Law of the Sea Studies, Exclusive Economic Zone (EEZ) Map of the World, 23 May 2021, https://iilss.net/exclusive-economic-zoneeez-map-of-the-world/; Michele Metych, 'Exclusive Economic Zone', in Encyclopaedia Britannica, last updated 13 July 2023, www.britannica.com/topic/exclusive-economic-zone; Churchill, Lowe and Sander (2022) 294–295.

[7] Myron H. Nordquist, Satya N. Nandan and Shabtai Rosenne (eds.), *United Nations Convention on the Law of the Sea 1982: A Commentary*, Vol. II (Martinus Nijhoff 1993) 508–509; Tommy Koh, *Building a New Legal Order for the Oceans* (NUS Press 2020) 32.

[8] See Tommy T. B. Koh and Shanmugam Jayakumar, 'The Negotiating Process of the Third United Nations Conference on the Law of the Sea', in Myron H. Nordquist (ed.), *United Nations Convention on the Law of the Sea 1982: A Commentary*, Vol. I (Martinus Nijhoff 1985) 29–134.

[9] UNCLOS, Articles 55–56, 58.

substantive rules to prevent and settle disputes.[10] The EEZ regime is maintained by two legal doctrines: the principles used to attribute rights and freedoms between the coastal State and other States; and the reciprocal due regard obligations relating to their excise. These two legal doctrines also guided the principles to resolve conflicts arising from the attribution of residual rights and the procedures to settle disputes among State parties. The legal framework is, however, incomplete or left open, not only to be worked out in more detailed agreements, but also to be governed by general rules and principles of international law. In this way, the EEZ regime will continue to evolve to meet new challenges and changed circumstances.

As provided in Article 56 of UNCLOS, the coastal State has 'sovereign rights for the purpose of exploring and exploiting, conserving and managing the natural resources' and 'with regard to other activities for the economic exploitation and exploration of the zone'. Moreover, the coastal State has specific jurisdiction with regard to 'the establishment and use of artificial islands, installations and structures', 'marine scientific research' and 'the protection and preservation of the marine environment' as provided for in the relevant provisions of UNCLOS. Article 58 states that all States, including the coastal State, enjoy the freedoms 'of navigation and overflight and of the laying of submarine cables and pipelines, and other internationally lawful uses of the sea related to these freedoms'. In sum, the general principle of allocating uses in the EEZ is to reserve those that may affect economic interests to the coastal States, while minimising the erosion of the communicational freedoms enjoyed by all States, and to preserve these freedoms to all States insofar as they are compatible with this specific legal regime. The rights of coastal States co-exist with those of other States.

The general principle of exercising these co-existing rights is the mutual obligation of due regard as explicitly required in both Articles 56(2) and 58(3), whereby no State may exercise their rights or freedoms in an absolute manner.[11] Both the coastal State and other States undertake the mutual obligation of having due regard to the rights and duties

[10] Barbara Kwiatkowska, *The 200 Mile Exclusive Economic Zone in the New Law of the Sea* (Martinus Nijhoff 1989) xx; Mohamed Dahmani, *The Fisheries Regime of the Exclusive Economic Zone* (Martinus Nijhoff 1987) 22; Natalie Klein, *Dispute Settlement in the UN Convention on the Law of the Sea* (Cambridge University Press 2005) 133.

[11] Bernard H. Oxman, 'The Principle of Due Regard', in ITLOS (eds.), *The Contribution of the International Tribunal for the Law of the Sea to the Rule of Law: 1996–2016* (Brill 2017) 108–113.

of the other party when exercising their rights and performing their duties within the EEZ, together with the general duty to fulfil their obligations in good faith and not to abuse their rights, jurisdiction and freedoms.[12]

Article 59 has been considered as a statement that UNCLOS has not fully attributed all rights and jurisdiction in the EEZ.[13] If a conflict arises between a coastal State and another State regarding the attribution of such a right or jurisdiction in the EEZ, it 'should be resolved on the basis of equity and in the light of all the relevant circumstances, taking into account the respective importance of the interests involved'.[14] This provision serves as a guide for resolving conflicts between the relevant States before the judicial settlement of a dispute. The basis of equity may also be adopted by a dispute settlement body to resolve the dispute *ex aequo et bono* if the parties agree.[15] This vague formula of 'relevant circumstances' echoes the general principle of allocating different uses in the EEZ. Moreover, the general principles for attributing and exercising co-existing rights and freedoms in the EEZ apply to all residual rights and jurisdiction. Combined, they create a dynamic system to assess and achieve a flexible balance of power between different user States in the EEZ, with each case to be decided on its own merits.

As a general principle of international law, State parties are obligated to settle disputes regarding the uses of the EEZ by peaceful means.[16] If the States parties cannot reach a settlement through the means of their choice, any party to the dispute may submit such dispute to the compulsory procedures entailing binding decisions established by Part XV of UNCLOS.[17] The application of the compulsory procedures to disputes relating to the EEZ is subject to specified limitations and exceptions that reflect the specific interests of the coastal State and other States.[18]

This delicate balance in the EEZ is not uncontroversial. The activities in the EEZ involve different, overlapping and often conflicting interests relating to the increasingly intensive use of the ocean and its resources by

[12] UNCLOS, Articles 56(2), 58(3), 300.

[13] Nordquist, Nandan and Rosenne (1993) 569; Churchill, Lowe and Sander (2022) 291–292.

[14] UNCLOS, Article 59.

[15] UNCLOS, Article 293(2).

[16] Charter of the United Nations (26 June 1945, in force 24 October 1945) 1 UNTS XVI, Article 2(3); UNCLOS, Article 279.

[17] UNCLOS, Articles 280–281, 286.

[18] UNCLOS, Articles 297, 298.

different States.[19] It is the intention here to analyse the general juridical nature of the EEZ and its residual status, and to determine if the EEZ legal regime established in UNCLOS is sufficiently flexible to allow the international community to respond to the new challenges created in subsequent State practice. The allocation of rights and duties between the coastal State and other States are analysed, and the manner in which a balance is struck between different interests in the light of State practice in the last four decades since the conclusion of UNCLOS is explored. The creation of the EEZ reflects the general agreement of States to sacrifice, at least to a certain degree, their long-established high seas freedoms in order to obtain exclusive economic rights in the extensive areas adjacent to their coasts. As a consequence, the freedoms of the high seas, as preserved in Article 58, cannot be viewed as an extension or a continuation of such freedoms within the EEZ. The preserved freedoms in the EEZ are subject to significant restrictions in an effort to accommodate the rights and jurisdiction of the coastal State. With this understanding in mind, States are developing a *sui generis* system for the attribution and exercise of rights and freedoms in the EEZ, in order to strike a dynamic balance between the two competing needs.

The analysis here is centred on the interpretation of the substantive provisions relating to the EEZ in UNCLOS. In doing so, the principles of treaty interpretation as recognised by international law are applied, with a particular focus on selected State practices that not only drove the development of the EEZ prior to the conclusion of UNCLOS but also influenced its interpretation and application over the past four decades.[20] Without going into details on the rules of treaty interpretation, which has a rich pool of literature, the general principles that have been used in this analysis are outlined below.[21]

19 Edward Duncan Brown, 'The Exclusive Economic Zone: Criteria and Machinery for the Resolution of International Conflicts between Different Users of the EEZ' (1977) 4 Marit Pol Mgmt 325, 326–327.

20 It should be made clear that the object of this book is not to provide an exhaustive account of State practice, nor indeed to present a prospectus on the current state of the implementation of the EEZ. Rather it selects those distinctive examples that contribute to the doctrinal construction of rules of the EEZ and represent the character of underlying discourses that structure the legal interventions.

21 See Alexander Orakhelashvili, *The Interpretation of Acts and Rules in Public International Law* (Oxford University Press 2008); Malgosia Fitzmaurice, Olufemi Elias and Panos Merkouris (eds.), *Treaty Interpretation and the Vienna Convention on the Law of Treaties: 30 Years* (Martinus Nijhoff 2011); Anthony Aust, *Modern Treaty Law and Practice* (Cambridge University Press 2013) 205–226; Sean D. Murphy, 'The Relevance

Treaty interpretation is a delicate matter. In order to understand the meaning of treaty provisions on the EEZ, one needs to be aware that there are fundamental rules of treaty interpretation. The key rules are set out in Articles 31 and 32 of the Vienna Convention.[22] Article 31(1) states that '[a] treaty shall be interpreted in good faith in accordance with the ordinary meaning to be given to the terms of the treaty in their context and in the light of its object and purpose'. Paragraph 2 makes it clear that the 'context' of a treaty includes the whole of the text and its preamble and annexes, as well as any agreement or instrument concerning the treaty which was made, or agreed to, by all the parties. Article 31(3) further provides that account shall also be taken, together with the context, of any subsequent agreement, subsequent practice and other rules of international law that are relevant to the parties. In addition to the ordinary meaning of the treaty provisions, according to Article 31(4), '[a] special meaning shall be given to a term if it is established that the parties so intended'. When the interpretation of treaty provisions, after applying the rules of Article 31, results in an undesirable result such as ambiguity or unreasonableness, other resources may be used to assist the interpretation. Article 32 provides that 'the preparatory work of the treaty and the circumstances of its conclusion' may be used to confirm or determine the meaning of the treaty provisions. It is also clear from Articles 31 and 32 that recourse to the preparatory work and the circumstances of the conclusion of the treaty is a supplementary means of interpretation only.

The negotiation of UNCLOS represented an effort in both codifying pre-existing customary law and progressively developing international law. With respect to the progressive development of international law, the consensus process that formed the basis of the treaty negotiation led to

of Subsequent Agreement and Subsequent Practice for the Interpretation of Treaties', in Georg Nolte (ed.), *Treaties and Subsequent Practice* (Oxford University Press 2013) 82–94; Eirik Bjorge, *The Evolutionary Interpretation of Treaties* (Oxford University Press 2014); Richard Gardiner, *Treaty Interpretation* (2nd ed., Oxford University Press 2015); Christian Djeffal, *Static and Evolutive Treaty Interpretation: A Functional Reconstruction* (Cambridge University Press 2015); Chang-Fa Lo, *Treaty Interpretation Under the Vienna Convention on the Law of Treaties: A New Round of Codification* (Springer 2017); Malcolm N. Shaw, *International Law* (8th ed., Cambridge University Press 2017) 706–711; Richard Gardiner, 'The Vienna Convention Rules on Treaty Interpretation', in Duncan B. Hollis (ed.), *The Oxford Guide to Treaties* (2nd ed., Oxford University Press 2020) 459–488; Eirik Bjorge and Robert Kolb, 'The Interpretation of Treaties over Time', in Hollis (2020) 489–503.

22 Vienna Convention on the Law of Treaties (23 May 1969, in force 27 January 1980) 1155 UNTS 331.

a situation where State practice and the formation of *opinio juris* went hand-in-hand in such a way that many of the rules of the EEZ were reflected in customary law by the time of the adoption of UNCLOS.[23] State practice, both unilateral and regional initiatives, relating to the claims over a jurisdictional zone beyond the territorial sea played a defining role in the development of the EEZ prior to the conclusion of UNCLOS in 1982.[24] Subsequent State practice since the adoption of UNCLOS, recognised as the authentic means of treaty interpretation, contributes to the formation of agreement among State parties regarding the interpretation of the provisions of the EEZ.[25] The State practice broadly speaking includes unilateral domestic implementation of the EEZ, implementation of rules involving another State, as well as multilateral decision-making and lawmaking processes that relate to the use of the EEZ.[26]

With such thoughts in mind, it is convenient to set out the structure of this book and the topics discussed. Besides the Introduction and Conclusion, this book is divided into three parts comprising seven chapters.

Part I, 'The Development and Status of the Exclusive Economic Zone', reviews the historical development and codification of the EEZ. Chapter 2 reflects on the origins and evolution of the notion of a functional maritime zone in favour of the coastal State for economic

[23] Statute of the International Court of Justice (26 June 1945, in force 24 October 1945) 1 UNTS 21, Article 38(1)(b); Vaughan Lowe, *International Law* (Oxford University Press 2007) 83–86; James Harrison, *Making the Law of the Sea* (Cambridge University Press 2011) 51–59; Shaw (2017) 412; Malcolm D. Evans, 'The Law of the Sea', in Malcolm D. Evans (ed.), *International Law* (5th ed., Oxford University Press 2018) 637–638; Churchill, Lowe and Sander (2022) 35–36.

[24] See L. D. M. Nelson, 'The Patrimonial Sea' (1973) 22 Int'l & Comp LQ 668; F. V. Garcia-Amador, 'The Latin American Contribution to the Development of the Law of the Sea' (1974) 68 Am J Int'l L 33; Lewis M. Alexander and Robert D. Hodgson, 'The Impact of the 200-Mile Economic Zone on the Law of the Sea' (1974–1975) 12(3) San Diego L Rev 569; Duke E. Pollard, 'The Exclusive Economic Zone: The Elusive Consensus' (1974–1975) 12(3) San Diego L Rev 600; Robert B. Krueger and Myron H. Nordquist, 'The Evolution of the 200-Mile Exclusive Economic Zone: State Practice in the Pacific Basin' (1978–1979) 19(2) Va J Int'l L 321; Lewis M. Alexander, 'The Ocean Enclosure Movement: Inventory and Prospect' (1983) 20(3) San Diego L Rev 561.

[25] Vienna Convention on the Law of Treaties, Article 31(3)(b); International Law Commission (ILC), 'Draft Conclusions on Subsequent Agreements and Subsequent Practice in Relation to the Interpretation of Treaties, with Commentaries, 2018' (2018) 2(2) YB ILC Conclusions 2, 3.

[26] Robin R. Churchill, 'The Impact of State Practice on the Jurisdictional Framework Contained in the LOS Convention', in Alex G. Oude Elferink (ed.), *Stability and Change in the Law of the Sea: The Role of the LOS Convention* (Brill 2005) 93–95; Lowe (2007) 42–46; Harrison (2011) 55–56; ILC (2018) Conclusions 4, 5.

purposes. Early expansion of the rights of the coastal State began with claims of jurisdiction over the natural resources found in the adjacent marine areas, both in the water column and on the seabed. The claim of a distance-based maritime zone gained strength after the Second World War associated with decolonisation and was supported by many newly independent States from Latin America, the Caribbean, Asia and Africa. The resulting concept of the EEZ is the culmination of this jurisdictional expansion over economic interests. Chapter 3 examines the jurisdictional framework of the EEZ as codified in UNCLOS. The coastal States' intention to claim exclusive rights in the EEZ was resisted by many maritime States in an effort to preserve the freedoms of navigation and overflight at the Third Conference. The negotiation resulted in a compromised *sui generis* legal regime consisting of substantive rules of the attribution and exercise of respective rights and duties and a dispute resolution mechanism to balance the competing demands of States.

Part II, 'Competing Uses of the Exclusive Economic Zone', examines how a dynamic balance of power between the coastal State and other States may be maintained through the two legal doctrines that guide the allocation and exercise of rights and duties in the EEZ. It analyses how the freedoms of navigation and overflight (Chapter 4) and the freedom to lay submarine cables and pipelines (Chapter 5) have been interpreted and implemented in the EEZ, with a focus on how the exercise of the coastal States' rights and jurisdiction may affect their enjoyment. Although there is a tendency to broaden the interpretation of the coastal State's rights and jurisdiction exercised in the EEZ, this is not sufficient to overturn the general freedoms preserved for all States. The communicational freedoms preserved in the EEZ are not absolute, and the primary obligation for all States exercising their freedoms is to have due regard for the interests of both the coastal State and the other States in exercising their rights and performing their duties within the EEZ. The same mandatory obligation is also laid on the coastal State to have due regard for the rights and duties of other States and to act in a manner compatible with UNCLOS as safeguards to the enjoyment of the preserved communicational freedoms.

Part III discusses means of 'Resolving Conflicts Regarding Unattributed Rights and Jurisdiction in the Exclusive Economic Zone'. It focuses on three issues over which there are unexplicitly attributed rights and jurisdiction in the EEZ: military activities (Chapter 6), maritime security (Chapter 7) and underwater archaeological and historical objects (Chapter 8). While applying the principles stated in Article 59 of UNCLOS, the general principles for allocating uses and exercising co-existing rights apply to these three issues. Chapter 6 addresses the complexities regarding the conduct of military activities in the EEZ with a focus on analysing the conflicts arising from the activities undertaken by a foreign State. Chapter 7 explores both the unilateral and multilateral responses taken by States to combat maritime security threats within the EEZ, and examines the emerging practice of promoting collaboration between the coastal State and other States to achieve collective security at sea. Chapter 8 discusses the protection of underwater archaeological and historical objects found in the EEZ, with a particular focus on a subsequent agreement that partially clarified the legal gap left by the UNCLOS.

Chapter 9 sets out the conclusions of this analysis. The establishment of the EEZ represents a success on the part of coastal States in securing their economic interests in the adjacent marine areas at the cost of encroaching, to some degree, on traditional high seas freedoms. However, the battle over freedom erosion and restraint continues as to other issues in an increasingly interdependent law of the sea environment. The overall balance between the economic interests of coastal States and the communicational interests of all States, as established in UNCLOS, represents a body of flexible prescriptions for dynamic adjustment, and State practice has for the most part been operating within, rather than significantly diverging from, the EEZ regime.

PART I

The Development and Status of the Exclusive Economic Zone

The historical roots of the exclusive economic zone (EEZ) lie in the earliest claims of national jurisdiction over marine resources of various types. The development of the EEZ is partly the result of widespread contemporary national practices and of the diplomatic negotiations that have been conducted at regional and global forums, particularly at the Third United Nations Conference on the Law of the Sea.[1] The two proclamations made in 1945 by the United States, one to fisheries in the areas beyond the territorial sea, the other to natural resources on the seabed of the continental shelf, marked the beginning of contemporary national practices.[2] These were closely followed by the resource-oriented extension of the territorial sea claims made first by the Latin American and subsequently African States, as well as by the perhaps better-known continental shelf claims.[3] Such claims to special interests on the part of the coastal State extending the traditional territorial sea limit soon spread to other parts of the world. This process was reflected in different ways in the three United Nations Conferences on the Law of the Sea – first as successful Western opposition, then as a stalemate, then as widespread and eventually universal acceptance of a compromise solution. The negotiated outcome gave effective priority to coastal States in resource matters within 200 nautical miles from the coast while preserving freedom of communication, including navigation and overflight, for all States.[4]

1 Francisco Orrego Vicuña, 'The Exclusive Economic Zone: A Latin American Perspective: An Introduction', in Francisco Orrego Vicuña (ed.), *The Exclusive Economic Zone: A Latin American Perspective* (Westview 1984) 1.

2 'Official Documents, United States: Proclamation by the President' (1946) 40 Am J Int'l L Sup 45.

3 Robin Churchill, Vaughan Lowe and Amy Sander, *The Law of the Sea* (4th ed., Manchester University Press 2022) 255–256.

4 Francisco Orrego Vicuña, *The Exclusive Economic Zone: Regime and Legal Nature under International Law* (Cambridge University Press 1989) 6–7; Myron H. Nordquist, Satya N.

This part begins by looking at the historical development and codification of the 200-mile maritime zone, and then considers the *sui generis* legal regime of the EEZ as codified in the 1982 United Nations Convention on the Law of the Sea.[5] The historical review confirms that the extended coastal State claims and jurisdiction beyond the limit of the territorial waters were primarily for economic benefits. The creation of the EEZ highlighted the gradual expansion of a coastal State's rights over economic interests in the coastal area after the Second World War.[6] The negotiated EEZ is specifically not a zone of sovereignty, but a special functional zone where the coastal State has sovereign rights over the natural resources and jurisdiction with regard to specific activities, while traditional freedoms of the high seas were well preserved. The delicate balance adopted in the EEZ regime is sustained by a body of flexible prescriptions for dynamic adjustment to prevent and resolve conflicts. These include the legal doctrines of attributing rights and freedoms to the coastal State and the other States, and the reciprocal due regard obligation relating to their exercise, as well as a mandatory dispute settlement mechanism that recognises the special features of the EEZ regime.

Nandan and Shabtai Rosenne (eds.), *United Nations Convention on the Law of the Sea 1982: A Commentary*, Vol. II (Martinus Nijhoff 1993) 491.

5 United Nations Convention on the Law of the Sea (10 December 1982, in force 16 November 1994) 1833 UNTS 3.

6 Alexander Proelss, 'Article 55', in Alexander Proelss (ed.), *United Nations Convention on the Law of the Sea: A Commentary* (Hart 2017) 411.

2

Origins and Evolution of the Exclusive Economic Zone

The foundation of the exclusive economic zone (EEZ) regime, which has gone through a long evolutionary process, goes back as far as the earliest unilateral national claims to various marine natural resources beyond the limit of the territorial sea. The purpose here is not to recite exhaustively this history but to highlight certain characteristic features of State practice that are relevant to the evolution of the fundamental regime of the EEZ. The essential aim of the national claims beyond the territorial sea was for economic benefits without the intention to interrupt navigation and communication.

2.1 Early Claims to Marine Living Resources

2.1.1 Preferential Rights to Sedentary Species

Not long after the Dutchman Huge De Grotius published his treatise, *Mare Liberum*, in 1609, the doctrine of 'freedom of the seas' came to be generally accepted as the principle applicable to the high seas for more than three centuries.[1] Coastal State sovereignty, in contrast, was limited within a three-mile territorial water belt as commonly adopted since the end of the eighteenth century, with some States claiming different breadths.[2] Consequently, coastal States' rights did not in general extend beyond the three-mile limit, though there was a consensus favouring the

[1] Percy Thomas Fenn, Jr, 'Justinian and the Freedom of the Sea' (1925) 19 *Am J Int'l L* 716, 716–717; James B. Morell, *The Law of the Sea: An Historical Analysis of the 1982 Treaty and Its Rejection by the United States* (McFarland & Company 1992) 2.

[2] Thomas Baty, 'The Three-Mile Limit' (1928) 22 Am J Int'l L 503, 503; Thorsten Kalijarvi, 'Scandinavian Claims to Jurisdiction over Territorial Waters' (1932) 26 Am J Int'l L 57, 69; Shigeru Oda, 'The Territorial Sea and Natural Resources' (1955) 4 Int'l & Comp LQ 415, 420–421.

coastal State to reserve the exclusive right to exploit resources of the seabed located beyond and adjacent to its territorial sea.[3]

Even before the doctrine of the three-mile limit was widely established, Britain had extended its right over the resources located on the surface of the seabed. By the Cornwall Submarine Mines Act, the Parliament had, in 1858, committed itself to the position that the seabed below the low-water mark was vested in the Crown 'as part of the soil and territorial possessions of the Crown'.[4] Without affecting the navigational and fishing rights in the superjacent water and 'restricted by the silent abandonment of more extended claims', the property right over sedentary fisheries was not considered inconsistent with the universal right of freedom of the seas, and was declared by Hurst as 'entitled to be recognized by other States'.[5] Other examples include the claims of pearl and chank fisheries in the Gulf of Mannar and Palk Bay by littoral successive masters, the Irish claim with regard to oyster beds and the claim of the Bey of Tunis respecting sponge banks.[6]

The essence of such claims rests on the unique nature of the sedentary fisheries. Oyster, pearl-oyster, chank and sponge fisheries or any other form of sedentary fisheries connected with the bottom of the seabed 'have always been considered as on a different footing from floating fish'.[7] They have also been compared to 'crops on land'; that these resources are considered to be the fruit of the seabed, to be harvested by the sovereign of the adjacent land rather than caught like swimming fish.[8] However, the most convincing theory was the principle enunciated by Lord Hall, who claimed the right over seabed resources depended on long and effective possession in order to be valid.[9] It follows that ownership over

[3] Richard Young, 'Sedentary Fisheries and the Convention on the Continental Shelf' (1961) 55 Am J Int'l L 359, 360–362; FV Garcia-Amador, 'The Origins of the Concept of an Exclusive Economic Zone: Latin American Practice and Legislation', in Francisco Orrego Vicuña (ed.), *The Exclusive Economic Zone: A Latin American Perspective* (Westview 1984) 8.

[4] Cecil J. B. Hurst, 'Whose Is the Bed of the Sea? Sedentary Fisheries Outside the Three-Mile Limit' (1923–1924) 4 Brit YB Int'l L 34, 34.

[5] Ibid 42–43.

[6] Ibid 40–41; Andrea Gioia, 'Tunisia's Claims over Adjacent Seas and the Doctrine of "Historic Rights"' (1984) 11(2) Syr J Int'l L & Com 327, 339; Robin Churchill, Vaughan Lowe and Amy Sander, *The Law of the Sea* (4th ed., Manchester University Press 2022) 223–224.

[7] Thomas Wemyss Fulton, *The Sovereignty of the Sea* (Blackwood 1911) 696–697.

[8] Young (1961) 360–361.

[9] Hurst (1923–1924) 39; Hersch Lauterpacht, 'Sovereignty over Submarine Areas' (1950) 27 Br YB Int'l L 376, 415–433.

the seabed can be established and maintained by the coastal State as long as effective occupation continues; the produce obtained from sedentary fisheries that are situated in the soil of the seabed can be owned by the coastal State as a product of the soil.[10]

The fact that these claims related to certain living resources rather than to the seabed did not retrench their significance. It was acknowledged that sedentary fisheries were an exception to the rule that navigation and fishing on the high seas were free to all alike and ownership can be claimed by the adjacent coastal State where the species are located.[11] Recognising coastal State preferential rights to sedentary fisheries was the first step in the long chain of development to endorse the exclusive rights over marine resources beyond the limit of territorial waters.

2.1.2 The Bering Sea Fur-Seals Arbitrations

Coastal fisheries are the oldest and most important use of the ocean. Jurisdictional claims over floating fisheries beyond territorial waters, however, were not accepted by international society until the twentieth century.

After purchasing the territory of Alaska from Russia in 1867, the United States unilaterally adopted strict conservation measures toward the fur-seals found there, as they were largely diminished in number and seemed threatened with extinction. These measures included some penal statutes prohibiting all persons from killing seals in the Bering Sea, and all vessels whose crews were found violating such statutes were liable to seizure and forfeiture and the crews liable to fine and imprisonment. The application of these statutes since 1886 involved the seizure of several vessels owned by citizens of Great Britain, which resulted in protests from the British who asserted that such seizures were wholly unjustified under international law because they took place outside the three-mile limit of US territorial waters. The two countries eventually agreed to submit the matter to arbitration by a treaty signed on 29 February 1892.[12] The core question that arose before the arbitral tribunal was whether the

[10] Hurst (1923–1924) 40.

[11] Ibid 40; Young (1961) 360.

[12] Bering Sea Fur-Seals Case (Great Britain/United States of America), (1999) 1 International Environmental Law Reports 44–52; Award between the United States and the United Kingdom relating to the Rights of Jurisdiction of United States in the Bering's Sea and the Preservation of Fur Seals, 15 August 1893, Reports of International Arbitral Awards, Volume XXVIII, 263–276 (United Nations, 2007) https://legal.un.org/riaa/cases/vol_XXVIII/263-276.pdf.

United States had the right to enforce its domestic laws beyond the three-mile territorial waters.[13]

The United States defended its actions on three main grounds: first, it was entitled to claim jurisdiction over the Bering Sea either as successor to Russia in sovereignty over Alaska or in its own right; second, the United States had 'a right of protection and property in the fur-seals frequenting the Pribilov Islands when found outside the ordinary three-mile limit'; and third, it had the right to protect fur-seals as trustee on behalf of the common interest of all nations.[14] The arbitral tribunal first found that Russia never in fact asserted or exercised any exclusive jurisdiction or right beyond the ordinary limit of its territorial waters in the Bering Sea, and neither did Great Britain recognise or concede any such claims. The arbitral tribunal then found that the United States 'had no right of protection or property in fur-seals frequenting US islands in the Bering Sea when such seals were found outside the limits of the territorial sea'.[15] Nevertheless, the arbitral tribunal recognised the necessity to protect and preserve the fur-seals outside the jurisdictional limits in the Bering Sea, and responded to the request of the two parties to lay down concurrent regulations for the United States and Great Britain to apply.[16] Those regulations were regarding prohibitions of fishing areas and periods, vessels types, fishing methods and tools, and application scope.[17] This award indicated that although the coastal State had no right to claim protective jurisdiction over fisheries beyond its territorial waters, this was not a legal vacuum; rather protection and preservation measures on the high seas could be applied through international agreements with the flag State.

At the end of the eighteenth century, the unilateral property claim over free swimming fisheries beyond the three-mile limit was novel, and there was no legal foundation to support such a claim against the better-established principle of freedom of the seas. As Arbitrator Morgan stated, these questions were 'to be decided upon the existing state of the law, and finding no existing precedent in the international law, they did not feel

[13] Great Britain–United States of America, Treaty for Submitting to Arbitration the Questions Relating to the Seal Fisheries in Bering Sea, Washington, 29 February 1892, (1999) 1 International Environmental Law Reports 63, Article I.

[14] Bering Sea Fur-Seals Case 54–58.

[15] Ibid 60–61.

[16] Ibid 61.

[17] Ibid 70–73.

warranted in creating one'.[18] It was not a surprise when Russia seized a number of British and American vessels for taking fur-seals in the Bering Sea in 1892 that these seizures had been declared illegal by a new arbitral tribunal, 'since the jurisdiction of the State could not be extended beyond the territorial sea, unless by express convention'.[19]

It was apparent that States were tempted to make inroads upon the general principle of the freedom of the seas. However, these desires were confronted with the difficulties of breaking the absolute dichotomy of 'territorial sea' and 'high seas'. The increasing awareness of protecting and conserving the living resources in waters adjacent but outside territorial waters created an urge for States to deliberately break the traditional rules to bring about these changes.[20]

2.2 The 1930 Hague Codification Conference

2.2.1 State Practice Pre-1930

Driven by the intention to protect the interests of neutrality, defence, surveillance and conservation, coastal States were concerned to extend their jurisdiction over foreign vessels to a broader belt of sea, in some cases upon the high seas adjacent to their territorial waters.[21] However, as the doctrine of the 'freedom of the seas' had been so deeply rooted in international law, there was a natural reluctance to admit that the coastal State had the right to do so.[22] In the absence of a rule of international law fixing a specific extent of coastal State competence over marine areas, States took various measures to meet their own needs.[23]

Several European States made no claim to a single belt of territorial waters, but instead claimed jurisdictions over different limits of adjacent waters for different purposes.[24] France, for example, claimed a cannon-

[18] Ibid 79.

[19] Note Concerning Russia–United States of America Fur-Seals Dispute, (1999) 1 International Environmental Law Reports 84–88.

[20] Daniel P. O'Connell, *The International Law of the Sea*, Vol. I (Clarendon Press 1982) ix.

[21] Percy Thomas Fenn Jr, 'Origins of the Theory of Territorial Waters' (1926) 20 Am J Int'l L 465, 465–471.

[22] Philip C. Jessup, *The Law of Territorial Waters and Maritime Jurisdiction* (GA Jennings 1927) 75.

[23] Ibid 3–71; Oscar R. Houston, 'Freedom of the Seas: The Present State of International Law' (1956) 42 ABA J 235, 235–236.

[24] Alan V. Lowe, 'The Development of the Concept of the Contiguous Zone' (1981) 52 Brit YB Int'l L 109, 133.

shot zone for general and fishing purposes, and jurisdiction up to six miles for neutrality and up to twelve kilometres for customs supervision.[25] The hypothesis behind these claims was the doctrinal position adopted by La Pradelle that a State's maritime jurisdiction was merely a 'bundle of servitudes' based on a 'solid juridical principle derived from the inherent quality of being a coastal State', but which did not amount to sovereignty.[26] Similar positions can be observed from the practice of Belgium, Greece, Italy, Portugal, Spain and Türkiye, all of which made multiple claims to jurisdictional zones of different widths for different purposes.[27]

For States that explicitly accepted the three-mile limit as the breadth of territorial waters, there were two opposite positions: some States denied the existence of jurisdiction beyond the normal limit of territorial waters, while others insisted on exercising such jurisdiction.

In 1736, the British Parliament adopted the Hovering Acts, 'by which vessels with certain cargoes on board, destined for British ports, might be seized within four leagues of the British coast'.[28] But the case of the *Petit Jules*, a French smuggling vessel seized by the British Revenue about twenty-three miles off the Isle of Wight in 1850, was the last occasion on which Britain exercised jurisdiction beyond the three-mile limit over foreign vessels.[29] However, there were inconsistent practices respecting the limits of bays, where coastal State jurisdiction extended to a ten-mile-wide diameter measured between headlands.[30] In 1892, the Fishery Board of Scotland made a by-law closing the Moray Firth and prohibited the use of beam-trawl and otter-trawl by any person for herring fisheries therein. Conviction was obtained and upheld against Danish fisherman Mortensen in 1906, whose violation was found 'at a point within the Moray Firth, more than three miles from the shore, but to the west of a line drawn from Duncansby Head in Caithness to Rattray Point in Aberdeenshire, that being thereafter found within British Territory'.[31] In general, since mid-nineteenth century, British 'national policy had been to uphold the three-mile limit, and to protect against and resist the pretension of any foreign country to enforce its own jurisdiction on the

[25] O'Connell (1982) 121–122.
[26] Ibid 68–70.
[27] Lowe (1981) 135–137.
[28] Fulton (1911) 593.
[29] Lowe (1981) 111–113.
[30] O'Connell (1982) 367.
[31] 'Mortensen v. Peters (High Court of Justiciary of Scotland)' (1907) 1 Am J Int'l L 532.

sea beyond the three-mile limit'.[32] The above-discussed *Bering Sea Arbitration* was one of those examples.

Nevertheless, the steadfast British position was not without exceptions. Traditionally, the strict three-mile jurisdictional competence could be extended in very limited circumstances. It was admitted that the doctrine of 'constructive presence' allowed a wider application of the three-mile rule; for self-defence reasons, the British government reserved its right to extend its jurisdiction; and lastly, the doctrine of 'hot pursuit' was also recognised within a confined scope.[33] Furthermore, as the time drew near to an imminent international law codification conference, Britain softened its position by conditionally agreeing to several extended zones claimed by France and Spain.[34] In the Schedule of Points circulated in advance of the Hague Conference, the British reply indicated that it was prepared to recognise the extended jurisdiction beyond territorial waters through bilateral or multilateral agreements.[35]

The other tendency among the three-mile territorial sea group was that the coastal State in addition claimed a jurisdictional zone within which at least the exercise of certain rights touching on vital interests was reserved.[36] A good example was the liquor laws adopted by the United States in 1920s. By the Eighteenth Amendment to the Constitution, the United States prohibited the importation and exportation of intoxicating liquors for beverage purposes and enforced it on both US nationals and foreigners.[37] Although the US government vigorously maintained the three-mile limit as the extent of territorial waters, it nonetheless seized numerous hovering vessels beyond that limit.[38] Moreover, Congress passed the Tariff Act in 1922 claiming customs control over all ships, whether bound for US ports or not, within four leagues of the coast.[39] Other examples include various extended customs zones or policing zones claimed by Argentina, Chile, Ecuador, Egypt, Estonia and Norway.[40]

[32] O'Connell (1982) 367.
[33] Lowe (1981) 117–122.
[34] Ibid 129.
[35] Ibid 130–131.
[36] Winston Conrad Extavour, *The Exclusive Economic Zone: A Study of the Evolution and Progressive Development of the International Law of the Sea* (Institut universitaire de hautes études internationales 1979) 32.
[37] Jessup (1927) 211.
[38] Ibid 241–242.
[39] Ibid 212–213.
[40] Lowe (1981) 134–135.

Thus, by the 1900s there was a certain tendency towards endorsing the coastal State's extended jurisdiction beyond territorial waters with at least a certain enforcement jurisdiction recognised. That tendency had been observed, analysed and finally incorporated into the formal agenda of the 1930 Hague Conference.

2.2.2 *Failure to Secure an International Agreement*

The First Conference for the Codification of International Law, held at The Hague under the auspices of the League of Nations in 1930, appointed Committee II to study the bases of discussion drawn up by the Preparatory Committee regarding territorial waters.[41] Due to wide divergences among delegations, Committee II was unable to reach an agreement in respect of the fundamental question of the breadth of territorial waters, which necessarily affected the results of the examination of other points.[42] The work of Committee II, however, did not go to waste, as it clarified the legal status of the territorial sea and paved the way for continuing development on this issue.

During the discussions of Committee II, it was recognised that 'international law attributes to each Coastal State sovereignty over a belt of sea round its coasts' which is essential for protecting the legitimate interests of the coastal State.[43] It also adopted the term 'territorial sea' to describe the belt of sea over which the 'sovereignty' extends.[44] Such 'sovereignty' was subject to conditions prescribed by international law, and one important condition resulted from the right of innocent passage granted to the vessels of all States.[45] However, 'outside the one of sovereignty no right of exclusive economic enjoyment may be exercised'.[46]

41 'Official Documents: Conference for the Codification of International Law (Hague Conference), The Hague, 13 March 1930, Draft Rules of Procedure for the First Conference for the Codification of International Law, Article VI' (1930) 24(1) Am J Int'l L Sup 74, 75; Hunter Miller, 'The Hague Codification Conference' (1930) 24 (4) Am J Int'l L 674, 674–675.

42 'Official Documents: Hague Conference, Report of the Second Committee (Territorial Sea), Rapporteur: M. Francois' (1930) 24(3) Am J Int'l L Sup 234, 236.

43 Francois (1930) 234.

44 'Official Documents: Hague Conference, The Legal Status of the Territorial Sea, Article 1' (1930) 24(3) Am J Int'l L Sup 184, 184.

45 Ibid 'The Legal Status of the Territorial Sea, Article 3' 185.

46 Proelss, 'Article 55' (2017), 411.

Correspondent with the divergent State practice as discussed above, Committee II was sharply divided on the question of the breadth of territorial sea and the associated question of coastal States' jurisdiction in adjacent waters.[47] Freedom of navigation was of utter importance to all maritime powers, 'in their own interests they ought to favour the application of the principle by all possible means'.[48] Consequently, the conciliatory approach of acknowledging a jurisdictional zone beyond territorial waters to achieve wider acceptance of the three-mile rule proposed by the Preparatory Committee was not well received at Committee II.[49] Among those States that favoured an additional jurisdictional zone beyond the territorial sea, the purposes of customs and defence were mostly accepted; only four delegations advocated extension of the scope to include fishing interests, namely Portugal, Belgium, Iceland and Denmark.[50] As a result, the Hague Conference merely adopted a recommendation that recognised the necessity of protecting the various products of the sea in the waters beyond the territorial sea, and affirmed the importance of measures of protection and collaboration to safeguard 'the riches constituting the common patrimony'.[51]

When Committee II concluded that it was unable to reach a convention on the territorial sea, the intention was to invite various States to continue exploring the question further and to reconvene a new conference as soon as was opportune.[52] At that time, the idea of certain jurisdictions existing separately from the notion of the territorial sea had emerged but was not widely accepted at the international level. As subsequent State practice showed, the divisions arising from previous claims over the adjacent waters would continue until an acceptable agreement was reached.

[47] 'Official Documents: Hague Conference, Territorial Waters, Extract from the Provisional Minutes of the Thirteenth Meeting Held on Thursday, April 3, 1930' (1930) 24(3) Am J Int'l L Sup 253.

[48] Francois (1930) 234.

[49] 'Official Documents: Hague Conference, Bases of Discussion Drawn up for the Conference by the Preparatory Committee, II Territorial Waters, Point III Breadth of the Territorial Waters' (1930) 24(1) Am J Int'l L Sup 25, 27–29.

[50] Garcia-Amador (1984) 11–12.

[51] 'Official Documents: Hague Conference, Conference for the Codification of International Law Final Act, Recommendation Concerning the Protection of Fisheries' (1930) 24(3) Am J Int'l L Sup 169, 187–188.

[52] 'Official Documents: Hague Conference, Conference for the Codification of International Law Final Act, Resolution' (1930) 24(3) Am J Int'l L Sup 169, 184.

2.3 Early Initiatives for a 200-Mile Maritime Zone

2.3.1 The Truman Proclamations

Aware of the necessity for preserving 'an augmented supply of natural resources' and conserving near-shore fisheries and acknowledging the inadequacy of the narrow extent of territorial waters for such purposes, the United States took unilateral measures to create new rules.[53] Two proclamations issued simultaneously by US President Truman on 28 September 1945, the Continental Shelf Proclamation and the Fisheries Proclamation, which opened the door for claims of coastal State jurisdiction over the high seas.[54]

The Continental Shelf Proclamation asserted jurisdiction and control over 'the natural resources of the subsoil and seabed of the continental shelf beneath the high seas but contiguous to the coasts of the [United States]', as they were regarded as 'appertaining to' the coastal State.[55] The United States had adopted the three-mile limit as the breadth of territorial waters and did not show any desire to challenge it before the late 1930s, except by enforcing jurisdiction under the liquor laws adopted during the Prohibition period in the 1920s.[56] Thus, it was admitted from the beginning that this proposal was 'to evolve new concepts of maritime territorial limits beyond three miles, and of rights to occupy and exploit the surface and subsoil of the open sea'.[57] The United States claimed to base its policy on the propositions that the continental shelf may be regarded as *ipso jure* appurtenant to its territory on geographic and geomorphological grounds, and that the resources therein were affected

[53] United States Department of State (US DOS), 'Formulation of United States Policy on the Resources of the Continental Shelf and on Coastal Fisheries', Foreign Relations of the United States: Diplomatic Papers, 1945, General: Political and Economic Matters, Volume 2, 1481–1482, 1521, http://digital.library.wisc.edu/1711.dl/FRUS.FRUS1945v02; David J Attard, *The Exclusive Economic Zone in International Law* (Clarendon Press 1987) 1.

[54] 'Official Documents – United States (US): Proclamation by the President with Respect to the Natural Resources of the Subsoil and Seabed of the Continental Shelf', 'Proclamation by the President with Respect to Coastal Fisheries in Certain Areas of the High Seas' (1946) 40(1) Am J Int'l L Sup 45–47; George V. Galdorisi and Alan G. Kaufman, 'Military Activities in the Exclusive Economic Zone: Preventing Uncertainty and Defusing Conflict' (2001–2002) 32 Cal W Int'l L J 253, 258.

[55] United States, 'Proclamation by the President with Respect to the Natural Resources of the Subsoil and Seabed of the Continental Shelf' 46.

[56] James R. Crawford, 'International Law on a Given Day', in James Crawford, *International Law as An Open System: Selected Essays* (Cameron May 2002) 80–81.

[57] US DOS, 'Formulation of United States Policy' 1481.

by and dependent upon coastal State activities; therefore, it was reasonable for the United States to exercise 'special jurisdictional and property rights in particular areas of the bed or subsoil of the high seas', as well as for the purposes of 'self-protection and as a matter of national defense'.[58]

The effect of the Fisheries Proclamation was to assert 'the policy of establishing conservation zones for the protection of fishery resources' in certain areas of the high seas contiguous to the coasts of the United States 'wherein fishing activities have been or in the future may be developed and maintained on a substantial scale'.[59] The United States reserved exclusive regulation and control over such conservation zones where fishing activities were conducted by its nationals only, while establishing and applying joint regulation and control in areas where fishing activities were conducted by nationals of other States.[60] Bearing in mind previous failed claims over the Bering Sea fur-seals discussed above, the Fisheries Proclamation was asserted on 'the premise that reasonable and just bases for the exercise of jurisdiction over the fisheries of an area of the high seas in the vicinity of the coasts of a state' exist.[61] It not only recognised the right of other States to establish conservation zones off their coasts on a reciprocal basis, but also explicitly ensured that the high seas status of the areas in which such zones were established and freedom of navigation were in no way affected.[62]

In order to prevent protests from other States, the United States conducted international consultations with twelve foreign governments whose interests might be affected before the proclamations were made.[63] For the Fisheries Proclamation in particular, the United States emphasised that it had no intention of extending the breadth of territorial waters or excluding foreign nationals, but rather was establishing clearly defined conservation zones in areas of the high seas contiguous to the coasts for conservation and protection purposes.[64] Iceland and Cuba gave definitive replies regarding the Fisheries Proclamation; the British

[58] Ibid 1500–1502.

[59] Ibid 1503; United States, 'Proclamation by the President with Respect to Coastal Fisheries in Certain Areas of the High Seas' 47.

[60] United States, 'Proclamation by the President with Respect to Coastal Fisheries in Certain Areas of the High Seas' 47.

[61] US DOS, 'Formulation of United States Policy' 1498.

[62] United States, 'Proclamation by the President with Respect to Coastal Fisheries in Certain Areas of the High Seas' 47.

[63] US DOS, 'Formulation of United States Policy' 1486–1487.

[64] Ibid 1499, 1507, 1515.

reluctantly accepted the Fisheries Proclamation, but welcomed the Continental Shelf Proclamation; Canada did not reply due to an imminent election, but from earlier dealings and the special relationship with the United States, it would likely have accepted the Fisheries Proclamation.[65] Therefore, although such proclamations were clearly tantamount to an infringement of the existing general freedom of the high seas, they were not met by widespread protests.

Other factors contributed to the success of the Truman Proclamations. As technology advanced, methods of industrial-scale fishing developed progressively, resulting in more intensified exploitation, which caused a rapid depletion of certain marine resources, such as tuna, salmon and whales in the Pacific.[66] In contrast, under the then international law, coastal State competence was limited to a narrow belt of territorial waters, which precluded coastal States from excluding foreign fishing vessels from the waters further offshore. Moreover, with modern technological progress, the utilisation of submarine areas for oil wells and mines was already practicable in the 1940s. The need for a basis for the extension of jurisdiction for a reasonable distance beyond territorial waters was accordingly recognised by coastal States.[67] Furthermore, far away from the European battlefield, the United States was able to develop its national economy, science and technology, thereby building up its strength to take the lead in post-war reconstruction.[68] As a result, when these two ground-breaking proclamations were published, they were generally accepted and widely followed.[69]

2.3.2 Latin American Practice

Unlike their moderate precedent, the maritime claims made by Latin American States following the Truman Proclamations were more

[65] Ibid 1493–1495, 1511–1514, 1523–1524, 1527.

[66] Ann L. Hollick, 'US Ocean Policy: The Truman Proclamations' (1976) 17(1) Va J Int'l L 23, 25.

[67] Robert B. Krueger and Myron H. Nordquist, 'The Evolution of the 200-Mile Exclusive Economic Zone: State Practice in the Pacific Basin' (1978-1979) 19(2) Va J Int'l L 321, 325.

[68] Crawford (2002) 91.

[69] Lewis M. Alexander, 'The Ocean Enclosure Movement: Inventory and Prospect' (1982–1983) 20(3) San Diego L Rev 561, 565; Attard (1987) 2–3; Krueger and Nordquist (1978–1979) 325–328; Daniel Margolies, 'Jurisdiction in Offshore Submerged Lands and the Significance of the Truman Proclamation in Post war U.S. Foreign Policy' (2020) 44(3) Diplomatic History 447, 448–451.

ambitious. With the end of the Second World War, Latin American States were facing resumed competition from industrial-scale fishing and whaling by foreign fleets in the South Pacific Ocean and the Antarctic Zone.[70] In addition, the geographical fact that a deep abyss along the west coast of South America causes the seabed to plunge abruptly before it rises to an offshore plateau, made the ordinary doctrine of the continental shelf irrelevant to some States.[71] In searching for alternative protections, some of the national decrees and proclamations attempted to claim sovereignty over the continental shelf and the superjacent waters to a minimum distance of 200 nautical miles (NM) measured from the baselines.[72]

As an immediate successor, the Mexican Presidential Declaration in 1945 laid claim to 'the whole of the continental platform or shelf adjoining its coastline and to each and all of the natural resources existing there, whether known or unknown' based on the grounds that the land forming the continental plateau rests on the continental shelf that 'clearly forms an integral part of the continental countries'.[73] With regard to fishing resources, with which the coastal State has been 'endowed by nature', their protection 'should consist in the extension of control and supervision by the State to the places and zones . . . irrespective of their distance from the coast'.[74] Mexico claimed exclusive rights over the fisheries resources and incorporated the continental shelf into its territory, rather than merely claiming jurisdiction and control of the natural resources therein. Nonetheless, it still recognised the lawful rights of third parties on a reciprocal basis and preserved the freedom of navigation.[75]

In order to protect the offshore fisheries effectively, Chile took the initiative in proclaiming a 200 NM sovereign maritime zone by Presidential Declaration in 1947, which was immediately followed by Peruvian Presidential Decree No. 781.[76] Both Chile and Peru asserted 'national sovereignty', or (in the language of the Peruvian Decree)

[70] Pilar Armanet, 'The Economic Interest Underlying the First Declaration on a Maritime Zone', in Orrego Vicuña (1984) 28.

[71] O'Connell (1982) 555.

[72] The claims were not consistent with the use of unit of measurement, this chapter only use nautical miles (NM) when the original documents so indicate.

[73] 'Mexico – Presidential Declaration with Respect to Continental Shelf, 29 October 1945', in Laws and Regulations on the Regime of the High Seas (United Nations, ST/LEG/SER.B/1, 11 January 1951), 13–14.

[74] Ibid.

[75] Ibid.

[76] 'Chile – Presidential Declaration Concerning Continental Shelf, 23 June 1947', 'Peru – Presidential Decree No. 781, Concerning Submerged Continental or Insular Shelf,

'national sovereignty and jurisdiction', over the continental shelf and the adjacent seas, regardless of depth, for preserving, protecting and exploiting the natural resources.[77] By virtue of these proclamations, coastal protection and control over the adjacent seas were immediately extended to a distance of 200 NM measured from the coastlines without affecting 'the rights of free navigation on the high seas'.[78] This single comprehensive claim of sovereignty over the continental shelf and its superjacent waters clearly went beyond the scope of the Truman Proclamations.[79] Nevertheless, similar claims beyond the limit of the territorial waters were declared by Argentina, Costa Rica, Cuba, El Salvador, Honduras, Iceland, Nicaragua, Panama, and Saudi Arabia.[80]

In order to consolidate their positions with respect to the new 200 NM maritime zone, Chile, Ecuador and Peru, all countries which had no continual continental shelf, signed a joint Declaration on the Maritime Zone in 1952 (Santiago Declaration) to claim sole right based on distance.[81] They declared that each State 'possesses exclusive sovereignty and jurisdiction over the sea along the coasts of their respective countries to a minimum distance of 200 nautical miles from the coasts', including 'the seabed and the subsoil thereof'.[82] There were controversial

1 August 1947', in Laws and Regulations on the Regime of the High Seas (United Nations, ST/LEG/SER.B/1, 11 January 1951), 6–7, 16–17.

77 'Chile – Presidential Declaration Concerning Continental Shelf', para (1); 'Peru – Presidential Decree No. 781', para 1.

78 'Chile – Presidential Declaration Concerning Continental Shelf', para (3); 'Peru – Presidential Decree No. 781', para 3.

79 Attard (1987) 6; Maritime Dispute (Peru v. Chile), Judgment, ICJ Reports 2014, p. 3, para 26.

80 'Costa Rica – Decree-Law No. 803, Concerning Continental and Insular Shelf, 2 November 1949', 'El Salvador – Political Constitution, 7 September 1950', 'Honduras – Congressional Decree No. 25, 17 January 1951', 'Iceland – Law No.44 Concerning the Scientific Conservation of the Continental Shelf Fisheries, 5 April 1948', in Laws and Regulations on the Regime of the High Seas (United Nations, ST/LEG/SER.B/1, 11 January 1951) 9–10, 300–303, 12–13; Richard Young, 'Recent Developments with respect to the Continental Shelf' (1948) 42 Am J Int'l L 849, 850–855; 'Rights Claimed by Littoral States in Adjacent Seas: Claims to the Continental Shelf' (1948–1949) 46 Int'l Law Stud 182 https://digital-commons.usnwc.edu/ils/vol46/iss1/29/.

81 Statement by HS Amerasinghe, 'The Third United Nations Conference on the Law of the Sea', in Myron H Nordquist (ed), *United Nations Convention on the Law of the Sea 1982: A Commentary*, Vol. I (Martinus Nijhoff 1985) 2.

82 Declaration on the Maritime Zone (Santiago Declaration), 18 August 1952, Articles II–IV, www.un.org/Depts/los/LEGISLATIONANDTREATIES/PDFFILES/TREATIES/CHL-ECU-PER1952MZ.PDF.

interpretations with regard to the character of the 'maritime zone' established by this Santiago Declaration. Although it used the phrase 'exclusive sovereignty and jurisdiction', the purpose of establishing such zones was solely for 'the conservation, development and exploitation of these resources, to which the coastal countries are entitled'.[83] In addition, the Santiago Declaration allowed 'innocent and inoffensive passage through the area indicated for ships of all nations', which was different from the preserved freedom of navigation beyond the limit of the territorial sea made in their individual national decrees.[84] This supports the assumption that the Santiago Declaration was proposing a special maritime zone that incorporates exclusive rights over all resources found in this area, with limited recognition for the freedom of navigation that is inoffensive to such economic purposes.[85]

The Latin American practices appeared to diverge significantly in scope and character from the Truman Proclamations, in particular with regard to the claims of sovereignty and jurisdiction to a 200 NM maritime zone. These unilateral claims, as well as the first international instrument in this respect, the Santiago Declaration, served as the foundation for subsequent developments in the international law of the sea and constituted a major source of inspiration for the concept of the EEZ.[86]

2.4 Development of the Exclusive Economic Zone Concept

2.4.1 The 1958 and 1960 Law of the Sea Conferences

The trend of extending coastal State jurisdiction up to a 200-mile maritime zone, which emerged and developed after the Second World War, gained little support at both the First and Second United Nations Conferences on the Law of the Sea, held in Geneva in 1958 and 1960 respectively.[87]

At its first session in 1949, the International Law Commission (ILC) incorporated the high seas and the territorial waters as topics whose codification were considered as 'necessary or desirable'.[88] The

[83] Ibid Article I.
[84] Ibid Article V.
[85] Francisco Orrego Vicuña, The Exclusive Economic Zone: Regime and Legal Nature under International Law (Cambridge University Press 1989)
[86] Garcia-Amador (1984) 7, 23; Extavour (1979) 57.
[87] United Nations, Codification Division Publications, Diplomatic Conferences, https://legal.un.org/diplomaticconferences/.
[88] 'Report of the International Law Commission to the United Nations General Assembly' (1949) 1 YB ILC 280.

Chairman observed the emerging State practice of establishing reserved zones for the preservation of fisheries that may affect 'the sea approaches to various territories' in spite of 'the time-honoured principle of the freedom of the high seas'.[89] The ILC's work accumulated into a draft of Articles Concerning the Law of the Sea adopted in 1956 (ILC Draft Articles), comprising 73 articles dealing with territorial waters and high seas (including high seas fisheries), as well as the continental shelf.[90]

At the ILC, the idea of endorsing a separate exclusive fishery right to the coastal State beyond the territorial sea limit was strongly resisted, while the freedom of fishing was explicitly preserved.[91] Nevertheless, the concept of the continental shelf was accepted. It was defined as 'the seabed and subsoil of the submarine areas adjacent to the coast but outside the area of the territorial sea, to a depth of 200 meters or, beyond that limit, to where the depth of the superjacent waters admits of the exploitation', where the coastal State had 'sovereign rights for the purpose of exploring and exploiting its natural resources'.[92] It was also confirmed that the sovereign rights 'over the continental shelf do not affect the legal status of the superjacent waters as high seas'.[93] The ILC Draft Articles demonstrated the tension between the coastal State claims and the freedom of the seas in the 1950s, which denied the previous proclamations of sovereignty and exclusive jurisdiction made by Latin American States and paved the way for the 1958 First Geneva Conference.

Among the four Conventions adopted at the 1958 First Geneva Conference, there was no recognition of a separate jurisdictional zone for fishery interests. The Territorial Sea and the Contiguous Zone Convention adopted a 12-mile contiguous zone as an independent regime of the territorial sea, where the coastal State has enforcement jurisdiction to prevent and punish 'infringement of its customs, fiscal, immigration or sanitary regulations within its territory or territorial sea'.[94] This provision signified that the contiguous zone was unrelated to fisheries. In addition, the High Seas Convention defined the high seas as 'all parts of the sea that are not included in the territorial sea or in the

[89] Ibid 43; Extavour (1979) 101.

[90] 'Report of the International Law Commission to the United Nations General Assembly, A/3159, Articles Concerning the Law of the Sea' (1956) 2 YB ILC 265.

[91] Ibid Article 27.

[92] Ibid Articles 67–68.

[93] Ibid Article 69.

[94] Convention on the Territorial Sea and the Contiguous Zone (29 April 1958, in force 10 September 1964) 516 UNTS 205, Article 24.

internal waters of a state', plainly declaring that the water column of the contiguous zone and above the continental shelf has the same legal status as the high seas.[95] Therefore, within the contiguous zone 'no state may validly purport to subject any part of them to its sovereignty', thereby preserving the freedoms of navigation and fishing.[96] Nevertheless, the Fisheries Convention recognised that the coastal State has 'a special interest in the maintenance of the productivity of the living resources in any area of the high seas adjacent to its territorial sea' and that it could 'adopt unilateral measures of conservation' to this end when fulfilling the requirements of prior consultation, urgent need, scientific support and non-discrimination.[97] Though this 'special interest' was significantly different from the extensive claims made by some Latin American States, it was the first modification of the freedom of fishing on the high seas and to some degree paved the way for extended coastal State jurisdiction over fisheries beyond the territorial sea.

In contrast, the emerging doctrine of the continental shelf had matured to be accepted on the international level and provided a victory for those seeking extended coastal State competence. The Continental Shelf Convention recognised the coastal State's sovereign rights over the continental shelf 'for the purpose of exploring it and exploiting its natural resources', including 'the mineral and other non-living resources of the seabed and subsoil together with living organisms belonging to sedentary species'.[98] Moreover, such rights 'do not affect the legal status of the superjacent waters as high seas', which undoubtedly did not constitute the right as one of 'sovereignty'.[99]

It is noteworthy that the 1958 First Geneva Conference took a tentative move to recognise certain rights of the coastal State beyond the territorial sea, but State practice was not yet mature enough to reach a consensus except for on the matter of the continental shelf. As the 1958 First Geneva Conference adjourned, there was a general understanding that there should be a second law of the sea conference to continue to work on the two unsolved questions, namely, the breadth of the territorial sea and

95 Convention on the High Seas (29 April 1958, in force 30 September 1962) 450 UNTS 11, Article 1.
96 Ibid Article 2.
97 Convention on Fishing and Conservation of the Living Resources of the High Seas (29 April 1958, in force 20 March 1966) 559 UNTS 285, Articles 6(1), 7.
98 Convention on the Continental Shelf (29 April 1958, in force 10 June 1964) 499 UNTS 311, Articles 2(1), 2(4).
99 Ibid Article 3.

the extent of the exclusive fisheries jurisdiction beyond the territorial sea.[100] Most proposals received at the 1960 Second Geneva Conference envisaged a narrow breadth of the territorial sea accompanied by a narrow fishery zone that was beyond and adjacent to the territorial sea, 'coupled with a phasing out of foreign fishing activity' therein.[101] One notable proposal was a so-called six-and-six formula co-sponsored by the United States and Canada that proposed a six-mile territorial sea with a further six-mile fishing zone where the coastal State 'shall have the same rights in respect of fishing and exploitation of the living resources of the sea as it has in its territorial sea'.[102] However, this proposal fell one vote short of the two-thirds majority necessary for adoption.[103]

It is clear that, after the Second World War, State practice took a shift towards the acceptance of extended coastal State rights over the maritime areas beyond and adjacent to the territorial sea, in particular the recognition of the doctrine of the continental shelf. Although exclusive fisheries jurisdiction beyond the territorial sea was not accepted, neither was the 200-mile single maritime zone claimed by the Latin American States. The work of the two Geneva Conferences was decisive for the development of the law of the sea in the period thereafter.

2.4.2 Post-Geneva Developments

The law of the sea was developed in the broader context of the international relations that witnessed the political, social and economic changes after the Second World War. One of the most decisive events has been the disintegration of the colonial empires and the birth of scores of a large number of new States that carry with them a legacy of resentment over their past status and a host of issues relating to their development.[104] In seeking to establish their national identity on the international stage,

[100] United Nations General Assembly (UNGA), Res 1307 (XIII), 10 December 1958, Convening of A Second United Nations Conference on the Law of the Sea.

[101] Nordquist, Nandan and Rosenne (1993) 495.

[102] Ibid; Second United Nations Conference on the Law of the Sea, A/CONF.19/L.11, 22 April 1960, 'Canada and United States of America: proposal'.

[103] Second United Nations Conference on the Law of the Sea, Official Records, Vol. I: Summary Records, Annexes and Final Act, A/CONF.19/SR.13, 26 April 1960, Thirteenth Plenary Meeting, 30.

[104] UNGA, Res 1514 (XV), 14 December 1960, Declaration on the Granting of Independence to Colonial Countries and Peoples; Malcolm N Shaw, *International Law* (8th ed., Cambridge University Press 2017) 28.

these new States were eager to embrace the ideas of the sovereignty and equality of States, and to support the right of permanent sovereignty over natural resources.[105] Their needs are manifested in the issues of national claims over natural resources in the adjacent maritime areas that came to shape the legal order for the ocean.[106]

Following the two Geneva Conferences, there was a renewed trend of coastal States to extend their claims of the breadth of the territorial sea or over specific rights or jurisdiction in the areas beyond the territorial sea.[107] For most coastal States that were actively engaged in this process, the primary drive was to preserve their fishing rights from the growing interests of distant-water fishing States.[108] A few notable practices emerged in this period. First, States quickly adopted the practice of extending the breadth of their territorial sea to 12 NM.[109] Second, in the absence of general rules regulating fishery rights, States' claims diverged between a 12-mile fishery zone up to 200-mile fishery zone, with numerous different breadths in between, for the purpose of asserting fisheries jurisdiction or other extensive rights.[110] Third, States concluded bilateral and multilateral instruments to secure recognition of their claims.

In Europe, there were emerging attempts to increase fisheries jurisdiction beyond the territorial sea. The inconsistent national practice, however, had led to the arrest of a number of fishing vessels and provoked conflicts among several States with some of the disputes been brought to the International Court of Justice (ICJ). In 1964, twelve European States signed a Fisheries Convention, *inter alia*, providing that each 'coastal State has the exclusive right to fish and exclusive jurisdiction in matters of fisheries within the belt of six miles measured from the baseline of its

105 UNGA, Res 1803 (XVII), 14 December 1962, Permanent Sovereignty over Natural Resources; Shaw (2017) 29.

106 Satya N. Nandan with Kristine E. Dalaker, *Reflections on the Making of the Modern Law of the Sea* (National University of Singapore 2021) 31–32.

107 Nordquist, Nandan and Rosenne (1993) 495.

108 Tommy Koh, *Building a New Legal Order for the Oceans* (National University of Singapore 2020) 270–282; Margaret A. Yong, 'A Quiet Revolution: The Exclusivity of Exclusive Economic Zone', in Kim Rubenstein (ed.), *Traversing Divides: Honouring Deborah Cas's Contribution to Public and International Law* (Australian National University Press 2021) 62–63.

109 Extavour (1979) 128.

110 Ibid 165–167; David Harris and Sandesh Sivakumaran, *Cases and Materials on International Law* (8th ed, Sweet & Maxwell 2015) 391–392; Churchill, Lowe and Sander (2022) 522–526.

territorial sea', and reserving the right to fish to only the coastal State and certain habitual fishing contracting parties in the belt between six and twelve miles from the baseline.[111] This was an effort to reconcile the desire of coastal States to extend their jurisdiction over a greater portion of the sea but still preserve the fishing rights of other interested States on a regional level.

More extensive claims emerged in Latin America, where States had extended their jurisdiction over the adjacent seas to distances greater than 12 miles. Brazil, for instance, extended its territorial sea to 200 NM, while granting ships of all other nations the right of innocent passage.[112] Similar claims to a 200-mile jurisdictional zone were made by Ecuador,[113] El Salvador,[114] Nicaragua[115] and Panama.[116] Among the 200 miles claimants, Uruguay established two well-distinguished legal regimes in this zone. By Decree 604/969 and the Fisheries Act Law No. 13833, both adopted on 3 December 1969, Uruguay extended its territorial sea to 200 miles: within the inner zone of 12 miles, it reserved the exclusive right to exploit the natural resources, and ships of all nations enjoyed the right of innocent passage; in the remaining 188 miles, the freedom of navigation and overflight were retained and fishing activities were permitted under certain conditions.[117] This regime served as an example of the functional approach to claim maritime jurisdiction, and it became the closest approximation to the nascent concept of the EEZ.

[111] Fisheries Convention (adopted London, 9 March/10 April 1964, entered into force 15 March 1966) Articles 2–3, Contracting Parties are Austria, Belgium, Denmark, the French Republic, the Federal Republic of Germany, Ireland, Italy, Luxembourg, the Netherlands, Portugal, Spain, Sweden and the United Kingdom of Great Britain and Northern Ireland, https://assets.publishing.service.gov.uk/media/5a7c6f4bed915d696ccfcc12/Fisheries_Conv_March-April_1964.pdf.

[112] 'Brazil, Decree Law No. 1098 of 25 March, 1970', in S Houston Lay, Robin Churchill and Myron Nordquist (eds), New Directions in the Law of the Sea, Documents Volume I (New York 1973) 15.

[113] Ecuador, Civil Code as amended by Decree No.256-CLP of 27 February 1970 (1), Article 628, www.un.org/Depts/los/LEGISLATIONANDTREATIES/PDFFILES/ECU_1970_Code.pdf.

[114] El Salvador, Constitution of 13 December 1983, Article 84, www.un.org/Depts/los/LEGISLATIONANDTREATIES/PDFFILES/SLV_1983_Constitution.pdf.

[115] Nicaragua, Act No. 205 of 19 December 1979 on the Continental Shelf and Adjacent Sea, Article 2, www.un.org/Depts/los/LEGISLATIONANDTREATIES/PDFFILES/NIC_1979_Act.pdf.

[116] Panama, Act No.31 of 2 February 1967, Article 1, www.un.org/Depts/los/LEGISLATIONANDTREATIES/PDFFILES/PAN_1967_Act.pdf.

[117] Extavour (1979) 139–140; Attard (1987) 17–18.

The claimant States supplemented their unilateral claims by a series of regional declarations to consolidate their positions in response to the movement within the United Nations towards the convocation of a third law of the sea conference.[118] The States involved in this revival were mainly newly independent developing countries of Latin America, Africa and Asia. For the Latin American States, this was an inevitable phase in the continuous process of evolution of their unilateral claims, while most newly independent States in Africa and Asia were making their first contribution to the development of international law that could meet their special needs and even form part of a new international economic order.[119]

The Latin American States consolidated their positions on the 200-mile zone in two multilateral declarations adopted in 1970. The first meeting, attended by nine States that claimed a 200-mile zone, unanimously adopted the Montevideo Declaration.[120] The subsequent meeting was intended to embrace all the States of the Latin America and Caribbean regions, with the aim of co-ordinating a common position based on the maritime policy agreed upon at the previous meeting, and 14 of the 20 participating States signed the Lima Declaration.[121] Both Declarations recognised the 'geographical, economic and social link between the sea, the land, and man who inhabits it', expressed concern over the 'abusive practice in the extraction of marine resources' and the 'disturbance of the ecological balance', and affirmed that each coastal State has the sovereign right over its natural resources.[122] Accordingly, the coastal State had the right to establish the limits of its maritime sovereignty or jurisdiction in accordance with reasonable criteria, to take control of the marine resources within, and to exercise other jurisdiction without prejudice to the freedom of navigation and overflight enjoyed by all States.[123] The Declarations endowed the coastal State with the right to decide its maritime jurisdiction limit – not to seek sovereignty for the sake of territorial expansion, but to accomplish the need to protect and utilise the natural resources for its own economic benefit.

118 Attard (1987) 15–17.
119 Extavour (1979) 143–145; Shaw (2017) 30.
120 Montevideo Declaration on the Law of the Sea, 8 May 1970, signed by Argentina, Brazil, Chile, Ecuador, El Salvador, Panama, Peru, Nicaragua, and Uruguay, (1970) 9(5) ILM 1081 (Montevideo Declaration).
121 Declaration of the Latin American States on the Law of the Sea, 8 August 1970, (1971) 10 (2) ILM 207 (Lima Declaration).
122 Montevideo Declaration, Preamble; Lima Declaration, Preamble.
123 Montevideo Declaration, paras 2, 6; Lima Declaration, paras 2–3.

The 200-mile maritime zone was refined in the Santo Domingo Declaration by a number of Caribbean States as the 'patrimonial sea', extending to a maximum of 200 NM, in which the coastal State had 'sovereign rights over the renewable and non-renewable natural resources, which are found in the waters, in the seabed and in the subsoil', instead of sovereignty over the sea itself.[124] Freedom of navigation, overflight and the laying of submarine cables and pipelines of all States were recognised 'with no restrictions other than those resulting from the exercise by the Coastal State of its rights within the area'.[125] The concept of 'patrimonial sea' was one of the immediate precursors of the EEZ, in the sense that it emphasised the economic interests of the coastal State over the natural resources, rather than the extension of jurisdiction for territorial purposes, while maintaining respect for the high seas freedoms of all other States.[126]

The newly independent States in Africa also faced a serious threat to their offshore fisheries due to over-exploitation by foreign distant-water fishing fleets, which brought them closer to the Latin American practice of protecting such natural resources.[127] Inspired by their participation in the Lima Conference, State members of the Asian-African Legal Consultative Committee included the subject of the law of the sea on the agenda for the 1971 Colombo session that set up a working group to consider related issues.[128] At the 1972 Lagos session, Kenya presented a working paper on 'the Exclusive Economic Zone Concept', which attempted to safeguard the coastal State's economic interests without interfering unduly in other States' legitimate interests in navigation.[129] This concept embodied a relatively narrow belt of territorial sea of 12 miles, supplemented by the exclusive right of coastal States for economic purposes in a wider zone up to a maximum distance of 200 NM from the

[124] Declaration of Specialized Conference on Problems of the Sea, 9 June 1972, (1972) 11(4) ILM 892, Patrimonial Sea, paras 1, 3 (Santo Domingo Declaration).

[125] Ibid Patrimonial Sea, para 5.

[126] Satya N. Nandan, 'The Exclusive Economic Zone: A Historical Perspective', in *The Law and the Sea: Essays in Memory of Jean Carroz* (United Nations Food and Agriculture Organization 1987), www.fao.org/docrep/s5280t/s5280t0p.htm.

[127] Attard (1987) 20–21; Koh (2021) 280–282.

[128] 'Report on the 13th Session of the Asian-African Legal Consultative Committee, 17 May 1972' (1972) 2 YB ILC 216; Julio Cesar Lupinacci, 'The Legal Status of the Exclusive Economic Zone in the 1982 Convention on the Law of the Sea', in Orrego Vicuña (1984) 88; Nandan (1987).

[129] 'Kenyan Draft Articles on the Concept of an Exclusive Economic Zone beyond the Territorial Sea, 7 August 1972' (1973) 12(1) ILM 33.

baselines.[130] This proposal received widespread support within the meeting, and encouraged States to explore this pattern further.[131]

A unified position on this economic zone was presented in the final Report of the African States Regional Seminar on the Law of the Sea in 1972.[132] This Report acknowledged that the coastal State has the right to determine the limits of its maritime jurisdiction, where it has the right to establish beyond the 12 NM territorial sea an economic zone over which it will have an exclusive jurisdiction for the exploitation of the living resources and pollution control, while other States enjoy the freedom of navigation, overflight and the laying of submarine cables and pipelines.[133]

The EEZ concept was further strengthened by the Declaration of the Organization of African Unity on the Issues of the Law of the Sea (OAU Declaration) as the general position of the African States at the newly convened conference on the law of the sea.[134] The OAU Declaration recognised 'the right of each coastal State to establish an [EEZ] beyond their territorial seas whose limits shall not exceed 200[NM]', within which it 'shall exercise permanent sovereignty over all the living and mineral resources and shall manage the zone without undue interference with the other legitimate uses of the sea, namely, freedom of navigation, overflight and laying of cables and pipelines'.[135] The OAU Declaration was incorporated into a proposal entitled Draft Articles on Exclusive Economic Zone and presented to the Sea-Bed Committee in 1973.[136]

2.5 Conclusion

The origins and evolution of the EEZ concept demonstrated beyond doubt that the intention of the extended coastal State claims is to satisfy economic interests while not unduly interrupting the high seas freedoms.

[130] Ibid Articles I–II, VII; Shigeru Oda, *The Law of the Sea in Our Time II: The United Nations Seabed Committee, 1968–1973* (Sijthoff Leyden 1977) 215–216.

[131] Report on the 13th Session of the Asian-African Legal Consultative Committee 217.

[132] 'African States: Conclusions of the Regional Seminar on the Law of the Sea, 30 June 1972' (1973) 12(1) ILM 210.

[133] Ibid para 1(a)(1)–(3).

[134] Third United Nations Conference on the Law of the Sea, Official Records, Vol. III: Documents, A/CONF.62/33, 19 July 1974, Declaration of the Organization of African Unity on the Issues of the Law of the Sea.

[135] Ibid Articles 6–7.

[136] UNGA, A/AC.138/SC.II/L.40, 16 July 1973; 'Draft Articles on the Exclusive Economic Zone' (1973) 12(5) ILM 1246.

Nevertheless, the challenge to the long established dichotomy between territorial waters and high seas met with strong resistance from different States over time.

The idea of claiming an additional zone beyond the territorial waters for fishery protection and conservation gained strength after the Second World War in association with the decolonisation movement. The claim of a 200-mile zone originated from a group of Latin American States, refined by the Caribbean States as the patrimonial sea, and defined explicitly by the African States as the exclusive economic zone. This process was supplemented by State practice in Europe and other regions to claim fisher jurisdictions to varying distances and under different terminologies.

By the early 1970s, State practice showed an accelerated trend towards the extension of coastal State jurisdiction over sea areas beyond the territorial sea limit.[137] These developments were such that in the 1974 *Fisheries Jurisdiction* cases, the ICJ stated that two concepts had crystallised as customary law arising out of State practice and the general consensus revealed at the two Geneva Conferences. The first was the concept of a 12-mile fishery zone measured from the baselines where the coastal State may claim exclusive fishery jurisdiction, and the second was the concept of a coastal State's preferential rights of fishing in adjacent waters in a situation of special dependence on its coastal fisheries.[138] However, ICJ declined to pronounce on the general validity in international law of Iceland's 50 NM exclusive fishing zone except to recognise its preferential position.[139] Against this background, the concept of the EEZ became a crucial item on the agenda of the Third United Nations Conference on the Law of the Sea which commenced in 1973, with the hope of completing the process of negotiation to become a widely-accepted legal regime.[140]

137 Harris and Sivakumaran (2015) 392; Myron Nordquist and Kenneth R Simmonds (eds.), *New Directions in the Law of the Sea*, Documents Volume X (New York 1973) 472.

138 Fisheries Jurisdiction (United Kingdom v. Iceland), Merits, Judgment, ICJ Reports 1974, p. 3, para 52; Fisheries Jurisdiction (Federal Republic of Germany v. Iceland), Merits, Judgment, ICJ Reports 1974, p. 175, para 44.

139 Fisheries Jurisdiction (UK v. Iceland), paras 67–68; Fisheries Jurisdiction (Germany v. Iceland), paras 59–60.

140 Nordquist, Nandan and Rosenne (1993) 498; Koh (2020) 3–10; Nandan (2021) 41–42.

3

The Exclusive Economic Zone in the United Nations Convention on the Law of the Sea

State practice following the Truman Proclamations revealed that the international community had reached a general consensus for coastal States to establish a separate maritime zone beyond the territorial sea to protect and preserve their economic interests over natural resources. Such consensus also extended to the preservation of vital high seas freedoms of all States in the same maritime zone. Hence, the maritime zone was to be established as a multifunctional zone in which the rights of the coastal State and the freedoms of other States would co-exist.

The basic concept of the exclusive economic zone (EEZ) was accepted early on during the Third United Nations Conference on the Law of the Sea (Third Conference), leaving negotiators the main task of making this new maritime zone a balanced legal regime that could accommodate States' competing, conflicting and overlapping demands.[1] A compromise was eventually achieved on the legal status of the EEZ. It is a *sui generis* legal regime under which the rights and duties of different States are governed by the relevant provisions of the United Nations Convention on the Law of the Sea (UNCLOS or the Convention).[2] The principle rights and jurisdiction of the coastal State and the freedoms of other States are enumerated in Articles 56 and 58, which also include the reciprocal due regard obligations for all relevant parties in order to maintain a balance in the uses of the EEZ. Article 59 acknowledges the existence of residual rights in the EEZ and lays down the criteria for resolving conflicts arising from their attribution, with no presumption in

[1] Myron H. Nordquist, Satya N. Nandan and Shabtai Rosenne (eds.), *United Nations Convention on the Law of the Sea 1982: A Commentary*, Vol. II (Martinus Nijhoff 1993) 498; James B. Morell, *The Law of the Sea: An Historical Analysis of the 1982 Treaty and Its Rejection by the United States* (McFarland 1992) 53; Alexander Proelss, 'Article 55', in Alexander Proelss (ed.), *United Nations Convention on the Law of the Sea: A Commentary* (Hart 2017) 414–415.

[2] United Nations Convention on the Law of the Sea (10 December 1982, in force 16 November 1994) 1833 UNTS 3, Article 55 (UNCLOS).

favour of either the coastal State or other States. As an integrated part of UNCLOS, any disputes concerning the interpretation or application of the EEZ regime must be settled, albeit subject to important exclusions, according to the dispute settlement mechanism established in Part XV.

This chapter is divided into three main sections. Section 3.1 reviews the process of codification of the EEZ at the Third Conference and the recognition of its *sui generis* character as a new functional zone involving a compromise between different States and groups of States. Section 3.2 analyses the jurisdictional framework of the EEZ as established by UNCLOS. It identifies the two legal doctrines that formulate the body of flexible prescriptions to maintain a delicate balance of the jurisdictional framework. These are the principles used to attribute rights and freedoms between the coastal State and other States, and the reciprocal due regard obligations relating to their excise. These two legal doctrines also guided the principles to resolve conflicts arising from the attribution of residual rights and the procedures to settle disputes among State parties. Section 3.3 examines the customary law status of the EEZ as achieved through State practice and consensus.

3.1 The Exclusive Economic Zone as a New Legal Regime

3.1.1 Codification History

Despite the absence of a general rule of international law fixing the maximum breadth of the territorial sea or the limit of coastal State jurisdiction over fisheries, it was largely the concern over deep seabed mining that triggered the convocation of a new law of the sea conference.[3] Initiated by a Maltese proposal, the United Nations General Assembly (UNGA) established the *ad hoc* Committee on the Peaceful Uses of the Sea-Bed and the Ocean Floor beyond the Limits of National Jurisdiction (Sea-Bed Committee) in 1968, consisting of 42 member States to study all related issues.[4] In 1970, the UNGA decided by

[3] Daniel P. O'Connell, *The International Law of the Sea*, Vol. I (Oxford University Press 1982) 25; Myron H. Nordquist (ed), *United Nations Convention on the Law of the Sea 1982: A Commentary*, Vol. I (Martinus Nijhoff 1985) xxvi; Third United Nations Conference on the Law of the Sea (Third Conference) (1973–1982), Official Records, https://legal.un.org/diplomaticconferences/1973_los/.

[4] United Nations General Assembly (UNGA) Res 2467.A (XXIII), 21 December 1968, Examination of the Question of the Reservation Exclusively for Peaceful Purposes of the Sea-Bed and the Ocean Floor, and the Subsoil Thereof, Underlying the High Seas beyond

Resolution 2759 C (XXV) to convene the Third United Nations Conference on the Law of the Sea in 1973 and instructed the Sea-Bed Committee to act as the preparatory body for the Third Conference.[5] The issues of coastal States' rights and jurisdiction over the natural resources in areas beyond the territorial sea were assigned to Sub-Committee II under Item 6: Exclusive Economic Zone beyond the Territorial Sea and Item 7: Coastal State Preferential Rights or other Non-Exclusive Jurisdiction over Resources beyond the Territorial Sea.[6]

During the consideration of substantive issues in the 1972 session of the Sea-Bed Committee, developing countries seeking exclusive rights over living and non-living resources widely supported the concept of the 200-mile economic zone, while developed States favoured only the preferential rights of the coastal State to fisheries to an adequate distance beyond the territorial sea.[7] Controversy with regard to different approaches continued in the 1973 session with a proliferation of proposals for a 200-mile zone.[8] However, the landlocked and geographically disadvantaged States (LL/GDS), which were also developing States, formed another group that resisted the approach of an additional maritime zone under the coastal States' jurisdiction, asserted their position of seeking access to and from the sea, and sought to participate in resource exploitation in the proposed area.[9] Therefore, when the Third Conference commenced its first session in 1973, the positions of States and groups of States in respect to an economic zone beyond the territorial sea were interrelated, overlapping and sometimes conflicting.[10]

the Limits of Present National Jurisdiction, and the Use of Their Resources in the Interest of Mankind, paras 1–2.

5 UNGA Res 2750.C (XXV), 17 December 1970, Reservation Exclusively for Peaceful Purposes of the Sea-Bed and the Ocean Floor, and the Subsoil Thereof, Underlying the High Seas beyond the Limits of Present National Jurisdiction, and the Use of Their Resources in the Interest of Mankind, and Convening of a Conference on the Law of the Sea, paras 2, 6.

6 Shigeru Oda, *The Law of the Sea in Our Time II: The United Nations Seabed Committee, 1968–1973* (Sijthoff Leyden 1977) 156–157, 201–203.

7 Oda (1977) 211, 214–218; Nordquist, Nandan and Rosenne (1993) 496–497.

8 Oda (1977) 269–276; Proelss 'Article 55' (2017) 414.

9 UNGA, Committee on the Peaceful Uses of the Sea-Bed and the Ocean Floor beyond the Limits of National Jurisdiction, A/AC.138/93, 2 August 1973, Draft Articles Relating to Land-Locked States submitted by Afghanistan, Bolivia, Czechoslovakia, Hungary, Mali, Nepal and Zambia; Oda (1977) 276–278.

10 John R. Stevenson and Bernard H. Oxman, 'Preparations for the Law of the Sea Conference' (1974) 68 Am J Int'l L 1, 13–23.

At the first substantive session of the Third Conference in Caracas in 1974, the concept of an economic zone, with specific attribution of rights between the coastal State and other States, was virtually accepted.[11] In fact, the formula of a 12 nautical miles (NM) territorial sea and an economic zone to a maximum distance of 200 NM was the most 'acceptable accommodation for those who favored extending coastal control over resources beyond the territorial sea but were opposed to any extension of national territorial sovereignty'.[12] The real issue was how to clarify the juridical status of the zone. Major maritime States sought to characterise the zone as part of the high seas, assigning only resource-related rights to coastal States; some developing States sought to characterise it as territorial sea, with no more than navigational and related rights granted to other States; and a third grouping intended to create a new legal regime that formed neither part of the highs seas nor of the territorial sea.[13]

The negotiations under Sub-Committee II were assisted by an informal working group of juridical experts, known as the Evensen Group after its chairperson Minister Jens Evensen of Norway, to resolve the competing politics and interests of various States and groups of States with respect to the EEZ.[14] Before the third session in 1975, the Evensen Group produced a cohesive set of draft articles on this zone. The draft articles proposed to give the coastal State sovereign rights and jurisdiction for economic purposes, to reserve to all States the fundamental navigational freedoms and to require both parties to observe the due regard obligation when exercising their rights and performing their duties.[15] However, this proposal was rejected by the Group of 77 and the LL/GDS Group mainly because it failed to meet their specific needs

[11] Third United Nations Conference on the Law of the Sea (Third Conference), Official Records, Vol. III: Documents, A/CONF.62/L.8/Rev.1, 17 October 1974, Statement of Activities of the Conference during Its First and Second Sessions, Annex II, Appendix I: Working Paper of the Second Committee: Main Treads; Nordquist, Nandan and Rosenne (1993) 498; Morell (1992) 53.

[12] Nordquist, Nandan and Rosenne (1993) 550.

[13] Julio Cesar Lupinacci, 'The Legal Status of the Exclusive Economic Zone in the 1982 Convention on the Law of the Sea', in Francisco Orrego Vicuña (ed.), *The Exclusive Economic Zone: A Latin American Perspective* (Westview 1984) 93; Nordquist, Nandan and Rosenne (1993) 499; Proelss 'Article 55' (2017) 414.

[14] Tommy TB Koh, 'Negotiating Process of the Third United Nations Conference on the Law of the Sea', in Nordquist (1985) 106; Satya N. Nandan with Kristine E. Dalaker, *Reflections on the Making of the Modern Law of the Sea* (National University of Singapore 2021) 95–96.

[15] Renate Platzöder (ed.), *Third United Nations Conference on the Law of the Sea: Documents*, Vol. IV (Ocean Publications 1983) 210–211.

and because it reflected a strong coastal State orientation by reserving to it sovereign rights over the resources.[16] The draft articles of the Evensen Proposal were incorporated into the Informal Single Negotiation Text (ISNT) Part II, under the title 'The Exclusive Economic Zone', adopted at the third session.[17] Essentially, it consolidated the general balance of competing interests between different States within the new maritime zone and established the extent and character of the zone.[18]

ISNT Part II had been discussed on an 'article-by-article' basis under 'a rule of silence' and revised during the fourth session in 1976 into the Revised Single Negotiating Text (RSNT) Part II.[19] There was a general agreement on the concept and breadth of the EEZ, but delegates remained divided with regard to the definition and status of the zone.[20] In the RSNT, the Chairman of Sub-Committee II stated that 'an accommodation could be found' and no changes to the text should be made to avoid upsetting the balance implicit in the ISNT, and he further declared that 'nor is there any doubt that the [EEZ] is neither the high seas nor the territorial sea. It is a zone *sui generis*'.[21] This approach was in line with the third grouping of the State negotiation positions, that of treating the economic zone as a separate maritime zone that contained no presumption in favour of either coastal States or other user States.

During the fifth session in 1976, the President of the Third Conference 'identified as a key issue the question of the definition and status of the [EEZ]' where 'a compromise must be reached', and noted the purpose of Negotiating Group No. 1 within Sub-Committee II was to 'consider the questions of the legal status of the [EEZ] and of the rights and duties of

[16] Ibid 224, 227; Nordquist, Nandan and Rosenne (1993) 500; Proelss 'Article 55' (2017) 414.

[17] Third Conference, Official Records, Vol. V: Revised Single Negotiating Text (Part II), A/CONF.62/WP.8/PartII, 7 May 1975, Text presented by the Chairman of the Second Committee; Renate Platzöder (ed.), *Third United Nations Conference on the Law of the Sea: Documents*, Vol. I (Ocean Publications 1982) 27–30.

[18] Nordquist, Nandan and Rosenne (1993) 501.

[19] Third Conference, Official Records, Vol. V: Revised Single Negotiating Text (Part II), A/CONF. 62/WP. 8/Rev. I/PartII, 6 May 1976, Text presented by the Chairman of the Second Committee; Platzöder (1982) 183–184: 'Early in its work the Committee agreed to follow "a rule of silence", whereby delegations would refrain from speaking on an article if they were essentially in agreement with the single text'.

[20] Nordquist, Nandan and Rosenne (1993) 501.

[21] Third Conference, Official Records, Vol. V: Revised Single Negotiating Text (Part II), A/CONF. 62/WP. 8/Rev. I/PartII, 6 May 1976, Introductory Note, paras 14–17; Platzöder (1982) 185; Nordquist, Nandan and Rosenne (1993) 501.

the coastal State and other States in that zone'.[22] However, no practical results were achieved, and the issue was eventually resolved through the work of a private group with 17 delegations formed at the sixth session in 1977, known as the Castañeda-Vindenes Group.[23] The Castañeda-Vindenes Group produced a comprehensive draft of articles to address the outstanding issues of the economic zone that reinforced the sovereign rights of coastal States and clarified the relative freedoms preserved for other States, emphasised the mutual obligation of due regard and suggested the inclusion of 'a new provision setting out the specific legal regime of the [EEZ]'.[24] The draft articles produced by the Castañeda-Vindenes Group provided a better basis for further negotiations and were integrated into the Informal Composite Negotiating Text (ICNT) Part V, along with the progress made on other maritime regimes at the Third Conference as a whole.[25] By then, a negotiated draft article recognising the *sui generis* legal status of the EEZ made its first appearance at the Third Conference, which was retained in subsequent revised texts and adopted in Part V of UNCLOS.[26]

3.1.2 A Sui Generis *Functional Zone*

A mini-package deal was achieved among the negotiated provisions on the EEZ, with a core provision that defines the legal status of the new economic zone. Article 55 of UNCLOS defined the EEZ as 'an area beyond and adjacent to the territorial sea, subject to the specific legal regime established in this Part, under which the rights and jurisdiction of the coastal State and the rights and freedoms of other States are governed by the relevant provisions of this Convention'.[27] This provision was paralleled by Article 86, a definition of the high seas that excluded its

[22] Nordquist, Nandan and Rosenne (1993) 502.

[23] Koh (1985) 108; Rolf Einar Fife, 'Obligations of "Due Regard" in the Exclusive Economic Zone: Their Context, Purpose and State Practice' (2019) 34(1) Int'l J Marine & Coast L 43, 53.

[24] Nordquist, Nandan and Rosenne (1993) 503; Platzöder (1983) 419, 424, 426.

[25] Third Conference, Official Records, Vol. VIII: Informal Composite Negotiating Text, A/CONF.62/WP.10/Add.1, 22 July 1977, Memorandum by the President of the Conference on Document A/CONF.62/WP.10; Platzöder (1983) 313–317.

[26] Third Conference, Official Records, Vol. VIII: Informal Composite Negotiating Text, A/CONF.62/WP.10, 15 July 1977, Informal Composite Negotiating Text; Nordquist, Nandan and Rosenne (1993) 503–504.

[27] UNCLOS Article 55.

application to the EEZ.[28] Article 55 decisively rules out the possibility that the new maritime zone be assimilated into either the territorial sea or the high seas, and confirmed the *sui generis* status of the EEZ as a new legal regime of the law of the sea.[29]

The EEZ shares the feature of a functional zone with those that have been established before, such as the fishery zone and the contiguous zone, where the coastal State exercises certain specialised powers in a maritime area beyond the territorial sea.[30] But these previous zones differ in not affecting the high seas status where rights that were not attributed to the coastal States are continually enjoyed by all other States.[31] For example, the coastal State's right to exercise control to prevent and punish certain infringements in the contiguous zone is an exceptional power restricted in scope, a necessary extension of its enforcement jurisdiction in the territory or the territorial sea.[32] The contiguous zone and the EEZ, although overlapping in the geographical aspect, are two distinctive regimes whereby the coastal State may exercise different powers therein.[33]

The EEZ is also different from the continental shelf, which derived from the idea of the innateness of State sovereignty over the land extension to the submarine terrain. The coastal State's rights over the continental shelf are exclusive in the sense that if it does not explore the continental shelf or exploit its natural resources, no one may undertake these activities without its express consent.[34] In contrast, the establishment of the EEZ is optional, and its existence depends on an actual claim made by the coastal State.[35] Where the coastal State chooses not to claim

[28] UNCLOS Article 86; Alexander Proelss, 'The Law on the Exclusive Economic Zone in Perspective: Legal Status and Resolution of User Conflicts Revisited' (2012) 26 Ocean YB 87, 88–90; Proelss 'Article 55' (2017) 416–418.

[29] Case Concerning the Continental Shelf (Tunisia v. Libyan Arab Jamahiriya), Judgment of 24 February 1982, ICJ Reports 1982, p. 18, Dissenting Opinion Oda, para 118; Nordquist, Nandan and Rosenne (1993) 514–515.

[30] Lupinacci (1984) 99; Maria Gavouneli, *Functional Jurisdiction in the Law of the Sea* (Martinus Nijhoff 2007) 59–60.

[31] Barbara Kwiatkowska, *The 200 Mile Exclusive Economic Zone in the New Law of the Sea* (Martinus Nijhoff 1989) 5.

[32] UNCLOS Article 33(1).

[33] Third Conference, Official Records, Document A/CONF.62/C.2/SR.31, Summary Records of the 31st Meeting of the Second Committee, 7 August 1974, 233–234. Alleged Violations of Sovereign Rights and Maritime Spaces in the Caribbean Sea (Nicaragua v. Colombia), Judgment of 21 April 2022, ICJ Reports 2022, p. 266, paras 161.

[34] UNCLOS Article 77(1)–(2).

[35] O'Connell (1982) 570–572; Edward Duncan Brown, *The International Law of the Sea Volume I: Introductory Manual* (Dartmouth 1994) 218; James Crawford, *Brownlie's*

an EEZ, the water column above its continental shelf continues to be the high seas. When claimed, the EEZ co-exists with the contiguous zone out to 24 NM and with the continental shelf to the maximum of 200 NM from the baselines from which the breadth of the territorial sea is measured.[36]

The EEZ breaks the dichotomy between the territorial sea and the high seas. It grants the coastal State sovereign rights over the natural resources and specified jurisdiction, preserves the right of communication to all States, and recognises the right of LL/GDS to participate in the exploitation of an appropriate part of the surplus of the living resources.[37] Additionally, it clearly recognises the existence of residual rights and declares that such rights will not be automatically attributed to either the coastal State, based on the territorial sea presumption, or to other States, based on the high seas presumption.[38] In this *sui generis* zone, States' rights and duties are attributed and exercised in a balanced manner where no one enjoys absolute authority but must give due regard to the rights and duties of others.

The functional character of the EEZ is concisely reaffirmed by international jurisprudence. For example, in the 2001 *Qatar v. Bahrain*, the International Court of Justice (ICJ) stated that '[m]ore to the north . . . the delimitation to be carried out will be one between the continental shelf and [EEZ] belonging to each of the Parties, areas in which States have only sovereign rights and functional jurisdiction'.[39] In the 2006 *Barbados v. Trinidad and Tobago*, both parties recognised that the EEZ is 'an optional elected zone' where the coastal State possesses only sovereign rights.[40] These statements confirmed that the EEZ is a specific legal regime where coastal States only have sovereign rights and functional jurisdiction.

Principles of Public International Law (9th ed., Oxford University Press 2019) 262, 264–265; Proelss 'Article 55' (2017) 409–410; Robin Churchill, Vaughan Lowe and Amy Sander, *The Law of the Sea* (4th ed., Manchester University Press 2022) 226–227, 293.

[36] UNCLOS Articles 33(2), 57, 76(1).

[37] UNCLOS Articles 56(1), 58(1), 69–70.

[38] UNCLOS Article 59; Brown (1994) 218–220.

[39] Case Concerning Maritime Delimitation and Territorial Questions between Qatar and Bahrain (Qatar v. Bahrain), Merits, Judgment of 16 March 2001, ICJ Reports 2001, p. 40, para 170.

[40] Arbitral Tribunal Constituted Pursuant to Article 287, and in Accordance with Annex VII, of the United Nations Convention on the Law of the Sea in the Matter of an Arbitration between Barbados and the Republic of Trinidad and Tobago, Award, 11 April 2006, PCA Case No. 2004-02, paras 175, 182 (Barbados v. Trinidad and Tobago).

The establishment of the EEZ was considered the most significant outcome of the Third Conference.[41] It first needs to be acknowledged that the codification of the EEZ was only achieved within the broader context of the Third Conference that negotiated all subjects and issues as a package deal.[42] Bearing in mind the subjects and issues are interrelated, the package deal approach allowed States to weigh their interests and make compromises and trade-offs in order to secure their core interests. The acceptance of the provisions on the EEZ as a whole was reached in the context of satisfactory outcomes on the limit of the territorial sea, the navigational issues in straits used for international navigation and archipelagic waters, the access and transit rights of LL/GDS and the continental shelf.[43] Secondly, within the mini-package deal of the EEZ, a delicate balance is maintained by its functional character. As a *sui generis* zone, the rights and freedoms are attributed between the coastal State and other States following a general principle and their exercise are guided by a mutual mandatory due regard obligation. The balance between the sovereign rights and jurisdiction of coastal States and the freedoms of all State in the EEZ is maintained in a dynamic manner and needs to be assessed in a given situation.[44]

3.2 The Jurisdictional Framework of the Exclusive Economic Zone

Two legal doctrines guide the attribution and exercise of the rights and freedoms between the coastal State and other States in the jurisdictional framework of the EEZ. On attribution of rights and freedoms, in principle, all activities relating to the economic exploitation of the zone and its resources fall within the rights pertaining to the coastal State, whereas all activities relating to the communication uses of the zone fall

[41] Horace B. Robertson, 'Navigation in the Exclusive Economic Zone' (1983–1984) 24(4) Va J Int'l L 865, 865.

[42] Deborah Cass, 'The Quiet Revolution: The Development of the Exclusive Economic Zone and Implications for Foreign Fishing Access in the Pacific' (1987–1988) 16 Melb UL Rev 83, 87; Tommy Koh, *Building a New Legal Order for the Oceans* (National University of Singapore 2020) 70–71; Nandan (2021) 47–66.

[43] Tommy Koh, 'A Constitution for the Oceans', in Nordquist (1985) 14–15; John R. Stevenson and Bernard H. Oxman, 'The Third United Nations Conference of the Law of the Sea: The 1975 Geneva Session' (1975) 69 Am J Int'l L 763, 764–765, 770.

[44] Ivan A. Shearer, 'Ocean Management Challenges for the Law of the Sea in the First Decade of the 21st Century', in Alex G. Oude Elferink and Donald R. Rothwell (eds.), *Ocean Management in the 21st Century: Institutional Frameworks and Responses* (Martinus Nijhoff 2004) 10.

within the freedoms pertaining to all States.[45] On the exercise of rights and freedoms, both the coastal State and other States undertake the reciprocal mandatory due regard obligations, as well as the general obligations of peaceful uses of the sea and non-abuse of rights. These two legal doctrines are also applied in resolving conflicts regarding the residual rights in the EEZ, and the settlement of disputes relating to the uses of the EEZ.

3.2.1 *The Attribution of Rights and Freedoms*

3.2.1.1 Economic Interests Consideration

Article 56 states in general terms the rights, jurisdiction and duties of the coastal State, supplemented by other provisions in different Parts of the Convention. Article 56 is the essence of the EEZ, as it confirms the original purpose of establishing this zone, which is to reserve the economic interests, present or future, exclusively to the coastal State. Additionally, it indicates that the sovereign rights of the coastal State pertain only to the natural resources of the zone rather than to the zone itself.[46]

The notion of 'sovereign rights' of the coastal State over natural resources in adjacent maritime zones beyond the territorial sea limit appeared in the Articles Concerning the Law of the Sea developed by the International Law Commission in 1956 (ILC Draft Articles), and was retained in the 1958 Convention on the Continental Shelf and later in UNCLOS.[47] The coastal State's sovereign rights in the EEZ refer in the first instance to the conservation and management of the living resources of the water column superjacent to the seabed. In exercising such rights, the coastal State is expected to take the measures necessary to maintain the sustainable use of these natural resources, and to share the surplus with LL/GDS of the same subregion or region on an equitable basis.[48] The coastal State's sovereign rights with respect to the exploration and

[45] Tullio Scovazzi, '"Due Regard" Obligations, with Particular Emphasis of Fisheries in the Exclusive Economic Zone' (2019) 34 Int'l J Marine & Coast L 56, 59.

[46] J. C. Phillips, 'The Exclusive Economic Zone as a Concept in International Law' (1977) 26 Int'l & Comp LQ 585, 587; Alexander Proelss, 'Article 56', in Proelss (2017) 420–421.

[47] 'Report of the International Law Commission to the United Nations General Assembly, A/3159, Articles Concerning the Law of the Sea' (1956) 2 YB ILC 256, Article 68 (ILC Draft Articles); Convention on the Continental Shelf (29 April 1958, in force 10 June 1964) 499 UNTS 311, Article 2(1); UNCLOS Article 56(1)(a).

[48] UNCLOS Articles 62(1)–(3), 69–70.

exploitation of the natural resources of the seabed and its subsoil are to be exercised in accordance with the regime of the continental shelf.[49]

The exclusive nature of the coastal State's sovereign rights over living and non-living natural resources demonstrates a clear presumption in favour of the plenary powers and jurisdiction of the coastal State. It also became the founding principle for allocating rights between the coastal State and other States, whereas activities that directly relate to natural resources rest with the coastal States.

Moreover, the coastal State has been given jurisdiction over certain specific matters. The connotational difference between 'sovereign rights' and 'jurisdiction' represents the grading in the intensity of the rights of the coastal State. Jurisdiction is a central feature of State sovereignty, for it describes the limits of the legal competence of a State to adopt and enforce rules of conduct upon persons and entities under international law.[50] The change of terminology also reflects a change in the balance between the coastal State and other States whereas considerable safeguards are written into the exercise of the jurisdiction in the interests of protecting the communicational freedoms.[51]

The coastal State has jurisdiction 'as provided for in the relevant provisions of this Convention' with regard to the establishment and use of artificial islands, installations and structures, marine scientific research and the protection and preservation of the marine environment.[52] The content, scope, exercise and safeguards in relation to these jurisdictions are further illustrated in other provisions of, *inter alia*, Parts V, VI, XII and XIII of UNCLOS. In addition, many of these provisions are supplemented and implemented by international rules and standards contained in other international instruments developed by States through the competent international organisation or diplomatic conferences.[53]

Furthermore, the coastal State has 'other rights and duties provided for' in UNCLOS.[54] This refers to those contained in other provisions of UNCLOS that are applicable and compatible with the EEZ regime, which provide for the maximum benefit for the coastal State to enjoy and

49 UNCLOS Article 56(3).
50 Malcolm N. Shaw, *International Law* (8th ed., Cambridge University Press 2017) 483; Christopher Staker, 'Jurisdiction', in Malcolm D. Evans (ed.), *International Law* (5th ed., Oxford University Press 2018) 289.
51 Brown (1977) 334.
52 UNCLOS Article 56(1)(b).
53 Nordquist, Nandan and Rosenne (1993) 542–543.
54 UNCLOS Article 56(1)(c).

exercise its economic rights and jurisdiction. For example, coastal States are entitled to exercise the right of visit to ensure the orderly use of the sea, and to adopt and enforce special rules for vessel-source pollution in ice-covered areas within the limits of the EEZ to better protect the ecological balance.[55]

In order to safeguard the exercise of sovereign rights and specific jurisdictions, the coastal State may exercise enforcement jurisdiction over alleged violations.[56] The enforcement jurisdiction of sovereign rights over living resources and jurisdiction over the protection and preservation of the marine environment are explicitly provided under UNCLOS.[57] The coastal State's enforcement jurisdiction for the exploration and exploitation of non-living resources and other economic activities is derived from the competence of its sovereign rights and jurisdiction and has been widely accepted in State practice.[58] The coastal State's enforcement jurisdiction is secured by the right of hot pursuit that applies *mutatis mutandis* to violations in the EEZ.[59]

3.2.1.2 Communicational Interests Consideration

As the concept of the EEZ was developed, many of the early proposals that described the adjacent jurisdictional zone emphasised establishing the rights of the coastal State first, with a requirement that it must be carried out 'with reasonable regard' and/or 'without prejudice to' the rights and freedoms of other States as a safeguard.[60] At the same time, the need to safeguard the right of free communication within practicable limits has been a constant theme throughout the evolution of the EEZ.[61] The protection of communication interests is primarily afforded in

55 UNCLOS Articles 110–111, 234.

56 ILC Draft Articles Article 68 Commentary 2; Churchill, Lowe and Sander (2022) 271.

57 UNCLOS Articles 73(1), 213–216, 220–221.

58 Nordquist, Nandan and Rosenne (1993) 791–794; Gemma Andreone, 'The Exclusive Economic Zone', in Donald R. Rothwell, Alex G. Oude Elferink, Karen N. Scott and Tim Stephens (eds.), *The Oxford Handbook of the Law of the Sea* (Oxford University Press 2015) 170; Churchill, Lowe and Sander (2022) 244, 263; M/V 'Virginia G' Case (Panama/ Guinea-Bissau), Judgment of 14 April 2014, ITLOS Reports 2014, p. 4, para 211; In the Matter of the Arctic Sunrise Arbitration before An Arbitral Tribunal Constituted under Annex VII to the 1982 United Nations Convention on the Law of the Sea between the Kingdom of the Netherlands and the Russian Federation, Award on the Merits, 14 August 2015, PCA Case No. 2014-02, paras 283–284, 324.

59 UNCLOS Article 111(2).

60 Nordquist, Nandan and Rosenne (1993) 556.

61 Ibid; Alexander Proelss, 'Article 58', in Proelss (2017) 445.

Article 58, which addresses the freedoms and duties of other States that co-exist with the rights and duties of the coastal State in the EEZ.

It first needs to be acknowledged that the so-called *jus communicationis* is something in which all States, including the coastal State and landlocked States, have an interest.[62] The coastal State, as a member of 'all States', would rely on Article 58 to enjoy the freedoms of navigation and overflight and of the laying of submarine cables and pipelines, and other internationally lawful uses of the sea related to these freedoms in the EEZ. The formulation of 'other internationally lawful uses of the sea' is intended to accommodate other possible uses of the ocean by all States in the EEZ, but embraces only those related to the exercise of these named freedoms. Nevertheless, there is no universal agreement on what uses may be considered 'other internationally lawful uses', and there is significant variation in State practice.[63] These freedoms, though customarily recognised, are not absolute in scope and must be compatible with the EEZ regime as well as other relevant provisions of UNCLOS.[64]

By cross-reference in Article 58(2), Articles 88–115 apply to the EEZ insofar as they are compatible with this legal regime. The effect is preservation of the right of all States to engage in a series of non-economic activities in the EEZ. These activities relate to the assistance and recue of persons and ships, the repression of piracy, the suppression of illicit trade in narcotic drugs and psychotropic substances, the suppression of unauthorised broadcasting, the right of hot pursuit, the right of visit and the protection of submarine cables and pipelines.

In sum, the basic principle to attribute rights and freedoms in the EEZ is assessing whether or not the essential interests at question link with the natural resources and economic interests. If affirmed in the positive, the balance of principles weighs heavily in favour of the coastal State. It is also worth noting that States can have rights in the EEZ other than those listed in Articles 56 and 58 of UNCLOS if they derive from other conventions and international agreements or customary international law compatible with UNCLOS, or have been agreed to by the parties of concern through bilateral or regional arrangements.[65] These rights and

[62] Nordquist, Nandan and Rosenne (1993) 496; Proelss 'Article 58' (2017) 449.

[63] Proelss 'Article 58' (2017) 452–454; J. Ashley Roach, *Excessive Maritime Claims* (4th ed., Brill 2021) 442–482.

[64] UNCLOS Article 58(1).

[65] UNCLOS Article 311; In the Matter of the Chagos Marine Protected Area Arbitration before an Arbitral Tribunal Constituted under Annex VII to the United Nations Convention on the Law of the Sea between the Republic of Mauritius and the United

freedoms are, nevertheless, not absolute, but must be exercised with a number of duties with the aim to maintain the dynamic balance of the jurisdictional framework of the EEZ.

3.2.2 *The Exercise of Rights and Freedoms*

Both Articles 56 and 58 contain an obligation that the acting State, while exercising its rights and performing its duties, 'shall have due regard to the rights and duties' of the other party. For the coastal State, the obligation extends to 'shall act' in a manner compatible with UNCLOS, and for the other State, they 'shall comply with' the laws and regulations duly adopted by the coastal State.[66] Additionally, all activities taking place in the EEZ must comply with the general obligations of use of the sea, including acting in good faith and non-abuse of rights, and for peaceful purposes.[67]

3.2.2.1 The Reciprocal Obligations of Due Regard

The phrase 'due regard' was first used as 'reasonable regard' in Article 2 of the Convention on the High Seas, and later was incorporated into UNCLOS to balance different uses among States by introducing a basic principle of self-restraint.[68] However, nowhere does UNCLOS give a clear definition of the phrase 'due regard', and there are no agreed criteria to determine whether the acting State has fulfilled this obligation. It is unclear what kind of activities may have such an effect of breaching this obligation, and the level of interference they may cause, from potential interference to minor or substantive damage, to the concerned State's rights and interests to determine the breach.

There are a number of judicial decisions that addressed the due regard obligation within a given context that would contribute to the understanding of the phrase. In the *Fisheries Jurisdiction* cases, upon

Kingdom of Great Britain and Northern Ireland, Award, 18 March 2015, PCA Case No. 2011-03, paras 293–294 (Chagos MPA Arbitration); Churchill, Lowe and Sander (2022) 273–276, 286–287.

66 UNCLOS Articles 56(2), 58(3).

67 UNCLOS Articles 300–301.

68 Convention on the High Seas (29 April 1958, in force 30 September 1962) 450 UNTS 11, Article 2; UNCLOS Preamble, Articles 27(4), 39(3)(a), 56(2), 58(3), 60(3), 66(3), 79(5), 87 (2), 142(1), 147(1) and (3), 148, 234, 267; Bernard H. Oxman, 'The Principle of Due Regard', in ITLOS (eds.), *The Contribution of the International Tribunal for the Law of the Sea to the Rule of Law: 1996–2016* (Brill 2017) 108–113.

recognising the co-existence of the preferential rights of the coastal State and the traditional rights of other fishing States, the ICJ emphasised the duty of both parties to have due regard to the rights of the other party, and declared that neither right is an absolute one; rather, such rights are limited according to the special considerations of the circumstances and the needs of conservation.[69]

In the *Chagos Marine Protected Area* case, the arbitral tribunal declined to find in the formulation of due regard any universal rule of conduct. Instead, it stated that the extent of the regard required would depend upon the nature of the rights held by one side, their importance, the extent of the anticipated impairment, the nature and importance of the activities contemplated by the other side, and the availability of alternative approaches.[70] Most importantly, the tribunal indicated that in the majority of cases, the assessment of regard by the acting State would 'necessarily involve at least some consultation with the rights-holding state'.[71]

The same consideration of the due regard obligation was applied by the arbitral tribunal in the *Enrica Lexie* case. The tribunal observed that the ordinary meaning of due regard 'does not contemplate priority for one activity over another'; rather, its object and purpose was to 'ensure balance between concurrent rights belonging to coastal and other States'.[72] The tribunal further declared that the 'extent of the "regard" required by the Convention depends, among others, upon the nature of the rights enjoyed by a State', and the reciprocal obligations 'are structured so as to guarantee observance of the concurrent respective rights of coastal and other States'.[73]

As highlighted in these judicial decisions, there are a few key elements that could be identified as requirements of the due regard obligation. First, the due regard obligations are imposed upon States as a compulsory

[69] Fisheries Jurisdiction Case (United Kingdom of Great Britain and Northern Ireland v. Iceland), Merits, Judgment of 25 July 1974, ICJ Reports 1974, p. 3, paras 67–72; Fisheries Jurisdiction Case (Federal Republic of Germany v. Iceland), Merits, Judgment of 25 July 1974, ICJ Reports 1974, p. 175, paras 60–64.

[70] Chagos MPA Arbitration para 519.

[71] Ibid.

[72] In the Matter of an Arbitration before an Arbitral Tribunal Constituted under Annex VII to the 1982 United Nations Convention on the Law of the Sea the Italian Republic and the Republic of India concerning the 'Enrica Lexie' Incident, Award, 21 May 2020, PCA Case No. 2015-28, paras 973, 975.

[73] Ibid para 978.

duty, as indicated by the word 'shall'. Second, both Articles 56(2) and 58 (3) require due regard only to the relevant State's 'rights and duties', but not to its interests more generally. Third, the due regard obligation represents an express recognition of the general need to accommodate different uses and to balance the rights, jurisdiction and duties of the coastal State with the freedoms and duties of other States in the EEZ.[74] Hence, neither the rights nor the freedoms exercised in the EEZ are absolute and neither side has the power to prohibit activities undertaken by the other party unilaterally.

The due regard obligation is triggered when there is a collision of rights and duites that requires accommodation.[75] It functions as a modifying norm to establish the relationship between the two principle norms, suh as the particular rights and freedoms as held by two State parties when they are in conflict.[76] The obligation requires, at a minimum, that the acting States be cognisant of the rights of others and to 'refrain from activities that unreasonably interfere with the exercise of the rights' of the other State.[77] It also could be argued that the due regard obligation presents both procedural and substantive aspects. The acting State, in principle, should not engage unilaterally in the 'balancing exercise' in assessing without any exchange or consultation with the counter State whether the activity in question may or may not infringe its right.[78] When balancing the collision of rights, the due regard obligation imports the notions of equity, fairness, reasonableness and justice which contribute to the assessment of the level of regard required in light of the

[74] Julia Gaunce, 'On the Interpretation of the General Duty of "Due Regard"' (2018) 32 Ocean YB 27, 37–38.

[75] Fife (2019) 45.

[76] Vaughan Lowe, 'Sustainable Development and Unsustainable Arguments', in Alan Boyle and David Freestone (eds.), *International Law and Sustainable Development* (Oxford University Press 1999) 33–35.

[77] Message from the President of the United States Transmitting United Nations Convention on the Law of the Sea, with Annexes, Done at Montego Bay, December 10, 1982 (The "Convention"), and the Agreement Relating to the Implementation of Part XI of The Convention, Adopted at New York, July 28, 1994, and Signed by the United States, Subject to Ratification, on July 29, 1994, Senate 103rd Congress 2nd Session, Treaty Doc 103-39, 26, www.foreign.senate.gov/imo/media/doc/treaty_103-39.pdf; Moritaka Hayashi, 'Military and Intelligence Gathering Activities in the EEZ: Definition of Key Terms' (2005) 29(2) Marine Policy 123, 133; Albert J Hoffmann, 'Freedom of Navigation', in *Max Planck Encyclopedia of Public International Law* (April 2011) para 15.

[78] Scovazzi (2019) 63; Ioannis Prezas, 'Foreign Military Activities in the Exclusive Economic Zone: Remarks on the Applicability and Scope of the Reciprocal 'Due Regard' Duties of Coastal and Third States' (2019) 34(1) Int'l J Marine & Coast L 97, 105–107.

circumstances and by the nature of those rights.[79] However, since there is no definite order of priority with respect to coastal and other States' rights and freedoms in the EEZ, 'it is only when due regard obligations can be subjected to third-party procedures that the possibility exists for these duties to have a meaningful application that would take into account the differing circumstances'.[80]

The significance of the reciprocal due regard obligations is that they serve to emphasise that the EEZ is not an instrument that grants a large bundle of undefined rights to either the coastal State or other States, but rather is a set of precisely defined rights that cannot be separated from a corresponding set of international obligations.[81] Together with the general principle to attribute rights and freedoms among States, they confirm the *sui generis* character of the EEZ. The object and purpose of the due regard obligation contributes to the establishment of the 'legal order for the seas' and is 'a fundamental principle on which the Convention is built'.[82]

3.2.2.2 Other Obligations for Uses of the Sea

Article 56(2) further requires the coastal State to 'act in a manner compatible with the provisions of this Convention'. This could be viewed from two perspectives. First, the exercise of its sovereign rights and jurisdiction must be compatible with relevant provisions that give content to these rights in Parts V, VII, XII and XIII. Second, the coastal State must comply with the other general obligations for uses of the sea that are applicable to all States.

On the second point, these obligations apply to any State undertaking activities in the EEZ. These general obligations include that all 'States Parties shall fulfil in good faith the obligations assumed under this Convention and shall exercise the rights, jurisdiction and freedoms recognized in this Convention in a manner which would not constitute an abuse of right'.[83] Historically, this obligation 'has a remote origin in

[79] Edward Duncan Brown, 'The Exclusive Economic Zone: Criteria and Machinery for the Resolution of International Conflicts between Different Users of the EEZ' (1977) 4 Marit Pol Mgmt 325, 334, 340.

[80] Natalie Klein, *Dispute Settlement in the UN Convention on the Law of the Sea* (Cambridge University Press 2005) 139.

[81] Robertson (1983–1984) 883.

[82] UNCLOS, Preamble; Case concerning Land Reclamation by Singapore in and around the Straits of Johor (Malaysia v. Singapore), Provisional Measures, Order of 8 October 2003, ITLOS Reports 2003, p. 10, Joint declaration of Judges ad hoc Hossain and Oxman.

[83] UNCLOS Article 300.

the negotiations on the status of the [EEZ] conducted in the Castañeda-Vindenes Group in 1977 and the settlement of disputes thereon'.[84] These general obligations further include that all 'States Parties shall refrain from any threat or use of force against the territorial integrity or political independence of any State, or in any other manner inconsistent with the principles of international law embodied in the Charter of the United Nations'.[85] As the negotiation history indicates, there are disagreements about the meaning and scope of this obligation. Particular with regard to the EEZ, it is unclear whether the obligation of 'peaceful purposes' would prohibit all military activities in the EEZ.[86]

Article 58(3) requires other States to 'comply with the laws and regulations adopted by the coastal State in accordance with the provisions of this Convention and other rules of international law in so far as they are not incompatible with this Part'. Compared with the reciprocal due regard obligation where there is no hierarchy between the rights and freedoms of the coastal State and other States, this obligation explicitly recognises the higher status of the coastal State's rights. However, this is not a blank authorisation to the coastal State that would render the freedoms preserved in the EEZ meaningless.

There are two preconditions embedded in this obligation. First, the coastal State may adopt and implement laws and regulations in accordance with 'other rules of international law' such as rules contained in other treaties, customary international law or non-binding instruments. These would primarily include the 'generally accepted international rules and standards' on ship-source pollution established under the auspice of the International Maritime Organization.[87] Second, these domestic laws and regulations must be compatible with the EEZ and be complementary to the coastal State's sovereign rights and specified jurisdiction. As stated by the International Tribunal for the Law of the Sea (ITLOS) in the *M/V Saiga* case, the coastal State does not have the right to enforce general custom laws in the EEZ by characterising such activities as affecting 'its

[84] Myron H. Nordquist, Shabtai Rosenne and Louis B. Sohn (eds.), *United Nations Convention on the Law of the Sea 1982: A Commentary*, Vol. V (Martinus Nijhoff 1989) 151.

[85] UNCLOS Articles 58(2), 88, 301; Charter of the United Nations (26 June 1945, in force 24 October 1945) 1 UNTS XVI, Article 2(4).

[86] Myron H. Nordquist, Satya N. Nandan and Shabtai Rosenne (eds.), *United Nations Convention on the Law of the Sea 1982: A Commentary*, Vol. III (Martinus Nijhoff 1995) 88–91; see also Chapter 6 of this volume.

[87] UNCLOS Article 211(5); see also Chapter 4 of this volume.

economic "public interest" or entail "fiscal losses" for it' because this would 'curtail the rights of other States' in the EEZ.[88]

It could be argued that this obligation under Article 58(3) is a confirmation that the reserved freedoms are subject to restrictions to accommodate the demands of the coastal State. Such restrictions must be reasonable and proportionate, and the extent of impact is determined according to the 'purpose for which the question is asked'.[89] For example, a foreign fishing vessel may be subject to boarding, inspection or detention if the coastal State has reasonable grounds to suspect such vessel violated its laws or regulations governing the conservation and management of the living resources in the EEZ.[90] Moreover, the foreign ship is subject to the coastal State's jurisdiction of pollution prevention and control, regulation of marine scientific research, and may be affected by the presence and use of offshore infrastructure.[91]

The obligation of all States to comply with duly adopted coastal laws and regulations has been regarded as a duty of conduct, not result, thus there is a due diligence obligation for States to take all necessary measures to ensure compliance by their nationals and ships flying their flags.[92] ITLOS in the Fishery Advisor Opinion read Article 58(3) together with other provisions laying down the general obligation of the flag State to determine that the flag State carries a 'responsibility to ensure . . . compliance by vessels flying its flag with the laws and regulations concerning conservation measures adopted by the coastal State'.[93] ITLOS further declared that the responsibility 'to ensure' may be characterised as an obligation of 'due diligence' such that the flag State must take all necessary measures to ensure compliance, including 'a certain level of vigilance in their enforcement and the exercise of administrative control applicable

[88] M/V 'Saiga' (No. 2) (Saint Vincent and the Grenadines v. Guinea), Judgment of 1 July 1999, ITLOS Reports 1999, p. 10, paras 127, 129, 131; see also Chapter 4 of this volume.

[89] Bernard H. Oxman, 'The Third United Nations Conference on the Law of the Sea: the 1977 New York Session' (1978) 72 Am J Int'l L 57, 74.

[90] UNCLOS Articles 60(6), 62(4), 63–67, 73(1); see also Chapter 4 of this volume.

[91] UNCLOS Articles 56(1)(b), 210, 211(5)–(6), 214, 216, 220–221, 248–249; see also Chapter 4 of this volume.

[92] Proelss 'Article 58' (2017) 456–457.

[93] Request for An Advisory Opinion submitted by the Sub-regional Fisheries Commission (SRFC), Advisory Opinion of 2 April 2015, ITLOS Reports 2015, p. 4, paras 111, 115, 122–127. The provisions that contain these obligations are Articles 62, 91, 92, 94, 192 and 193.

to public and private operators'.[94] It should be highlighted that the obligation of due diligence entails an evolving standard of rules and regulations as they are continually developed by the coastal State and relevant international regulatory bodies.[95]

It is important to remember that the rights and freedoms in the EEZ are not absolute, but are subject to a number of limitations and corresponding duties upon which their legal exercise is preconditioned. These conditions are designed not to limit or restrict the rights or freedoms, but to safeguard their exercise in the interests of the entire international community.[96] Unfortunately, these duties and conditions tend to be forgotten or manipulated.[97] As will be discussed in subsequent chapters, many of the activities taking place in the EEZ are facing competition and challenges from concurrent activities, and it is crucial for all States to diligently fulfil their obligations to ensure the peaceful use of the sea.

3.2.3 Resolving Conflicts Regarding Residual Rights

Recognising that the EEZ is a *sui generis* zone in which not all uses of the zone could be clearly attributed to either the coastal State or other States, Article 59 was introduced to provide a formula to resolve conflicts regarding the attribution of residual rights and jurisdiction in the EEZ.[98] Article 59 requires that 'the conflict should be resolved on the basis of equity and in the light of all the relevant circumstances, taking into account the respective importance of the interests involved to the parties as well as to the international community as a whole'. This formula is often considered to be the main evidence of the *sui generis* character of the EEZ and the cornerstone of the construction of the EEZ legal regime.[99] It represents the ultimate exposition that UNCLOS does not attribute the residual rights to either the coastal State or the other

[94] Ibid paras 128–140.

[95] Alan Boyle and Catherine Redgwell, *Birnie, Boyle and Redgwell's International Law and the Environment* (4th ed., Oxford University Press 2021) 165–167.

[96] ILC Draft Articles Article 27 Commentary.

[97] David Freestone, 'Modern Principles of High Seas Governance: The Legal Underpinnings' (2009) 39(1) Environmental Policy and Law 44, 45.

[98] Kwiatkowska (1989) 5; Extavour (1979) 266; Alexander Proelss, 'Article 59', in Proelss (2017) 459.

[99] Kwiatkowska (1989) 228; Erik Franckx, 'American and Chinese Views on Navigational Rights of Warships' (2011) 10 Chinese J Int'l L 187, 200–201.

State, but rather each case, as it arises, will have to be decided on its own merits on the basis of the criteria set out in Article 59.[100]

If interpreted strictly, Article 59 may only be applicable in situations where UNCLOS does not attribute rights or jurisdiction, hence referring to uses that cannot be assimilated to any attributed uses of the EEZ.[101] Taken together, Articles 56 and 58 constitute the essence of the regime of the EEZ, and it is clear that most of the conventional uses have been covered.[102] However, there may be new uses of the sea resulting from future scientific and technological developments. More importantly, it could be argued that the formula and criteria contained in Article 59 could be used to resolve conflicts regarding various uses or activities that have not been explicitly included in Part V. Thus, Article 59 may play a role in resolving conflict regarding the conduct of military activities, the use of installations and structures that are not for the purpose of the exercise of coastal State rights, ship wrecks, the recovery of archaeological and historical objects, the designation of traffic separation schemes and other activities to enhance maritime safety, pure marine scientific research and the promotion of maritime security.[103]

In contrast to the due regard obligation that is guided towards the 'rights and duties' of the counter State, Article 59 applies to a conflict that arises between the 'interests' of the coastal State and any other State or States, and the resolution involves taking into account the respective importance of the 'interests' involved to the parties. The negotiation history does not illustrate a particular discussion on why the term 'interests' was chosen. 'Interests' is a more general term that could be used to include any activities or connections with something that affects the State, especially if it may benefit from them in some way that invokes its willingness to protect them. The interests of a State could be grouped into political, security, historical, economic, social and cultural perspectives, and a certain activity may involve multiple perspectives of interests.

Article 59 is the only provision in UNCLOS that directly refers to '"equity" in a normative text for the resolution of conflicts regarding the

[100] Tommy Koh, 'The Exclusive Economic Zone' (1988) 30 Malayan L Rev 1, 32–33; Churchill, Lowe and Sander (2022) 292.

[101] Proelss 'Article 59' (2017) 460.

[102] Nordquist, Nandan and Rosenne (1993) 556.

[103] Brown (1994) 239–240; Kwiatkowska (1989) 228; Churchill, Lowe and Sander (2022) 291–293.

attribution of rights and jurisdiction in the [EEZ]'.[104] However, the meaning of the term 'equity' is not clear.[105] The term has been interpreted by the ICJ as 'a matter of abstract justice'[106] and 'a general principle directly applicable as law'[107] as opposed to the phrase 'equitable principles', which are 'actual rules of law' based on 'a foundation of very general precepts of justice and faith'.[108] Thus 'equity', when used as an independent basis of decision, must be understood in the light of the circumstances peculiar to the case in question in order to fulfil the requirements of justice to a given dispute.[109] The application of 'equity' as a basis to resolve conflicts calls for the consideration of fairness, reasonableness and individualised justice that is specific to that conflict.[110]

In Article 59, the norm of 'equity' is qualified by substantive criteria for finding the most appropriate solution, among which are the assessment of 'all the relevant circumstances' and 'the respective importance of the interests' for the parties involved and for the international community.[111] This assessment should take into consideration the parallel existence of the reciprocal due regard obligation and the general principle of attributing rights and freedoms laid down in Articles 56 and 58.[112] As such, as a precondition, there is no general presumption in favour of either the coastal State or any other State in a specific circumstance. It is reasonable to argue that, since all the resource and economic originated rights are exclusively attributed to the coastal State, the Article 59 formula would tend to favour the coastal State if the rights and jurisdiction in dispute are of economic interests or concern, and would tend to favour the interests

104 Nordquist, Nandan and Rosenne (1993) 569. A similar phrase 'equitable basis' is used in Articles 69–70 for the right of landlocked and geographically disadvantaged States, and in Article 266 for the promotion of the transfer of marine technology; another phrase 'equitable solution' is used in Articles 74 and 83 for the delimitation of the EEZ/continental shelf between States with opposite or adjacent coasts.

105 Masahiro Miyoshi, *Considerations of Equity in the Settlement of Territorial and Boundary Disputes* (Martinus Nijhoff 1993) 11–12.

106 North Sea Continental Shelf Cases (Federal Republic of German v. Netherlands; Federal Republic of Germany v. Denmark), Judgment of 20 February 1969, ICJ Reports 1969, p. 3, para 85.

107 Continental Shelf (Tunisia v. Libyan Arab Jamahiriya) para 71.

108 North Sea Continental Shelf para 85.

109 Miyoshi (1993) 13, 17; Continental Shelf (Tunisia v. Libyan Arab Jamahiriya) para 71.

110 Francesco Francioni, 'Equity in International Law', in *Max Planck Encyclopedia of International Law* (November 2020); Proelss 'Article 59' (2017) 461.

111 UNCLOS Article 59; Nordquist, Nandan and Rosenne (1993) 569.

112 Proelss (2012) 95; Boyle and Redgwell (2021) 133.

of other States or the international community if the issue does not involve the exercise of resource rights.[113]

It is noteworthy that States hold different interpretations of the formula adopted in Article 59. For example, Ecuador declared that 'it has the exclusive right to regulate uses or activities not expressly provided for in the Convention (residual rights and jurisdiction) that relate to its rights within the 200 nautical miles, as well as any future expansion of the said rights'.[114] Both Cabo Verde and Uruguay claimed jurisdiction over 'the uses and activities not provided for expressly' but are related to the sovereign rights and jurisdiction of the coastal State.[115] Some States, notably Belgium, Germany, Italy, the Netherlands, Sweden and the United Kingdom, refute arguments that the coastal State enjoys other residual rights in the EEZ.[116]

Article 59 is a due-regard-type provision that can be considered 'a skillful diplomatic device which tries to reconcile opposing positions by means of an elastic formulation'.[117] It has been described as 'surely the most loosely worded [provision] of the entire Convention' and can only be clarified through subsequent State practice.[118] In circumstances where a conflict arises regarding the attribution of rights or jurisdiction in the EEZ, the parties must attempt to reach a solution based on the criteria provided under Article 59. If this is unsuccessful, then they may resolve such dispute using the dispute settlement procedures provided in Part XV of UNCLOS. Third-party adjudication will be critical to determining the normative content of Article 59 and thus the limits of the rights and duties of any specific State in the EEZ.[119]

3.2.4 Settlement of Disputes

Historically, international disputes have been settled through diplomatic efforts, economic sanctions or by force, and only submitted to third-party

[113] Nordquist, Nandan and Rosenne (1993) 504, 569; Proelss 'Article 59' (2017) 461–463.

[114] UNCLOS, Declarations and Statements, Ecuador, https://treaties.un.org/Pages/ViewDetailsIII.aspx?src=TREATY&mtdsg_no=XXI-6&chapter=21&Temp=mtdsg3&clang=_en.

[115] UNCLOS, Declarations and Statements, Cabo Verde and Uruguay.

[116] UNCLOS, Declarations and Statements, Germany, Italy, the Netherlands and the United Kingdom.

[117] Scovazzi (2019) 60; Churchill, Lowe and Sander (2022) 292.

[118] Shearer (2004) 10.

[119] Klein (2005) 140; Nordquist, Nandan and Rosenne (1993) 569; Proelss 'Article 59' (2017) 459; Churchill, Lowe and Sander (2022) 293.

processes with the expressed consent of the State parties involved.[120] UNCLOS is one of the few international conventions that provide mandatory jurisdiction entailing binding decisions for disputes arising from its interpretation and application.[121] This has been hailed 'as one of the most significant developments in dispute settlement in international law'.[122] The achievement has, nonetheless, been somewhat undercut by the embedded exceptions and limitations to the compulsory procedure, in particular with regard to those relating to the EEZ.[123]

At an early stage of the negotiations during the Third Conference, it was recognised that the dispute resolution system would only be acceptable on the condition that certain issues be excluded from the obligation to submit to a compulsory procedure entailing binding decisions.[124] Moreover, the controversy relating to the exercise of the coastal States' sovereign rights in the EEZ was one of the 'hard-core' issues in the negotiation of the dispute settlement procedures.[125] The compromise achieved in UNCLOS is that disputes relating to the coastal State's 'sovereign right or jurisdiction' in the EEZ are *ipso facto* excluded from the compulsory dispute settlement procedures and disputes relating to the freedoms of navigation, overflight and the laying of submarine cables and pipelines are subject to compulsory procedures.[126] Such a formula essentially reflects the delicate balance between the rights and freedoms of the coastal State and other States in the EEZ.

The choice of forum follows the general provisions whereby the dispute will be submitted to the same procedure chosen by both parties, otherwise to arbitration in accordance with Annex VII, unless otherwise agreed.[127] The introduction of arbitral tribunals as the default

[120] Charter of the United Nations Article 33(1); Klein (2005) 2.

[121] UNCLOS Articles 279–280, 286.

[122] Klein (2005) 2; Alan E. Boyle, 'Dispute Settlement and the Law of the Sea Convention: Problems of Fragmentation and Jurisdiction' (1997) 46 Int'l & Com LQ 37, 37; Louis B. Sohn, 'Settlement of Law of the Sea Disputes' (1995) 10(2) Int'l J Marine & Coastal L 205, 205–206.

[123] Klein (2005) 3; Shigeru Oda, 'Dispute Settlement Prospects in the Law of the Sea' (1995) 44 Int'l & Comp LQ 863, 863.

[124] Nordquist, Rosenne and Sohn (1989) 87–88; Andrew Serdy, 'Article 297', in Proelss (2017) 1911.

[125] Nordquist, Rosenne and Sohn (1989) 91–103; Chagos MPA Arbitration para 309.

[126] UNCLOS Articles 297, 298(1)(b); Günther Jaenicke, 'Dispute Settlement under the Convention on the Law of the Sea' (1983) 43 Heidelberg J Int'l L 813, 817; Klein (2005) 140–141; Churchill, Lowe and Sander (2022) 866; Serdy 'Article 297' (2017) 1908–1909.

[127] UNCLOS Article 287(3)–(5).

compulsory procedure, where the composition of the tribunal is determined in consultation with the parties, presumably gives parties more confidence in using the compulsory third-party dispute settlement.[128] Such flexibility as to the choices of fora and the priority of consent of the parties mirrors States' general position toward dispute settlement, and serves to narrow down the scope of compulsory procedures.[129]

The core to the comprised formula is articulated in Article 297. It first acknowledges that three types of disputes concerning the interpretation or application of the EEZ regime with regard to the exercise of a coastal State's rights and jurisdiction are subject to compulsory procedures. Not only may the coastal State confront other States' wrongful use of the preserved freedoms, but Article 297 also enables other States to challenge the actions of the coastal State if they have unduly affected the exercise of preserved freedoms in the EEZ.[130] In addition, the coastal State's actions to implement and enforce specified international rules and standards for the protection and preservation of the marine environment may also be challenged.[131]

Article 297 further states that disputes concerning the interpretation and application of relevant provisions relating to marine scientific research and fisheries shall be subject to the compulsory procedures except in certain cases. In the case of marine scientific research, the exercise by the coastal State of a right or discretion to grant or withhold consent, or a decision by the coastal State to order suspension or cessation of a research project in its EEZ, is exempted.[132] In the case of fisheries, disputes relating to the coastal State's sovereign rights with respect to the living resources in the EEZ or their exercise' are exempted.[133] Only in limited cases, where there is alleged manifest non-compliance with UNCLOS or abuse of a right by the coastal State, and the parties cannot reach a settlement, may the dispute be submitted to conciliation.[134] The scope of the exemption for fisheries has been interpreted to be narrow and closely linked with the utilisation and management of the living resources rather than excluding all disputes concerning living resources.[135]

128 Kwiatkowska (1989) 224; UNCLOS Annex VII, Article 3; Annex VIII, Article 3.
129 Oda (1995) 863.
130 UNCLOS Article 297(1)(a)–(b); M/V Saiga (No. 2) para 30.
131 UNCLOS Articles 56(1)(b)(iii), 192, 211(5)–(6), 220(3), (5)–(6), 297(1)(c).
132 UNCLOS Articles 246, 253, 297(2)(a)(i)–(ii).
133 UNCLOS Article 297(3)(a).
134 UNCLOS Article 297(2)(b), (3)(b).
135 Serdy 'Article 297' (2017) 1918; Chagos MPA Arbitration, Dissenting and Concurring Opinion, Judge James Kateka and Judge Rüdiger Wolfrum, paras 58–60.

It is important to recognise that the enumerated types of cases in Article 297 do not restrict a court or tribunal from considering disputes concerning the coastal State's exercise of sovereign rights and jurisdiction in other cases. Where a dispute concerns 'the interpretation or application' of relevant provisions of UNCLOS, and 'provided that none of the express exceptions to jurisdiction set out in Article 297(2) and 297(3) are applicable, jurisdiction for the compulsory settlement of the dispute flows from Article 288(1)'.[136] Although it is recognised that certain sovereign rights and exclusive jurisdiction of the coastal States in the EEZ are not to be questioned by a third party, the manner of their exercise 'should be [justiciable] before an appropriate forum' to avoid unreasonable interference with the *jus communicationis* of other States.[137]

Additionally, Article 298 gives all States the right to make optional exceptions to the compulsory dispute settlement procedure by unilateral declaration.[138] In relation to the exercise of rights and duties in the EEZ, States may declare that they do not accept compulsory jurisdiction regarding disputes concerning military activities, disputes concerning coastal State's law enforcement activities over living resources and marine scientific research, and disputes in respect of which the United Nations Security Council is exercising its assigned functions.[139] Consequently, the coastal State further secures sole discretion over a number of important uses of the EEZ. With an effective declaration under Article 298, the coastal State may argue that disputes of whether military activities or security matters fall under attributed rights or residual rights (and in the latter case, how to attribute such rights) are exempted from the compulsory third-party settlement procedures. It is likely that such an argument would be successful. However, a complication may arise when the exception relates to law enforcement powers of the coastal State, as this may clash with the freedom of navigation of other States.[140] The coastal State is given explicit enforcement jurisdiction over living resources in the EEZ and is entitled to board, inspect, arrest and institute judicial proceedings against a suspected foreign

136 Chagos MPA Arbitration para 317.

137 Nordquist, Rosenne and Sohn (1989) 91–92; Francisco Orrego Vicuña, *The Exclusive Economic Zone: Regime and Legal Nature under International Law* (Cambridge University Press 1989) 123–124.

138 UNCLOS Article 298(1).

139 UNCLOS Article 298(1)(b)–(c).

140 Klein (2005) 310–311.

vessel.[141] The exercise of such powers has a direct impact on the freedom of navigation and disputes relating to the interference of freedom of navigation are explicitly included under Article 297. UNCLOS does not provide a direct solution on how to harmonise conflicts between Articles 297 and 298, but it would seem there is support for the view that navigation disputes are included under the compulsory procedures, since the exceptions to law enforcement activities are only optional and should be interpreted narrowly.[142]

In order to limit the impact of coastal States' enforcement jurisdiction over foreign vessels in the EEZ, coastal States are obligated to promptly release arrested vessels and their crews for violations of laws and regulations with regard to fishery or environmental protection upon the posting of reasonable bond or other security.[143] If the detaining State fails to comply with prompt release procedures, the flag State may submit such a dispute to any mutually agreed court or tribunal, or to ITLOS, unless otherwise agreed.[144] The court or tribunal will 'deal only with the question of release, without prejudice to the merits of any case before the appropriate domestic forum against the vessel, its owner or its crew'.[145] Although prompt release is an independent procedure, the issue of detention is 'inevitably linked with the content of the rules and regulations of the coastal State concerning the fisheries in its [EEZ], and the way in which these rules are enforced'.[146] This requires that the court or tribunal must exercise 'restraint' in examining these interlinked merits to the extent that is necessary for it to reach a decision on the question of release.[147]

The elaborate system for the settlement of disputes is at the heart of the UNCLOS package deal to provide some assurance that the delicate equilibrium of rights and duties established in the Convention will be respected in practice.[148] Within the *sui generis* EEZ system, where there

[141] UNCLOS Article 73(1).

[142] Klein (2005) 310–311; Serdy 'Article 297' (2017) 1917–1918; Andrew Serdy, 'Article 298', in Proelss (2017) 1930.

[143] UNCLOS Articles 73(2), 226(1)(b); Tullio Treves, 'Article 292', in Proelss (2017) 1882; see also Chapter 4 in this volume.

[144] UNCLOS Article 292(1).

[145] UNCLOS Article 292(3).

[146] Oda (1995) 866.

[147] Treves 'Article 292' (2017) 1891–1892; M/V 'Saiga' Case (Saint Vincent and the Grenadines v. Guinea), Prompt Release, Judgment of 4 December 1997, ITLOS Reports 1997, p. 16, para 50.

[148] Churchill, Lowe and Sander (2022) 851.

is no explicit order of priorities between the rights of the coastal State and those of other States, a compulsory dispute settlement scheme entailing binding decisions is 'an important procedural guarantee for maintaining a proper balance'.[149] The dispute settlement procedures as applicable to the EEZ essentially reflect the compromise of power achieved in the substantive provisions of Part V. On the one hand, issues that touch on the interests of all States, namely navigational freedoms and marine environmental protection, are subject to compulsory procedures entailing binding decisions. On the other hand, the establishment of the EEZ regime itself 'signals a prevalent trend in favour of coastal State authority over the traditional *mare liberum* system', which resulted in the exclusion of a range of coastal State discretions from the compulsory third-party processes.[150]

3.3 The Status of the Exclusive Economic Zone

The comprehensive legal framework established by UNCLOS, comprising 320 articles and nine annexes, known as 'a Constitution for the Oceans', is the result of the codification and progressive development of the international law of the sea.[151] In order to maintain the integrity of UNCLOS, States must exercise their rights and perform their duties in good faith and cannot make any reservations or exceptions except those expressly permitted.[152] As of July 2024, there are 170 parties to UNCLOS, of which many States have made declarations or statements upon signing, ratifying or acceding, but none of them could validly 'exclude or modify the legal effect of the provisions of this Convention in their application to that State'.[153] The concept of the EEZ is one of the most important pillars of UNCLOS, and the legal regime created for the EEZ is perhaps the most complex and multifaceted in the whole Convention.[154]

149 Klein (2005) 139; Kwiatkowska (1989) 223.

150 Kwiatkowska (1989) 146; Klein (2005) 225; Natalie Klein, 'Legal Implications of Australia's Maritime Identification System' (2006) 55 Int'l & Com LQ 362.

151 Koh (1985) 14–15.

152 Vienna Convention on the Law of Treaties (23 May 1969, in force 27 January 1980) 1155 UNTS 331, Article 26; UNCLOS Articles 300, 309; Crawford (2019) 363.

153 UNCLOS Article 310; United Nations Treaty Collection, United Nations Convention on the Law of the Sea, Status as at 25 July 2024, https://treaties.un.org/Pages/ViewDetailsIII.aspx?src=TREATY&mtdsg_no=XXI-6&chapter=21&Temp=mtdsg3&clang=_en.

154 Nordquist, Nandan and Rosenne (1993) 508; Crawford (2019) 259.

There is a wide and growing area of overlap between customary law and UNCLOS, in particular with regard to the EEZ regime.[155] As defined in Article 38 of the Statute of the ICJ, international custom refers to the 'evidence of a general practice accepted as law'.[156] The existence of custom is determined by three elements: widely adopted practice among States, general acceptance of the legal binding force of the practice (*opinio iuris sive necessitatis*) and consistency of such practice over a considerable period of time.[157] The issue of whether the *sui generis* EEZ has found acceptance in customary international law is also decided by these three elements. The material sources of custom are manifold and include diplomatic correspondence, official statements, executive decisions and orders, domestic legislation, treaties and other international agreements, and national and international judicial decisions and awards.[158]

The customary law status of the EEZ has been discussed and stated by numerous judges, counsels and scholars.[159] As early as in the 1982 *Tunisia v. Libya* case, the ICJ declared that the concept of the EEZ 'may be regarded as part of modern international law'.[160] In the 1984 *Gulf of Maine Area* case, the Chamber stated that the dispute was 'a delimitation between the different forms of partial jurisdiction, i.e., the "sovereign rights" which, under current international law, both treaty-law and general law, coastal States are recognized to have in the marine and submarine areas lying outside the outer limit of their respective territorial seas, up to defined limits'.[161] Furthermore, in the 1985 *Libya v. Malta* case, the ICJ asserted firmly that '[i]t is in the Court's view incontestable that … the institution of the [EEZ], with its rule on

155 Tullio Treves, 'UNCLOS at Thirty: Open Challenges' (2013) 27 Ocean YB 49, 51; Attard (1987) 287.

156 Statute of the International Court of Justice (in force 24 October 1945) Article 38(1)(b), www.icj-cij.org/statute.

157 Crawford (2019) 21–25.

158 Ibid 23; Attard (1987) 278.

159 Barbara Kwiatkowska, *Decisions of the World Court Relevant to the UN Convention on the Law of the Sea: A Reference Guide* (Kluwer Law International 2002) 42–43; Charles Quince, *The Exclusive Economic Zone* (Vernon Press 2019) 199–217; Shani Friedman, 'The Concept of Entitlement to an Exclusive Economic Zone as Reflected in International Judicial Decisions' (2020) 53(1) Israel Law Review 101, 104–108.

160 Continental Shelf (Tunisia v. Libyan Arab Jamahiriya) para 100.

161 Case Concerning Delimitation of the Maritime Boundary in the Gulf of Maine Area (Canada/United States of America), Judgment of 12 October 1984, ICJ Reports 1984, p. 246, para 19.

entitlement by reason of distance, is shown by the practice of States to have become a part of customary law'.[162] After the entering into force of UNCLOS in 1994, the domestic implementation of the Convention became the reference points of the EEZ.[163] For example, the ICJ in *Nicaragua v. Honduras* acknowledged that both parties had established their maritime zones through legislation.[164] Similarly, the arbitral tribunal in *Barbados v. Trinidad and Tobago* recognised that both parties had claimed an EEZ through domestic legislation.[165] Most recently, in *Nicaragua v. Colombia*, the ICJ declared that '[c]ustomary rules on the rights and duties in the [EEZ] of coastal States and other States are reflected in several articles of UNCLOS, including Articles 56, 58, 61, 62 and 73'.[166]

The entry into force of UNCLOS and the subsequent enactment of national legislation on the EEZ by a large number of States have provided further evidence of a general practice accepted as customary law, at least in its essentials.[167] As of 2024, 140 States have claimed an EEZ (see Table 3.1), with more than 100 of them claimed for the full distance of 200 NM.[168] Most States established the EEZ regime verbatim as set out in Part V of UNCLOS, which balances the sovereign rights and jurisdic-

162 Case Concerning the Continental Shelf (Libyan Arab Jamahiriya/Malta), Judgment of 3 June 1985, ICJ Reports 1985, p. 13, para 34.

163 Friedman (2020) 116–119.

164 Case Concerning Territorial and Maritime Dispute between Nicaragua and Honduras in the Caribbean Sea (Nicaragua v. Honduras), Judgment of 8 October 2007, ICJ Reports 2007, p. 659, paras 50–51.

165 Barbados v. Trinidad and Tobago paras 47, 49.

166 Nicaragua v. Colombia (2022) paras 57, 61.

167 Attard (1987) 308; Brown (1994) 245; Kwiatkowska (1989) 27–28; David Harris and Sandesh Sivakumaran, *Cases and Materials on International Law* (8th ed., Sweet & Maxwell 2015) 391–392; Tim Stephens and Donald R Rothwell, 'The LOSC Framework for Maritime Jurisdiction and Enforcement 30 Years On' (2012) 27 Int'l J Marine & Coastal L 701, 704; Robin R Churchill, 'The Impact of State Practice on the Jurisdictional Framework Contained in the LOS Convention', in Alex G. Oude Elferink (ed.), *Stability and Change in the Law of the Sea: The Role of the LOS Convention* (Martinus Nijhoff 2005) 96; Churchill, Lowe and Sander (2022) 256; Proelss 'Article 55' (2017) 410.

168 There are currently 193 Member States (two observer States) of the United Nations, of which 43 are landlocked States. Member States of the United Nations, www.un.org/en/about-us/member-states. List of Landlocked Developing Countries, https://unctad.org/topic/landlocked-developing-countries/list-of-LLDCs; United States Central Intelligence Agency, 'The World Factbook: Countries', www.cia.gov/the-world-factbook/countries/.

Table 3.1 *Table of claims to the EEZ*[a]

State	Breadth (NM)	State	Breadth (NM)	State	Breadth (NM)
Albania	DLM	Algeria	COORD	Angola	200
Antigua and Barbuda	200	Argentina	200	Australia	200
Bahamas	200	Bahrain	DLM[a1]	Bangladesh	200
Barbados	200	Belgium	COORD	Belize	200
Benin	200	Brazil	200	Brunei Darussalam	200
Bulgaria	200	Cabo Verde	200	Cambodia[c]	200
Cameroon	DLM[a2]	Canada	200	Chile	200
China, People Republic of	200	Colombia[c]	200	Comoros	200
Congo	200	Cook Islands[b]	200	Costa Rica	200
Côte d'Ivoire	200	Croatia	DLM	Cuba	200
Cyprus	200	Democratic People's Republic of Korea[c]	200	Democratic Republic of the Congo	200
Denmark	200	Djibouti	200	Dominica	200
Dominican Republic	200	Ecuador	200	Egypt	DLM
El Salvador[c]	200	Equatorial Guinea	200	Eritrea[c]	DLM[a3]
Estonia	COORD	Fiji	200	Finland	DLM
France	200	Gabon	200	Gambia, Republic of the	200, DLM
Georgia	DLM	Germany	COORD, DLM	Ghana	200
Greece	COORD, DLM	Grenada	200	Guatemala	200
Guinea	200	Guinea-Bissau	200	Guyana	200
Haiti	200	Honduras	200	Iceland	200

Table 3.1 (*cont.*)

State	Breadth (NM)	State	Breadth (NM)	State	Breadth (NM)
India	200	Indonesia	200	Iran, Islamic Republic of[c]	DLM
Iraq	DLM	Ireland	200	Israel[c]	DLM
Italy	DLM	Jamaica	200	Japan	200
Jordan	DLM	Kenya	200	Kiribati	200
Kuwait	DLM	Latvia	DLM	Lebanon	COORD
Liberia	200	Libyan Arab Jamahiriya[c]	200	Lithuania	COORD
Madagascar	200	Malaysia	200	Maldives	200
Malta	DLM	Marshall Islands	200	Mauritania	200
Mauritius	200	Mexico	200	Micronesia, Federated States of	200
Monaco	DLM	Montenegro	COORD	Morocco	200
Mozambique	200	Myanmar	200	Namibia	200
Nauru	200	Netherlands, Kingdom of the	COORD	New Zealand	200
Nicaragua	200	Nigeria	200, DLM[a2]	Niue[b]	200
Norway	200	Oman	200	Pakistan	200
Palau	200	Panama	200	Papua New Guinea	200
Peru[c]	200[d]	Philippines	200	Poland	DLM
Portugal	200	Qatar	DLM[a1]	Republic of Korea	200
Romania	200	Russian Federation	200	Saint Kitts and Nevis	200

Saint Lucia	200	Saint Vincent and the Grenadines	200	Samoa	200
São Tomé and Príncipe	200	Saudi Arabia	DLM	Senegal	200
Seychelles	200	Sierra Leone	200	Singapore	DLM
Slovenia	DLM	Solomon Islands	200	Somalia	200
South Africa	200	Spain	200	Sri Lanka	200
Sudan	DLM	Suriname	200	Sweden	DLM
Syrian Arab Republic[c]	200	Tanzania, United Republic of	200	Thailand	200
Timor-Leste	200	Togo	200	Tonga	200
Trinidad and Tobago	200	Tunisia	DLM	Türkiye, Republic of[c]	200
Tuvalu	200	Ukraine	200	United Arab Emirates[c]	200
United Kingdom of Great Britain and Northern Ireland	200	United States of America[c]	200	Uruguay	200
Vanuatu	200	Venezuela, Bolivarian Republic of[c]	200	Viet Nam	200
Yemen	200, DLM[a3]				

[a] This reference table also includes claims made by States to only certain elements of the EEZ that are indicated in the respective footnotes. Robin Churchill and Vaughan Lowe, *The Law of the Sea* (3rd ed., Manchester University Press 1999), Appendix 1: Claims to Maritime Zones, 463–472; Brown (1994) 246–247; UN DOALOS, *The Law of the Sea: National Legislation on the Exclusive Economic Zone*; UN DOALOS, Table of Claims to Maritime Jurisdiction (as at 15 July 2011, currently under review); UN DOALOS, *Maritime Space: Maritime Zones and Maritime Delimitation*; Barbara Kwiatkowska, '200-Mile Exclusive Economic/Fishery Zone and the Continental Shelf – An Inventory of Recent State Practice: Part 1' (1994) 9 Int'l J Marine & Coastal L 199; Barbara Kwiatkowska,

‘200-Mile Exclusive Economic/Fishery Zone and the Continental Shelf – An Inventory of Recent State Practice: Part 2’ (1994) 9 Int’l J Marine & Coastal L 337; Barbara Kwiatkowska, ‘200-Mile Exclusive Economic/Fishery Zone and the Continental Shelf – An Inventory of Recent State Practice: Part 3’ (1995) 10 Int’l J Marine & Coastal L 53; Robert W. Smith, *Exclusive Economic Zone Claims: An Analysis and Primary Documents* (Martinus Nijhoff 1986) 29–40; United States Department of State, Bureau of Oceans and International Environmental and Scientific Affairs, Limits in the Seas, No. 36 National Claims to Maritime Jurisdictions (8th Revision, 2000), www.state.gov/wp-content/uploads/2020/01/LIS-36.pdf; Roach (2021) 160.

Legend: COORD: defined by coordinates; DLM: delimitation

[a1] *Case Concerning Maritime Delimitation and Territorial Questions between Qatar and Bahrain (Qatar v. Bahrain)*, Merits, Judgment, ICJ Reports 2001, p. 40

[a2] *Land and Maritime Boundary between Cameroon and Nigeria (Cameroon v. Nigeria: Equatorial Guinea intervening)*, Judgment, ICJ Reports 2002, p. 303.

[a3] *Sovereignty and Maritime Delimitation in the Red Sea (Eritrea v. Yemen)*, Award of the Arbitral Tribunal in the Second Stage – Maritime Delimitation of 17 December 1999, PCA Case No. 1996-04.

[b] Not a party of the United Nations as at 2024.

[c] Not a party to UNCLOS as at 2024.

[d] *Maritime Dispute (Peru v. Chile)*, Judgment, ICJ Reports 2014, p. 3.

tion of the coastal State with preserved freedoms by all other States.[169] In addition, there are approximately twenty States and territories, including some of which have claimed an EEZ, an exclusive fisheries zone or an ecological protection zone with only some of the rights accorded to coastal States in the EEZ under UNCLOS.[170]

The EEZ has come a long way since the United States made revolutionary claims through the Truman Proclamations to the natural resources in the marine areas beyond and adjacent to the narrow limit of the territorial sea.[171] Nearly eight decades of State practice, particularly through national legislation and international juridical decisions, and the codification and development of UNCLOS have safely proven that the EEZ, as a *sui generis* functional zone, forms part of international customary law.[172]

3.4 Conclusion

With the establishment of the EEZ, it is anticipated that the preserved freedoms applicable in the *sui generis* regime, as compared to those exercised on the high seas, are circumscribed to varying extents to allow for the exercise of the coastal State's sovereign rights and specific jurisdiction. The EEZ has become a specific model to address, and it may be hoped to resolve, the classic *mare liberum/mare clausum* controversy, where rights and duties of different users co-exist in a dynamic balance and no rights or freedoms can be exercised in an absolute manner. For current or foreseen uses of the EEZ, UNCLOS attempts to prescribe limits that allow accommodation with other uses by other States. In the case of uses that are not explicitly included, provisions of Part V provide a set of general criteria and procedures for resolving conflicts that might occur.

169 Churchill (2005) 127; United Nations Division for Ocean Affairs and the Law of the Sea (UN DOALOS), *The Law of the Sea: National Legislation on the Exclusive Economic Zone* (United Nations 1993); UN DOALOS, *Maritime Space: Maritime Zones and Maritime Delimitation*, www.un.org/Depts/los/LEGISLATIONANDTREATIES/regionslist.htm; Churchill, Lowe and Sander (2022) 293–295.

170 Roach (2021) 161; Churchill, Lowe and Sander (2022) 295–297.

171 'Official Documents – United States: Proclamation by the President with Respect to the Natural Resources of the Subsoil and Seabed of the Continental Shelf', 'Proclamation by the President with Respect to Coastal Fisheries in Certain Areas of the High Seas' (1946) 40 Am J Int'l L Sup 45–47.

172 Shaw (2017) 434; Crawford (2019) 262; UNCLOS, Declarations and Statements, Slovenia.

The body of flexible prescriptions to maintain such a delicate balance can be summarised as follows. As a general rule of attributing rights and freedoms, all economic-related activities and interests are reserved exclusively to the coastal State while essential communicational freedoms are preserved to all States. By way of a mechanism for preventing and resolving potential conflicts between the different categories of co-existing rights, all States are required to exercise their rights and perform their duties in good faith, and to have due regard to the rights and duties of another party or parties. Moreover, as a safeguard, the integrity of the balanced legal system is protected by compulsory third-party dispute resolution which recognises the special interests of both the coastal State and other States. If applied in good faith, these prescriptions should provide acceptable solutions that will accommodate the conflicting interests of coastal and other States.[173]

In addition to the treaty law provisions, the concept of the EEZ has been widely accepted and recognised as part of customary law that is binding on all States. However, the interpretation and implementation of detailed aspects of the *sui generis* regime have shown significant diversity in State practice. Both coastal States and other States have on occasion stretched this special legal regime to accommodate their own needs. State practice has shown examples of States making excessive claims on their rights or freedoms within the EEZ and/or exercising their rights and duties without paying due regard to the other party. It is important for States to find a certain flexibility to accommodate different interests in a given context, which will in turn further develop the EEZ legal regime. The following chapters will examine how the body of flexible prescriptions have worked in practice in specific circumstances.

[173] Robertson (1983–1984) 888.

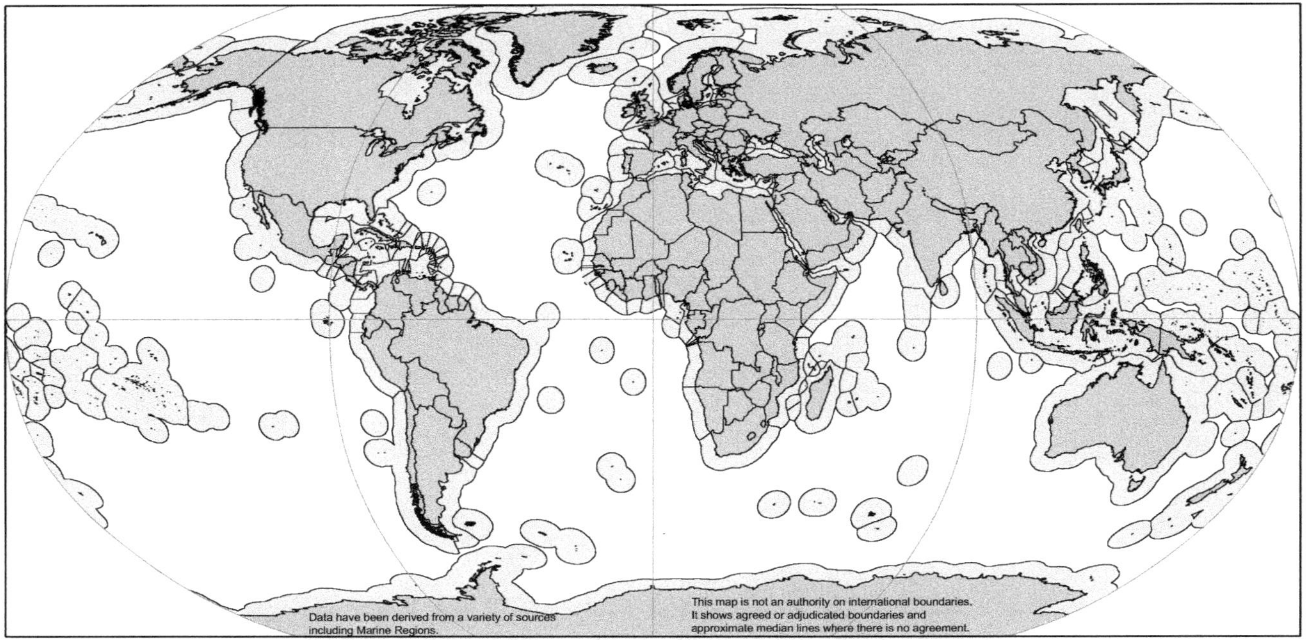

Figure 3.1 Map showing 200 NM maritime zones and associated boundaries.
Source: Dr Robin Cleverly, Marbdy Consulting Ltd

PART II

Competing Uses of the Exclusive Economic Zone

As discussed in Part I, after nine years of intensive negotiations, the Third United Nations Conference on the Law of the Sea (Third Conference) concluded a comprehensive United Nations Convention on the Law of the Sea (UNCLOS) that – in so far as verbal formulae can do so – successfully encompassed a series of dedicated compromises into an integral whole package deal.[1] The legal status of the exclusive economic zone (EEZ) proved to be one of the most controversial issues at the Third Conference, and it has continued to be controversial in State practice.[2] There are various reasons contributing to the disagreements on the competing uses of the zone between different States, and the less-than-definitive language of Part V of UNCLOS is one of them. The provisions of Part V represent a comprehensive version of the EEZ concept and set out the essential juridical configuration of the legal regime, which must be read in line with pertinent provisions of other parts of UNCLOS as well as other relevant rules of international law. But treaty texts, however final and definitive they are intended to be, do not have the last word; that lies with the interpreters and appliers of the regime.

Part II examines in detail how this *sui generis* legal regime has been implemented in State practice, in particular whether, and to what degree, coastal State rights and jurisdiction have affected the exercise of the freedoms of navigation and overflight and of the laying of submarine cables and pipelines, and other internationally lawful uses of the sea

[1] United Nations, 'Third United Nations Conference on the Law of the Sea, 1973–1982' https://legal.un.org/diplomaticconferences/1973_los/; Tommy TB Koh and Shanmugam Jayakumar, 'The Negotiating Process of the Third United Nations Conference on the Law of the Sea', in Myron H Nordquist (ed.), *United Nations Convention on the Law of the Sea 1982: A Commentary*, Vol. I (Martinus Nijhoff 1985) 29–134.

[2] Third United Nations Conference on the Law of the Sea (Third Conference), Note by the President of the Conference, A/CONF.62/L.12/Rev.1, 2 August 1976, para 12; Barbara Kwiatkowska, *The 200 Mile Exclusive Economic Zone in the New Law of the Sea* (Martinus Nijhoff 1989) 230–234.

related to these freedoms, in the EEZ. The balance of this regime relies on the continual assessment of the importance of the interests at stake and diligent obedience to the due regard obligation. Subsequent State practice indicates that the balance has shifted slightly in favour of the coastal State's interests, particularly in connection with its sovereign rights over living resources and jurisdiction for environmental protection. On the other hand, the overall balance has been maintained in that international freedoms of navigation and overflight and of the laying of submarine cables and pipelines in the EEZ have not been seriously, or in most contexts even materially, impaired.

4

The Impact of Coastal State's Rights on the Navigational Freedoms

After the establishment of the exclusive economic zone (EEZ) regime in the United Nations Convention on the Law of the Sea (UNCLOS),[1] the struggle between the tendency of the coastal State to extend its rights and jurisdiction and the desire of all States to maintain high seas freedoms has continued. In the course of this process, navigational freedoms have been affected to varying degrees by broadened coastal State rights and jurisdiction. In particular, foreign vessels and aircraft are obliged to have due regard for coastal State rights and duties and must observe the laws and regulations established by the coastal State in conformity with UNCLOS and other applicable rules of international law.[2] There is considerable potential for conflict between the rights and duties of the coastal State and those of other States.[3] Since most of the seaborne routes in widespread use for navigation and overflight are within the limit of the EEZ, the manner in which the navigational freedoms are exercised is of vital importance.[4]

This chapter examines how the exercise of a coastal State's sovereign rights and specific jurisdiction may affect foreign navigation and overflight and other related internationally lawful uses of the sea in the EEZ, both prescriptive and enforcement jurisdiction, and explores the safeguard measures established by UNCLOS to protect these freedoms. The limitations of the navigational freedoms emplaced by the coastal State can only be justified if they are made in accordance with the general principles of the attribution and exercise of rights and jurisdiction in the EEZ. In other words, a coastal State's claims must be made within the limits of its

[1] United Nations Convention on the Law of the Sea (10 December 1982, in force 16 November 1994) 1833 UNTS 3 (UNCLOS).

[2] UNCLOS Article 58(3).

[3] Robin Churchill, Vaughan Lowe and Amy Sander, *The Law of the Sea* (4th ed., Manchester University Press 2022) 287–288.

[4] Barbara Kwiatkowska, *The 200 Mile Exclusive Economic Zone in the New Law of the Sea* (Martinus Nijhoff 1989) 198.

sovereign rights or specific jurisdiction and must be exercised in good faith and by giving due regard to other States' navigational freedoms.

This chapter is divided into five main sections. Section 4.1 reviews the scope of the preserved navigational freedoms of all States in the EEZ, including other related internationally lawful uses of the sea, such as those associated with the operation of ships and aircraft. Their non-absolute character and the duty of having due regard to the coastal State's rights and duties and obeying applicable domestic laws are highlighted. Section 4.2 examines how a coastal State's sovereign rights over natural resources would affect navigational freedoms. The coastal State has been given broad authority to exercise its sovereign rights, including adopting navigational measures and regulating activities ancillary to fishing. Section 4.3 addresses the impacts caused by the coastal State's jurisdiction to preserve and protect the marine environment. The coastal State's jurisdiction is limited to implementing applicable international rules and standards that reflect the predominance of navigational interests over coastal interests. Section 4.4 focuses on the impact of coastal jurisdiction and rights with regard to artificial islands, installations and structures. Although the use of such infrastructure and the surrounding safety zones may restrict navigational freedoms, the coastal State is obliged to act with due diligence and not to unreasonably interfere with international navigation. Section 4.5 discusses the dispute settlement mechanisms that could be used to resolve potential disputes between the coastal State and other States. Of particular interest are the limitations and optional exceptions to the applicability of the compulsory procedures that were included to further ensure a balance of rights and freedoms in the EEZ.

4.1 The Scope of the Navigational Freedoms

Article 58 of UNCLOS guarantees the navigational freedom for all States in the EEZ.[5] Although it was the intention of some maritime powers during the negotiation that 'the high-seas freedoms exercised in the zone are qualitatively and quantitatively the same as the traditional high-seas freedoms recognised by international law', they are nevertheless restricted by several provisions of UNCLOS and other rules of

[5] Delimitation of the Maritime Boundary in the Atlantic Ocean (Ghana/Côte d'Ivoire), Judgment of 23 September 2017, ITLOS Reports 2017, p. 4, para 426.

international law.[6] Only the freedoms that are 'essentially concerned with international communications', in particular the freedom of navigation and overflight and other internationally lawful uses related to these freedoms, remain open to all States, but they are subject to important limitations to accommodate the economic interests of the coastal State.[7]

When discussing the scope of navigational freedoms, the first issue is to clarify that they are not limited to any particular category of ships and aircraft. All ships and aircraft registered with all States, including those of military nature and used for other public service, as well as those registered in landlocked countries, have been granted the freedom of navigation and overflight in the EEZ.[8] This refers to the unrestricted transit of a ship or aircraft through the EEZ of a coastal State en route between two destinations.[9] UNCLOS used 'ship' and 'vessel' interchangeably, and offered no definition of either term. According to conventions developed under the auspices of the International Maritime Organisation (IMO), ship 'means a vessel of any type whatsoever operating in the aquatic environment and includes submersibles, floating craft, floating platforms, Floating Storage Units (FSUs) and Floating Production Storage and Offloading Units (FPSOs)', but exempts or modifies the application of the floating platforms when they are on location engaged in seabed activities.[10]

The second issue is to determine the 'other internationally lawful uses of the sea related to these freedoms'.[11] Article 58 gives an example, 'such as those associated with the operation of ships, [and] aircraft ... and compatible with the other provisions of this Convention'. This example remains vague as to whether such use should be essential to the operation of a ship or aircraft, such as a hydrographic survey that collects data to support navigation, or distantly support their operations, such as the exchange of ballast waters and bunkering, which are occasional activities

[6] Bernard H. Oxman, 'The Third United Nation's Conference on the Law of the Sea: The 1977 New York Session' (1978) 72 Am J Int'l L 57, 68–69, 72–73; Kwiatkowska (1989) 199–200.

[7] Churchill, Lowe and Sander (2022) 276.

[8] For military navigation and overflight, see Chapter 6 in this volume.

[9] Churchill, Lowe and Sander (2022) 276.

[10] Protocol of 1978 relating to the International Convention for the Prevention of Pollution from Ships, 1973 (17 February 1978, in force 2 October 1983) 1340 UNTS 61, Article 2(4) (MARPOL); International Convention for the Control and Management of Ship's Ballast Water and Sediments (13 February 2004, in force 8 September 2017) 3282 UNTS I-55544, Article 1(12) (BWM Convention).

[11] UNCLOS Article 58(1).

but not essential. State practice and judicial decisions seem to support a broader interpretation. The exchange of ballast water in the EEZ is discouraged but generally tolerated, especially in areas beyond 50 nautical miles (NM) from the nearest land.[12] The International Tribunal for the Law of the Sea (ITLOS) in both the *Norstar* case and *M/T San Padre Pio* case stated that the argument that bunkering activities in the EEZ (not to fishing vessels as confirmed in the *Virginia G* case) came within the high seas freedom of navigation is plausible.[13] Furthermore, according to the arbitral tribunal in *Arctic Sunrise*, protest at sea by ships is also included in the scope of internationally lawful uses of the sea, as it is 'necessarily exercised in conjunction with freedom of navigation'.[14] There are also ongoing debates and conflicting State practice on whether military manoeuvres and espionage fall within the scope of 'other internationally lawful uses'.[15]

Article 58 guarantees the unhampered navigation by foreign ships and aircraft through the EEZ of the coastal States, while the regulation of navigation and overflight are developed under other international instruments, including the rules and standards adopted by competent international organisations and diplomatic conferences. IMO is the global standard-setting authority for the safety, security and environmental performance of international shipping, and many of its rules and regulations have been universally adopted and implemented.[16] Rules for

[12] BWM Convention Annex, Regulation B-4.

[13] M/V 'Norstar' Case (Panama v. Italy), Judgment of 10 April 2019, ITLOS Reports 2018–2019, p. 10, paras 219–220; M/T 'San Padre Pio' Case (Switzerland v. Nigeria), Provisional Measures, Order of 6 July 2019, ITLOS Reports 2018–2019, p. 375, paras 107–108.

[14] In the Matter of the Arctic Sunrise Arbitration before an Arbitral Tribunal Constituted under Annex VII to the 1982 United Nations Convention on the Law of the Sea between the Kingdom of the Netherlands and the Russian Federation, Award on the Merits, 14 August 2015, PCA Case No. 2014-02, paras 227, 328 (Arctic Sunrise Arbitration); Joanna Mossop, 'Protests against Oil Exploration at Sea: Lessons from the Arctic Sunrise Arbitration' (2016) 31 Int'l J Marine & Coastal L 60, 66-67; Churchill, Lowe and Sander (2022) 277.

[15] Churchill, Lowe and Sander (2022) 280–283. For further discussion, see Chapter 6 in this volume.

[16] International Maritime Organization (IMO) LEG/MISC.8, 30 January 2014, Implications of the United Nations Convention on the Law of the Sea for the International Maritime Organization, 7; United Nations Division for Ocean Affairs and the Law of the Sea (UN DOALOS), '"Competent or Relevant International Organizations" under the United Nations Convention on the Law of the Sea' (1996) 31 Law of the Sea Bulletin 79; Zhen Sun, 'UNCLOS Part XII and IMO Instruments on Regulating Environmental Impacts of Shipping: Towards an Effective Regulatory Synergy' (2021) 35 Ocean YB 473, 482–483.

overflight are mainly contained in the Convention on International Civil Aviation (Chicago Convention) developed under the auspices of the International Civil Aviation Organization.[17] Under the Chicago Convention, the rules of the air apply to the high seas and to the EEZ through cross-reference under UNCLOS Article 58(2).[18]

The freedoms of navigation and overflight in the EEZ, like all other high seas freedoms, are subject to a number of limitations. First, the exercise of freedoms of navigation and overflight in the EEZ must be for peaceful purposes.[19] Second, States exercising such freedoms are required to have 'due regard to the rights and duties of the coastal State and shall comply with the laws and regulations adopted by the coastal State' in accordance with UNCLOS and other compatible rules of international law.[20] Moreover, it can be argued that the general obligation to have 'due regard' applies to the interests of other States in their exercise of the recognised freedoms in the EEZ.[21] The essential element of the due regard obligation is to define the non-absolute character of the right it attached.[22] The extent of the 'regard' required in each case will depend upon the nature of the rights held by the other State, their importance, the extent of the anticipated impairment, the nature and importance of the activities contemplated by the operations of the State, and the availability of alternative approaches.[23]

UNCLOS has, nevertheless, laid down detailed provisions to protect the navigational freedoms as applicable in the EEZ. First, a flag State enjoys exclusive jurisdiction over ships flying its flag navigating in a foreign EEZ except as otherwise authorised.[24] Second, warships and ships used only in government non-commercial service have 'complete

[17] Convention on International Civil Aviation (7 December 1944, in force 4 April 1947) 15 UNTS 295.

[18] Ibid Article 12; Kay Hailbronner, 'Freedom of the Air and the Convention on the Law of the Sea' (1983) 77 Am J Int'l L 503, 490–520; Churchill, Lowe and Sander (2022) 284.

[19] UNCLOS Articles 88, 301.

[20] UNCLOS Article 58(3).

[21] UNCLOS Article 87(2); Churchill, Lowe and Sander (2022) 288.

[22] See discussion in Chapter 3 in this volume.

[23] In the Matter of the Chagos Marine Protected Area Arbitration Before an Arbitral Tribunal Constituted under Annex VII to the United Nations Convention on the Law of the Sea between the Republic of Mauritius and the United Kingdom of Great Britain and Northern Ireland, Award, 18 March 2015, PCA Case No. 2011-03, para 519 (Chagos MPA Arbitration).

[24] UNCLOS Articles 58(2), 92(1), 94.

immunity from the jurisdiction of any State other than the flag State' and are specifically exempted from a coastal State's jurisdiction over environmental protection.[25] Moreover, the coastal State is explicitly obliged to 'have due regard to the rights and duties of other States' and to 'act in a manner compatible with provisions of [UNCLOS]',[26] whereby it cannot exercise its rights and jurisdiction in an absolute manner and must refrain from unreasonably interfering with foreign navigation and overflight. Furthermore, it is expressly stated that any disputes concerning an allegation where a coastal State has acted in contravention of the provisions in regard to the navigational freedoms will be subjected to a compulsory dispute procedure.[27]

The following sections examine how different measures taken by the coastal State in exercising its rights and jurisdiction might affect the exercise of the preserved navigational freedoms in the EEZ.

4.2 Sovereign Rights over Natural Resources and Other Economic Activities

The phrase 'sovereign rights', first used in the context of the continental shelf regime, suggests that the coastal State's rights are exclusive in the sense that although the coastal State does not have sovereignty, it has 'all rights necessary for and connected with the exploration and exploitation of the natural resources', including 'jurisdiction in connexion with the prevention and punishment of violations of the law'.[28] The notion of 'sovereign rights' must be seen as constituting an extract of the broader concept of sovereignty – the mode of exercise is no different from that exercised by the coastal State within its territorial sea on the development of the natural resources and other economic activities.[29]

[25] UNCLOS Articles 58(2), 95–96, 236.

[26] UNCLOS Article 56(2).

[27] UNCLOS Article 297(1)(a).

[28] 'Report of the International Law Commission to the United Nations General Assembly, A/3159, Articles Concerning the Law of the Sea with Commentaries' (1956) 2 YB ILC 297, Article 68 Commentary 2 (ILC Draft Articles); M/V 'Virginia G' Case (Panama/Guinea-Bissau), Judgment of 14 April 2014, ITLOS Reports 2014, p. 4, para 211.

[29] Case Concerning the Continental Shelf (Tunisia v. Libyan Arab Jamahiriya), Judgment of 24 February 1982, ICJ Reports 1982, p. 18, Dissenting Opinion of Judge Oda, para 124; Alexander Proelss, 'Article 56', in Alexander Proelss (ed), *United Nations Convention on the Law of the Sea: A Commentary* (Hart 2017) 424–425.

4.2.1 *Living Resources*[30]

The EEZ can be regarded as the direct result of developments in the law of the sea concerning coastal State fisheries jurisdiction in adjacent sea areas.[31] As of 2024, among the 151 listed coastal States, more than 110 States have claimed the full distance of a 200 NM EEZ, subject to delimitation with States with opposite or adjacent coasts, together with another 4 States that have only claimed fisheries zones of various breadths.[32] These claimed EEZ regimes encompass approximately 90 per cent of the world's marine fisheries, which remain a major source of food and a key provider of employment and economic benefits.[33]

'Living resources' in the EEZ refers to non-sedentary species found in the water column superjacent to the seabed, including all fisheries, marine mammals, highly migratory species, shared and straddling stocks, anadromous and catadromous species and seabirds.[34] Sedentary species have been explicitly exempted from the EEZ regime under Article 68 but are subject to the coastal State's sovereign rights and jurisdiction under the continental shelf regime.[35] The different legal basis has certain implications for the scope of rights and obligations possessed by the coastal State.[36] First, Article 68 was included for historical reasons, as sedentary species were protected under the continental shelf regime before the establishment of the EEZ and their protection extends to the extended continental shelf.[37] Second, the exemption was meant to ensure

[30] A preliminary draft of this section was published under the title 'Conservation and Utilization of the Living Resources in the Exclusive Economic Zone – How Far Can We Go?' by Berkeley Law Publications in July 2013, www.law.berkeley.edu/files/Sun-final.pdf.

[31] Shigeru Oda, *International Control of Sea Resources* (2nd ed., Martinus Nijhoff 1989) xvii–xix; Churchill, Lowe and Sander (2022) 255–256.

[32] See examination in Chapter 3, Table 3.1.

[33] Food and Agriculture Organization of the United Nations (FAO), 1995 Code of Conduct for Responsible Fisheries (FAO 1995) Preface, paras 1–2.

[34] UNCLOS Articles 61–68, 77(4); Philippe Sands and Jacqueline Peel, with Adriana Fabra and Ruth MacKenzie, *Principles of International Environmental Law* (4th ed., Cambridge University Press 2018) 506.

[35] UNCLOS Articles 68, 77(4): 'sedentary species' refers to 'organisms which, at the harvestable stage, either are immobile on or under the seabed or are unable to move except in constant physical contact with the seabed or the subsoil'.

[36] James Harrison, 'Article 68', in Proelss (2017) 540.

[37] UNCLOS Article 76(4)–(8); Myron H. Nordquist, Satya N. Nandan and Shabtai Rosenne (eds.), *United Nations Convention on the Law of the Sea 1982: A Commentary*, Vol. II (Martinus Nijhoff 1993) 687–688, 897–898; Convention on the Continental Shelf (29 April 1958, in force 10 June 1964) 499 UNTS 311, Article 2(4).

that the coastal State is not subject to the obligation of giving excess of the surplus to other States where it does not have the capacity to harvest the entire allowable catch.[38] Third, the coastal State has no express obligation to conserve and manage sedentary species of the continental shelf in the same way as non-sedentary living resources in the EEZ.[39] However, the coastal State may do so in the exercise of its sovereign rights over the continental shelf and to fulfil its obligations under other international law such as the 1992 Convention on Biological Diversity.[40]

Coastal State sovereign rights relate not only to the management of these species and other natural resources but also to their conservation for economic utilisation.[41] These rights, together with certain duties imposed on the coastal State, are further elaborated in Articles 61–73. The coastal State's sovereign rights encompass two main aspects as listed in Articles 61 and 62 (respectively): conservation and utilisation, with the objective of the conservation measures being to reach the goal of optimum utilisation.[42] In order to do this, the coastal State must take into account the best available scientific evidence and cooperate with competent international organisations as appropriate, whether sub-regional, regional or global.[43] Additionally, States have the sovereign right to exploit their natural resources pursuant to their environmental policies and in accordance with their duty to protect and preserve the marine environment.[44] This reflects a general principle of international law that States have a legal obligation to promote the conservation and sustainable use of natural resources within the limits of their jurisdiction, including in the EEZ.[45]

[38] UNCLOS Article 77(2).

[39] Churchill, Lowe and Sander (2022) 531–532.

[40] Harrison 'Article 68' (2017) 542–543; Convention on Biological Diversity (5 June 1992, in force 29 December 1993) 1760 UNTS 79, Article 10.

[41] Thomas Dux, *Specially Protected Marine Areas in the Exclusive Economic Zone: The Regime for the Protection of Specific Areas of the EEZ for Environmental Reasons under International Law* (LIT Berlin 2011) 90.

[42] Nordquist, Nandan and Rosenne (1993) 608; M/V 'Virginia G' Case para 212.

[43] UNCLOS Article 61(2). Request for An Advisory Opinion submitted by the Commission of Small Island States on Climate Change and Internaitonal Law, Advisory Opinion of 21 May 2024, ITLOS List of cases: No. 31, para 414 (Climate Change Advisory Opinion).

[44] UNCLOS Article 193; Case Concerning Pulp Mills on the River Uruguay (Argentina v. Uruguay), Judgment of 20 April 2010, ICJ Reports 2010, p. 14, para 175; Alan Boyle and Catherine Redgwell, *Birnie, Boyle and Redgwell's International Law and the Environment* (4th ed., Oxford University Press 2021) 137.

[45] Rio Declaration on Environment and Development (Rio de Janeiro, June 1992), UN Doc A/CONF.151/26 (Vol. I) (12 August 1992), Principles 4–5, 8; Sands and Peel (2018) 222–223.

It is also acknowledged that, in exercising its sovereign rights over the living resources, the coastal State undertakes a mutual obligation of having 'due regard' to the rights and duties of other States in the EEZ.[46] This general obligation is inserted to balance the rights and interests in the EEZ between the coastal State and other States. It requires that the coastal State must be aware of other States' interests and give them sufficient consideration when planning or conducting any activities that may affect the exercise of the freedom of navigation and overflight and other related freedoms, and refrain from activities that unreasonably impede the exercise of these freedoms.[47] The effects imposed on navigational freedoms by coastal conservation and management measures are examined in more detail below.

4.2.1.1 Protection of Marine Species, Habitats and Ecosystem

Coastal States have, based on their sovereign rights, the authority to determine the extent and the limits of conservation and utilisation measures of the living resources in the EEZ.[48] However, there is a correlative obligation for each coastal State to 'ensure through proper conservation and management measures that the maintenance of the living resources in the [EEZ] is not endangered by over-exploitation'.[49] These measures should be designed to 'maintain or restore populations of harvested species at levels which can produce the maximum sustainable yield, as qualified by relevant environmental and economic factors, including the economic needs of coastal fishing communities'.[50] It is both a right and an obligation for the coastal State to sustainably manage the natural resources in the EEZ. As subsequent development in the environmental law field has demonstrated, the effective conservation of marine species must also take into account the protection of associated or

46 UNCLOS Article 56(3).

47 George K. Walker, 'Defining Terms in the 1982 Law of the Sea Convention IV: The Last Round of Definitions Proposed by the International Law Association (American Branch) Law of the Sea Committee' (2005) 36 Cal West Int'l L J 133, 174-177; Moritaka Hayashi, 'Military and Intelligence Gathering Activities in the EEZ: Definition of Key Terms' (2005) 29 Marine Policy 123, 132–133.

48 William T. Burke, *The New International Law of Fisheries: UNCLOS 1982 and Beyond* (Oxford University Press 1994) 39; Boyle and Redgwell (2021) 732–733.

49 UNCLOS Article 61(2). Climate Change Advisory Opinion para 414.

50 UNCLOS Article 61(3).

dependent species, their associated habitats and interlocking ecosystems, and the impacts of climate change and ocean acidification.[51]

In circumstances where shipping and other collateral activities may cause considerable damage to spawning grounds or nurseries, the coastal State arguably has a wide margin of discretion to restrict navigation for the purpose of conservation, subject to the fulfilment of its due regard obligation.[52] These conservation measures may affect foreign vessels navigating through or within the EEZ under two circumstances. First, the coastal State may prescribe navigational measures, primarily through IMO, to regulate the movement of all foreign vessels in order to protect certain marine species or their habitats. Second, the coastal State may prescribe specific regulations towards foreign fishing vessels to protect such exclusive use. In the case where foreign fishing vessels[53] are given access to fish the surplus of the allowable catch through agreements or other arrangement with the coastal State, they must comply with the conservation measures established in that State's coastal laws and regulations.[54]

Vessels may pose various threats to marine lives and habitats, *inter alia*, pollution including greenhouse gas emissions, aquatic nuisance species transferred through ballast water, and physical damages through grounding and collisions.[55] Measures that aim to reduce such impacts primarily relate to the use of ships' routeing systems developed and monitored under the auspices of IMO.[56] If the coastal State has sufficient reason to believe that the density of traffic is hazardous to the safety of navigation and/or protection of the marine environment in or around a specific area, it may submit a proposal to IMO for approval to adopt

[51] UNCLOS Article 194(5); Sands and Peel (2018) 515; Boyle and Redgwell (2021) 750–752. Climate Change Advisory Opinion para 414.

[52] Dux (2011) 38–40.

[53] Agreement to Promote Compliance with International Conservation and Management Measures by Fishing Vessels on the High Seas (24 November 1995, in force 24 April 2003) 2221 UNTS 91, Article 1(a): 'Fishing vessel' means any vessel used or intended for use for the purposes of the commercial exploitation of living marine resources, including mother ships and any other vessels directly engaged in such fishing operations.

[54] UNCLOS Articles 62(2) and (4), 73; Request for an Advisory Opinion Submitted by the Sub-Regional Fisheries Commission (SRFC), Advisory Opinion of 2 April 2015, ITLOS Reports 2015, p. 4, para 102 (Fisheries Advisory Opinion); Churchill, Lowe and Sander (2022) 543; Sands and Peel (2018) 515.

[55] UNCLOS Article 1(1)(4); IMO Res A.982(24), 1 December 2005, Annex: Revised Guidelines for the Identification and Designation of Particularly Sensitive Sea Areas (PSSA), para 2.1 (IMO Revised PSSA Guidelines); Climate Change Advisory Opinion para 179.

[56] IMO, 'Ships' Routeing' www.imo.org/en/OurWork/Safety/Pages/ShipsRouteing.aspx.

ships' routeing systems.[57] These systems may be made voluntary or mandatory for 'all ships, certain categories of ships, or ships carrying certain cargoes' in the designated sea areas.[58] The proposed ships' routeing systems must 'reasonably be expected to significantly prevent or reduce the risk of pollution or other damage to the marine environment of the area concerned'.[59] The precise measures will depend upon the particular circumstances it is intended to alleviate, but may include some or all of the following: traffic separation schemes, two-way routes, recommended tracks, areas to be avoided, roundabouts, precautionary areas and deep-water routes.[60] For instance, in a coral reef area where anchoring is hazardous or could result in unacceptable damage to the marine habitat, the coastal State may establish through IMO a clearly defined no-anchoring area where anchoring is prohibited by all ships or certain classes of ships. In addition, it is very common for a coastal States to establish closed areas during spawning seasons to preserve and improve the spawning of domestic species, and it may be worth considering using similar conservation measures for species found in the EEZ to protect marine habitats.[61]

Further, many coastal States are taking various measures to prevent and deter illegal, unreported and unregulated (IUU) fishing in their EEZs, with some regulating the navigation of foreign fishing vessels in their EEZs.[62] IUU fishing undermines the objective of sustainable use of fisheries, which is considered one of the major threats to coastal State efforts to conserve and manage the living resources in the EEZ and is

[57] International Convention for the Safety of Life at Sea, as amended (1 November 1974, in force 25 May 1980) 1184 UNTS 2, Chapter V, Regulation 10, paras 1–2 (SOLAS); IMO LEG/MISC.8 (2014) 34.

[58] IMO MSC/Circ.1060, 6 January 2003, Annex: Guidance Note on the Preparation of Proposals on Ships' Routing Systems and Ship Reporting Systems for Submission to the Sub-Committee on Safety of Navigation, para. 2.1.

[59] Ibid Annex, para 3.5.2.

[60] IMO Res A.572(14), 20 November 1985, General Provisions on Ships' Routeing, para 2.1.

[61] Douglas M. Johnston, *The International Law of Fisheries: A Framework for Policy-Oriented Inquires* (Yale 1965) 61, 65; UNCLOS Article 62(4)(c); IMO MEPC 43/6/2, 31 March 1999, Identification and Protection of Special Areas and Particularly Sensitive Sea Areas, Relationship between the 1982 United Nations Convention on the Law of the Sea and the IMO Guidelines for the Designation of Special Areas and the Identification of Particularly Sensitive Sea Areas, Submitted by the Division for Ocean Affairs and the Law of the Sea, Office of Legal Affairs, United Nations, para 4; Churchill, Lowe and Sander (2022) 291.

[62] William T. Burke, 'Exclusive Fisheries Zones and Freedom of Navigation' (1982) 20(3) San Diego L Rev 595, 606–622; Fisheries Advisory Opinion para 106.

responsible for the depletion of many fish stocks.[63] It has also been identified as one of the main causes of the overfishing that has 'constrained progress in achieving food security for dependent populations and supporting sustainable livelihoods' and has indirectly threatened international peace and security.[64]

Costa Rica, for example, requires foreign fishing vessels without fishing permits transiting its EEZ to 'communicate entry and departure' to local authorities with information on the characteristics of the vessel, proposed course, place of entry and exit, and time required for passage.[65] Similar legislation was adopted by Canada whereby 'no foreign fishing vessel shall enter Canadian fisheries waters for any purpose unless authorized'.[66] In addition to setting specific regulations for foreign fishing vessels, Maldives extended restrictions to all types of foreign vessels by asserting that 'no foreign vessels shall enter the [EEZ] of Maldives except with prior authorization from the Government of Maldives in accordance with the laws of Maldives'.[67] These unilateral domestic laws create obligations for foreign fishing vessels (all vessels, in the case of Maldives) transiting through the EEZ, which effectively places a condition on the freedom of navigation that seems to be contrary to the freedom of navigation preserved in Article 58(1) of UNCLOS.[68]

Ship reporting systems, which are commonly used for monitoring the movement of foreign vessels, must be adopted and implemented through IMO.[69] The coastal State may propose establishing a ship reporting

[63] FAO, 'Illegal, Unreported and Unregulated Fishing' www.fao.org/iuu-fishing/en/; International Plan of Action to Prevent, Deter and Eliminate Illegal, Unreported and Unregulated Fishing (FAO 2001) para 1.

[64] United Nations General Assembly (UNGA) A/63/63, 10 March 2008, Oceans and the Law of the Sea: Report of the Secretary-General, paras 98–99.

[65] Costa Rica, Law No. 6267/1978, Article 7; Decree No. 9996-S of 16 April 1979, at FAO Corporate Document Repository, 'Table C: Coastal State Requirements for Foreign Fishing' www.fao.org/docrep/V9982E/v9982e10.htm.

[66] Canada, Coastal Fisheries Protection Act, RSC 1985, c C-33, Article 3. According to Article 2, 'Canadian fisheries waters' include 'all waters in the fishing zones of Canada, all waters in the territorial sea of Canada and all internal waters of Canada'; Canada, Oceans Act, SC 1996, c 31 Article 16: 'The fishing zones of Canada consist of areas of the sea adjacent to the coast of Canada that are prescribed in the regulations'.

[67] Maldives, Maritime Zones of Maldives Act No.6/96, Article 14, www.un.org/Depts/los/LEGISLATIONANDTREATIES/PDFFILES/MDV_1996_Act.pdf; Fisheries Act of the Maldives, No. 14/2019, Articles 25–26, https://faolex.fao.org/docs/pdf/mdv195984.pdf.

[68] J. Ashley Roach, *Excessive Maritime Claims* (4th ed., Brill 2021) 463–467.

[69] SOLAS Chapter V, Regulation 11, para 1.

system in a specific area to address issues relating to 'the safety and efficiency of navigation and/or to increase the protection of the marine environment', including marine habitats.[70] Under a duly established ship reporting system, a foreign vessel may be required to provide its identity, position, course and other related information to the shore-based authority through the automatic identification system, long-range identification and tracking system or other applicable ship reporting systems.[71] The information required should be restricted to that essential for the proper operation of the system.[72] IMO has approved mandatory ship reporting systems in areas that partially cover an EEZ of a coastal State for navigation safety and environmental protection purposes.[73] The coastal State could arguably, through IMO, require foreign fishing vessels to provide identification information upon entering or leaving certain areas of its EEZ based on its sovereign rights over living resources, provided that it has given due regard to a foreign vessel's right of free navigation.

There are also safeguards to preserve navigational freedoms when the coastal State attempts to adopt protective measures in the EEZ. For example, when delineating ships' routeing systems, the coastal State must ensure that routes follow existing patterns of traffic flow as closely as possible and should allow optimum use of aids to navigation; when proposing a ship reporting system, the coastal State should limit the requested information to that which is essential to achieving the objectives of the system.[74] These navigation regulations, when duly adopted through IMO and implemented by the coastal State, could be used to support the protection of living resources and the marine environment in the EEZ.[75]

It is worth noting that State practice and a number of judicial decisions have regarded the conservation and management of living resources as one of the major components of the comprehensive approach to preserving and protecting the marine environment.[76] ITLOS stated in the

[70] IMO Res MSC.43 (64), 9 December 1994, Guidelines and Criteria for Ship Reporting Systems, para 2.1.

[71] SOLAS Chapter V, Regulation 19.

[72] IMO MSC/Circ.1060 Annex, para 6.2.2.

[73] IMO Res MSC.126(75), 20 May 2002, Mandatory Ship Reporting Systems (in Greenland waters); IMO Res MSC.190(79), 6 December 2004, Adoption of Mandatory Ship Reporting System in the Western European Particularly Sensitive Sea Area.

[74] IMO MSC/Circ.1060 Annex, paras 3.4, 6.2.

[75] Markus Detjen, 'The Western European PSSA: Testing a Unique International Concept to Protect Imperilled Marine Ecosystems' (2006) 30 Marine Policy 442, 453.

[76] Kwiatkowska (1989) 56–57; Sands and Peel (2018) 558–564.

Southern Bluefin Tuna cases that 'the conservation of the living resources of the sea is an element in the protection and preservation of the marine environment'.[77] This was confirmed in the *Fisheries Advisory Opinion* in which ITLOS further stated that

> the flag State is under an obligation to ensure compliance by vessels flying its flag with the relevant conservation measures concerning living resources enacted by the coastal State for its [EEZ] because, as concluded by the Tribunal, they constitute an integral element in the protection and preservation of the marine environment.[78]

This approach was reconfirmed by the arbitral tribunal in the *South China Sea* case, where it found China breached its environmental obligations under Article 192 of UNCLOS because of its failure to prevent its fishing vessels from taking turtles and giant clams.[79] And additionaly by ITLOS in the *Climate Change Advisory Opinion*, where it observed that 'the conservation of living resources and marine life, which falls within the general obligation to protect and preserve the marine environment, requires measures that may vary over time depending on the activities involved and the threats to the marine environment'.[80] Accordingly, the protection of rare and endangered species, as well as vulnerable marine habitats and areas, became the primary basis for the designation of specially protected marine areas in the EEZ under the environmental protection realm, which will be discussed in Section 4.3.2.2.

4.2.1.2 Regulation of Activities Ancillary to Fishing

The categories of coastal regulations listed in Article 62(4) are illustrative rather than exhaustive, as signified by the term '*inter alia*' in the introduction.[81] The list establishes guidelines for the coastal State to adopt fisheries laws and regulations that are designated to avoid over-exploitation of the

[77] Southern Bluefin Tuna Cases (New Zealand v. Japan; Australia v. Japan), Provisional Measures, Order of 27 August 1999, ITLOS Reports 1999, p. 280, para 70.

[78] Fisheries Advisory Opinion para 120.

[79] In the Matter of the South China Sea Arbitration before an Arbitral Tribunal Constituted under Annex VII to the 1982 United Nations Convention on the Law of the Sea between the Republic of the Philippines and the People's Republic of China, Award, 12 July 2016, PCA Case No 2013-19, para 960.

[80] Climate Change Advisory Opinion paras 169, 409.

[81] Francisco Orrego Vicuña, *The Exclusive Economic Zone: Regime and Legal Nature under International Law* (Cambridge University Press 1989) 66; Nordquist, Nandan and Rosenne (1993) 637; M/V 'Virginia G' Case para 213.

resources and to meet the coastal State's 'environmental, social and economic goals'.[82] But it does not clearly define the scope of fishing activities that are subject to regulation by the coastal State. In the 1977 Portuguese law, 'fishing means the search for, the catch, the harvesting or the utilisations of any living resources' in the EEZ, as well as activities 'preparatory to fishing' or 'adversely affecting to the exercise of fishing'.[83] This broad interpretation is supported by subsequent State practice and judicial decisions, which shows the tendency of the coastal State to regulate a wide array of activities connected with fishing activities.

In January 1985, Canadian authorities refused to grant a licence for fishing in the Gulf of St Lawrence to the French vessel *La Bretagne*, which was equipped with on-board fish-filleting equipment. French authorities challenged this decision on the basis of a bilateral agreement and submitted the dispute to arbitration.[84] The arbitral tribunal considered the phrase 'fishery regulations' in Canadian law as covering all the rules applicable to fishing activities, taking into consideration future developments, and determined that it refers not only to 'those setting technical standards for the physical conditions in which the fishing is carried on but also those requiring the completion of certain formalities prior to the performance of these activities'.[85] Accordingly, coastal States may adopt and enforce laws to regulate all fishing activities to maintain order on fishing grounds as well as to protect and conserve the living resources, albeit subject to UNCLOS (as adopted) and general international law. First, although the list in Article 62(4) is not exhaustive, it does not authorise coastal States to regulate subjects of a different nature other than those described; for example, 'fishing equipment' should not be interpreted to include processing equipment that is beyond the ordinary meaning of this term.[86] Second, the exercise of coastal States' rights subject to the rule of 'reasonableness' requires that the regulations must be proportional to the aim legally pursued and gives reasonable regard to the rights of other States.[87] Furthermore, such rights are also subject to the rule of 'relativity', whereby the prohibition of an activity could only

[82] UNCLOS Article 61(3); Nordquist, Nandan and Rosenne (1993) 635, 637.

[83] Portugal, Act No. 33/77, 28 May 1977, Regarding the Juridical Status of the Portuguese Territorial Sea and the EEZ, Article 4(3), www.un.org/Depts/los/LEGISLATIONANDTREATIES/PDFFILES/PRT_1977_Act.pdf.

[84] La Bretagne Arbitration (Canada v. France), Summary (1990) 82 Int'l L Reports 591–592.

[85] Ibid 618–620 (paras 37–38).

[86] Ibid 630 (para 52).

[87] Ibid 631 (para 54).

be legislated and enforced if the coastal State can prove that the practice of this activity would inevitably lead to an infringement of the law.[88]

ITLOS had its first opportunity to address the scope of Article 62(4) in the *M/V Saiga* case, where Guinea arrested a vessel for supplying oil to three fishing vessels in the Guinean EEZ as a violation of its customs law.[89] During the prompt release phase, ITLOS stated that

> it has already been indicated that laws or regulations on bunkering of fishing vessels may arguably be classified as laws or regulations on activities within the scope of the exercise by the coastal State of its sovereign rights to explore, exploit, conserve and manage the living resources in the [EEZ].[90]

But it did not come to a clear conclusion. At the merits phase, ITLOS avoided making any findings on this question by examining a broader question of the application of customs laws in the Guinean EEZ.[91] When denying Guinea's argument to apply customs laws in the EEZ, ITLOS seems to have applied the same rule of 'reasonableness' and 'relativity': first, it pointed out that recourse to the principle of 'public interest' to apply customs law in the EEZ would entitle a coastal State to prohibit any activities that it considers as affecting its economic interests and would unreasonably curtail the rights of other States; second, there was no evidence showing that Guinea's 'essential interests were in grave and imminent peril' or that the application of the customs laws was the only means to protect those interests.[92]

In 2011, ITLOS received another case regarding a coastal State's ability to regulate the passage of foreign vessels through its EEZ based on its assertion of natural resource protection measures. The Panamanian-flagged fuel oil tanker *M/V Virginia G* was arrested and detained by the maritime authorities of Guinea-Bissau for supplying fuel to four fishing vessels that had initially been authorised to carry out refueling services in Guinea-Bissau's EEZ through a third local party.[93] ITLOS interpreted Article 62(4) as 'for all activities that may be regulated by a

[88] Ibid 637 (para 63).

[89] M/V 'Saiga' Case (Saint Vincent and the Grenadines v. Guinea), Prompt Release, Application Submitted by Saint Vincent and the Grenadines, 11 November 1997 www.itlos.org/en/main/cases/list-of-cases/case-no-1/.

[90] M/V 'Saiga' Case (Saint Vincent and the Grenadines v. Guinea), Prompt Release, Judgment of 4 December 1997, ITLOS Reports 1997, p. 16, para 63.

[91] M/V 'Saiga' (No. 2) (Saint Vincent and the Grenadines v. Guinea), Judgment of 1 July 1999, ITLOS Reports 1999, p. 10, paras 137–138.

[92] Ibid paras 129–136.

[93] M/V 'Virginia G' Case para 58–63.

coastal State there must be a direct connection to fishing', and it observed that 'such connection to fishing exists for the bunkering of foreign vessels fishing in the [EEZ]'.[94] It went on to declare that

> the regulation by a coastal State of bunkering of foreign vessels fishing in its [EEZ] is among those measures which the coastal State may take in its [EEZ] to conserve and manage its living resources under article 56 of the Convention read together with article 62, paragraph 4, of the Convention. This view is also confirmed by State practice which has developed after the adoption of the Convention.[95]

As mentioned earlier, in the subsequent *Norstar* case, ITLOS held that bunkering on the high seas came within the high seas freedom of navigation, which it noted also applies in the EEZ under Article 58(1) of UNCLOS.[96] This suggested that bunkering of ships other than fishing vessels in the EEZ was not subject to coastal State regulation. ITLOS confirmed this finding shortly afterwards in the *San Padre Pio* case at the provisional measures phase when it observed that Switzerland's 'claims that bunkering activities carried out by the *M/T San Padre Pio* in the EEZ of Nigeria are part of the freedom of navigation and that it has exclusive jurisdiction as flag State with respect to such bunkering activities' appeared to be 'plausible'.[97] ITLOS gave no reasons to support this view other than noting that it took into account the legal arguments of the parties and the evidence available to it. By agreement of the two parties in December 2021, the proceedings of the merits of the *San Padre Pio* case was discontinued and ITLOS did not have the chance to confirm its provisional view on the merits.[98]

In *La Bretagne*, the arbitral tribunal did not accept Canada's claim that it could regulate fish-processing equipment because the prohibition of using on-board filleting equipment was not explicitly included in its national law, and it was not a 'long-standing policy', but not because Canada did not have the right to prescribe such regulations.[99] In *M/V Saiga*, ITLOS rejected the application of customs law in the EEZ but suggested reclassifying the bunkering of fishing vessels as an activity

[94] Ibid para 215.
[95] Ibid para 217.
[96] M/V 'Norstar' Case paras 219–220.
[97] M/T 'San Padre Pio' Case paras 107–108.
[98] Churchill, Lowe and Sander (2022) 272–273; M/T 'San Padre Pio' (No. 2) Case (Switzerland v. Nigeria), Order, 29 December 2021.
[99] La Bretagne Arbitration 622–626 (paras 42–46).

ancillary to fishing.[100] Later in *M/V Virginia G*, ITLOS stated expressly that the coastal State has the right to regulate bunkering of foreign vessels fishing in its EEZ as an activity ancillary to fishing.[101]

There is a tendency for a coastal State to claim jurisdiction over a broad range of activities that may affect its sovereign rights over the living resources in the EEZ. The Canadian Coastal Fisheries Protection Act defines a fishing vessel in a broad scope. It includes the vessel that is used or equipped for fishing; processing or transporting fish; taking, processing or transporting marine plants; provisioning, servicing, repairing or maintaining any vessels of a foreign fishing fleet while at sea; and transhipping fish or marine plants.[102] Whether or not the activity concerned is sufficiently connected to the sovereign rights of the coastal State ought to be decided on a case-by-case basis, taking into account the circumstances under which the activity is conducted and depending on the type of legislation applied by the coastal State.[103] But such laws need to be compatible with UNCLOS and must not unreasonably impede other States' freedoms in the EEZ. Compliance with coastal States' laws and regulations would inevitably increase the burden of foreign vessels traversing these waters; more importantly, violation of these laws could lead to enforcement measures being taken by coastal States.

4.2.2 Non-Living Resources

The coastal State's 'sovereign rights for the purpose of exploring and exploiting, conserving and managing the natural resources' in the EEZ also cover the non-living resources of the seabed and subsoil as well as the superjacent waters.[104] The indication of non-living resources of 'the waters superjacent to the seabed' refers to the various minerals which can be extracted from sea waters.[105] Generally, the reference to 'conserving

100 M/V 'Saiga' Case para 63.
101 M/V 'Virginia G' Case para 217.
102 Canada, Coastal Fisheries Protection Act, Article 2(1).
103 David Anderson, 'Coastal State Jurisdiction and High Seas Freedoms in the EEZ in the Light of the Saiga Case', in Clive R. Symmons (ed.), *Selected Contemporary Issues in the Law of the Sea* (Martinus Nijhoff 2011) 113.
104 UNCLOS Article 56(1)(a).
105 Churchill, Lowe and Sander (2022) 264.

and managing' applies primarily, if not exclusively, to the living resources, and the phrase 'exploring and exploiting' is intended to apply to non-living resources.[106]

In respect of the non-living resources found on the seabed and of its subsoil, the EEZ overlaps in its entirety with the continental shelf regime within the 200 NM limit from the baseline.[107] Coastal States thus enjoy essentially unrestricted rights in the sense that no one has the right to share these resources even if the coastal State does not undertake such exploration and exploitation.[108] Coastal States also have exclusive right to authorise, use and regulate any means to conduct the exploration and exploitation, including drilling for all purposes and tunnelling.[109] The primary facilities from which exploration and exploitation take place are artificial islands, offshore installations and structures, all of which the coastal State has exclusive right to construct and to authorise and regulate.[110]

All States, in exercising their freedoms and performing their duties, must have due regard to the rights and duties of the coastal State and must comply with duly adopted domestic laws and regulations.[111] It would be impossible for coastal States to undertake economic exploration and exploitation of the non-living resources unless other States admit some slight encroachment on high seas freedoms.[112] In exercising its sovereign rights over non-living resources, the coastal State undertakes the same obligation to have due regard to other States' rights and duties and shall not unduly affect their implementation. The use of the infrastructure to support the exploration and exploitation will be the primary concern that may interfere with foreign navigation and overflight, which will be discussed in Section 4.4.

4.2.3 Other Activities for Economic Uses

According to Article 56(1)(a), the coastal State's sovereign rights also extend to 'other activities for the economic exploitation and exploration of the zone, such as the production of energy from the water, currents and winds'. The examples are not exhaustive, as indicated by the phrase

106 Proelss 'Article 56' (2017) 426; Churchill, Lowe and Sander (2022) 263–264.
107 UNCLOS Articles 56(3), 77.
108 UNCLOS Article 77(1).
109 UNCLOS Articles 81, 85.
110 Nordquist, Nandan and Rosenne (1993) 928; UNCLOS Articles 60(1)(b)–(c), 80.
111 UNCLOS Article 58(3).
112 Churchill, Lowe and Sander (2022) 242.

'such as', and are intended to cover all of the economic activities that may emerge, including the production of solar energy or thermal energy from the ocean, the utilisation of minerals dissolved in marine waters, offshore aquaculture activities, ocean fertilization and other marine geoengineering activities, the exploitation of icebergs as freshwater reservoirs and the desalination of sea water.[113] This provision permits the coastal State to take advantage of technological developments to further its economic interests through any new means to utilise or exploit the natural resources of the EEZ.[114] It also, arguably, gives the coastal State jurisdiction over activities affiliated with such emerging uses. The construction and utilisation of the supporting infrastructure to these economic exploitation and exploration activities must be read in conjunction with the coastal State's jurisdiction over artificial islands, installations and structures that will be discussed in Section 4.4.

Most coastal States have asserted such rights by incorporating Article 56(1) verbatim without specifying these activities.[115] It is not entirely clear from such national legislation and subsequent State practice what activities may be included in 'other activities for the economic exploitation and exploration of the zone'. However, reserving such activities to the coastal State's rights ultimately prevented them from being classified as unattributed rights, and as such facilitated the determination and attribution of other residual rights of the EEZ under Article 59.[116]

The exercise of the sovereign rights over these potential economic activities would be subject to the same rules as other economic uses of the EEZ. On the one hand, the coastal State has both legislative and enforcement jurisdiction over these economic activities. On the other hand, while carrying out these economic activities, coastal States are obliged to have due regard to the freedoms of other States and must refrain from activities that cause unreasonable interference with these freedoms.

[113] Kwiatkowska (1989) 105–106; Dux (2011) 54; Proelss 'Article 56' (2017) 427. GESAMP (2019). 'High level review of a wide range of proposed marine geoengineering techniques' (P. W. Boyd and C. M. G. Vivian, eds.). (IMO/FAO/UNESCO-IOC/UNIDO/WMO/IAEA/UN/UN Environment/UNDP/ISA Joint Group of Experts on the Scientific Aspects of Marine Environmental Protection). Rep. Stud. GESAMP No. 98, 144, 42–77.

[114] Churchill, Lowe and Sander (2022) 266.

[115] UN DOALAS, *The Law of the Sea: National Legislation on the Exclusive Economic Zone* (United Nations, 1993); Robin R. Churchill, 'The Impact of State Practice on the Jurisdictional Framework Contained in the LOS Convention', in Alex G. Oude Elferink (ed.), *Stability and Change in the Law of the Sea: The Role of the LOS Convention* (Martinus Nijhoff 2005) 127–128.

[116] Orrego Vicuña (1989) 72.

4.2.4 *Enforcement Jurisdiction*

Coastal States' enforcement powers[117] came a long way during the negotiation of UNCLOS, as many major long-distance fishing States preferred exclusive flag State enforcement jurisdiction or jurisdiction through regional or international organisations with regard to violations in the EEZ.[118] The International Law Commission (ILC) recognised, when it first introduced the term 'sovereign rights' into the context of the continental shelf in the 1956 Draft Articles, that enforcement powers must be included to guarantee the exercise of such rights.[119] This authorisation is explicitly included in Article 73 of UNCLOS where a foreign vessel is found fishing without a licence, or acting in a way contrary to its licence, or infringing any other applicable laws and regulations in the EEZ, the coastal State may board, inspect, arrest and initiate juridical proceedings as appropriate against the vessel to ensure compliance.[120] The precondition of the enforcement jurisdiction is that the coastal State has established relevant laws and regulations on fishing that are compatible with UNCLOS.[121] Although coastal States are given broad enforcement jurisdiction as 'in the exercise of its sovereign rights' over the living resources, they must act in 'good faith' and have 'due regard to the rights and duties of other States'.[122]

It is noteworthy that the coastal State does not have explicit enforcement jurisdiction for exploration and exploitation of the non-living resources or other economic activities, in contrast to the clear authorisation for living resources provided in Article 73.[123] Nevertheless, the coastal State should have the competence to prevent and punish such violations of foreign vessels based on the extensive scope of its sovereign rights.[124] This competence is further recognised in Article 111 of

[117] Enforcement jurisdiction over IUU fishing and the general right of hot pursuit are also discussed in Chapter 7 in this volume.

[118] Nordquist, Nandan and Rosenne (1993) 786–791; James Harrison, 'Article 73', in Proelss (2017) 557–558.

[119] ILC Draft Articles Article 68 Commentary 2.

[120] UNCLOS Article 73(1); M/V 'Virginia G' Case para 266.

[121] M/V 'Saiga' (No. 2) paras 122, 136.

[122] UNCLOS Articles 56(2), 73(1), 300; M/V 'Virginia G' Case para 347.

[123] Nordquist, Nandan and Rosenne (1993) 791–794; Gemma Andreone, 'The Exclusive Economic Zone', in Donald R. Rothwell, Alex G. Oude Elferink, Karen N. Scott and Tim Stephens (eds.), *The Oxford Handbook of the Law of the Sea* (Oxford University Press 2015) 170; Churchill, Lowe and Sander (2022) 244.

[124] M/V 'Virginia G' Case para 211; Arctic Sunrise Arbitration paras 283–284, 324; Churchill, Lowe and Sander (2022) 263.

UNCLOS where the right of hot pursuit applies to violations of the EEZ or continental shelf laws and regulations.[125] The coastal State would have the right to take 'appropriate' measures to prevent interference with its sovereign rights to non-living resources in the EEZ or on the continental shelf, provided that such measures 'fulfil the tests of reasonableness, necessity and proportionality'.[126] There are coastal States that clearly claim enforcement jurisdiction over violations with regard to the exploration and exploitation of non-living resources in the EEZ or on the continental shelf. Canada, for example, applies federal laws 'on or under any marine installation or structure ... attached or anchored to the continental shelf of Canada in connection with the exploration of that shelf or exploitation of its mineral or other non-living resources'.[127] A Canadian court would have jurisdiction 'in respect of any such matter involving a federal law' that arises in the EEZ, and the court may 'make any order or exercise any power it considers necessary' in respect of such matter.[128] The enforcement officer is authorised to exercise the powers to stop, inspect, search and seize any suspected conveyance, on reasonable grounds, to ensure compliance with applicable Canadian laws.[129]

It is significant that the right of hot pursuit applies to violations in the EEZ.[130] If the coastal State has 'good reason to believe that the ship has violated the laws and regulations' applicable in the EEZ, it may approach the ship and verify its flag and other basic information.[131] Hot pursuit may only be commenced when the foreign ship is in the EEZ and refuses to stop voluntarily after being given a visual or auditory signal to do so.[132] It is not necessary that the order to stop is given when the foreign ship is undertaking the activities that violated the applicable law. As confirmed in the *M/V Saiga*, the fact that the pursuit commenced after the alleged illegal activity took place was not challenged by either the flag State or ITLOS.[133] Hot pursuit must be continuous and

125 UNCLOS Article 111(2); Myron H. Nordquist, Satya N. Nandan and Shabtai Rosenne (eds.), *United Nations Convention on the Law of the Sea 1982: A Commentary*, Vol. III (Martinus Nijhoff 1995) 257.

126 M/V 'Virginia G' Case paras 284, 326–327; Arctic Sunrise Arbitration para 326; Churchill, Lowe and Sander (2022) 264.

127 Canada, Oceans Act Article 20(1).

128 Ibid Article 22(1) and (3).

129 Ibid Article 39(1).

130 UNCLOS Articles 58(2), 111(1); Arctic Sunrise Arbitration para 244.

131 UNCLOS Articles 73(1), 111(1), 214, 216(1), 220(3) and (5)–(6), 226(1).

132 UNCLOS Article 111(4).

133 M/V 'Saiga' (No. 2) paras 140, 142, 147.

uninterrupted in order for it to be continued outside the EEZ, and such right ceases when the foreign ship pursued 'enters the territorial sea of its own State or of a third State'.[134] These conditions for the exercise of the right of hot pursuit are 'cumulative; each of them has to be satisfied for the pursuit to be legitimate under the Convention'.[135]

The term 'boarding' implies that coastal authorities may board the vessel and may use force if it is necessary and not in violation of UNCLOS and the Charter of the United Nations.[136] 'Inspection' is normally limited to the examination of various certificates, records or other documents that the vessel is required to carry; further inspection may be undertaken if the circumstances so warrant.[137] The word 'arrest' is used in relation to both the vessel and the crew, signifying the initiation of detention with the purpose of invoking judicial proceedings.[138] These necessary enforcement procedures must be applied on reasonable grounds and be proportional to the circumstances to ensure that the legal rights of the foreign vessel and the fishers are not unduly interfered with.[139]

The coastal State must apply lawful enforcement measures to board and arrest the foreign vessel, particularly in cases where the use of force was involved. First, these 'enforcement activities can be exercised only by duly authorized identifiable officials of a coastal State and . . . their vessels must be clearly marked as being on government service'.[140] Second, enforcement activities should not 'endanger the safety of navigation or otherwise create any hazard to a vessel, or bring a vessel to an unsafe port or anchorage, or expose the marine environment to an unreasonable risk'.[141] Third, although the use of force is not prohibited, it 'must be avoided as far as possible and, where force is unavoidable, it must not go beyond what is reasonable and necessary under the circumstances.

[134] UNCLOS Article 111(1) and (3).
[135] M/V 'Saiga' (No. 2) para 146.
[136] Charter of the United Nations (6 June 1945, in force 24 October 1945) 1 UNTS XVI, Article 2(4); UNCLOS Article 225; Nordquist, Nandan and Rosenne (1993) 794; Harrison 'Article 73' (2017) 559.
[137] UNCLOS Article 226(1); Nordquist, Nandan and Rosenne (1993) 794; Harrison 'Article 73' (2017) 558.
[138] Nordquist, Nandan and Rosenne (1993) 795.
[139] M/V 'Virginia G' Case para 270; Churchill, Lowe and Sander (2022) 546.
[140] M/V 'Virginia G' Case para 342.
[141] UNCLOS Article 225; M/V 'Virginia G' Case para 373.

Considerations of humanity must apply in the law of the sea, as they do in other areas of international law'.[142]

The coastal State's enforcement measures will predictably affect the activities of foreign vessels in the EEZ. In order to minimise the potential impacts and protect the flag State's jurisdiction, UNCLOS has laid down further safeguards for the exercise of coastal State enforcement jurisdiction. Coastal States are obliged to promptly notify the flag State, through appropriate channels, of the arrest or detention of its vessels, of the actions taken and any subsequently imposed penalties.[143] It is worth noting that the coastal State is not required to suspend its proceedings to impose penalties if the flag State takes actions, and its right to institute proceedings is not subject to a prosecution period as in the case of vessel-source pollution in the EEZ, which is discussed in Section 4.3.3.

Moreover, a coastal State must promptly release the arrested fishing vessels and their crews upon the posting of reasonable bond or other security.[144] This obligation includes 'elementary considerations of humanity and due process of law' as well as 'a concern for fairness'.[145] The coastal State should, based on its domestic law, determine the reasonable bond or security that is of a financial nature in light of the assessment of relevant factors.[146] In the case where the flag State challenges the release of the detained vessel and crews by the coastal State, it may bring the dispute under a special compulsory procedure known as prompt release as discussed in Section 4.5.[147] The question of release will be dealt with by a court or tribunal that has jurisdiction 'without prejudice to the merits of any case before the appropriate domestic forum against the vessel, its owner or its crew'.[148]

[142] Agreement for the Implementation of the Provisions of the United Nations Convention on the Law of the Sea of 10 December 1982 Relating to the Conservation and Management of Straddling Fish Stocks and Highly Migratory Fish Stocks (4 August 1995, in force 11 December 2001) 2167 UNTS 3, Article 22(1)(f) (Fish Stocks Agreement); M/V 'Saiga' (No. 2) paras 155–156; M/V 'Virginia G' Case para 360.

[143] UNCLOS Article 73(4); M/V 'Virginia G' Case para 328.

[144] UNCLOS Article 73(2); The 'Monte Confurco' Case (Seychelles v. France), Prompt Release, Judgment of 18 December 2000, ITLOS Reports 2000, p. 86, para 70.

[145] The 'Juno Trader' Case (Saint Vincent and the Grenadines v. Guinea-Bissau), Prompt Release, Judgment of 18 December 2004, ITLOS Reports 2004, p. 17, para 77.

[146] The 'Volga' Case (Russian Federation v. Australia), Prompt Release, Judgment of 23 December 2002, ITLOS Reports 2002, p. 10, para 77; The 'Hoshinmaru' Case (Japan v. Russian Federation), Prompt Release, Judgment of 6 August 2007, ITLOS Reports 2005–2007, p. 18, para 88.

[147] UNCLOS Article 292(1); Harrison 'Article 73' (2017) 560.

[148] UNCLOS Article 292(3); M/V 'Saiga' Case para 86.

Furthermore, where the violations are established, the coastal State may impose appropriate penalties as applicable in its domestic law based on its sovereign rights in the EEZ.[149] These sanctions are expected to be 'adequate in severity to be effective in securing compliance and to discourage violations wherever they occur and shall deprive offenders of the benefits accruing from their illegal activities'.[150] ITLOS has confirmed that, 'in the light of the practice of coastal States on the sanctioning of violations of fishing laws and regulations', penalties imposed under Article 73(1) may include the confiscation of fishing vessels.[151] However, the imposed penalties 'may not include imprisonment, in the absence of agreements to the contrary by the States concerned, or any other forms of corporal punishment'.[152] Nevertheless, there are around twenty States that apply imprisonment penalties for violations of their EEZ laws.[153] For example, under Indian law, offences of the EEZ regulations may be punished with imprisonment of up to three years with or without fines.[154] Similar provisions can be found in the EEZ laws of Bangladesh,[155] Barbados,[156] the Philippines[157] and Portugal.[158] These domestic laws have clearly exceeded the enforcement rights permitted under UNCLOS.[159]

149 M/V 'Virginia G' Case, Dissenting Opinion of Vice-President Hoffmann, Judges Marotta Rangel, Chandrasekhara Rao, Kateka, Gao and Bouguetaia, para 49; Harrison 'Article 73' (2017) 562.

150 Fish Stocks Agreement Article 19(2).

151 The 'Tomimaru' Case (Japan v. Russian Federation), Prompt Release, Judgment of 6 August 2007, ITLOS Reports 2005–2007, p. 74, para 72; M/V 'Virginia G' Case para 253.

152 UNCLOS Article 73(3); M/V 'Virginia G' Case para 305.

153 Roach (2021) 170.

154 India, The Territorial Waters, Continental Shelf, Exclusive Economic Zone and other Maritime Zones Act, 1976, Act No. 80 of 28 May 1976, Article 11, www.un.org/Depts/los/LEGISLATIONANDTREATIES/PDFFILES/IND_1976_Act.pdf.

155 Bangladesh, Territorial Waters and Maritime Zones Act, No. XXVI of 1974, Article 9(3), www.un.org/Depts/los/LEGISLATIONANDTREATIES/PDFFILES/BGD_1974_Act.pdf.

156 Barbados, Marine Boundaries and Jurisdiction Act, 1978-3, 25 February 1978, Article 6(3), www.un.org/Depts/los/LEGISLATIONANDTREATIES/PDFFILES/BRB_1978_3.pdf.

157 Philippines, Presidential Decree No. 1599 of 11 June 1978 Establishing an Exclusive Economic Zone and for other Purposes, Section 5(b), www.un.org/Depts/los/LEGISLATIONANDTREATIES/PDFFILES/PHL_1978_Decree.pdf.

158 Portugal, Act No. 33/77, Territorial Sea and the EEZ, Article 8(2).

159 Nordquist, Nandan and Rosenne (1993) 795; Harrison 'Article 73' (2017) 561.

It is a considerable challenge for many coastal States to maintain effective surveillance and enforcement of vast EEZs, especially for developing States and small islands States.[160] Hence, many States have engaged in increasing co-operation through regional or international fishery management organisations or bodies to share information, conduct joint surveillance or undertake reciprocal enforcement activities.[161] In the South Pacific region, for example, seventeen States established the Pacific Islands Forum Fisheries Agency (FFA) in 1979 to provide monitoring, control and surveillance activities, policy and services for members to strengthen national capacity, and regional solidarity to achieve sustainable use of fisheries within their EEZs.[162] The FFA developed a Regional Monitoring, Control and Surveillance Strategy since 2010 and established a Regional Fisheries Surveillance Centre to coordinate the regional efforts to prevent, deter and eliminate IUU fishing in the Pacific with particular emphasis on optimised use of existing and innovative surveillance and enforcement assets from the member States.[163]

The EEZ regime gives coastal States sovereign rights and extensive competence over natural resources. Such powers were deemed necessary to protect the legitimate interests granted to the coastal State, notwithstanding corresponding curtailment of the navigational freedoms of other States. It is inevitable that the freedoms of navigation and overflight will be affected to a certain degree, especially by IMO approved navigational measures and those directly connected with fishing activities. Nevertheless, the coastal State's sovereign rights in the EEZ are confined to the functional 'purpose of exploring and exploiting, conserving and managing the natural resources', which is different from the rigorous term 'sovereignty'.[164] When exercising its rights and performing its duties, the coastal State must 'fulfil in good faith' the mutual obligation

160 Churchill, Lowe and Sander (2022) 548.

161 FAO, 'Fisheries and Aquaculture, Regional Fishery Bodies (RFB)' www.fao.org/fishery/en/rfb.

162 Pacific Islands Forum Fisheries Agency (FFA), 'About the Pacific Islands Forum Fisheries Agency' www.ffa.int/about-us/#.

163 FFA, Regional Monitoring, Control and Surveillance Strategy 2010–2015 (adopted by FFC74, May 2010), https://macbio-pacific.info/wp-content/uploads/2017/08/RMCSS-adopted-FFC-74-in-2010_0.pdf; FFA, Regional Monitoring, Control and Surveillance Strategy 2018-2023, www.ffa.int/download/regional-monitoring-control-and-surveillance-mcs-strategy-2018-2023/.

164 UNCLOS Article 56(1); Proelss 'Article 56' (2017) 424.

of 'due regard', and act 'in a manner which would not constitute an abuse of right'.[165] The exercise of the coastal State's sovereign rights must be closely related to the purposes for which the EEZ was established and must not cause unreasonable obstruction of other States' navigational freedoms.

4.3 Jurisdiction to Protect and Preserve the Marine Environment

4.3.1 General Obligation of Environmental Protection

In the wake of increasing concern about the environment, a general obligation of all States, whether coastal or landlocked, to protect and preserve the marine environment has been incorporated in Article 192 of UNCLOS. It is primarily an obligation to diligently prevent and control threats for the irreversible damage that may be caused to the marine environment, echoing the general environmental law principle, namely the precautionary approach.[166] The consensus reached at the Third Conference, the degree of acceptance of UNCLOS and subsequent State practice support the conclusion that the provisions on the protection and preservation of the marine environment represent an agreed codification of existing principles which are now part of customary international law and apply to both Party and non-Party States.[167] UNCLOS remains the only global treaty to address all matters relating to the protection and preservation of the marine environment, which is implemented and complemented by other relevant environmental treaties.[168]

The two main elements of the law relating to the protection of the marine environment are the conservation of marine biodiversity and the control of marine pollution, with the former being addressed mainly through fisheries management and conservation and the latter dominating the major provisions in Part XII of UNCLOS.[169] In the EEZ, this general environmental obligation needs to be read in conjunction with the coastal State's sovereign rights over the living resources and its

[165] UNCLOS Articles 56(3), 300.

[166] UNCLOS Article 194; Rio Declaration on Environment and Development, Principle 15; UNGA A/CONF.151/26 (Vol. I), 12 August 1992, Report of the United Nations Conference on Environment and Development (UNCED), Rio de Janeiro, 3–14 June 1992, Annex 2: Agenda 21, Chapter 17, para 17.22(a) (Agenda 21).

[167] Boyle and Redgwell (2021) 510–511.

[168] Churchill, Lowe and Sander (2022) 604–607; Climate Change Advisory Opinion, paras 223, 385.

[169] Churchill, Lowe and Sander (2022) 620–627.

jurisdiction as provided for in the relevant provisions of UNCLOS. As discussed earlier, conservation of the living resources in the EEZ has been given specific content by Article 61, which ties it to measures coastal States take to establish allowable catches, and conservation should not include a general competence for pollution control in the EEZ.[170]

Pollution is defined under UNCLOS as 'the introduction by man, directly or indirectly, of substances or energy into the marine environment' that may result in deleterious effects to marine resources or activities.[171] This definition is extensive enough to cover any human activity that satisfies these criteria, including shipping.[172] Pollution from ships takes the form of both catastrophic events and chronic pollution from regular operational discharges and can include oil and oily mixtures, noxious liquid substances, sewage, garbage, noxious solid substances, anti-fouling systems, harmful aquatic organisms and pathogens, underwater noise, air pollution and greenhouse gas emissions.[173] These substances and energy may cause serious or irreversible degradation of the marine environment. It has been recognised that shipping represents a significant contribution to the cumulative pressures that humans are imposing on the marine environment, which affects the harvest from the sea and the maintenance of biodiversity.[174]

Both the flag State and the nationality State have the primary responsibility to ensure that the ships flying their flags or under their jurisdiction comply with environmental regulations and standards.[175] Within the EEZ, the coastal State may claim concurrent jurisdiction over a foreign vessel or activity as authorised by UNCLOS and other international law.

[170] Horace B. Robertson, 'Navigation in the Exclusive Economic Zone' (1983–1984) 24(4) Va J Int'l L 865, 897.

[171] UNCLOS Article 1(4).

[172] Agenda 21, Chapter 17, para 17.18; Amit A. Pandya and Rupert Herbert-Burns with Junko Kobayashi, *Maritime Commerce and Security: The Indian Ocean* (Stimson Center 2011) 55. Climate Change Advisory Opinion, para 161.

[173] Agenda 21, Chapter 17, para 17.20; UNGA A/70/112, 22 July 2015, Summary of the First Global Integrated Marine Assessment, paras 138–143; IMO Revised PSSA Guidelines para 2.2; Timothy Fileman, Stephen de Mora and Thomas Vance, 'Physical Effects of Ships on the Environment', in Stephen de Mora, Timothy Fileman and Thomas Vance (eds.), *Environmental Impact of Ships* (Cambridge University Press 2020) 216–222. Climate Change Advisory Opinion paras 179.

[174] Alan Simcock and Osman Keh Kamara, 'Chapter 17: Shipping', in United Nations, *The First Global Integrated Marine Assessment: World Ocean Assessment I* (Cambridge University Press 2017).

[175] UNCLOS Articles 94(1), 194(2), 211(2), 217(1).

4.3.2 *Prescriptive Jurisdiction*

According to Article 56, the coastal State's environmental jurisdiction is 'as provided for in the relevant provisions of [UNCLOS]' contained in Part XII.[176] Coastal States shall take 'all measures consistent with [UNCLOS] that are necessary', using 'the best practicable means at their disposal and in accordance with their capabilities' to prevent, reduce and control pollution of the marine environment in the EEZ.[177] While taking these environmental regulation measures, the coastal State 'shall refrain from unjustifiable interference with activities carried out by other States in the exercise of their rights and in pursuance of their duties in conformity with [UNCLOS]'.[178] These requirements are intended to balance environmental protection needs and navigational interests in the EEZ.[179]

4.3.2.1 Regulation of Ships and Shipping

Under UNCLOS, jurisdiction over the prevention, reduction and control of vessel-source pollution is divided between the flag State, the coastal State and the port State.[180] The extension of coastal State jurisdiction over foreign ships for environmental issues was one of the innovative features of the EEZ regime, which from very early in the negotiations was linked to the idea of internationally accepted rules.[181] This linkage is highlighted through the notion of 'generally accepted international rules and standards' which 'reflected the crux of a delicately weighed balance of power arrived at between coastal states and shipping nations'.[182] Thus, the competence of a coastal State is limited to applying international rules and standards established by the competent international

[176] UNCLOS Article 56(1)(b)(iii).

[177] UNCLOS Article 194(1) and (3)(b); Myron H. Nordquist, Shabtai Rosenne and Alexander Yankov (eds.), *United Nations Convention on the Law of the Sea 1982: A Commentary*, Vol. IV (Martinus Nijhoff 1991) 65.

[178] UNCLOS Article 194(4).

[179] Nordquist, Rosenne and Yankov (1991) 200.

[180] UNCLOS Articles 56(1)(b)(iii), 94, 211, 217–218, 220.

[181] James Harrison, *Making the Law of the Sea* (Cambridge University Press 2011) 170; Kristin Bartenstein, 'Article 211', in Proelss (2017) 1434; Churchill, Lowe and Sander (2022) 270.

[182] International Law Association (ILA), 'Report of the Committee on Coastal State Jurisdiction relating to Marine Pollution' (ILA 2000) 45; Erik Franckx, *Vessel-Source Pollution and Coastal State Jurisdiction: The Work of the ILA Committee on Coastal State Jurisdiction Relating to Marine Pollution* (1991–2000) (Kluwer Law International 2001) 11.

organisation, the IMO, or a general international conference over foreign ships.[183] The rules of reference also allows State to implement those subsequently adopted or amended international rules and standards.[184] It should be acknowledged that there are no unified criteria to determine which international rules and standards have reached the status of 'generally accepted'.[185] It could be argued that this reference should not be limited to customary international law or binding agreements, but also include non-binding rules and standards that have been widely followed in State practice.[186] Of particular interest, the resolutions of the IMO Assembly and other main technical bodies are normally adopted by consensus of all 176 IMO Member States and accordingly reflect global agreement.[187] These resolutions often incorporate recommendations on the implementation of technical rules and standards not included in IMO treaties that can be adopted by national legislations to apply to foreign ships.[188] In addition, these resolutions may later be developed into mandatory instruments, either as an amendment to an existing treaty or as an independent treaty.[189]

Essentially, vessel-source pollution is caused by either operational (intentional) discharges or accidental (unintentional) discharges.[190] Measures to prevent, reduce and control vessel-source pollution are consequently divided into two categories: rules and standards relating to the characteristics and management of the vessel to reduce and regulate operational discharges; and regulation of the vessel and naviga-

[183] Nordquist, Rosenne and Yankov (1991) 200–201, 204; IMO LEG/MISC.8 (2014) 7–10.

[184] Climate Change Advisory Opinion paras 130–131.

[185] Bartenstein 'Article 211' (2017) 1434–1437; Sun (2021) 480; Roach (2021) 623–626. Climate Change Advisory Opinion para 280.

[186] Bernard H. Oxman, 'The Duty to Respect Generally Accepted International Standards' (1991) NYU J Int' L & Pol 109, 146–147; ILA, 'Report of the Committee on Coastal State Jurisdiction relating to Marine Pollution' (2000) 37–38. James Harrison, *Saving the Oceans through Law: The International Legal Framework for the Protection of the Marine Environment* (Oxford University Press, 2017), 140–141.

[187] Convention on the International Maritime Organization (6 March 1948, in force 17 March 1958) 289 UNTS 3, Articles 15, 28, 38; IMO, 'Member States, IGOs and NGOs' www.imo.org/en/About/Membership/Pages/Default.aspx.

[188] IMO LEG/MISC.8 (2014) 10.

[189] Zhen Sun, 'Unconventional Lawmaking in the Compliance Mechanism for the International Regulation of Shipping', in Natalie Klein (ed.), *Unconventional Lawmaking in the Law of the Sea* (Oxford University Press 2022) 99.

[190] Boyle and Redgwell (2021) 523–524.

tion to prevent and counter accidental discharges.[191] Recognising safer ships will reduce vessel-source pollution and lead to cleaner seas means that regulations to improve navigational safety positively contribute to the protection of the marine environment.[192] It is further recognised that ships contribute to air pollution and global emissions of carbon dioxide which are subject to regulations developed under the International Convention for the Prevention of Pollution from Ships (MARPOL).[193] The coastal State may regulate pollution of the marine environment from or through the atmosphere, applicable to the air space under its sovereignty and to vessels flying its flag or vessels or aircraft of its registry.[194] Therefore, the coastal State may adopt laws to regulate air pollution from foreign ships by giving effect to relevant international rules and standards, but may not regulate air pollution from foreign aircraft in its EEZ.

It is noteworthy that subsequent State practice also granted the coastal State additional rights to locate, mark and remove shipwrecks found in its EEZ if they pose a hazard to navigation or the marine environment.[195] The Nairobi International Convention on the Removal of Wrecks (RWC) was concluded under the auspice of IMO and applies only to the EEZ, or to an equivalent coastal area of up to 200 NM where no EEZ is claimed.[196] The primary responsibility for removing a wreck rests with the registered owner, who is liable for the costs of locating, marking and removing the wreck and is obliged to maintain compulsory insurance or other financial security for such purposes.[197] The coastal State in whose

[191] UNCLOS Article 194(3)(b); Erik J. Molenaar, *Coastal State Jurisdiction over Vessel-Source Pollution* (Kluwer Law International 1998) 21–25; IMO, 'Marine Environment' www.imo.org/en/OurWork/Environment/Pages/Default.aspx.

[192] *Safer Ships, Cleaner Seas – Report of Lord Donaldson's Inquiry into the Prevention of Pollution from Merchant Shipping, presented to Parliament by the Secretary of State for Transport by Command of Her Majesty, May 1994* (HM Stationery Office 1994).

[193] IMO, 'Climate Action and Clean Air in Shipping' www.imo.org/en/OurWork/Environment/Pages/Decarbonization%20and%20Clean%20air%20in%20shipping.aspx; MARPOL Annex VI: The Prevention of Air Pollution from Ships. Climate Change Advisory Opinion paras 280, 291.

[194] UNCLOS Article 212(1).

[195] Churchill, Lowe and Sander (2022) 275–276; Nairobi International Convention on the Removal of Wrecks (18 May 2007, in force 14 April 2015) 3283 UNTS I-55565, Article 1 (1) (RWC). For shipwrecks of archaeological and historical nature, see Chapter 8 in this volume.

[196] IMO, 'Nairobi International Convention on the Removal of Wrecks' www.imo.org/en/About/Conventions/Pages/Nairobi-International-Convention-on-the-Removal-of-Wrecks.aspx; RWC Article 1(1).

[197] RWC Articles 10–12.

EEZ the wreck is located has been given the status as 'affected State' and a number of associated rights, such as determining whether a wreck poses a hazard, setting a deadline for removing the wreck of concern, and removing the wreck if the registered owner fails to meet that deadline.[198] Flag States to the RWC are deemed to have consented to such actions.[199] The preamble and Article 16 of RWC state that it is to be implemented consistently with UNCLOS and does not prejudice rights and obligations under UNCLOS.

The RWC represents a modest extension to the EEZ rights of coastal States bestowed by UNCLOS by expanding the legal basis to protect navigational safety and to prevent marine environmental harm from a wreck. Given the lack of explicit reference in UNCLOS, the rights granted to the coastal State in the RWC can be seen as a specific agreement in line with Article 59, attributing rights in respect of a matter not addressed in UNCLOS.[200] The coastal State is given the right to locate, mark and remove wrecks to protect its 'related interests' that are directly affected or threatened by a wreck. The 'related interests' are connected to the economic uses of the area, including fisheries activities and offshore infrastructures, and the wellbeing of the area concerned, including 'conservation of marine living resources and of wildlife'.[201] The exercise of coastal State rights is also guided by the principle of necessity and reasonableness, and giving due regard to the rights of other States.[202] The attribution and the exercise of the rights under RWC affirms the two legal doctrines under the EEZ regime of UNCLOS.

There are examples whereby the coastal State goes beyond the existing generally accepted international rules and standards to regulate foreign ships navigating in its EEZ. The conflicting State practice can be observed from the declarations and objections made by States when ratifying the Basel Convention.[203] Colombia, Ecuador, Egypt, India, Mexico, Portugal, Uruguay and Venezuela were of the view that they could require prior notification of all transboundary movements of hazardous wastes across their EEZ, whereas Finland, Germany, Italy, Japan, the Netherlands, Singapore, Sweden, the United Kingdom and the United States were

198 RWC Articles 1(10), 6, 9(6)–(7).

199 RWC Article 9(10).

200 Churchill, Lowe and Sander (2022) 275–276.

201 RWC Article 1(6).

202 RWC Articles 7(2), 8(3), 9(1) and (5)–(8).

203 Basel Convention on the Control of Transboundary Movements of Hazardous Wastes and their Disposal (22 March 1989, in force 5 May 1992) 1673 UNTS 57 (Basel Convention).

against such a position.[204] Moreover, Argentina, Brazil, Chile, Kiribati, Nauru, New Zealand and South Africa all have regulated the movement of nuclear ships or nuclear cargos in their EEZs, which was criticised by Japan, the United Kingdom and the United States on various occasions.[205] Ten States in the Pacific region also adopted the Waigani Convention to reduce and eliminate transboundary movements of hazardous and radioactive waste, including in their EEZs.[206] It is difficult to reach a definite conclusion on whether the relevant practice is sufficiently widespread and uniform to have given coastal States the right to regulate foreign ships based on the nature of the ship and its cargo.[207] These State practices have, nevertheless, promoted the development of both binding and non-binding instruments on the transport of dangerous goods and radioactive materials under the auspice of IMO and the International Atomic Energy Agency.[208]

Coastal States have been able to advance their unilateral legislation to the status of international rules and standards through appropriate channels. This process was demonstrated by the IMO's legislative process with regard to double-hull requirement for oil tankers, which was very much dictated by domestic developments in the United States following the *Exxon Valdez* incident of 1989, and in France, Spain and the European Communities following the sinking of the tankers *Erika* and *Prestige* in 1999 and 2002, respectively.[209] In particular, as a result of the breakup of the oil tanker *Prestige* in November 2002, Spain and France unilaterally asserted that they would require information and impose rigorous inspections on single-hull oil tankers in excess of 15 years old passing through their EEZs; if the vessels were found to be unseaworthy, they would be expelled from their EEZs.[210] This action was joined shortly

[204] Roach (2021) 467–471; Basel Convention, 'Declarations and Objections' https://treaties.un.org/Pages/ViewDetails.aspx?src=IND&mtdsg_no=XXVII-3&chapter=27&clang=_en.

[205] Jon M. Van Dyke, 'The Disappearing Right to Navigational Freedom in the Exclusive Economic Zone' (2005) 29 Marine Policy 107, 111–112; Roach (2021) 471–478.

[206] Convention to Ban the Importation in Forum Islands Countries of Hazardous Wastes and Radioactive Wastes and to Control the Transboundary Movement and Management of Hazardous Wastes within the South Pacific Region (16 September 1995, in force 21 October 2001) Articles 1, 4, 6 (Waigani Convention) www.sprep.org/convention-secretariat/waigani-convention.

[207] Churchill, Lowe and Sander (2022) 278–279.

[208] UNGA A/RES/76/72, 20 December 2021, Oceans and the Law of the Sea, paras 172–175.

[209] Alan Khee-Jin Tan, *Vessel-Source Marine Pollution: The Law and Politics of International Regulation* (Cambridge University Press 2006) 139–155.

[210] Emma Daly, 'After Oil Spill, Spain and France Impose Strict Tanker Inspection', *The New York Times*, 27 November 2002 (online); UNGA A/58/65, 3 March 2003, Oceans and the Law of the Sea, Report of the Secretary-General, para. 57.

after by Portugal and Morocco, who urged the European Union to ban large single-hull tankers carrying heavy-grade oil from entering any European port.[211] These unilateral actions exceeded the coastal States' environmental jurisdiction in their EEZ and generated difficult debates at IMO.[212] However, over time, these unilateral actions effectively contributed to the acceleration of the gradual phasing-out of single-hull tankers within Europe[213] and then worldwide,[214] changing perceptions and the governing standards for the design and construction of oil tankers.

There are a large number of international conventions and instruments concerning vessel-source pollution that could arguably be considered 'generally accepted international rules and standards' and become applicable in the EEZ through domestic legislation.[215] It can be observed that all of the conventions and instruments are consistent with the jurisdiction allocated between the flag State and coastal State without giving additional right to the coastal State, except the RWC.[216] Should the coastal State choose to give effect to these rules and standards

211 Jon M. Van Dyke, 'Balancing Navigational Freedom with Environmental and Security Concerns' (2004) 15 Colo J Int'l Env L & Pol'y 19, 22–23.

212 UNCLOS Articles 56(1)(b)(iii), 211(5)–(6); IMO MSC 76/23, 16 December 2002, Report of the Maritime Safety Committee on Its Seventy-Sixth Session, paras 1.13–1.28; Churchill, Lowe and Sander (2022) 645.

213 Regulations (EC) No 1726/2003 of the European Parliament and of the Council of 22 July 2003 amending Regulation (EC) No 417/2002 on the accelerated phasing-in of double-hull or equivalent design requirements for single-hull oil tankers, OJ L 249/1 (2003).

214 IMO Res MEPC.111(50), 4 December 2003, Amendments to the Annex of the Protocol of 1978 Relating to the International Convention for the Prevention of Pollution from Ships, 1973.

215 UN DOALOS, The Law of the Sea: Obligations of State Parties under the United Nations Convention on the Law of the Sea and Complementary Instruments (United Nations 2004); IMO LEG/MISC.8 (2014) 56–61; Gorana Jelic Mrcelic, Nikola Mandic and Ranka Petrinovic, 'International Legislative Framework', in De Mora, Fileman and Vance (2020) 336–344; IMO, 'List of IMO Conventions' www.imo.org/en/About/Conventions/Pages/ListOfConventions.aspx; IMO, 'Status of IMO Treaties: Comprehensive information on the status of multilateral Conventions and instruments in respect of which the International Maritime Organization or its Secretary-General performs depositary or other functions, 24 July 2024' www.imo.org/en/About/Conventions/Pages/StatusOfConventions.aspx; IMO, 'Global Integrated Shipping Information System (GISIS): Non-mandatory Instruments (registration required)' https://gisis.imo.org/Public/INSTR/Default.aspx.

216 IMO LEG/MISC.8 (2014) 12–13, 59.

through its domestic laws, they could be the legal basis to hold the flag State responsible if a pollution incident does occur in the EEZ.

4.3.2.2 Specially Protected Areas

In addition to giving effect to the implementation of generally accepted international rules and standards, the coastal State may adopt, through appropriate channels, special measures to regulate ships and shipping in a particular area within its EEZ in association with various concepts of specially protected areas. The rationale of designating specially protected areas is that the general standards of protection may be inadequate due to the ecological or biological vulnerability of certain marine areas; therefore, a tailored regime with higher protection may be desirable.[217] The effective use of specially protected areas can contribute to the conservation of biodiversity, the protection of marine habitats and species, and the preservation of the marine environment.[218]

(1) Special Areas under MARPOL If the discharge of certain harmful substances by ships, even when operating in compliance with generally applicable international standards, becomes unacceptable in a certain area, the coastal State may, through IMO, define such area as a Special Area under the MARPOL annexes, and restrict and monitor the discharge more closely.[219] A Special Area may be designated within the EEZ and 'may encompass the maritime zones of several States, or even an entire enclosed or semi-enclosed area'.[220]

The IMO is the only competent organisation to approve the designation of a Special Area under MARPOL.[221] In the proposal for designation, the coastal State must prove that the proposed area satisfies the detailed criteria of oceanographic conditions, ecological conditions and vessel traffic characteristics.[222] The ecological conditions of the proposed area are directly linked to the subjects that fall under the sovereign rights of the coastal State, such as depleted, threatened or endangered marine species, spawning, breeding and nursery areas and critical habitats for

217 Dux (2011) 19, 35.

218 Graeme Kelleher, *Guidelines for Marine Protected Areas* (IUCN 1999) xiii, xvii.

219 Dux (2011) 264–265; IMO Res A.1087(28), 4 December 2013, Guidelines for the Designation of Special Areas under MARPOL, Annex, para 2.1. Special Areas designated under MARPOL Annex VI are known as Emission Control Areas.

220 IMO Res A.1087(28) Annex, para 2.2.

221 Ibid para 3.1.

222 Ibid paras 2.3–2.6.

marine resources, including fish stocks.[223] Other elements, such as threats to amenities, the influence of other sources of pollution and existing management regimes, may also be taken into account.[224]

Under the MARPOL annexes, there are four types of Special Areas addressing pollution from oil (ten designated Special Areas), noxious liquid substances (one designated Special Area), sewage (one designated Special Area) and garbage (eight designated Special Areas) and seven designated Emission Control Areas dealing with prevention of air pollution.[225] Many of these designated areas cover marine areas under the EEZ claims of coastal States in the Mediterranean Sea, the Baltic Sea, the North Sea, the Arctic waters, North West European Waters, the Wider Caribbean region, including the Gulf of Mexico and the Caribbean Sea, and North America.[226]

The more restrictive discharge requirements of these Special Areas may 'only become effective when adequate reception facilities are provided for ships in accordance with the provisions of MARPOL 73/78'.[227] Ships navigating in an enforced Special Area must obey such discharge restrictions.

(2) Particularly Sensitive Sea Areas If the 'recognized ecological, socio-economic, or scientific attributes' of an area are such that it 'may be vulnerable to damage by international shipping activities', coastal States may designate it through IMO as a 'Particularly Sensitive Sea Area (PSSA)', where associated protective measures could be adopted to 'prevent, reduce, or eliminate the threat or identified vulnerability'.[228] A PSSA can be designated in the EEZ 'with the view to the adoption of international protective measures regarding pollution and other damage caused by ships'.[229]

Coastal States, however, do not have unilateral legislative jurisdiction in the PSSA. Any proposed protective measures must be 'already

[223] Ibid para 2.5.

[224] Ibid paras 2.8–2.10.

[225] IMO, 'Special Areas under MARPOL' www.imo.org/en/OurWork/Environment/Pages/Special-Areas-Marpol.aspx. In December 2022, MEPC approved the proposal to designate the Mediterranean Sea Emission Control Area. See MEPC 79/15, 8 February 2023, Report of the Marine Environment Protection Committee on its Seventy-Ninth Session, para 3.32, Annex 3. In April 2024, MEPC approved the proposals to designate two Emission Contral Areas for the Canadian Arctic waters and Norwegian Sea covering EEZ of both States. See MEPC 81/16, 8 April 2024, Report of the Marine Environment Protection Committee on its Eighty-First Session, para 11.13.2.

[226] Ibid.

[227] IMO Res A.1087(28) Annex, para 2.7.

[228] IMO Revised PSSA Guidelines para 1.2.

[229] Ibid para 4.3.

available under an existing IMO instrument', or could be developed within the competence of IMO or pursuant to UNCLOS Article 211(6) concerning special areas.[230] Measures for the designated PSSAs must be adequate and clearly linked with the identified vulnerability of the area, which may include the designation of Special Areas under MARPOL, ships' routeing and reporting systems, areas to be avoided, pilotage schemes and other vessel traffic management systems.[231]

There are currently eighteen designated PSSAs worldwide, with many covering marine areas under the EEZ claims of coastal States.[232] For instance, the entire western coasts of the United Kingdom, Ireland, Belgium, France, Spain and Portugal, from the Shetland Islands in the North to Cape S. Vicente in the South, covering large areas of the territorial seas and the EEZs, were designated as a single PSSA in 2004.[233] In addition to the existing protective measures in this area, including various deep-water routes, areas to be avoided, traffic separation schemes and ships' routeing measures, a mandatory ship reporting system was adopted for 'every kind of oil tanker of more than 600 tonnes deadweight' carrying heavy crude oil, heavy fuel oils, bitumen and tar and their emulsions navigating in this PSSA.[234]

(3) **Special Areas under Article 211(6)** UNCLOS recognises the coastal State's right to establish special areas in the EEZ for the purpose of preventing and combatting vessel-source pollution. Where the generally accepted international rules and standards on vessel-source pollution are inadequate to meet the special circumstances, the coastal State may, through IMO, adopt special mandatory measures as 'required for recognized technical reasons in relation to its oceanographical and ecological conditions, as well as its utilisation or the protection of its resources and the particular character of its traffic' to a particular, clearly defined area of its EEZ.[235]

These additional protective measures seem to have considerable potential to enhance the level of stringency for regulating vessel-source

[230] Ibid para 7.5.2.3.
[231] Ibid paras 6.1, 7.5.2.1, 7.5.2.4.
[232] IMO, 'Particularly Sensitive Sea Areas' www.imo.org/en/OurWork/Environment/Pages/PSSAs.aspx.
[233] IMO MEPC.121(52), 15 October 2004, Designation of the Western European Waters as a Particularly Sensitive Sea Area, Annex 1: Description of the PSSA.
[234] IMO MSC.190(79).
[235] UNCLOS Article 211(6)(a).

pollution in comparison to the general international rules and standards applicable in the EEZ. Moreover, Article 211(6) provides the necessary prescriptive power for the coastal State to fulfil its general obligation to take measures 'necessary to protect and preserve rare or fragile ecosystems as well as the habitat of depleted, threatened or endangered species and other forms of marine life'.[236] However, as at 2024, no State has established a special area in the EEZ under Article 211(6).[237]

One reason for the limited use of Article 211(6) may be that some States consider this provision to not give the coastal State sufficient independence because of the lengthy requirement of obtaining approval from IMO.[238] At the Fourth Session of the Third Conference in 1976, India made a proposal to give coastal States the independent right to establish designated areas in the EEZ 'in which the coastal States may prohibit or regulate the entry and passage of foreign ships . . . and take such other measures as it may deem necessary or appropriate for the purpose of . . . protecting the marine environment' along with other purposes.[239] After this proposal had been rejected, India proclaimed such rights in its domestic law.[240] Similar legislation has been adopted by Bangladesh,[241] Guyana,[242] Nigeria,[243] Pakistan[244] and Sri Lanka.[245] These claims have given the coastal State wide

[236] UNCLOS Article 194(5).

[237] Churchill (2005) 130; Dux (2011) 209; Bartenstein 'Article 211' (2017) 1438; Nicola R Wheen, 'Marine Protected Areas in the Exclusive Economic Zone: UNCLOS or the TPPA's Looming Presence (2016) 14(2) Otago L Rev 351, 354–358.

[238] IMO MEPC 43/6/2 paras 18–22; Bartenstein 'Article 211' (2017) 1439–1442.

[239] 'Informal Proposal of India of 7 April 1976', in Renate Platzöder, Third United Nations Conference on the Law of the Sea: Documents, Vol. IV (Oceana Publications 1983) 294.

[240] India, The Territorial Waters, Continental Shelf, Exclusive Economic Zone and other Maritime Zones Act, 1976, Article 7(6).

[241] Bangladesh, Territorial Waters and Maritime Zones Act, No. XXVI of 1974, Article 6; Bangladesh specifies its right to establish conservation zones in the EEZ for the maintenance of the productivity of the living resources of the sea, where it may take such conservation measures so adopted as it may deem appropriate for the purpose, including measures to protect the living resources of the sea from indiscriminate exploitation, depletion or destruction.

[242] Guyana, Maritime Boundaries Act, 1977, Act No.10 of 30 June 1977, Articles 12, 18, www.un.org/Depts/los/LEGISLATIONANDTREATIES/PDFFILES/GUY_1977_Act.pdf.

[243] Nigeria, Exclusive Economic Zone Decree No.28 of 5 October 1978, Article 3(1) and (4),where associated protective measures could be adopte www.un.org/Depts/los/LEGISLATIONANDTREATIES/PDFFILES/NGA_1978_Decree.pdf.

[244] Pakistan, Territorial Waters and Maritime Zones Act, 1976, Article 6(4), www.un.org/Depts/los/LEGISLATIONANDTREATIES/PDFFILES/PAK_1976_Act.pdf.

[245] Sri Lanka, Maritime Zones Law No.22 of 1976, Article 7, www.un.org/Depts/los/LEGISLATIONANDTREATIES/PDFFILES/LKA_1976_Law.pdf.

discretionary power over the designated areas where navigational rights may be threatened. However, the comprehensive authority claimed by these States has drawn criticism to the creeping jurisdiction within the EEZ regime and has put their legitimacy into question.[246]

Another reason for the limited use of Article 211(6) would be that subsequent State practice has shown a preference to establish other types of specially protected areas. The most commonly used ones are Special Areas under MARPOL and PSSAs, which seem to have served the purpose of protecting special oceanographic and ecological conditions of areas within the EEZ.[247]

(4) Ice-Covered Areas Another UNCLOS-authorised special regime for environmental protection purposes in the EEZ is the coastal State's unilateral prescriptive jurisdiction in ice-covered areas.[248] It is recognised that the 'particularly severe climatic conditions and the presence of ice covering such areas for most of the year create obstructions or exceptional hazards to navigation, and pollution of the marine environment could cause major harm to or irreversible disturbance of the ecological balance', which makes such areas even more vulnerable to vessel-source pollution.[249]

In contrast with the general environmental jurisdiction and the special areas under Article 211(6), under Article 234 the coastal State has the right to unilaterally prescribe laws and regulations for ice-covered areas, with no restrictions to implement international rules and standards, nor do they need approval of IMO. Consequently, the coastal State has the competence to determine what type of standard vessels may enter and which sea lanes they must follow in its ice-covered EEZ. One of the uncertain elements of this special authorisation is that there is no general agreement on the definition of 'the presence of ice covering such areas for

[246] William T. Burke, 'National Legislation on Ocean Authority Zones and the Contemporary Law of the Sea' (1981) 9(3-4) Ocean Dev Int'l L 289, 295–296; Fabio Spadi, 'Navigation in Marine Protected Areas: National and International Law' (2000) 31 (3) Ocean Dev Int'l L 285, 294.

[247] IMO MEPC 43/6/2 paras 26–38; Harrison (2011) 187–189; Robin Churchill, 'Under-Utilized Coastal State Jurisdiction: Causes and Consequences', in Henrik Ringbom (ed.), *Jurisdiction over Ships: Post-UNCLOS Developments in the Law of the Sea* (Brill 2015) 295–296.

[248] Churchill, Lowe and Sander (2022) 646.

[249] UNCLOS Article 234.

most of the year', which is increasingly challenging due to the impact of climate change and the reduction of ice cover in the polar regions.[250]

This special authorisation to the coastal State, however, does not alter the fact that the ice-covered areas remain subject to the general EEZ legal regime established by UNCLOS.[251] And there are safeguards put in place to balance the environmental interests of coastal State in these areas with the navigational interests of all States.[252] In such areas, the coastal State is obliged to ensure that these measures are 'non-discriminatory' and 'based on the best available scientific evidence', and that they 'have due regard to navigation'.[253]

As the negotiating history indicates, Article 234 was negotiated directly among the Arctic littoral States – Canada, the Soviet Union (USSR) and the United States – and was intended to apply primarily to the Arctic.[254] Canada, for example, adopted the Arctic Waters Pollution Prevention Act and Arctic Shipping Pollution Prevention Regulations, among others, to ensure that navigation in Arctic waters is conducted in a way to preserve and protect the natural resources of the Canadian Arctic.[255] The special regulations include the establishment of shipping safety control zones where special construction, design, equipment and manning (CDEM) standards and requirements apply, and the use of ice navigators and Arctic Pollution Prevention Certificates are mandatory.[256]

The regulations for navigation in ice-covered areas have been unified through the international rules and standards developed by IMO, particularly the mandatory Polar Code that applies to both the Arctic and the Antarctic.[257] The Polar Code covers the full range of CDEM,

[250] Viatcheslav Gavrilov, Roman Dremliuga and Rustambek Nurimbetov, 'Article 234 of the 1982 United Nations Convention on the Law of the Sea and Reduction of Ice Cover in the Arctic Ocean' (2019) 106 Marine Policy 103518.

[251] Christopher C. Joyner, 'Ice-Covered Regions in International Law' (1991) 31 Nat Res J 213, 217.

[252] Nordquist, Rosenne and Yankov (1991) 392–393; Erik Franckx and Laura Boone, 'Article 234', in Proelss (2017) 1569.

[253] UNCLOS Article 234; IMO MEPC 43/6/2 para 14.

[254] Nordquist, Rosenne and Yankov (1991) 393; Franckx and Boone (2017) 1569–1570.

[255] Canada, Arctic Waters Pollution Prevention Act, RSC 1985, c A-12 (AWPPA); Canada, Arctic Shipping Pollution Prevention Regulations, CRC, c 353 (ASPPR) [Repealed, SOR/2017-286, s 34].

[256] Canada, AWPPA ss 11–12; Canada, ASPPR ss 4–6, 12–13, 26.

[257] IMO, 'International Code for Ships Operating in Polar Waters (Polar Code)' www.imo.org/en/OurWork/Safety/Pages/polar-code.aspx.

operational, training, search and rescue, and environmental protection matters relevant to ships operating in the inhospitable polar waters.[258] The Polar Code has been made mandatory through amendments to MARPOL and other relevant conventions.[259] Despite being without the official title, the Polar Code effectively designated Arctic Waters as a Special Area under MARPOL with special mandatory measures for the prevention of pollution.[260] Another contribution of the Polar Code is a generally agreed geographic scope of Arctic Waters, in contrast to the different interpretations of 'within the limits' of the EEZ and covered by ice 'most of the year' under Article 234.[261] With the entry into force of the Polar Code in 2017, the three major coastal States in the Arctic – Canada, Russia and the United States – all amended their domestic legislations to enhance their compatibility with these international rules and regulations.[262]

In sum, these specially protected areas, once duly designated, must be respected by all applicable vessels navigating through or within these areas. The rationale for giving such competence is to protect the coastal State's special interests in the EEZ and to assist it in fulfilling its obligation to protect and preserve the marine environment. However, both the designation of the area and the adoption of special protective measures, though initiated by the coastal State, need to be approved by IMO except for ice-covered areas. These procedural requirements confirm the superior status of the generally accepted international rules and standards in relation to environmental protection in the EEZ.

[258] IMO Res MEPC.264(68), 15 May 2015, International Code for Ships Operating in Polar Waters (Polar Code).

[259] IMO Res MEPC.265(68), 15 May 2015, Amendments to the Annex of the Protocol of 1978 Relating to the International Convention for the Prevention of Pollution from Ships, 1973, Amendments to MARPOL Annexes I, II, IV and V (to make use of environment-related provisions of the Polar Code mandatory).

[260] Roach (2021) 586–587.

[261] IMO Res MEPC.265(68), MARPOL Annex I, reg 46.2; Annex II, reg 21.2; Annex IV, reg 17.3; Annex V, reg 13.2; Franckx and Boone (2017) 1575–1578.

[262] Canada, Arctic Shipping Safety and Pollution Prevention Regulations, SOR/2017-286; Jan Jakub Solski, 'The Northern Sea Route in the 2010s: Development and Implementation of Relevant Law' (2020) 11 Arctic Rev on L & Pol 383, 390; Drummond Fraser, 'A Change in the Ice Regime: Polar Code Implementation in Canada', in Aldo Chircop, Floris Goerlandt, Claudio Aporta and Ronald Pelot (eds.), *Governance of Arctic Shipping: Rethinking Risk, Human Impacts and Regulation* (Springer 2020) 296–297; Roach (2021) 589–599; Sian Prior, 'Review of Perceived Gaps and Challenges in the Implementation of the Polar Code' (WWF's Arctic Programme 2022) https://apiwwfarcticse.cdn.triggerfish.cloud/uploads/2022/04/12144330/22-4372_polar_code_220408_links-3.pdf.

4.3.2.3 Pollution from Seabed Activities and by Dumping

The coastal State's jurisdiction to protect and preserve the marine environment extends to two further activities, seabed activities including the use of artificial islands, installations and structures subject to national jurisdiction, and dumping. The coastal State has a broader scope of prescriptive jurisdiction over these two activities compared to its jurisdiction over vessel-source pollution.

Most, if not all, seabed activities including the use of artificial islands, installations and structures are connected with the exploration of the seabed and exploitation of its natural resources that are subject to the sovereign right of the coastal State.[263] Within the EEZ, the most common activities are connected with the exploration and exploitation of oil and gas, which may give rise to both intentional and accidental pollution.[264] The coastal State also has jurisdiction to prevent, reduce and control pollution from pipelines that are not associated with an activity under its jurisdiction.[265] The coastal State is obliged to take all necessary measures to prevent, reduce and control pollution from the offshore activities subject to its jurisdiction with the constraint that such laws, regulations and measures must be 'no less effective than international rules, standards and recommended practices and procedures'.[266] As at 2024, States have not developed any binding international agreement to regulate pollution from these offshore activities.

Dumping within the EEZ is subject to the prior approval of the coastal State, which has the right to permit, regulate and control such dumping after due consideration with other relevant States.[267] The laws, regulations and measures adopted by the coastal State must be 'no less effective in preventing, reducing and controlling such pollution than the global rules and standards'.[268] The 1972 London Convention and 1996 London Protocol, which have been accepted by 87 and 53 contracting parties, respectively, are the only global treaties regulating dumping at sea.[269]

263 UNCLOS Articles 56(1), 77(1).

264 Churchill, Lowe and Sander (2022) 682.

265 UNCLOS Article 79(2). For activities related to the laying of submarine pipelines, see Chapter 5 in this volume.

266 UNCLOS Article 208(1)–(3).

267 UNCLOS Article 210(5).

268 UNCLOS Article 210(6).

269 Convention on the Prevention of Marine Pollution by Dumping of Wastes and Other Matter (29 December 1972, in force 30 August 1975) 1046 UNTS 120 (London Convention); 1996 Protocol to the London Convention (7 November 1996, in force

Any foreign ships or aircraft that have obtained approval from the coastal State to engage in seabed activities or dumping in its EEZ are subject to the coastal State's environmental regulations. Compared with the coastal State's jurisdiction over vessel-source pollution, the reference to 'international rules' and 'global rules and standards' is not subject to the requirement that they have been 'generally accepted'. This arguably widens the scope of the applicable global rules and standards. Nonetheless, the coastal State's jurisdiction to regulate pollution from seabed activities and dumping is less likely to directly affect the freedom of navigation and overflight in the EEZ. In the event of an accidental pollution incident, such as the 2009 Montara oil spill and the 2010 Deepwater Horizon accident, ships might need to alter their navigation route to avoid an area.[270]

4.3.3 *Enforcement Jurisdiction*

It should be acknowledged that the enforcement provision in Article 73 of UNCLOS refers only to the exercise of coastal State's 'sovereign rights to explore, exploit, conserve and manage the living resources'. The coastal State's explicit enforcement jurisdiction[271] over the protection and preservation of the marine environment is provided in Part XII. Such jurisdiction is framed around the primary subject, namely ships and aircraft, including those flying foreign flags.

It is significant that coastal States are given enforcement jurisdiction over vessel-source pollution in the EEZ. This represents an attempt to respond to the ineffectiveness of a regime based on exclusive flag State enforcement over such an issue.[272] Following the limited scope of the prescriptive jurisdiction, the coastal State may only enforce those environmental laws 'conforming to and giving effect to generally accepted

24 March 2006) (London Protocol); IMO, 'Convention on the Prevention of Polllution by Dumping of Wastes and Other Matter' www.imo.org/en/OurWork/Environment/Pages/London-Convention-Protocol.aspx.

270 Australian Government, Department of Climate Change, Energy, the Environment and Water, 'Montara Oil Spill' www.dcceew.gov.au/environment/marine/marine-pollution/montara-oil-spill; Julien Rochette, Matthieu Wemaëre, Lucien Chabason and Sarah Callet, Seeing beyond the Horizon for Deepwater Oil and Gas: Strengthening the International Regulation of Offshore Exploration and Exploitation (IDDRI Studies N° 01/14 2014).

271 Activities that intentionally cause severe damage to the marine environment has been considered as threat to maritime security, see Chapter 7 in this volume.

272 Nordquist, Rosenne and Yankov (1991) 282.

international rules and standards' established through IMO or general diplomatic conference.[273] Coastal States are given a graded enforcement competence depending on the amount of the discharge and the perceived or anticipated severity of the damage to the marine environment. As clearly stated in Article 111, the right of hot pursuit applies to violations of environmental laws and regulations in the EEZ.[274]

If the coastal State has 'clear grounds for believing' that the vessel has committed a violation of applicable laws and regulations in its EEZ, the first step in exercising enforcement jurisdiction is to require the suspected foreign vessel navigating in the EEZ or the territorial sea to give information about its identity and other relevant information.[275] Second, if the vessel has failed to provide such information and the coastal State has 'clear grounds for believing' that there is danger of such violation 'resulting in a substantial discharge causing or threatening significant pollution of the marine environment', it may conduct physical inspection of the vessel for matters relating to the violation.[276] Third, if the inspection leads to 'clear objective evidence' that the violation will result in 'a discharge causing major damage or threat of major damage to the coastline or related interests of the coastal State, or to any resources of its territorial sea or [EEZ]', the coastal State may, 'provided that the evidence so warrants, institute proceedings, including detention of the vessel, in accordance with its laws'.[277] These enforcement measures apply to violations of 'applicable international rules and standards for the prevention, reduction and control of pollution from vessels or laws and regulations of that State conforming and giving effect to such rules and standards'.[278] The word 'or' seems to indicate that the coastal State could exercise enforcement jurisdiction over violations of applicable international rules and standards even if it has not adopted domestic laws to implement them. These would include violations of CDEM standards, discharge and emission control, ships' routeing systems, other operational practices, as well as protective measures applicable to specially protected areas. The three progressive steps of enforcement measures by the coastal State, each qualified by an increased level of threat to the

[273] UNCLOS Article 211(5).
[274] UNCLOS Article 111(2).
[275] UNCLOS Article 220(3).
[276] UNCLOS Article 220(5).
[277] UNCLOS Article 220(6).
[278] UNCLOS Article 220(3).

marine environment, will have an increasing impact on the freedom of navigation if the foreign vessel has committed a violation in the EEZ.

It is worth noting that within ice-covered areas the coastal State is given a wide margin of discretion of enforcement jurisdiction, in contrast to its limited competence with regard to specially protected areas established under UNCLOS Article 211(6), MARPOL or the PSSA.[279] As indicated in the Canadian Arctic Waters Pollution Prevention Act, a pollution prevention officer may 'board any ship that is within a shipping safety control zone and conduct such inspections thereof as will enable the officer to determine whether the ship complies with standards prescribed by any regulations' that are applicable in such a zone and may order the ship to proceed outside the zone on reasonable grounds.[280] Violations under the Act are punishable offences, and the suspected person and ship are liable to pay a fine on summary conviction.[281] However, this broader competence needs to be exercised in accordance with the coastal State's due regard obligation and the other general requirements applied in the process of enforcement activities, such as acting in a non-discriminatory, reasonable, proportionate and non-abusive manner.[282] For example, the coastal State may only take actions based on clear, or at least reasonable, grounds for believing that a foreign vessel has acted in contravention of its applicable laws or regulations and must avoid causing unnecessary interference with the vessel.

In addition to their general enforcement jurisdiction, coastal States also have the right to take and enforce proportionate measures to avoid pollution arising from accidental discharge due to maritime casualties in the EEZ.[283] The supertanker *Torrey Canyon*, after running aground on rocks outside the territorial sea of the United Kingdom in 1967, caused devastating environmental effects and was eventually bombed by the Royal Navy to avoid further damage.[284] At that time, the United Kingdom had no right to intervene with foreign vessels on the high seas, but it claimed to act according to the right of self-protection or self-help

[279] UNCLOS Articles 220(8), 234.

[280] Canada, AWPPA s 15(4).

[281] Ibid ss 18–19.

[282] UNCLOS Articles 226, 300.

[283] UNCLOS Article 221. 'Maritime casualty' means a collision of vessels, stranding or other incident of navigation, or other occurrence on board a vessel or external to it resulting in material damage or imminent threat of material damage to a vessel or cargo.

[284] Marine Management Organisation, 'Torrey Canyon 1967' https://webarchive.nationalarchives.gov.uk/ukgwa/20140305104626/http://www.marinemanagement.org.uk/protecting/pollution/incidents_torreycanyon.htm (archived content).

under general law, whereby a State, when one of its vital interests is affected or is likely to be affected by certain events, can respond with extreme measures.[285] This incident inspired the adoption of the 1969 Intervention Convention, which permitted the coastal State to take actions against foreign vessels on the high seas as 'may be necessary to prevent, mitigate or eliminate danger to its coastline or related interests from pollution by oil or other substances or the threat thereof, following upon a maritime casualty'.[286] This practice has been incorporated into Article 221 of UNCLOS, which permits the coastal State, subject to other rules of international law, to 'take and enforce measures' in the EEZ 'proportionate to the actual or threatened damage' to avoid pollution or threat of pollution arising from maritime causalities.[287]

UNCLOS also lays down detailed procedural and other safeguards to ensure that the freedom of navigation in the EEZ is not unduly restricted from enforcement jurisdiction by the coastal State.[288] There are general obligations of coastal States to take measures to facilitate proceedings, to exercise their enforcement powers through qualified government entities or officials, to avoid endangering the safety of navigation or human lives, to refrain from discrimination against foreign vessels, to duly notify the flag State and other States concerned, to limit itself to monetary penalties and to be liable for damages arising from improper enforcement measures.[289]

In addition, there are essential safeguards that reflect the dominant interests of the freedom of navigation over the environmental jurisdiction of the coastal State. Article 226 spells out the main procedures for investigating foreign vessels to minimise unnecessary physical inspection.[290] The initial physical inspection provided in Article 220(3) 'shall be limited to an examination of such certificates, records or other documents as the vessel is required to carry' by international law.[291] Further inspection is only permitted when 'there are clear grounds for believing' that these documents are misleading or when they are inadequate or

[285] Tan (2006) 70; Nordquist, Rosenne and Yankov (1991) 305; James Crawford, *Brownlie's Principles of Public International Law* (9th ed., Oxford University Press 2019) 446, 463–464.
[286] International Convention relating to Intervention on the High Seas in cases of Oil Pollution Casualties (29 November 1969, in force 6 May 1975) 970 UNTS 211 (Intervention Convention). Nordquist, Rosenne and Yankov (1991) 305–306.
[287] UNCLOS Article 221(1).
[288] Nordquist, Rosenne and Yankov (1991) 321.
[289] UNCLOS Articles 223–225, 227, 230–232.
[290] Vasco Becker-Weinberg, 'Article 226', in Proelss (2017) 1539.
[291] UNCLOS Article 226(1)(a).

invalid.[292] Where the violation is confirmed and the vessel is accordingly detained, coastal States are obliged to release it promptly upon the posting of a bond or other financial security.[293] However, if the release of the vessel may pose an unreasonable threat of damage to the marine environment, the coastal State may refuse or make its release conditional upon appropriate repair.[294] Additionally, States are required to cooperate to develop detailed investigation procedures to avoid unnecessary inspection of vessels at sea, which is intended to limit the power of coastal States to apply domestic laws.[295]

Furthermore, Article 228 implies that the disciplinary action imposed by a coastal State in response to a violation relating to vessel-source pollution in its EEZ can be overridden by instituting a flag State proceeding.[296] The flag State has the right to request such suspension within six months of the date on which the coastal State instituted the proceedings, and is obliged to disclose its proceedings to the coastal State in due course.[297] However, if the violation has caused 'major damage to the coastal State' or the flag State has 'repeatedly disregarded' its enforcement obligation, the privilege of the flag State does not stand.[298] The reference to 'major damage' echoes Article 220(6) but has not been elaborated, and it is also not clear what actions would constitute 'repeatedly disregarded' behaviour, which leaves ample room for differing interpretations.[299] The coastal State is barred from instituting proceedings to impose penalties on foreign vessel if the flag State has taken corresponding charges, or after three years since the violation was committed.[300] Article 228 indicates the clear intention to give priority to flag State jurisdiction over vessel-source pollution.[301]

It is recognised that the increasing volume of shipping traffic poses a serious threat to the coastal marine environment and may cause irreversible damage to marine habitats and fragile ecosystems. Consequently, there is growing awareness of the need to prevent, reduce and control

292 UNCLOS Article 226(1)(a)(i)–(iii).
293 UNCLOS Article 226(1)(b).
294 UNCLOS Articles 219, 226(1)(c).
295 UNCLOS Article 226(2); Nordquist, Rosenne and Yankov (1991) 344.
296 UNCLOS Article 228(1).
297 Ibid.
298 Ibid.
299 Nordquist, Rosenne and Yankov (1991) 358–359; Jean-Pierre Cot, 'Pollution in the EEZ' (2010) 104 Am J Int'l L 265, 266, 270.
300 UNCLOS Article 228(1).
301 Nordquist, Rosenne and Yankov (1991) 358; Vasco Becker-Weinberg, 'Article 228', in Proelss (2017) 1548.

vessel-source pollution.[302] UNCLOS has, in fact, altered the exclusive jurisdiction of flag States in respect of vessel-source pollution, but the concurrent jurisdiction granted to the coastal State is onerous and retrospective and does not substantially encroach upon international navigation.[303] It has been pointed out that this is the most complex modification to the regime governing the coastal State and other States in the exercise of their rights and jurisdiction.[304] Freedom of navigation is further protected by ensuring uniformity of applicable international rules and standards, which are the normal limit of coastal State competence.[305] In addition, State practice, although limited, indicates that most coastal States have only made a general claim to environmental jurisdiction in the EEZ and few of them have enacted specific domestic laws, let alone undertaken enforcement actions.[306] These situations perhaps reflect the predominance of internationalism over unilateralism and navigational interests over coastal States' environmental concerns in the EEZ. Nevertheless, the marginal coastal State jurisdiction provides extra protection to its coastal marine environment and may pressure flag States to enhance compliance by their vessels with applicable international rules and standards. As IMO has been pushed by States to adopt initiatives to address vessel-source pollution, coastal States' prescriptive jurisdiction should gradually expand in the EEZ through the implementation of international rules and standards.[307]

4.4 Rights and Jurisdiction with Regard to Artificial Islands, Installations and Structures

4.4.1 General Scope of Coastal State Rights

Similar to the regime of protection and preservation of the marine environment, coastal States only have 'jurisdiction' to establish and use

[302] Lindy S. Johnson, *Coastal State Regulation of International Shipping* (Oceana Publications 2004) 17–19.

[303] Bartenstein 'Article 211' (2017) 1434; Yaodong Yu, Yue Zhao and Yen-Chiang Chang, 'Challenges to the Primary Jurisdiction of Flag States Over Ships' (2018) 49(1) Ocean Dev & Int'l L 85, 93–95.

[304] Orrego Vicuña (1989) 84.

[305] UNCLOS Articles 56(1)(b)(iii), 211(5), 220(3).

[306] Molenaar (1998) 398–399; Shotoro Hamamoto, 'Article 220', in Proelss (2017) 1511–1512.

[307] Tim Stephens and Donald R. Rothwell, 'The LOSC Framework for Maritime Jurisdiction and Enforcement 30 Years On' (2012) 27 Int'l J Marine & Coastal L 701, 705.

artificial islands, installations and structures in the EEZ, which is a narrower concept than 'sovereign rights'.[308] The exercise of such jurisdiction is elaborated in Article 60, which addresses it in two formulations. In the first place, coastal States have the 'exclusive right to construct and to authorize and regulate the construction, operation and use of artificial islands' and of 'installations and structures for the purposes provided for in Article 56 and other economic purposes' or those 'which may interfere with the exercise of the rights of the coastal State in the zone'.[309] In the second place, coastal States have 'exclusive jurisdiction over such artificial islands, installations and structures, including jurisdiction with regard to customs, fiscal, health, safety and immigration laws and regulations'.[310] Moreover, the coastal State has jurisdiction over marine scientific research in the EEZ, thus the deployment and use of any type of scientific research installation or equipment are subject to the coastal State's jurisdiction.[311] Furthermore, as discussed earlier, the coastal State has the jurisdiction to prevent, reduce and control pollution from seabed activities including the use of artificial islands, installations and structures under their jurisdiction.[312] These rights and jurisdiction apply *mutatis mutandis* to the artificial islands, installations and structures built in and upon the continental shelf.[313]

The three categories of infrastructures are broad enough to cover broadcasting facilities, deep-water ports, offshore airports, offshore surveillance structures, seabed drilling platforms and other exploitation facilities, scientific research installations and even almost self-contained industrial towns.[314] Article 60 distinguishes artificial islands from installations and structures, with the former falling under the exclusive right and jurisdiction of the coastal State while the latter are subject to certain qualifications. However, UNCLOS does not provide any definition of the three terms, which renders the distinction difficult to determine, as an installation or structure could eventually be assimilated into an artificial island.[315] Except for the common feature of having to be human-made

[308] UNCLOS Article 56(1)(a) and (b)(i); Proelss 'Article 56' (2017) 424–425, 429.
[309] UNCLOS Article 60(1).
[310] UNCLOS Article 60(2).
[311] UNCLOS Articles 56(1)(b)(ii), 246(1), 258.
[312] UNCLOS Articles 208, 214; Nordquist, Nandan and Rosenne (1993) 588.
[313] UNCLOS Article 80.
[314] Kwiatkowska (1989) 104; Kent M. Keith, 'Floating Cities: A New Challenge for Transnational Law' (1977) 1 Marine Policy 190, 201–204.
[315] Churchill, Lowe and Sander (2022) 267–268.

objects, it seems that the main criteria for differentiation the three terms are size and permanency, and possibly the method of construction.[316]

One consequence of the lack of definitions is that the legal status of floating platforms and other structures in the EEZ, which can move by their own power but will become stable once they reach the operation site, is not entirely clear.[317] At the early stage of the negotiations, Belgium and the United States proposed to exclude floating artificial islands from coastal States jurisdiction because they were 'theoretically mobile' and could be 'treated as vessels'.[318] This proposal was rejected, as both scientific evidence and State practice support the conclusion that floating structures operate in different ways from ships.[319] However, the definition of ships adopted in some IMO instruments includes floating platforms except when they are on location engaged in seabed activities.[320] Under Canadian law, at least some floating structures are included in the definition of 'marine installation or structure'.[321] Based on the fact that they are mainly used for economic purposes or scientific research in the EEZ, it is plausible to treat floating structures as artificial islands, installations or structures under Article 60, especially when they become stationary and operate in one particular area.[322]

Although Article 60 limits coastal States' rights with regard to specific installations and structures, it leaves coastal States with broad discretion to decide the scope of their jurisdiction. When referring to 'other economic purposes', in addition to those provided in Article 56, which

[316] UN DOALOS, *The Law of the Sea: Baselines* (United Nations 1989), Appendix I: Consolidated Glossary of Technical Terms used in the United Nations Convention on the Law of the Sea, 56; Alex G. Oude Elferink, 'Artificial Islands, Installations and Structures', last updated September 2013 *Max Planck Encyclopedia of Public International Law: South China Sea Arbitration* (2016) paras 996–1009, 1036–1037.

[317] Kwiatkowska (1989) 108; Churchill, Lowe and Sander (2022) 266.

[318] Shigeru Oda, *The Law of the Sea in Our Time II: The United Nations Seabed Committee, 1968–1973* (Sijthoff Leyden 1977) 359.

[319] Kwiatkowska (1989) 108; Hayley Farr, et al., 'Potential Environmental Effects of Deepwater Floating Offshore Wind Energy Facilities' (2021) 207 Ocean and Coastal Management 105611.

[320] MARPOL Article 2(4); BWM Convention Article 1(12).

[321] Canada, Oceans Act, Article 2: 'marine installation or structure' includes (a) any ship and any anchor, anchor cable or rig pad used in connection therewith, (b) any offshore drilling unit, production platform, subsea installation, pumping station, living accommodation, storage structure, loading or landing platform, dredge, floating crane, pipelaying or other barge or pipeline and any anchor, anchor cable or rig pad used in connection therewith, and (c) any other work or work within a class of works prescribed pursuant to paragraph 26(1)(a).

[322] Kwiatkowska (1989) 108–109; Alexander Proelss, 'Article 60', in Proelss (2017) 470.

already includes 'other activities for the economic exploitation and exploration', Article 60 indicates that it is 'a matter that can also influence the assignment of residual rights' under Article 59.[323] It has been argued that the exclusion of installations and structures for non-economic purpose from coastal States' exclusive rights represents a successful effort to exempt installations and structures used for military purposes.[324] However, the coastal State may still argue that such installations or structures 'may interfere [with] the exercise of' its rights on a case-by-case basis. This again will affect the interpretation and application of Article 59, as it gives a clear preference for the coastal State to decide which non-economic installations and structures will be subject to its jurisdiction.[325] Therefore, most installations and structures that may possibly be erected within the EEZ, including those used for scientific research projects, are subject to the coastal State's exclusive authority.[326]

Coastal States can exercise 'exclusive jurisdiction' over such artificial islands, installations and structures 'with regard to customs, fiscal, health, safety and immigration laws and regulations'.[327] Consequently, no vessels may load or unload any commodity, currency or person onto these infrastructures without coastal State authorisation. It would thus follow that coastal States should have criminal jurisdiction with regard to offences committed on or against such artificial islands, installations and structures.[328] According to the Protocol for the Suppression of Unlawful Acts against the Safety of Fixed Platforms Located on the Continental Shelf (SUA Platforms Protocol), coastal States may criminalise offences of unlawful seizures or exercises of control over a fixed platform, or performance of violence against a person on board, or any other activities that may endanger its safety.[329] The exclusive jurisdiction is particularly important considering the growing size and capacities of such infrastructure used within the EEZ.

Many States have claimed exclusive right and jurisdiction over artificial islands, installations and structures in the EEZ by incorporating the

[323] UNCLOS Articles 56 (1)(a), 60(1)(b); Orrego Vicuña (1989) 74.
[324] Nordquist, Nandan and Rosenne (1993) 584–585; Proelss 'Article 60' (2017) 471. For military installations, structures and other devices, see Chapter 6 in this volume.
[325] Proelss 'Article 60' (2017) 472.
[326] UNCLOS Article 246(5)(c).
[327] UNCLOS Article 60(2).
[328] Nordquist, Nandan and Rosenne (1993) 585; Proelss 'Article 60' (2017) 473.
[329] Protocol of 2005 to the Protocol for the Suppression of Unlawful Acts against the Safety of Fixed Platforms Located on the Continental Shelf (14 October 2005, in force 28 July 2010) 1678 UNTS 304, Articles 2–3.

general scope of Article 56 into their domestic laws, with few of them including the detailed rules of Article 60.[330] It is noteworthy that Brazil,[331] Cambodia,[332] Guyana,[333] India,[334] Indonesia,[335] Myanmar,[336] Pakistan[337] and Sri Lanka[338] have specified that their rights and jurisdiction extend to artificial islands, installations and structures for any purposes. It is also interesting to note that Honduras,[339] Maldives,[340] Mauritius,[341] the Seychelles[342] and Vanuatu[343] have retreated from their excessive claims and have amended their domestic laws to be consistent with UNCLOS.

330 Kwiatkowska (1989) 113–115; Robert W. Smith, *Exclusive Economic Zone Claims: An Analysis and Primary Documents* (Martinus Nijhoff 1986) 35–37; UN DOALOS, *The Law of the Sea: National Legislation on the Exclusive Economic Zone*; Sophia Kopela, 'The "Territorialisation" of the Exclusive Economic Zone: Implications for Maritime Jurisdiction' (2009) 6–7, in 20th Anniversary Conference of the International Boundary Research Unit on 'The State of Sovereignty'; 1–3 April 2009, Durham, UK. (Unpublished).

331 Brazil, Law No.8.617 of 4 January 1993, on the Territorial Sea, the Contiguous Zone, the Exclusive Economic Zone and the Continental Shelf, Article 8, www.un.org/Depts/los/LEGISLATIONANDTREATIES/PDFFILES/BRA_1993_8617.pdf.

332 Cambodia, Decree of the Council of State of 13 July 1982, Article 6, www.un.org/Depts/los/LEGISLATIONANDTREATIES/PDFFILES/KHM_1982_Decree.pdf.

333 Guyana, Maritime Boundaries Act No. 10 of 30 June 1977, Articles 16(b), 17.

334 India, The Territorial Waters, Continental Shelf, Exclusive Economic Zone and other Maritime Zones Act, 1976, Article 7(4)(b).

335 Indonesia, Act No. 5 of 1983 on the Indonesian Exclusive Economic Zone, Article 6, www.un.org/Depts/los/LEGISLATIONANDTREATIES/PDFFILES/IDN_1983_Act.pdf.

336 Myanmar, Territorial Sea and Maritime Zones Law, 1977, Article 18(b), www.un.org/Depts/los/LEGISLATIONANDTREATIES/PDFFILES/MMR_1977_Law.pdf.

337 Pakistan, Territorial Waters and Maritime Zones Act, 1976, Article 6(2)(b).

338 Sri Lanka, Maritime Zones Law No. 22 of 1976, Article 5(3)(c).

339 Honduras, Decree No. 921 of 13 June 1980 on the Utilization of Marine Natural Resources, Article 1(b); Maritime Areas of Honduras Act – Legislative Decree 172-99, 30 October 1999, Article 7(3)(a), www.un.org/Depts/los/LEGISLATIONANDTREATIES/STATEFILES/HND.htm.

340 Maldives, Law No. 30/76 Relating to the EEZ, Article 2; Maritime Zones of Maldives Act No. 6/96, Article 9, www.un.org/Depts/los/LEGISLATIONANDTREATIES/STATEFILES/MDV.htm.

341 Mauritius, Maritime Zones Act No. 13 of 1977, Article 7(b); Maritime Zone Act 2005, Articles 15(1)(b)(i), 17(d). However, Article 16(2) also emphasises that 'the law of Mauritius shall apply to artificial islands, installations and structures in the EEZ as if they were in the territorial sea', www.un.org/Depts/los/LEGISLATIONANDTREATIES/STATEFILES/MUS.htm.

342 Seychelles, Maritime Zones Act 1977, Article 7(1)(b); Maritime Zones Act 1999, Article 10 (b)–(d), www.un.org/Depts/los/LEGISLATIONANDTREATIES/STATEFILES/SYC.htm.

343 Vanuatu, Maritime Zones Act No. 23 of 1981, Article 10(b), UN DOALOS, National Legislation on the EEZ, 393; Maritime Zones Act No. 6 of 2010, Article 10(2)(a), www.un.org/Depts/los/LEGISLATIONANDTREATIES/PDFFILES/vut_2010_Act06.pdf.

4.4.2 *Safety Zones*

In order to protect the safety of both navigation and the artificial islands, installations and structures, where necessary, the coastal State may establish reasonable safety zones around such infrastructure and take appropriate measures.[344] Coastal States have the independent right to establish these safety zones in contrast to other specially protected areas in the EEZ that have to be approved by IMO. This leaves coastal States broad discretionary power to decide when it is necessary to establish, and how to justify the reasonableness, of the safety zones.

The coastal State's rights are, nevertheless, subject to a number of constraints. Coastal States must determine the breadth of safety zones 'taking into account applicable international standards'.[345] 'Taking into account' is a rather vague requirement and much less demanding than 'conforming to and giving effect to generally accepted international rules and standards' used to limit the coastal State's jurisdiction over vessel-source pollution.[346] The designation of safety zones must be 'reasonably related to the nature and function of the artificial islands, installations or structures', and the breadth 'shall not exceed a distance of 500 meters around them, . . . except as authorised by generally accepted international standards or as recommended by the competent international organization'.[347] Where the installations are used for scientific research, the breadth must not exceed a distance of 500 metres with no exceptions.[348]

Coastal States may 'take appropriate measures' to ensure safety of both navigation and the infrastructure within the safety zones 'in the nature of the enactment of laws or regulations, and of the enforcement of such laws and regulations'.[349] Although UNCLOS does not indicate which measures may be considered appropriate, it requires all ships to 'comply with generally accepted international standards regarding navigation in the vicinity of artificial islands, installations and structures and safety zones'.[350] This seems to limit these 'appropriate measures' to those adopted by IMO or other international conferences regarding the safety of navigation. These measures may include ships' routeing systems, ship

344 UNCLOS Article 60(4).
345 UNCLOS Article 60(5).
346 UNCLOS Article 211(5).
347 UNCLOS Article 60(5); Proelss 'Article 60' (2017) 477.
348 UNCLOS Article 260.
349 UNCLOS Article 60(4); Arctic Sunrise Arbitration para 211.
350 UNCLOS Article 60(6).

reporting systems, vessel traffic services, navigational aids, automatic identification systems, long-range identification and tracking system, pilotage and other operational measures for shipping.[351] Foreign vessels are required to respect the applicable measures, to navigate with caution and, where appropriate, to take precautionary actions when approaching such infrastructure or safety zones.[352] It is not completely clear, however, whether the coastal State may extend its entire jurisdiction applicable to the safety zones to include customs, fiscal, health, immigration and environmental regulations.[353]

4.4.3 Safeguards

UNCLOS confers extensive authority on coastal States to establish and use artificial islands, installations and structures and safety zones for economic purposes. Given that the existence of these offshore infrastructures will have an impact on the navigational freedoms, it is important that coastal States exercise such rights and jurisdiction in a non-abusive manner and have due regard to other States' rights and freedoms.[354] These general obligations are strengthened by detailed procedural requirements and safeguards, particularly with respect to the preservation of the freedom of navigation. As State practice stands, the height of most offshore infrastructures do not pose a major threat to the freedom of overflight.

First of all, coastal States must give 'due notice' of the construction of any artificial islands, installations and structures.[355] The 'due notice' is only relevant to the 'construction' of the infrastructure and serves to notify other States of the intention of the coastal State to begin the construction process.[356] The notice should be given in the format of notices to mariners, radio warnings and markings on all appropriate navigational charts.[357] It is not clear how far in advance the coastal State should give such notice, but it should be before the actual

351 SOLAS, Chapter V: 'Safety of Navigation'; IMO, 'Safety of Navigation' www.imo.org/en/OurWork/Safety/Pages/NavigationDefault.aspx.

352 IMO Res A.671(16), 19 October 1989, Safety Zones and Safety of Navigation around Offshore Installations and Structures, Annex, Article 2.

353 Proelss 'Article 60' (2017) 476–477.

354 Nordquist, Nandan and Rosenne (1993) 587; UNCLOS Articles 56(2), 60(4), 300.

355 UNCLOS Article 60(3).

356 Proelss 'Article 60' (2017) 473.

357 IMO Res A.671(16) Annex, Articles 1(1), 4(2), 5.

construction take place. The coastal State is also not under an obligation to consult with other States regarding the impending location or construction of such infrastructure.

Secondly, the construction of such infrastructure and the establishment of the safety zones around them 'may not be established where interference may be caused to the use of recognized sea lanes essential to international navigation'.[358] However, the tentative word 'may' indicates that, where necessary, a coastal State could still establish such infrastructure and the safety zones around them, even if interference is caused. Moreover, the rigid requirements of 'recognized' and 'essential' imply that when normal sea lanes are not recognised as essential to international navigation, or even when there are alternative sea lanes which can be used, interference is permissible. This interpretation of the limited effect of such a requirement is reaffirmed by the more stringent language used in relation to scientific research installations in the EEZ, where they 'shall not constitute an obstacle to established international shipping routes'.[359] In practice, in order to avoid potential interruption to navigation, IMO calls on coastal States to study the pattern of shipping traffic through the intended exploration areas to avoid serious obstruction of sea approaches or shipping routes.[360]

Thirdly, coastal States must maintain 'permanent means for giving warning of their presence'.[361] Installations or equipment used for scientific research in the EEZ must have 'adequate internationally agreed warning signals to ensure safety at sea'.[362] The permanent means are generally implemented by using navigational marks and lights.

Lastly, any abandoned or disused installations or structures

> shall be removed to ensure safety of navigation, taking into account any generally accepted international standards established in this regard by the competent international organization. Such removal shall also have due regard to fishing, the protection of the marine environment and the rights and duties of other States.[363]

This obligation is different from the strict rule contained in the 1958 Convention on the Continental Shelf whereby 'any installations

[358] UNCLOS Article 60(7).
[359] UNCLOS Article 261.
[360] IMO Res A.671(16) Preamble, para 1(a); Proelss 'Article 60' (2017) 478–479.
[361] UNCLOS Article 60(3).
[362] UNCLOS Article 262.
[363] UNCLOS Article 60(3).

which are abandoned or disused must be entirely removed'.[364] UNCLOS altered the complete removal requirement and left it to the coastal State (with generally accepted international standards in mind) to determine the extent of the removal of installations and structures in specific circumstances. As the competent international organisation, IMO has adopted guidelines to address these issues.[365]

The removal of abandoned or disused installations and structures must be based on consideration of 'any potential effect on safety of surface or subsurface navigation or of other uses of the sea', any potential effect on the marine environment, and any other advantages or disadvantages that may be caused by such removal.[366] If the structure is located in an area where higher traffic volume is anticipated in the future, or in the proximity of designated or customary sea lanes or port access routes, complete removal would be expected.[367] If it is located in 'approaches to or in straits used for international navigation or routes used for international navigation through archipelagic waters, in customary deep-draught sea lanes, or in, or immediately adjacent to, routeing systems', then it should be entirely removed with no exceptions.[368] Also, if the structure is 'standing in less than 75m (or 100m if it was emplaced on the sea-bed on or after 1 January 1998) of water and weighing less than 4,000 tonnes in air, excluding the deck and superstructure, should be entirely removed', but it is subject to certain exceptions.[369] Such removal, entirely or partially, should be undertaken in the manner so as not to cause 'significant adverse effects upon navigation or the marine environment'.[370]

If an abandoned or disused installation or structure has not been entirely removed, a coastal State must give the depth, position and dimensions through appropriate publicity and clearly indicate such on nautical charts.[371] Coastal States are also required to monitor 'the accumulation and deterioration of material left on the sea-bed to ensure there

[364] Convention on the Continental Shelf Article 5(5).

[365] IMO Res A.672(16), 19 October 1989, Annex: Guidelines and Standards for the Removal of Offshore Installations and Structures on the Continental Shelf and in the Exclusive Economic Zone.

[366] Ibid Annex, Article 2.1.

[367] Ibid Annex, Article 2.2.

[368] Ibid Annex, Article 3.7.

[369] Ibid Annex, Articles 3.1–3.2, 3.4.

[370] Ibid Annex, Article 3.3.

[371] UNCLOS Article 60(3).

is no subsequent adverse impact on navigation, other uses of the sea or the marine environment'.[372]

4.4.4 *Enforcement Jurisdiction*

The counterpart of coastal State's exclusive right and jurisdiction over artificial islands, specific installations and structures is that other States have the mutual obligation of having due regard to the rights and duties of the coastal State and must comply with duly adopted domestic legislation.[373] The coastal State's enforcement jurisdiction is trigged when the requirements of hot pursuit are satisfied.[374] The coastal State's jurisdiction to enforce its legislation to implement the SUA Platforms Protocol follows the general enforcement jurisdiction contained in UNCLOS.

Compared with the three progressive steps of enforcement procedures over vessel-source pollution, it is not entirely clear what powers and competence coastal States may exercise following the hot pursuit. It could be argued that the coastal State may undertake boarding, inspection and detention of the suspected foreign vessel following a similar approach to that used for vessel-source pollution if justified by the circumstances.[375] Since these alleged violations mainly relate to the safety of navigation, the flag State's exclusive jurisdiction prevails over that of the coastal State, unless severe damage is caused to the infrastructure. IMO recommends that coastal States should first take actions to notify and provide evidence to the flag State of the infringement, and it is the latter's responsibility to take appropriate measures to ensure that suitable procedures are brought against the reported vessel.[376] This recommendation reflects the strong intention of preserving exclusive flag State jurisdiction over vessels with regard to infringement of safety zones in the EEZ.

In the *Arctic Sunrise Arbitration*, the tribunal considered that the coastal State may justify 'some form of preventive action against a vessel' if the circumstances 'give rise to a reasonable belief that the vessel may be involved in a terrorist attack on an installation or structure of the coastal State'.[377] If the coastal State has 'reasonable grounds to suspect' the vessel

[372] IMO Res A.672(16) Annex, Article 2.4.
[373] UNCLOS Articles 56(1)(b)(i), 58(3), 60(1)–(2).
[374] UNCLOS Article 111(1)–(2); Arctic Sunrise Arbitration para 244.
[375] UNCLOS Articles 73, 220, 228.
[376] IMO Res A.671(16) Annex, Article 3.
[377] Arctic Sunrise Arbitration para 314.

within the safety zone is engaged in terrorist offences against offshore infrastructure, it may take measures to board, seize and detain the vessel.[378]

The establishment and use of artificial islands, installations and structures, and the safety zones around them, will inevitably impede the freedom of navigation to some degree.[379] The framework proposed by Article 60 attempts to create a balance between the interests of the coastal State and other States. While interference with navigation is predictable, it is to be minimised and must be eliminated once such infrastructure or safety zones no longer serve the primary purpose for which they were originally established.[380]

4.5 Resolving Disputes Concerning the Navigational Freedoms

The dispute settlement mechanism contained in Part XV of UNCLOS provides further assurance that the delicate equilibrium of rights and duties established between the coastal State and other States will be respected in practice. Like all disputes concerning the interpretation and application of UNCLOS, State parties must settle their disputes concerning the navigational freedoms by any peaceful means chosen by them.[381] Where no settlement has been reached by the peaceful means of their choice, any party may submit such dispute to the court or tribunal having jurisdiction under UNCLOS Part XV, which are known as compulsory dispute settlement procedures.[382] In addition, an UNCLOS court or tribunal may also have jurisdiction over any disputes concerning the interpretation and application of other relevant international agreements related to the purposes of UNCLOS.[383] For example, both the London Protocol and RWC confer the UNCLOS court and tribunal jurisdiction over disputes regarding their interpretation and application.[384]

There are also special procedures and limitations applicable to disputes concerning the navigational freedoms in the EEZ. Article 297 introduces certain automatic limitations to the application of the compulsory dispute settlement procedures to disputes relating to the uses of the EEZ

378 Arctic Sunrise Arbitration para 278.
379 Churchill, Lowe and Sander (2022) 243, 268–269, 278.
380 UNCLOS Article 60(3).
381 UNCLOS Articles 279–280.
382 UNCLOS Articles 281, 286–287.
383 UNCLOS Article 288(2).
384 London Protocol, Article 16; RWC Article 15.

that resemble the balance between the coastal State and other States.[385] Article 297 starts with an assertion of jurisdiction phrased in affirmative terms to include disputes that are subject to the compulsory dispute settlement procedures, and then exempts certain categories of disputes that touch upon important interests of the coastal State.

On the affirmed jurisdiction, it has been explicitly stated that disputes concerning the interpretation or application of provisions relating the navigational freedoms are subject to the compulsory dispute settlement procedures of Part XV.[386] This includes both when the coastal State allegedly has acted in contravention of the relevant provisions and when other States allegedly have acted in contravention of the relevant provisions of UNCLOS and duly adopted national laws and regulations.[387] In both *M/V Saiga (No.2)* and the *Arctic Sunrise Arbitration*, the applicants relied on Article 297(1) on matters relating to the freedom of navigation in the EEZ.[388]

In addition, the compulsory jurisdiction extends to disputes relating to when the coastal State allegedly acted in contravention of specified international rules and standards for the protection and preservation of the marine environment that are applicable to it.[389] This ensures that other States may challenge the coastal State's exercise of its environmental jurisdiction within the EEZ, including disputes relating to the contravention of rules and standards found in IMO instruments such as MARPOL or the London Convention.[390] In the *Chagos Marine Protected Area Arbitration*, the arbitral tribunal accepted jurisdiction based on the argument that the dispute in respect of the marine protected area (MPA) established by the United Kingdom relates to the preservation of the marine environment that falls under Article 297(1)(c).[391]

[385] Andrew Serdy, 'Article 297', in Proelss (2017) 1908–1909; Myron H. Nordquist, Shabtai Rosenne and Louis B Sohn (eds.), *United Nations Convention on the Law of the Sea 1982: A Commentary*, Vol. V (Martinus Nijhoff 1989) 105–106.

[386] UNCLOS Article 297(1)(a)–(b).

[387] Serdy 'Article 297' (2017) 1914–1916.

[388] M/V 'Saiga' (No. 2) (Saint Vincent and the Grenadines v. Guinea), Provisional Measures, Order of 11 March 1998, ITLOS Reports 1998, p. 24, para 30; In the Matter of the Arctic Sunrise Arbitration before an Arbitral Tribunal Constituted under Annex VII to the 1982 United Nations Convention on the Law of the Sea between the Kingdom of the Netherlands and the Russian Federation, Award on Jurisdiction, 26 November 2014, PCA Case No. 2014-02, paras 52, 61.

[389] UNCLOS Article 297(1)(c).

[390] Chagos MPA Arbitration, paras 321–322; Serdy 'Article 297' (2017) 1916.

[391] Chagos MPA Arbitration para 319.

It should be acknowledged that the list contained in Article 297(1) does not restrict an ITLOS court or tribunal from considering disputes concerning the exercise of sovereign rights and jurisdiction in other cases.[392] It would have rendered the following limitations to jurisdiction redundant if the ITLOS court or tribunal could only consider three types of cases relating to the exercise of sovereign rights and jurisdiction. Where a dispute concerns the interpretation or application of relevant provisions of the EEZ, and provided that the dispute is not subject to the express limitations set out in Article 297(2) and (3), jurisdiction for compulsory dispute settlement flows from the general provisions of Article 288(1).[393]

On the relevant limitations to jurisdiction, Article 297(3)(a) first confirms that disputes concerning the interpretation and application of the provisions with regard to fisheries shall be subject to compulsory dispute settlement procedures, then exempts certain categories of disputes in the EEZ. Coastal States are not obliged to accept the submission to such settlement procedures for disputes

> relating to its sovereign rights with respect to the living resources in the [EEZ] or their exercise, including its discretionary powers for determining the allowable catch, its harvesting capacity, the allocation of surpluses to other States and the terms and conditions established in its conservation and management laws and regulations.[394]

These disputes may be submitted to conciliation at the request of any party to the dispute if no settlement has been reached through other peaceful means chosen by the parties.[395] Article 298(1)(b) further permits the coastal State to opt out of the compulsory dispute settlement procedures with respect to 'disputes concerning law enforcement activities in regard to the exercise of sovereign rights or jurisdiction excluded from the jurisdiction of a court or tribunal' under Article 297(3). However, the coastal State's enforcement jurisdiction of its sovereign rights with respect to other economic activities and non-living resources falls outside the limitations of Article 297(3)(a) and therefore is subject to the compulsory dispute settlement procedures.[396]

[392] Ibid para 317.
[393] Ibid para 317.
[394] UNCLOS Article 297(3)(a).
[395] UNCLOS Article 297(3)(b).
[396] Arbitral Tribunal Constituted Pursuant to Article 287, and in Accordance with Annex VII, of the United Nations Convention on the Law of the Sea in the Matter of an

The effect of Articles 297(3)(a) and 298(1)(b), is not, however, to exclude all disputes relating to fisheries in the EEZ from the compulsory mechanism.[397] Disputes relating to fisheries that are not connected to sovereign rights granted to coastal States or their exercise are not exempted. For example, a dispute concerning the legality of imprisonment penalty for violations of fisheries laws in the EEZ could not be automatically excluded from the compulsory dispute settlement procedures.[398] When the implementation of conservation measures of the living resources unduly impair navigational freedoms, other States may also challenge the coastal State's actions.

In practice, a dispute often involves multiple elements of the rights and duties of the State parties involved. Therefore, how to characterise a dispute could play a crucial role in the application of the compulsory dispute settlement procedures. The *Chagos Marine Protected Area Arbitration* between Mauritius and the United Kingdom illustrates this point whereby the arbitral tribunal examined the 'far from clear' relationship between Article 297 paragraph 1 on the affirmation of jurisdiction and paragraph 3 on the limitations to jurisdiction.[399] The dispute relating to the establishment of a MPA around the Chagos Archipelago by the United Kingdom could cover both the marine environment and the coastal State's sovereign rights over the living resources and their exercise in the EEZ. After an examination of the scope of the MPA and the rights invoked by Mauritius, the arbitral tribunal came to the conclusion that the MPA reflected 'environmental concerns that extend well beyond the management of fisheries' and that the submission of Mauritius could not 'be excluded entirely by the exception from jurisdiction set out in Article 297(3)(a)'.[400] The arbitral tribunal considered that the dispute 'relates to the preservation of the marine environment and that Mauritius has alleged a violation of international rules and standards in this area', therefore the dispute is subject to the compulsory dispute settlement procedures asserted under Article 297(1)(c).[401]

Arbitration between Guyana and Suriname (Guyana v. Suriname), Award, 17 September 2007, PCA Case No. 2004-04, paras 413–416.

397 Nordquist, Rosenne and Sohn (1989) 105, 137.

398 UNCLOS Article 73(3); Serdy 'Article 297' (2017) 1909; P. Chandrasekhara Rao and Philippe Gautier, *The International Tribunal for the Law of the Sea: Law, Practice and Procedure* (Edward Elgar 2018) 95.

399 Chagos MPA Arbitration para 314; Chandrasekhara Rao and Gautier (2018) 95–96.

400 Chagos MPA Arbitration para 304.

401 Ibid para 319.

The application of Article 297 is subject to an additional safeguard, contained in Article 294, which restricts an UNCLOS court or tribunal from considering relevant disputes under certain circumstances. Article 294 permits a party to seek a preliminary determination, or by initiative of the court or tribunal to determine, in advance of other stages in the procedure concerning a dispute referred to in Article 297, as to 'whether the claim constitutes an abuse of legal process or whether *prima facie* it is well founded'.[402] If the claim constitutes an abuse of legal process or is *prima facie* unfounded, the court or tribunal should take no further action in the case.[403] The preliminary proceedings under Article 294 are independent from the general right of any party to a dispute to make preliminary objections to the jurisdiction of an UNCLOS court or tribunal.[404] Under the Rules of ITLOS, there are two provisions designed to implement these two specific procedures, namely preliminary proceedings and preliminary objections.[405] Objections to the jurisdiction of ITLOS based on Article 297 may also be dealt with under the more general procedure contained in preliminary objections which covers '[a]ny objection to the jurisdiction of the Tribunal or to the admissibility of the application'.[406]

In addition to the affirmed jurisdiction in Article 297, Arctic 292 establishes that the prompt release requirement is subject to a special compulsory dispute settlement procedure.[407] Where it is alleged that the coastal State has not complied with the relevant provisions for 'the prompt release of the vessel or its crew upon the posting of a reasonable bond or other financial security, the question of release from detention' may be submitted to ITLOS unless the parties have agreed otherwise.[408] Therefore, the right to bring a dispute before a court or tribunal about the detention of a foreign vessel is restricted to the cases expressly provided for in UNCLOS with respect to the enforcement of the living resources and environmental regulations.[409] The application for release

[402] UNCLOS Article 294(1); Churchill, Lowe and Sander (2022) 866–867.
[403] UNCLOS Article 294(1).
[404] UNCLOS Article 294(3); Pablo Ferrara, 'Article 294', in Proelss (2017) 1899.
[405] Rules of the Tribunal (ITLOS/8), adopted 28 October 1997, as amended, Articles 96, 97.
[406] Chandrasekhara Rao and Gautier (2018) 96, 233.
[407] Rainer Lagoni, 'The Prompt Release of Vessels and Crews Before the International Tribunal for the Law of the Sea: A Preparatory Report' (1996) 11(2) Int'l J Marine & Coastal L 147, 147; Tullio Treves, 'Article 292', in Proelss (2017) 1882.
[408] UNCLOS Article 292(1).
[409] UNCLOS Articles 73(2), 226(1)(b)–(c), 292(1); Nordquist, Rosenne and Sohn (1989) 69; Treves 'Article 292' (2017) 1885–1886.

may be made only by or on behalf of the flag State invoking its independent rights under UNCLOS, and the court or tribunal shall deal only with the question of release without prejudice to the merits of any case before the relevant domestic forum.[410] These obligations and proceedings are included to balance the interests of the detaining coastal State against that of the flag State in order to avoid an excessive detention of its vessels.[411] Up until 2024, 10 out of 30 contentious cases brought to ITLOS since it was established in 1996 were related to prompt release.[412] These cases have assisted in establishing the procedures and requirements of prompt release, particularly the criteria for assessing the reasonableness of bonds or other financial security, and providing judicial remedies for flag States to avoid unreasonable detention of their vessels.[413]

In sum, disputes concerning the basic navigational freedoms and the protection of the marine environment in the EEZ retain the complete protection of the compulsory dispute settlement procedures provided in Part XV. The main limitations to compulsory jurisdiction are disputes concerning the sovereign right and discretion of the coastal State over living resources and their exercise, which generally do not have a direct bearing on the exercise of the navigational freedoms.

4.6 Modified Freedoms in the Exclusive Economic Zone

Navigational freedoms have been a central concept of the law of the sea for hundreds of years, albeit increasing restrictions have more recently been imposed on them with the expansion of coastal State's rights.[414] The survey in this chapter illustrates that it is unavoidable that navigational freedoms be curtailed to some degree so as to accommodate coastal

410 UNCLOS Article 292(2)–(3); Nordquist, Rosenne and Sohn (1989) 70–71; The 'Camouco' Case (Panama v. France), Prompt Release, Judgment of 7 February 2000, ITLOS Reports 2000, p. 10, para 58.

411 'Monte Confurco' Case paras 71–72; Donald R. Rothwell and Tim Stephens, 'Illegal Southern Ocean Fishing and Prompt Release: Balancing Coastal and Flag State Rights and Interests' (2004) 53(1) Int'l & Compar LQ 171, 183; 'Tomimaru' Case para 74; Churchill, Lowe and Sander (2022) 546–547.

412 ITLOS, 'Contentious Cases' www.itlos.org/en/main/cases/contentious-cases/.

413 M/V 'Saiga' Case para 82; 'Camouco' Case para 67; 'Monte Confurco' Case para 76; 'Volga' Case para 77; 'Juno Trader' Case para 85; 'Hoshinmaru' Case para 88.

414 Maria Gavouneli, *Functional Jurisdiction in the Law of the Sea* (Martinus Nijhoff 2007) 1–2.

States' sovereign rights and jurisdiction in the EEZ as compared to the traditional high seas freedoms.[415]

As far as the economic utilisation of the zone is concerned, particularly with respect to the living resources, the balance of the EEZ generally supports accepting a 'shift of emphasis in favour of the coastal State'.[416] State practice has also developed to allow coastal State to regulate navigation through their EEZs under certain circumstances based on their interactions with the exercise of the coastal State's sovereign rights and jurisdiction.[417] This is particularly noticeable with respect to activities that can be considered as ancillary to fishing and navigational regulations developed under the auspice of IMO to protect living resources or the marine environment.

Important safeguards have been introduced to protect the international community's interest to continue using the EEZ for navigation and overflight. This is highlighted through the limitations to coastal State jurisdiction over foreign vessels, including due process at IMO, generally accepted international rules and standards, the due regard obligation, non-abuse of rights, restricted enforcement powers and other safeguards. Moreover, disputes concerning the exercise of navigational freedoms are subject to compulsory dispute settlement procedures, where both the coastal State and other States may submit their allegation to an UNCLOS court or tribunal.

The international law of the sea is in a period of reassessment and transition with regard to how to maintain a balance between protecting the essential navigational freedoms and the expansion of the rights of coastal States.[418] The fact that the coastal State is given expanded concurrent jurisdiction in relation to foreign vessels means that certain restraints on the navigational freedoms are acceptable, but such development is not enough to entirely alter the jurisdictional framework of the EEZ established under UNCLOS.[419] The less than definitive language of

[415] J. C. Phillips, 'The Exclusive Economic Zone as a Concept in International Law' (1977) 26 Int'l & Compar LQ 585, 589–590; Yoshifumi Tanaka, *The International Law of the Sea* (3rd ed., Cambridge University Press 2019) 159.

[416] David J Attard, *The Exclusive Economic Zone in International Law* (Clarendon Press 1987) 75; Alexander Proelss, 'The Law on the Exclusive Economic Zone in Perspective: Legal Status and Resolution of User Conflicts Revisited' (2012) 26 Ocean YB 87, 92–97; Tullio Scovazzi, '"Due Regard" Obligations, with Particular Emphasis of Fisheries in the Exclusive Economic Zone' (2019) 34 Int'l J Marine & Coastal L 56, 69.

[417] Van Dyke (2005) 121; Boyle and Redgwell (2021) 506, 544–545.

[418] Stephens and Rothwell (2012) 708–709.

[419] Churchill, Lowe and Sander (2022) 278.

Part V, on the positive side, has given both sides sufficient flexibility to find a dynamic balance.

It is important to acknowledge that the tension between navigational freedoms and coastal interests will continues to exist within the framework of this *sui generis* regime, with occasional developments trending to advantage either the coastal State or other States. In most cases, the tension can be managed if both sides respect the attribution of rights and duties, and exercise their due regard obligations diligently. It is also important that disputes relating to the basic navigational freedoms are subject to the compulsory dispute settlement procedures. Among other implications, the juridical process could contribute to legal certainty on some crucial provisions to prevent potential conflicts. This is illustrated by the contribution made by ITLOS in making a firm statement that, while the coastal State has the right to regulate bunkering of fishing vessels in its EEZ, the bunkering of non-fishing vessels falls within the freedom of navigation.[420]

[420] M/V 'Virginia G' Case para 217; M/V 'Norstar' Case paras 219–220; M/T 'San Padre Pio' Case paras 107–108.

5

Coastal State Rights and the Freedom of the Laying of Submarine Cables and Pipelines

Submarine cables and pipelines laid on the seabed remain the foundation of the global communications network and the offshore energy transportation system that facilitate the increasing globalisation and interconnectedness of the world.[1] International law seeks to strengthen these systems by, *inter alia*, preserving the freedom to lay submarine cables and pipelines in the exclusive economic zone (EEZ).[2] Legal issues concerning submarine cables and pipelines are also guided by the two legal doctrines of the allocation and exercise of rights and freedoms in the EEZ. Coastal States are obligated not to impede such freedom relating to the realm of communications and transportation, except for exercising their sovereign rights and other authorised jurisdiction as permitted under international law.[3] Both the coastal State and the operating State undertake the mutual obligation of having due regard to each other's rights and duties when exercising their rights and freedoms with regard to activities related to submarine cables and pipelines. Considering that the coastal State has sovereign rights over activities for the economic exploitation and exploration of the EEZ, and jurisdiction over the use of offshore infrastructures, it can be expected that the primary subjects of the freedom to lay submarine cables and pipelines are those not associated with activities that are under the coastal State's jurisdiction.

The legal framework of submarine cables and pipelines established in the United Nations Convention on the Law of the Sea (UNCLOS),

[1] Douglas R. Burnett, Tara M. Davenport and Robert C. Beckman, 'Introduction: Why Submarine Cables?' in Douglas R. Burnett, Robert C. Beckman and Tara M. Davenport (eds.), *Submarine Cables: The Handbook of Law and Policy* (Martinus Nijhoff 2014) 1–2; M. Wynn Tranfield, 'Unspooling the Legacy of Submarine Cables' (2018) 46(3) Documents to the People 8, 8.

[2] United Nations Convention on the Law of the Sea (adopted 10 December 1982, in force 16 November 1994) 1833 UNTS 3, Article 58(1) (UNCLOS).

[3] UNCLOS Article 79.

however, appears to be under increasing pressure in the EEZ.[4] The challenges are coming from two directions. First, there is a growing trend among some coastal States to exceed the jurisdictional limits recognised by UNCLOS relating to submarine cables and pipelines in their EEZs; second, submarine cables and pipelines are subjected to challenges, as well as undue interference and damage, posed by competing uses of ocean space by both the coastal State and other user States, as well as intentional damages.[5]

This chapter addresses issues relating to the freedom to lay submarine cable and pipelines in the EEZ, as well as mechanisms for their protection. It is divided into five sections. Section 5.1 provides a brief overview of submarine cables and pipelines. Section 5.2 discusses the legal framework on submarine cables and pipelines as laid down in UNCLOS with the aim to clarify the scope of the freedom to lay them in the EEZ. Section 5.3 examines the limitations imposed by law and State practice relating to this freedom, particularly the scope of coastal States' rights and jurisdiction. Section 5.4 explores the means to protect submarine cables and pipelines provided under international law and as developed by State practice, with an emphasis on the potential active role of the coastal State in complying with the legal framework and regulating competing uses in the EEZ. Section 5.5 discusses the dispute settlement mechanisms that could be used to resolve potential disputes between the coastal State and the operating State.

5.1 Basic Facts about Submarine Cables and Pipelines

By function, there are two main types of submarine cables: submarine fibre-optic cables used to transmit data communications traffic; and submarine power cables used to transmit electricity.[6] Submarine fibre-optic cables,

[4] UNCLOS Articles 21(1)(c), 51(2), 58(1), 79, 81(1)(c), 112–115, 297(1).

[5] Tara Davenport, 'Submarine Communications Cables and Law of the Sea: Problems in Law and Practice' (2012) 43(3) Ocean Dev Int'l L 201, 202; Robert Beckman, 'Protecting Submarine Cables from Intentional Damage: The Security Gap', in Burnett, Beckman and Davenport (2014) 281–283; Nord Stream, 'Incident on the Nord Stream Pipeline (updated 14/11/2022)' www.nord-stream.com/press-info/press-releases/incident-on-the-nord-stream-pipeline-updated-14112022-529/.

[6] Max Planck Institute for Comparative Public Law and International Law, *Encyclopedia of Public International Law*, Vol. I (North-Holland 1992) 516–517: 'Cables, Submarine': high-voltage submarine power cables are mainly used to transmit electric energy to offshore installations on the continental shelf; George K. Walker (ed.), *Definitions for*

based on the type of data transmitted, can be further divided into telecommunication cables, scientific research cables and military cables.[7] Submarine cables are designed for underwater use and are usually laid on or buried under the seabed. The first submarine communication cable – a copper-based telegraph cable – was laid across the English Channel from Dover to Calais in 1851. Subsequently, submarine cable technology evolved through several distinct phases: the submarine telegraph cable in the mid- to late 1800s, the transoceanic telephone cable in the mid-1950s and then the lightweight fibre-optic submarine cable, which has been used since the 1980s.[8] Modern submarine cables are small in size. The typical deep-ocean fibre-optic cables are 17–22 millimetres (mm) in diameter without protective armour and up to 50 mm with armour; the power cables, comprising solid copper conductor cores, insulation and armouring, are normally between 70 and 150 mm and can be up to 300 mm in diameter.[9]

Broadband communications through submarine fibre-optic cables have become critically important to the world economy and to the security of all States. Today, more than 95 per cent of the world's international telecommunications are provided by submarine fibre-optic cables, including services such as the internet, e-mail, phones and internet banking, as well as support for offshore platforms, military activities and marine scientific research.[10] As the world continues to consume ever-increasing amounts of data, driven by the demand for cloud services and mobile technology like 5G, the demand for submarine fibre-optic

the Law of the Sea: Terms Not Defined by the 1982 Convention (Martinus Nijhoff 2012) 'Submarine Cable', 310–311.

7 International Cable Protection Committee (ICPC), 'Cable Data' www.iscpc.org/information/cable-data/; Lionel Carter and Alfred H. A. Soons, 'Marine Scientific Research Cables' and J. Ashley Roach, 'Military Cables', in Burnett, Beckman and Davenport (2014) 323–350. Cables used for military purpose are discussed in Chapter 6 in this volume.

8 ICPC and the United Nations Environment Programme (UNEP), Submarine Cables and the Oceans: Connecting the World (UNEP-WCMC 2009) 11–20 www.iscpc.org/publications/; ICPC, 'Information: Narrative History' www.iscpc.org/information/learn-about-submarine-cables/narrative-history/; ICPC, 'Information: Timeline History' www.iscpc.org/information/learn-about-submarine-cables/timeline-history/; History of the Atlantic Cables & Undersea Communications, www.atlantic-cable.com/.

9 ICPC and UNEP (2009) 18–19; Lionel Carter, Douglas Burnett and Tara Davenport, 'The Relationship between Submarine Cables and the Marine Environment', in Burnett, Beckman and Davenport (2014) 179–180.

10 ICPC and UNEP (2009) 3, 8; Submarine Telecoms Forum (STF), Industry Report 2023–2024, Forward https://subtelforum.com/industry-report/.

cables will continue to increase.[11] Between 1991 and 2021, the submarine telecommunication industry invested approximately 50.7 billion USD to build more than 1.3 million route kilometres (km) of cables, which is an annual average investment of 1.6 billion USD, and 41,600 km of deployed systems.[12] During the COVID-19 pandemic, the sharp increase in demand on remote communications demonstrated beyond doubt the crucial role that submarine telecommunication cables play in connecting the world.[13]

Submarine power cables supply offshore installations and islands with electrical power, and are used as transmission cables to connect power grids between countries.[14] The first underwater power cable was laid across the Isar River in Germany in 1811 and has since been widely used in the North Sea and Baltic Sea, among other regions.[15] The advancement in power cable technology has enabled more ambitious cable projects with increased capacity across great ocean distances and depths between States, including between continents.[16] It is estimated that around 25 per cent of electricity travels to the United Kingdom via power cables, and that figure 'is rapidly expanding'.[17] In 2021, the United

[11] STF, Industry Report 2023–2024, Section 2.1: Global Capacity.

[12] STF, Industry Report 2021-2022, Section 2: Ownership Financing Analysis https://subtelforum.com/industry-report/.

[13] Henry Lancaster, 'A Global Crisis: Showcasing Dependence on Submarine Cable Infrastructure after a Global Crisis' and Byron Clatterbuck, 'Beyond COCID-19: Reimaging the Future of Telecommunications', in Submarine Telecoms Forum Magazine Issue 112 (May 2020) 20–21, 26–28 https://subtelforum.com/magazine/.

[14] Malcolm Eccles, Joska Ferencz and Douglas Burnett, 'Submarine Power Cables', in Burnett, Beckman and Davenport (2014) 301–302; Renato Moreira Vidaurre and Márcio Zamboti Fortes, 'The Interaction of Submarine Cables and the Power Quality of an Oil Rig's Electrical System' (2020) 102 Electrical Engineering 1521, 1521–1522; Jeremy Firestone, Alison W. Bates, and Adam Prefer, 'Power Transmission: Where the Offshore Wind Energy Comes Home' (2018) 29 Environmental Innovation and Societal Transitions 90, 90–92.

[15] Eccles, Ferencz and Burnett (2014) 302–303; ICPC, 'Power Cable Systems' www.iscpc.org/information/cable-data/power-cable-systems/.

[16] Leslie Hook, 'UK Start-up Plans World's Longest Subsea Electric Cable with Morocco', Financial Times, 26 September 2021 (online); 'Octopus Backs 3.6GW Morocco-UK Renewables Cable', ReNews, 12 May 2022 https://renews.biz/77800/octopus-energy-backs-36gw-morocco-uk-renewables-cable/.

[17] United Kingdom, House of Lords, International Relations and Defence Committee, 2nd Report of Session 2021-22, UNCLOS: The Law of the Sea in the 21st Century, para 316 https://committees.parliament.uk/publications/9005/documents/159002/default/ (UK House of Lords 2021-22).

Kingdom and Norway completed the world's longest existing interconnector, which costs about 2 billion Euros and stretches 720 km across the North Sea.[18] As the global demand for energy interconnection and offshore wind power development continues to increase, there is a potential market for energy transmission of greater distances using submarine power cables.[19]

In recent years, as the importance of submarine cables to world economies and States has grown exponentially, damages to them from natural disasters, fishing and shipping activities, as well as intentional harm have increased considerably.[20] Major disruptions to the submarine communication network, as exemplified by the 2006 Hengchun subsea earthquake that damaged nine cables and disrupted international communications for up to seven weeks, has demonstrated the need for increased protection of submarine cables and for the rapid repair of damaged cables.[21] In 2010, the United Nations General Assembly (UNGA) recognised for the first time the critical importance of fibre-optic submarine cables to 'the global economy and the national security of all States' and that such cables are susceptible to accidental and intentional damages and called for States to take measures to protect them.[22]

Submarine pipelines refers to a pipeline that lies beneath the ocean that is 'used or intended to be used for the conveyance of gas (including

[18] Leslie Hook, 'UK and Norway Complete World's Longest Subsea Electricity Cable', Financial Times, 15 June 2021 (online).

[19] Xiaoling Zhao et al., 'Technical and Economic Demands of HVDC Submarine Cable Technology for Global Energy Interconnection' (2020) 3(2) Global Energy Interconnection 120, 121–122; Arturs Purvins et al., 'Submarine Power Cable between Europe and North America: A Techno-Economic Analysis' (2018) 186 Journal of Cleaner Production 131, 134–136; Annad veldi ehf Skuli Johannsson, 'IceLink Submarine Power Cable from Iceland to Britain', Reykjavik Iceland 25th of March 2014, https://2veldi.files.wordpress.com/2016/04/icelink-submarine-power-cable-from-iceland-to-britain.pdf; Alex Lawson, 'National Grid to Use Subsea Cable Cash to Help Struggling Energy Users', The Guardian, 11 May 2022 (online).

[20] 'About Submarine Telecommunication Cables', ICPC, 2011 www.iscpc.org/publications/; Douglas R. Burnett, 'Submarine Cable Security and International Law' (2021) 97 Int'l Law Stud 1659, 1675–1679; Group of Experts of the Regular Process, The Second World Ocean Assessment, Volume II, (United Nations, 2021) Chapter 14: Changes in Coastal and Marine Infrastructure, 206 (World Ocean Assessment II).

[21] ICPC and UNEP (2009) 9; Lionel Carter et al.,, 'Insights into Submarine Geohazards from Breaks in Subsea Telecommunication Cables', (2014) 27(2) Oceanography 58, 59–60.

[22] United Nations General Assembly (UNGA) Res A/RES/65/37, 17 March 2011, Oceans and the Law of the Sea, Preamble and para 121.

natural gas), petroleum, oil, water, or any other mineral, liquid, or substance; and includes all fittings, pumps, tanks, appurtenances, or appliances used in connection with a pipeline'.[23] Submarine pipelines in the EEZ can be divided into three types: intra-field pipelines that connect a well and the offshore platform, export pipelines that transport the gas and oil from the field to land, and transport pipelines that are not linked with an operating field.[24] The first commercial submarine pipeline was constructed in 1954, and was a 250-mm-diameter concrete-coated gas pipeline of 16 km in length, installed at a depth of 4–10 metres in the Gulf of Mexico.[25] Modern submarine pipeline inventory comprises rigid (steel) pipelines and flexible flowlines, which vary in diameter from 50 mm to 1,400 mm.[26] Submarine transport pipelines are located predominantly around the Mediterranean, the Baltic and North Seas, with many having been built after 2000.[27] Pipelines provide a safe and cost-effective method for transporting natural resources, particularly natural gas.[28] It is expected that the demand for submarine pipelines will continue to grow, driven by the global consumption of energy and the advancement of technologies to extract natural resources from the ocean floor at greater distances from land.[29]

Like submarine cables, offshore pipelines are susceptible to both natural and human hazards, including intentional harm.[30] Notably, since

[23] Agreement between the United States of America and the French Republic Regarding the Operation, Maintenance and Security of the Donges-Metz Pipeline System (in force 1 April 1967) (1967) 6(4) International Legal Materials 731, Article 1; New Zealand, Submarine Cables and Pipelines Protection Act 1996 (Version as at 28 October 2021), s 2; Rainer Lagoni, 'Pipelines', last updated April 2011, Max Planck Encyclopedias of International Law www.mpepil.com.

[24] Group of Experts of the Regular Process, The First Global Integrated Marine Assessment (United Nations 2016) Chapter 19: Submarine Cables and Pipelines, 10 (World Ocean Assessment I).

[25] O-Lay, 'History of Offshore Pipeline Installation' http://o-lay.net/history-pipe-laying-technology (accessed in December 2023).

[26] Oil & Gas UK, 'Decommissioning of Pipelines in the North Sea Region – Issue 1' (2013), 4 https://oeuk.org.uk/product/guidelines-on-decommissioning-of-pipelines-in-the-north-sea-region-issue-1/; World Ocean Assessment I, Chapter 21: Offshore Hydrocarbon Industries, 14.

[27] World Ocean Assessment I, Chapter 19: Submarine Cables and Pipelines, 10.

[28] John Crowley, 'International Law and Coastal State Control over the Laying of Submarine Pipelines on the Continental Shelf: The Ekofisk-Emden Gas Pipeline' (1987) 56 Nordic J Int'l L 39, 39.

[29] World Ocean Assessment II, Volume II, Chapter 19: Changes in Hydrocarbon Exploration and Extraction, 286.

[30] Patrick Edobor Igbinovia, *Oil Thefts and Pipeline Vandalization in Nigeria* (Safari Books Ltd 2014) 87–95; Säkerhetspolisen (Swedish Security Service), 'Confirmed Sabotage of the

pipelines are linked to the exploitation and transportation of natural resources, damage to pipelines has the potential to cause serious pollution of the marine environment. Due to these environmental concerns, as well as the linkage to the exploration and exploitation of non-living resources, certain aspects of the laws and regulations with regard to the laying and protecting of pipelines are different from those of submarine cables. The following discussion will begin with a review of the historical development of the legal framework and discuss the scope of the freedom to lay submarine cables and pipelines and their protection under the law of the sea.

5.2 The Legal Framework of Submarine Cables and Pipelines

5.2.1 The Freedom to Lay Submarine Cables and Pipelines

When submarine telegraph cables began to be laid across the seabed during the 1850s, coastal States' rights were generally limited to the three-mile territorial waters, with the rest of the vast ocean being freely used by all States.[31] It was in every State's interest that international communications should be developed as quickly and smoothly as possible.[32] As a result, under the general realm of the freedom of the high seas, some States asserted the right to lay submarine cables with minimum resistance from other States.[33]

The first international agreement addressing submarine cables was the 1884 Paris Convention for the Protection of Submarine Telegraph Cables (1884 Paris Convention), which 'applies outside territorial waters to all legally established submarine cables landed on the territories, colonies or possessions of one or more of the High Contracting Parties'.[34] It focused mainly on the preservation and protection of submarine cables, including

Nord Stream Gas Pipelines' (18 November 2022) https://sakerhetspolisen.se/ovriga-sidor/nyheter/nyheter/2022-11-18-bekraftat-sabotage-vid-gasledningarna.html.

31 James Crawford, *Brownlie's Principles of Public International Law* (9th ed., Oxford University Press 2019) 245–246, 281–282.

32 Crowley (1987) 48.

33 David Joseph Attard, *The Exclusive Economic Zone in International Law* (Oxford University Press 1987) 123.

34 Convention for the Protection of Submarine Telegraph Cables (14 March 1884), Article I (1884 Paris Convention) https://cil.nus.edu.sg/wp-content/uploads/2019/02/1884-Convention-for-the-Protection-of-Submarine-Telegraph-Cables-1.pdf; René-Jean Dupuy and Daniel Vignes, *A Handbook on the New Law of the Sea*, Vol. II (Brill | Nijhoff 1991) 977–979.

for post-construction purposes such as liability for damage and compensation for anchors and fishing gear sacrificed to avoid damaging the cables.[35] The 1884 Paris Convention seems to assume that the cables laid between the contracting parties crossing their territorial waters are 'legally established' without explicitly recognising the right of States to freely lay submarine cables on the seabed beneath the high seas.[36] The 1884 Paris Convention was later supplemented by a resolution for the guidance of the trawling industry adopted at the London Conference of 1913.[37] It is still in force for those States that are not parties to any of the subsequent international conventions. It is worth noting that the 2012 United Nations Secretary-General Report on the Oceans and Law of the Sea expressed the view that the 1884 Paris Convention as amended is 'relevant' with regard to 'the transmission and transport of the renewable energy produced' at sea.[38] It can be interpreted that the principle to protect and preserve telecommunication cables can be extended to include high-voltage power cables and pipelines beneath the high seas, which is consistent with the development of the law.[39]

The regulation of submarine cables was well developed by the time it became necessary and technically possible to lay pipelines for transporting petroleum or gas products across the ocean in the 1950s.[40] Their similarities to submarine cables made it inevitable that pipelines should share the same legal regime.[41] Therefore, much of the international law relating to offshore pipelines, including the freedom to lay, penalties and liability for damage, and compensation for sacrificed anchors and fishing gear, has been drawn by analogy from the long-established framework for submarine cables.[42] The legal frameworks of submarine cables,

[35] 1884 Paris Convention, Articles II–VII.

[36] Myres S. McDougal and William T. Burke, *The Public Order of the Oceans: A Contemporary International Law of the Sea* (Yale University Press 1962) 781.

[37] United Nations Conference on the Law of the Sea, Official Records, Vol. IV, Second Committee (High Seas: General Regime), Summary Records of Meetings and Annexes, Geneva, 21 February–27 April 1958, A/CONF.13/40, Thirtieth Meeting, 11 April 1958, 89.

[38] UNGA A/67/79, 4 April 2012, Oceans and the Law of the Sea Report of the Secretary-General, para 37.

[39] United Kingdom, Continental Shelf Act, 15 April 1964, Article 8.

[40] Stuart Kaye, 'International Measures to Protect Oil Platforms, Pipelines and Submarine Cables from Attack' (2006–2007) 31 Tul Mar LJ 396–397.

[41] Crowley (1987) 39.

[42] Max Planck Institute for Comparative Public Law and International Law, *Encyclopedia of Public International Law*, Vol. III (North-Holland 1997) 1035.

including power cables, and pipelines were officially combined after widespread support at the International Law Commission (ILC) session in 1956, and the freedom to lay submarine cables and pipelines on the high seas was included in the Draft Articles Concerning the Law of the Sea (ILC Draft Articles).[43]

Both the 1958 Convention on the High Seas and 1958 Convention on the Continental Self contain provisions on the freedom to lay submarine cables and pipelines and their protection, which were based largely on the ILC Draft Articles.[44] It was recognised that all States enjoy the freedom to lay submarine cables and pipelines on the seabed of the high seas and, except for taking 'reasonable measures for the exploration of the continental shelf and the exploitation of its natural resources, the coastal State may not impede the laying or maintenance of submarine cables or pipelines on the continental shelf'.[45] The ILC in 1951 suggested that the coastal State 'may not exclude' the establishment and maintenance of submarine cables by other States, which was changed to 'may not prevent' in 1953 and to 'may not impede' in 1956, which suggests a positive statement in favour of the freedom to lay submarine cables and pipelines on the continental shelf.[46]

With the establishment of the EEZ in UNCLOS, the freedom to lay submarine cables and pipelines, as one of the high sea freedoms for communications and connectivity, was explicitly preserved in Article 58 as a right of all States. The expression 'all States' should be interpreted as including nationals and private entities of the States that are in fact laying submarine cables and pipelines.[47] Moreover, the term 'other

[43] 'Report of the International Law Commission to the United Nations General Assembly, A/3159, Articles Concerning the Law of the Sea with Commentaries' (1956) 2 YB ILC 278, Article 27 Commentary (ILC Draft Articles).

[44] Ibid Articles 27, 61–65.

[45] Convention on the High Seas (29 April 1958, in force 30 September 1962) 450 UNTS 11, Articles 2(3), 26; Convention on the Continental Self (29 April 1958, in force 10 June 1964) 499 UNTS 311, Article 4.

[46] Daniel P. O'Connell, *The International Law of the Sea*, Vol. I (Oxford University Press 1982) 508; 'Document A/1858, Report of the International Law Commission Covering the Work of its Third Session, 16 May–27 July 1951' (1951) 2 YB ILC, Annex: Draft Articles on the Continental Shelf and Related Subjects, Article 5; 'Document A/CN.4/76, Report of the International Law Commission Covering the Work of its Fifth Session, 1 June–14 August 1953' (1953) 2 YB ILC, Draft Articles on the Continental Shelf, Article 5.

[47] Dorota Jadwiga Englender, 'Article 79', in Alexander Proelss (ed.), *United Nations Convention on the Law of the Sea: A Commentary* (Hart 2017) 623; Douglas Guilfoyle and Cameron Miles, 'Article 112', in Proelss (2017) 781; Myron H. Nordquist, Satya N. Nandan and Shabtai Rosenne (eds.), *United Nations Convention on the Law of the Sea 1982: A Commentary*, Vol. III (Martinus Nijhoff 1995) 264; International Law Association (ILA),

internationally lawful uses of the sea related to these freedoms' includes all other activities associated with the operation of such cables and pipelines.[48] In order to clarify what these associated activities are, it is important to understand the process of how these cables and pipelines are operated. Since these operational procedures are similar between submarine cables and pipelines, they will be described by using the example of telecommunication cable operations.[49]

When planning a cable route, the first step is to undertake a desktop study to design an optimal route based on available data, then a hydrographic ship will conduct a route survey to investigate detailed seabed and environmental conditions before confirming the route.[50] After the cables and other components are manufactured and tested on land, they will be loaded on a highly specialised cable ship that supports the laying of the cables.[51] In the event of a fault or damage, the submarine cable has to be retrieved from the seabed so that a replacement section can be spliced and re-laid in by the cable ship.[52] At the end of service, the cable can be reused for other purposes, salvaged or left on the seabed.[53] Essentially, the associated activities include all of those spanning across the life cycle of the cable, including the design and survey of routes, manufacture and assembly, laying and installation, inspection, maintenance, repair and salvage.[54]

Committee on Submarine Cables and Pipelines under International Law, Interim Report 2020, para 72 www.ila-hq.org/en_GB/committees/submarine-cables-and-pipelines-under-international-law.

48 UNCLOS Article 58(1); Myron H. Nordquist, Satya N. Nandan and Shabtai Rosenne (eds.), *United Nations Convention on the Law of the Sea 1982: A Commentary*, Vol. II (Martinus Nijhoff 1993) 564.

49 Stelios Kyriakides and Edmundo Corona, *Mechanics of Offshore Pipelines: Volume 1 Buckling and Collapse* (Elsevier 2007) 34–52; Boyun Guo, et al., *Offshore Pipelines: Design, Installation, and Maintenance* (2nd ed., Elsevier 2014) 1–10; Nord Stream, 'From Pipes to Pipeline' www.nord-stream.com/the-project/construction/.

50 ICPC and UNEP (2009) 21–22; Graham Evans and Monique Page, 'The Planning and Surveying of Submarine Cable Routes', in Burnett, Beckman and Davenport (2014) 94–108.

51 Zhen Sun, 'Protection of Cable Ships Engaged in Operations for Submarine Telecommunication Cables' (2018) 49(2) Ocean Dev Int'l L 118, 120–121.

52 Douglas R Burnett, 'Recovery of Cable Repair Ship Cost Damages from Third Parties That Injure Submarine Cables' (2010–2011) 35 Tul Mar LJ 103, 109.

53 Douglas Burnett, 'Out-of-Service Submarine Cables', in Burnett, Beckman and Davenport (2014) 214–217.

54 Douglas Burnett, Tara Davenport and Robert Beckman, 'Overview of the International Legal Regime Governing Submarine Cables', in Burnett, Beckman and Davenport (2014) 79–80; Michael N. Schmitt, *Tallinn Manual 2.0 on the International Law Applicable to Cyber Operations* (Cambridge University Press 2017) 255–256 (Tallinn Manual 2.0);

An important distinction must be made with regard to submarine cables used for marine scientific research, including specific purpose-built systems and those incorporating sensors in or attached to the repeaters of fibre-optic telecommunication cable systems.[55] States and competent international organisations that intend to lay scientific research cables in the EEZ and on the continental shelf must apply for a permit and comply with the conditions laid down by the coastal State and international law.[56] The coastal State should, under normal circumstances, grant such consent.[57] However, the legal distinction becomes blurry regarding the anticipated dual-purpose submarine cables, known as Science Monitoring And Reliable Telecommunications (SMART) cables, an initiative led by a Joint Task Force sponsored by three United Nations agencies.[58] Recognising the advantages of the global submarine fibre-optic network, SMART cables are expected to integrate sensors into future undersea telecommunications cables, creating the potential for seafloor-based global ocean observing systems for climate monitoring and disaster warning at a modest incremental cost.[59]

The first major SMART project was established in 2021 by Portugal and linked mainland Portugal, the Azores and Madeira, equipping the cable ring with environmental seismic detection.[60] The use of SMART cables has raised questions concerning the interpretation and application of the legal frameworks of marine scientific research and the laying of

Englender (2017) 624; Robin Churchill, Vaughan Lowe and Amy Sander, *The Law of the Sea* (4th ed., Manchester University Press 2022) 285.

55 Lionel Carter and Alfred HA Soons, 'Marine Scientific Research Cables', in Burnett, Beckman and Davenport (2014) 325–332; ICPC, 'Scientific Cables' www.iscpc.org/information/cable-data/scientific-cables/.

56 UNCLOS Articles 248–249.

57 UNCLOS Articles 56(1)(b)(ii), 246(3).

58 International Telecommunication Union (ITU), 'ITU/WMO/UNESCO IOC Joint Task Force' www.itu.int/en/ITU-T/climatechange/task-force-sc/Pages/default.aspx. The ITU, the Intergovernmental Oceanographic Commission of the United Nations Educational, Scientific and Cultural Organization (UNESCO/IOC) and the World Meteorological Organization (WMO) established the Joint Task Force (JTF) on SMART cable systems in late 2012.

59 Bruce M. Howe et al., 'SMART Cables for Observing the Global Ocean: Science and Implementation' (2019) 6 Frontiers in Marine Science 424, doi: 10.3389/fmars.2019.00424; Mike Clare, 'The Science Monitoring and Reliable Telecommunications (SMART) Cables Initiative' (March 2022) 4 Submarine Cable Protection and the Environment 13 www.iscpc.org/publications/submarine-cable-protection-and-the-environment/.

60 SMART Cables, 'SMART Systems - Launched: Atlantic CAM' www.smartcables.org/systems; 'ANACOM Promotes Debate on Submarine Cables', 27 May 2021 www.anacom.pt/render.jsp?contentId=1663595.

submarine cables in the EEZ.[61] The major difference would be whether the laying of SMART cables is subject to the consent of the coastal State or falls under the freedom available to all States. Given the lack of a definition of marine scientific research in UNCLOS, States hold different interpretations of whether ocean observing systems fall under the scope of marine scientific research.[62] The Argo programme, operated under the Global Ocean Observing System (GOOS), collects information from inside the ocean using a fleet of close to 4,000 active floats that drift with the ocean currents and move up and down between the surface and mid-water level.[63] The Argo Guidelines acknowledge that the coastal State must be informed in advance, through appropriate channels, of the deployment of any float that may enter its EEZ, and may request the implementer to withhold the public release of sensitive date obtained within the EEZ.[64] This is a compromise position that acknowledges neither that the ocean observing Argo programme is a marine scientific research activity nor a high seas freedom. By analogy, the coastal State could request certain notification or permission from the deployment of a SMART cable within its EEZ. The SMART cable does not fit neatly under the rubric of either marine scientific research or freedom to lay submarine cables; its legal status needs to be clarified by subsequent State practice. Nevertheless, it needs to be acknowledged that all scientific cables are subject to other provisions on submarine cables in UNCLOS, particularly those relating to their protection.

When laying submarine cables and pipelines, States must have due regard to those already in position and must not prejudice the possibilities of repairing the existing ones.[65] In addition, when exercising such

[61] UNGA A/74/350, 11 September 2019, Oceans and the Law of the Sea Report of the Secretary-General, para 60.

[62] J. Ashley Roach, *Excessive Maritime Claims* (Brill 2021) 495–496; Aurora Mateos and Montserrat Gorina-Ysern, 'Climate Change and Guidelines for Argo Profiling Float Deployment on the High Seas' (2010) 14(8) ASIL Insights www.asil.org/insights/volume/14/issue/8/climate-change-and-guidelines-argo-profiling-float-deployment-high-seas.

[63] Argo, Implementation Status https://argo.ucsd.edu/about/status/; National Oceanic and Atmospheric Administration, Atlantic Oceanographic and Meteorological Laboratory, 'Argo Program' www.aoml.noaa.gov/argo/.

[64] UNESCO Doc IOC/EC-XLI.4, Guidelines for the Implementation of Resolution XX-6 of the IOC Assembly Regarding the Deployment of Profiling Floats in the High Seas within the Framework of the Argo Programme (2008), Annex https://oceanexpert.org/document/21855.

[65] UNCLOS Article 79(5).

freedom, States must have due regard to the rights and duties of other States, particularly the coastal State in the EEZ and on the continental shelf, and must comply with applicable domestic laws and regulations, as well as reasonable measures and other applicable conditions adopted by the coastal State.[66] Furthermore, the laying of submarine pipelines is subject to the coastal State's right to take reasonable measures to prevent, reduce and control pollution, and to give consent to the delineation of the course.[67]

5.2.2 *The Protection of Submarine Cables and Pipelines*

The first international law on submarine cables, the 1884 Paris Convention, was developed to protect submarine telegraph cables.[68] It requires contracting parties to provide proper safety measures for the track of the cable and its dimensions, to punish those responsible for intentional damage to a cable, to provide for civil liability for accidental damage to a cable, and to provide compensation for ships that suffered a loss in order to avoid injuring a cable.[69] Notably, the 1884 Paris Convention prescribes obligations, including observing navigational rules and maintaining distance, for other marine activities such as fishing to avoid interfering with the operations of a cable ship and damaging a cable.[70]

Much of the protective provisions in the 1884 Paris Convention were incorporated and extended to the protection to power cables and pipelines in the ILC Draft Articles.[71] However, the ILC Draft Articles omitted the specific obligations for ships to observe navigational rules and to maintain an appropriate distance from the cable ship and buoys. The only reference to other marine activities is an obligation for States to 'regulate trawling so as to ensure that all the fishing gear used shall be so constructed and maintained as to reduce to the minimum any danger of fouling submarine cables or pipelines'.[72] The ILC stated that the omission of the matter of collisions was dealt with by the adoption of the 1952 International Convention for the Unification of Certain Rules Relating to Penal Jurisdiction in Matters of Collisions or Other Incidents of Navigation, and further

[66] UNCLOS Articles 56(3), 58(3), 79(2) and (4).
[67] UNCLOS Article 79(2)–(4).
[68] Burnett, Davenport and Beckman (2014) 66.
[69] 1884 Paris Convention Articles II–IV, VII.
[70] Ibid Articles V–VI.
[71] ILC Draft Articles 62–63, 65.
[72] Ibid Article 64.

acknowledged that damage to a submarine cable or a pipeline 'may be regarded as an "incident of navigation"'.[73]

The Convention on the High Seas inherited the obligations for States, through domestic legislation, to punish those responsible for intentional damage to a cable or pipeline, to provide for civil liability for accidental damage to a cable or pipeline, and to provide compensation for ships that suffer a loss in order to avoid injuring a cable or pipeline.[74] Albeit, it deleted the specific reference to any marine activities except for obligating States to ensure that ships under their flag comply with navigational rules to ensure safety at sea.[75]

Under UNCLOS, all States are required to protect submarine cables and pipelines as established under the high seas regime that applies to the EEZ by cross-reference in Article 58(2). The protections provided are in line with the three categories as developed in previous conventions, namely intentional damage, accidental damage and indemnity for loss.[76] It is notable that UNCLOS extends punishable breaking and injury of a submarine cable and pipeline to include 'conduct calculated or likely to result in such breaking or injury' that goes beyond results-based damage.[77] This language was introduced by the informal consultative group on the high seas to address the specific 'concerns with fishing vessels anchoring to pipelines in the North Sea and with exploration by researchers around cables,' an issue which remains alive today.[78]

The legal framework of the freedom to lay submarine cables and pipelines along with other associated activities, as well as the obligation to protect them, has been maintained in the EEZ. With increasing demands to accommodate the economic interests of coastal States, as well as the need to effectively protect submarine cables and pipelines, the freedom to lay submarine cables and pipelines is subject to specified limitations in the EEZ compared with on the high seas. In particular, the laying of pipelines is subject to coastal States' regulation of environmental protection and control of delineation of the course, which brings into doubt its classification as a preserved freedom.[79]

[73] Ibid Article 20 Commentary, Article 35 Commentary.
[74] Convention on the High Seas Articles 27–29.
[75] Ibid Article 10.
[76] UNCLOS Articles 113–115.
[77] UNCLOS Article 113.
[78] Nordquist, Nandan and Rosenne (1995) 268; Douglas Guilfoyle and Cameron Miles, 'Article 113', in Proelss (2017) 783.
[79] UNCLOS Article 79(2)–(3); Churchill, Lowe and Sander (2022) 244, 285.

5.3 Limitations on the Freedom to Lay Submarine Cables and Pipelines

5.3.1 Reasonable Measures Taken by the Coastal State

Consistent with the legal doctrine for allocating uses in the EEZ, without impeding the laying or maintenance of submarine cables and pipelines, coastal States may take 'reasonable measures for the exploration of the continental shelf, the exploitation of its natural resources and the prevention, reduction and control of pollution from pipelines'.[80] However, it is unspecified as to what 'reasonable measures' a coastal State could take and to what extent such measures might affect the freedom of the laying of submarine cables and pipelines.[81]

5.3.1.1 Exploration and Exploitation Considerations

Many States have recognised the freedom of all States to lay submarine cables and pipelines in their EEZs by incorporating Article 58(1) in their domestic legislation.[82] With respect to a coastal State's right over natural resources and the continental shelf, it can be argued that measures that impose restrictions to avoid damage to fishing grounds or significant marine habitats, or restrictions on the laying of such cables and pipelines in areas designated for the exploitation of oil, gas or other mineral resources, would be considered reasonable.[83] Pipelines, particularly those associated with an operational field, are closely linked with the exploration of the seabed and the exploitation of the natural resources that are usually subject to tighter regulations on delineation and pollution by the coastal State. However, there is some inconsistent State practice with regard to activities associated with the use of submarine cables, such as requiring permission for survey, laying, maintenance and repair activities.[84]

[80] UNCLOS Articles 56(1), 79(2).

[81] Englender (2017) 624–625.

[82] United Nations, Division for Ocean Affairs and the Law of the Sea, *The Law of the Sea: National Legislation on the Exclusive Economic Zone* (United Nations 1993).

[83] Robert Beckman, 'Submarine Cables – A Critically Important but Neglected Area of the Law of the Sea', International Conference on Legal Regimes of Sea, Air, Space and Antarctica, India, January 2010, 6 https://cil.nus.edu.sg/wp-content/uploads/2010/01/Beckman-PDF-ISIL-Submarine-Cables-rev-8-Jan-10.pdf; Englender (2017) 624.

[84] Evans and Page (2014) 119–122; ICPC Recommendation No. 10, The Minimum Requirements for Load and Lay Reporting and Charting, Issue 3A, 1 June 2014, available by request at www.iscpc.org or secretariat@iscpc.org; Roach (2021) 557–560.

One of the reasons for some States to require a permit for cable survey activities is that they consider the survey to be part of marine scientific research activity over which they have jurisdiction. There are no provisions in UNCLOS that define marine scientific research, nor are there provisions specifically governing survey activities in the EEZ or on the continental shelf.[85] Because of the lack of clarity in UNCLOS, State practice varies with regard to survey activities in the EEZ. Some States consider survey activities as part of the freedoms confirmed in Article 58 (1), while others argue that such activities are a form of marine scientific research and therefore subject to the coastal State's consent as provided for in Articles 56(1)(b)(ii) and 246 of UNCLOS.[86] For example, China has claimed jurisdiction over surveys in the EEZ, whereby foreign organisations or individuals that wish to undertake surveying and mapping must obtain approval from local authorities and observe relevant Chinese laws and regulations.[87]

It goes beyond the scope of this chapter to discuss the historical and contemporary debates on the definition and scope of marine scientific research and survey.[88] Rather it follows the legal doctrine of allocating uses in the EEZ by examining the purpose of the cable route survey. As discussed earlier, the survey is an integral part of the operations of submarine cables given its essential role in determining the delineation of the route and design of installation procedures and protection strategies.[89] Hence, the cable route survey is closely linked with the need to

[85] United Nations Division for Ocean Affairs and the Law of the Sea Office of Legal Affairs, *Marine Scientific Research: A revised guide to the implementation of the relevant provisions of the United Nations Convention on the Law of the Sea* (United Nations, 2010) 4–6.

[86] EEZ Group 21, Guidelines for Navigation and Overflight in the Exclusive Economic Zone (26 September 2005, Tokyo, Japan, Ocean Policy Research Foundation), Article IX www.spf.org/opri/en/news/05_7.html; Sam Bateman, 'Hydrographic Surveying in the EEZ: Differences and Overlaps with Marine Scientific Research' (2005) 29 Marine Policy 167; Davenport (2012) 211–212; Youri Van Logchem, 'Submarine Telecommunication Cables in Disputed Maritime Areas' (2014) 45(1) Ocean Dev Int'l L 107, 111–112.

[87] China, Surveying and Mapping Law of the People's Republic of China (amended in 2002), Article 7 www.asianlii.org/cn/legis/cen/laws/samlotproc506/.

[88] Roach (2021) 486–541; Nele Matz-Luck, 'Article 238', in Proelss (2017) 1609–1610.

[89] Alexander Lott, 'Marine Environmental Protection and Transboundary Pipeline Projects: A Case Study of the Nord Stream Pipeline' (2011) 27(73) Merkourios International and European Environmental Law 55, 58; Evans and Page (2014) 99–108; David Langlet, 'Transboundary Transit Pipelines: Reflections on the Balancing of Rights and Interests in Light of the Nord Stream Project' (2014) 63(4) Int'l & Compar LQ 977, 985–988; Roach (2021) 553–554.

facilitate international communications rather than direct economic benefit to the coastal State. Even if some States argue that a survey in general is a form of applied science,[90] the cable route survey could be exempted from coastal State jurisdiction because it is an ancillary activity, a lawful use of sea associated with the laying of submarine cables.

Another reason for some States to require a permit for cable survey activities is the concern that data obtained through the survey might be relevant to the exploitation of the seabed and its natural resources.[91] It is important to understand what data is collected during the survey to distinguish a cable route survey from a survey for natural resources. The main purpose of the cable route survey is to understand the hydrographic and geologic conditions of the pertinent region before laying a submarine cable. The survey ship usually employs a range of technologies to collect data along a narrow strip of seabed, typically ranging from 500 to 1,000 metres in shallow water and three times the water depth in deep water.[92] The cable route survey usually contains data components of bathymetry, seabed imagery, high-resolution seismic reflection profiling, seabed soils, submarine geology, electronic burial and plow assessment, and oceanography.[93] From a technical perspective, a cable route survey uses similar techniques and collects some of the same data as in surveys for exploration of natural resources.[94] However, the limited scanned area and data, both in terms of the width of the area and the depth of the seabed, determine that the data collected during a cable route survey is not sufficient to discover, evaluate or exploit economic resources on the seabed.[95] In other words, the cable route survey is not designed to perform systematic investigations into and study of the marine environment, but is merely to establish facts and provide information to confirm or amend the preliminary data for cable installation.

[90] 余敏友和周昱圻,《专属经济区海洋科学研究与测量活动的国际法分析》,时代法学,2021年6月,第19卷第3期,11–19,第14–15页 (YU Min-you and ZHOU Yu-qi, 'A Study on Marine Scientific Research and Survey Activities in the EEZ' (2021) 19(3) Presentday Law Science 11, 14–15).

[91] Evans and Page (2014) 111–113.

[92] Ibid 103.

[93] Ibid 103–106.

[94] Ibid 110–111.

[95] Ibid 111–113.

CAMBRIDGE
UNIVERSITY PRESS & ASSESSMENT

Packing List

Page	1
Copy Code	1

Document No.	0083494341
Date	03/03/26
Document Type	Gratis Order
Customer No.	0070251977

Sold To:
JUSTICE MICHAEL B. HYMAN
265 GRAEMERE STREET
NORTHFIELD, IL 60093-3132

Supply To:
JUSTICE MICHAEL B. HYMAN
265 GRAEMERE STREET
NORTHFIELD, IL 60093

ORD=Ordered Qty, SHP=Shipped Qty

QTY ORD	QTY SHP	TITLE	AUTHOR	ED/TD	ISBN	P.O. No.	PRICE	DISC %	NET VALUE
1	1	Finding a Balance in the Exclu	Sun	H/C	9781009471305	3027921Awards	140.00	100.0%	.00

This Document does not show any sales taxes or VAT. This is not a tax invoice.

Run No.	
Batch/Doc	142192303
Shipment No.	000302
Ship Via	
Op/Doc tp	
Seq. No.	

Lines	1
Quantity	1
Ship	1
Ship Charge	.00
Reg Wt. lbs.	1.84
Cartons	1

Carrier	UPS GROUND
Weight in Lbs.	1.84

U.S. Dollar

Subtotal	.00
Freight / Handling	.00
Total	.00

D334 - 22170V06

WC 729 #8K7LZ 20N9029 03/06/26 3027921Awards

In addition, some coastal States, notably China,[96] India[97] and Seychelles,[98] require permits for foreign vessels or nationals to undertake submarine cable laying, maintenance and repair activities in their EEZs.[99] The permission requirements for operational activities vary from State to State and range from straightforward application to highly complex with different associated conditions. These conditions includes a combination of annual fees, security checks for crew, a list of the nationalities of the crew, registration documents for the vessel, requirements for an on-board security officer or observer, pre-approved locations and a copy of the survey data and reports.[100] These conditions of permission can cause significant delays in cable operations and, in the case of repair activities, may lead to multiple cable failures and increased loss of revenue.[101] The situation will be even more complicated if the fault location is uncertain or if it spans the EEZ of more than one State or is in a disputed sea area.[102] If the attribution of jurisdiction over survey activity in the EEZ is unclear, the requirement of attaining permission to conduct the laying, maintenance or repair work on submarine cables is inconsistent with UNCLOS. Article 79(2) specifically states that 'the coastal State may not impede the *laying* or *maintenance* of such cables' (emphasis added). Additionally, the 2011 UNGA Resolution on the Oceans and the Law of the Sea clearly recognised the importance for States to act in

[96] China, Exclusive Economic Zone and Continental Shelf Act, 1998, Article 11 www.un.org/Depts/los/LEGISLATIONANDTREATIES/PDFFILES/chn_1998_eez_act.pdf; China, Provisions Governing the Laying of Submarine Cables and Pipelines 1989, Article 10 www.asianlii.org/cn/legis/cen/laws/pgtloscap600/; Surveying and Mapping Law of the People's Republic of China, 2002, Article 7. In the event of emergency repairs on China's continental shelf, foreign vessels may enter the site to start operations simultaneously with a report submitted to the competent authorities, and such operations must not impair China's sovereign rights and jurisdiction.

[97] India, The Territorial Waters, Continental Shelf, Exclusive Economic Zone and Other Maritime Zones Act, 1976, Act No. 80 of 28 May 1976, Article 7(8) www.un.org/Depts/los/LEGISLATIONANDTREATIES/PDFFILES/IND_1976_Act.pdf.

[98] Seychelles, Maritime Zones Act, 1999 (Act No. 2 of 1999), Article 14(1)(b) www.un.org/Depts/los/LEGISLATIONANDTREATIES/PDFFILES/SYC_1999_Act2.pdf.

[99] Keith Ford-Ramsden and Douglas Burnett, 'Submarine Cable Repair and Maintenance', in Burnett, Beckman and Davenport (2014) 169–176.

[100] Roach (2021) 557–560; Anjali Sugadev, 'India's Critical Position in the Global Submarine Cable Network: an Analysis of Indian Law and Practice on Cable Repairs' (2016) 56 Indian J Int'l L 173.

[101] ICPC, Submarine Cable Network Security (2009) 30–32 www.iscpc.org/information/Openly%20Published%20Members%20Area%20Items/Submarine_Cable_Network_Security_PDF.pdf.

[102] Van Logchem (2014) 113–114; UK House of Lords 2021-22 para 323.

conformity with UNCLOS with regard to the maintenance, including the repair, of submarine cables.[103]

Considering that the EEZ is for all intents and purposes a resource zone, the 'reasonable measures' taken by the coastal States must be closely linked to the exploration of the continental shelf or the exploitation of its natural resources and must be proportionate.[104] A measure would be unreasonable if it rendered the laying of a submarine cable or pipeline impossible or if it disproportionately increased the cost of laying them or is of a discriminatory character.[105] The practice of some State to require a permit for cable route survey, laying, maintenance and repair can hardly be justified as a reasonable measure or the execution of the due regard obligation. Alternatively, in order to reduce tension, the operating State may, as fulfilling its due regard obligation in good faith, provide the coastal State with notification of the purpose, route, timing and work plan of the cable operation activities.[106] The coastal State may require permits as a reasonable measure for pipeline operations in a direct link to its right over pollution control measures and the delineation of pipeline courses.

5.3.1.2 Environmental Considerations

Compared to the regime applicable to submarine cables, pipelines are subject to coastal States' jurisdiction over pollution control in the EEZ. This jurisdiction was only introduced during the negotiation of UNCLOS, as it did not exist in the 1958 Geneva Conventions.[107] Article 79(2) of UNCLOS specifies that the freedom of laying pipelines be subject to a coastal States' right to take 'reasonable measures ... for the prevention, reduction and control of pollution from pipelines'. This also gives the coastal State jurisdiction over transiting pipelines, often owned and operated by a foreign entity, that do not land on its coast or connect to its offshore operational fields. The exercise of this jurisdiction should be consistent with the rules established in Article 56 and Part XII Articles 208 and 214 with regard to pollution in connection with seabed activities that are subject to national jurisdiction, where such measures

[103] UNGA A/RES/66/231, 5 April 2012, Oceans and the Law of the Sea, Preamble, para 126.

[104] UNCLOS Articles 56(1), 79(2); Beckman (2010) 9; Sam Bateman, 'A Response to Pedrozo: The Wider Utility of Hydrographic Surveys' (2011) 10 Chinese J Int'l L 177, 180–181.

[105] Englender (2017) 624; Tallinn Manual 2.0 (2017) 254–255.

[106] Roach (2021) 558; Evans and Page (2014) 120; Van Logchem (2014) 112.

[107] Nordquist, Nandan and Rosenne (1993) 912.

'shall be no less effective than international rules, standards and recommended practices and procedures'.[108] It is important to point out that, unlike the international shipping regulations that have been developed under the auspice of the International Maritime Organization (IMO), States have not adopted any binding international rules and regulations for the use and operation of submarine pipelines.[109]

Coastal States must ensure that these pollution prevention and control measures meet the requirements of 'reasonableness' and the 'due regard' obligation in such a way as not to impede the laying or maintenance of pipelines. The German legislation on the continental shelf offers an example of such reasonable measures. Other States, through private entities, that intend to install and operate a transiting pipeline must seek authorisation from the German government, which may only be denied 'where there is reason to fear a danger to human life or health or to material property, or a threat to overriding public interests, which cannot be prevented or removed by means of conditions or restrictions'.[110] It further defines 'a threat to overriding public interests' to include activities hindering or impairing German rights on the continental shelf, causing pollution of the sea or threatening the security of Germany.[111] Other than these specified considerations, the German authority may not withhold its permission for the laying of pipelines on its continental shelf.

The environmental considerations for issuing permission for the laying of pipelines may also be affected by geopolitical situations and the broader economic context. The first Nord Stream twin pipeline system provides Europe with approximately 55 billion cubic metres of natural gas per year for at least 50 years from Russia through two 1,224-km offshore pipelines passing by the territorial sea and/or EEZ of Russia, Finland, Sweden, Denmark and Germany.[112] The operators provided an

[108] UNCLOS Articles 56(1)(b)(iii), 208(3), 214.

[109] Saeed Hashemi Lalehabadi, 'Legal Problems of Submarine Pipelines in the Continental Shelf and the Exclusive Economic Zone' (2018) 163 Ocean and Coastal Management 528, 528–529.

[110] Germany, Act of 24 July 1964 on Provisional Determination of Rights Relating to the Continental Shelf as Amended on 2 September 1974, Article 2(4) www.un.org/Depts/los/LEGISLATIONANDTREATIES/PDFFILES/DEU_1974_Act.pdf.

[111] Germany, Provisional Determination of Rights Relating to the Continental Shelf 1974, Article 2(4).

[112] Nord Stream, 'The Pipeline' www.nord-stream.com/the-project/pipeline/; Timo Koivurova and Ismo Pölönen, 'Transboundary Environmental Impact Assessment in the Cases of the Baltic Sea Gas Pipeline' (2010) 25 Int'l J Marine & Coastal L 151, 176–179; Lott (2011) 61–63.

extensive 2,585-page environmental impact assessment (EIA) report to the relevant coastal States on the environmental impacts of the construction, operation and decommissioning of the pipelines justifying that the design and routeing of the pipelines are safe and environmentally sound.[113] It took the operators five years after the announcement of the project to secure all the permits to begin construction in 2010, and the two pipelines have been in operation since 2011 and 2012, respectively.[114] A new Nord Stream 2 project, with two more pipelines that possess the same capacity, was proposed to run roughly parallel to the existing Nord Stream pipeline, and construction was completed by September 2021 at an estimated cost of 11 billion Euros.[115] The operators went through a similar process to obtain permits from the five coastal States and consulted with the other coastal States of the Baltic Sea.[116] However, despite meeting the legal requirements of obtaining permits from the coastal States to build the Nord Stream 2 pipeline, the project has been put on hold due to the change in geopolitics, most notably the relationship between Europe and Russia.[117]

[113] Nord Stream, Espoo Report – Nord Stream Environmental Impact Assessment Documentation for Consultation under the Espoo Convention (2009) www.nord-stream.com/press-info/library/; Nord Stream, 'Comprehensive Studies for Ecological Compatibility' www.nord-stream.com/environment/research/; Rolf Lidskog and IngemarElander, 'Sweden and the Baltic Sea Pipeline: Between Ecology and Economy' (2012) 36 Marine Policy 333, 334–335; David Langlet, 'Nord Stream, the Environment and the Law: Disentangling a Multijurisdictional Energy Project' (2014) 59 Scandinavian Stud L 79, 98–107.

[114] Nord Stream, 'Who We Are' www.nord-stream.com/about-us/.

[115] Nord Stream 2 www.nord-stream2.com/ (this website was taken down after March 2022); Holly Ellyatt, 'Nord Stream 2 Cost $11 Billion to Build. Now, the Russia-Europe Gas Pipeline Is Unused and Abandoned', CNBC, 31 March 2022 (online).

[116] Nord Stream 2, 'Environment' www.nord-stream2.com/environment/ (accessed in February 2022).

[117] Steve Wood and Otto Henke, 'Denmark and Nord Stream 2: A Small State's Role in Global Energy Politics' (2021) 148 Energy Policy 111991; 'Nord Stream 2: How Does the Pipeline Fit into the Ukraine-Russia Crisis?' BBC News, 22 February 2022 (online); 'Ukraine Crisis: Germany Halts Nord Stream 2 Approval'. Deutsche Welle, 22 February 2022 (online); Nord Stream, Press Statement, 4 March 2022 www.nord-stream.com/press-info/press-releases/press-statement-523/. In the Statement, Nord Stream distinguished itself from the Nord Stream 2 project in light of sanctions against Russia. See also Valerie Volcovici, 'Ukraine Lobbies for Cuts in Russian Nord Stream 1 Gas Shipments', Reuters, 21 April 2022 (online).

Article 79(2) of UNCLOS limits a coastal State's right to taking reasonable measures for pollution control to submarine pipelines. The omission of submarine cables, however, cannot be interpreted such that they are completely exempted from environmental protection considerations. When exercising the freedom to lay submarine cables, States must have due regard to the coastal State's rights and duties in the EEZ, including its rights to conserve and manage natural resources, and its jurisdiction and obligation to protect and preserve the marine environment.[118] The laying and use of submarine cables inevitably interact with the marine environment to varying degrees at different phases. For example, route surveys employ instruments that produce acoustic pulses that might affect marine mammals; the laying of cables requires mechanical plowing into the seabed for burial in shallow waters; cables laid on the surface of the seabed will interact with water, sediment and marine biota; and electromagnetic fields generated by power cables may have an impact on the marine environment.[119] Existing research and studies are not conclusive on the environmental impacts, particularly the cumulative impacts, that cables have on the marine environment through their lifespan. Nonetheless, the cable industry has lobbied that any threats are not detrimental to the marine environment.[120]

The operating State has the primary responsibility to address the environmental impacts of the laying and use of submarine cables. It has the general obligation to protect and preserve the marine environment, among which is to ensure that activities under its jurisdiction or control do not cause damage by pollution to other States and their

[118] UNCLOS Articles 56(1)(a) and (b)(iii), 58(3), 192.

[119] Carter, Burnett and Davenport (2014) 179–195; Magdalena Jakubowska et al., 'Effect of Low Frequency Electromagnetic Field on the Behavior and Bioenergetics of the Polychaete Hediste Diversicolor' (2019) 150 Marine Environmental Research 104766; Luana Albert et al., 'A Current Synthesis on the Effects of Electric and Magnetic Fields Emitted by Submarine Power Cables on Invertebrates' (2020) 159 Marine Environmental Research 104598.

[120] ICPC and UNEP (2009) 29–30; OSPAR Commission, 'Background Document on Potential Problems Associated with Power Cables other than those for Oil and Gas Activities' (2008) www.ospar.org/documents?v=7128; OSPAR Commission, 'Assessment of the Environmental Impacts of Cables' (2009) https://qsr2010.ospar.org/media/assessments/p00437_Cables.pdf; Bastien Taormina et al., 'A Review of Potential Impacts of Submarine Power Cables on the Marine Environment: Knowledge Gaps, Recommendations and Future Directions' (2018) 96 Renewable and Sustainable Energy Reviews 380, 388-389; UNGA A/67/79 paras 84, 87; ICPC, Intervention at BBNJ IGC-4 Opening Session, 7 March 2022 www.un.org/bbnj/statements.

environment, to monitor and to assess the environmental impact.[121] However, the decision to monitor the risk of pollution and to conduct an EIA is at the discretion of the operating State, such that only when it has 'reasonable grounds for believing' that the planned activities 'may cause substantial pollution of or significant and harmful changes to the marine environment', it is obligated to conduct an EIA.[122] The coastal State has limited ground to challenge or influence the operating State's assessment and monitoring of cable operations, particularly for transiting cables in the EEZ.

The balance of environmental concerns over submarine cables will fall back on the mutual due regard obligations. The fulfilment of the due regard obligations should be determinate by the circumstances and by the nature of those rights.[123] It could be argued that if the proposed cable operation occurs within an existing specially protected area or a critical marine habitat, the operating State should consult the coastal State in good faith in the laying of cables to minimise the risks to the marine environment. The coastal State, on the other hand, could arguably introduce restrictive measures on cable operations in such special marine areas in the EEZ.[124] For example, the United Kingdom sought to control the routing of a new cable system from entering a special conservation area, and the United States restricted access to a designated critical habitat area to protect the leatherback sea turtle.[125]

The right of the coastal State to adopt and apply these reasonable measures must meet the requirements imposed by other provisions of UNCLOS. First, these measures must be 'reasonable' as they must be kept within the limits of respect for the law and implemented impartially so as to 'not infringe or result in any unjustifiable interference with' the freedom of other States to lay submarine cables and pipelines.[126] Second, the coastal State must recognise such freedom and must have

[121] UNCLOS Articles 194(2), 204, 206.

[122] UNCLOS Articles 204–206.

[123] In the Matter of the Chagos Marine Protected Area Arbitration Before an Arbitral Tribunal Constituted under Annex VII to the United Nations Convention on the Law of the Sea between the Republic of Mauritius and the United Kingdom of Great Britain and Northern Ireland, Award, 18 March 2015, PCA Case No. 2011-03, para 519 (Chagos MPA Arbitration).

[124] UNCLOS Articles 194(5), 211(5)–(6); Yoshifumi Tanaka, *The International Law of the Sea* (3rd ed., Cambridge University Press 2019) 175–176.

[125] Carter, Burnett and Davenport (2014) 205–206.

[126] UNCLOS Articles 78(2), 79(2).

due regard for their interests to exercise this freedom.[127] Third, the coastal State must exercise its rights in a manner so as not to 'constitute an abuse of right'.[128] Hence, these measures should not amount to a right for a coastal State to require a permit or payment as a condition for other States to conduct operational activities related to the submarine cables in its EEZ. Where there is a dispute on the scope and application of measures adopted by the coastal State, the coastal State and the operating State should consult with one another in good faith to resolve their dispute before seeking settlement through other peaceful means.[129]

5.3.2 *Delineation of the Course of Submarine Cables and Pipelines*

Careful route planning is essential for effective laying and protection of submarine cables and pipelines. Planning must take into account all current and proposed marine activities, especially fishing and the exploitation of natural resources, and all relevant natural and cultural seabed features in the pertinent region in order to determine the most appropriate route.[130] The coastal State's jurisdiction over the delineation of the course of submarine cables and pipelines are different, with the latter falling under its jurisdiction.

The coastal State's jurisdiction to regulate the delineation of the course of pipelines was only introduced in Article 79(3) of UNCLOS.[131] This authorisation also gives coastal States rights over the delineation of transiting pipelines that do not land on their coast or connected with any offshore platforms under their jurisdiction. The extended coastal State jurisdiction was introduced by States that were in favour of restricted freedom to lay pipelines on their continental shelf, notably China and Denmark.[132] The Danish proposal provided that, considering the significant difference between the laying of submarine cables and the

127 UNCLOS Article 56(2).
128 UNCLOS Article 300.
129 UNCLOS Article 279.
130 ICPC and UNEP (2009) 21–22.
131 Convention on the Continental Self Article 4; Convention on the High Seas Article 26 (2); UNCLOS Article 79(3).
132 'Denmark: Continental Shelf' (Article 67 RSNT II) [1977], reproduced in Renate Platzöder (ed.), *The Third United Nations Conference on the Law of the Sea: Documents*, Vol. IV (Oceana Publications 1990) 470; Crowley (1987) 49; Nordquist (1993) 911, 914.

laying of pipelines, the laying of pipelines across the continental shelf/ EEZ should be subject to the coastal State's consent.[133] This Danish position was used in the negotiations with Norway relating to the delineation of a transiting gas pipeline across its continental shelf in the 1970s. The Ekofisk-Emden pipeline carries natural gas from the Ekofisk field on the Norwegian continental shelf in the North Sea to the operations plant at Emden in Germany, of which approximately 50 km passes through the Danish continental shelf.[134] Denmark granted permission for the construction and operation of such a pipeline on the condition that the pipeline was buried to a depth of one metre along the entire length.[135] Moreover, Denmark established a safety zone of 100 metres on each side of the pipeline in which fishing and anchoring were prohibited.[136]

As far as submarine cables are concerned, the intention of granting coastal States jurisdiction over the delineation of the laying of their course was implied in the ILC Draft Articles. Commenting on a coastal State's 'right to take reasonable measures for the exploration of the continental shelf and the exploitation of its natural resources', the ILC stated that Article 61(2) was added to 'make it quite clear that the coastal State is obliged to permit the laying of cables and pipelines ... but that it may impose conditions as to the route to be followed, in order to prevent undue interference with the exploitation of the natural resources of the seabed and subsoil'.[137] The comments to Article 70, which only dealt with submarine cables, repeated the statement that the coastal State 'may impose conditions concerning the route to be followed'.[138] These comments clearly illustrate that the coastal State's right to take 'reasonable measures' could include imposing conditions on the route of submarine cables.

During the negotiation of the Convention on the Continental Self, Venezuela stated that it was 'prepared to recognize the right of States to

[133] Third United Nations Convention on the Law of the Sea, Official Records, Vol. XIV: Resumed Ninth Session, Summary Records of the Plenary, A/CONF.62/SR.138, Plenary Meetings, 26 August 1980, 61–62.

[134] Crowley (1987) 50; Industrial Heritage EKOFISK, 'Platforms: Norpipe B11' https://ekofisk.industriminne.no/en/norpipe-gnsc-b11-2/.

[135] Crowley (1987) 53–55; Per A. Loeken, 'Engineered Backfilling on the 36" Ekofisk-Emden Gas Pipeline', Paper presented at the Offshore Technology Conference, Houston, Texas, May 1980 https://doi.org/10.4043/3741-MS.

[136] Crowley (1987) 56.

[137] ILC Draft Articles Article 61 Commentary 3.

[138] ILC Draft Articles Article 70 Commentary 1.

lay cables on the continental shelf, but considered that prior consultation with the coastal State and its consent were essential'.[139] Further,

> if the coastal State had the right to take reasonable measures for the exploitation of the continental shelf, it obviously had the right to make regulations on the laying of submarine cables on the continental shelf. In that way, the coastal State could protect the interests of States if a conflict arose regarding exploitation and the laying of submarine cables.[140]

Venezuela's proposal of inserting the phrase 'and to its right to make regulations ... concerning the routes to be followed,' however, was rejected by 22 votes to 18, with 15 abstentions.[141] Therefore, the Convention on the Continental Self only recognised the coastal State's right to take 'reasonable measures for the exploration of the continental shelf and the exploitation of its natural resources' without specifying delineation of the course of submarine cables and pipelines.[142] The negotiation records show that the delegations had different understandings of whether or not the right to take 'reasonable measures' included adopting regulations concerning cable and pipeline routes.[143]

Before the Third United Nations Conference on the Law of the Sea, China proposed to the Sea-Bed Committee that '[t]he delineation of the course for laying submarine cables and pipelines on the continental shelf by a foreign State is subject to the consent of the coastal State'.[144] However, this proposal was never incorporated into the negotiation text.[145] Article 79 of UNCLOS was adopted based on the text drafted by the Evensen Group that the right to take 'reasonable measures'

[139] United Nations Conference on the Law of the Sea, Official Records, Vol. VI, Fourth Committee (Continental Shelf), Summary Records of Meetings and Annexes, Geneva, 24 February - 27 April 1958, A/CONF.13/42, Tenth Meeting, 14 March 1958, 21.

[140] Ibid Twenty-Seventh Meeting, 1 April 1958, 79.

[141] Ibid Twenty-Seventh Meeting, 1 April 1958, 80; United Nations Conference on the Law of the Sea, A/CONF.13/C.4/L.34, 21 March 1958, 136, Venezuela: Proposal, Article 70.

[142] Convention on the Continental Self Article 4; Convention on the High Seas Article 26 (2).

[143] United Nations Conference on the Law of the Sea, Official Records, Vol. VI, Fourth Committee (Continental Shelf), A/CONF.13/42, Fourth Meeting, 4 March 1958, 3; Seventh Meeting, 11 March 1958, 9; Tenth Meeting, 14 March 1958, 22; Twenty-seventh Meeting, 1 April 1958, 79–81.

[144] UNGA A/AC.138/SC.II/L.34, 16 July 1973, Working Paper on Sea Area within the Limits of National Jurisdiction, Submitted by the Chinese Delegation; Dupuy and Vignes (1991) 985.

[145] Nordquist, Nandan and Rosenne (1993) 913–915; Englender (2017) 626.

provided the coastal State with an explicit right to give consent to the delineation of the course of pipelines.[146] Nevertheless, even without explicit authorisation under UNCLOS, subsequent national legislation of Cabo Verde,[147] China,[148] Guyana,[149] Grenada,[150] India,[151] Malaysia,[152] Mauritius,[153] Pakistan,[154] Poland,[155] Portugal,[156] Saint Kitts and Nevis,[157] Saint Lucia,[158] São Tomé and Príncipe,[159] Syria,[160] Russia[161] and Trinidad and Tobago[162] extended the coastal State's right to require consent to the delineation of the course for the laying of submarine cables in their EEZ.[163]

146 Nordquist, Nandan and Rosenne (1993) 912–914.

147 Cabo Verde, Law No.60/IC/92 of 21 December 1992, Article 21 www.un.org/Depts/los/LEGISLATIONANDTREATIES/PDFFILES/CPV_1992_Law.pdf.

148 China, Exclusive Economic Zone and Continental Shelf Act, 1998, Article 11.

149 Guyana, Maritime Boundaries Act, 1977, Act No.10 of 30 June 1977, Articles 14, 20 www.un.org/Depts/los/LEGISLATIONANDTREATIES/PDFFILES/GUY_1977_Act.pdf.

150 Grenada, Territorial Sea and Maritime Boundaries Act, 1989 (Act No. 25 of 1989), Article 14 (3) www.un.org/Depts/los/LEGISLATIONANDTREATIES/PDFFILES/grd_act_25_1989.pdf.

151 India, The Territorial Waters, Continental Shelf, Exclusive Economic Zone and Other Maritime Zones Act, 1976, Act No. 80 of 28 May 1976, Article 6(7).

152 Malaysia, Exclusive Economic Zone Act, Act No. 311, 1984, Article 22(1) www.un.org/Depts/los/LEGISLATIONANDTREATIES/PDFFILES/MYS_1984_Act.pdf.

153 Mauritius, Maritime Zones Act 2005 (Act No. 2 of 2005), (2006) 62 LOSB 56–57, Articles 17(b), 21(1)(b).

154 Pakistan, Territorial Waters and Maritime Zones Act, 1976 (22 December 1976), Articles 5 (6), 6(6) www.un.org/Depts/los/LEGISLATIONANDTREATIES/PDFFILES/PAK_1976_Act.pdf.

155 Poland, Act Concerning the Maritime Areas of the Polish Republic and the Marine Administration, 21 March 1991, Article 27 www.un.org/Depts/los/LEGISLATIONANDTREATIES/PDFFILES/POL_1991_Act.pdf.

156 Portugal, Act No. 33/77 of 28 May 1977 Regarding the Juridical Status of the Portuguese Territorial Sea and the Exclusive Economic Zone, Article 7 www.un.org/Depts/los/LEGISLATIONANDTREATIES/PDFFILES/PRT_1977_Act.pdf.

157 Saint Kitts and Nevis, The Maritime Areas Act No.3 of 30 August 1984, Article 13(2)(a) www.un.org/Depts/los/LEGISLATIONANDTREATIES/PDFFILES/KNA_1984_Act.pdf.

158 Saint Lucia, Maritime Areas Act, No.6 of 18 July 1984, Article 13(2)(a) www.un.org/Depts/los/LEGISLATIONANDTREATIES/PDFFILES/LCA_1984_Act.pdf.

159 Sao Tome and Principe, Law No.1/98 on Delimitation of the Territorial Sea and the Exclusive Economic Zone, Article 7(2) www.un.org/Depts/los/LEGISLATIONANDTREATIES/PDFFILES/STP_1998_Law.pdf.

160 Syria, Law No. 28 of 19 November 2003, (2004) 55 LOSB 16–17, Article 24(2).

161 Russia, Federal Act on the Exclusive Economic Zone of the Russian Federation 1998, Article 7 (20) www.un.org/Depts/los/LEGISLATIONANDTREATIES/PDFFILES/RUS_1998_Act_EZ.pdf.

162 Trinidad and Tobago, Archipelagic Waters and Exclusive Economic Zone Act, 1986, Act No. 24 of 11 November 1986, Article 20(c) www.un.org/Depts/los/LEGISLATIONANDTREATIES/PDFFILES/TTO_1986_Act.pdf.

163 Barbara Kwiatkowska, *The 200 Mile Exclusive Economic Zone in the New Law of the Sea* (Martinus Nijhoff 1989) 217; Keith Ford-Ramsden and Tara Davenport, 'The

Article 79(3) indicates that the delineation of the course for the submarine cables in the EEZ is not subject to the consent of the coastal State. However, the interpretation of 'reasonable measures' included in Article 79(2) seems to provide that the coastal State can place certain requirements on the laying of submarine cables, albeit such measures may not equal the requirement of consent for the delineation of the course. Coastal States may arguably require notification or pre-consultation regarding the proposed cable route, particularly in relation to its rights over natural resources and the protection of the marine environment, and as per the reciprocal due regard obligation of the operating State. It is also in the best interest of the cable operator to obtain all relevant information of the pertinent region to avoid potential conflicts with the coastal State's existing and planned exploration and exploitation activities when designing the route for a submarine cable. In case of a conflict – for example, where the route of a proposed submarine cable would interfere with the potential exploitation of an oil field – the coastal State and the operating State should consult with each other in good faith. It is arguable that the outcome would likely be a re-routeing of the cable to give priority to the sovereign rights of the coastal State, but the coastal State should not rely on potential interference with its rights in an abusive manner.[164]

5.3.3 *Regulations of Specific Submarine Cables and Pipelines*

Article 79(4) of UNCLOS gives coastal States additional rights and jurisdiction over two specific types of submarine cables and pipelines laid in its EEZ. The coastal State has the right to fix any conditions necessary relating to the laying of submarine cables and pipelines that enter its territory or territorial sea, and it has jurisdiction over those used in connection with the exploration and exploitation of the continental shelf and its natural resources, as well as the operation of artificial islands, installations and structures.[165]

With respect to cables and pipelines that enter the territory or territorial sea, the first unclarified issue is where these conditions apply. If a

Manufacture and Laying of Submarine Cables', in Burnett, Beckman and Davenport (2014) 148; Tanaka (2019) 175; Roach (2021) 559.

164 Alexander Proelss, 'The Law on the Exclusive Economic Zone in Perspective: Legal Status and Resolution of User Conflicts Revisited' (2012) 26 Ocean YB 87, 100.

165 UNCLOS Article 79(4).

submarine cable or pipeline were to be constructed between different States, or from offshore infrastructure to the coast, it would typically transit the EEZ or continental shelf, where the coastal State has sovereign rights, to the territorial sea or territory, where it has sovereignty.[166] Since a coastal State's rights over submarine cables and pipelines within its territory and territorial sea has been explicitly articulated in other provisions of UNCLOS, the authorisation in Article 79(4) is not merely repetitive.[167] The terminology used to supplement the coastal State's right is 'conditions', which imply much less authority than 'sovereignty'. The conditions are attachments to the coastal State's right to issue permits to lay cables and pipelines in the territorial sea. In addition, the fact that this authorisation is placed in Article 79 under the continental shelf regime suggests that it applies to this ocean area and within the EEZ.[168] Therefore, the additional conditions imposed by coastal States would apply to the sections, either the entire section or selected segment closer to the outer limit of the territorial sea, of the submarine cables and pipelines that lie on its continental shelf or within the EEZ. After the submarine cables and pipelines physically enter the territory or territorial sea of the coastal State, the more rigorous rules, which are a concomitant of sovereignty, would apply.

The second issue is the scope of these conditions. A guiding point could be that the scope is reasonable and proportionate, whereas the conditions themselves should be linked to protecting the sovereignty of the coastal State in the territorial sea and should not render the laying of cables and pipelines impractical. These conditions arguably may include pre-consultation on the delineation of the course for the laying of cables, burial requirements or other protective measures, and requirements to minimise interference with other marine activities. It is not clear whether such conditions may include levies or other charges. The Spanish Supreme Court, for example, decided that the Spanish Ministry of the Environment was not entitled to impose a fee on submarine telecommunication cables beyond Spain's territorial sea.[169]

With respect to the second category of cables and pipelines, UNCLOS confirms that the coastal State's jurisdiction over these infrastructures extends to the connected cables, notably power cables, and pipelines.[170]

[166] UNCLOS Articles 2(2), 56(1)(a), 77(1).
[167] UNCLOS Articles 2(1), 19(2)(l), 21(1)(c).
[168] UNCLOS Article 56(3).
[169] Englender (2017) 627.
[170] UNCLOS Articles 56(1)(b)(i), 60(1)–(2), 79(4).

First, this would make such submarine cables subject to the coastal State's right to adopt and enforce laws and regulations 'to prevent, reduce and control pollution of the marine environment arising from or in connection with seabed activities subject to their jurisdiction and from artificial islands, installations and structures under their jurisdiction'.[171] Second, it could be argued that the coastal State has the right to lay, authorise and regulate the laying, operation, maintenance and repair of such cables and pipelines connected to infrastructure, as well as regulate relevant matters on customs, fiscal, health, safety and immigration.[172]

The wording in Article 79(4) seems to suggest that the specific cables and pipelines are in supporting positions to infrastructure that is under the jurisdiction of the coastal State. It does not, however, include infrastructure that can be constructed or used to support the operation of cables and pipelines. It has been acknowledged that submarine cables and pipelines per se are not considered installations and structures that are under the jurisdiction of the coastal State,[173] but the operating State may arguably construct or use artificial islands, installations or structures to support their laying, operation or protection, or have a standalone purpose such as the establishment of underwater database installations.[174] Under Article 60, the coastal State has 'exclusive right to construct and to authorize and regulate the construction, operation and use of' artificial islands and installations and structures for economic purposes and those may interfere with the exercise of its rights. However, it is not clear whether it is the coastal State or the operating State that has to decide whether such use is for economic purposes or may interfere with the exercise of the coastal State's rights. While subject to debate and different State practices, given its potential interference with the marine environment and the jurisdiction of the coastal State, the operating State should be obliged to consult, if not apply for permission, to use

[171] UNCLOS Articles 208, 214.

[172] UNCLOS Articles 60(1)–(2), 80.

[173] UNCLOS Article 56(1)(b)(i); Yoshinobu Takei, 'Law and Policy for International Submarine Cables: An Asia-Pacific Perspective' (2012) 2 Asian J Int'l L 205, 209; Englender (2017) 623.

[174] John Roach, 'Microsoft Finds Underwater Datacenters are Reliable, Practical and Use Energy Sustainably', Microsoft, 14 September 2020 https://news.microsoft.com/innovation-stories/project-natick-underwater-datacenter/; Peter Judge, 'Project Natick: Microsoft's Underwater Voyage of Discovery', DCD, 5 January 2021 www.datacenterdynamics.com/en/analysis/project-natick-microsofts-underwater-voyage-discovery/.

permanently established infrastructure associated with submarine cables and pipelines.

Article 79(4) provides the coastal State with additional competence beyond the 'right to take reasonable measures' over these specific cables and pipelines.[175] The intention is to make it clear that the obligation of coastal States not to impede the laying or maintenance of submarine cables and pipelines on the continental shelf or in the EEZ will not affect the more intensified rights generated from their sovereignty over their territory and territorial sea and sovereign rights over the EEZ and the continental shelf.

5.3.4 Due Regard Obligation and Other Limitations

A general limitation on the freedom to lay submarine cables and pipelines is the 'due regard' obligation found in the regimes of the EEZ, the continental shelf and the high seas.[176] The operating State, when laying submarine cables and pipelines in the EEZ and on the continental shelf, is required to have due regard to both the coastal State and other user States as regards their rights and duties in the same marine area. Although the term 'due regard', together with 'reasonable regard', is repeatedly used in UNCLOS, there is no agreed definition of it.[177] As discussed in Chapter 3, due regard indicates not only a duty to refrain from activities that unreasonably interfere with the exercise of other internationally lawful uses of the same area but also a positive duty to consider the actual rights and interests involved in any given circumstance and aims to achieve a balance between parties.[178]

175 UNCLOS Article 79(2).

176 UNCLOS Articles 58(3), 79(5), 87(2).

177 'Due regard' is used in UNCLOS, Preamble, Articles 27(4), 39(3)(a), 56(2), 58(3), 60(3), 66(3)(a), 79(5), 87(2), 142(1), 148, 161(4), 162(2)(d), 163(2), 167(2), 234, 267; 'reasonable regard' is used in Article 147(1) and (3).

178 Fisheries Jurisdiction Case (United Kingdom of Great Britain and Northern Ireland v. Iceland), Merits, Judgment of 25 July 1974, ICJ Reports 1974, p.3, paras 68, 72; Fisheries Jurisdiction Case (Federal Republic of Germany v. Iceland), Merits, Judgment of 25 July 1974, ICJ Reports 1974, p. 175, paras 60, 64; Churchill, Lowe and Sander (2022) 288–290; Moritaka Hayashi, 'Military and Intelligence Gathering Activities in the EEZ: Definition of Key Terms' (2005) 29 Marine Policy 123, 133; Chagos MPA Arbitration para 519; Shotaro Hamamoto, 'The Genesis of the "Due Regard" Obligations in the United Nations Convention on the Law of the Sea' (2019) 34 Int'l J Marine & Coastal L 1, 23–24.

As discussed earlier, State practice is not consistent concerning, *inter alia*, the interpretation and application of the law on whether the coastal State may regulate cable survey and other operational activities, the delineation of cable routes and the environmental consideration of submarine cables. Based on the due regard obligation, the operating State is expected to take into consideration the rights and jurisdiction of the coastal State as specified in Articles 56 and 79 while laying and operating submarine cables. It could be argued that the operating State should provide the coastal State with information through notification or consultation about the planned activities to avoid misunderstandings or conflicts. However, this obligation by no means gives the coastal State a right to require a permit. It would be for a court or tribunal to decide whether the operating State has fulfilled the due regard obligation in case of a dispute.

In addition, when laying submarine cables or pipelines, the operating State must have due regard to cables or pipelines already in position, and must not prejudice the possibilities of repairing existing ones.[179] This obligation aims to resolve potential conflicts between proposed cables and pipelines and those already in position by giving priority to the latter. This is strengthened by the general obligation contained in Articles 78(2) and 87(2), where the freedom to lay submarine cables and pipelines must be exercised with due regard for further interests of other States and their internationally lawful uses of the sea area.[180]

A less-addressed issue relating to the laying of submarine cables and pipelines is the end of service arrangement. The design and commercial life of a submarine fibre-optic cable system is typically twenty to twenty-five years, and between forty and sixty-five years for power cables, with the possibility of further life extensions.[181] For pipelines associated with an operational platform, the commercial lifespan is between twenty and thirty years.[182] There is no general obligation under the law of the sea to remove cables and pipelines that are abandoned, decommissioned or out

[179] UNCLOS Article 79(5); Convention on the High Seas Article 26(3).

[180] Englender (2017) 627–628; Geneviève Bastid Burdeau, 'The Respect of Other States' Rights (Freedom of Navigation and Other Rights and Freedoms Set Out in the LOSC) as a Limitation to the Military Uses of the EEZ by Third States' (2019) 34 Int'l J Marine & Coastal L 117, 117, 120–122 Churchill, Lowe and Sander (2022) 288.

[181] Eccles, Ferencz and Burnett (2014) 308; Douglas Burnett, 'Out-of-Service Submarine Cables', in Burnett, Beckman and Davenport (2014) 213.

[182] Youna Lyons, 'The New Offshore Oil and Gas Installation Abandonment Wave and the International Rules on Removal and Dumping' (2014) 29 Int'l J Marine & Coastal L 480, 480–481.

of service.[183] Those that are connected with the use of installations or structures should be removed to ensure the safety of navigation, while having due regard to fishing, the protection of the marine environment and the rights and duties of other States.[184]

In practice, it is the cable or pipeline owners who decide on removal, unless the coastal State provides a valid jurisdictional basis for requiring such removal of the sections laid in its EEZ.[185] The jurisdictional basis can be found under the coastal State's right to take reasonable measures and the specific jurisdiction over certain cables or pipelines.[186] If the cables and pipelines in question have the potential to interfere with the coastal State's right to explore or exploit the continental shelf and its natural resources, or pose a threat to the marine environment, the coastal State may take measures to request such removal. The coastal State may also require the removal of cables and pipelines that enter its territorial sea and territory, are constructed or used in connection with the exploration and exploitation of the continental shelf and its resources, or with the operation of artificial islands, installations and structures under its jurisdiction. Moreover, the coastal State may make the removal of abandoned or disused pipelines a condition when giving consent to the delineation of the course of such pipelines.[187] However, the coastal State may at times find it less straightforward to establish such a jurisdictional basis, particularly with regard to submarine telecommunication cables and transiting pipelines.[188]

[183] J. M. Anderson, 'Decommissioning Pipelines and Subsea Equipment: Legislative Issues and Decommissioning Processes' (2002) 25(2) International Journal of the Society for Underwater Technology 105, 107.

[184] UNCLOS Article 60(3).

[185] Burnett (2014) 219–220; Mišo Mudrić, 'Rights of States Regarding Underwater Cables and Pipelines' (2010) 29 Australian Resources & Energy LJ 246, 251; ICPC Recommendation No. 1, Management of Decommissioned and Out-of-Service Cables, Issue 14A, 12 June 2020, available by request at www.iscpc.org; Mark J. Kaiser and Siddhartha Narra, 'A Hybrid Scenario-based Decommissioning Forecast for the Shallow Water U.S. Gulf of Mexico, 2018–2038' (2018) 163 Energy 1150, 1152–1153.

[186] UNCLOS Article 79(2)–(4).

[187] UNCLOS Article 79(3); Mudrić (2010) 251.

[188] Convention on the Continental Self Articles 5, 6; UNCLOS Articles 21(1), 56(1)(b)(i), 60, 78–79, 80, 87, 145, 147; Kaye (2006–2007) 403; Burnett (2014) 218–219; Anderson (2002) 107; Soheil Manouchehri, 'Subsea Pipelines and Flowlines Decommissioning – What We Should Know for a Rational Approach', Proceedings of the ASME 2017 36th International Conference on Ocean, Offshore and Arctic Engineering, OMAE2017, 25–30 June 2017, Trondheim, Norway, OMAE2017-61239.

There has been some practice of changing decommissioned telecommunication cables into scientific cables for various research purposes, or recovering for repurposing and recycling purposes.[189] These cables would normally change owners as they cease to be part of the telecommunications industry and are subsequently removed from charts or marked as out of service. Cable owners may also choose to salvage out-of-service cables for their scrap value. The International Cable Protection Committee (ICPC) recommends cable owners, when deciding whether or not to remove out-of-use cables, consider any potential effects on the safety of navigation or other marine uses, the effects on the marine environment, and the costs, benefits and technical feasibility associated with the removal of such cables.[190] Between 2013 and 2023, around 113 submarine telecommunications cable systems with a combined length of 257,000 kilometres of cable have been taken out of service.[191] It has been estimated that 85 cable systems are expected to reach their end of service by 2028 with an additional 53 expected by 2032.[192]

The current practice of decommissioning submarine pipelines is often associated with the decommissioning of offshore platforms. The United Kingdom, for example, requires a comprehensive assessment of all relevant factors, including decommissioning options, before making a decision on a case-by-case basis for any removal or partial removal of a pipeline on the continental shelf.[193] Although estimates vary, it is likely that between 2013 and 2022, it will cost more than 10 billion Pounds to decommission the end-of-life offshore oil and gas platforms on the continental shelf of the United Kingdom.[194] Among the common

[189] ICPC, 'Scientific Cables'; Burnett (2014) 214–215; STF, Industry Report 2023–2024, Section 1.5: Out of Service Systems Analysis.

[190] ICPC Recommendation No. 1, Management of Redundant and Out-Of-Service Cables.

[191] STF, Industry Report 2023–2024, Section 1.5: Out of Service Systems Analysis.

[192] Ibid.

[193] United Kingdom, Department for Business, Energy and Industrial Strategy, Guidance Notes Decommissioning of Offshore Oil and Gas Installations and Pipelines, November 2018, Chapter 10 www.gov.uk/guidance/oil-and-gas-decommissioning-of-offshore-installations-and-pipelines.

[194] Mick Borwell, 'UK Pipeline Decommissioning Provides Potential for Innovation', Offshore, 5 February 2014 www.offshore-mag.com/pipelines/article/16757230/uk-pipeline-decommissioning-provides-potential-for-innovation; Judith Aldersey-Williams, 'Chapter I-13 Decommissioning Security', in Greg Gordon, John Paterson and Emre Üşenmez (eds.), *UK Oil and Gas Law: Current Practice and Emerging Trends: Volume I: Resource Management and Regulatory Law* (Edinburgh University Press 2018) 297.

practices in the United Kingdom, trenched and buried pipelines are often decommissioned in situ whereas surface laid pipelines are returned to shore for reuse, recycling or disposal.[195]

There are different interpretations of whether pure abandonment of submarine cables and pipelines, where no new use is intended, could be considered dumping. Under UNCLOS, 'deliberate disposal' of 'man-made structures at sea' fall within the definition of 'dumping'.[196] The 1996 London Protocol further clarified this definition whereby the abandonment or toppling at site of 'man-made structures at sea' such as submarine cables and pipelines for 'the sole purpose of deliberate disposal' is considered dumping.[197] Such dumping could be permitted should the State party consider that this is consistent with the objective and obligation to protect and preserve the marine environment.[198] The regional practice of the North-East Atlantic through the OSPAR Convention presents another side of the argument.[199] Dumping is defined to include 'any deliberate disposal in the maritime area of . . . offshore pipelines', but it does not include 'the leaving wholly or partly in place of a . . . disused offshore pipeline, provided that any such operation takes place in accordance with any relevant provision of the Convention and with other relevant international law'.[200] Industry practice has shown a tendency to not classify the abandonment of cables or pipelines as dumping to avoid regulation by the coastal State.[201] It is worth noting that a cable or pipeline that is decommissioned or out of service does not change ownership rights, responsibilities and obligations under international law.[202] Hence, the owners remain liable for claims by coastal States for pollution from pipelines and claims for sacrificed fishing gear

[195] United Kingdom, Department for Business, Energy and Industrial Strategy, 'Draft Decommissioning Programmes under Consideration' www.gov.uk/guidance/oil-and-gas-decommissioning-of-offshore-installations-and-pipelines; Sally Rousea, Peter Hayesb, Ian M Daviesb, and Thomas A. Wildinga, 'Offshore Pipeline Decommissioning: Scale and Context' (2018) 129 Marine Pollution Bulletin 241, 242.

[196] UNCLOS Article 1(5)(a).

[197] 1996 Protocol to the 1972 Convention on the Prevention of Marine Pollution by Dumping of Wastes and Other Matter (London Protocol) (7 November 1996, in force 24 March 2006) 2006 ATS 11, Articles 1.4.1.4, 1.4.2.3.

[198] Ibid Articles 2–3, Annex 1 Article 1(4).

[199] Convention for the Protection of the Marine Environment of the North-East Atlantic (OSPAR Convention) (22 September 1992, in force 25 March 1998) 2354 UNTS 67.

[200] Ibid Article 1(f) and (g).

[201] Englender (2017) 626; Burnett (2014) 219–220; UNCLOS Article 210(5).

[202] ICPC Recommendation No. 1, Management of Redundant and Out-Of-Service Cables; Burnett (2014) 220.

or anchors in avoiding injury to a cable or pipeline.[203] It can also be argued that the owner should make the information on abandoned or out-of-service cables and pipelines available to other marine users and mark them on nautical charts.[204] The limited examples of decommissioning cables and pipelines during the past few decades have not been sufficient to establish any customary practices.[205]

The freedom to lay submarine cables and pipelines has been expressly preserved in the EEZ. The exercise of such a freedom is, however, subject to a number of explicit limitations, most notably from the coastal State. The limitations imposed by the coastal State must meet its due regard obligation and must not amount to any infringement or unjustifiable interference with the laying of such cables and pipelines. Nevertheless, as State practice indicates, the growing interest of coastal States in preserving natural resources and protecting the marine environment in the EEZ, particularly by some unilateral excessive claims for permits for cable operations, have, to varying degrees, eroded this preserved freedom.

5.4 Protecting Submarine Cables and Pipelines

The fact that the EEZ is a multifunctional zone means that the freedom to lay submarine cables and pipelines needs to co-exist with other uses of the same area.[206] With the increase in competing uses in the EEZ, submarine cables and pipelines often have been interfered with or damaged by other marine uses, particularly in water depths less than 1,000 metres. For example, the laying, maintenance and repairing activities by the cable-laying ship often are interrupted by fishing vessels or other marine activities, and cables and pipelines are also at risk of being damaged by ship anchoring, fish trawling, dredging, dumping, sand extraction, oil or gas exploitation and other offshore activities.[207]

203 UNCLOS Articles 79(2), 115.

204 Mudrić (2010) 247; ICPC, 'Cable Data'; TeleGeography, 'Submarine Cable Map' www.submarinecablemap.com.

205 Seline Trevisanut, 'Decommissioning of Offshore Installations: A Fragmented and Ineffective International Regulatory Framework', in Catherine Banet (ed.), *The Law of the Seabed: Access, Uses, and Protection of Seabed Resources* (Brill 2020) 452–453.

206 Kwiatkowska (1989) 4.

207 ICPC and UNEP (2009) 45–47; Stephen C. Drew and Alan G. Hopper, *Fishing and Submarine Cables: Working Together* (ICPC 2009) 19–33; ICPC, Submarine Cable Network Security (2009) 8; ICPC, About Submarine Telecommunications Cables (2011) 37.

Natural effects, including submarine earthquakes, density currents and waves, tsunami, hurricanes and volcanic activities, may also dislocate, break or bury cables or pipelines.[208] Moreover, there are growing concerns that critical submarine cables and pipelines might be subject to security threats from intentional harm for varying purposes.[209]

Unlike the territorial sea, where the coastal State has the right to adopt laws and regulations to protect submarine cables and pipelines,[210] the coastal State has neither the right nor the obligation to protect those laid in its EEZ beyond regulating activities under its jurisdiction, particularly with regard to transiting cables and pipelines. Nevertheless, there is an emerging trend for all States to treat fibre-optic submarine cables as 'critical communications infrastructure' that deserves stronger protection and to take effective measures to promote their safety and security in accordance with international law.[211]

5.4.1 Protecting Operational Activities Ancillary to the Laying of Submarine Cables and Pipelines

The surveying, laying, maintenance and repair of submarine cables and pipelines require a ship to physically operate on site. These specialised ships are often limited in speed and are at risk of being interfered with by other marine activities, especially fishing.[212] Neither the 1958 Geneva Conventions nor UNCLOS have any provisions offering special protection to these ships, such as authorising the use of floating safety zones around ships engaged in cable or pipeline operations or requiring other vessels to keep a minimum distance away from such ships. Nevertheless,

[208] ICPC, About Submarine Telecommunications Cables (2011) 37; ICPC, 'Subsea Landslide is Likely Cause of SE Asian Communications Failure', Press Release, 21 March 2007 www.iscpc.org; Cuiwei Fu et al., 'Effects of Parameter Uncertainties on Interaction between Submarine Telecommunication Cables and Lateral Seabed Movements' (2020) Advances in Civil Engineering Article ID 8824391; Shantanu Joshi, Amit Prashant, Arghya Deb and Sudhir K. Jain, 'Analysis of Buried Pipelines Subjected to Reverse Fault Motion' (2011) 31 Soil Dynamics and Earthquake Engineering 930, 930–931.

[209] Kaye (2006–2007) 377–379; Stuart Kaye, 'Threats from the Global Commons: Problems of Jurisdiction and Enforcement' (2007) 8(1) Melb J Int'l L 185, 190–191.

[210] UNCLOS Article 21(1)(c).

[211] UNGA A/RES/65/37 para 121; UNGA A/70/74, 30 March 2015, Oceans and the Law of the Sea Report of the Secretary-General, paras 53–55.

[212] Drew and Hopper, Fishing and Submarine Cables (2009) 5.

all vessels must obey the international navigation rules and regulations to enhance maritime safety, including 'the use of signals, the maintenance of communications and the prevention of collisions'.[213]

Insofar as submarine cables are concerned, the 1884 Paris Convention contains requirements for other vessels to maintain a minimum distance from cable ships or buoys. Under Article V, cable ships that are engaged in laying or repair operations are required to exhibit signals that are agreed among contracting member States, while 'other vessels which see them, or are able to see them, shall withdraw to or keep beyond a distance of one nautical mile at least from the ship in question, so as not to interfere with her operations' and must keep the fishing gear and nets at the same distance. Article VI further states that vessels which see, or are able to see, the buoys showing the position of a cable that is being laid, is broken or out of order, must keep a minimum distance of one-quarter nautical mile and must keep their fishing nets and gear at the same distance. However, the 1884 Paris Convention is limited in efficacy because it only has thirty-six parties, and there is no clear evidence showing that its rules have gained the status of customary international law binding on all States.[214]

With respect to the international rules on navigation, the 1972 Convention on the International Regulations for Preventing Collisions at Sea (COLREG) is the main international agreement with 164 contracting States representing approximately 98.91 per cent of the gross tonnage of the world's merchant fleet.[215] These rules are applicable to 'all vessels upon the high seas and in all waters connected therewith navigable by seagoing vessels' regardless of its size, including the EEZ.[216] COLREG provides that 'a vessel engaged in laying, servicing, or picking up a … submarine cable or pipeline' is considered a 'vessel restricted in her ability to manoeuvre … and is therefore unable to keep out of the way of another vessel'.[217] A vessel that is restricted in her ability to

[213] UNCLOS Article 94(3)(c).

[214] 1884 Paris Convention; Burnett, Davenport and Beckman (2014) 64.

[215] Convention on the International Regulations for Preventing Collisions at Sea, 1972 (20 October 1972, in force 15 July 1977) 1050 UNTS 16 (COLREG); International Maritime Organization (IMO), 'Status of IMO Treaties: Comprehensive information on the status of multilateral Conventions and Instruments in respect of which the International Maritime Organization or its Secretary-General performs depositary or other functions, 24 July 2024', 110 www.imo.org/en/About/Conventions/Pages/StatusOfConventions.aspx.

[216] COLREG Rule 1(a).

[217] COLREG Rule 3(g).

manoeuvre is required to exhibit specific visual and sound signals to warn other vessels so they are aware of its operations.[218] Other vessels, including power-driven vessels, sailing vessels, and fishing vessels, must 'keep out of the way' of the vessel restricted in its ability to manoeuvre.[219] In contrast to the 1884 Pairs Convention, which specifies the minimum distance between other ships and the cable ship, COLREG does not provide clarification on the meaning of 'keep out of the way'.

The practical issue is that, even though vessels engaged in cable or pipeline operations strictly comply with the COLREG rules, other vessels often ignore them, especially when the operations are taking place near a fishing ground.[220] The United States and Marshall Islands, supported by other States, unsuccessfully attempted to introduce specific distance requirements for the phrase 'keep out of the way' in the relevant rules of COLREG.[221] The main opposing argument for introducing specific distance requirements is that as a goal-based standard, the responsibility for interpretation and application of the requirement to 'keep out of the way' is a matter for a mariner to decide under the circumstances, and a strict distance requirement might not be practical in narrow waterways.[222] When encountering a ship engaged in cable or pipeline operations, mariners may choose the most effective manner to keep out of the way by shifting course, keeping a distance or reducing speed. The basic requirement is to ensure that the cable or pipeline ship is not interrupted, and hence reduce the chance of a collision.

The flag State has the primary duty to take all necessary measures for ships flying its flag to ensure safety at sea, including 'the use of signals, the maintenance of communications and the prevention of collisions'.[223] Since most marine activities in the EEZ, particularly fishing, involve

[218] COLREG Rules 27(b), 35(c).

[219] COLREG Rule 18(a)–(c).

[220] ICPC, Submarine Cable Network Security (2009) 28–29.

[221] IMO, Sub-Committee on Navigation, Communications and Search and Rescue (NCSR), NCSR 2/22/3, 2 January 2015, Protection of Cable Ships and Repair Operations for International Submarine Cables, Submitted by the United States; IMO NCSR 3/25/1, 16 November 2015, Interpretation of COLREG 1972 rule 18 – Protection of Cable Ships, Submitted by the Republic of the Marshall Islands; IMO NCSR 3/29, 22 March 2016, Report to the Maritime Safety Committee, para 25.17; Sun (2018) 125–126.

[222] COLREG Rule 2; IMO NCSR 3/WP.4, 3 March 2016, Report of the Navigation Working Group, para 5.2.

[223] UNCLOS Article 94(3)(c).

coastal vessels, it is important for the coastal State to enforce navigation rules with due diligence. Such measures taken by the flag State include enforcing penal jurisdiction in matters of collision or any other incident of navigation.[224] The phrase 'incident of navigation' has been interpreted as including 'damage to a submarine telegraph, telephone or high-voltage power cable or to a pipeline'.[225] This jurisdiction over navigation rules is complementary to the jurisdiction provided to States regarding the breaking or injury to submarine cables and pipelines discussed below.

5.4.2 *Protecting Submarine Cables and Pipelines from Competing Uses*

Submarine cables and pipelines are exposed to natural and human hazards in all water depths. Generally speaking, submarine cables are more vulnerable than pipelines. The breaking strength of modern submarine cables of 17–50 mm in diameter ranges from only a few tonnes to more than 40 tonnes.[226] In contrast, a pipeline of up to 550 mm in diameter will not be damaged by trawling activities, even without burial.[227] However, managing the risks related to these threats is equally important for maintaining the integrity and efficiency of submarine cable and pipeline systems. On average, there are approximately 200 submarine cable faults worldwide every year, and the average cost of a single repair is between 1 million and more than 3 million USD, and the loss of revenue and costs of using alternative satellite communication are often higher.[228] Although less frequent, interruptions to offshore pipelines pose serious threats to the marine environment if the damage leads to a rupture. There are various ways to protect submarine cables and pipelines from damage, ranging from calculated route planning, to burial and other measures to increase the safety of the cables and pipelines, to providing incentive measures to avoid damage, and to promoting collaboration among different maritime users.[229]

224 UNCLOS Article 97.
225 ILC Draft Articles Article 35 Commentary; Nordquist, Nandan and Rosenne (1995) 168.
226 ICPC and UNEP (2009) 44.
227 Crowley (1987) 51.
228 Burnett (2010–2011) 108.
229 Eric Wagner, 'Submarine Cables and Protections Provided by the Law of the Sea' (1995) 19(2) Marine Policy 127, 132–133.

5.4.2.1 Burial of Submarine Cables and Pipelines

Submarine cables and pipelines have the potential to be interrupted by other marine activities operated on or near the seabed. Approximately 65–75 per cent of all submarine cable failures recorded between 1959 and 2000 were caused by fishing and shipping activities within water depths shallower than 200 metres.[230] A study of pipeline incidents in the North Sea between 1971 and 2001 showed that among 65 incidents reported that resulted in a leakage, 17 per cent were related to anchoring and 14 per cent were caused by trawling.[231]

In order to reduce potential conflicts with other marine activities, submarine cables and pipelines are often buried to a certain depth (from 1 metre and exceptionally up to 10 metres), according to the type of cable and pipeline involved and the seabed conditions, in areas up to approximately 2,000 metres water depth.[232] However, even with the latest technology, there are areas of the seabed where burial is either impractical or impossible, for example in rugged rocky areas or zones of high sediment mobility. The cable industry has introduced other forms of protection including the use of covers of rocks, concrete mattresses and steel or plastic conduits where practical and environmentally sound.[233]

5.4.2.2 Designation of Protection Zones

In order to minimise the threats of human activities to submarine cables and pipelines, some coastal States impose restrictions on the conduct of activities in areas where cables and pipelines are at risk. The proposal to establish 'safety zones' that preclude anchoring and trawling within 250 metres of each side of a submarine pipeline was rejected by the ILC in 1956, as it was considered impractical and 'would constitute a further encroachment on the freedom of navigation and fishing and that it is consequently unjustified'.[234] Instead, the ILC Draft Articles required States to take the necessary measures to punish deliberate and negligent breaking or injuring of submarine cables and pipelines beneath the high

230 ICPC and UNEP (2009) 34, 39.

231 Det Norske Veritas (DNV), Recommended Practice DNV-RP-F116, Integrity Management of Submarine Pipeline Systems (DNV, October 2009) 39 https://rules.dnv.com/docs/pdf/dnvpm/codes/docs/2009-10/RP-F116.pdf.

232 ICPC, About Submarine Telecommunications Cables (2011) 21–22; Ford-Ramsden and Davenport (2014) 135–136; DNV (2009) 28, 39.

233 ICPC and UNEP (2009) 23–24; Eccles, Ferencz and Burnett (2014) 314–315.

234 'Regime of the High Seas and Regime of the Territorial Sea, Doc A/CN.4/97, Report by JPA Francois, Special Rapporteur, 27 January 1956' (1956) 2 YB ILC 12, para 67.

seas,[235] a provision which was later included in both the Convention on the High Seas and UNCLOS.

Several States have taken the initiative to establish protective zones in which certain activities are prohibited or restricted to protect submarine cables or pipelines.[236] New Zealand, for example, has claimed the right to establish protected areas in the EEZ to regulate potentially harmful activities to submarine cables and pipelines.[237] Fishing operations and anchoring are generally prohibited within these protected areas, and both the owner and the master of a ship who commit an offence are liable for monetary penalties.[238] However, this legislation has limited effects on foreign nationals or foreign ships in the EEZ, since it only applies to a person on board or by means of a New Zealand ship, and by a New Zealand citizen on board or by means of a foreign ship.[239] Australia separated submarine cables from pipelines and adopted protection zones for the former.[240] In 2007, Australia declared three submarine cable protection zones, two off the coast of Sydney and one off the coast of Perth, which stretch up to 50 NM into its EEZ.[241] Within these zones, certain activities are prohibited, including bottom trawling, demersal gill net fishing, sand mining and dumping, and other activities are restricted, such as line fishing and constructing or maintaining navigational aids and installations.[242] Engaging in conduct that contravenes a prohibition or restriction in the protected zone is a punishable offence, subject to

[235] Ibid 12.

[236] China, Provisions on the Protection of Submarine Cables and Pipelines, Order of the Ministry of Land and Resources of the People's Republic of China (No. 24), effective from 1 March 2004, Articles 7–8.

[237] New Zealand, Submarine Cables and Pipelines Protection Order 2009 (SR 2009/41) (as at 2016), 'Schedule Protected areas', www.legislation.govt.nz/regulation/public/2009/0041/latest/whole.html?search=ts_act%40bill%40regulation%40deemedreg_submarine_resel_25_a&p=1#DLM1847701; New Zealand, Submarine Cables and Pipelines Protection Act 1996, s 12.

[238] New Zealand, Submarine Cables and Pipelines Protection Act 1996, s 13(1), 15.

[239] Ibid s 4(b)–(c).

[240] Australia, Telecommunications Act 1997 as amended up to June 2024, Schedule 3A Protection of Submarine Cables, Part 2 Protection Zones; Telecommunications and other Legislation Amendment (Protection of Submarine Cables and Other Measures) Act 2005, No. 104, 2005.

[241] Australia, Telecommunications Legislation Amendment (Submarine Cable Protection) Bill 2013, paras 1.22–1.27 www.aph.gov.au/parliamentary_business/committees/senate/environment_and_communications/submarine_cable_protection/report/c01.

[242] Australia, Telecommunications Act 1997, Schedule 3A, Part 2, Division 2, Clauses 10–11.

monetary penalties and imprisonment.[243] Similar to the New Zealand law, the application of the Australian legislation, despite being applicable to activities within the EEZ, exempts foreign nationals and foreign ships.[244]

While international law provides a sufficient basis for cable protection zones within the territorial sea,[245] there is no equivalent clear norm with respect to either the EEZ or the continental shelf, and certainly not for the high seas. The establishment of protection zones of submarine cables and pipelines within their EEZs by Australia and New Zealand is not without controversy.[246] However, since both States established these protection zones for cables or pipelines landed on their shore, and restricted their application to activities done by nationals and national ships in the EEZ, it should not impede the exercise of the freedom to lay submarine cables and pipelines by other States. These unilateral actions may be seen as good practice to protect submarine cables and pipelines from competing uses, and can rectify a legal gap in their protection in the EEZ.

The coastal State may adopt navigation rules that apply to foreign ships in certain parts of the EEZ if it can justify them within the current legal framework. For example, through IMO, the coastal State may adopt ships' routeing systems, in particular precautionary areas and no-anchoring areas, within its EEZ if it can justify that damage to submarine cables and pipelines poses a danger to the safety of navigation or causes pollution to the marine environment.[247] When discussing the flag State's jurisdiction over collisions on the high seas, the ILC recognised that 'damage to a submarine … cable or to a pipeline may be regarded as an "incident of navigation"'.[248] Hence, the coastal State may argue that the existence of submarine cables and pipelines in converging areas forms an unfavourable condition to navigation, where certain marine activities need to be carried out with great caution or need to be avoided

243 Ibid, Schedule 3A, Part 2, Division 4, Subdivision B, Clauses 40–41, 44.

244 Ibid, Schedule 3A, Part 2, Division 4, Subdivision B, Clause 44A.

245 UNCLOS Article 21(1)(c).

246 Robert Wargo and Tara Davenport, 'Protecting Submarine Cables from Competing Uses', in Burnett, Beckman and Davenport (2014) 275–276.

247 International Convention for the Safety of Life at Sea, as amended (1 November 1974, in force 25 May 1980) 1184 UNTS 2, Chapter V, Regulation 10; IMO, 'Ships' Routeing' www.imo.org/en/OurWork/Safety/Pages/ShipsRouteing.aspx.

248 ILC Draft Articles Article 35 Commentary 2.

completely.[249] In the case of pipelines, the intention of protecting the marine environment could be another reason for the coastal State to propose a routeing system.[250] The implementation of navigation rules in specific risk areas could reduce potential damage to submarine cables and pipelines in the EEZ.

5.4.2.3 Collaboration between Marine Users

Another measure that could promote effective protection of submarine cables and pipelines is to enhance collaboration between industries and between operators within the same industry. This requires coordination in planning and routing and cooperation in the protection, maintenance and repair of cables and pipelines in areas of multiple marine uses. Moreover, there is an appeal for States to adopt laws and regulations, as well as establish a dedicated government agency or department, to coordinate all competing marine uses to minimise external interruptions of submarine cables and pipelines.

The operating State undertakes the obligation to have 'due regard to cables or pipelines already in position,' particularly to the possibility to repair them, when laying new ones.[251] Under Article 114 of UNCLOS, all States are further obligated to adopt laws and regulations to provide that the owners of a submarine cable or pipeline who, in laying or repairing their cable or pipeline, break or injure an existing one are liable for the cost of the repairs. The combination of the obligation to avoid damages and to provide civil liability by the owner fills the gap to cover both accidental and incidental damage to existing cables and pipelines. However, the owner's liability is limited to bearing 'the cost of the repairs' that excludes the cost of alternative uses and any profit loss incurred as a result of the damage, or the cost associated with restoration of the marine environment.[252] This liability was first included in the 1884 Paris Convention, which provides that where 'the owner of a cable who, on

[249] IMO Res A.572(14), 20 November 1985, General Provisions on Ships' Routeing, Annex, para 1.

[250] IMO MSC/Circ.1060, 6 January 2003, Guidance Note on the Preparation of Proposals on Ships' Routeing Systems and Ship Reporting Systems for Submission to the Sub-Committee on Safety of Navigation, Annex, para 3.5.

[251] UNCLOS Article 79(5).

[252] Nordquist, Nandan and Rosenne (1995) 272–273; Douglas Guilfoyle and Cameron Miles, 'Article 114', in Proelss (2017) 786–787; Dupuy and Vignes (1991) 983.

laying or repairing his own cable, breaks or injures another cable, must bear the cost of repairing the breakage or injury'.[253] This phrase seemed to be broadened when it was considered by the ILC, which obliged the owner who caused such damage to 'bear the cost,' implying the cost of all collateral damage.[254] The phrase was changed back to 'the cost of repairing' in the Convention on the High Seas based on a Danish proposal[255] and was maintained in UNCLOS. Nevertheless, the cable or pipeline owner responsible for such a damage may be liable for economic or other consequential loss under the tort law of the relevant State.[256]

Moreover, Article 115 of UNCLOS requires all States to adopt laws and regulations concerning the indemnification by the owner of a submarine cable or pipeline to the owner of a ship who was forced to sacrifice an anchor, a net or any other fishing gear in order to avoid injuring a submarine cable or pipeline. The claim for indemnity is conditioned on the shipowner taking 'all reasonable precautionary measures beforehand' and being able to prove that they have suffered a loss to avoid injury to the cable or pipeline.[257] This is in line with the ILC's statement that 'compensation cannot be claimed if there has been any negligence on the part of the ship'.[258] Guaranteeing the indemnification of the shipowner's sacrifice encourages the shipowner to choose to protect submarine cables and pipelines in case of an emergency.

UNCLOS does not specify what precautionary measures need to be taken or what procedures are required to make the indemnity claim, but such a claim should be balanced against the obligation of all ships to avoid damaging submarine cables and pipelines in the first place.[259] In the case of submarine cables and fishing, the ICPC has published detailed guidance on how to avoid catching a cable, including improving communication between the cable industry and fishers.[260] The premise

253 1884 Paris Convention Article IV.

254 ILC Draft Articles Article 63.

255 United Nations Conference on the Law of the Sea, Official Record, Vol. IV: Second Committee (High Seas: General Regime), A/CONF.13/42, 13th Meeting, 11 April 1958, 89, 95.

256 Guilfoyle and Miles 'Article 114' (2017) 788.

257 UNCLOS Article 115.

258 ILC Draft Articles Article 65 Commentary 2.

259 Nordquist, Nandan and Rosenne (1995) 277; Douglas Guilfoyle and Cameron Miles, 'Article 115', in Proelss (2017) 790.

260 Drew and Hopper, Fishing and Submarine Cables (2009) 50–54.

for fishers to avoid catching a cable is to know where it is and to act with caution to prevent disrupting it.[261] Hence, access to updated submarine cable and pipeline charts and electronic data services, which rely on the information provided by the cable and pipeline industries, is essential. Claim procedures, including the standard of proof, are to be decided by the applicable municipal law system.[262] The procedure provided in the 1884 Paris Convention could provide some guidance:

> [I]n order to establish a claim to such compensation, a statement, supported by the evidence of the crew, should, whenever possible, be drawn up immediately after the occurrence; and the master must, within 24 hours after his return to or next putting into port, make a declaration to the proper authorities.[263]

Increasingly, coastal States are using marine spatial planning as a tool to proactively plan activities in maritime waters under national jurisdiction to coordinate the expanding range of conflicts of maritime uses.[264] For example, Germany developed maritime spatial plans for its EEZ in the North Sea and the Baltic Sea in 2009 that were revised in 2021 following an extensive process that included national and international consultations.[265] The German plans contain provisions aimed at coordinating the individual uses and functions of shipping, the exploitation of resources, laying of submarine cables and pipelines, marine scientific research, wind power production, fisheries and mariculture, as well as protection of the marine environment.[266] Similar State practice can be observed in other European countries in their surrounding seas,[267] in Canada regarding the area of the Scotian Shelf[268] and in South Africa, which divides its EEZ into western, eastern and southern marine areas

[261] Ibid 50–51.

[262] Guilfoyle and Miles'Article 115' (2017) 790.

[263] 1884 Paris Convention Article VII.

[264] World Ocean Assessment II, Volume II, Chapter 26: Developments in Marine Spatial Planning, 434.

[265] Bundesamt für Seeschifffahrt und Hydrographie, 'Maritime Spatial Planning' www.bsh.de/EN/TOPICS/Offshore/Maritime_spatial_planning/maritime_spatial_planning_node.html.

[266] Ibid.

[267] European MSP Platform, 'Projects' https://maritime-spatial-planning.ec.europa.eu/msp-practice/msp-projects.

[268] Canada, Oceans Act, SC 1996, c 31, Preamble para 8, s 31; Heather Breeze and Tracy Horsman (eds.), Scotian Shelf: An Atlas of Human Activities (Fisheries and Oceans Canada 2005) www.dfo-mpo.gc.ca/oceans/publications/scotian-atlas-ecossais/page08-eng.html.

and the Prince Edward Islands, for which statutory marine spatial plans are to be developed.[269]

It also worth emphasising the importance of international cooperation in protecting submarine cables and pipelines. The submarine cable industry, through the ICPC, has for more than half a century provided a forum for government administrations and private entities to work on relevant technical, legal and environmental issues.[270] There is also emerging regional cooperation in Europe to promote marine safety and protect cable installations[271] and in Southeast Asia to promote good practices to reduce conflicts between the coastal State and the operating State, and to protect submarine cables and pipelines from competing uses and intentional damage.[272]

In addition to the protective measures taken by the industry, States can play an active role in protecting submarine cables and pipelines from competing uses. This includes implementing legislation to provide clear legal obligations for operators to avoid damage to submarine cables and pipelines, to impose civil liabilities on those who have caused accidental and incidental damages, and to offer indemnification to those operators who suffered a loss to avoid damaging such cables and pipelines. It is worth noting that since most of the competing uses in the EEZ are conducted by locals, it is particularly important for the coastal State to diligently exercise these rights over its nationals and ships flying its flag.

5.4.3 Protecting Submarine Cables and Pipelines from Intentional Damage

All States are required to adopt laws and regulations to ensure that it is a punishable offence for their ships or nationals that wilfully, or through

[269] South Africa, National Framework for Marine Spatial Planning in South Africa, 26 May 2017 https://cer.org.za/wp-content/uploads/2016/08/National-Framework-for-Marine-Spatial-Planning-in-South-Africa.pdf; South Africa, Marine Spatial Planning Act, Act No. 16 of 2018 https://www.gov.za/documents/acts; Marine Spatial Planning Global, South Africa, www.mspglobal2030.org/msp-roadmap/msp-around-the-world/africa/south-africa/.

[270] ICPC, 'About the ICPC' www.iscpc.org/about-the-icpc/.

[271] European Subsea Cables Association www.escaeu.org/.

[272] Association of Southeast Asian Nations (ASEAN), ASEAN Guidelines for Strengthening Resilience and Repair of Submarine Cables (2019) https://asean.org/wp-content/uploads/2012/05/ASEAN-Guidelines-for-Strengthening-Resilience-and-Repair-of-Submarine-Ca....pdf; Utpal Kumar Raha and Raju KD, 'Submarine Telecommunication Cable Infrastructure in South Asia under International Law: Opportunity for Sri Lanka and India' (2018) 26 Sri Lanka J Int'l L 79, 97–101; Beckman (2014) 290–295.

culpable negligence, break or injure a submarine cable or pipeline beneath the high seas or in the EEZ.[273] The history of this obligation in UNCLOS Article 113 can be traced to Article II of the 1884 Paris Convention, which formed the basis for Article 27 of the Convention on the High Seas. UNCLOS extended the scope of States' jurisdiction to include conduct that is 'calculated or likely to result in' the breaking or injury of a submarine cable or pipeline, excluding actions taken by the persons who were acting merely with the purpose of saving their lives or their ship, after having taken all necessary precautions to avoid such break or injury.[274] As a result, the intention or attempt to break or injure a cable or pipeline associated with such conduct is also a punishable offence, even without the conduct resulting in an actual break or injury.[275]

Both acts that result in damage and are likely to result in damage are punishable only when performed 'wilfully or through culpable negligence'.[276] However, Article 113 does not specify which party bears the burden of proof. According to general criminal procedures, the prosecution is responsible for proving all the essential elements to justify the crime charged.[277] Therefore, the ship or person involved will not be punished unless the prosecution can prove, *prima facie*, that their acts were performed with wilful intent or culpable negligence. The interpretation of what constitutes wilful intent or negligence is largely a decision of domestic courts, and State practices vary. Under Australian law, for instance, it is an offence 'if the person engages in conduct, and the conduct results in damages to a submarine cable', but the penalty is lighter when 'the person is negligent as to the fact that the conduct results in that damage'.[278] This legislation disregards whether or not the person was 'wilful' when engaged in

273 UNCLOS Articles 58(2), 113.

274 UNCLOS Article 113.

275 Nordquist, Nandan and Rosenne (1995) 270.

276 UNCLOS Article 113.

277 Barton L. Ingraham, 'The Right of Silence, the Presumption of Innocence, the Burden of Proof, and a Modest Proposal: A Reply to O'Reilly' (1995–1996) 86 J Crim L & Criminology 559, 562; Alleged Violations of Sovereign Rights and Maritime Spaces in the Caribbean Sea (Nicaragua v. Colombia), Judgment of 21 April 2022, ICJ Reports 2022, p. 266, para 64.

278 Australia, Telecommunications and Other Legislation Amendment (Protection of Submarine Cables and Other Measures) Act 2005, Schedule 1, Part 1, Division 4, Subdivision A, Clauses 36–37.

such conduct but focuses on actual damage, and the offender is subjected to a lighter punishment if proven 'negligent'. It also excludes conduct that is 'calculated or likely to result in' such damages.

Article 113 of UNCLOS in effect obligates States to adopt legislation for an offence by their nationals, including ships flying their flags, for activities that may have occurred outside of their territorial jurisdiction.[279] By limiting the jurisdictional basis to nationality and registration, Article 113 did not create universal jurisdiction over such an offence.[280] However, it is not difficult to anticipate the insufficiency of the implementation of such jurisdiction. States are reluctant to adopt legislation for offences committed outside their territories, and for those that have legislated, enforcement is very limited.[281] This situation is even more worrying when it comes to States with open registration that lack both the willingness and capacity to enforce such legislation for the large fleet. It worth noting that the 1884 Paris Convention provided State parties a right of visit over other parties' vessels suspected of offences of the Convention and obliged such States to report offences to the State has jurisdiction.[282] This police power was omitted from both the Convention on the High Seas and UNCLOS.[283]

The coastal State has the same obligation to punish intentional damage to submarine cables and pipelines by its nationals and ships flying its flag. However, it has no straightforward jurisdiction over damage to such cables and pipelines caused by foreign nationals or ships in its EEZ. Coastal State jurisdiction over suspected foreign ships may only be established on its sovereign rights or specific jurisdiction claimed in the

[279] Christopher Staker, 'Jurisdiction', in Malcolm D. Evans (ed.), *International Law* (5th ed., Oxford University Press 2018) 289, 296–298.

[280] Dupuy and Vignes (1991) 982.

[281] Takei (2012) 216–217; Davenport (2012) 219; Beckman (2010) 13–14; UNGA A/65/69, 29 March 2010, Oceans and the Law of the Sea Report of the Secretary-General, para 71.

[282] 1884 Paris Convention Article X.

[283] Douglas Guilfoyle, 'Article 110', in Proelss (2017) 769; Guilfoyle and Miles 'Article 113' (2017) 783; Tallinn Manual 2.0 (2017) 257. In 1959, the United States invoked Article X of the 1884 Paris Convention to board and investigate the Soviet trawler *Novorossiisk* for damaging five transatlantic cables. With the master's consent, a US warship inspected the vessel and determined that there was a 'strong presumption' that the *Novorossiisk* violated the proscription in Article II of the Convention against intentional, wilful or culpably negligent breaking or injuring a submarine cable. See The Novorossiisk, Department of State Bulletin (20 April 1959), Vol. 40, No. 1034, 555.

EEZ. For instance, if the damaged cable or pipeline was 'used in connection with the exploration of its continental shelf or exploitation of its resources', the coastal State could exercise jurisdiction over the foreign ship that caused such damage.[284] Further, if the damage resulted in pollution from a pipeline, the coastal State may assert jurisdiction over the foreign ship for the protection and preservation of the marine environment.[285] However, such claims could be challenged, since coastal State jurisdiction over foreign vessels in the EEZ is limited to 'pollution from vessels'.[286] Pollution caused by a collision between a vessel and a pipeline, which could be considered incident of navigation, would, *prima facie*, remain under the jurisdiction of the flag State, and the coastal State may only assert concurrent jurisdiction.

There has been increasing discussion about the security issues associated with intentional damage to submarine cables and pipelines.[287] Submarine communication cables are susceptible to being physically tapped, for instance by purpose-built submarines, whereas the data transmitted through them can be collected, altered or jammed.[288] In response to an incident of stolen cable and an optical amplifier by Vietnamese vessels in 2007, arguments were made to treat the incident as piracy under international law because it was an 'act of depredation' committed for private end by a private ships against 'property in a place outside the jurisdiction of any State'.[289] In September 2022, three out of the four pipelines of the Nord Stream and Nord Stream 2 were torn open by explosives and released over 220,000 tonnes of methane into the

[284] UNCLOS Articles 56(3), 77(1), 79(4).
[285] UNCLOS Articles 56(1)(b)(iii), 79(2).
[286] UNCLOS Article 220(3) and (5)–(6).
[287] STF, Industry Report 2023–2024, Section 9.1: Legal and Regulatory Matters Year Review. Tara Davenport, 'Intentional Damage to Submarine Cable Systems by States, Hoover Working Group on National Security, Technology, and Law, Aegis Series' Paper No. 2305 (October 26, 2023) www.lawfaremedia.org/article/intentional-damage-to-submarine-cable-systems-by-states.
[288] Tallinn Manual 2.0 (2017) 253; Marcia Wendorf, 'Operation Ivy Bells: The U.S. Top-Secret Program That Wiretapped a Soviet Undersea Cable', Interesting Engineering, 3 January 2022 https://interestingengineering.com/innovation/operation-ivy-bells-the-us-top-secret-program-that-wiretapped-a-soviet-undersea-cable.
[289] Mick P. Green and Douglas R. Burnett, 'Security of International Submarine Cable Infrastructure: Time to Rethink?' in Myron H. Nordquist, Rüdiger Wolfrum and Ronán Long (eds.), *Legal Challenges in Maritime Security* (Brill 2008) 557; Robert Beckman, 'Protecting Submarine Cables from Intentional Damage: The Security Gap', in Burnett, Beckman and Davenport (2014) 289.

atmosphere.[290] The damaged pipelines were located on the seabed of the EEZs of Denmark and Sweden where both States have limited jurisdiction over these transiting pipelines.[291] While Denmark, Germany, Sweden and Russia all initiated investigations over the alleged acts of sabotage against the Nord Stream pipelines, with Russia been isolated from the collaboration among the other three States, it remains unclear how to categorise such intentional damage under international law.[292] There has been discussion on whether or not the act of attacking submarine communication cables or pipelines amounts to an armed attack such that the affected State could invoke the right of self-defence to use force.[293] Moreover, it is questionable whether the attack on this infrastructure could be treated as an international crime, including maritime terrorism, if it was done for the purpose of intimidating a population, or compelling a government or an international organisation to act in a certain way or to abstain from any act.[294] With respect to submarine cables, the Global Maritime Crime Programme lead by the United Nations Office on Drugs and Crime has been developing a framework to assist States in ensuring the protection and resilience of submarine

[290] Nord Stream, 'Incident on the Nord Stream Pipeline (updated 14/11/2022)' Press Release, 14 November 2022 www.nord-stream.com/press-info/press-releases/incident-on-the-nord-stream-pipeline-updated-14112022-529/; Mengwei Jia et al., 'The Nord Stream Pipeline Gas Leaks Released Approximately 220,000 Tonnes of Methane into the Atmosphere' (2022) 12 Environmental Science and Ecotechnology 100210.

[291] Åklagarmyndigheten Swedish Prosecution Authority, 'The prosecutor closes the Swedish investigation concerning gross sabotage against Nord Stream', 7 February 2024 www.aklagare.se/en/media/press-releases/2024/february/the-prosecutor-closes-the-swedish-investigation-concerning-gross-sabotage-against-nord-stream/.

[292] United Nations Security Council S/PV.9266, 21 February 2023, Threats to International Peace and Security; United Nations, Meeting Coverage, Security Council, SC/15206, 21 February 2023, 'Avoid Speculation' about Responsibility for 2022 Nord Stream Pipeline Incident, Official Urges Security Council, Stressing United Nations Cannot Verify Claims https://press.un.org/en/2023/sc15206.doc.htm.

[293] Blair Shepherd, 'Cutting Submarine Cables: the Legality of the Use of Force in Self-Defense' (2020) 31 Duke J Compar & Int'l L 199, 208–216; Yusuke Saito, 'Reviewing Law of Armed Conflict at Sea and Warfare in New Domains and New Measures: Submarine Cables, Merchant Missile Ships, and Unmanned Marine Systems' (2019) 44(107) Tul Mar LJ 107, 112–116; Danae Azaria and Geir Ulfstein, 'Are Sabotage of Submarine Pipelines an "Armed Attack" Triggering a Right to Self-defence?', EJIL:Talk!, 18 October 2022 www.ejiltalk.org/are-sabotage-of-submarine-pipelines-an-armed-attack-triggering-a-right-to-self-defence/; Davenport (2023), 10-13.

[294] Kaye (2006–2007) 378; Beckman (2014) 290–295.

cables within their maritime zones.[295] Another potential channel to address crimes against submarine cables or pipelines is to incorporate such offences under the international agreements on the suppression of unlawful acts against the safety of maritime navigation, or fixed platforms located on the continental shelf.[296]

The laying and operation of submarine cables and pipelines need to be protected even at the expense of putting certain limitations on other marine uses. The need for protection is expected to continue, because most nations are increasingly dependent on submarine fibre-optic cables for international communications and on pipelines for transporting offshore and inland resources. Although UNCLOS requires States to develop domestic legislation related to the protection of submarine cables and pipelines, many States still have not done so.[297] It is particularly important for the coastal State to adopt and enforce effective measures because its nationals and ships conduct most of the competing uses in the EEZ.

5.5 Resolving Disputes Concerning the Laying of Submarine Cables and Pipelines

As one of the preserved freedoms in the EEZ, it is essential that disputes on the interpretation and application of provisions on the laying of submarine cables and pipelines be subject to the compulsory dispute

[295] United Nations Office on Drugs and Crime (UNODC), 'Key Actions to Protect Submarine Cables from Criminal Activity Identified at UNODC Global Expert Meeting', 7 February 2019 www.unodc.org/unodc/en/frontpage/2019/February/key-actions-to-protect-submarine-cables-from-criminal-activity-identified-at-unodc-global-expert-meeting.html; UNGA A/74/350, para 44; UNODC, 'Protecting submarine cables in the Indian Ocean', 13 January 2021 www.unodc.org/easternafrica/en/Stories/protection-of-submarine-cables-in-indian-ocean.html.

[296] Convention for the Suppression of Unlawful Acts against the Safety of Maritime Navigation (10 March 1988, in force 1 March 1992) and Protocol for the Suppression of Unlawful Acts against the Safety of Fixed Platforms Located on the Continental Shelf (14 October 2005, in force 28 July 2010) 1678 UNTS 221; see also IMO, 'Convention for the Suppression of Unlawful Acts Against the Safety of Maritime Navigation, Protocol for the Suppression of Unlawful Acts Against the Safety of Fixed Platforms Located on the Continental Shelf' www.imo.org/en/About/Conventions/Pages/SUA-Treaties.aspx.

[297] UK House of Lords 2021-22 para 321; 王赞，《破坏海底电缆、管道罪国内法化研究》2013年第1期，学术论坛，111–115，第112页 (WANG Zan, 'Studies on Domestic Implementation of the Crime to Damage Submarine Cables and Pipelines' (2013) 1 Academic Forum 111, 112).

settlement procedures under UNCLOS.[298] When it is alleged that either a coastal State or the operating State has acted in contravention of the provisions relating to their respective rights and duties in relation to the laying of submarine cables and pipelines, the other party may initiate the dispute settlement procedures where the parties have reached no agreement.[299]

The practical issue is that, under the international law of the sea, States are the right holders that normally delegate the exercise of the freedom to lay submarine cables and pipelines to corporations or other private entities through the link of nationality or registration.[300] These corporations and private entities are precluded from using the dispute settlement procedures under UNCLOS, which are only open to State parties.[301] Hence, the difficulty lies both in how to identify which State has a legitimate stand and in how to provide it with sufficient incentives to initiate procedures on behalf of these private actors. For example, international submarine cables and pipelines are usually owned by a large consortium of companies incorporated in different States, and the suppliers, operators and end users could be located in many different countries and territories.[302] Determining which States may represent the cable or pipeline for a particular case can be challenging. As demonstrated in the above-mentioned Nord Stream incidents, both pipeline systems are operated by an independent consortium, based in Switzerland, of multiple companies, among which the Russian State-owned Gazprom Group company holds over 50 per cent of the shares.[303] Nearly two years after the incidents, there is no public report indicating that Switzerland, as the State where the consortiums are registered, has taken any action.[304]

The challenge of lack of State-level representation is particularly evident in the case of submarine fibre-optic cables. Take, for example, the case where the coastal State requires a permit for repair work of a transiting fibre-optic cable that is located in its EEZ, which *prima facie*

[298] UNCLOS Article 279(1); Kwiatkowska (1989) 216–217; Dupuy and Vignes (1991) 986.

[299] UNCLOS Articles 281, 286, 297(1)(a)–(b).

[300] Nordquist, Nandan and Rosenne (1995) 264; Mudrić (2010) 238–239; Guilfoyle and Miles 'Article 112' (2017) 781; ILA, Committee on Submarine Cables and Pipelines under International Law, Interim Report 2020, para 207.

[301] UNCLOS Article 286.

[302] Mick Green, 'The Submarine Cable Industry: How Does It Work?' in Burnett, Beckman and Davenport (2014) 41–45; Nord Stream, 'Our Shareholders' www.nord-stream.com/about-us/our-shareholders/; UK House of Lords 2021-22 para 322.

[303] The operators of Nord Stream 2 were Gazprom, Shell and ENGIE.

[304] United Nations Security Council SC/15206 (2023).

is inconsistent with the rights and jurisdiction of the coastal State over such cables. Under normal practice, the cable owner, a large consortium, would charter a specialised cable ship to undertake the repair work, whose flag State is usually not the same as the national State of the cable owner. It may be more straightforward if the flag State of the cable ship could challenge the coastal State's requirement of permission. However, the flag State of the cable ship often does not have the political will or interest to challenge a coastal State on behalf of the cable owner.[305] The cable owner, which often consists of multiple telecom or content companies from different States and territories that co-own the cable system's capacity and operate the cable system according to a commercial agreement, can hardly avail itself of a representing State for the dispute settlement procedures.[306] Submarine cables are, unlike ships, neither registered under any flag nor operated under the auspice of any international organisation or agency.[307] Should States be willing to establish a formal registration process for international fibre-optic cables, it would provide legal clarity as to which State may represent the cable operator's and owner's interest when a coastal State has acted in contravention of the provisions concerning the freedom of the laying of submarine cables in the EEZ.

Apart from disputes directly related to the coastal State's conduct, submarine cables and pipelines may face challenges from competing uses and intentional damage. These cases are often resolved at the domestic level through procedures between the two private parties over commercial claims, or through procedures brought by a government agency to prosecute intentional damage. Only when such cases exhaust local remedies and do not resolve the dispute may the claimant State bring an international claim over its counterpart under UNCLOS or other relevant fora.

The parties to the dispute have the right to decide which procedure applies to the settlement of their dispute.[308] Both parties could accept the same procedure, or go to arbitration if they cannot agree on the procedure.[309] A court or arbitral tribunal would clarify the interpretation and application of a number of provisions, including the scope of the

[305] Van Logchem (2014) 117.

[306] Burnett, Davenport and Beckman (2014) 88–89.

[307] Robert Beckman and Tara Davenport, Workshop Report – Workshop on Submarine Cables and Law of the Sea, 14–15 December 2009, Singapore (Centre for International Law, National University of Singapore 2010) https://cil.nus.edu.sg/wp-content/uploads/2009/10/Workshop-Report-29-Jan-2010.pdf.

[308] UNCLOS Article 280.

[309] UNCLOS Article 287(4)–(5).

reasonable measures and conditions that could be taken by the coastal State, and the due regard obligation that could be invoked by both parties under various scenarios. The court or tribunal, when finding jurisdiction *prima facie*, may prescribe appropriate provisional measures to preserve the respective rights of the parties or to prevent serious harm to the marine environment.[310] As of 2024, no State has pursued dispute settlement procedures under UNCLOS relating to the freedom of the laying of submarine cables or pipelines.

5.6 Conclusion

With the increasing demand for submarine cables and pipelines worldwide, it is critically important to preserve the freedom of the laying of such cables and pipelines and to protect their operation and use. The exercise of such freedom in the EEZ, however, is under growing pressure to accommodate the coastal State's sovereign rights and jurisdiction, as well the challenges and threats posed by competing uses and intentional damage.

In terms of the legal framework, the freedom to lay submarine cables, in theory, has been well preserved in the EEZ, with limited interference from the coastal State in taking reasonable measures for the exploration and exploitation of the seabed and its natural resources. It is notable that submarine pipelines are subject to additional regulation by the coastal State compared to submarine cables. The delineation of the course of a pipeline is subject to the coastal State's consent, and the laying of pipeline is subject to its jurisdiction over pollution control. This is mainly because the use of pipelines is often associated with the exploitation of natural resources or offshore infrastructures, and it is well known that materials transported by pipelines have the potential to cause harm to the marine environment. Hence, the freedom to lay pipelines in the EEZ is further restricted compared with submarine cables to give priority to the sovereign rights and jurisdiction granted to the coastal State.

In terms of State practice, some coastal States have made excessive claims over activities related to the laying of submarine cables and pipelines in the EEZ, particularly with regard to communication cables. Many of these excessive claims were based on the coastal State's broad interpretation of its sovereign rights and jurisdiction. States exercising the freedom to lay submarine cables and pipelines are required under

[310] UNCLOS Article 290(1).

UNCLOS to give due regard to the coastal State's rights and to comply with their laws, but this does not give the coastal State the right to decide how such an obligation is undertaken or to adopt laws and regulations contrary to UNCLOS. The excessive coastal State claims, particularly with regard to permits for cable operations and the delineation of cable routes, may not only erode the freedom to lay submarine cables but may also interfere with the freedom of navigation. This constitutes a threat to the delicate balance of rights and duties in the EEZ. A possible solution is for these coastal States to retreat from excessive claims that are inconsistent with UNCLOS and to act with due regard to other State's rights and duties. The operating State could facilitate the transition of such coastal State practice by voluntarily providing information and consultation to ensure that their operations will not interfere with the coastal State's exercise of its sovereign rights or jurisdiction.

It needs to be emphasised that the coastal State can play an important role in protecting the safety and security of submarine cables and pipelines in the EEZ. In addition to the obligation to have due regard to the exercise of such freedom, the coastal State has an interest in protecting these cables and pipelines in light of their importance to global communications and energy security, particularly if such cables and pipelines are landed on its coast. The coastal State should actively fulfil its duty to adopt the laws and regulations necessary to punish those who damage a cable or pipeline wilfully or through culpable negligence, impose civil liability for damages caused by non-criminal acts, and provide indemnity for loss incurred to avoid injury to the cable or pipeline. Moreover, the coastal State should diligently regulate competing uses by its nationals and ships flying its flag, and promote cooperation between different marine uses to avoid unnecessary interference with submarine cables and pipelines.

PART III

Resolving Conflicts Regarding Unattributed Rights and Jurisdiction in the Exclusive Economic Zone

Overall, the whole package deal of the legal order of the ocean as adopted in the United Nations Convention on the Law of the Sea (UNCLOS) is the result of a trade-off of negotiations and compromises.[1] The *sui generis* exclusive economic zone (EEZ) legal regime established at the margin between the two distinctive regimes – the territorial sea and the high seas – is an area of compendium rights and duties between the coastal State and other States.[2] As discussed in Part II, UNCLOS has covered the more obvious uses of the EEZ.[3] However, not all potentially relevant rights and jurisdiction have yet been attributed, at least explicitly.

Part III discusses three subjects that UNCLOS has not stipulated specifically as pertaining to either the coastal State or other States, namely military activities, maritime security and underwater archaeological and historical objects. State practice and scholarly writings show different interpretations of whether these three subjects fall under the scope of unattributed rights and jurisdiction in the EEZ, particularly those relating to military activities. Following a strict reading of the provisions of UNCLOS, these three subjects are not automatically associated with either the sovereign rights or jurisdiction granted to the coastal States or the preserved communicational freedoms available to all States. Nevertheless, it is clear that some of the activities relating to these subjects are more clearly affiliated with a specific State than others, such as law enforcement activities over certain threats to maritime security in the EEZ.

1 United Nations Convention on the Law of the Sea (adopted 10 December 1982, in force 16 November 1994) 1833 UNTS 3 (UNCLOS); Arnd Bernaerts, Bernaerts' Guide to the 1982 United Nations Convention on the Law of the Sea (Fairplay 1988), 8; Tommy Koh, *Building A New Legal Order for the Oceans* (NUS Press, 2020), 25–47; Robin Churchill, Vaughan Lowe and Amy Sander, *The Law of the Sea* (4th ed., Manchester University Press, 2022), 23–24.

2 UNCLOS, Articles 55 and 57.

3 UNCLOS, Articles 56 and 58; Churchill, Lowe and Sander (2022), 262–291.

By giving these three subjects the status as unattributed rights and jurisdiction in the EEZ, it leaves room for both the coastal State and other States to discuss their attribution based on the general principle applied to this *sui generis* legal regime: that is, to reserve the rights and jurisdiction over those activities that may affect economic interests to the coastal States while minimising the erosion of the communicational freedoms enjoyed by all States, and to preserve these freedoms for all States insofar as they are compatible with the EEZ. The exercise of these rights and jurisdiction will continue to be guided by the mutual obligation of due regard as explicitly required in both Articles 56(2) and 58(3) of UNCLOS, whereby no State may exercise their rights or freedoms in an absolute manner. The principle of equity and other circumstances as set out in Article 59 will be drawn on when a conflict arises between States on the attribution of rights and jurisdiction over these three subjects.

In the age of globalisation and interdependency, the former primary objective of winning command of the sea has gradually given way to the peaceful and secure use of the ocean by the international community. The implication is that instead of competing for exclusive jurisdiction, the coastal State and other States must recognise the need and right of each other to pursue their interests in the same marine area, and prepare to make compromises if the respective importance of the interests of the other party or the international community outweighs its own interest.

6

Military Activities

Among the rights that have not been explicitly attributed in the exclusive economic zone (EEZ), States disagree in particular on the law governing military activities. On the one hand, although some maritime powers view the United Nations Convention on the Law of the Sea (UNCLOS) as permitting navies to operate in a foreign EEZ essentially the same way as they operate on the high seas, some coastal States argue that different rules apply.[1] On the other hand, it is not clear as to what extent the coastal State can use its EEZ for military purposes, particularly when such use may affect the exercise of freedoms by other States. Moreover, States hold different views on what constitutes military activities. The conflicting interpretations and applications of UNCLOS and customary international law between coastal States and other military-user States have led to a stalemate where both groups believe that their actions are justified and lawful.[2]

This chapter examines the issue of whether or not the establishment of the 200 nautical miles (NM) EEZ affects the conduct of military activities,

[1] United Nations Convention on the Law of the Sea (10 December 1982, in force 16 November 1994) 1833 UNTS 3 (UNCLOS).

[2] George V. Galdorisi and Alan G. Kaufman, 'Military Activities in the Exclusive Economic Zone: Preventing Uncertainty and Defusing Conflict' (2001) 32 Cal W Int'l LJ 253; Jon M. Van Dyke, 'Military Ships and Planes Operating in the Exclusive Economic Zone of Another Country' (2004) 28 Marine Policy 29; Brian Wilson, 'An Avoidable Maritime Conflict: Disputes Regarding Military Activities in the Exclusive Economic Zone' (2010) 41 J Mar L & Com 425; Raul (Pete) Pedrozo, 'Preserving Navigational Rights and Freedoms: The Right to Conduct Military Activities in China's Exclusive Economic Zone' (2010) 9 Chinese J Int'l L 9; Haiwen Zhang, 'Is It Safeguarding the Freedom of Navigation or Maritime Hegemony of the United States? – Comments on Raul (Pete) Pedrozo's Article on Military Activities in the EEZ' (2010) 9 Chinese J Int'l L 31; Peter Dutton, Military Activities in the EEZ: A U.S.-China Dialogue on Security and International Law in the Maritime Commons' (China Maritime Studies Institute, US Naval War College, Red Books Study No. 7 2010) https://digital-commons.usnwc.edu/cmsi-red-books/3/; Erik Franckx, 'American and Chinese Views on Navigational Rights of Warships' (2011) 10 Chinese J Int'l L 187; Raul Pedrozo, 'Military Activities in the Exclusive Economic Zone' (2021) 97 Int'l L Stud Ser US Naval War Col 45.

and if so, what international rules apply to such activities. Given the lack of clarity of jurisdiction, this analysis applies the two legal doctrines of the attribution and exercise of rights and duties in the EEZ. On the attribution issue, the conduct of military activities in the EEZ is considered an unattributed right such that jurisdiction is assessed on the particular activity within a given circumstance. In exercising such a residual right, the operating State must maintain a peaceful purpose and must have due regard to other States' rights and duties in using the same maritime zone. This means that, when using the EEZ for military purposes, the coastal State must not impede the freedoms enjoyed by other States, while other States must not impair the sovereign rights and jurisdiction of the coastal State.

This chapter is divided into four sections. Section 6.1 reflects on the history of military uses of the sea, acknowledges the right of all States to conduct military activities on the high seas and identifies the general obligations for conducting peacetime military activities under international law. Section 6.2 discusses military security interests in the EEZ. Although security interests are not explicitly included in Part V of UNCLOS, they nonetheless exist, have been claimed and are protected by both the coastal State and other States from different perspectives. Section 6.3 examines conflicting opinions and practices with regard to the conduct of specific military activities in the EEZ as a means to protect military security interests. The attribution of rights to conduct these activities has provoked conflicts between the operating State and other States, mainly the coastal State. Neither side has any general priority in exercising co-existing rights, but each must act in good faith and give due regard to the other party. Section 6.4 reviews State practice relating to the regulation of military activities at sea and explores a mechanism to build trust and confidence to improve mutual understanding and avoid conflicts.

6.1 Military Uses of the Sea in Peacetime

6.1.1 Freedom of the Seas

The ocean has traditionally been divided into two legal regimes: territorial waters, where the coastal State has sovereignty, and the high seas, which is dominated by the principles of freedom and the exclusivity of flag State jurisdiction.[3] The freedom of the high seas, as a rule of

[3] Daniel P. O'Connell, *The International Law of the Sea*, Vol. I (Oxford University Press 1982) 1; Robin Churchill, Vaughan Lowe and Amy Sander, *The Law of the Sea* (4th ed., Manchester University Press 2022) 372.

customary law as well as treaty law, is a cornerstone of the international law of the sea.[4] Although its meaning and content have undergone change and refinement over time, the freedom of the high seas has traditionally included the freedom to conduct military activities in times of both peace and war, either defensive or offensive.[5] In theory, subject to the principle of peaceful purposes, the high seas can be used by all ships and aircraft for activities that are not explicitly prohibited under customary or conventional international law.[6]

Broadly speaking, military uses of the sea embrace a wide and complex range of peacekeeping and wartime activities conducted not only on the water surface and in the column, on the seabed and subsoil but also in superjacent air space, by warships, support vessels, military aircraft and tactical and ballistic missile submarines.[7] In addition, military uses of the sea include cyber operations conducted from or through cyber infrastructure located in seas, including infrastructure mounted on ships and submarines, aircraft above the seas, offshore installations and through submarine communication cables.[8] The military uses of the sea serve a variety of purposes for governments.[9] First, in order to protect a State's interests at sea, warships and military aircraft commonly conduct manoeuvres at sea to maintain readiness of engagement, with or without weapons testing.[10] Second, duly authorised government entities perform law enforcement duties with respect to activities occurring within their

[4] O'Connell (1982) 9–10; Churchill, Lowe and Sander (2022) 375–380.

[5] David Joseph Attard, *The Exclusive Economic Zone in International Law* (Clarendon Press 1987) 86; Daniel P. O'Connell, *The International Law of the Sea*, Vol. II (Oxford University Press 1988) 809, 1094–1096; James C. F. Wang, *Handbook on Ocean Politics & Law* (Greenwood 1992) 367–388; Robin R. Churchill and A. Vaughn Lowe, *The Law of the Sea* (3rd ed., Manchester University Press 1999) 421–431; Donald R. Rothwell and Tim Stephens, *The International Law of the Sea* (Hart 2010) 258–284.

[6] Edward D. Brown, 'Freedom of the Sea versus the Common Heritage of Mankind: Fundamental Principles in Conflict' (1982–1983) 20(3) San Diego L Rev 521, 533; Douglas Guilfoyle, 'The High Seas', in Donald R. Rothwell, Alex G. Oude Elferink, Karen N. Scott and Tim Stephens (eds.), *The Oxford Handbook of the Law of the Sea* (Oxford University Press 2015) 203, 206–208.

[7] Charles E. Pirtle, 'Military Uses of Ocean Space and the Law of the Sea in the New Millennium' (2000) 31(1) Ocean Dev Int'l L 7, 8; James Kraska and Raul Pedrozo, *International Maritime Security Law* (Martinus Nijhoff 2013) 236.

[8] Michael N. Schmitt, *Tallinn Manual 2.0 on the International Law Applicable to Cyber Operations* (Cambridge University Press 2017) 232 (Tallinn Manual 2.0).

[9] Naval Operations Concept 2010: Implementing the Maritime Strategy (Joint Publication of the US Marine Corps, the US Navy and the US Coast Guard 2010) 9–10 https://irp.fas.org/doddir/navy/noc2010.pdf.

[10] Churchill and Lowe (1999) 426.

jurisdictional sea areas, over ships flying the same flag on the high seas, and over certain international crimes at sea.[11] Third, warships and military aircraft customarily conduct hydrographic surveys and other data-gathering activities through seabed devices or other onboard structures to improve navigational safety and to obtain strategic information about the targeted area.[12] Fourth, States routinely conduct intelligence collection activities or espionage, which may include the use of airborne and ship-based maritime surveillance systems and military devices, installations and structures on the seabed.[13]

Any maritime State, large or small, may use its sea power to secure legitimate uses of ocean space to provide national security, in terms of both self-defence and the capacity to deploy military force overseas for warfare and peaceful purposes.[14] In fact, the use of military force to project power and influence over international relations has long been a traditional weapon in the diplomatic arena – the very term 'gunboat diplomacy' confirms the historic use of naval forces as a coercive element in achieving national goals.[15] Therefore, States possessing strong maritime forces have always favoured more liberal legal regimes for the ocean. The United States, for example, has 'traditionally maintained a strong Navy to preserve the freedom of the seas and to support the global commitments associated with its forward defense strategy' with the aim to ensure political persuasion, reassure allies, deter political adversaries and influence regional events.[16] These political imperatives have pushed maritime powers to seek the greatest freedom for military uses of the sea when developing the legal regimes of maritime zones.

The freedom to use ocean space for military purposes has never been without challenges and contradictions. The presence of a foreign navy in

[11] UNCLOS Articles 110(1) and (5), 111(5).

[12] Sam Bateman, 'Hydrographic Surveying in the EEZ: Differences and Overlaps with Marine Scientific Research' (2005) 29 Marine Policy 163, 163–164.

[13] Desmond Ball, 'Intelligence Collection Operations and EEZs: The Implications of New Technology' (2004) 28 Marine Policy 67, 68–77.

[14] Wang (1992) 367; Arthur W. Westing, 'Military Impact on Ocean Ecology' (1978) 1 Ocean YB 436, 439; Scott C. Truver, 'The Law of the Sea and the Military Use of the Oceans in 2010' (1984) 45 La L Rev 1221, 1226.

[15] Dale G .Stephens, 'The Impact of the 1982 Law of the Sea Convention on the Conduct of Peacetime Naval/Military Operations' (1998–1999) 29 Cal W Int'l LJ 283, 285.

[16] Truver (1984) 1228; Andrew S. Erickson, 'America's Security Role in the South China Sea (Testimony before a Hearing of the US House Foreign Affairs Committee, Subcommittee on Asia and the Pacific, 23 July 2015)' (2016) 69(1) Naval War Col Rev 7, 18.

a nearby sea area is considered to pose a threat to the security and integrity of the coastal State and has provoked conflicts between the coastal State and the operating State.[17] Restrictions on military activities in coastal areas were commonly used in times of crisis and international confrontation. For example, during the Falkland/Malvinas conflict in 1982, the United Kingdom declared a 200 NM maritime exclusion zone around the islands and then replaced it by a total exclusion zone that banned the entry of all Argentine warships, naval auxiliaries and aircraft.[18]

Within adjacent sea areas, the competition has always been between the coastal State's intention to control all military activities for its exclusive use and the desire of other States to freely use the sea for their own or common interests.[19] Over time, the freedom to use the sea for military purposes has been affected by the elongation of the extent of the territorial sea and the creation of various functional jurisdiction zones.

6.1.2 *Codification of the Law of Military Uses of the Sea*

The development of international law in the twentieth century has witnessed the growth of an international consensus in support of increasing restrictions on the use of force in international relations.[20] The broad prohibition on the threat or use of force in the Charter of the United Nations (UN Charter) represents an achievement of profound importance for the strengthening of international law.[21] This development,

[17] Zhang (2010) 47; 邹立刚,《论国家对专属经济区内外国平时军事活动的规制权》,中国法学,2012年第6期,49–57页,第52–53页 (ZOU Ligang, 'On Coastal State's Jurisdiction over Foreign Military Activities in the EEZ in Peacetime' (2012) 6 China Legal Science 49, 52–53).

[18] 'The Falklands Conflict – Chronology of Events' www.falklandswar.org.uk/chron.htm; Lawrence Freedman, *The Official History of the Falklands Campaign* (Routledge 2005) 257–258.

[19] Myres S. McDougal and William T. Burke, *The Public Order of the Oceans: A Contemporary International Law of the Sea* (Martinus Nijhoff 1985) 17; James Kraska, 'Military Operations', in Rothwell, Oude Elferink, Scott and Stephens (2015) 865, 885.

[20] Paul B. Stephan III and Boris M. Klimenko (eds.), *International Law and International Security: Military and Political Dimensions* (ME Sharpe 1991) 2; David Harris and Sandesh Sivakumaran, *Cases and Materials on International Law* (8th ed., Sweet and Maxwell 2015) 725–727; Christine Gray, *International Law and the Use of Force* (4th ed., Oxford University Press 2018) 9–10.

[21] Charter of the United Nations (26 June 1945, in force 24 October 1945), 557 UNTS 143, Article 2(4) (UN Charter).

although it goes beyond the scope of the codification of the law of the sea, influenced the discussion of military uses of ocean space at the three United Nations Conferences on the Law of the Sea.[22]

The historical claims of a coastal State's sovereign rights over the continental shelf was formalised in the 1958 Convention on the Continental Shelf, and refined in UNCLOS.[23] The law of the sea acknowledges the sovereign rights of coastal States over the continental shelf, including the outer continental shelf that extends beyond 200 NM from the baselines, for the exploration and exploitation of the seabed and its natural resources, while preserving the freedom to lay submarine cables and pipelines for all States.[24] The emplacement of military objects on or beneath the seabed floor and subsoil, one of the most important military uses of the sea, is not explicitly permitted or prohibited by these two conventions.[25]

When the 1958 Convention on the Continental Shelf was being negotiated, India proposed that the continental shelf should not be used by any State for the purpose of building military bases or installations, but this was rejected by thirty-one votes to eighteen.[26] Although the final articles did not include an explicit permission, it was believed that, at least in 1958, the traditional high seas freedoms included the right to emplace military installations and devices on or in the seabed of the continental shelf.[27] The additional coastal States' sovereign rights over the continental shelf, as intrusions on the high sea freedoms, are limited to 'the purpose of exploring it and exploiting its natural resources' without affecting the legal status of the superjacent waters or airspace

22 R. W. G. de Muralt, 'The Military Aspects of the UN Law of the Sea Convention' (1985) 32 Netherlands Int'l L Rev 78, 79.

23 Convention on the Continental Shelf (29 April 1958, in force 10 June 1964) 499 UNTS 311; UNCLOS Part VI. For the historical background of the development of the coastal State jurisdiction, see Chapter 2 in this volume.

24 Convention on the Continental Shelf Articles 2, 4; UNCLOS Articles 77, 79.

25 Tullio Treves, 'Military Installations, Structures, and Devices on the Seabed' (1980) 74 Am J Int'l L 808, 831.

26 United Nations Conference on the Law of the Sea, Official Records, Vol. VI: Fourth Committee (Continental Shelf) Summary Records of Meetings and Annexes, Geneva, 24 February – 27 April 1958, A/CONF.13/C.4/L.57, Thirtieth Meeting, Consideration of the Draft Articles adopted by the International Law Commission at its Eighth Session (A/3159), India: Proposal, 91, 141.

27 Rex J. Zedalis, '"Peaceful Purposes" and Other Relevant Provisions of the Revised Composite Negotiating Text: A Comparative Analysis of the Existing and Proposed Military Regime for the High Seas' (1979) 7 Syracuse J Int'l L & Com 1, 14; Treves (1980) 834–835.

above those waters.[28] The coastal State's sovereign rights do not automatically apply to the military field, which remains to be governed by the high seas regime.[29] There are, however, limitations on the freedom to use the continental shelf for military purposes. As a traditional high seas freedom, States wishing to emplace weapons, installations and other military devices on the continental shelf are obliged to do so with reasonable regard to the interests of other States in the exercise of their freedom of the high seas.[30] Additionally, it can be argued that the use of the continental shelf for military purposes by a foreign State, similar to the laying or maintenance of submarine cables or pipelines, is subject to the coastal State's right to 'take reasonable measures for the exploration of the continental shelf and the exploitation of its natural resources'.[31]

The freedom to use the seabed for military purposes is further restricted by the 1971 Seabed Treaty, which came into force in 1972 and has ninety-four State parties.[32] The 1971 Seabed Treaty recognises the common interest of humankind to promote the peaceful use of the seabed and the ocean floor, and contributes to the process of general and complete disarmament under strict and effective international control.[33] All State parties are obligated

> not to implant or emplace on the seabed and the ocean floor and in the subsoil thereof beyond the [12-mile outer limit] any nuclear weapons or any other types of weapons of mass destruction as well as structures, launching installations or any other facilities specifically designed for storing, testing or using such weapons.[34]

Nevertheless, the 1971 Seabed Treaty only concerns the prohibition on the use of nuclear weapons and other types of weapons of mass destruction, which were considered to have special verification procedures.[35] The freedom to use other, less destructive weapons or military devices on

[28] Convention on the Continental Shelf, Articles 2(1), 3.
[29] O'Connell (1982) 488.
[30] Convention on the High Seas (29 April 1958, in force 30 September 1962) 450 UNTS 11, Article 2.
[31] Ibid Article 26(2); Convention on the Continental Shelf Article 4.
[32] Treaty on the Prohibition of the Emplacement of Nuclear Weapons and Other Weapons of Mass Destruction on the Sea-bed and Ocean Floor and in the Subsoil Thereof (11 February 1971, in force 18 May 1972) 955 UNTS 115 (1971 Seabed Treaty).
[33] Ibid Preamble.
[34] Ibid Articles 1(1), 2.
[35] David L. Larson, 'Security, Disarmament and the Law of the Sea' (1979) 3 Marine Policy 40, 43.

the seabed and ocean floor was not affected by the 1971 Seabed Treaty so long as their use did not interfere with international navigation or other legitimate uses of the ocean.

During the negotiation of the 1971 Seabed Treaty in 1970, the United Nations General Assembly (UNGA) adopted the Declaration of Principles Governing the Seabed and the Ocean Floor (Declaration of Principles).[36] The Declaration of Principles explicitly reserves the seabed and the ocean floor and subsoil thereof beyond the limits of national jurisdiction exclusively for peaceful purposes, 'without prejudice to any measures which have been or may be agreed upon in the context of international negotiations undertaken in the field of disarmament and which have be applicable to a broader area'.[37] Although UNCLOS does not contain any provisions on disarmament or arms control in ocean space, the thrust of discussion at the Third United Nations Conference on the Law of the Sea (Third Conference) and the final provisions are premised upon the guidelines established by the Declaration of Principles and the 1971 Seabed Treaty.[38]

Safeguarding free naval movement was one of the primary motivations of the major maritime powers in negotiating UNCLOS in light of the irreversible trend of extended coastal States' claims.[39] Meanwhile, contrasting proposals were made by Malta and other States at an early stage to include coastal States' security rights and jurisdiction in the EEZ.[40] Since it was not possible to reconcile this disagreement, military uses were left out from the formal debate and consequently not expressly addressed in UNCLOS.[41]

[36] United Nations General Assembly (UNGA) Res 2749(XXV), Declaration of Principles Governing the Sea-Bed and Ocean Floor, and the Sub-Soil thereof, beyond the Limits of National Jurisdiction, 17 December 1970.

[37] Ibid para. 8.

[38] Larson (1979) 44.

[39] Bernard H. Oxman, 'The Regime of Warships under the United Nations Convention on the Law of the Sea' (1983–1984) 24 Va J Int'l L 809, 831–832, 835–841; Satya N. Nandan with Kristine E. Dalaker, *Reflections on the Making of the Modern Law of the Sea* (National University of Singapore Press 2021) 93.

[40] Shigeru Oda, *The Law of the Sea in Our Time II: The United Nations Seabed Committee, 1968–1973* (Sijthoff Leyden 1977) 284–285; UNGA, Committee on the Peaceful Uses of the Sea-bed and the Ocean Floor beyond the Limits of National Jurisdiction, Sub-Committee II, A/AC.138/SC.II/L.28, 16 July 1973, Malta.

[41] Francisco Orrego Vicuña, *The Exclusive Economic Zone: Regime and Legal Nature under International Law* (Cambridge University Press 1989) 108; Boleslaw A. Boczek, 'Peaceful Purposes Provisions of the United Nations Convention on the Law of the Sea' (1989) 20 (4) Ocean Dev & Int'l L 359, 368–370.

With the establishment of the EEZ, there is an important difference between the legal regimes of the areas within and beyond the 200 NM limit. As its name indicates, the primary purpose of establishing the EEZ is to maximise the economic benefits of the coastal State in the adjacent sea area. Consequently, the rights over natural resources, including fishing, jurisdiction to construct artificial islands for all purposes and installations or structures for economic purposes, and to conduct marine scientific research in the EEZ, have been drastically curtailed compared to those on the high seas, and are subject to the jurisdiction of the coastal State.[42] However, the important high seas freedoms for communication have been explicitly preserved. All States enjoy the freedoms of 'navigation and overflight and of the laying of submarine cables and pipelines, and other internationally lawful uses of the sea related to these freedoms'.[43] There was no explicit reference to military activities in the current attribution of rights and freedoms in the EEZ, which veraciously fall under the realm of unattributed rights and duties based on the *sui generis* character of the EEZ.

On the one hand, the coastal State has sovereign rights and functional jurisdiction in the EEZ, as well as over the continental shelf. These are 'sovereign rights' exercised 'for the purpose of exploring and exploiting, conserving and managing the natural resources' and 'jurisdiction' in respect of certain other specified activities and purposes in conjunction with consequential duties.[44] Military uses, however, are not automatically included in these sovereign rights and jurisdiction. This is consistent with the drafting history of the provisions concerning the coastal State's sovereign rights over the continental shelf.[45]

On the other hand, States hold different views with regard to whether the freedom to conduct military activities in a foreign EEZ was automatically included in Article 58(1) during the negotiation of UNCLOS and after its adoption.[46] The original version of Article 58, which preserves

42 UNCLOS Articles 56(1), 60(1), 87(1).

43 UNCLOS Article 58(1).

44 UNCLOS Articles 56(1), 77(1); Myron H. Nordquist, Satya N. Nandan and Shabtai Rosenne (eds.), *United Nations Convention on the Law of the Sea 1982: A Commentary*, Vol. II (Martinus Nijhoff 1993) 525.

45 O'Connell (1982) 488; Nordquist, Nandan and Rosenne (1993) 895–896.

46 R. Galindo Pohl, 'The Exclusive Economic Zone in the Light of Negotiations of the Third United Nations Conference on the Law of the Sea', in Francisco Orrego Vicuña (ed.), *The Exclusive Economic Zone: A Latin American Perspective* (Westview Press 1984) 55; Francesco Francioni, 'Peacetime Use of Force, Military Activities, and the New Law of

the freedoms for all States in the EEZ, appeared in the 1975 text produced by the Evensen Group, and read as 'the freedoms of navigation and overflight and of the laying of submarine cables and pipelines and other internationally lawful uses of the sea related to navigation and communication'.[47] The Castañeda-Vindenes Group replaced 'navigation and communication' with 'these freedoms' and added 'such as those associated with the operation of ships, aircraft and submarine cables and pipelines, and compatible with the other provisions of [UNCLOS]'.[48] Subsequent attempts to limit the scope of the proposed high seas freedoms in the EEZ were not accepted.[49] The formula proposed by the Castañeda-Vindenes Group was adopted as part of the final text of Article 58(1). The change to 'related to these freedoms' considerably clarified and possibly expanded the freedoms preserved in the EEZ.[50] It has been argued that international law historically considers military activity a lawful use of the high seas associated with the operation of warships and military aircraft exercising the freedoms of navigation and overflight.[51] Therefore, these changes served the intention of preserving the maritime State's military uses rights in the EEZ and arguably included naval operations under 'other internationally lawful uses of the sea'.[52]

However, a number of States made declarations when signing UNCLOS to express their opinion on these controversial aspects of military uses of the sea. Brazil declared that 'the provisions of the Convention do not authorise other States to carry out in the exclusive economic zone military exercises or manoeuvres, in particular those that imply the use of weapons or explosives, without the consent of the coastal

the Sea' (1985) 18 Cornell Int'l LJ 203, 213–216; A. V. Lowe, 'Some Legal Problems Arising from the Use of the Seas for Military Purposes' (1986) 10 Marine Policy 171, 179–180; YannHuei (Billy) Song, 'China and the Military Use of the Ocean' (1990) 21(2) Ocean Dev & Int'l L 213, 216–217; 王泽林,《论专属经济区内的外国军事活动》,法学杂志,2010年第3期,123–125,第123–124 (WANG Zelin, 'On Foreign Military Operation In Exclusive Economic Zone' (2010) 3 Law Science Magazine 123, 123–124); Moritaka Hayashi, 'Military Activities in the Exclusive Economic Zones of Foreign Coastal States', in David Freestone (ed.), *The 1982 Law of the Sea Convention at 30: Successes, Challenges and New Agendas* (Martinus Nijhoff 2013) 121–129.

47 Nordquist, Nandan and Rosenne (1993) 558.

48 Ibid 561–562.

49 Ibid 563.

50 Galdorisi and Kaufman (2001) 272.

51 Brown (1982–1983) 533.

52 Barbara Kwiatkowska, 'Military Uses in the EEZ – A Reply' (1987) 11 Marine Policy 249, 249.

State'.[53] Similar declarations and positions are maintained by Bangladesh, Cabo Verde, Ecuador, India, Malaysia, Pakistan, Thailand and Uruguay.[54] In contrast, other maritime States have expressly rejected such limitations on the traditional freedom of navigation. For example, Germany specifically stated:

> [a]ccording to the Convention, the coastal State does not enjoy residual rights in the exclusive economic zone. In particular, the rights and jurisdiction of the coastal State in such zone do not include the rights to obtain notification of military exercises or manoeuvres or to authorize them.[55]

Italy, the Netherlands and the United Kingdom made similar statements.[56]

The question of military uses of the sea touches on political sensitivities and balance of power paradigms that were deliberately avoided during the negotiations at the three UN Conferences on the Law of the Sea. As a result, there is no provision in UNCLOS that clearly states whether the EEZ can be used for military purposes by either the coastal State or other States. The negotiation history and subsequent State practice fail to reveal a unified interpretation of relevant provisions in Part V. Regardless of the attribution of the right to use the EEZ for military purposes, there are certain rules to follow when conducting military activities therein. The general requirement is that the EEZ is reserved for peaceful purposes only, and all States must refrain from any threat or use of force inconsistent with general international law.[57]

53 UNCLOS, Declarations and Statements, Brazil, Declaration upon Signature (10 December 1982), https://treaties.un.org/Pages/ViewDetailsIII.aspx?src=TREATY&mtdsg_no=XXI-6&chapter=21&Temp=mtdsg3&clang=_en.

54 UNCLOS, Bangladesh, Declaration made upon Ratification (27 July 2001) para 1; Cabo Verde, Declaration made upon Signature (10 December 1982) and confirmed upon Ratification (19 August 1987) para v; Ecuador, Declaration made upon Ratification (24 September 2012) para XVIII; India, Declaration made upon Ratification (29 June 1995) para (b); Malaysia, Declaration made upon Ratification (14 October 1996) para 3; Pakistan, Declaration made upon Ratification (26 February 1997) para (iii); Thailand, Declaration made upon Ratification (15 May 2011) para I(4); Uruguay, Declaration made upon Signature (10 December 1982) para (D).

55 UNCLOS, Germany, Declaration upon Accession (14 October 1994).

56 UNCLOS, Italy, Declarations made upon Signature (7 December 1984) and confirmed upon Ratification (13 January 1995); the Netherlands, Declaration upon Ratification (28 June 1996) para B(II)(2) and (4); UK, Declaration upon Accession (25 July 1997) para (a).

57 UNCLOS Articles 58(2), 88, 301.

In addition, States must have due regard to each other when exercising their legitimate rights and performing their duties.[58]

6.1.3 *Obligations in Conducting Peacetime Military Activities*

6.1.3.1 The Reservation for Peaceful Purposes/Uses

The concept of peaceful purposes was introduced into the law of the sea by the Declaration of Principles, and repeatedly has been referred to as 'peaceful uses' or 'peaceful purposes' in the Preamble and various provisions of UNCLOS.[59] Among these, three provisions are relevant to the EEZ. Article 88 provides that the high seas and, through cross-reference by Article 58(2), the EEZ 'shall be reserved for peaceful purposes'. Article 240(3) requires that the coastal State give consent for marine scientific research projects in its EEZ that will be conducted by other States 'exclusively for peaceful purposes'. Finally, Article 301 on 'peaceful uses of the sea' is applicable to all aspects of the rights and duties of State parties in the maritime context.

A general debate on the 'peaceful uses of ocean space: zones of peace and security' took place at the fourth session of the Third Conference in 1976, which centred on whether military activities in the ocean were permitted.[60] Many States, including Peru, Ecuador and Madagascar, interpreted 'peaceful purposes' as prohibiting all military activities; other States, the United States among them, interpreted it as prohibiting all military activities for aggressive purposes only, but not for the use of military means of communication; a third group argued that the test of whether an activity is 'peaceful' depends on whether it is consistent with the UN Charter and other rules of international law.[61] The formulation adopted in UNCLOS Article 301 echoes the view of the third group:

[58] UNCLOS Article 58(3).

[59] UNGA Res 2749(XXV) paras 5, 8; UNCLOS Articles 88, 141, 143(1), 147(2), 155(2), 240 (a), 242(1), 246(3), 301.

[60] Third United Nations Conference on the Law of the Sea (Third Conference), Official Records, Vol. V: Fourth Session, Summary Records of Meetings, Plenary Meetings: A/CONF.62/SR.66, Sixtieth Meeting (19 April 1976); A/CONF.62/SR.68, Sixty-eighth Meeting (26 April 1976), 54–68; De Muralt (1985) 79.

[61] Third Conference, Official Records, Vol. V: Fourth Session, Summary Records of Meetings, Plenary Meetings: A/CONF.62/SR.68, Sixty-eighth Meeting (26 April 1976) 65–66 (Iran: para 24); United States, Message from the President of the United States Transmitting United Nations Convention on the Law of the Sea and the Agreement on

> In exercising their rights and performing their duties under this Convention, States Parties shall refrain from any threat or use of force against the territorial integrity or political independence of any State, or in any other manner inconsistent with the principles of international law embodied in the Charter of the United Nations.

Thus, military activities that are consistent with the principles of international law embodied in the UN Charter, in particular with Article 2(4) and Article 51, are not *prima facie* prohibited by UNCLOS.[62]

This interpretation of Article 301 is supported by the fact that numerous provisions of UNCLOS either acknowledge legitimate military activities or enumerate non-acceptable ones.[63] Warships and governmental non-commercial ships are not only recognised but are also granted complete immunity from the jurisdiction of any State other than their flag State.[64] This indicates that, in UNCLOS at least, the use of warships or military aircraft does not equate to non-peaceful purposes.[65] Moreover, the prohibition of certain military activities that are incompatible with innocent passage within the territorial sea implies that these activities may be permissible in other parts of the sea if not explicitly prohibited.[66] Furthermore, the optional exclusion of military activities from compulsory judicial settlement is another example indicating the existence, if not the recognition, of military uses of the sea.[67]

Therefore, the requirement of 'peaceful purposes/uses' means that the use of ocean space or the purpose of activities conducted therein or thereabove must not involve a threat or use of force against the territorial integrity or political independence of a State, or in any manner inconsistent with the principles of international law embodied in the UN Charter. 'Peaceful purposes/uses' per se does not exclusively curb military

Implementation of Part XI, Senate Treaty Doc. 103–39, 7 October 1994, 94 www.foreign.senate.gov/imo/media/doc/treaty_103-39.pdf (US Commentary (1994)).

62 Report of the Secretary-General, 'General and Complete Disarmament: Study on the Naval Arms Race', para. 188, A/40/535 (17 September 1985)' (1985) 1 Int'l Org & L Sea Documentary YB 1; Charlotte Beaucillon, 'Limiting Third States' Military Activities in the EEZ: "Due Regard Obligations" and the Law on the Use of Force Applied to Nuclear Weapons' (2019) 34 Int'l J Marine & Coastal L 128, 131–132.

63 Oxman (1983–1984) 814–815; Boleslaw Adam Boczek, 'Peacetime Military Activities in the Exclusive Economic Zone of Third Countries' (1988) 19 Ocean Dev Int'l L 445, 457–458.

64 UNCLOS Articles 32, 95, 96, 236.

65 Kwiatkowska (1989) 204.

66 UNCLOS Article 19(2).

67 UNCLOS Article 298(1)(b).

activities on the high seas or in the EEZ. Therefore, military activities at sea are not *prima facie* prohibited by UNCLOS. The question thus hinges on what constitutes a 'threat or use of force' as codified in Article 301.

6.1.3.2 The Prohibition on the Threat or Use of Force

The phrase 'threat or use of force' in UNCLOS Article 301 is drawn from Article 2(4) of the UN Charter to provide an answer to the question of what criteria are required to qualify as 'peaceful purpose/uses'. Article 2 (4) provides that '[a]ll Members shall refrain in their international relations from the threat or use of force against the territorial integrity or political independence of any State, or in any other manner inconsistent with the Purpose of the United Nations'. Although not identical, UNCLOS Article 301 echoes the obligation laid down in Article 2(4) of the UN Charter. The replacement of 'the' by 'any' in front of the phrase 'threat or use of force' and the expression of 'the principles of international law embodied in the [Charter]' instead of 'the purposes of the United Nations' arguably broadens the scope of the 'threat or use of force' covered by Article 301.[68] It would cover all the principles of international law that are embodied in the UN Charter and not simply be limited to the four purposes of the UN identified in the UN Charter.[69] Subsequent UN resolutions and juridical decisions have contributed to clarifying the legal meaning of the phrase 'threat or use of force', although States remain divided on the interpretation of the vital subject of the phrase, and the application of the law varies depending on the facts of the episode itself.[70]

The term 'use of force' is relatively clear in referring to armed force used directly or indirectly by a State against another State that excludes 'political or economic coercion'.[71] Foremost, it prohibits 'the most serious and dangerous form of the illegal uses of force' – aggression – 'being

[68] Myron H. Nordquist, Shabtai Rosenne and Louis B. Sohn (eds.), *United Nations Convention on the Law of the Sea 1982: A Commentary*, Vol. V (Martinus Nijhoff 1989) 154.

[69] Ibid; UN Charter Article 1.

[70] Gray (2018) 10–11; James Crawford, *Brownlie's Principles of Public International Law* (9th ed., Oxford University Press 2019) 719–720; Olivier Corten, 'The Controversies over the Customary Prohibition on the Use of Force: A Methodological Debate' (2005) 16(5) European J Int'l L 803, 803; Harris and Sivakumaran (2015) 727–730.

[71] Crawford (2019) 720; UNGA A/Res/2625(XXV), 24 October 1970, Declaration on Principles of International Law Concerning Friendly Relations and Co-Operation among States in Accordance with the Charter of the United Nations, Preamble; Harris and Sivakumaran (2015) 727–728.

fraught, in the conditions created by the existence of all types of weapons of mass destruction, with the possible threat of world conflict and all its catastrophic consequences'.[72] Any invasion, attack or other action by the armed forces of a State against the sovereignty, territorial integrity or political independence of another State constitutes *prima facie* evidence of an act of aggression and falls under the prohibition of the use of force.[73] Moreover, as the International Court of Justice (ICJ) stated in the advisory opinion on the *Legality of the Threat or Use of Nuclear Weapons*, 'if the envisaged use of force is itself unlawful, the stated readiness to use it would be a threat prohibited under Article 2, paragraph 4'.[74] Furthermore, the focus is the verb 'use' to define the occurrence of the action without a requirement of consequences or the period of how long the force was used.

The term 'threat of force' in the context of armed force is disputed, especially when State practice shows a certain tolerance of it.[75] It has been interpreted that any such 'threat' must be closely tied to what the target State perceives as the 'readiness' of another State to use armed force, which is 'a state of extreme aggravation of contradictions, an immediate pre-conflict state' for an attempt to compel the targeted State to take or not to take certain actions.[76] In 1994, when 'Iraqi artillery and tanks were deployed in positions pointing towards and within range of Kuwait, with ammunition at the ready' on the Iraqi side of the border, this situation was argued at the UN Security Council debate to be a 'threat to Kuwait and a breach of the provisions of the Charter'.[77]

The meaning of the phrase 'territorial integrity or political independence' is also unclear.[78] The preparatory work for the UN Charter and the ICJ jurisprudence have demonstrated that this phrase was not intended to have a restrictive effect as 'respect for territorial sovereignty is an essential foundation of international relations', and international law requires political integrity to be respected.[79] Some States have used the

[72] UNGA A/Res/3314(XXIX), 14 December 1974, Definition of Aggression, Preamble.
[73] Ibid paras 1–3.
[74] Legality of the Threat or Use of Nuclear Weapons, Advisory Opinion of 8 July 1996, ICJ Reports 1996, p. 226, para 47.
[75] Crawford (2019) 720.
[76] Alexander S. Skaridov, 'Naval Activity in the Foreign EEZ: The Role of Terminology in Law Regime' (2005) 29 Marine Policy 153, 153–154.
[77] Harris and Sivakumaran (2015) 729.
[78] Beaucillon (2019) 135–136.
[79] Crawford (2019) 720; The Corfu Channel Case, Merits, Judgement of 9 April 1949, ICJ Reports 1949, p. 4, 35; Case Concerning Military and Paramilitary Activities in and

right of 'humanitarian intervention' as a justification to allow the threat or use of force against another State to establish democracy or another preferred political system.[80] However, such practice is limited in number and support, thus it neither presages nor constitutes a change in the customary law that prohibits intervention.[81] Meanwhile, many States insist that any form of use of armed force, whatever the purpose or duration, violates the prohibition on all use of force against another State.[82] If there is ambiguity on the interpretation and application of the phrase, the principle of effectiveness should be applied.[83] Arguably, it is the targeted State that has the right to claim that it is under such threat.

The alternative qualifier is when the threat or use of force is in any other manner inconsistent with the principles of international law embodied in the UN Charter. The language of Article 301 therefore covers all the principles of international law that are embodied in the Charter. This broad coverage was a compromise between two ideologically diverse groups at the Third Conference, where one side aimed for complete demilitarisation of the sea whereas the other side wanted to have limited application of the prohibition of the use of force.[84] Among those principles brought in by UNCLOS Article 301, the inherent right of self-defence, as set out in Article 51 of the Charter, 'is unimpaired and may require adaptation to the new concepts introduced by the Convention'.[85]

In *Guyana/Suriname*, the arbitral tribunal was of the view that the order given by the Surinamese official by radio to the Guyanese rig 'constituted an explicit threat that force might be used if the order was not complied with', based primarily on the testimony of witnesses to the incident that they were convinced of 'unspecified consequences'.[86] The

Against Nicaragua (Nicaragua v. United States of America), Merits, Judgement of 27 July 1986, ICJ Reports 1986, p. 14, para 202.

[80] Gray (2018) 30–33; Oscar Schachter, 'The Legality of Pro-Democratic Invasion' (1984) 78 Am J Int'l L 645, 648–649.

[81] Crawford (2019) 726–729; Military and Paramilitary Activities (Nicaragua v. United States of America) (1986) para 209.

[82] Gray (2018) 30–33; Schachter (1984) 648–649.

[83] Harris and Sivakumaran (2015) 730.

[84] Killian O'Brien, 'Article 301', in Alexander Proelss (ed.), United Nations Convention on the Law of the Sea: A Commentary (Hart 2017) 1947.

[85] Nordquist, Rosenne and Sohn (1989) 154.

[86] Arbitral Tribunal Constituted Pursuant to Article 287, and in Accordance with Annex VII, of the United Nations Convention on the Law of the Sea in the Matter of an Arbitration between Guyana and Suriname (Guyana v. Suriname), Award, 17 September 2007, PCA Case No. 2004-04, 143–144, para 439.

tribunal accepted that 'force may be used in law enforcement activities provided that such force is unavoidable, reasonable and necessary', but concluded that Suriname's action 'seemed more akin to a threat of military action rather than a mere law enforcement activity'.[87] Since it is 'illegal for a State to threaten force to secure territory from another State, or to cause it to follow or not follow certain political or economic paths', the Surinamese threat of the use of force to expel the Guyanese rig from the disputed area breached Article 2(4) of the UN Charter and general international law.[88]

The decision of the arbitral tribunal was criticised for setting a low threshold for determining whether a specific act constitutes the threat of force in violation of Article 2(4).[89] The order was given by a Surinamese navy vessel to a Guyanese private rig and drill ship operated by CGX, Guyana's licensee for commercial activities, within an area that was approximately 50 NM from the baseline.[90] Therefore, such an action cannot be considered as a threat of force directly against the 'political independence' of Guyana, the sovereign State. In addition, this incident took place in the disputed area of the continental shelf, where neither Suriname nor Guyana has territorial rights.[91] Hence, the threat given by the Surinamese navy was not against the 'territorial integrity' of Guyana. An alternative argument could be that the Surinamese navy's threat of unspecified consequences was a threat 'inconsistent with the purposes of the United Nations', which include the settlement of dispute by peaceful means and therefore violated Article 2(4).[92] Contrary to the tribunal's assessment, such a threat should be categorised as a law enforcement activity that violated the safeguards laid down in UNCLOS and general international law whereby 'the use of force must be avoided as far as

[87] Ibid 147, para 445.

[88] Ibid 143–144, paras 439–440.

[89] Gray (2018) 30; Tom Ruys, *'Armed Attack' and Article 51 of the UN Charter: Evolutions in Customary Law and Practice* (Cambridge University Press 2010) 121, 210; Atsuko Kanehara, 'A Legal and Practical Arrangement of Disputes Concerning Maritime Boundaries Pending Their Final Solution and Law Enforcement: From a Japanese Perspective', in Norman A. Martínez Gutiérrez (ed.), *Serving the Rule of International Maritime Law: Essays in Honour of Professor David Joseph Attard* (Routledge 2010) 109.

[90] Guyana v. Suriname 30, para 140; Memorial of the Republic of Guyana, Volume 1, 22 February 2005, 5.9.

[91] Guyana v. Suriname 32–33, paras 150–151.

[92] Harris and Sivakumaran (2015) 729.

possible and, where force is unavoidable, it must not go beyond what is reasonable and necessary in the circumstances'.[93]

Directly incorporating the obligation under the UN Charter has the effect of emphasising its implementation in the context of the law of the sea. Particularly in view of Article 103 of the UN Charter, obligations under the Charter have the highest priority in the event of a conflict between the obligations of different international agreements.[94] UNCLOS Article 301 has not introduced any additional obligations beyond Article 2(4) whereby the prohibition of the threat or use of force is limited in international relations.[95] The 'threat or use of force' prohibited in Article 2(4) must be applied restrictively and distinctively from activities that constitute 'breach of peace', 'armed attack' or mere 'law enforcement'.[96] Military activities that do not involve the threat or use of force against the territorial integrity or political independence of another State, or violate the principles of international law recognised in the UN Charter, are not prohibited under Article 301.[97]

6.1.3.3 Obligation of Due Regard

Another limitation on using ocean space for military purposes is that the operating State must have due regard for the interests of other States in exercising their rights and obligations.[98] More broadly, in fulfilling their

[93] M/V 'Saiga' (No. 2) (Saint Vincent and the Grenadines v. Guinea), Judgment of 1 July 1999, ITLOS Reports 1999, p. 10, para. 155. See opposite opinion and discussion in Patricia Jimenez Kwast, 'Maritime Law Enforcement and the Use of Force: Reflections on the Categorisation of Forcible Action at Sea in the Light of the Guyana/Suriname Award' (2008) 13 J Conflict & Security L 77; Jianjun Gao, 'Comments on Guyana v. Suriname' (2009) 8 Chinese J Int'l L 199.

[94] UN Charter Article 103.

[95] Boczek (1989) 370–371.

[96] Gray (2018) 36–40; Bruno Simma (ed.), *The Charter of the United Nations: A Commentary*, Vol. I (2nd ed., Oxford University Press 2002) 117–125; 金永明,《中美专属经济区内军事活动争议的海洋法剖析》,太平洋学报,第19卷第11期,2011年11月,74–81,第76页 (JIN Yongming, 'A Dissection of Disputes between China and the United States over Military Activities in Exclusive Economic Zone by the Law of the Sea' (2011) 19(11) Pacific Journal 74, 76).

[97] Myron H. Nordquist, Satya N. Nandan and Shabtai Rosenne (eds.), *United Nations Convention on the Law of the Sea 1982: A Commentary*, Vol. III (Martinus Nijhoff 1995) 91; James Kraska, *Maritime Power and the Law of the Sea: Expeditionary Operations in World Politics* (Oxford University Press 2011) 253; O'Brien (2017) 1944.

[98] UNCLOS Articles 58(2)–(3), 87(2).

reciprocal due regard obligation, States must act in good faith and exercise their rights, jurisdiction and freedoms 'in a manner which would not constitute an abuse of right'.[99]

The drafting history of the provisions of the EEZ show that early proposals first established the new sovereign rights and jurisdiction of coastal States as intrusions to the high seas freedoms and then made efforts to preserve certain freedoms for all States.[100] As discussed in Chapter 3, the inclusion of a mutual due regard obligation emphasises that both parties' rights and freedoms are not absolute, but must be exercised in a reasonable and fair way so as not to infringe another State's freedoms or rights.[101] The reciprocal duties of due regard contain both substantive and procedural aspects concerning the actions of both sides.[102] In respect to conducting military activities in the EEZ, the operating State must recognise, consider and balance the legitimate rights and obligations of other States, and act in good faith to consult and negotiate in the event of a conflict.[103]

The reciprocal due regard obligation reflects the basic principle of establishing and maintaining an appropriate balance of rights and freedoms between the coastal State and other States in the EEZ. However, there are no agreed specific criteria for States to measure whether their conduct of military activities has fulfilled the due regard obligation. The question of whether an activity is conducted in accordance with the due regard obligation therefore must be decided on a case-by-case basis by the States involved. In some cases, other relevant provisions will assist with the interpretation of the connotation of the due regard obligation. For example, the coastal State may not establish military artificial islands, installations and structures 'where interference may be caused to the use

[99] UNCLOS Article 300.

[100] Nordquist, Nandan and Rosenne (1993) 556.

[101] See discussion in Chapter 3 in this volume. Moritaka Hayashi, 'Military and Intelligence Gathering Activities in the EEZ: Definition of Key Terms' (2005) 29 Marine Policy 123, 133.

[102] Tullio Scovazzi, '"Due Regard" Obligations, with Particular Emphasis of Fisheries in the Exclusive Economic Zone' (2019) 34 Int'l J Marine & Coastal L 56, 63.

[103] Ibid; Ioannis Prezas, 'Foreign Military Activities in the Exclusive Economic Zone: Remarks on the Applicability and Scope of the Reciprocal 'Due Regard' Duties of Coastal and Third States' (2019) 34 Int'l J Marine & Coastal L 97, 105–107; George K. Walker, 'Defining Terms in the 1982 Law of the Sea Convention IV: The Last Round of Definitions Proposed by the International Law Association (American Branch) Law of the Sea Committee' (2005) 36 Cal West Int'l LJ 133, 174–175.

of recognised sea lanes essential to international navigation'.[104] Also, one can confidently say that activities of any kind that could cause significant damage to the natural resources being exploited by the coastal State or deny access to the area of such exploitation would be contrary to the due regard obligation.[105]

Moreover, it has been argued that the reciprocal obligations of due regard flow also 'from the States Parties' obligation to protect and preserve the marine environment, a fundamental principle underlined in Articles 192 and 193 of the Convention'.[106] Although a military entity is exempted from the environmental provisions of UNCLOS, the operating State must adopt appropriate measures, on the basis of not impairing operations or operational capabilities of such entities, to ensure that they act in a manner consistent, so far as is reasonable and practicable, with the environmental provisions.[107] In particular, the operating State has the responsibility to ensure that activities within its jurisdiction or control, including military activities, do not cause damage to the environment of other States.[108]

In conclusion, even on the high seas, the freedom to conduct military activities is neither absolute nor static, but is a balanced right that subjects States to the duty of having due regard for the interests of other States and for peaceful purposes.[109] Moreover, States may conclude bilateral or multilateral agreements to regulate conflicting uses of the sea.[110] Additional restrictions on the freedom to use ocean spaces for military purposes are predictable according to the legal regime of the specific sea area where such activities take place. States have been conducting military activities for various purposes within their own EEZ and

[104] UNCLOS Article 60(7).

[105] Oxman (1983–1984) 838; Sam Bateman, 'The Regime of the EEZ: Military Activities and the Need for Compromise?' in Tafsir M. Ndiaye and Rüdiger Wolfrum (eds.), *Law of the Sea, Environmental Law and Settlement of Disputes* (Martinus Nijhoff 2007) 569, 573.

[106] Request for an Advisory Opinion submitted by the Sub-regional Fisheries Commission (SRFC), Advisory Opinion of 2 April 2015, ITLOS Reports 2015, p. 4, para 216; Prezas (2019) 107–108.

[107] UNCLOS Articles 192, 194(4), 236, 300; Pascale Ricard, 'The Limitations on Military Activities by Third States in the EEZ Resulting from Environmental Law' (2019) 34 Int'l J Marine & Coastal L 144, 151–152.

[108] UNCLOS Article 194(2); Declaration of the United Nations Conference on the Human Environment (Stockholm, 16 June 1972), UN Doc A/Conf.48/14/Rev.1 (1973), Principle 21; Rio Declaration on Environment and Development (Rio de Janeiro, June 1992), UN Doc A/CONF.151/26 (Vol. I) (12 August 1992), Principle 2; Ricard (2019) 155–157.

[109] UNCLOS Articles 87(2), 88; O'Connell (1988) 796–797.

[110] UNCLOS Article 311.

in another State's EEZ, but the extent to which rights and duties are modified or affected remains a controversial matter.

6.2 Military Security in the Exclusive Economic Zone

UNCLOS has established the EEZ as a *sui generis* zone that is neither subject to coastal State sovereignty nor possessing high seas status.[111] UNCLOS grants the economic interests exclusively to the coastal State and reserves communication freedoms to all States. Military security interests, in general, are not explicitly attributed to either the coastal State or other States.[112] Nonetheless, a diverse group of States have asserted security claims beyond the limit of the territorial sea to varying degrees. Essentially, this phenomenon reflects the fact that maritime space is commonly linked with the concept of global security, which inevitably affects territorial interests.[113]

6.2.1 National Security Interests at Sea

Freedom of the seas, especially the free movement of military forces, has come to be regarded as essential for maintaining and advancing the national security interests of States.[114] However, national security interests alone are not a solid foundation for seeking to qualify the freedom to use the sea under the jurisdiction of another State for military purposes, as security interests are adjusted according to the changing international environment and are often confronted by the extension of national jurisdiction by the coastal State for security purposes.[115] The scope and meaning accorded to the notion of national security at sea – however different according to the coastal State or other States – influence which interests need to be protected and which activities need to be regulated.

States, coastal or landlocked, large or small, use ocean space for a great variety of purposes under many different circumstances.[116] The ocean is

[111] UNCLOS Article 55.
[112] Tallinn Manual 2.0 (2017) 240.
[113] Kraska (2011) 302; Natalie Klein, *Maritime Security and the Law of the Sea* (Oxford University Press 2011) 4.
[114] Kraska (2011) 153.
[115] O'Connell (1988) 796–797.
[116] McDougal and Burke (1985) 14–15.

not only the place for natural resource development but also the centre of sea lanes communication and other human activities, including military activities.[117] Ensuring the use of the ocean for military training and planning, manoeuvres, weapons testing or other military operations is essential for maintaining and enhancing the capability of States to protect their security interests at sea.[118] Consequently, the adjacent sea areas are of crucial importance to promoting States' strategic and military interests. For these purposes, States are advancing claims not only to the use of ocean space under their jurisdiction but also to securing effective and efficient access to the ocean space of others, as well as to sharing in the benefits of using the high seas.[119]

On the one hand, coastal States have concerns in relation to national security interests and the protection of natural resources and the marine environment in the adjacent sea areas and tend to extend their control as far as possible to prevent threats coming from the sea.[120] This includes placing limitations on foreign military activities in the EEZ.[121] The development of new military technologies has enabled the proliferation of a number of small and medium-sized navies to control their immediate maritime domains, which contributes to an overall trend in which more States are in favour of limiting the freedom of use of the seas.[122] China, for example, has on various occasions protested and challenged foreign military activities, especially reconnaissance conducted within its EEZ, and asserted that such activities endangered China's national security interests.[123]

117 Kraska (2011) 139.

118 Peter A. Dutton, 'Caelum Liberum: Air Defense Identification Zones Outside Sovereign Airspace' (2009) 103 Am J Int'l L 691, 707–708.

119 McDougal and Burke (1985) 17–18.

120 Klein (2011) 26–27.

121 Kraska (2011) 214; 郑雷，《论中国对专属经济区内他国军事活动的法律立场—以"无暇号"事件为视角》，法学家，2011年第1期，137–146，第140–144页 (ZHENG Lei, 'The Chinese Legal Position on Foreign Military Activities in the EEZ – from the Perspective of the USNS Impeccable Incident' (2011) 1 The Jurist 137, 140–144); 贺赞，《专属经济区内的有限军事活动自由》，政法论坛，第33卷第4期，2015年07月，160–167，第161–162页 (HE Zan, 'The Limited Freedom of Military Activities in the Exclusive Economic Zone' (2015) 33(4) Tribune of Political Science and Law 160, 161–162).

122 Kerry Lynn Nankivell, 'A Review of "Maritime Power and the Law of the Sea: Expeditionary Operations in World Politics"' (2011) 42(4) Ocean Dev Int'l L 383, 384.

123 Xiaofeng Ren, 'Commentary on Guidelines for Military and Intelligence Gathering Activities in the EEZ: Freedom of Navigation and Over-Flight does not Equal to Freedom of Military and Intelligence Gather', EEZ Group 21 Honolulu Meeting, East-West Center, Hawaii, USA, 9–10 December 2003; Guangqian Peng, 'China's Maritime

On the other hand, some States, notably powerful maritime States such as the United States, continue to consider maximising mobility in ocean space to be a fundamental national interest.[124] These States argue that ensuring a naval power retains the authority for unimpeded access to the global commons will help to prevent the emergence of security threats on and above the ocean, especially in regions where coastal States have insufficient maritime capacity to maintain order without external assistance.[125] This authority is known as 'expeditionary sea power', a military operation 'to accomplish a specific objective on the periphery or in a foreign country', which relies on the rapid deployment of naval forces.[126] This concern reflects the situation in the Horn of Africa, where international authorities have been brought in to assist the coastal States, primarily Somalia, in gathering military forces for preventing and combatting piracy and international terrorists and for providing security and order at sea.[127]

A somewhat mixed set of policies towards security interests at sea shows that most States pursue policies that enhance their national security while simultaneously fighting to limit the strategic capabilities of their opponents. However, no State can, or should, simply assert control in its own maritime neighbourhood by restraining a foreign presence while seeking unlimited and unimpeded access to areas under the jurisdiction of another State. In addition, the race for control may lead to a situation where States are suspicious of each other's intention in asserting power, and in return seek to accumulate increased power, but not necessarily feel more secure.[128] Unless there is a self-sustaining process built on mutual

Rights and Interests', in Dutton (2010) 15–21; 郑雷 (2011),第143页 (ZHENG (2011) 143); 周忠海和张小奕,《论专属经济区中的军事研究和测量活动》,法学杂志,2012年第10期,101–105,第103–104页 (ZHOU Zhonghai and ZHANG Xiaoyi, 'On Military Research and Military Survey in Exclusive Economic Zone' (2012) 10 Law Science Magazine 101, 103–104).

124 James Kraska, 'The Law of the Sea Convention: A National Security Success – Global Strategic Mobility Through the Rule of Law' (2007) 39 Geo Wash Int'l L Rev 543, 547–548; The Law of the Sea Convention (Treaty Doc. 103-39), Hearings before the Committee on Foreign Relations United States Senate, 112 Congress, Second Session, June 14 2012, 'Perspectives from the U.S. Military', S. HRG. 112–654.

125 Dutton (2009) 707–708.

126 Kraska (2011) 179.

127 United Nations Security Council S/RES/1816 (2008), 2 June 2008, Preamble.

128 Shiping Tang, *A Theory of Security Strategy for Our Time: Defensive Realism* (Palgrave Macmillan 2010) 39.

understanding, this situation will become a vicious cycle that may provoke unnecessary conflicts, especially in times of political intensity.

It is inevitable that States want to pursue their national security interests at sea, but their approaches to achieving security vary significantly since they have different perspectives on what constitutes their prioritised interests at a given time. Although contributing to 'the strengthening of peace, security, co-operation and friendly relations among all nations' is a goal of the codification and progressive development of the law of the sea, security interests have never been clearly recognised in the EEZ under UNCLOS.[129] However, the recognition of coastal States' sovereign rights in the EEZ has given them a broader capacity to regulate activities taking place within adjacent sea areas and to prevent threats to their economic interests. It is often in this respect that some coastal States use creative interpretations of their granted rights to incorporate security interests in their EEZ.

6.2.2 Security Claims over the Exclusive Economic Zone

Within the territorial sea, foreign vessels must not act in a manner 'prejudicial to the peace, good order or security of the coastal State', but such language was not included in the provisions concerning either the contiguous zone or the EEZ.[130] The desire to protect sovereignty and national interests has driven some States to become more creative and expansive in their definition and interpretation of national security interests, most frequently beyond the limit of their territorial seas.[131] State practice reveals three main approaches: claiming security interests in the contiguous zone; claiming jurisdiction over military surveys or the use of military structures or installations in the EEZ; and requiring consent for the conduct of military activities in the EEZ, especially military manoeuvres involving the use of weapons or explosives (Table 6.1).

It is notable that some States have retreated from their security claims in the EEZ in association with broader territorial sea claims. Chile, for example, was the first Latin American State to proclaim a 200 NM sovereign maritime zone in 1947, but brought its claims in line with

[129] UNCLOS Preamble, para 7.
[130] UNCLOS Articles 19, 33(1), 55–56.
[131] Kraska (2011) 302–304.

Table 6.1 *Security claims over the EEZ*

State	Claims
Bangladesh	Consent required for military exercises or manoeuvres, especially with weapons or explosives, in the EEZ or on the continental shelf[a]
Brazil	Consent required for military exercises and manoeuvres, in particular those involving the use of weapons or explosives; claims exclusive rights to the establishment, operation and use of all types of artificial islands, installations and structures in the EEZ without exception, whatever their nature or purpose[b]
Myanmar	Claims security interest in the contiguous zone; claims jurisdiction to establish a security area for offshore infrastructure in the EEZ[c]
Cabo Verde	Claims exclusive jurisdiction to any other rights not recognised by third States in the EEZ; claims jurisdiction over all installations and structures of any other nature; prohibits military exercises 'with weapons'[d]
Cambodia	Claims security interests in the contiguous zone and control of all foreign activities on the continental shelf irrespective of purpose[e]
China	Enforces security laws in the contiguous zone; requires authorisation for the laying of submarine cables and pipelines on the continental shelf; consent required to conduct any surveying and mapping activities in the EEZ[f]
DPR of Korea	Prohibits any foreign person, vessel or aircraft from installing facilities, taking photographs, investigating or surveying in the EEZ[g]
Ecuador	Claims exclusive right to all types of artificial islands, installations and structures within the 200 NM of its maritime territory; exercises all residual rights and jurisdiction; requires prior notification and authorisation for the entry of any warships, naval auxiliaries or other vessels or aircraft, or ships powered by nuclear energy; requires consent for any military exercises or manoeuvres of any type[h]
Egypt	Claims security jurisdiction to a further 6 NM zone beyond and contiguous to the territorial sea; regulates all matters relating to its EEZ[i]
El Salvador	Claims sovereignty and jurisdiction over the sea and its bed and subsoil to a distance of 200 NM[j] (In the *El Salvador v. Honduras* case, the ICJ judgment refers to the territorial sea, continental shelf and exclusive economic zone of El Salvador[k])

Table 6.1 (*cont.*)

State	Claims
Guyana	Claims exclusive rights and jurisdiction over artificial islands, offshore terminals, installations and other structures and devices for all purposes[l]
India	Claims security jurisdiction out to 24 NM; requires consent for military exercises or manoeuvers, especially those involving the use of weapons or explosives;[m] claims right to verify, inspect, remove or destroy any weapon, device, structure, installation or facility which might be implanted or emplaced on or beneath its continental shelf by any other country[n]
Indonesia	Broadly defines marine scientific research; claims jurisdiction over any artificial islands or installations or other structures within the EEZ[o]
Iran	Claims jurisdiction over other installations and structures, the laying of submarine cables and pipelines, and any kid of research; prohibits foreign military activities and practices, collection of information in the EEZ[p]
Kenya	Claims jurisdiction over military surveillance installations and any structures; claims the right to regulate passage of warships and the conduct of any military manoeuvres in the EEZ[q]
Libya	Claimed the Gulf of Sidra (Surt) as Libyan internal waters with a closing line measuring approximately 300 NM[r]
Malaysia	Requires consent to conduct military exercises or manoeuvres, particularly those involving the use of weapons or explosives, in the EEZ[s]
Maldives	Purports to grant ships of all States innocent passage in the EEZ and requires all foreign vessels to attain prior authorisation before entering the EEZ[t]
Mauritius	Applies domestic laws to artificial islands, installations and structures in the EEZ and on the continental shelf as if they were in the territorial sea; claims jurisdiction over the laying of submarine cables and pipelines[u]
Mexico	Claims the right to verify, inspect, remove, or destroy any military weapon, structure, installation, device or equipment placed on its continental shelf[v]
Nicaragua	Claims over all survey activities[w]
Pakistan	Consent required for military exercises and manoeuvres in the EEZ[x]
Peru	Claims sovereignty and jurisdiction up to a distance of 200 NM 'maritime domain'[y]

Table 6.1 (*cont.*)

State	Claims
Saudi Arabia	Claims security interests in the contiguous zone; applies security laws over artificial islands, installations and structures in the EEZ[z]
Sudan	Claims security interests to a further distance of 6 NM beyond the territorial sea[aa]
Syria	Claims security interests in the contiguous zone; requires a permit for the laying of submarine cables and pipelines[bb]
Thailand	Requires consent for military exercises in the EEZ[cc]
Uruguay	Claims exclusive jurisdiction over all artificial islands, installations and structures in the EEZ; requires authorisation for foreign military exercises and any other military activity in the EEZ[dd]
Viet Nam	Prohibits any acts against the sovereignty, defence and security of Vietnam in the EEZ[ee]
Yemen	Claims security interests in the contiguous zone[ff]

[a] UNCLOS, *Declarations and Statements*, Bangladesh, Declaration made upon Ratification (27 July 2001), para 1

[b] Brazil, Law No. 8617 of 4 January 1993, on the Territorial Sea, the Contiguous Zone, the Exclusive Economic Zone and the Continental Shelf, (1993) 23 LOSB 19, Articles 8–9; UNCLOS, *Declarations and Statements*, Brazil, Declaration made upon Signature (10 December 1982), para IV; Upon Ratification (22 December 1988), para II

[c] Myanmar, Territorial Sea and Maritime Zones Law, 17 July 2017, Articles 18(a), 20(b) www.un.org/Depts/los/LEGISLATIONANDTREATIES/PDFFILES/Myanmar_MZL_2017.pdf

[d] Cabo Verde, Law No. 60/IV/92 Delimiting the Maritime Areas of the Republic of Cape Verde and Revoking Decree-Law No. 126/77 and all Legal Provisions which contravene this Law, (1994) 26 LOSB 26, Article 13(b)(iv); UNCLOS, *Declarations and Statements*, Cabo Verde, Declaration made upon Signature (10 December 1982) and confirmed upon Ratification (19 August 1987), paras IV–VI

[e] People's Republic of Kampuchea, Decree of the Council of State of 13 July 1982, Articles 4, 6, www.un.org/Depts/los/LEGISLATIONANDTREATIES/PDFFILES/KHM_1982_Decree.pdf

[f] China, Exclusive Economic Zone and Continental Shelf Act (26 June 1998), Article 11, www.un.org/Depts/los/LEGISLATIONANDTREATIES/PDFFILES/chn_1998_eez_act.pdf; China, Surveying and Mapping Law of the People's Republic of China, 1 December 2002, Article 7 www.asianlii.org/cn/legis/cen/laws/samlotproc506/

[g] Decree by the Central People's Committee Establishing the Economic Zone of the People's Democratic Republic of Korea, 21 June 1977 www.un.org/Depts/los/LEGISLATIONANDTREATIES/PDFFILES/PRK_1977_Decree.pdf
[h] UNCLOS, *Declarations and Statements*, Ecuador, Declaration made upon Ratification (24 September 2012), paras IV(3), X–XI, XVIII
[i] Decree concerning the Territorial Waters of the Arab Republic of Egypt of 15 January 1951, as amended by Presidential Decree of 17 February 1958, Article 9 www.un.org/Depts/los/LEGISLATIONANDTREATIES/PDFFILES/EGY_1958_Decree.pdf; UNCLOS, *Declarations and Statements*, Egypt, Declarations upon Ratification (26 August 1983).
[j] El Salvador, Constitution of 13 December 1983, Article 84 www.un.org/Depts/los/LEGISLATIONANDTREATIES/PDFFILES/SLV_1983_Constitution.pdf
[k] *Land, Island and Maritime Frontier Dispute (El Salvador/Honduras: Nicaragua intervening)*, Judgment, ICJ Reports 1992, p. 351, General List No. 75.
[l] Guyana, Maritime Boundaries Act, 1977, Act No. 10 of 30 June 1977, Article 16 www.un.org/Depts/los/LEGISLATIONANDTREATIES/PDFFILES/GUY_1977_Act.pdf
[m] India, The Territorial Waters, Continental Shelf, Exclusive Economic Zone and other Maritime Zones Acts, 1976, Act No. 80 of 28 May 1976, Articles 5(4)(a), 7(5) www.un.org/Depts/los/LEGISLATIONANDTREATIES/PDFFILES/IND_1976_Act.pdf; UNCLOS, *Declarations and Statements*, India, Declaration made upon Ratification (29 June 1995), para (b)
[n] 1971 Seabed Treaty, Declaration by India, https://2009-2017.state.gov/documents/organization/74105.pdf (archived content)
[o] Indonesia, Act No. 5 of 1983 on the Indonesia Exclusive Economic Zone (18 October 1983), (1986) 7 LOSB 26, 28, Articles 1(c), 6
[p] Iran, Act on the Marine Areas of the Islamic Republic of Iran in the Persian Gulf and the Oman Sea, (1993) 24 LOSB 12, 14, Articles 14, 16
[q] Kenya, Chapter 371 – The Maritime Zones Act 1989, Articles 1(2), 9(1)(e) www.un.org/Depts/los/LEGISLATIONANDTREATIES/PDFFILES/KEN_1989_Maritime.pdf
[r] Libya, Information Concerning the Jurisdiction of the Gulf of Surt, www.un.org/Depts/los/LEGISLATIONANDTREATIES/PDFFILES/LBY_1973_Information.pdf
[s] UNCLOS, *Declarations and Statements*, Malaysia, Declaration made upon Ratification (14 October 1996), para 3
[t] Maldives, Law No. 32/76 of 5 December 1976 relating to the Navigation and Passage by Foreign Ships and Aircrafts through the Airspace, Territorial Waters and the Economic Zone of the Republic of Maldives, Article 1; Maritime Zones of Maldives Act No. 6/96, Article 14 www.un.org/Depts/los/LEGISLATIONANDTREATIES/STATEFILES/MDV.htm
[u] Maiuritius, Maritime Zones Act 2005 (Act No. 2 of 2005), (2006) 62 LOSB 56–57, Articles 16(2), 17(b), 20(2)
[v] 1971 Seabed Treaty, Declaration by Mexico, https://2009-2017.state.gov/documents/organization/74105.pdf (archived content)

[w] J Ashley Roach, *Excessive Maritime Claims* (4th ed, Brill 2021) 459
[x] UNCLOS, *Declarations and Statements*, Pakistan, Declaration made upon Ratification (26 February 1997), para (iii)
[y] Peru, Peruvian Maritime Dominion Baselines Law, (2007) 64 LOSB 15, Article 1; *Maritime Dispute (Peru v. Chile)*, Judgment, ICJ Reports 2014, p. 3, para 178; 'Peru's Agent formally declared on behalf of his Government that "[t]he term 'maritime domain' used in [Peru's] Constitution is applied in a manner consistent with the maritime zones set out in the 1982 Convention"'
[z] Saudi Arabia, Translation of Royal Decree No. 6 dated 18/1/1433H, Statute of Maritime Delimitation of the Kingdom of Saudi Arabia (13 December 2011), Articles 11(2), 13(2)(c) www.un.org/Depts/los/LEGISLATIONANDTREATIES/PDFFILES/SAU_2011_Decree.pdf
[aa] Sudan, Territorial Waters and Continental Shelf Act, 1970, Article 9 www.un.org/Depts/los/LEGISLATIONANDTREATIES/PDFFILES/SDN_1970_Act.pdf
[bb] Syria, Law No. 28 of 19 November 2003, (2004) 55 LOSB 16–17, Articles 20, 24(2)
[cc] UNCLOS, *Declarations and Statements*, Thailand, Declaration made upon Ratification (15 May 2011), para I(4)
[dd] Uruguay, Act No.17.033 of 20 November 1998 Establishing the Boundaries of the Territorial Sea, the Adjacent Zone, the Exclusive Economic Zone, and the Continental Shelf, Articles 6(A), 8 www.un.org/Depts/los/LEGISLATIONANDTREATIES/PDFFILES/URY_1998_Act.pdf; UNCLOS, *Declarations and Statements*, Uruguay, Declaration made upon Signature (10 December 1982), para (D)
[ee] Viet Nam, The Law on Vietnamese Sea, Law No. 18/2012/QH13, 21 June 2012, Article 37(1) https://lawnet.vn/en/vb/Law-No-18-2012-QH13-on-Vietnamese-sea-23278.html
[ff] Yemen, Act No. 45 of 17 December 1977 Concerning the Territorial Sea, Exclusive Economic Zone, Continental Shelf and Other Marine Areas, Article 12 www.un.org/Depts/los/LEGISLATIONANDTREATIES/PDFFILES/YEM_1977_Act.pdf

UNCLOS in 1986.[132] Nicaragua, which once claimed sovereignty and jurisdiction over the adjacent sea to 200 NM that was only open to the innocent passage of foreign merchant vessels, has since adjusted its

[132] Chile, Presidential Declaration Concerning Continental Shelf, 23 June 1947, Laws and Regulations on the Regime of the High Seas (United Nations ST/LEG/SER.B/1, 11 January 1951) 6–7; Chile, Law No. 18.565 Amending the Civil Code with Regard to Maritime Space, 13 October 1986 (1), Article 1(1)–(2) www.un.org/Depts/los/LEGISLATIONANDTREATIES/PDFFILES/CHL_1986_18565.pdf.

claims in accordance with UNCLOS.[133] The same practice is observed by Liberia and Somalia, which rolled back from a claim of 200 NM territorial sea and established maritime zones according to UNCLOS.[134]

No fewer than thirty coastal States have explicitly sought to apply restrictions to the movement or operations of foreign warships, military aircraft or military devices in the EEZ for the purpose of safeguarding their security interests. These claims have been alleged as being inconsistent with UNCLOS and have been challenged and protested by other States, most notably the United States.[135] In addition, eleven States made objecting declarations for those coastal States that prohibited foreign military activities in the EEZ without permission. These include Belgium, Finland, Germany, Ireland, Italy, Latvia, the Netherlands, Italy, Sweden, the United Kingdom and the United States, with some arguing that the coastal State's rights and jurisdiction in the EEZ 'do not include the rights to obtain notification of military exercises or manoeuvres or to authorize them'.[136]

6.2.3 Protection of Security Interests as a Residual Right in the Exclusive Economic Zone

It is clear that security interests exist in maritime areas and a number of States have claimed security interests in the EEZ without specifying the

[133] Nicaragua, Act No. 205 of 19 December 1979 on the Continental Shelf and Adjacent Sea, Articles 2, 4 www.un.org/Depts/los/LEGISLATIONANDTREATIES/PDFFILES/NIC_1979_Act.pdf; Case concerning Territorial and Maritime Dispute between Nicaragua and Honduras in the Caribbean Sea (Nicaragua v. Honduras), Judgment of 8 October 2007, ICJ Reports 2007, p. 659; United Nations Division for Ocean Affairs and the Law of the Sea (UN DOALOS), Table of Claims to Maritime Jurisdiction (as at 15 July 2011, under review as of 2024), www.un.org/Depts/los/LEGISLATIONANDTREATIES/claims.htm.

[134] Liberia, Executive Order No. 48 of 10 January 2013 Extension of Executive Order No. 39 Delimiting the Maritime Zones of the Republic of Liberia www.un.org/Depts/los/LEGISLATIONANDTREATIES/PDFFILES/LBR_10Jan2013_Act_EO48.pdf; Proclamation by the President of the Federal Republic of Somalia, 30 June 2014 www.un.org/Depts/los/LEGISLATIONANDTREATIES/PDFFILES/SOM_2014_Proclamation.pdf.

[135] J. Ashley Roach, *Excessive Maritime Claims* (4th ed., Brill 2021) 442–458; US Commentary (1994) 24–25.

[136] UNCLOS, Declarations and Statements; Third Conference, Official Records, Vol. XVII: Resumed Eleventh Session, Written Statements of the Plenary, A/CONF.62/WS/37 and ADD.1–2, 8 March 1983, United States of America, 244.

legal basis for their claims. As discussed earlier, there are different approaches to protecting a State's security interests in the EEZ. While several coastal States have adopted the position that they have been granted jurisdiction over all military activities to prevent security threats in the EEZ, other States insist that the right to conduct military activities is included in the preserved high seas freedoms.[137] As both sides argue for their right to claim or prohibit military activities in the EEZ, it is uncertain which side will prevail.[138] At the debate on 'peaceful uses of ocean space: zones of peace and security' in 1976, Madagascar declared that it

> could not accept a situation where its sovereignty, independence and security were subordinate to the defence interests of others, and where the rich countries used their technological superiority to weaken further the position of the developing countries in the fields of exploration and exploitation of marine resources and, in particular, in the political and military fields.[139]

Many developing States at the meeting echoed this position. However, this debate did not reach any conclusion on whether military activities should be permitted or prohibited in the EEZ. Nearly half-a-century later, the situation that Madagascar could not accept continues.

A possible solution to resolve these conflicting positions is to treat the protection of security interests, including the core element of asserting the right to conduct military activities, as a residual right in the EEZ given the lack of explicit reference in UNCLOS.[140] The conflict is primarily between the need to conduct certain military activity to achieve the protection of the security interest of one State and the interests of another State. As such, whether a State has the right to conduct certain military activity in a given context is determined in such a way to ensure a balance between different States for protecting their respective

137 Churchill and Lowe (1999) 427.

138 Yoshifumi Tanaka, *The International Law of the Sea* (3rd ed., Cambridge University Press 2019) 469–472.

139 Fourth Session, Plenary Meetings, 67th Meeting (23 April 1976), 57 (Madagascar: para 13).

140 Lowe (1986) 179; Barbara Kwiatkowska, *The 200 Mile Exclusive Economic Zone in the New Law of the Sea* (Martinus Nijhoff 1989) 228; Alexander Proelss, 'Article 59', in Proelss (2017) 460; Scovazzi (2019) 60–62; Eduardo Cavalcanti de Mello Filho, 'The Legal Regime of the Exclusive Economic Zone and Foreign Military Exercises or Maneuvers' (2021) Storia Militare Contermporanea 361, 373–375.

interests.[141] Among the declarations and statements made by States upon ratification of and accession to UNCLOS, Belgium, Ecuador, Germany, Italy, the Netherlands, Sweden and Uruguay made explicit references to the residual rights in the EEZ that are linked with the right to conduct military activities.[142]

The guidance provided for resolving conflicts of residual rights in UNCLOS Article 59 is that it is to be 'resolved on the basis of equity and in the light of all the relevant circumstances, taking into account the respective importance of the interests involved to the parties as well as to the international community as a whole'. Article 59 reaffirms the characteristic of the EEZ as a *sui generis* zone, which provides no presumption in favour of either party, but rather a basis for both sides to argue for rights and jurisdiction over military activities, as discussed in Chapter 3.[143]

Security interests at sea present an overlapping situation where different States can advance their claim over the same military activity for different purposes. The prospect of classifying the protection of security interests in the EEZ as a residual right means that such rights are not automatically assigned to either the coastal State or other States, and the conflict arising from their exercise should be resolved 'on the basis of equity and in the light of all the relevant circumstances' within a given context.[144] When reviewing 'all the relevant circumstances', one must take into consideration the formula of attributing rights and freedoms between the coastal State and other States. As such, those favouring the coastal State must be adequately associated with their sovereign rights over natural resources and explicitly recognised jurisdiction whereas those favouring other States are closely associated with the recognised freedoms. Exercising the right to conduct military activities for security purposes, as with the exercise of other rights and freedoms, must be for peaceful purpose only and with due regard to other States' co-existing rights and duties.

[141] Tim Stephens and Donald R. Rothwell, 'The LOSC Framework for Maritime Jurisdiction and Enforcement 30 Years On' (2012) 27 Int'l J Marine & Coastal L 701, 705; Robin R. Churchill, 'The Impact of State Practice on the Jurisdictional Framework Contained in the LOS Convention', in Alex G. Oude Elferink (ed.), *Stability and Change in the Law of the Sea: The Role of the LOS Convention* (Martinus Nijhoff 2005) 134–135.

[142] UNCLOS, Declarations and Statements.

[143] Churchill, Lowe and Sander (2022) 292–293; Proelss 'Article 59' (2017) 462–463.

[144] UNCLOS Article 59.

6.3 Conflicts Regarding Military Activities in the Exclusive Economic Zone

The lack of specific attribution of the right to protect security interests in the EEZ, crucially the conduct of military activities, has led to controversial interpretations and State practice that has resulted in conflicts. The controversies are focussed on two main issues: whether certain activities can be categorised as military activities, and who has the right to conduct these activities. The discussion here follows the formula set out in Article 59, and more broadly Part V of UNCLOS, concerning the attribution of rights to conduct military activities in the EEZ while taking into consideration the debate over their categorisation from both perspectives. However, it appears to be impossible to give a definitive attribution of the right to conduct military activities in the EEZ given the wide range of activities involved.[145] Four main types of activities can be identified that involve the operation of military vessels, aircraft and devices to analyse the attribution and the exercise of rights between the coastal State and other States.

6.3.1 *Navigation, Overflight and Military Manoeuvres*

Every State, whether coastal or landlocked, has the right to sail ships and fly aircraft entitled to fly its flag in and above the EEZ.[146] As customarily recognised, the freedom of navigation and overflight has never been absolute, in that it must be exercised for peaceful purposes only and with reasonable regard to the interests of other States in exercising their rights and freedoms, as well as fulfilling other conditions laid down in international law.[147] Such freedoms are subject to further restrictions in the EEZ as they need to be compatible with the *sui generis* legal regime.[148]

The right of all States to navigate a military ship or fly a military aircraft in the EEZ must be exercised for peaceful purposes only. The desire to establish a legal order for the seas that will facilitate international communication and promote peaceful use of the seas is clearly recognised in the Preamble and repeated in various provisions of UNCLOS.[149] As discussed earlier, the 'peaceful purposes/uses'

[145] Scovazzi (2019) 61.
[146] UNCLOS Articles 58(1)–(2), 90.
[147] Convention on the High Seas Article 2; UNCLOS Articles 87(2), 88, 300, 301.
[148] UNCLOS Article 58(3). For discussion on the freedoms of navigation and overflight in the EEZ, see Chapter 4 in this volume.
[149] UNCLOS Preamble, Articles 88, 141, 143(1), 147(2), 155(2), 240(a), 242(1), 246(3), 301.

obligation does not exclude the simple movement of any military ships or aircraft in the EEZ.[150]

In exercising the freedoms of navigation and overflight in the EEZ, States must give due regard to the rights and duties of other States using the same area. In terms of freedoms exercised by a foreign State, it must comply with the laws and regulations adopted by the coastal State in accordance with UNCLOS and other rules of international law.[151] However, military entities enjoy immunity from coastal State jurisdiction in the EEZ, especially laws and regulations on the protection and preservation of the marine environment.[152] This immunity is based on the grounds of State sovereignty and the principle of equity, because one State is not to be subjected to the jurisdiction of another.[153] When a foreign military entity violates a coastal State's rights and jurisdiction, the coastal State may require the vessel to leave the operational site immediately and the flag State assumes responsibility for any loss or damage resulting from its activities.[154]

There is emerging State practice challenging the freedom of navigation for military vessels powered by nuclear sources because of concerns about radioactive ocean contamination.[155] For instance, a nuclear-powered submarine with a 35 megawatt reactor produces about 22.4 grams of mixed fission products daily during operation, which after 100 days of disintegrating at the rate of 14.7 kilocuries, releases the equivalent amount of short-lived isotopes as a 0.42 kiloton atomic bomb.[156] Despite the relatively good safety record of nuclear-powered vessels, there are concerns over irreversible damage to the ocean environment that might be caused by a large amount of radioactive release

150 UNCLOS Article 301. See Section 6.1.3.1 in this chapter.

151 UNCLOS Article 58(3).

152 UNCLOS Articles 58(2), 95, 236.

153 UN Charter Article 2(1).

154 UNCLOS Articles 30–31; The 'ARA Libertad' Case (Argentina v. Ghana), Provisional Measures, Order of 15 December 2012, ITLOS Reports 2012, p. 332, para 64: 'although article 32 is included in Part II of the Convention entitled "Territorial Sea and Contiguous Zone", and most of the provisions in this Part relate to the territorial sea, some of the provisions in this Part may be applicable to all maritime areas, as in the case of the definition of warships provided for in article 29 of the Convention' (emphasis added). By analogy, Articles 30–31 apply to the EEZ.

155 Westing (1978) 448; Ian Hore-Lacy, *Nuclear Energy in the 21st Century* (World Nuclear University Press 2007) 93–110; United States Environmental Protection Agency, 'Nuclear Submarines and Aircraft Carriers' www.epa.gov/radtown/nuclear-submarines-and-aircraft-carriers.

156 Westing (1978) 452–453.

resulting from either intentional or accidental damage or sinking of such vessels.[157] Numerous States restrict or forbid the movement of nuclear warships in their territorial sea and some have extended these restrictions to the EEZ.[158] However, the fact that nuclear-powered warships pose a potential environmental threat is not sufficient grounds to deprive them of the freedom of navigation in the EEZ. It remains the flag State's right and obligation to implement the appropriate preventative measures for these vessels.

Traditionally, military exercises and manoeuvres are considered operational activities as part of the freedom of movement and communication on the high seas.[159] However, it is unclear, since the establishment of the EEZ, whether these activities are considered an internationally lawful use of the sea related to the freedom of navigation that are compatible with the EEZ legal regime, or are prohibited as incompatible with the EEZ regime, or are unattributed rights.[160] State practice also shows great divergence on this issue, particularly those manoeuvres involving weapons testing or live fire exercise.[161] As stated earlier, upon signing or ratifying UNCLOS, Bangladesh, Brazil, Cabo Verde, Ecuador, India, Malaysia, Pakistan, Thailand and Uruguay explicitly declared that military exercises and manoeuvres, particularly those involving the use of weapons, are not permitted in the EEZ without the consent of the coastal State. Meanwhile, opposing declarations were made by Belgium, Finland, Germany, Italy, Sweden, the Netherlands and the United Kingdom.

It is a matter of fact that States routinely conduct military exercises and manoeuvres at sea, including in their own EEZ and in foreign EEZs, as well as on the high seas, either individually or jointly with the

157 T. J. Mueller, J. M. Steele and A. C. Gellender, *Environmental Monitoring and Disposal of Radioactive Wastes from U.S. Naval Nuclear-Powered Ships and Their Support Facilities* (Naval Nuclear Propulsion Program, Department of the Navy, Report NT-19-1, May 2019) 7–9; International Atomic Energy Agency (IAEA), Inventory of Accidents and Losses At Sea Involving Radioactive Material (IAEA, 2001) www-pub.iaea.org/MTCD/Publications/PDF/te_1242_prn.pdf.

158 Kraska (2011) 115, 303.

159 Attard (1987) 86.

160 Churchill and Lowe (1999) 427; Tanaka (2019) 469–472.

161 Mark J. Valencia, 'Foreign Military Activities in Asia EEZs: Conflict Ahead?' in The National Bureau of Asian Research, Special Report No. 27 (May 2011) 14; United States Department of Defense, 'Military and Security Developments Involving the People's Republic of China', 2023 Annual Report to Congress (2023 China Military Power Report) 19 www.defense.gov/CMPR/.

participation of the coastal State and a third State.[162] These exercises, including missile testing and launching weapons and planes from an aircraft carriers or other warships, are important for military forces to test their strategic deployment and fighting skills in a broad range of scenarios, including evolving crisis and conflict situations.[163] For example, the North Atlantic Treaty Organization (NATO) routinely conducts large-scale military training and exercises.[164] NATO regularly deploys maritime forces in the Baltic Sea in order to exhibit forward presence, maintain a credible and capable defensive capability, and contribute to operational coherence among allied naval forces to support greater regional security and stability.[165]

The coastal State, when conducting military exercises and manoeuvres within its EEZ, must have due regard to the rights and duties of other States and must maintain peaceful purposes. UNCLOS is silent on whether the coastal State may close a certain sea area to navigation for such activities, in contrast to the explicit reference to the right to suspend innocent passage temporarily 'for the protection of its security, including weapons exercise'.[166] It may be argued that the coastal State could close a specified area within its EEZ for military exercises and manoeuvres provided that such closure has been duly published and is not impeding normal passage routes used for international navigation and overflight. NATO allies, for example, have used the Baltic Sea and the region surrounding it as a maritime training ground for over five decades. Known as the Baltic Operations (BALTOPS), the annual military exercise is aimed at delivering high-end training across the entire spectrum of naval warfare.[167]

Military exercises and manoeuvres conducted in the EEZ by a foreign State are likely to be challenged by the coastal State, particularly if such activities involve the use of weapons, and/or take place in disputed areas,

[162] Kraska (2011) 269.

[163] Naval Operations Concept 2010 (2010) 41; United Kingdom Ministry of Defence, 'Huge Military Exercise Underway', 16 April 2013 www.gov.uk/government/news/largest-european-military-exercise-underway.

[164] North Atlantic Treaty Organization (NATO), 'NATO Exercises', 28 March 2022 www.nato.int/cps/en/natohq/topics_49285.htm.

[165] NATO, 'Steadfast Defender 2021' www.nato.int/cps/en/natohq/173840.htm; NATO, 'NATO navies hold annual Northern Coasts collective defence exercise in the Baltic Sea', 9 September 2023 www.nato.int/cps/en/natohq/news_218241.htm?selectedLocale=en.

[166] UNCLOS Article 25(3).

[167] NATO, 'The 50th BALTOPS Kicks off in June', 24 May 2021 https://sfn.nato.int/newsroom/2021/the-50th-baltops-kicks-off-in-june.

and/or during periods of political tension. Numerous examples exist. The military exercises jointly conducted by the United States and South Korea were often denounced by the Democratic People's Republic of Korea as 'an irresponsible and dangerous action' and a 'rehearsal for war', which they responded to with threats of nuclear war.[168] China has firmly protested the annual joint military exercise between the Philippines and the United States, known as 'Balikatan' (shoulder-to-shoulder), and asserts that such activities have raised the risk of armed confrontation over the disputed South China Sea.[169] Such protests concerning foreign military activities are also common in the Baltic Sea, the Black Sea and the Mediterranean Sea, particularly in relation to the tension between NATO and Russia. Both Latvia and Sweden protested Russia's missile tests and military drills in the Baltic Sea in 2018 and 2020, respectively.[170] With an acceleration of tension between Türkiye and Greece over their long-standing dispute concerning maritime rights and natural resources in 2020, both sides brought in allies to conduct military exercises and drills with the intention to demonstrate strength, and issued protests over the other side's activities.[171] Despite these ongoing challenges by the

[168] KJ Kwon, 'South Korea: Joint Military Drills with US over, but Vigilance on North Remains', CNN, 30 April 2013 (online); Reuters, 'U.S., South Korea conduct joint Navy drills to counter North Korea threat', 16 October 2017, (online).

[169] Peter Symonds, 'US-Philippine Military Exercises Directed against China', World Socialist Web Site, 26 April 2012, www.wsws.org/en/articles/2012/04/usph-a26.html; Guifen Zhang, 'US-Philippines Joint Military Exercise Means Nothing for Philippines', People's Daily Online, 15 April 2013, http://english.peopledaily.com.cn/90786/8207055.html (Accessed in December 2022); Renato Cruz de Castro, 'Balikatan 2019 and the Crisis in Philippine-China Rapprochement', Asia Maritime Transparency Initiative, 23 April 2019 https://amti.csis.org/balikatan-2019-and-the-crisis-in-philippine-china-rapprochement/; Brad Lendon, 'US and Philippine Forces Fire on Mock Enemy Warship in South China Sea Military Exercise', CNN, 26 April 2023 (online); Bree Megivern, 'Why China Is Wary of US 'Ironclad' Alliance With the Philippines', The Diplomat, 2 May 2024 (online).

[170] Gederts Gelzis, 'Russian Rocket Tests Force Partial Closing of Baltic Sea, Airspace', Reuters, 4 April 2018 (online); Thomas Erdbrink and Andrew E Kramer, 'Sweden Raises Alarm over Russian Military Exercises', The New York Times, 26 August 2020 (online).

[171] 'France Joins Military Exercises in East Mediterranean', Reuters, 26 August 2020 (online); 'Tensions Rise in Eastern Mediterranean after Turkey Launches New Military Drills', Euronews, 29 August 2020 (online); Monique O'Neill, 'Greece, Cyprus and the U.S. join forces for naval SOF exercise in the Mediterranean Sea', 10 February 2021 www.eucom.mil/article/41100/greece-cyprus-and-the-us-join-forces-for-naval-sof-exercise-in-the-mediterranean-sea.

coastal States, the ICJ concluded in *Nicaragua (Merits)* that the conduct of military manoeuvres closer to a coastal State's border is not in breach of 'the principle of forbidding recourse to the threat or use of force'.[172]

The operating State, either the coastal State or a foreign State, is obligated to adopt appropriate measures to ensure that its military entities act in a manner consistent with the environmental protection and preservation provisions in UNCLOS.[173] Such measures must not impair operations or operational capabilities of such entities and must be reasonable and practicable.[174] Such measures may include the assessment of environmental impacts and subsequent communication with potentially affected States.[175] However, the vague language and general obligation leaves a coastal State little to no means to challenge foreign military activity based on environmental obligations. Likewise, it would be difficult for any foreign State to challenge a coastal State's military activity conducted in its own EEZ on the basis of environmental obligation.

In summary, warships and military aircraft of all States enjoy the freedom of navigation and overflight in the EEZ, including the freedom to conduct military manoeuvres despite the lack of consensus in relation to their legalities among States.[176] As long as these activities are conducted consistent with the due regard obligation and peaceful purposes, they are not prohibited in principle.[177] Up until a certain point, foreign military presence and exercises are to be tolerated in the EEZ of a coastal State. In the problematic situation where weapons are used, there are a range of factors that would be applicable in determining whether their use fulfils these requirements, particularly the due regard obligation. These would include whether such use causes undue restriction on the freedoms of navigation and overflight, or causes harm to natural resources. The operating State must ensure that it fulfils these obligations and assumes responsibility if such exercises damage the rights and

[172] Military and Paramilitary Activities (Nicaragua v. United States of America) (1986) paras 92, 227.

[173] UNCLOS Articles 192, 194, 236.

[174] UNCLOS Article 236.

[175] UNCLOS Articles 204–206, 300; Case Concerning Pulp Mills on the River Uruguay (Argentina v. Uruguay), Judgment of 20 April 2010, ICJ Reports 2010, p. 14, para 204; Ricard (2019) 160–162.

[176] Rothwell and Stephens (2010) 280.

[177] Churchill, Lowe and Sander (2022) 280–281.

jurisdiction of the coastal State, or the freedoms of other States. In order to reduce tension, it would be a good practice for the operating State to give notice to the coastal State or other interested States and provide information of what, when and where such military exercises will take place. Moreover, given the circumstances and by the nature of the rights that could be affected by the military exercise, the operating State should initiate a certain level of consultation with the rights-holding State to fulfil their due regard obligation.[178]

6.3.2 *Espionage, Intelligence Gathering and Surveillance*

States have advanced the need to acquire knowledge of maritime areas, mainly through intelligence gathering activities, to make decisions about their national defence strategies.[179] There is no general rule in international law that prohibits or limits activities of intelligence gathering beyond the limit of the territorial sea.[180] Despite different interpretations on the legality of military intelligence gathering in the EEZ, in practice, States have tolerated such activities for a long time.[181] Peacetime military intelligence gathering, also known as reconnaissance or espionage, is principally conducted by space-based, airborne, ship-based and seabed-attached maritime surveillance systems, including cyber infrastructure.[182] Although peacetime military intelligence gathering does not per se violate international law, the method by which it is carried out might do so.

[178] In the Matter of the Chagos Marine Protected Area Arbitration Before an Arbitral Tribunal Constituted under Annex VII to the United Nations Convention on the Law of the Sea between the Republic of Mauritius and the United Kingdom of Great Britain and Northern Ireland, Award, 18 March 2015, PCA Case No. 2011-03, para 519 (Chagos MPA Arbitration).

[179] Klein (2011) 214–215; Asaf Lubin, 'The Liberty to Spy' (2020) 61(1) Harv Int'l LJ 185, 233–235.

[180] UNCLOS Article 19(2)(c); Inaki Navarretet and Russell Buchan, 'Out of the Legal Wilderness: Peacetime Espionage, International Law and the Existence of Customary Exceptions' (2019) 51 Cornell Int'l LJ 897, 909–910.

[181] Dieter Fleck, 'Individual and State Responsibility for Intelligence Gathering' (2006-2007) 28 Mich J Int'l L 687, 688–689.

[182] Ball (2004) 67–68; Efthymios Papastavridis, 'Intelligence Gathering in the Exclusive Economic Zone' (2017) 93 Int'l Law Stud 446, 450; Tallinn Manual 2.0 (2017) 168. The use of seabed-attached devices are discussed in Section 6.3.4 in this chapter.

Satellite-based reconnaissance was initiated by the United States in 1958 to spy on the Union of Soviet Socialist Republics (USSR) and its allies.[183] The Galactic Radiation and Background satellite system, the first satellite system for signal surveillance, detected radar as it passed within the line of sight of a transmitting radar system; it then beamed down the radar signals it intercepted to a network of ground stations and transferred them to magnetic tape, which was then taken by courier to the United States for analysis.[184] The technology of the Galactic Radiation and Background satellite system is now obsolete, but conducting electronic surveillance from orbit continues to be a primary technique.[185] Except in cases that use artificial islands, installations and structures for on-land stationing, conducting satellite-based reconnaissance in another State's EEZ is less likely to interfere with the coastal State's sovereign rights or jurisdiction.

Airborne surveillance systems are operated by military aircraft that collect both signal and electronic intelligence, which has the advantage of providing regular, real-time surveillance of the electromagnetic emissions in important parts of the spectrum that are undetectable from ground sites.[186] Traditional manned aircraft can intercept and record the emissions of radar and other radio/electronic systems, as well as signals of computer-to-computer data traffic, and even phone traffic, to map air defence networks, airfields and missile batteries for target planning purposes.[187] The advanced airborne facility involves unmanned aerial vehicles, which can be launched outside the EEZ on a pre-programmed mission without the launching ship or aircraft actually entering the zone itself.[188] Since the coastal State's jurisdiction in the airspace above the EEZ is limited to activities for the economic exploitation and exploration of the zone, such as the production of energy from wind, it would be difficult to challenge foreign airborne surveillance unless it interferes with these economic activities.[189]

Likewise, military surveillance ships are widely used to collect intelligence at sea. For example, the United States maintains six ocean surveillance ships as part of the twenty-one ships under the Military Sealift

[183] Mark F. Moynihan, 'The Scientific Community and Intelligence Collection' (2000) 53 Physics Today 51, 53.

[184] Ibid 54–56.

[185] Ibid 55; Marco Giulio Barone, 'Maritime Surveillance Radars: Eyes on the Seas' (2020) 4 Military Technology 49, 49. 2023 China Military Power Report 97-103.

[186] Ball (2004) 69; Naval Operations Concept 2010 (2010) 83–84.

[187] Ball (2004) 69.

[188] Ibid 71; Naval Operations Concept 2010 (2010) 83–84.

[189] UNCLOS Article 56(1)(a).

Command's Special Mission programme,[190] which routinely collects intelligence on the high seas and in foreign EEZs, despite diplomatic protests from China, India, Brazil and other States.[191] The surveillance ships conduct a variety of missions, including collecting signal and electronic intelligence; monitoring naval exercises, communications, or combatant surveillance; monitoring the movement of ballistic missile–carrying submarines; and using passive and active low-frequency sonar arrays to detect and track undersea threats.[192] Some of the detection techniques used by the surveillance ships – high-powered sonar arrays, for example – may disorient or injure whales and other marine mammals,[193] which arguably could interfere with the coastal State's sovereign rights to explore, conserve and manage such resources.

There have been increasing concerns regarding the legitimacy of certain highly advanced technologies used in intelligence gathering and surveillance. Particularly relevant in this context are active signals intelligence activities, some of which are deliberately provocative and are intended to generate responses from the targeted coastal State, while others may involve intercepting naval radar and emitters to locate, identify and track surface ships in the targeted areas.[194] These activities do not have a direct impact on natural resources and appear to cause far greater interference with communication and defence systems of the targeted State. These highly provocative activities may cause or exacerbate conflicts, since many coastal States consider them hostile and incompatible with the peaceful purposes obligation.[195]

190 United States Navy's Military Sealift Command, 'Special Mission (PM2)', Oceanographic Surveillance Ships: USNS Able, USNS Effective, USNS Impeccable, USNS Loyal, HOS Red Rock and USNS Victorious www.msc.usff.navy.mil/Ships/Special-Mission-PM2/.

191 Pedrozo (2010) 12–15.

192 Ball (2004) 73–76.

193 Supreme Court of the United States, 'Winter, Secretary of the Navy, et al. v. Natural Resources Defense Council, Inc., Et Al.', Certiorari to the United States Court of Appeals for the Ninth Circuit, No.07-1239, decided on 12 November 2008, 5–6; Douglas P Nowacek and Brandon L Southall, Effective Planning Strategies for Managing Environmental Risk Associated with Geophysical and other Imaging Surveys (IUCN 2016); Erica Fleishman et al., 'Current Status of Development of Methods to Assess Effects of Cumulative or Aggregated Underwater Sounds on Marine Mammals', in Arthur N Popper and Anthony Hawkins (eds), The Effects of Noise on Aquatic Life II (Springer, 2016) https://doi.org/10.1007/978-1-4939-2981-8_36.

194 Ball (2004) 69; Papastavridis (2017) 471.

195 Hayashi (2005) 126, 130; Klein (2011) 220; 周忠海和张小奕 (2012), 第103–104页 (ZHOU and ZHANG (2012), 103–104).

The lack of legal clarity in relation to espionage, intelligence gathering and surveillance in the EEZ has been problematic, especially in situations where such activities are conducted in a foreign EEZ.[196] Alongside the firm position held by the United States, the United Kingdom also considers the airspace above the EEZ as international airspace, in which military aircraft of another State may lawfully fly 'for the purpose of surveillance and observation of activities within that other state's national airspace or territory'.[197] China, on the other hand, constantly challenges unauthorised foreign intelligence-gathering and surveillance activities in its EEZ.[198] China recognises that all States enjoy 'the freedom of navigation and overflight and of laying submarine cables and pipelines, and shall enjoy other legal and practical marine benefits associated with these freedoms' within the Chinese EEZ.[199] However, the phrase 'other legal and practical marine benefits associated with these freedoms' is different from the expression of 'other internationally lawful uses of the sea related to these freedoms' used in UNCLOS Article 58(1). The phrase in the Chinese law only equals the expression of 'such as those associated with the operation of ships, aircraft and submarine cables and pipelines' that was used to exemplify 'other internationally lawful uses'.[200] This language would narrow the scope of the associated freedoms enjoyed by other States, which is arguably intended to restrict foreign military activities in China's EEZ.

The debate over foreign intelligence-gathering activities was highlighted in April 2001 when a US Navy EP-3 surveillance plane collided with a Chinese F-8 fighter jet approximately 70 NM southeast of Hainan Island, killing the Chinese pilot and making a forced landing at Lingshui Military Airport.[201] The Chinese view was that the intelligence collected

[196] Mark J. Valencia, 'Introduction: Military and Intelligence Gathering Activities in the Exclusive Economic Zones: Consensus and Disagreement II' (2005) 29 Marine Policy 98. Amaani Lyle, 'DoD Registers Concern to China for Dangerous Intercept', 22 August 2014, www.defense.gov/News/News-Stories/Article/Article/603111/dod-registers-concern-to-china-for-dangerous-intercept/.

[197] United Kingdom, Ministry of Defence, The Joint Service Manual of the Law of Armed Conflict (JSP 383, 2004) Chapter 12: Air Operations, para 12.14, www.gov.uk/government/organisations/ministry-of-defence/series/jsp-383.

[198] Christopher J. Castelli, 'Clashing Views Exchanged in Sino-U.S. Maritime Safety Talks' (2010) 26(46) Inside the Pentagon 11, 11–12.

[199] China, Exclusive Economic Zone and Continental Shelf Act Article 11.

[200] UNCLOS Article 58(1).

[201] Shirley A Kan et al., 'China-US Aircraft Collision Incident of April 2001: Assessments and Policy Implications', CRS Report for Congress (10 October 2001) 1 www.fas.org/

could be used for hostile purposes and such activity went far beyond the scope of overflight and abused such a freedom, breaching the due regard obligation and peaceful purposes, which constituted an infringement upon China's sovereignty.[202] The United States claimed it was engaging in a traditional military activity over international waters, which was legally permissible and conducted with due regard of China's rights as a coastal State.[203] It is generally recognised that the airspace above the EEZ is governed by the 'specific legal regime' as established in UNCLOS, which is different from the international space asserted by the United States.[204] Thus, the United States military plane flying above the Chinese EEZ must fulfil the obligation of operating for peaceful purposes and have due regard to the rights and duties of China.[205] However, the mere assertion that performing reconnaissance in the EEZ constitutes an abuse of the right of overflight seems too weak to support China's position of prohibiting the entrance of US aircraft altogether. The Chinese position is further weakened by its own increased surveillance activities in the East and South China Sea, particularly around disputed islands with Japan, as well as observing a US missile defence test off Alaska in 2017 and 2021.[206]

There have been many incidents involving coastal States and foreign surveillance ships in Asian waters. In December 2001, the Japanese Coast Guard chased an alleged North Korean spy ship out of its EEZ using at least twenty-five vessels and fourteen aircraft, attacking and eventually

sgp/crs/row/RL30946.pdf; Eric Donnelly, 'The United States-China EP-3 Incident: Legality and Realpolitik' (2004) 9(1) J Conflict & Sec L 25, 25–26; Robert T. Kline, 'The Pen and the Sword: The People's Republic of China's Effort to Redefine the Exclusive Economic Zones through Maritime Lawfare and Military Enforcement' (2013) 216 Mil L Rev 122, 125.

202 发言人谈美国军用侦察机撞毁中国军用飞机事件真相和中方有关立场 (Spoke's Person on the Facts and China's Position on the Incident of United States Military Surveillance Plan Crushed Chinese Military Plan) 3 April 2010, www.mfa.gov.cn/web/ziliao_674904/zt_674979/ywzt_675099/2355_676073/2379_676137/200104/t20010403_9289942.shtml.

203 Kan (2001) 20; Roach (2021) 413–420.

204 UNCLOS Articles 55, 86.

205 UNCLOS Articles 58(2)–(3), 88, 300–301.

206 Sui-Lee Wee and Linda Sieg, 'China Surveillance Ships near Islands Disputed with Japan', Reuters, 14 September 2012 (online); Martin Fackler, '日本抗议中国战机再次威胁日方侦察机 (Japan Protested over Chinese Military Plan threating Japanese Surveillance Aircraft)', The New York Times, 12 June 2014 (online); Roach (2021), 454; 2023 China Military Power Report v, 19, 52–53.

sinking the suspected ship in China's EEZ, killing the fifteen crewmembers on board.[207] The United States and China continue to have confrontations in the Yellow Sea, the East China Sea and the South China Sea, with China challenging the activities of US surveillance ships. Most notably, on 8 March 2009, five Chinese vessels surrounded the USNS *Impeccable* approximately seventy-five miles south of Hainan Island in the South China Sea and forced it to stop operating and leave the area.[208] The United States made a formal complaint, labelling the Chinese actions as reckless, unprofessional and unlawful; China responded that *Impeccable* had illegally engaged in intelligence data gathering and was in violation of Chinese domestic law and international law.[209] Given the ongoing tension around disputed islands in the East and South China Seas and the battle for maritime dominance between China and the United States in the Asia-Pacific region, the suspicion over foreign military surveillance activities will continue to provoke conflicts among the coastal State and operating States.[210]

The need to obtain intelligence in the EEZ seems even more important for the coastal State based on its security concerns. Coastal States are also not prohibited from conducting espionage, intelligence-gathering and surveillance activities in their EEZs provided that they are not impeding the freedoms of navigation and overflight and such activities are for peaceful purposes. In addition to the often secret espionage activities, coastal States are increasingly using air defence identification zones (ADIZ) and maritime identification zones to obtain information that could further complicate the debate on military intelligence gathering

[207] James Conachy, 'Japan Militarisation Accelerates after Sinking of Alleged North Korean Spy Ship', World Socialist Web Site, 9 January 2002 www.wsws.org/en/articles/2002/01/jap-j09.html.

[208] Thom Shanker and Mark Mazzetti, 'China and US Clash on Naval Fracas', The New York Times, 10 March 2009 (online).

[209] 'Raw Data: Pentagon Statement on Chinese Incident with US Navy', Fox News, 9 March 2009 (online); 'China Hits out at US on Navy Row', BBC News, 10 March 2009 (online).

[210] Felix K. Chang, 'China's Maritime Intelligence, Surveillance, and Reconnaissance Capability in the South China Sea', Foreign Policy Research Institute, 5 May 2021 www.fpri.org/article/2021/05/chinas-maritime-intelligence-surveillance-and-reconnais sance-capability-in-the-south-china-sea/; Mark J. Valencia, 'US-China Race for Surveillance Supremacy in South China Sea Risks a Needless Clash', South China Morning Post, 14 May 2021 (online); 2023 China Military Power Report 138-139.

and surveillance activities in the EEZ.[211] These coastal surveillance regulations should have limited impacts on foreign military aircraft and ships, since they should be exempted given their immunity status. However, there has been some questionable State practice on the applicable regulations that were adopted with an aim to limit foreign espionage activities. China, for example, requires all aircraft entering the East China Sea ADIZ to submit flight plans and maintain communications through radio and radar, and will assert necessary armed response to non-compliant aircraft.[212]

Unlike in the territorial sea, where 'any act aimed at collecting information to the prejudice of defence or security of the coastal States' is forbidden, such activities are not specifically outlawed in the EEZ.[213] Despite the ongoing debates, both the coastal State and other States have been conducting espionage, intelligence-gathering and surveillance activities in the EEZ. In general, these activities have the essential feature that the data generated are used for military purposes only and are not released to the public. It is often accepted that the operating State has the right to determine if a certain activity is of military nature and for military purposes, with other States having less means to question this categorisation.[214] The coastal State, for instance, would have to accept that the data allegedly collected for military purposes does not have direct economic value and would not impede the normal exercise of its sovereign rights and jurisdiction. Nevertheless, the increasing sophistication of surveillance capabilities has put the appropriate balance between the

[211] See further discussion in Chapter 8 in this volume.

[212] 中华人民共和国东海防空识别区航空器识别规则公告, 2013年11月23日 (Announcement of the Aircraft Identification Rules of the East China Sea Air Defense Identification Zone of the People's Republic of China, 23 November 2013), www.gov.cn/jrzg/2013-11/23/content_2533101.htm; 中华人民共和国政府关于划设东海防空识别区的声明(Statement by the Government of the People's Republic of China on the Establishment of the East China Sea Air Defense Identification Zone)，23 November 2013 www.gov.cn/jrzg/2013-11/23/content_2533099.htm; 王崇敏和邹立刚，《我国在专属经济区建立防空识别区的探讨》，法学杂志，2013年第1期，95–99，第99页 (WANG Chongmin and ZOU Ligang, 'Discussion on Building Air Defence Identification Zone in Our Exclusive Economic Zone' (2013) 1 Law Science Magazine 95, 99).

[213] UNCLOS Article 19(2)(c).

[214] In the Matter of the South China Sea Arbitration before an Arbitral Tribunal Constituted under Annex VII to the 1982 United Nations Convention on the Law of the Sea between the Republic of the Philippines and the People's Republic of China, Award, 12 July 2016, PCA Case No 2013-19, paras 1027–1028.

coastal State and the operating State to a test, as the security interests recognised and protected in the territorial sea or even the territory of the coastal State may be infringed upon without the offender physically entering these areas.[215] However, until the right to protect security interests is recognised in the EEZ, the coastal State does not have a strong legal position to challenge the legality of intelligence gathering and surveillance by a foreign State, other than the vague mutual due regard obligation and the prohibition on the threat or use of force.

6.3.3 *Military Survey and Research*

The military survey is another type of military activity that has been routinely conducted in the EEZ irrespective of the controversy over its legitimacy.[216] It is closely related to the hydrographic survey, oceanographic survey and marine scientific research activities. UNCLOS has relatively clear rules on jurisdiction over marine scientific research in the EEZ, but since it does not provide definitions for any of these activities, States employ differing interpretations that may confuse the attribution of jurisdiction over a specific activity. Thus, there is often disagreement over whether surveys are a marine scientific research activity, and whether military surveys and research should be exempted from coastal State jurisdiction.

Marine scientific research, in general, refers to 'any study or related experimental work designed to increase man's knowledge of the marine environment' that falls under coastal State jurisdiction in the EEZ.[217]

[215] Klein (2011) 220–221.

[216] UN DOALOS, Marine Scientific Research: A Revised Guide to the Implementation of the Relevant Provisions of the United Nations Convention on the Law of the Sea (United Nations 2010) 5–6; Kraska (2011) 270–271; 金永明 (2011) 第76–77页 (JIN (2011) 76–77); 王传剑和李军,《中美南海航行自由争议的焦点法律问题及其应对》,东南亚研究,2018年第5期,132–158,第147页 (WANG Chuanjian and LI Jun, 'The Focal Legal Issues of Sino-US Dispute over the Freedom of Navigation in South China Sea and Their Countermeasures' (2018) 5 Southeast Asian Studies 132, 147).

[217] Alfred H. A. Soons, *Marine Scientific Research and the Law of the Sea* (TMC Hague 1982) 6; UNCLOS Articles 246, 253; United Nations Division for Ocean Affairs and the Law of the Sea Office of Legal Affairs, *Marine Scientific Research: A revised guide to the implementation of the relevant provisions of the United Nations Convention on the Law of the Sea* (United Nations, 2010) 4–6; United States, Department of the Navy, 'Diplomatic Clearance for U.S. Navy Marine Data Collection Activities in Foreign Jurisdictions', OPNAV INSTRUCTION 3128.9G, 22 April 2021, para 4(d) (OPNAV INSTRUCTION 3128.9G) www.secnav.navy.mil/doni/Directives/03000%20Naval%20Operations%20and%20Readiness/03-100%20Naval%20Operations%20Support/3128.9G.pdf.

Hydrographic survey is defined by the International Hydrographic Organization as

> [a] SURVEY having for its principal purpose the determination of DATA relating to bodies of water. A hydrographic survey may consist of the determination of one or several of the following classes of DATA: DEPTH of water; configuration and NATURE OF THE BOTTOM; directions and force of CURRENTS; HEIGHTS and TIMES of TIDES and water stages; and location of topographic features and fixed objects for survey and navigation purposes (emphasis in the original).[218]

Oceanographic survey is defined as '[a] study or examination of any physical, chemical, biological, geological or geophysical condition in the OCEAN, or any part of it. An expedition to gather DATA, samples or information to conduct such studies or examination' (emphasis in the original).[219]

The 1958 Convention on the Continental Shelf distinguished between 'purely scientific research into the physical or biological characteristics of the continental shelf' and other resource-oriented research.[220] The former refers to activities that are solely intended to increase human knowledge about the ocean with the results made internationally available, regardless of their subsequent application, while the latter refers to those undertaken primarily for specific practical purposes, commonly known as applied scientific research.[221] The coastal State may not normally withhold its consent for pure scientific research, but may reserve authorisation over applied scientific research.[222]

UNCLOS does not distinguish survey from scientific research, but various articles refer to research and survey activities separately, and Part XIII deals solely with marine scientific research.[223] A close reading of the provisions shows that the separation only occurs in the context of special passage regimes, including innocent passage, transit passage and archipelagic sea lanes passage, to ensure such passage is 'continuous and expeditious'.[224] It is unclear why survey activities

[218] International Hydrographic Organization (IHO), S-32 IHO - Hydrographic Dictionary, (Hydrographic Dictionary Working Group (HDWG) 2019), Eng ID 5244, https://iho.int/en/standards-and-specifications.
[219] Ibid Eng ID 5250.
[220] Convention on the Continental Shelf Article 5(8).
[221] Soons (1982) 6.
[222] Convention on the Continental Shelf Article 5(8).
[223] UNCLOS Articles 19(2)(j), 21(1)(g), 40, and Part XIII.
[224] UNCLOS Articles 18(2), 19(2)(j), 21(1)(g), 39(1)(c), 40, 54.

have been singled out in these provisions, but State practice remains divided on whether UNCLOS established a separate legal regime for surveying.[225]

UNCLOS nevertheless implies its acceptance of the different treatment between pure and applied scientific research as adopted in the 1958 Convention on the Continental Shelf. It requires that coastal States should normally 'grant their consent for marine scientific research projects' in their EEZs or on their continental shelves to be carried out 'in order to increase scientific knowledge of the marine environment for the benefit of all mankind', emphasising the right to reserve consent for projects for any specific practical purposes.[226] Surveys, both hydrographic and oceanographic, serve the purpose of obtaining knowledge of the condition of the waters and the seabed. Some survey activities also employ the same methods and equipment as scientific research, in particular oceanographic sampling, mid-water and ocean floor parameters, launch and recovery of hydrographic survey launches or other scientific packages, including the handling, monitoring and servicing of remotely operated vehicles.[227] Hence, surveys in general should be considered part of the broader scope of marine scientific research as a type of applied scientific research. However, certain specific survey activities may be exempted from coastal State jurisdiction if they can be assimilated to other preserved freedoms, such as cable surveys, which are regarded as activities associated with the operation of submarine cables.[228] Jurisdiction over hydrographic and oceanographic surveys is more controversial because they provide vital information to determine the geographical features of the seabed that facilitates the exploration and exploitation

[225] Klein (2011) 222–223; Bateman (2005) 165; Sam Bateman, 'A Response to Pedrozo: The Wider Utility of Hydrographic Surveys' (2011) 10 Chinese J Int'l L 117, 179; Roach (2021) 486–493.

[226] UNCLOS Article 246(3) and (5); Myron H. Nordquist, Shabtai Rosenne and Alexander Yankov (eds.), *United Nations Convention on the Law of the Sea 1982: A Commentary*, Vol. IV (Martinus Nijhoff 1991) 517–518.

[227] Australian Government, Geoscience Australia, 'Marine and Coastal Survey Techniques' www.ga.gov.au/scientific-topics/marine/survey-techniques; Sam Bateman, 'Hydrographic Surveying in Exclusive Economic Zones: Is it Marine Scientific Research?', in Myron H Nordquist, Tommy Koh, and John Norton Moore (eds.), *Freedom of Seas, Passage Rights and the 1982 Law of the Sea Convention* (Brill 2009) 105, 111–114.

[228] UNCLOS Article 58(1). See also discussion in Chapter 5 in this volume.

of natural resources, which are of great concern for coastal States' economic interests.[229]

The US Navy has adopted the definition of military survey as

> activities undertaken in territorial seas, archipelagic waters, straits for navigation, the EEZ, high seas and on the continental shelf involving marine data collection (whether or not classified) for military purposes (not normally available to the general public or scientific community). Military surveys can include oceanographic, hydrographic, marine geological, geophysical, chemical, biological, acoustic and related data.[230]

Most of these activities can be classified under the category of hydrographic survey, subordinate to a broader definition of marine scientific research.[231] The key element that the US Navy uses to differentiate military surveys from marine scientific research is the 'military purposes' whereby data is not made available to the public.[232] The information generated during a military survey is essential for 'effective submarine operations, anti-submarine warfare, mine warfare and mine countermeasures', particularly in waters where 'oceanographic and underwater acoustic conditions vary widely with uneven bottom topography, fast tidal streams and a relatively high level of marine life'.[233] Similar to the data collected by intelligence gathering and surveillance activities, a military survey provides the operating State important knowledge to make decisions about their defence strategies.

The United States routinely conducts military surveys and research seaward of foreign territorial seas and has continued to do so since the establishment of the EEZ.[234] It has also clearly stated that hydrographic

[229] UNCLOS Article 246(5)(a); Soons (1982) 118–125; Alfred H. A. Soons, 'The Legal Regime of Marine Scientific Research: Current Issues', in Myron Nordquist, Ronán Long, Tomas Heidar and John Norton Moore (eds.), *Law, Science & Ocean Management* (Brill 2007) 139, 160; Bateman (2011) 180–181; Haiwen Zhang, 'The Conflict between Jurisdiction of Coastal States on MSR in EEZ and Military Survey', in Myron Nordquist, John Norton Moore and Kuen-Chen Fu (eds.), *Recent Developments in the Law of the Sea and China* (Brill 2006) 317, 328.

[230] OPNAV INSTRUCTION 3128.9G para 4(b).

[231] Mohammad Hanif Hamden and Ami Hassan Md Din, 'A Review of Advancement of Hydrographic Surveying towards Ellipsoidal Referenced Surveying Technique', (2018) IOP Conf Ser: Earth Environ Sci 169 012019.

[232] Roach (2021) 541; OPNAV INSTRUCTION 3128.9G para 4(d).

[233] Bateman (2005) 166.

[234] Pedrozo (2010) 12–13; Roach (2021) 538–539.

surveys and military surveys are not marine scientific research.[235] The US Navy has eight ships dedicated to surveying and research. Two are general-purpose oceanographic research vessels that are manned by contracted commercial crews.[236] It also maintains six oceanographic survey ships as part of the twenty-one ships under the Military Sealift Command's Special Mission programme.[237] These survey ships perform acoustic, biological, physical and geophysical surveys using multi-beam, wide-angle, precision sonar systems that are the same as used for hydrographic surveys to collect data on the ocean environment.[238] However, the United States insists that these naval operations are required not to be combined with marine scientific research activities.[239]

In contrast, both China and India take the position that military hydrographic surveys fall under the scope of marine scientific research that is subject to the coastal State's jurisdiction in the EEZ.[240] China requires foreign organisations or individuals that wish to conduct such activities in its EEZ to obtain approval from the competent authorities and observe the provisions of relevant Chinese laws, administrative rules and regulations.[241] This requirement would forbid any foreign entity from conducting military surveys without explicit consent from the Chinese government. China has frequently confronted US military survey and research ships in its EEZ. For example, in September 2009, USNS *Bowditch* was confronted and followed by Chinese patrol planes and vessels in the Yellow Sea while doing oceanographic surveys, which led to a collision between a Chinese fishing vessel and *Bowditch* that

235 United States, Department of State, Office of Ocean and Polar Affairs, 'Marine Scientific Research Consent Overview' www.state.gov/marine-scientific-research-consent-overview/.

236 Roach (2021) 538.

237 United States Navy's Military Sealift Command, 'Special Mission (PM2)', Oceanographic Survey Ships: USNS Bowditch, USNS Bruce C. Heezen, USNS Henson, USNS Pathfinder, USNS Mary Sears, USNS Marie Tharp.

238 United States Navy's Military Sealift Command, 'Special Mission (PM2)'; Melvin J Umbach, *Hydrographic Manual* (4th ed., United States, Department of Commerce, National Oceanic and Atmospheric Administration, 4 July 1976) Part One, https://nauticalcharts.noaa.gov/publications/docs/standards-and-requirements/hydrographic-manual/hydro-man-4th-edition.pdf; IHO, *Manual on Hydrography* (IHO 2005) chapter 1 http://acls-aatc.ca/wp-content/uploads/2017/06/iho-manual.pdf.

239 OPNAV INSTRUCTION 3128.9G paras 6.a.(8)–(10); Roach (2021) 539.

240 China, Exclusive Economic Zone and Continental Shelf Act Article 9; India, Act No. 80 (1976) Article 7(5).

241 China, Surveying and Mapping Law, Article 7.

damaged its sonar system.[242] India also has restricted foreign military activities in its EEZ.[243] It challenged the USNS *Bowditch* for conducting military surveys in its EEZ in 2004, with India claiming that 'the warship gathered data that could reveal much military information on the ocean environment, including identifying possible underground nuclear facilities and submarines. Such data helps reorient technology in undersea warfare and enemy ship detection'.[244]

There is no general consensus in relation to military surveys and research in the EEZ.[245] It could be argued that surveys are a type of marine scientific research that should be regulated by the coastal State in the EEZ except those that can be exempted. The crucial issue is whether military surveys and research should be exempted from coastal State jurisdiction due to their military purpose. The data collected could be used to support the safety of navigation, increase the knowledge of the marine environment for economic purposes, or assist with warfare planning. In practice, the coastal State cannot be certain of the type and purpose of the survey or research that military entities are conducting in its EEZ, which tends to raise suspicions and provoke conflicts.[246] The coastal State may only challenge such activities if they violate its sovereign rights over natural resources or jurisdiction over marine scientific research, but they lack a legal basis to challenge such vessels for constituting a threat to its security interests.

Due to the highly political nature and sensitivity of the data collected, it seems unlikely that disputes on this matter will be easily resolved between States or settled by international courts and tribunals in the

242 魏庆, '美间谍船潜伏中国近海 助侦察攻击中国核潜艇', 2015年03月04日 (WEI Qing, 'US Spy Ship Lurks in China's Coastal Waters to help Detect and Attack Chinese Nuclear Submarines' 4 March 2015), www.xinhuanet.com/mil/2015-03/04/c_127541834.htm; '2001–2009 South China Sea Developments' www.globalsecurity.org/military/world/war/south-china-sea-2009.htm; 李广义，万彬华和朱宏杰，《论专属经济区军事活动的权利与义务》，中国海洋法评论，2011年第1期，134–147，第138–140页 (LI Guangyi, WAN Binhua and ZHU Hongjie, 'On the Rights and Obligations of Military Activities in the Exclusive Economic Zone', (2011) 1 China Oceans Law Review 134, 138–140).

243 UNCLOS, Declarations and Statements, India, Declaration made upon Ratification (29 June 1995), para (b).

244 Ranjit Bhushan, 'Port Hole: An American Warship Is Caught Spying in the Indian Waters under the Pretext of Research', Outlook, 7 June 2004 https://outlookindia.com/magazine/story/port-hole/224131 (last visited in December 2023).

245 Franckx (2011) 198; Pedrozo (2021) 48.

246 Zhang (2010) 37–38; Moritaka Hayashi, 'Military Activities in the Exclusive Economic Zones of Foreign Coastal States' (2012) 27(4) Int'l J Marine & Coastal L 795, 797–799.

near future.[247] It would help to ease tensions if the operating State obeyed the due regard obligation and refrained from collecting data vital to the coastal State's economic interests and gave assurances through notification of the survey time and location. The operating State may also release the data collected, wholly or partially, after a period of time when the secrecy is no longer needed. In particular, if the military research can 'increase scientific knowledge of the marine environment for the benefit of all mankind', the research data should be made available to the public.[248]

6.3.4 *Military Installations, Structures and Other Devices*

Many maritime powers have deployed various military devices, installations and structures in and onto the ocean floor, including the seabed of foreign EEZs, that play a significant role in military uses of the sea.[249] These objects can be placed on the seabed directly, or through storage and other facilities, including submarines, submarine cables, platforms or installations fixed onto the seabed.[250] Examples of these objects include undersea data centres, espionage equipment, sonar monitoring and surveillance systems, navigation aids for submarines and warships, armed mines and other weapon systems.[251] Given the lack of explicit attribution of the right to deploy military objects in the EEZ, the attribution and exercise of such a right should follow the rules established in Article 59 of UNCLOS and the obligations of exercising co-existing rights. Each type of military object will be discussed below to determine whether they are more closely associated with the communication freedoms under Article 58, or with the sovereign rights and jurisdiction of the coastal State, particularly its jurisdiction over 'installations and structures' under Article 60.

Submarines and other warships deploy listening equipment and other detection and communication devices to monitor the positions, movement and numbers of submarines or other military forces in the targeted

[247] Franckx (2011) 199; Tanaka (2019) 442–444.
[248] Tallinn Manual 2.0 (2017) 240; UNCLOS Article 244.
[249] Treves (1980) 808–809.
[250] Ibid; Tallinn Manual 2.0 (2017) 253.
[251] Hayashi (2005) 129–130; Tallinn Manual 2.0 (2017) 234–235.

area.[252] They are essential components of anti-submarine warfare, which dates back to the First World War when 'the British effectively used listening devices (hydrophones) and aircraft to detect German U-boats, and depth charges and mines to sink them'.[253] The continental slope is an ideal area to place anti-submarine warfare sonar devices, as they can pick up sounds at a greater distance over the deep seabed, and the advancement of technology over the past five decades provides a high degree of accuracy.[254] These data provide important information to assist with targeting and navigation, as well as scouting another State's military capability and movements, which could be essential in avoiding surprise attacks.[255] It seems that these monitoring and surveillance devices are more closely associated with the operation of ships than the exploration and exploitation of natural resources. States often argue that the use of such devices is essential to protect their security interests, but many of them still challenge the deployment of these devices by a foreign State within their EEZ or on their continental shelf.

States are also deploying various expendable marine instruments to collect data about the water column for a variety of purposes, including modelling global warming and other hydrologic changes, locating natural resources and monitoring the movement of submarines and other naval operations.[256] Both warships and scientific research ships routinely deploy expendable instruments into the ocean, with an estimated deployment of millions of such instruments worldwide between the 1960s and 1990s.[257] Underwater explosions or disposal of unwanted explosives at sea can have harmful effects on marine living creatures and the environment due to the shock waves and release of toxic chemicals.[258] When such expendable instruments are used as part of a marine scientific

[252] Treves (1980) 810–811.

[253] Frank Barnaby, 'Strategic Submarines and Antisubmarine Warfare' (1978) 1 Ocean YB 376, 378.

[254] Larson (1979) 53; Brian Taddiken, '66 Years of Undersea Surveillance' (2021) 35(1) Naval History Magazine www.usni.org/magazines/naval-history-magazine/2021/february/66-years-undersea-surveillance; James Kraska and Raul Pedrozo, 'Seabed Warfare', in James Kraska and Raul Pedrozo, *Disruptive Technology and the Law of Naval Warfare* (Oxford University Press 2022) 174–179.

[255] Treves (1980) 810.

[256] James Kraska, 'Oceanographic and Naval Deployments of Expendable Marine Instruments under US and International Law' (1995) 20 Ocean Dev Int'l L 314, 337; Hayashi (2005) 130.

[257] Kraska (1995) 314.

[258] Wang (1992) 373.

research project in the EEZ, they must be authorised by the coastal State.[259] Given that their use is mainly for navigation and survey purposes, military forces of all States may deploy such instruments in the EEZ. Their use must observe the obligations set out in UNCLOS for military activities at sea. In particular, the use of expendable instruments in the EEZ must not interfere with the exercise of another States' rights and duties, including the coastal State's sovereign rights and jurisdiction.[260] The operating State should also adopt appropriate measures to ensure that their normal uses are consistent, as far as is reasonable and practicable, with environmental protection and preservation requirements.[261]

States have traditionally deployed armed mines and other weapon systems on the seabed. The 1971 Seabed Treaty prohibits the emplacement of nuclear weapons and other weapons of mass destruction and of installations specially designed to store, test or use them on the seabed beyond 12 miles from shore.[262] But the treaty is silent on other conventional weapons. It could be argued that, in peacetime, the emplacement of weapons on the continental shelf by both the coastal State and other States is not in full compliance with the peaceful purposes obligation except for legitimate self-defence as recognised by the UN Charter.[263] In addition, deploying weapon systems by a foreign State in a nearby marine area poses direct threats to a coastal State's security interests, along with the possibility of causing irreparable damage to the marine environment, and interferes with the exercise of the rights and freedoms by other States in the EEZ.[264]

Submarine cables, including the repeaters, could also be used for military purposes.[265] The military may build, purchase or lease a submarine fibre optic cable for a variety of purposes, including telecommunications, acoustic monitoring and bilateral communications.[266] The US

[259] UNCLOS Articles 56(1)(b)(ii), 246(1)–(2).
[260] UNCLOS Articles 56(1)(b)(iii), 192.
[261] UNCLOS Article 236.
[262] 1971 Seabed Treaty Articles 1–2.
[263] UNCLOS Articles 88, 301; UN Charter Article 51.
[264] Lowe (1986) 180.
[265] For the freedom to lay submarine cables and their protection, see Chapter 5 in this volume.
[266] J. Ashley Roach, 'Military Cables', in Douglas R. Burnett, Robert C. Beckman and Tara M. Davenport (eds.), *Submarine Cables: The Handbook of Law and Policy* (Brill 2014) 339, 339–343.

Navy, for example, maintains two cable laying/repair ships to transport, deploy, retrieve and repair undersea cables.[267] Moreover, the military could use a purpose-built submarine or unmanned underwater vehicle to physically tap communication cables in order to collect, alter or jam any traffic transmitted through them, particularly in relation to cyber operations.[268] Furthermore, as technology develops, the military could build undersea data centres associated with or without a submarine cable.[269] The freedom to lay submarine cables, including uses associated with the operation of cables, should apply to military cables.[270] Tapping operations of submarine cables in the EEZ do not constitute a violation of the rights of the coastal State unless they interfere with the exploration and exploitation of the seabed and its natural resources.[271] The establishment of military undersea data centres, either an installation or structure, by a foreign State in the EEZ would be questionable if it interferes with exercise of the rights of the coastal State.[272]

It is relevant to clarify the scope of a coastal State's jurisdiction under Article 60 over the use of installations and structures in the EEZ.[273] The coastal State's 'exclusive right to construct and to authorize and regulate the construction, operation and use of' installations and structures is limited to those 'for the purposes provided for in Article 56 and other economic purposes' and those that 'may interfere with the exercise of the rights of the coastal State in the zone'.[274] Apart from resource-related activities, these economic purposes include 'other activities for the economic exploration and exploitation of the zone, such as the production of energy from the water, currents and winds', marine scientific research, and the protection and preservation of the marine environment.[275] A plain reading of this provision may lead to the conclusion that the

[267] United States Navy's Military Sealift Command, 'Special Mission (PM2)', Cable Laying & Repair Ships: USNS Zeus and CS Global Sentinel.

[268] Tallinn Manual 2.0 (2017) 168–169, 253; Marcia Wendorf, 'Operation Ivy Bells: The U.S. Top-Secret Program That Wiretapped a Soviet Undersea Cable', Interesting Engineering, 17 August 2019 https://interestingengineering.com/innovation/operation-ivy-bells-the-us-top-secret-program-that-wiretapped-a-soviet-undersea-cable.

[269] Tallinn Manual 2.0 (2017) 234–235.

[270] UNCLOS Article 58(1).

[271] Tallinn Manual 2.0 (2017) 257; UNCLOS 79(2).

[272] Tallinn Manual 2.0 (2017) 235; UNCLOS Article 60(1)(c).

[273] For the coastal State's jurisdiction over artificial islands, installations and structures, see Chapter 4 in this volume.

[274] UNCLOS Article 60(1)(b)–(c).

[275] UNCLOS Article 56(1)(a)–(b).

use of military objects on the seabed, which generally are not for resource-related purposes, is exempted from the exclusive right of the coastal State. However, a coastal State may find legitimate grounds to challenge the use of foreign military installations or structures if they interfere with the exercise of its rights and jurisdiction in the EEZ. The extension to potential interference expands and strengthens the legal basis for the coastal State to challenge the deployment of these military objects.[276]

Under the 1958 Convention on the Continental Shelf, the coastal State is entitled to construct and maintain or operate on the continental shelf 'installations and other devices' necessary for the exploration and exploitation of its natural resources.[277] Under UNCLOS, the language was changed to 'installations and structures' and the term 'devices' is used separately elsewhere.[278] This distinction indicates that the two terms have a different connotation. The term 'devices'[279] refers to objects that operate in certain mechanical or chemical ways or have attributes permitting their use for the performance of certain tasks, while the term 'structures'[280] refers only to those lacking operative characteristics or functional attributes.[281] The term 'structures' is a narrower concept than 'devices'.[282] This interpretation is confirmed in Article 209, where the two terms are phrased as 'vessels, installations, structures and other devices', indicating that the term 'devices' includes 'structures'.[283] Consequently, 'devices' that cannot be considered as 'structures' are not objects that fall under the exclusive rights and jurisdiction of the coastal State.[284]

Under contemporary international law, it is arguable that any State can use the ocean floor of the EEZ and the continental shelf to deploy and service military devices, installations and structures that do not fall under the jurisdiction of the coastal State, even with the contrary argument from a coastal State that is often backed by political objections.[285]

276 Treves (1980) 841.
277 Convention on the Continental Shelf Article 5(2).
278 UNCLOS Articles 56(1)(b)(i), 79(4), 80.
279 UNCLOS Articles 19(2)(f), 145(a), 194(3)(c)–(d), 209(2), 274(b).
280 UNCLOS Articles 1(5)(a)-(b), 56(1)(b)(i), 60, 79(4), 80, 207(1), 208(1), 209(2), 214, 246 (5)(c), 268(c), 269(a).
281 Rex J Zedalis, 'Military Installations, Structures, and Devices on the Continental Shelf: A Response' (1981) 75 Am J Int'l L 926, 930.
282 Treves (1980) 841.
283 UNCLOS Article 209(2).
284 Treves (1980) 841.
285 O'Connell (1982) 488.

Nevertheless, the uses of these military objects must fulfil important obligations. First, such uses of the seabed must be for peaceful purposes only, and weapons systems should not be deployed unless for legitimate self-defence purposes. Second, the operating State must comply with the due regard obligation, whereby there should not be any unreasonable interruption to the exercise of rights and freedoms of other States, particularly those of the coastal State. However, there is a considerable difference between the operating State fulfilling its obligations and the coastal State forbidding these activities, as the latter denies such uses as a freedom.

6.3.5 *Remarks on Conflicting Practices*

The preceding discussion demonstrates that, even though there is no clear attribution of jurisdiction over military activities in the EEZ, both coastal States and other States routinely conduct such activities. The key controversies are that States have different interpretations of whether a foreign State may conduct certain military activities in the EEZ of another State, and what kind of restrictions are placed on the operating State.

The resolution of conflicts regarding the conduct of military activities in the EEZ should follow the formula provided by Article 59. Certain foreign military activities would be restricted to give priority to the coastal State's economic interests in the EEZ.[286] For example, foreign military activities must not involve the exploration and exploitation of natural resources in the EEZ, nor can they unduly interfere with the exercise of the EEZ-related rights of the coastal State.[287] Military manoeuvres, especially those that involve the use of weapons, should be balanced with the coastal State's sovereign rights either through notification or consultation. However, military activities that do not interfere with the coastal State's sovereign rights can be carried out by all States. These activities include military navigation and overflight, espionage, intelligence gathering, surveillance, military survey and the use of military devices.

The exercise of the right to conduct all peacetime military activities, by both the coastal State and other States, must fulfil the reciprocal due

[286] Nordquist, Nandan and Rosenne (1993) 560.
[287] UNCLOS Articles 56(1), 58(3).

regard obligation to other States. Military activities that have a severe impact on natural resources or cause irreparable damage to the marine environment could be considered as violating the coastal State's rights and jurisdiction.[288] For example, if foreign military manoeuvres and ballistic exercises take place in a fishing area, or in close proximity to an active offshore oil platform, or as near as 13 NM from the coast, the coastal State may oppose or impose certain requirements.[289] In turn, the coastal State should not conduct any military activities that unduly impair the freedoms of navigation and overflight, the laying of submarine cables and pipelines, and other internationally lawful uses of the sea related to these freedoms.

In cases where the coastal State determines that the foreign warship or military aircraft has abused its rights in the EEZ, the coastal State, even though it cannot exercise enforcement jurisdiction, may require the departure of foreign military entities from this maritime area.[290] In addition, if the alleged wrongful act has caused any loss or damage to the coastal State, the flag State must bear international responsibility for such wrongdoings.[291] In cases where the foreign State asserts that its freedoms have been affected by the coastal State's conduct of a military activity, it may challenge such conduct initially through diplomatic channels. States must be cautious as to what measures are used against another State's warship or military aircraft. As a warship is 'an expression of the sovereignty of the State whose flag it flies', 'any action affecting the immunity of warships is capable of causing serious harm to the dignity and sovereignty of a State' and hence 'imping[e] on the maintenance of international peace and security'.[292]

[288] UNCLOS Article 56(1)–(2).

[289] Oxman (1983–1984) 826–827.

[290] Julio Cesar Lupinacci, 'The Legal Status of the Exclusive Economic Zone in the 1982 Convention on the Law of the Sea', in Vicuna (1984) 103; 金永明,《专属经济区内军事活动问题与国家实践》,法学,2008年第3期,118–126,第125–126页 (JIN Yongming, 'Foreign Military Activities in the EEZ and State Practice' (2008) 3 Legal Science 118, 125–126).

[291] UNCLOS Article 31; International Law Commission (ILC), 'Draft Articles on Responsibility of States for Internationally Wrongful Acts', (2001) 2(2) YB ILC 31, Articles 1, 2, 36.

[292] 'ARA Libertad' Case, paras 44, 46–47, 94, 97; Separate Opinion of Judge Chandrasekhara Rao, para 16; Detention of Three Ukrainian Naval Vessels (Ukraine v. Russian Federation), Provisional Measures, Order of 25 May 2019, ITLOS Reports 2018–2019, p. 283, para 110.

It is noteworthy that disputes concerning military activities are optional exceptions to the compulsory third-party dispute settlement procedures established by UNCLOS. Upon signing, ratifying or acceding to UNCLOS, or at any time thereafter, any State may declare in writing that it does not accept the compulsory procedures with respect to 'disputes concerning military activities, including military activities by government vessels and aircraft engaged in non-commercial service'.[293] As of 2024, twenty-four States have made declarations to exclude themselves from the compulsory procedures with regard to this exception.[294] Moreover, the United States holds the opinion that, under Article 298(1)(b), each State party has the exclusive right to determine whether its activities are or were 'military activities' and that such determinations are not subject to review.[295] The distinction between certain military activities and non-military activities, particularly survey, research and law enforcement activities has blurred considerably. The distinctive feature of a military activity is based 'primarily on an objective evaluation of the nature of the activities in question, taking into account the relevant circumstances in each case'.[296] Given the political nature of disputes concerning military activities, it is not very likely that this kind of dispute will soon come before an international tribunal. It is highly recommended that States reconcile their differences through mutual understanding and confidence-building measures to avoid escalation of disputes over military activities in the EEZ.

293 UNCLOS Article 298(1)(b).

294 UNCLOS, Declarations and Statements. The 24 States are: Algeria, Argentine, Belarus, Cabo Verde, Canada, Chile, China, Cuba, Ecuador, Egypt, France, Greece, Guinea-Bissau, Kenya, Mexico, Portugal, Republic of Korea, Russian Federation, Saudi Arabia, Thailand, Togo, Tunisia, Ukraine and the United Kingdom. Argentina withdrew its declaration of optional exception in 2012. Denmark, Nicaragua, Slovenia and Norway declared specific choices on the forum with regard to disputes concerning military activities and law enforcement activities.

295 United States Senate, Committee on Foreign Relations, Executive Report 110-09: Convention on the Law of the Sea, 19 December 2007, 19 www.foreign.senate.gov/treaties/103-39.

296 Detention of Three Ukrainian Naval Vessels (Ukraine v. Russian Federation) (Order of 25 May 2019) paras 64–66.

6.4 International Efforts to Reconcile Conflicts over Military Activities

6.4.1 Agreements to Prevent Incidents at Sea

As political tensions kept rising during the Cold War, the USSR concluded a number of bilateral agreements with Western maritime powers to prevent incidents between their military entities at sea beyond the limit of the territorial sea.[297] These agreements were formulated to reduce misunderstanding between the parties and to promote safety at sea for all interested States.

In order to prevent the accidental outbreak of nuclear war in light of several close incidents between naval forces in the 1960s, the United States and the USSR concluded the 1972 Agreement on Prevention of Incidents on and over the High Seas (US-USSR Agreement), which came into force on the same day.[298] The US-USSR Agreement obligates the parties to 'take measures to instruct commanding officers of their respective ships to observe strictly the letter and spirit of the International Regulations for Preventing Collision at Sea' and the principles with respect to conducting operations at sea as recognised in the 1958 Convention on the High Seas.[299] Specifically, it provides detailed guidelines for preventing accidents on the high seas while conducting naval operations.[300] In an amendment made by an exchange of notes between the two States in 1998, the US-USSR Agreement applies to 'waters outside the limits of the territorial sea'.[301] Consequently, these operational guidelines are applicable to both parties' navies, where each is operating in the other's EEZ.

The USSR concluded similar bilateral agreements for the purpose of reducing provocative or risky behaviour of armed forces and military aircraft beyond the limit of the territorial sea with the United Kingdom in

[297] Churchill, Lowe and Sander (2022) 282–283.

[298] Agreement between the Government of the United States of America (US) and the Government of the Union of Soviet Socialist Republics (USSR) on the Prevention of Incidents On and Over the High Seas, 25 May 1972 (US-USSR Agreement) https://2009-2017.state.gov/t/isn/4791.htm (archived content).

[299] Ibid Article II.

[300] Ibid Article III.

[301] Russian Federation (12957), Agreement Amending the Agreement of May 25, 1972, on the Prevention of Incidents On and Over the High Seas, Treaties and Other International Acts Series 12957 (in force 28 May 1998) www.state.gov/12957.

1986,[302] with Germany in 1988[303] and with France, Canada and Italy in 1989[304] (USSR Prevention of Incidents at Sea Agreements). It is notable that all of these agreements have adopted practical measures to assist the State parties in fulfilling their obligations, including the requirements for an annual meeting to review the implementation of the terms, and the use of mutually agreed special signals for communication or marks to be used by the ships and aircraft.[305]

The USSR Prevention of Incidents at Sea Agreements suggest that, at least among contracting parties, all States have an unfettered right to conduct weapons exercises, naval manoeuvres and other military activities beyond the territorial sea, including in a foreign EEZ. Moreover, it is important for States to exchange information and clarify their intentions when conducting military activities, not out of a legal obligation of general international law but for good faith, political and security purposes, in order to promote mutual trust and avoid misunderstandings and thus reduce the chance of potential conflicts.

Since the end of the Cold War, China has been a consistent challenger to the military activities conducted by the United States within its EEZ through operational means.[306] By 'recognizing the need to promote common understanding regarding activities undertaken by their respective maritime and air forces when operating in accordance with

[302] Agreement between the Government of the United Kingdom of Great Britain and Northern Ireland and the USSR Concerning the Prevention of Incidents at Sea beyond the Territorial Sea, 15 July 1986, (1987) 10 LOSB 97–102 (Agreement between the UK and USSR).

[303] Agreement between the Government of the Federal Republic of Germany and the USSR Concerning the Prevention of Incidents at Sea outside Territorial Waters, 25 October 1988, (1989) 14 LOSB 15–27 (Agreement between Germany and USSR).

[304] Agreement between the USSR and the Government of the French Republic Concerning the Prevention of Incidents at Sea Outside Territorial Waters of 4 July 1989, (1990) 16 LOSB 23–34 (Agreement between USSR and France); Agreement between the Government of Canada and the USSR Concerning the Prevention of Incidents at Sea beyond the Territorial Sea, 20 November 1989, (1991) 18 LOSB 25–32 (Agreement between Canada and USSR); Agreement between the Government of the Italian Republic and the USSR Concerning the Prevention of Incidents at Sea Outside Territorial Waters of 30 November 1989, (1990) 16 LOSB 35–46 (Agreement between Italy and USSR).

[305] US-USSR Agreement, Articles III(5), IX; Agreement between the UK and USSR Articles IX and Annex; Agreement between Germany and USSR Article 9 and Annex; Agreement between USSR and France Article IX and Annex; Agreement between Canada and USSR Article IX and Annex; Agreement between Italy and USSR Article IX and Annex.

[306] Pedrozo (2010) 13; Pedrozo (2021) 49–50.

international law, including the principles and regimes reflected in the [UNCLOS]', the United States and China concluded the Agreement on Establishing a Consultation Mechanism to Strengthen Military Maritime Safety in 1998 (US-China Agreement).[307] It establishes a stable channel for consultations between the two States consisting of three mechanisms, namely annual meetings, working groups of subject matter experts and special meetings for consulting on specific matters.[308] The US-China Agreement has played a momentous role in dealing with incidents between the two States. For instance, the two sides held several special meetings in Beijing after the April 2001 collision discussed earlier in the chapter, which led to an agreement on compensation, the release of the crew and the return of the EP-3 plane, resolving this incident without causing serious setbacks to the relationship between the United States and China.[309] In 2014, the two States signed two memoranda of understanding (MOUs) establishing voluntary confidence-building measures intended to manage risk, enhance mutual understanding and avoid miscalculation between the two militaries: the Notification of Major Military Activities MOU and the Rules of Behavior for Safety of Air and Maritime Encounters MOU.[310] The actual value of the US-China Agreement and MOUs, however, might not have been fully realised, since it has not prevented conflicts from arising.[311] In particular, the bilateral dialogue has been interrupted by the tension in the South China Sea and the Taiwan Strait where both sides blame the other State of provoking actions that threat the stability of the region.[312]

[307] China (12924), Agreement on Establishing a Consultation Mechanism to Strengthen Military Maritime Safety, Treaties and Other International Acts Series 12924 (in force 19 January 1998), Article 1 (US-China Agreement) www.state.gov/12924.

[308] Ibid Article II.

[309] Kan (2001) 21–23.

[310] Caitlin Campbell, 'China Primer: U.S.-China Military-to-Military Relations', Congressional Research Service, In Focus, 4 January 2021 https://crsreports.congress.gov/product/pdf/IF/IF11712.

[311] Pedrozo (2010) 28–29; Zhang (2010) 46; 刘惠荣和田杨洋,《沿海国专属经济区内外国军事活动管辖权辨析》,中国海洋大学学报,社会科学版,2014年第3期,14–19,第18–19页 (LIU Huirong and TIAN Yangyang, 'The Analysis of Jurisdiction over Foreign Military Activities in the EEZ of the Coastal State'(2014) 3 Journal of Ocean University of China, Social Science Edition 14, 18–19).

[312] Campbell (2021); 余敏友和雷筱璐,《评美国指责中国在南海的权利主张妨碍航行自由的无理性》,江西社会科学,2011年第9期,13–19,第17页 (YU Minyou and LEI Xiaolu, 'Comment on the Irrationality of the United States' Accusation that China's Rights Claims in the South China Sea Impede the Freedom of Navigation' (2011)

It is noteworthy that an agreement to prevent an escalation of tensions between militaries at sea would have more influence if it was agreed to and obeyed by many State parties. In 2014, at the Western Pacific Naval Symposium, a series of biennial meetings of Pacific nations to discuss naval matters, naval chiefs of twenty-one States adopted a non-binding Code for Unplanned Encounters at Sea (CUES) that has been subsequently amended.[313] CUES is a set of rules-of-the-road standardising safety protocols, basic communications and basic manoeuvring at sea for ships and aircraft to avoid misjudgement, misunderstanding and mismanoeuvring among navies.[314] Despite of its non-binding nature, CUES may contribute to the improvement of good order at sea and prevent accidental conflicts should the navies follow these rules.

Given that the most controversial practice is between the coastal State that seeks to halt foreign military operations in its EEZ and other States that continue to conduct them, a bilateral agreement or arrangement to prevent conflicts and avoid escalatory events seems necessary and appropriate. An agreement to avoid accidents is one of the confidence-building mechanisms that enhances mutual knowledge and understanding of military activities at sea between the State parties, consequently reducing the possibility of conflict by accident, miscalculation, or failure of communication.[315] These practices provide a functional framework for States

9 Jiangxi Social Sciences 13, 17); Niharika Mandhana, 'How Beijing Boxed America Out of the South China Sea', The Wall Street Journal, 11 March 2023 (online); 2023 China Military Power Report 5-6, 125, 136-137, 184 .

313 Australian Navy, Western Pacific Naval Symposium (WPNS), as of 2023 WPNS includes 22 Member States and 8 observer nations. The Member States are: Australia, Brunei, Cambodia, Canada, Chile, China, Fiji, France, Indonesia, Japan, Malaysia, New Zealand, Papua New Guinea, Peru, Philippines, Republic of Korea, Russia, Singapore, Thailand, Tonga, United States of America and Vietnam. www.navy.gov.au/media-room/publications/semaphore-14-06 (last visited in December 2023); 'Document: Code for Unplanned Encounters at Sea', USNI News, 17 June 2014 https://news.usni.org/2014/06/17/document-conduct-unplanned-encounters-sea.

314 'Western Pacific Naval Symposium, Workshop 2014, Nanjing, China, 14–17 January 2014, Minutes', para 41 http://img.mod.gov.cn/reports/201310/bzdd/site21/20140213/4437e6581cab14667a2734.pdf; Wang Xinjuan, 'The Western Pacific Naval Symposium serves as an important platform for countries to deepen friendship, promote exchanges and enhance mutual trust' 25 April 2014 http://eng.mod.gov.cn/xb/News_213114/NewsRelease/16303567.html.

315 US-USSR Agreement, Preamble; US-China Agreement, Preamble.

to pay mutual respect to military uses of the sea, and should be implemented effectively and efficiently.

6.4.2 *Regional Disarmament Efforts*

The international community is moving steadily towards peace and security, including global nuclear non-proliferation and disarmament through strengthening political and legal frameworks.[316] Global disarmament efforts affect the general acceptance and use of weapons at sea. States have adopted a number of regional arrangements and treaties that indicate their support for limiting the use of weapons at sea, particularly nuclear weapons, weapons of mass destruction and other strategic weapons.[317] These regional frameworks not only apply to the territorial sea and the EEZ of the State parties but also extend to the high seas. These agreements should be compatible with UNCLOS without affecting the enjoyment of rights or the performance of obligations by States but, nevertheless, may to varying degrees affect the conduct of military activities involving nuclear-armed warships.[318]

The Antarctic Treaty was adopted in 1959 with the aim to reserve the Antarctic for peaceful purposes only and to promote scientific research.[319] It covers the area south of 60° South latitude, within which State parties shall prohibit 'any measures of a military nature, such as the establishment of military bases and fortifications, the carrying out of military maneuvers, as well as the testing of any type of weapons'.[320] The demilitarisation of the Antarctic has eliminated potential armed conflicts or military incidents arising from the complex territorial disputes in the region.[321] By acceding to the Antarctic Treaty, State parties agreed to abolish the military use of

[316] United Nations Office for Disarmament Affairs (UNODA), 'Areas of Work' https://disarmament.unoda.org/.

[317] Securing Our Common Future: An Agenda for Disarmament (United Nations 2018) 61–65 www.un.org/disarmament/sg-agenda/en/.

[318] UNCLOS Article 311(2).

[319] 'The Antarctic Treaty Explained', www.bas.ac.uk/about/antarctica/the-antarctic-treaty/the-antarctic-treaty-explained/; Antarctic Treaty (1 December 1959, in force 23 June 1961) 402 UNTS 71, Articles I–V.

[320] Antarctic Treaty Articles I(1), VI.

[321] Seven States claimed territory in Antarctica (claimants): Argentina, Australia, Chile, France, New Zealand, Norway, and the United Kingdom. See Australian Antarctic Program, 'Antarctic Territorial Claims' www.antarctica.gov.au/about-antarctica/law-and-treaty/history/antarctic-territorial-claims/.

the treaty area, including their frozen maritime zone claims.[322] The Antarctic Treaty remains in force indefinitely, and as of 2024 has twenty-nine Consultative Parties and another twenty-eight Non-Consultative Parties that have no decision-making power.[323]

The efforts of the littoral States to establish the Indian Ocean as a zone of peace date back to the 1970s as a response to the military rivalry between the United Kingdom, the United States and the USSR in the region.[324] This led to the adoption of UNGA Resolution 2832 (1971), which recognises this movement and declared the Indian Ocean, together with the air space above and the sea floor subjacent thereto, to be a 'zone of peace'.[325] It called on all superpowers to enter into immediate consultations with the littoral States with a view to 'halting the further escalation and expansion of their military presence' and to remove 'all bases, military installations and logistical supply facilities, the disposition of nuclear weapons and weapons of mass destruction and any manifestation of great Power military presence' from the region.[326] It also called on States to make efforts to establish 'a system of universal collective security without military alliances and strengthening international security through regional and other co-operation'.[327] The *Ad Hoc* Committee on the Indian Ocean was established in 1972 to study the implications of Resolution 2832 (1971).[328] However, these efforts did not stop the steady escalation of the arms race and the competitive military presence in the region.[329] On the contrary, the United States established a military base on the atoll of Diego Garcia, a British Indian Ocean Territory, in 1971 and maintains its presence to date.[330] Due to the non-participation of many military powers (especially France, the United Kingdom and the United States), the *Ad Hoc* Committee was not been able to embark on any discussions on practical measures to implement the declaration of a

[322] Antarctic Treaty Article VI; UNCLOS Article 311(3).

[323] Secretariat of the Antarctic Treaty, 'Parties' www.ats.aq/devAS/Parties?lang=e.

[324] Rasul B Rais, *The Indian Ocean and the Superpowers: Economic, Political and Strategic Perspectives* (Croom Helm 1986) 29–33, 40–46, 172–173.

[325] UNGA A/RES/2832(XXVI), 16 December 1971, Declaration of the Indian Ocean as a Zone of Peace, Preamble and Article 1.

[326] Ibid Article 2.

[327] Ibid Article 3.

[328] UNGA A/RES/2992 (XXVII), 15 December 1972, Declaration of the Indian Ocean as a Zone of Peace, Article 2.

[329] Rais (1986) 184–185.

[330] Peter H Sand, 'Diego Garcia: British-American Legal Black Hole in the Indian Ocean?' (2009) 21(1) J Env't L 113, 114–115; Chagos MPA Arbitration paras 70–71.

'zone of peace' in the Indian Ocean.[331] In recent years, given the changes in the political environment and security priorities in the region, the *Ad Hoc* Committee has discussed changing its mandate to address non-traditional maritime threats and challenges and continued to call for all permanent members of the Security Council and the major maritime users of the Indian Ocean to support its work.[332]

States have also adopted several regional treaties that, broadly stated, prohibit the testing, use, manufacture, production or acquisition of nuclear weapons through establishing nuclear-free zones and nuclear weapon–free zones covering parts of Latin America and the Caribbean, the South Pacific, Southeast Asia, Africa and Central Asia.[333] For example, in the wake of the Cuban Missile Crisis in 1967, twenty-one Latin American States signed the multilateral Treaty for the Prohibition of Nuclear Weapons in Latin America (Treaty of Tlatelolco).[334] All State parties undertake the obligation to prohibit and prevent in their respective territories, including the territorial sea, the testing, use, manufacture, production, acquisition or any form of possession by any means whatsoever of any nuclear weapons.[335] Through Additional Protocol II, all five nuclear weapon States have committed themselves to respect the status of the nuclear-free zone and not use or threaten to use

[331] UNGA A/60/29, 26 July 2005, Report of the Ad Hoc Committee on the Indian Ocean; UNGA A/RES/64/23, 2 December 2009, Implementation of the Declaration of the Indian Ocean as a Zone of Peace.

[332] UNGA A/74/29, 31 May 2019, Report of the Ad Hoc Committee on the Indian Ocean; UNGA A/78/401, 10 November 2023, Implementation of the Declaration of the Indian Ocean as a Zone of Peace.

[333] UNODA, 'Nuclear-Weapon-Free Zones' https://disarmament.unoda.org/wmd/nuclear/nwfz/.

[334] Treaty for the Prohibition of Nuclear Weapons in Latin America (14 February 1967, in force 22 April 1968) 634 UNTS 281 (Treaty of Tlatelolco). In the first amendment of the Tlatelolco Treaty in 1990, the words 'and the Caribbean' were added to the legal name of the Treaty. See Agency for the Prohibition of Nuclear Weapon in Latin America and the Caribbean, CG/E/Res.267 (E-V), 3 July 1990, Modification to the Treaty for the Prohibition of Nuclear Weapons in Latin America, para 1 www.opanal.org/wp-content/uploads/2015/12/CGE05res267i.pdf. See also Paul D. Beamont and Thomas Rubinsky, 'An Introduction to the Issue of Nuclear Weapons in Latin America and the Caribbean', ILPI Nuclear Weapons Project Background Paper No. 2, December 2012, 3 www.academia.edu/7707739/Nuclear_Weapons_Project_Background_Paper_Nuclear_Weapons_In_Latin_America_and_the_Carribean.

[335] Treaty of Tlatelolco Articles 1–4; Nuclear Threat Initiative (NTI), 'Tlatelolco Treaty' www.nti.org/learn/treaties-and-regimes/treaty-prohibition-nuclear-weapons-latin-america-and-caribbean-lanwfz-tlatelolco-treaty/.

nuclear weapons against any State parties to the Treaty of Tlatelolco.[336] This Treaty created the first nuclear weapon-free zone, which promoted the development of nuclear non-proliferation within this region and beyond, and served as a model for four other nuclear weapon-free zones in the South Pacific (1985), Southeast Asia (1995), Africa (1996) and Central Asia (2006).[337] These zones have been recognised as contributing to 'the security of members of such zones, to the prevention of the proliferation of nuclear weapons and to the goals of general and complete disarmament'.[338]

In summary, States' efforts to regulate military activities at the international level are limited to establishing guidelines to prevent misunderstandings and promote co-operation, and the only agreed prohibition is with regard to the use of nuclear weapons on a regional basis that are largely restricted to areas under the sovereignty of the contracting parties. This confirms that not only is there no general prohibition on conducting military activities in the EEZ under international law[339] but also that States are unable to develop precise legal obligations to regulate such uses. In order to prevent further conflicts at sea, States must take further steps to build mutual trust, including the adoption of good practices for military activities at sea, especially in regions where such activities are most frequently challenged.

6.5 The Way Forward

States regularly conduct a wide range of military activities at sea to protect their respective security interests. The proposal to include coastal State security interests in the EEZ was raised but rejected during the Third Conference, as was the proposal to include military activities as a preserved freedom for all States. As a result, UNCLOS intentionally left military issues out of the EEZ regime. Moreover, the optional exceptions

336 NTI, 'Tlatelolco Treaty: Additional Protocol II'.

337 Susan F. Burk, 'OPANAL Commemoration of 45th Anniversary of the Treaty of Tlatelolco', Panel on Lessons Learned and Good Practices in the Creation and Consolidation of Tlatelolco, Mexico City, 14 February 2012 https://2009-2017.state.gov/t/isn/rls/rm/187535.htm (archived content); IAEA, 'Nuclear-Weapon-Free-Zones' www.iaea.org/topics/nuclear-weapon-free-zones.

338 UNGA A/RES/3472(XXX) A/B, 11 December1975, Comprehensive Study of the Question of Nuclear-weapon-free zones in All Its Aspects, Preamble.

339 Churchill and Lowe (1999) 427.

in the dispute settlement mechanism make it possible for States to exempt any disputes concerning military activities from compulsory adjudication. Given the absence of clear attribution of jurisdiction, the right to conduct an activity with military elements falls under the residual rights provisions in the EEZ and the resolution of associated conflicts following the formula contained in Article 59 and the general principles of attributing and exercising rights and duties in this *sui generis* regime.

Conflicts with regard to military activities in the EEZ need to be resolved on 'the basis of equity and in the light of all the relevant circumstances, taking into account the respective importance of the interests involved to the parties as well as to the international community as a whole'.[340] The formula provided by Article 59 gives no priority to either the coastal State or other States. According to the general rules of attributing rights and duties in the EEZ, it is recognised that the EEZ was established to reserve vital economic interests to the coastal States. Hence, when a military activity concerns economic interests, the priority is inevitably vested with the coastal State; when it is closely associated with the operation of ships or aircraft without impairing the coastal State's economic interests, the priority is granted to the operating State.[341] According to the general rules of exercising co-existing rights in the EEZ, the operating State must ensure military activity is conducted for peaceful purpose only and must have due regard to the rights and obligations of other States.[342] As a result, most military activities are tolerated within the EEZ and only in limited circumstance may they be legally challenged. For example, the coastal State may challenge a foreign military activity in its EEZ if it harms its sovereign rights to natural resources, whereas a non-coastal State may challenge the coastal State's military activity if it unduly impedes its exercise of the freedoms of navigation or overflight.

The international legal system, including the law of the sea, develops in parallel with the changing demands of States. There are certain developments in the international arena that may influence the law on military uses of the sea. The first is the changing balance of power among States in the international arena over the last half century. Fundamentally, the rules of military uses of ocean space serve the military interests of the

340 UNCLOS Article 59.

341 UNCLOS Articles 56, 58; Nordquist, Nandan and Rosenne (1993) 569; Klein (2011) 209.

342 UNCLOS Articles 56(2), 58(3), 88, 301.

States that have the capability to utilise them.[343] Emerging maritime States such as China, India and Brazil, which had previously strongly opposed and challenged these rules, have now gained the capability to use them. For example, the Chinese navy started to conduct military intelligence collection operations in the EEZ of the United States in 2012, and is in the process of expanding its global presence and influence.[344] As these emerging States put increasing emphasis on their security interests at sea, they face the dilemma of restricting foreign military activities in the adjacent area of their coast on the one hand while seeking free and open access to other States' EEZs for military purposes on the other.

Secondly, there has been an international movement of disarmament and non-proliferation of nuclear weapons, and the promotion of confidence-building measures to facilitate collaboration among States rather than reinforcing their separation, showing the universal need for peace management and demilitarisation of the ocean.[345] However, the momentum built after the Cold War is under increasing pressure with the breakout of the war between the Russian Federation and Ukraine, the growing assentation of the Democratic People's Republic of Korea, as well as the mounting tension between China and the United States in the South China Sea and the Strait of and Taiwan.

Thirdly, military forces have been given increasingly diverse functions at sea, including law enforcement, disaster relief assistance, escorting civilian vessels through dangerous areas and engaging in international co-operation programmes in foreign EEZs.[346] While these activities will increase the presence of military forces in foreign EEZs, they may not

[343] Pirtle (2000) 7–8.

[344] Kathrin Hille, 'Chinese Navy Begins US Economic Zone Patrols', Financial Times, 2 June 2013 (online); Kimberly Hsu and Craig Murray, 'China's Expanding Military Operations in Foreign Exclusive Economic Zones', U.S.-China Economic and Security Review Commission Staff Research Backgrounder Paper, 19 June 2013 www.uscc.gov/sites/default/files/Research/Staff%20Backgrounder_China%20in%20Foreign%20EEZs.pdf; 2023 China Military Power Report 52–53, 149–163.

[345] Kraska and Pedrozo (2013) 9; Securing Our Common Future: An Agenda for Disarmament (2018).

[346] G. Lammons and J. Ervin, 'Naval Oceanography Turns Data into Decisions' (2011) 17(2) Ocean News & Technology 34, 35–36; United Nations Security Council, 'Security Council Renews Authorization for International Naval Forces Fighting Piracy off Somali Coast, Unanimously Adopts Resolution 2554 (2020)', Press Release, 4 December 2020 www.un.org/press/en/2020/sc14373.doc.htm.

necessarily cause tension with the coastal States, since they primarily have a civilian purpose.

States will continue to use the EEZ for military purposes despite different interpretations and practices on its legality. It is in the interests of all States to find a balance between maximising their individual maritime rights and jurisdiction in adjacent maritime areas and maintaining the common interest of all States to use the multi-functional EEZ.[347] Subject to observing the peaceful purpose requirement, States could avoid conflicts if both sides obeyed the mutual due regard obligation in good faith and refrained from provoking activities that raise tensions with concerned States. For many of the coastal States that frequently challenge foreign military activities in their EEZs, which challenges are determined from a pure coastal State perspective, might gradually change when their navies are capable of conducting the same activities in a foreign EEZ.

Given the political sensitivity of military activities and the lack of clear legal framework, States will maintain different interpretations of the legitimacy of certain military activities in a given situation. Further, States should not take an all-or-nothing approach, whereby all military activities are either subject to the prior consent of the coastal State or subject to an absolute right of all States without any form of prior notification and consultation with the coastal State.[348] This is an approach that both the rules to attribute residual rights and the reciprocal due regard obligations were apparently designed to prevent. To avert destabilising incidents, it is important for States to take the necessary measures to improve mutual understanding and build trust and confidence in order to increase stability, international peace and security at sea.

[347] Stephens and Rothwell (2012) 705–706; Tanaka (2019) 471–472.
[348] Prezas (2019) 115–116.

7

Maritime Security

Security interests at sea have traditionally related to military interests and naval power.[1] While this remains fundamental to the security of States, there is an increasing urgency to address other diverse security threats in and from the maritime domain by non-State actors.[2] Non-military or non-traditional maritime security goes back to early maritime history under the rubrics of piracy and barratry, but now includes illegal immigrants; maritime terrorism; people, weapon and drug trafficking; information security; and environmental security, among others.[3]

The right to protect maritime security is not explicitly included in the exclusive economic zone (EEZ) regime, albeit the United Nations Convention on the Law of the Sea (UNCLOS) addresses the specific threats to maritime security in some way or another.[4] From the perspective of resolving conflicts regarding maritime security interests, based on the criteria provided in Article 59 and the general rules of attributing rights and duties in the EEZ, States could assert jurisdiction over activities that are related to their endowed rights or freedoms in this *sui generis* zone, or are otherwise provided by international instruments. The claims of jurisdiction over maritime security in the EEZ by different States often overlap and sometimes compete with one another. This is because States have both shared interests in maintaining the security of navigation and other

[1] Linton F. Brooks, 'Naval Power and National Security: The Case for the Maritime Strategy' (1986) 11(2) Int'l Sec 58, 58–60; Natalie Klein, *Maritime Security and the Law of the Sea* (Oxford University Press 2011) 1.

[2] Natalie Klein, 'Maritime Security', in Donald R. Rothwell, Alex G. Oude Elferink, Karen N. Scott and Tim Stephens (eds.), *The Oxford Handbook of the Law of the Sea* (Oxford University Press 2015) 582–583; Jun Zhao, 'Non-traditional Maritime Security and International Cooperation' (2015) 45(3) Hong Kong LJ 743, 744–745.

[3] Vinh V. Thai, 'Effective Maritime Security: Conceptual Model and Empirical Evidence' (2009) 36(2) Marit Pol Mgmt 147, 147–148; Christian Bueger, 'What Is Maritime Security?' (2015) 53 Marine Policy 159, 160–161.

[4] United Nations Convention on the Law of the Sea (10 December 1982, in force 16 November 1994) 1833 UNTS 3, Articles 99–111 (UNCLOS).

communication rights, as well as competing interests in protecting their respective priorities. From the perspective of exercising the right to protect maritime security interests, the general rules of exercising co-existing rights and duties continue to apply with regard to measures to address threats to maritime security. In the case where different States share concurrent jurisdiction over certain threats to maritime security, they are required to respect each other's rights and duties and are expected to cooperate to promote mutual security.

This chapter examines the current and emerging State practice in respect of preventing and combatting maritime security threats, it discusses the respective interests involved in attributing specific rights and jurisdiction and explores the rules for States in exercising them. It is divided into four sections. Section 7.1 discusses the concept of maritime security and the security interests as shown in the EEZ. The protection of maritime security in the EEZ refers to the right of States to address various threats to their legitimate rights and interests as recognised in this zone. Section 7.2 reviews the current international legal framework for combatting specific threats to maritime security. In the attribution of jurisdiction, it remains the flag State that has exclusive jurisdiction over vessels flying its flag, but other States share concurrent jurisdiction over certain international crimes or have been granted authorisation in international agreements to deal with such threats. Section 7.3 explores the implementation by coastal States of measures, including self-help measures, to protect their maritime security interests in the EEZ. There are limited mechanisms under the current international legal framework for the coastal State to effectively combat imminent threats to maritime security in its EEZ, which are often of a transnational nature. Section 7.4 examines the regional and international efforts to combat threats to maritime security and discusses an emerging practice of protecting collective security interests to promote collaboration between States to meet the jurisdiction gap.

7.1 The Concept of Maritime Security

7.1.1 Defining Maritime Security

The very word 'security' is a commonly used term in international relations that does not have a clear definition.[5] Although it may have

[5] Ken Booth, *Theory of World Security* (Cambridge University Press 2007) 96; Ramesh Thakur, *The United Nations, Peace and Security: From Collective Security to the Responsibility to Protect* (2nd ed., Cambridge University Press 2017) 35–36.

different meanings in different contexts, 'security' may simply be understood as an emotive term referring to 'a sense of safety and hence freedom from fear'.[6] Security in the maritime context is closely linked with what may be called 'territorial security', indicating that activities at sea may impinge on actions taken on land.[7] Maritime security refers to a condition in which the maritime rights and interests of a State, recognised by international law, are free from harm or danger from the threat of direct attack and other crimes at sea.[8] Following the decrease in direct military confrontations after the Second World War and the expansion of the security agenda in the twenty-first century, the term 'maritime security' is often used to describe the non-military dimension of security at sea, namely counter-piracy, counter-terrorism, all sorts of counter-trafficking activities and other crimes at sea.[9]

Maritime security is often refered to as a buzzword that enables international cooperation on actions absent a consensus on its definition.[10] As such, maritime security could be analysed through its relations to others terms, the aspects of security of a particular State and how such threats to security have been addressed in practice.[11] Such a conceptual framework proposes to analyse specific threats to a particular State's maritime security based on its relations with national security, economic development, the marine environment and human resilience.[12] This framework analysis methodology concurs with the approach adopted in the 2008 United Nations Secretary-General's Report on Oceans and the

[6] Klein (2011) 2; Lisa Otto, 'Introducing Maritime Security: The Sea as a Geostrategic Space', in Lisa Otto (ed.), *Global Challenges in Maritime Security: An Introduction* (Springer 2020) 6–7.

[7] Klein (2011) 4. For discussions on traditional security interest in the EEZ, see Chapter 6 in this volume.

[8] United Nations General Assembly (UNGA) A/63/63, 10 March 2008, Oceans and the Law of the Sea: Report of the Secretary-General, para 39; 国家海洋局海洋发展战略研究所课题组，中国海洋发展报告 2009 (海洋出版社，2009)，第115页 (China Institute for Marine Affairs, China's Ocean Development Report: 2009) (Ocean Press 2009) 115; Dirk Siebels, *Maritime Security in East and West Africa: A Tale of Two Regions* (Palgrave Macmillan 2020) 19–21.

[9] Klein (2015) 582–583; Donald R. Rothwell and Natalie Klein, 'Maritime Security and the Law of the Sea', in Natalie Klein, Joanna Mossop and Donald R. Rothwell (eds.), *Maritime Security: International Law and Policy Perspectives from Australia and New Zealand* (Routledge 2010) 22–23.

[10] Bueger (2015) 159–160.

[11] Ibid 160–163; Natalie Klein, Joanna Mossop and Donald R. Rothwell, 'Australia, New Zealand and Maritime Security', in Klein, Mossop and Rothwell (2010) 5–9.

[12] Bueger (2015) 160; Christian Bueger, Timothy Edmunds and Barry J. Ryan, 'Maritime Security: The Uncharted Politics of the Global Sea' (2019) 95(5) Int'l Aff 971, 971–974.

Law of the Sea (2008 UN SG Report) and the approaches taken by many States to define their maritime security strategies.

The 2008 UN SG Report, recognising that there is no universally accepted definition of the concept of maritime security and that it can only be analysed in relation to the context and users, identified seven specific activities that are commonly perceived as threats to maritime security.[13] The seven categories of activities include piracy and armed robbery against ships; terrorist attacks on vessels, offshore installations and the people and property on board; illicit trafficking in arms and weapons of mass destruction (WMD); illicit trafficking of drugs and psychotropic substances; smuggling and human trafficking; illegal, unreported and unregulated (IUU) fishing; and intentional and unlawful harm to the marine environment.[14]

Another comprehensive example is the 2014 European Union Maritime Security Strategy (EUMSS), which conceptualises maritime security as 'a state of affairs of the global maritime domain, in which international law and national law are enforced, freedom of navigation is guaranteed and citizens, infrastructure, transport, the environment and marine resources are protected'.[15] EUMSS further defines the strategic maritime security interests of the European Union and its Member States, and then identifies a list of risks and threats to those interests, before articulating how to strengthen the responses to such risks and threats.[16] In addition to the seven specific activities identified in the 2008 UN SG Report, EUMSS's list includes the threat or use of force, maritime disputes, threats to freedom of navigation, natural or human-made disasters including climate change, and illegal pillage of archaeological objects.[17]

Both lists cover various threats to the safety of navigation, national defense strategies, the marine environment, law enforcement activities, fishing and other maritime issues, but this list is not exhaustive. Other harmful acts occurring at sea may also threaten the security of a State's territory, economy, environment and society. For example, with the development of operational technology and automatic vessels, cyber

[13] UNGA A/63/63 paras 39–40.

[14] UNGA A/63/63 paras 54–113.

[15] Council of the European Union, European Union Maritime Security Strategy, Brussels, 24 June 2014, 11205/14, s II (EUMSS).

[16] Ibid ss IV–VI.

[17] Ibid s V.

security is a growing concern of maritime security.[18] Cyber operations could directly target the vessel or network systems within a coastal State, or cyber means could be used to facilitate threats to maritime security.[19] The importance of submarine cables and pipelines to international communications and energy supply may warrant further review of the effectiveness of regulations concerning potential threats to the operation and protection of cables and pipelines lying on the ocean floor.[20]

To discuss maritime security in the EEZ, it is important to first identify which State is the right holder, the security interests of the State that need to be protected and then the means to address existing or potential threats to these interests. Since the Cold War, the security paradigm has undergone a shift from conventional and military interests to non-conventional and non-military interests.[21] Security interests have expanded to include political, economic, societal and ecological concerns that focus on development rights and go beyond the basic needs of survival.[22] As a result, threats to maritime security extend to any events or processes that lead to significant damage to the rights and interests of the coastal State as well as other user States.

7.1.2 Maritime Security in the EEZ

UNCLOS provides for the peaceful use of the sea by setting out a delicately balanced legal framework to accommodate the maritime activities of States.[23] However, there is no provision in UNCLOS that has particular relevance for assessing maritime security in general in the EEZ. Commonly perceived threats to maritime security, including piracy, terrorism, transnational crimes, marine pollution and marine resource management, are all correlative to the EEZ. Therefore, within the EEZ, any State whose legitimate interests are threatened is of relevance when addressing threats to maritime security.

[18] International Maritime Organization (IMO), 'Maritime Cyber Risk' www.imo.org/en/OurWork/Security/Pages/Cyber-security.aspx.

[19] Michael N. Schmitt (ed.), *Tallinn Manual 2.0 on the International Law Applicable to Cyber Operations* (Cambridge University Press 2017) 243 (Tallinn Manual 2.0).

[20] International Law Association (ILA), Committee on Submarine Cables and Pipelines under International Law, Interim Report 2024 on Intentional Damage to Submarine Cables and Pipelines www.ila-hq.org/en_GB/committees/submarine-cables-and-pipelines-under-international-law. See discussion in Chapter 5 in this volume on submarine cables and pipelines.

[21] Suk Kyoon Kim, 'Maritime Security Initiatives in East Asia: Assessment and the Way Forward' (2011) 42 Ocean Dev Int'l L 227, 227.

[22] Booth (2007) 110; UNGA A/63/63 para 40.

[23] UNCLOS Preamble, Articles 88, 138, 141, 301; Rothwell and Klein (2010) 27–29.

From the perspective of threats to maritime security, there are two sets of States' interests to be protected in the EEZ. On the one hand, all States share a collective interest in promoting the safety of navigation, securing the unobstructed transportation of goods and passengers, improving the quality of the marine environment, preventing crimes at sea and maintaining the sustainability of marine resources.[24] All these collective interests are the concern of maritime user States in general. States that undertakes activities in the EEZ of another State have the right to ensure that their nationals or entities are not threatened or harmed. On the other hand, the coastal State has an individual interest in ensuring that its adjacent sea area is not used in a way that could jeopardise its territorial integrity or political independence, or endanger its rights or jurisdiction in the EEZ as recognised by international law.

Protecting lawful maritime interests from imminent threats is different from asserting a special security right in the EEZ. The attempt to assert such a right beyond the territorial sea was rejected by the International Law Commission (ILC) in 1956, where

> [i]t considered that the extreme vagueness of the term "security" would open the way for abuses and that the granting of such rights was not necessary. . . . In so far as measures of self-defence against an imminent and direct threat to the security of the State are concerned, the Commission refers to the general principles of international law and the Charter of the United Nations.[25]

By excluding security interests in the EEZ, it avoided granting the coastal State unbridled discretion, as its determination of a security threat could be unilateral and subjective. This statement did not preclude the coastal State from protecting its security interests from specific threats, which could be addressed according to the rules of general international law.

In addition, protecting non-traditional maritime security interests in the EEZ is different from the practice, as has been used during armed

[24] Leticia M. Diaz and Barry Hart Dubner, 'An Examination of the Evolution of Crimes at Sea and the Emergence of the Many Legal Regimes in Their Wake' (2008–2009) 34 NC J Int'l L & Com Reg 521, 544; Scott Edwards, 'Fragmentation, Complexity and Cooperation: Understanding Southeast Asia's Maritime Security Governance' (2022) 44 (1) Contemporary Southeast Asia: A Journal of International and Strategic Affairs 87, 94–99.

[25] 'Report of the International Law Commission to the United Nations General Assembly, A/3159, Commentary to the Articles Concerning the Law of the Sea' (1956) 2 YB ILC 295, Article 66 Commentary (4) (ILC Draft Articles).

conflicts at sea, of asserting various maritime security zones and maritime exclusion zones.[26] A security/exclusion zone,

> also referred to as a military area, barred area, war zone, or operational zone, is an area of water and superjacent air space in which a party to an armed conflict purports to exercise control and to which it denies access to ships and aircraft without permission.[27]

It explicitly interferes with the freedom of navigation and overflight of other States. The non-traditional security interests in the EEZ relate to the protection of the normal rights of transit and economic exploitation. Moreover, within a security/exclusion zone, the primary responsibility for maintaining security rests with navies. Protecting non-traditional maritime security (in which not only shipping but the entire maritime system is at risk) involves a collective effort of multiple agencies, such as coast guards, marine police forces, customs and immigration organisations, intelligence agencies, port authorities, other law enforcement authorities and commercial entities throughout the maritime sector.[28]

Therefore, combatting threats to maritime security in the EEZ refers to the protection of navigation, overflight, economic exploration and exploitation, the marine environment and other lawful uses from piracy, terrorist acts and other international crimes at sea, in which all States' interests are correlated. The right to address these threats to maritime security, however, is limited based on the legal framework provided by UNCLOS and other international instruments. In addition, States may take significantly different positions with regards to threat perception, the seriousness of a particular threat and the countermeasures necessary to address it. To effectively prevent and combat threats to maritime security in the EEZ, States are expected to exercise their rights in good faith and with due regard to other States' interests, and to cooperate and coordinate with respect to threats that endanger the collective interests of all maritime user States.

[26] Frederick C. Leiner, 'Maritime Security Zone: Prohibited Yet Perpetuated' (1983–1984) 24 Va J Int'l L 967, 968; Daniel P. O'Connell, *The International Law of the Sea, Volume II* (Oxford University Press 1988) 1109–1112.

[27] W. J. Fenrick, 'The Exclusion Zone Device in the Law of Naval Warfare' (1986) 24 Can YB Int'l L 91, 92.

[28] Chris Rahman, The Global Maritime Partnership Initiative: Implications for the Royal Australian Navy (Papers in Australian Maritime Affairs No. 24, Sea Power Centre Australia 2008) 8–9; J. Ashley Roach, *Excessive Maritime Claims* (4th ed., Brill 2021) 691–692.

7.2 Legal Framework to Address Maritime Security Threats

This section provides a brief overview of existing international law that applies to the different threats to maritime security in the EEZ. At the outset of this chapter, the meaning of maritime security was posited as a condition in which the maritime rights and interests of a State, in the context of national security, economic development, the marine environment and human resilience, are free from harm or danger from threats at sea. The most commonly addressed harmful acts are those identified by the 2008 UNSG's Report. Given the extensive literature on these threats, definition of various terms, the factual situation or the level of threats posed by these threats in different regions will not be discussed in detail here. Rather, the focus is on identifying the key international instruments that address these threats, and discussing the attribution of jurisdiction between States. A more comprehensive list of relevant international instruments is illustrated in the Annex to this chapter (Table 7.1).

7.2.1 International Instruments and Marine Security Threats

The first category of threat is pirate activities that endanger the safety and welfare of seafarers, disrupt navigation and commerce, and cause financial losses to ship and cargo owners.[29] The international law of piracy developed gradually throughout the nineteenth century and was codified in Articles 14–22 of the 1958 High Seas Convention, and almost literally restated in Articles 100–107 and 110 of UNCLOS.[30] These provisions apply to the EEZ by reference of Article 58(2). Pirates are criminals subject to universal jurisdiction because their acts pose a threat to all States and their interests in the freedom of navigation.[31] As pirates are

[29] UNGA A/63/63 para 54–62; Klein (2011) 303; Türk (2012) 71; Sami Bensassi and Inmaculada Martinez-Zarzoso, 'How Costly Is Modern Maritime Piracy to the International Community?' (2012) 20(5) Rev of Int'l Economics 869, 869–870.

[30] Donald R. Rothwell and Tim Stephens, *The International Law of the Sea* (Oxford University Press 2010) 162; Douglas Guilfoyle and Rob McLaughlin, 'The Crime of Piracy', in Charles C. Jalloh, Kamari M. Clarke and Vincent O. Nmehielle (eds.), *The African Court of Justice and Human and Peoples' Rights in Context: Development and Challenges* (Cambridge University Press 2019) 389–391.

[31] Paul Hallwood and Thomas J. Miceli, 'An Examination of Some Problems with International Law Governing Maritime Piracy' (2013) 40(1) Marit Pol Mgmt 65, 68–69; James Crawford, *Brownlie's Principles of Public International Law* (9th ed., Oxford University Press 2019) 286; Malcolm D. Evans, 'The Law of the Sea', in Malcolm D. Evans (ed.), *International Law* (5th ed., Oxford University Press 2018) 650; Malcolm D. Evans and Sofia Galani, 'Piracy and the Development of International Law', in Panos

outlawed, ships that are engaged in piratical activities are denied the protection of the flag State whereby any State may capture them on the high seas and in the EEZ and punish them.[32] It is not only a 'long established right' but also a duty for States to 'cooperate to the fullest possible extent in the repression of piracy'.[33]

The second category of threat is terrorist acts that endanger the safety of seafarers, the security of ports, offshore facilities, the ship, the people and property on board and other maritime interests.[34] While the definition of terrorism, including in the maritime context, has never been free from controversy, there is an extensive body of law applicable to specific terrorist acts that threaten security at sea.[35] Unlike piracy that is under universal jurisdiction, the right to address a vessel suspected of terrorism is not permitted in the absence of the flag State's consent.[36] A State other than the flag State, including a coastal State, may only assert the right for intervention to respond to maritime terrorism concerns based on the jurisdictional links provided by international conventions or bilateral agreements, or by the authorisation of the United Nations Security Council (UNSC).[37]

Koutrakos and Achilles Skordas (eds.), *The Law and Practice of Piracy at Sea: European and International Perspectives* (Hart 2014) 344–345.

32 UNCLOS Article 105; Myron H. Nordquist, Satya N. Nandan and Shabtai Rosenne (eds.), *United Nations Convention on the Law of the Sea 1982: A Commentary*, Vol. III (Martinus Nijhoff 1995) 215; Yoshifumi Tanaka, *The International Law of the Sea* (3rd ed., Cambridge University Press 2019) 456; Douglas Guilfoyle, *Shipping Interdiction and the Law of the Sea* (Cambridge University Press 2009) 28–29.

33 ILC Draft Articles Article 38 Commentary (2); UNCLOS Article 100; Nordquist, Nandan and Rosenne (1995) 184; Tullio Treves, 'Piracy and the International Law of the Sea', in Douglas Guilfoyle (ed.), *Modern Piracy: Legal Challenges and Responses* (Edward Elgar 2013) 122; Robin Churchill, Vaughan Lowe and Amy Sander, *The Law of the Sea* (4th ed., Manchester University Press 2022) 383.

34 E. K. J. Pladdet, 'A Report on the Symposium 'Interference with Navigation: Modern Challenges', International Tribunal for the Law of the Sea, Hamburg, Germany, March 15, 2003' (2003) 5 Int'l LF D Int'l 137, 137–138; UNGA A/63/63 paras 63–71.

35 Samuel Pyeatt Menefee, 'Maritime Terror in Europe and the Mediterranean' (1988) Marine Policy 143, 143; Klein (2011) 305; Crawford (2019) 454–455; UNGA A/77/185, 18 July 2022, Measures to Eliminate International Terrorism, Report of the Secretary-General, para 123.

36 UNCLOS Article 92(1); Nordquist, Nandan and Rosenne (1995) 126.

37 Malvina Halberstam, 'Terrorism on the High Seas: The Achille Lauro, Piracy and the IMO Convention on Maritime Safety' (1988) 82(2) Am J Int'l L 269, 295–302; Christopher Staker, 'Jurisdiction', in Evans (2018) 299–306; Crawford (2019) 462–464.

The third category of threat is the illicit trafficking of arms and WMD, particularly for its interlinkage with other violence and crimes at sea.[38] There are several international instruments to suppress and regulate the illicit trafficking or transfer of certain arms and weapons, including through the maritime domain.[39] In addition to strengthening flag State and port State controls, States have also concluded bilateral agreements, including ship-boarding agreements, to provide a treaty basis for the right of visit of vessels reasonably suspected of being engaged in illicit trafficking of arms and WMD material.[40] However, the main challenge to addressing this threat is that there is no widespread consensus among States as to the inherent illegality of possession or trade in conventional arms and WMD material, particularly a common interpretation of the standards for import, export and transfer assessment.[41]

The forth category of threat is illicit trafficking in narcotic drugs and psychotropic substances. Approximately 70 per cent of illicit drugs seized are confiscated either during or after transportation by sea.[42] The flag State has the primary obligation, as well as exclusive jurisdiction, to act against drug trafficking on board its vessels.[43] The authority available to States to act against a foreign-flagged vessel suspected of drug trafficking in the EEZ is limited, however. Despite calling for full cooperation between States to suppress drug trafficking on the high seas, UNCLOS fell short on granting States the right of visit over ships suspected of drug trafficking unless the ship is without nationality.[44] States subsequently

[38] UNGA A/63/63 paras 72–81; United Nations Security Council (UNSC) Res 1549 (2004), 28 April 2004.

[39] UNGA A/63/63 paras 75–78; Arms Trade Treaty (2 April 2013, in force 24 December 2014) 3013 UNTS 269.

[40] United States, Department of State (US DOS), 'Ship Boarding Agreements' https://2009-2017.state.gov/t/isn/c27733.htm (archived content). Participating States include Antigua and Barbuda, Bahamas, Belize, Croatia, Cyprus, Liberia, Malta, Marshall Islands, Mongolia, Panama and St. Vincent and the Grenadines.

[41] UNGA A/63/63 para 75; Guilfoyle (2009) 233; Klein (2011) 309; Arms Trade Treaty Articles 6–8.

[42] UNGA A/63/63 paras 82–88; Guilfoyle (2009) 79; United Nations Office on Drugs and Crime (UNODC), 'Drug Trafficking' www.unodc.org/unodc/en/drug-trafficking/index.html.

[43] UNCLOS Articles 92, 94, 108(2); Nordquist, Nandan and Rosenne (1995) 126, 152, 228.

[44] UNCLOS Articles 108, 110(1)(d); Efthymios Papastavridis, 'Enforcement Jurisdiction in the Mediterranean Sea: Illicit Activities and the Rule of Law on the High Seas' (2010) 25 Int'l J Marine & Coastal L 569, 588–589; Efthymios Papastavridis, *The Interception of Vessels on the High Seas: Contemporary Challenges to the Legal Order of the Oceans* (Hart 2013) 206–207.

adopted international conventions, regional and bilateral agreements to facilitate enforcement related to drug trafficking by sea, particularly with respect to requesting flag State consent to take appropriate measures against a suspected vessel.[45]

The fifth category of threat is human trafficking and migrant smuggling, which usually entails considerable risk to human life and human rights, and poses serious challenges to border and immigration control.[46] The international legal framework that applies to such threats is multifaceted and includes international human rights law, refugee law, criminal law, immigration law and the law of the sea.[47] UNCLOS requires the flag State to exercise effective control over ships flying its flag, including taking appropriate measures to prevent criminal acts at sea. Subsequent international agreements have developed procedures for State parties to request authorisation from the flag State to board, search or take other actions against a vessel that is suspected of being engaged in the smuggling of persons.[48] Some academic literature and State practice treat human trafficking as a modern version of the traditional 'slave trade' or 'practices similar to slavery'.[49] This interpretation would put human trafficking under the universal jurisdiction as recognised in UNCLOS, whereby every State has the right of visit for any vessel suspected of engaging in human trafficking on the high seas and in the EEZ.[50]

The sixth category of threat is IUU fishing, which threatens marine biodiversity, food security and the social and economic development of the coastal State.[51] Unlike the previous five types of threats, the coastal State is accorded explicit right and jurisdiction to enforce its

[45] UNGA A/63/63 paras 84–86; Guilfoyle (2009) 79–91; Carina Bruwer, 'Smuggling and Trafficking of Illicit Goods by Sea', in Otto (2020) 65–66.

[46] UNGA A/63/63 paras 89–97; UNGA A/61/515, 13 October 2006, Summary of the High-Level Dialogue on International Migration and Development, paras 10–11; UNODC 'Human Trafficking'.

[47] UNGA A/63/63 para 91; Klein (2011) 313–314.

[48] United Nations Convention against Transnational Organized Crime and the Protocols Thereto, UNGA A/RES/55/25, 15 November 2000 (in force 29 September 2003), Annex I: United Nations Convention against Transnational Organized Crime, Article 15; Annex III: Protocol against the Smuggling of Migrants by Land, Sea and Air, Article 8.

[49] US DOS, 'What Is Modern Slavery?' www.state.gov/j/tip/what/index.htm; Crawford (2019) 299; Guilfoyle (2009) 228–231.

[50] UNCLOS Articles 58(2), 99, 110(1)(b); Churchill, Lowe and Sander (2022) 398.

[51] UNGA A/63/63 paras 98–106; Klein (2011) 314–315.

laws relating to fisheries in the EEZ under UNCLOS.[52] The greater challenge to the coastal State's fishery jurisdiction concerns the conservation and management of highly migratory species and straddling stocks that are threatened by IUU fishing on the high seas.[53] There is still a reliance on the flag State, and increasingly the port State, to take the necessary actions to ensure the concerned vessel complies with the rules and legislation intended to protect living resources on the high seas.[54]

The seventh category of threat is the intentional and unlawful damage to the marine environment that may harm marine life, damage marine habitats and the ecosystem and affect the social and economic interests of the coastal State.[55] While it remains open how to assess which intentional breach of environmental law may amount to a threat to maritime security, the coastal State has enforcement jurisdiction over vessel-source pollution and dumping in the EEZ.[56] However, the coastal State's enforcement jurisdiction is limited to giving effect to generally accepted international rules and standards, and remains supplementary to the exclusive flag State jurisdiction. Moreover, the damages to the marine environment could arise beyond the scope of vessel-source pollution. For example, the sea could be used to traffick protected species of wild marine fauna and flora, which contributes to the extinction of endangered marine species.[57] There has also been increasing concern over sea shipments of highly radioactive or other ultra-hazardous materials and the risk they pose of causing irreversible damage to the marine environ-

[52] UNCLOS Articles 56(1)(a), 73; Myron H. Nordquist, Satya N. Nandan and Shabtai Rosenne (eds.), *United Nations Convention on the Law of the Sea 1982: A Commentary*, Vol. II (Martinus Nijhoff 1993) 794. See also Chapter 4 in this volume.

[53] Klein (2011) 316–317; Mary Ann Palma-Robles, 'Tightening the Net: The Legal Link between Illegal, Unreported and Unregulated Fishing and Transnational Crime under International Law' (2015) 29 Ocean YB 144, 147–148.

[54] UNGA A/63/63 paras 101–113.

[55] UNGA A/63/63 para 107; Basil Germond, *The Maritime Dimension of European Security Seapower and the European Union* (Palgrave MacMillan 2015) 85.

[56] UNCLOS Articles 56(1)(b)(III), 210(5), 211(5), 216(1)(a), 220(3); UNGA A/63/63 para 108; Klein (2011) 318. See also Chapter 4 in this volume.

[57] Chris Trelawny, 'Tackling the Trafficking of Illegal Wildlife Products: How Can Maritime Transport Contribute?' (2015) 2 IMO News 40, 42 (online); R. L. Castaneda, C. Condit and B. Wilson, 'Legal Authorities for Maritime Law Enforcement, Safety, and Environmental Protection', in Michael A. McNicholas (ed.), *Maritime Security: An Introduction* (Elsevier 2016) 456.

ment.[58] Given the nexus between climate change impacts, ocean acidification, marine life, social vulnerabilities and the occurrence of maritime criminality, there is a growing recognition of a link between climate change effects and threats to maritime security.[59]

7.2.2 *Remarks on Attribution of Jurisdiction*

In sum, States have established a comprehensive legal framework to address specific threats to maritime security. However, the current international legal framework for preventing and combatting maritime security threats reveals an overwhelming reliance on exclusive flag State jurisdiction in areas beyond the territorial sea.[60] The nationality nexus remains the primary foundation for States to assert jurisdiction over unlawful acts at sea irrespective of where the activities took place. The role of the coastal State in the EEZ for combatting threats to maritime security has been effectively marginalised in most scenarios as it has been set against that of the flag State.[61]

From the coastal State's perspective, there are two approaches to enhance the effectiveness of the maritime security international legal framework. First, the coastal State must maximise its opportunities to exercise jurisdiction, to the extent allowed under international law, over suspected offenders in order to protect its maritime security in the EEZ. Second, efforts should be made towards strengthening cooperation and coordination with flag States in responding to maritime security threats, both on bilateral and multilateral levels.

UNCLOS and other international conventions provide for the legislative and enforcement jurisdiction of coastal States with respect to some

[58] Jon M. Van Dyke, 'The Legal Regime Governing Sea Transport of Ultrahazardous Radioactive Materials' (2002) 33 Ocean Dev Int'l L 77, 78; Suzette V. Suarez, 'Post September 11 Security Challenges to the Legal Regime of the Maritime Carriage of Nuclear and Radioactive Materials' (2003) 18 Int'l J Marine & Coastal L 423, 425–426; Jon M. Van Dyke, 'Balancing Navigational Freedom with Environmental and Security Concerns' (2004) 15 Colo J Int'l Env L & Pol'y 19, 22; Stuart Kaye, 'Freedom of Navigation in a Post 9/11 World: Security and Creeping Jurisdiction', in David Freestone, Richard Barnes and David M. Ong (eds.), *The Law of the Sea: Progress and Prospects* (Oxford University Press 2006) 361.

[59] Klein (2011) 319–320; Basil Germonda and Antonios D. Mazaris, 'Climate Change and Maritime Security' (2019) 99 Marine Policy 262, 263–265.

[60] UNCLOS Articles 58(2) 92(1), 94(1) and (6).

[61] UNCLOS Articles 73(1), 77, 111(1)–(2), 220(3) and (5)–(6).

specific threats to maritime security such as piracy, unlawful acts against the safety of navigation, IUU fishing and vessel-source pollution. Coastal States need to take actions to exercise such jurisdiction. Using piracy as an example, international law allows for States to exercise universal jurisdiction but does not demand it.[62] It is up to individual States to domesticise piracy acts under their national laws, exercise enforcement jurisdiction and decide whether to put suspects on trial, to extradite them for prosecution by another State, or not to undertake judicial procedures at all.[63] It can be observed that many coastal States have not exercised the legislative jurisdiction to criminalise piracy under their domestic law, let alone exercise enforcement jurisdiction over suspected pirate ships.[64]

The coastal State may also seek consent from the flag State, through multilateral and bilateral agreements, to exercise concurrent jurisdiction over certain illegal activities in its EEZ, such as smuggling of drugs and trafficking of arms or people. When considering such a request for consent, the flag State should be mindful of its due regard obligation to the rights and duties of the coastal State in the EEZ.[65] In other words, the flag State must recognise the coastal State's interests in combatting various maritime security threats and act with due diligence when considering the coastal State's request for boarding suspect vessels flying its flag.

Therefore, both the flag State and the coastal State may exercise enforcement jurisdiction over specific threats to maritime security by officials or by warships and military aircraft, or other entities clearly marked and identified as being on government service in the EEZ.[66] However, States maintain different positions on whether a foreign State

[62] Douglas Guilfoyle, 'Prosecuting Somali Pirates: A Critical Evaluation of the Options' (2012) 20 J Int'l Crim Just 767, 775; Jan Klabbers, 'Piracy in Global Law and Global Governance', in Panos Koutrakos and Achilles Skordas (eds.), *The Law and Practice of Piracy at Sea: European and International Perspectives* (Hart 2014) 334.

[63] UNCLOS Article 105; Tullio Treves, 'Piracy, Law of the Sea, and Use of Force: Developments off the Coast of Somalia' (2009) 20(2) Eur J Int'l L 399, 402; Türk (2012) 81; Tanaka (2019) 457.

[64] Ilja Van Hespen, 'Developing the Concept of Maritime Piracy: A Comparative Legal Analysis of International Law and Domestic Criminal Legislation' (2016) 31 Int'l J Marine & Coastal L 279, 293; United Nations Division for Ocean Affairs and the Law of the Sea, 'National Legislation on Piracy' www.un.org/depts/los/LEGISLATIONANDTREATIES/piracylegislation.htm; UNGA A/74/10, 20 August 2019, Report of the International Law Commission, Seventy-first Session (29 April–7 June and 8 July–9 August 2019), Annex C: Prevention and Repression of Piracy and Armed Robbery at Sea, National Legislations on Piracy and Armed Robbery at Sea, 386–388.

[65] UNCLOS Article 58(3).

[66] UNCLOS Article 224.

can exercise enforcement jurisdiction in the EEZ of a coastal State and what measures the operating State may take.[67] Besides obeying the general obligations of peaceful purposes and due regard for exercising a co-existing right, the operating State must follow the safeguard measures that are part of law enforcement activities, principally in relation to the use of force.[68]

Many international conventions and non-binding resolutions or guidelines adopted by major international bodies call on all States to cooperate and coordinate to prevent and combat maritime security threats. Such cooperation and coordination should extend on two levels. The first level is between different States, including bilateral cooperation between a coastal State and a flag State, and recognises that threats to maritime security that occurred in a particular EEZ can cause damage to multilateral interest holders. The second level recognises the interconnections between different unlawful activities, such as illicit trafficking of arms to support pirate or terrorist acts, which requires that different enforcement agencies coordinate their responses and actions. In the end, it is in everyone's best interest that the relevant States explore the necessary measures to maintain a secure ocean space for all user States and actors.

7.3 Coastal State Implementation under the Current Legal Framework

The recognition of the coastal State's sovereign rights in the EEZ gives it broad capacity to regulate the economic activities taking place within its EEZ but does not award it jurisdiction over security interests in general. The coastal State's capability to defend and protect its recognised

[67] 王勇，《应当赋予他国在沿海国专属经济区内打击海盗的管辖权—以修改《联合国海洋法公约》为视》，政治与法律，2012年第8期，94-101，第95页 (WANG Yong, 'Should other States be Granted the Jurisdiction to Counter Piracy in the Exclusive Economic Zone of A Coastal State – From the Perspective of Amending the United Nations Convention on the Law of the Sea' (2012) 8 Politics and Law 94, 95.); Tallinn Manual 2.0 (2017) 235; Alleged Violations of Sovereign Rights and Maritime Spaces in the Caribbean Sea (Nicaragua v. Colombia), Judgment of 21 April 2022, ICJ Reports 2022, p. 266, paras 100–101.

[68] UNCLOS Articles 56(2), 58(3), 225, 301; M/V 'Saiga' (No. 2) (Saint Vincent and the Grenadines v. Guinea), Judgment of 1 July 1999, ITLOS Reports 1999, p. 10, para 156; Douglas Guilfoyle, *Shipping Interdiction and the Law of the Sea* (Cambridge University Press 2009) 271; Klein (2011) 116–117; David Harris and Sandesh Sivakumaran, *Cases and Materials on International Law* (8th ed., Sweet and Maxwell 2015) 375.

interests in the EEZ must be exercised in line with the rights and jurisdiction to which they attach. Under the current legal framework, the coastal State can strengthen its ability to combat maritime security threats through two types of actions: enhanced awareness of the situation within the maritime domain through gaining information of the sea area, and improved response capacity, including exercise enforcement jurisdiction.

7.3.1 Maritime Domain Awareness

A critical element for the coastal State in protecting maritime security is to obtain the necessary information at its disposal to take preventative and responsive actions. In the aftermath of 9/11, States have increasingly demanded comprehensive knowledge of their coastal maritime areas, especially with regard to information on vessels, their cargoes and crews for the protection of their maritime security,[69] as well as for the purposes of search and rescue and disaster relief. This trend has led to the development of a policy framework of maritime domain awareness (MDA).

The United States considers the secure use of the world ocean a fundamental element of its territorial safety and economic security. It established a Maritime Security Policy Coordinating Committee to oversee the development of the National Strategy for Maritime Security and eight supporting implementation plans to better integrate efforts to address maritime threats.[70] It redefined the concept of MDA, which emerged from the US Coast Guard in the late 1990s, in the National Plan to Achieve MDA as 'the effective understanding of anything associated with the maritime domain that could impact the security, safety, economy, or environment of the United States'.[71] This concept is further

[69] Chris Rahman, 'Maritime Domain Awareness in Australia and New Zealand', in Klein, Mossop and Rothwell (2010) 202–203.

[70] United States, National Security Presidential Directive NSPD-41, Homeland Security Presidential Directive HSPD-13, 21 December 2004, 'Maritime Security Policy' https://irp.fas.org/offdocs/nspd/nspd41.pdf; United States, Homeland Security, The National Strategy for Maritime Security (NSMS), 20 September 2005 http://georgewbush-whitehouse.archives.gov/homeland/maritime-security.html; Richard R. Yong and Gary A. Gordon, '9/11, Maritime Transportation Security Act (MTSA), and How We Got to Where We Are?' in Gary A. Gordon and Richard R. Yong (eds.), *Intermodal Maritime Security: Supply Chain Risk Mitigation* (Elsevier 2021) 12.

[71] United States, Department of Homeland Security (US DOHS), National Plan to Achieve Maritime Domain Awareness for the National Strategy for Maritime Security, October 2005, 'Key Definitions', 1 www.dhs.gov/xlibrary/assets/HSPD_MDAPlan.pdf (US National Plan to Achieve MDA); Rahman (2011) 202.

exemplified by the definition of maritime domain, which comprises 'all areas and things of, on, under, relating to, adjacent to, or bordering on a sea, ocean, or other navigable waterway, including all maritime related activities, infrastructure, people, cargo, and vessels and other conveyances'.[72] Thus, the United States seeks to obtain knowledge of all activities occurring at sea, including all maritime areas under its jurisdiction, and arguably beyond.

Other countries and international organisations have further developed the policy of MDA with similar definitions and formats.[73] Australia, for example, adopted the same concept as the United States but defines its maritime domain as '[t]he series of jurisdictional zones that surrounds the coast of a State. It includes territorial seas and the EEZ'.[74] Canada considers MDA to mean

> having true and timely information about everything on, under, related to, adjacent to, or bordering a sea, ocean or other navigable waterway. This includes all related activities, infrastructure, people, cargo, vessels, or other means of transport. For marine security, it means being aware of anything in the marine domain that could threaten Canada's national security.[75]

The International Civil Aviation Organization (ICAO) and the International Maritime Organization (IMO) also accepted the US definition of MDA for the purpose of search-and-rescue operations.[76]

[72] US National Plan to Achieve MDA 'Key Definitions' 1.

[73] Christian Bueger, 'From Dusk to Dawn? Maritime Domain Awareness in Southeast Asia' (2015) 37(2) Contemporary Southeast Asia 157, 159–160; I. Gusti Bagus Dharma Agastia and Anak Agung Banyu Perwita, 'Building Maritime Domain Awareness as an Essential Element of the Global Maritime Fulcrum: Challenges and Prospects for Indonesia's Maritime Security' (2017) 6 Jurnal Hubungan Internasional 113, 115–117; David Brewster, 'Give Light, and the Darkness Will Disappear: Australia's Quest for Maritime Domain Awareness in the Indian Ocean' (2018) 14(3) Journal of the Indian Ocean Region 296. 298; Christian Bueger and Anthony Bergin, 'Uniting Nations: Developing Maritime Domain Awareness for the "Blue Pacific"', Australian Strategic Policy Institute, 8 May 2018 www.aspistrategist.org.au/uniting-nations-developing-maritime-domain-awareness-for-the-blue-pacific/.

[74] Australian Maritime Doctrine, RAN Doctrine 1, (2nd ed, Royal Australian Navy 2010) 198 https://seapower.navy.gov.au/sites/default/files/documents/Amd2010.pdf; Australian Government Civil Maritime Security Strategy (Australian Government 2021) 10–11 www.homeaffairs.gov.au/about-us/our-portfolios/national-security/civil-maritime-security.

[75] Government of Canada, Transport Canada, 'Maritime Domain Awareness' www.tc.gc.ca/eng/marinesecurity/initiatives-235.htm.

[76] International Aeronautical and Maritime Search and Rescue Manual, Volume III Mobile Facilities (International Civil Aviation Organization and IMO 2016) xvi.

MDA is essentially an enabler for the formulation and implementation of maritime policy. In practice, achieving MDA depends on three steps. First, collecting a comprehensive set of data of all relevant activities at sea from all agencies, partners and stakeholders; second, analysing the data and information in such a way to identify trends and anomalies, including potential threats; and third, reacting in a timely manner to address identified suspected activities, including law enforcement activities.[77]

One critical component to achieving MDA is to obtain timely and adequate information within the respective maritime domain. Facilitating data collection and information sharing for the purpose of MDA requires cooperation and coordination not only among domestic government departments but also with the private sector, as well as regional and international partners.[78] The United States, for example, established a National MDA Implementation Team to provide a forum for inter-agency coordination of each MDA implementation action to ensure they are consistent with other component plans of the National Strategy for Maritime Security.[79] At the international level, the United States promotes global maritime partnerships to expand MDA capabilities globally and enhance regional enforcement capacities through information sharing, cooperation and capacity-building.[80]

The coastal State needs to establish a comprehensive MDA policy to achieve maritime security, including in the EEZ. The coastal State should utilise various information sources and technologies to seek information about activities in its maritime domain, to coordinate with relevant partners and international organisations to share information, and to reach agreements with major flag States to promote accountability.[81]

[77] US National Plan to Achieve MDA 'Strategic Environment' 2–3; United States, Department of the Navy, 'Navy Maritime Domain Awareness Concept', 29 May 2007 https://apps.dtic.mil/sti/citations/ADA502494.

[78] US National Plan to Achieve MDA 'Key Organizations' 5–6; EUMSS Section VI; Marin Chintoan-Uta and Joaquim Ramos Silva, 'Global Maritime Domain Awareness: A Sustainable Development Perspective' (2017) 16 WMU Journal of Maritime Affairs 37.

[79] US National Plan to Achieve MDA 'Implementation' 18.

[80] United States, Global Maritime Intelligence Integration Plan for the NSMS, October 2005 https://irp.fas.org/offdocs/nspd/gmii-plan.pdf; US DOHS, 'International Outreach and Coordination Strategy for the NSMS', November 2005 www.hsdl.org/c/; Rahman (2008) 7–8.

[81] Renato Cruz De Castro, 'The Philippines Discovers Its Maritime Domain: The Aquino Administration's Shift in Strategic Focus from Internal to Maritime Security' (2016) 12(2) Asian Security 111, 116–124; Agastia and Perwita (2017) 115–117; Tom Abke, 'Indo-Pacific Countries Turn to Unmanned Vessels to Patrol Region's Waters' (Indo-Pacific Defence Forum, 25 January 2019).

7.3.2 Means to Collect Information

It is essential for coastal States to have accurate and sufficient information at their disposal in order to take proper measures to address maritime security threats.[82] UNCLOS and other international instruments provide the coastal State with a number of tools and channels to collect pertinent information on foreign vessels navigating within the EEZ. Moreover, some coastal States take unilateral actions to require data of the vessels traversing their EEZs, with or without entering their ports or other offshore terminals.

Requesting information to monitor the movement of vessels is by no means a new phenomenon in the maritime field. The coastal State may adopt, under the auspice of IMO, several commonly used systems to monitor vessels in the EEZ for safety and security purposes.

Where the volume of traffic, level of navigational risk or environmental considerations justify, the coastal States may adopt, through IMO, ship reporting systems in a clearly defined area.[83] A reporting system may be mandatory for all vessels, or certain types of vessels, or vessels with certain cargoes.[84] On entering such areas, vessels subject to reporting are required to provide information essential to achieving the objectives of the reporting system, including the vessel's name, call sign, IMO identification number, position and other supplementary information, if appropriately requested.[85] It is also possible, if the circumstances justify, for the coastal State to adopt such reporting systems through IMO as a special mandatory measure for the prevention of pollution from vessels within a special area of its EEZ.[86]

In an amendment to Chapter V of SOLAS in 2000, 'ships of 300 gross tonnage and upwards engaged on international voyages and cargo ships of 500 gross tonnage and upwards not engaged on international voyages and passenger ships irrespective of size' were required to be fitted with an

[82] Klein (2011) 211.

[83] International Convention for the Safety of Life at Sea, as amended (1 November 1974, in force 25 May 1980) 1184 UNTS 2, Chapter V, Regulation 11 (SOLAS); IMO MSC/Circ.1060, 6 January 2003, Guidance Note on the Preparation of Proposals on Ships' Routeing Systems and Ship Reporting Systems for Submission to the Sub-Committee on Safety of Navigation, Annex, paras 6.2.1, 6.2.3.

[84] IMO MSC/Circ.1060, Annex, para 5.1; SOLAS Chapter V, Regulation 11, para 1.

[85] IMO MSC/Circ.1060, Annex, paras 5.1, 6.2.2.

[86] UNCLOS Article 211(6). For coastal State's jurisdiction over foreign vessels in the EEZ, see Chapter 4 in this volume.

automatic identification system (AIS) no later than 31 December 2004.[87] AIS is a shipboard very high-frequency (VHF) radio broadcast system, standardised by the International Telecommunication Union, that allows automatic exchange of navigation and other vessel information between appropriately equipped aircraft or shore stations and other vessels.[88] The information provided by AIS includes the ship's identity, type, position, course, speed, navigational status and other voyage- and safety-related information.[89] Although AIS was initially a tool to promote navigational safety, it also facilitates the coastal State's ability to identify vessels navigating in adjacent areas, assist in tracking target vessels and enhance situation awareness.[90]

There have been growing concerns over the security of AIS data due to its open access by all appropriately equipped transponders and publication on the World Wide Web, both of which may be exploited by organised crime.[91] Another limitation is that the typical range of AIS transmissions at sea is nominally 20 NM, with further coverage dependent on the use of repeater stations.[92] Since 2008, IMO has been considering the use of improved satellite detection of AIS in order to continue tracking vessels when they are out of range of coastal stations.[93] Norway, for instance, launched its first satellite AIS in 2010 and has full operational capability with an unprecedented ability to monitor ship traffic on a global scale.[94]

Another ship monitoring system is the satellite-based Long-Range Identification and Tracking (LRIT) System, adopted in a 2006 amendment to Chapter V of SOLAS, which enables the global identification and

[87] SOLAS Chapter V, Regulation 19, para 2.4.1–2.4.4.

[88] IMO SN/Circ.227, 6 January 2003, Guidelines for the Installation of a Shipborne Automatic Identification System (AIS), Annex, para 1; United States Coast Guard, Navigation Center, 'Automatic Identification System (AIS) Overview' www.navcen.uscg.gov/automatic-identification-system-overview.

[89] SOLAS Chapter V, Regulation 19, para 2.4.5; IMO Res A.1106(29), 2 December 2015, Revised Guidelines for the Onboard Operational Use of Shipborne Automatic Identification Systems (AIS), paras 12–14.

[90] IMO Res A.1106(29) para 4.

[91] IMO Res A.1106(29) para 22; IMO, 'AIS Transponders, Maritime Security – AIS Ship Data www.imo.org/en/OurWork/Safety/Pages/AIS.aspx.

[92] US DOHS, Navigation Center, 'How AIS Works' www.navcen.uscg.gov/how-ais-works.

[93] IMO MSC.85/11/1, 26 August 2008, Safety of Navigation: Improved Satellite Detection of AIS, Note by the Secretariat; International Telecommunication Union (ITU), Improved Satellite Detection of AIS, Report ITU-R M.2169 (ITU December 2009) www.itu.int/pub/R-REP-M.2169-2009.

[94] Andreas Nordmo Skauen, 'Ship Tracking Results from State-of-the-art Space-based AIS Receiver Systems for Maritime Surveillance' (2019) 11 CEAS Space Journal 301, 301–302.

tracking of ships.[95] LRIT applies to passenger ships and cargo ships (including high-speed craft) of and above 300 gross tonnage that are engaged on international voyages and mobile offshore drilling units.[96] Ships that have been fitted with AIS and operate exclusively within 'an area within the radio telephone coverage of at least one VHF coast station in which continuous DSC (Digital Selective Calling) alerting is available' are exempted from this regulation.[97] The LRIT system consists of

> the shipborne LRIT information transmitting equipment, the Communications Service Provider(s), the Application Service Provider (s), LRIT Data Center(s), including any related Vessel Monitoring System (s), the LRIT Data Distribution Plan and the International LRIT Data Exchange.[98]

Subject vessels are required to automatically transmit their identity, position (latitude and longitude) and the date and time of the position provided.[99]

Each contracting State must nominate a data centre to which ships flying its flag may transmit LRIT information, and all contracting governments may request the information through the established national or participating regional or cooperative LRIT data centres using the International LRIT Data Exchange system.[100] A coastal State may receive the information about foreign ships under two circumstances: first, when the ships have communicated an intent to enter a port facility or a place under its jurisdiction irrespective of where such ships may be located; second, when the ships are navigating within a distance not exceeding 1,000 NM of its coast, provided that under both circumstances the ships are not located within the waters landward of the baselines of another contracting State.[101] The LRIT operates under a private data centre that only releases the information about a specific vessel to a contracting government, who must bear all costs associated with any information it receives.[102]

[95] IMO, 'Long-Range Identification and Tracking (LRIT)' www.imo.org/en/OurWork/Safety/Pages/LRIT.aspx.

[96] IMO Res MSC.202(81), 19 May 2006, Adoption of Amendments to the International Convention for the Safety of Life at Sea, 1974, as Amended, para 2.1.

[97] Ibid para 4.2; SOLAS Chapter IV 'Radio Communications', Regulations 2.1.3, 2.1.12.

[98] IMO, 'Long-Range Identification and Tracking'.

[99] IMO Res MSC.202(81) para 5.

[100] IMO, 'Long-Range Identification and Tracking'.

[101] IMO Res MSC.202(81) paras 8.1.2–8.1.3.

[102] Ibid para 11.1.

States may also adopt a specific ship monitoring system on a regional level. Member States of the European Union, Norway and Iceland established a vessel traffic monitoring and information system, SafeSeaNet, in 2002 to enhance the safety and efficiency of navigation and to improve the response of coastal States to potential threats to their maritime security.[103] SafeSeaNet requires all vessels of and above 300 gross tonnage bound for a port of participating States to notify the port authority with general information about the vessel, its voyage and persons on board at least 24 hours in advance, or at the time it leaves the previous port.[104] Vessels carrying dangerous or polluting goods, irrespective of their size, must notify the port authority at the latest at the moment of departure, giving detailed information of the cargo, as well as the foregoing general information.[105] Participating States are required to monitor and take all necessary and appropriate measures to ensure that all duly established maritime systems, including ship reporting systems, AIS, vessel traffic services, ships' routeing systems and voyage data recorder systems, are being observed.[106] Participating States may also exchange computerised data on the ship and the dangerous or polluting goods on board for the purpose of maritime security and the protection of the marine environment.[107]

At the national level, Australia, with a total estimated coastline length of 59,681 kilometres, has been investing heavily to protect the civil maritime security, safety, economy and environment interests associated with Australia's maritime domain.[108] It proposed a Maritime Identification Zone of up to 1,000 NM from its coast in 2004, which was reformulated to the Australian Maritime Identification System in

[103] Directive 2002/59/EC of the European Parliament and of the Council of 27 June 2002, Establishing a Community Vessel Traffic Monitoring and Information System and Repealing Council Directive 93/75/EEC, as amended, Article 1, OJ L 208, 5 August 2002, pp. 10–27.

[104] Ibid Article 4(1) and Annex I (1). According to Article 2(2): 'This Directive shall not apply to: (a) warships, naval auxiliaries and other ships owned or operated by a Member State and used for non-commercial public service; (b) fishing vessels, traditional ships and recreational craft with a length of less than 45 meters; (c) bunkers below 5,000 ton, ship's stores and equipment for use on board ships'.

[105] Ibid Articles 4(2), 13, and Annex I (3).

[106] Ibid Articles 5–10.

[107] Ibid Article 14.

[108] Australian Government, Geoscience Australia, 'Coastline Lengths – States and Territories' www.ga.gov.au/scientific-topics/national-location-information/dimensions/border-lengths; Australian Government Civil Maritime Security Strategy (2021) III.

2005 following a torrent of criticism from neighbouring States.[109] After more than a decade of operation, the system was consolidated into the Modernised Australian Ship Tracking and Reporting System (MASTREP), which came into force in 2016.[110] MASTREP implements Australia's treaty obligations under both SOLAS and the International Convention on Maritime Search and Rescue that apply to the Australian search and rescue region, including the high seas.[111] Within the MASTREP area, position reports are mandatory for all Australian-flagged vessels and foreign vessels that are transiting between Australian ports.[112] All vessels navigating within the MASTREP area are required to report a marine incident, and to submit special reports involving the carriage of dangerous goods, harmful substances and marine pollutants as set out by IMO regulations.[113]

Similar to the establishment of maritime identification zones, some coastal States have adopted an air defence identification zone (ADIZ) in the airspace over their EEZs. Initially, an ADIZ was a military concept adopted by the United States after the Second World War and was reconsidered after the 9/11 attack when threats from the air re-emerged as a great concern.[114] The ICAO defines an ADIZ as '[s]pecial designated

[109] News Room, Prime Minister of Australia: John Howard, Media Release, 15 December 2004, 'Strengthening Offshore Maritime Security' http://pandora.nla.gov.au/pan/10052/20050221-0000/www.pm.gov.au/news/media_releases/media_Release1173.html; Phil Goff, 'Australian Maritime Identification Zone', 17 December 2004 www.beehive.govt.nz/release/australian-maritime-indentification-zone; Natalie Klein, 'Legal Implications of Australia's Maritime Identification System' (2006) 55(2) Int'l & Compar LQ 337, 339; Clive Schofield, Martin Tsamenyi and Mary Ann Palma, 'Securing Maritime Australia: Developments in Maritime Surveillance and Security' (2008) 39(1) Ocean Dev Int'l L 94, 101–104; Donald R. Rothwell and Cameron Moore, 'Australia's Traditional Maritime Security Concerns and Post 9/11 Perspectives', in Klein, Mossop and Rothwell (2010) 42–43.

[110] Australian Maritime Safety Authority, 'Modernised Australian Ship Tracking and Reporting System', last updated: 23 December 2020 www.amsa.gov.au/safety-navigation/navigation-systems/modernised-australian-ship-tracking-and-reporting-system.

[111] Ibid.

[112] MASTREP and Australian Mandatory Reporting Guide (2nd ed, Australian Maritime Safety Authority, February 2016) www.amsa.gov.au/safety-navigation/navigation-systems/mastrep-guide-2016.

[113] Ibid.

[114] United States Code of Federal Regulations, Title 14: Aeronautics and Space, Part 99 – Security Control of Air Traffic (up to date as of 7/24/2024), paras 99.3, 99.41–99.47 www.ecfr.gov/current/title-14/chapter-I/subchapter-F/part-99; Peter A. Dutton, 'Caelum Liberum: Air Defense Identification Zones Outside Sovereign Airspace' (2009) 103 Am J Int'l L 691, 691–692; 袁发强, 张磊, 王秋雯, 郑雷, 高俊涛,《航行自由的国际

airspace of defined dimensions within which aircraft are required to comply with special identification and/or reporting procedures additional to those related to the provision of air traffic services'.[115] Currently, more than twenty States have established an ADIZ beyond the limit of the territorial sea extending to various breadths, including Bangladesh, Canada, China, India, Japan, Pakistan, the Philippines, the United Kingdom and the United States.[116] The regulations adopted in these identification zones vary from State to State, but most include a request for information to identify the aircraft for security purposes.[117] Although there is no explicit authorisation for the establishment of the ADIZ over the airspace beyond the territorial sea under UNCLOS, such practice is not necessarily inconsistent with existing international law.[118]

法理论与实践研究》(北京大学出版社，2018)，第三章，航行自由的国际法限制，第三节，防空识别区与海洋飞越自由 (YUAN Faqiang, ZHANG Lei, WANG Qiuwen, ZHENG Lei and GAO Juntao, *Research on the Theory and Practice of International Law on the Freedom of Navigation* (Beijing University Press, 2018), Chapter 3 International Law Limitations on the Freedom of Navigation, Section 3 Air Defence Identification Zone and the Freedom of Overflight.).

115 Convention on International Civil Aviation (7 December 1944, in force 4 April 1947) 15 UNTS 295, Annex 15: Aeronautical Information Services, Chapter 1, para 1.1.

116 王崇敏和邹立刚，《我国在专属经济区建立防空识别区的探讨》，法学杂志·2013 年第1 期，95–99，第96页 (WANG Chongmin and ZOU Ligang, 'Discussion on Building Air Defence Identification Zone in Our Exclusive Economic Zone' (2013) 1 Law Science Magazine 95, 96); Matthias Vanhullebusch and Wei Shen, 'China's Air Defence Identification Zone: Building Security through Lawfare' (2016) 16(1) The China Review 121, 126–131; Raul (Pete) Pedrozo, 'Air Defense Identification Zones' (2021) 97 Int'l L Stud Ser US Naval War Col 7, 8; Transport Canada, Designated Airspace Handbook, Issue No 301, effective 20 April 2023, M6: ADIZ www.navcanada.ca/en/dah20230223.pdf.

117 Jinyuan Su, 'The Practice of States on Air Defense Identification Zones: Geographical Scope, Object of Identification, and Identification Measures' (2019) 18 Chinese J Int'l L 811, 821–824; US Code of Federal Regulations, Title 14: Aeronautics and Space, Part 99 – Security Control of Air Traffic (up to date as of 7/29/2022), paras 99.7, 99.9, 99.11; Australia Defence Force, Flight Information Handbook Australia (effective 17 June 2021), ENR 1.12: Interception of Civil Aircraft, para 3.1.3 https://ais-af.airforce.gov.au/sites/default/files/current-cycle-products/2106%20FIHA.pdf; United Kingdom, The Joint Service Manual of the Law of Armed Conflict (Joint Service Publication 383, 2004 ed), para 12.15 https://assets.publishing.service.gov.uk/government/uploads/system/uploads/attachment_data/file/27874/JSP3832004Edition.pdf.

118 Ruwantissa Abeyratne, 'In Search of Theoretical Justification for Air Defence Identification Zones' (2012) 5 J Transp Secur 87, 88; James Kraska and Raul Pedrozo, *International Maritime Security Law* (Martinus Nijhoff 2013) 178; Crawford (2019) 265–266; Jinyuan Su, 'Is the Establishment of Air Defence Identification Zones Outside National Airspace in Accordance with International Law?' (2021) 32(4) Eur J Int'l L 1309, 1133–1134.

There is controversy around what type of information the coastal State is seeking and whether the subject aircraft is bound for the territorial airspace of the coastal State.[119]

These tools and channels to collect information about ships and aircraft in the EEZ, although mainly developed for navigation safety and search and rescue purposes, have the potential to provide valuable knowledge to enhance MDA and protect maritime security. The coastal State is encouraged to use these available tools and channels to enhance maritime awareness for its security purposes in accordance with international law. It is worth noting that, although coastal States are entitled to request information of foreign vessels entering their EEZs, they are not entitled to any additional direct enforcement jurisdiction over non-compliance with such requests except for notifying the flag State, and may take action when the ship enters its port.

7.3.3 Law Enforcement, Right of Hot Pursuit and Right of Visit

The basic principle of the high seas freedoms remains that the vessels sail under the exclusive jurisdiction of the flag State without interruption, with the exceptions conferred by UNCLOS and general international law that other States share legislative or/and enforcement jurisdiction under certain circumstances.[120] The coastal State has the right to prescribe and enforce certain laws and regulations for foreign vessels in the EEZ, supported by the right of hot pursuit.[121] The right of visit is an exceptional power of all States that challenges the exclusive jurisdiction of the flag State for certain international crimes on the high seas and in the EEZ for the benefit of the international community.[122]

The coastal State's authority to carry out law enforcement power rests in its exercise of sovereign rights and jurisdiction over the EEZ.[123] The coastal State has the power, in exercising its sovereign rights, to 'explore, exploit, conserve and manage the living resourses' in the EEZ, to 'take such measures, including boarding, inspection, arrest and judicial

119 Roach (2021) 406, 416–417.

120 Maria Gavouneli, *Functional Jurisdiction in the Law of the Sea* (Martinus Nijhoff 2007) 33; Churchill, Lowe and Sander (2022) 381.

121 UNCLOS Articles 56, 73, 111(2), 211(5)–(6), 220(3)–(6); Nicholas M Poulantzas, *The Right of Hot Pursuit in International Law* (2nd ed., Martinus Nijhoff 2002) 39.

122 UNCLOS Articles 58(2), 110; Papastavridis (2013) 33–39; Crawford (2019) 291–292.

123 See Chapters 4 and 5 in this volume.

proceedings, as may be necessary to ensure compliance' with its laws.[124] Such enforcement jurisdiction could apply to suspected terrorist acts, IUU fishing[125] and other criminal matters affecting the economic resources and economic exploitation of the zone. Where there are clear grounds for believing that a vessel navigating in the EEZ has intentionally polluted the marine environment, causing major damage or threat of major damage to the environment or its resources, the coastal State may take enforcement measures against the suspected vessel.[126] Although the coastal State has not been given explicit enforcement jurisdiction over non-living resources, artificial islands, installations and structures, it could be argued that such a right is implicit in connection with the prevention and punishment of violations of the law.[127] Hence, if a coastal vessel or offshore infrastructure was under violent attack in the EEZ, such as from pirates, terrorists or smugglers, the coastal State can take enforcement measures to protect its maritime security based on protective jurisdiction.[128]

Where the coastal State has good reason to believe that a foreign vessel, when within the EEZ, has violated that State's applicable laws and regulations, it may continue pursuit of the vessel outside the EEZ if the vessel ignored the visual or auditory signal to stop and tried to escape.[129] The requirement of a signal to stop must be interpreted in light of modern use of technology to include radio broadcast, VHF messages and potentially maritime autonomous vehicles.[130] Such pursuit must be

124 UNCLOS Article 73(1); James Harrison, 'Article 73', in Alexander Proelss (ed.), *United Nations Convention on the Law of the Sea: A Commentary* (Hart 2017) 557.

125 Request for an Advisory Opinion submitted by the Sub-Regional Fisheries Commission (SRFC), Advisory Opinion of 2 April 2015, ITLOS Reports 2015, p. 4, para 106.

126 UNCLOS Article 220(3) and (5)–(6); Myron H. Nordquist, Shabtai Rosenne and Alexander Yankov (eds.), *United Nations Convention on the Law of the Sea 1982: A Commentary*, Vol. IV (Martinus Nijhoff 1991) 300–301; Shotaro Hamamoto, 'Article 220', in Proelss (2017) 1509–1510.

127 ILC Draft Articles Article 77 Commentary; Nordquist, Nandan and Rosenne (1993) 896; In the Matter of the Arctic Sunrise Arbitration before an Arbitral Tribunal Constituted under Annex VII to the 1982 United Nations Convention on the Law of the Sea between the Kingdom of the Netherlands and the Russian Federation, Award on the Merits, 14 August 2015, PCA Case No. 2014-02, para 284 (Arctic Sunrise Arbitration).

128 UNCLOS Articles 56(1), 60; Poulantzas (2002) 135–137; Staker (2018) 301–302; M/V 'Virginia G' Case (Panama/Guinea-Bissau), Judgment of 14 April 2014, ITLOS Reports 2014, p. 4, para 211.

129 UNCLOS Article 111(1)–(2) and (4); Nordquist, Nandan and Rosenne (1995) 256.

130 M/V 'Saiga' (No. 2) paras 147–148; Arctic Sunrise Arbitration para 259; Natalie Klein, 'Maritime Autonomous Vehicles within the International Law Framework to Enhance Maritime Security' (2019) 95 Int'l Law Stud 244, 254.

commenced when the vessel or one of its boats is within the EEZ of the pursuing State, may only be continued outside the EEZ if the pursuit has not been interrupted and ends as the vessel enters the territorial sea of its flag State or a third State.[131] State practice appears to support the idea that hot pursuit by relay may be conducted by multiple vessels of the coastal State, and may even be continued or concluded with the assistance of vessels of a third State.[132] The vessel under pursuit may be stopped, arrested and escorted to a port of the coastal State for inquiries and proceedings if the circumstances justify.[133] The right of hot pursuit is deemed necessary to enable coastal jurisdiction to be efficiently exercised.[134]

UNCLOS also provides the coastal State the right of visit over foreign merchant vessels in the EEZ if they are suspected of being engaged in piracy, the slave trade, unauthorised broadcasting or being without nationality.[135] Under these circumstances, the coastal State may proceed to verify the vessel's flag, and if suspicion remains, it may proceed to a further examination on board the vessel.[136] As technology advances, it has been argued that the right of visit could be carried out virtually using cyber means.[137] However, the right of visit is not automatically followed by the right of seizure.[138] The coastal State is authorised to seize the foreign vessel only in cases of piracy based on universal jurisdiction, and unauthorised broadcasting if that State has a connection with the person or ship or is affected by such activity.[139] In the other three circumstances, UNCLOS is silent on seizure. In most cases, the coastal State that has conducted an onboard examination and found incriminating evidence may only report the facts to the flag State and leave it in the latter's hands to exercise enforcement jurisdiction.[140]

131 UNCLOS Article 111(1) and (3); Nordquist, Nandan and Rosenne (1995) 257–258.
132 Warwick Gullett and Clive Schofield, 'Pushing the Limits of the Law of the Sea Convention: Australian and French Cooperative Surveillance and Enforcement in the Southern Ocean' (2007) 22(4) Int'l J Marine & Coastal L 545, 569; Natalie Klein, Douglas Guilfoyle, Md Saiful Karim and Rob McLaughlin, 'Maritime Autonomous Vehicles: New Frontiers in the Law of the Sea' (2020) 69 Int'l & Compar LQ 719, 731.
133 UNCLOS Article 111(7).
134 Arctic Sunrise Arbitration para 245; Crawford (2019) 294.
135 UNCLOS Articles 58(2), 109, 110(1).
136 UNCLOS Article 110(1)–(2).
137 Tallinn Manual 2.0 (2017) 238–239.
138 Crawford (2019) 292.
139 UNCLOS Articles 105, 109(3).
140 UNCLOS Article 94(6).

In respect of addressing maritime security threats, there are several *lex specialis* treaties providing the coastal State the jurisdiction, or the right to request authorisation, to interdict a suspect foreign vessel in its EEZ. For example, a coastal State that is a party to the SUA Convention and Protocol may claim concurrent jurisdiction over a number of unlawful acts based on the nationality of the victim, the nationality or the habitual residence of the perpetrator, when it is the target of the act, or when the perpetrator is present within its territorial jurisdiction.[141] Under the 1988 UN Narcotics Convention, the 2000 Migrants Smuggling Protocol and the 2016 IMO Interim Measures, a contracting State with reasonable suspicions that the foreign vessel is engaged in a violation may request permission from the flag State to board, search the suspected vessel and take appropriate actions.[142]

Moreover, flag State consent ship interdiction is widely used in WMD-related non-proliferation operations.[143] The most notable example is the Proliferation Security Initiative (PSI) launched by the United States in 2003.[144] States participating in PSI are required to take actions to board and search vessels flying their flag in 'their internal waters or territorial seas, or areas beyond the territorial seas of any other State' that are suspected of carrying WMD, and to consider authorising other States to board, search and seize their vessels with reasonable suspicion.[145] By 2024, PSI had developed into a global security regime with 113 participating countries on six continents.[146] PSI is further strengthened by eleven bilateral ship boarding agreements, under which either one of the parties can request the other to authorise the boarding, search and possible detention

[141] Convention for the Suppression of Unlawful Acts against the Safety of Maritime Navigation (10 March 1988, in force 1 March 1992) 1678 UNTS 221, Article 6; SUA Protocol (14 October 2005, in force 28 July 2010), Article 3.

[142] United Nations Convention against Illicit Traffic in Narcotic Drugs and Psychotropic Substances Narcotics Convention, (20 December 1988, in force 11 November 1990) 1582 UNTS 164, Article 17(3); Protocol against the Smuggling of Migrants by Land, Sea and Air, supplementing the United Nations Convention against Transnational Organized Crime (15 December 2000, in force 28 January 2008) 2241 UNTS 507, Article 8 (2000 Migrants Smuggling Protocol); IMO MSC.1/Circ.896/Rev.2, 26 May 2016, IMO Interim Measures for Combating Unsafe Practices Associated with the Trafficking, Smuggling or Transport of Migrants by Sea, Article 12.

[143] Guilfoyle (2009) 243–246.

[144] US DOS, 'Proliferation Security Initiative' www.state.gov/proliferation-security-initiative/.

[145] US DOS, 'PSI Interdiction Principles' www.state.gov/psi-interdiction-principles/.

[146] US DOS, 'PSI Participants' www.state.gov/proliferation-security-initiative/.

of the vessel and its cargo.[147] There are also practices in some bilateral treaties to arrange a 'ship-rider' on board the other party's law enforcement vessel to provide on-the-spot consent to the interdiction of vessels flying its flag and to exercise the flag State's enforcement jurisdiction.[148]

The coastal State must not discriminate in form or in fact against foreign-flagged vessels and must respect safeguards measures when exercising enforcement jurisdiction.[149] When taking enforcement measures, the coastal State must ensure the safety and humane treatment of the persons on board, take due account of the need not to endanger the security of the vessel or its cargo, and not prejudice the commercial or legal interests of the flag State or any other interested parties.[150] In all circumstances, force must be avoided and may only be used in a way proportionate and necessary according to the specific circumstances.[151] When using direct force, all efforts must be made to ensure that human life is not endangered, and the level and type of force must be proportionate to the targeted ship, where use of force with an intention to sink the vessel is not acceptable.[152] Further, where the suspicions upon boarding prove to be unfounded or when the enforcement measures are proven unlawful or 'exceed those reasonably required in the light of available information', the coastal State shall be liable for damage or losses arising from such measures.[153]

With respect to enforcement of fishery laws and pollution regulations, the coastal State should promptly release the arrested vessel and its crew upon the posting of bond, and take reasonable efforts to avoid unduly detaining or delaying the vessel.[154] The coastal State should only impose monetary penalties for these two types of violations by a foreign-flagged vessel, and should promptly notify the flag State of the actions taken.[155]

147 US DOS, 'Ship Boarding Agreements'.

148 Guilfoyle (2009) 91; Robin Geiss and Anna Petrig, *Piracy and Armed Robbery at Sea: The Legal Framework for Counter-Piracy Operations in Somalia and the Gulf of Aden* (Oxford University Press 2011) 87–90.

149 UNCLOS Article 227.

150 UNCLOS Articles 225, 226(1)(a); Guilfoyle (2009) 266–271.

151 M/V 'Saiga' (No. 2) paras 156–158; Guilfoyle (2009) 271–272; Christine Gray, *International Law and the Use of Force* (4th ed., Oxford University Press 2018) 150.

152 M/V 'Saiga' (No. 2), paras 155–156; M/V 'Virginia G' Case paras 361–362; Klein (2011) 116–117; Harris and Sivakumaran (2015) 375.

153 UNCLOS Articles 110(3), 111(8), 232.

154 UNCLOS Articles 73(2), 220(7), 226(1)(a)–(b). For coastal State's enforcement jurisdiction concerning natural resources in the EEZ, see discussions in Chapters 4 in this volume.

155 UNCLOS Articles 73(3)–(4), 230(1).

Subject to justifications, the coastal State should suspend its proceedings to impose penalties in respect of pollution violations if the flag State takes action to impose penalties of the corresponding charges within six months.[156]

Regardless of the imminent alleged threats coming from the sea, the international law of the sea offers limited means for the coastal State to achieve maritime security in the EEZ.[157] The collection of information is considered a passive activity, and it has limited enforcement jurisdiction over suspected activities by foreign-flagged vessels. The coastal State must be prepared to cooperate with the flag State in combatting, suppressing and investigating suspected threats at sea. In fact, when coping with multifaceted threats to maritime security, which have a strong transboundary influence, all States must take collaborative approaches to be effective and to reduce the risk of long-term or irreversible adverse effects on human life and the maritime environment.

7.4 International Efforts to Enhance Maritime Security

7.4.1 Maritime Security as Collective Security

The preamble of UNCLOS recognises that 'the problems of ocean space are closely interrelated and need to be considered as a whole' and that the legal framework 'achieved in this Convention will contribute to the strengthening of peace, security, cooperation and friendly relations among all nations'.[158] Efforts to enhance maritime security in the EEZ not only protect the security interests of a specific coastal State but also contribute to the secure use of ocean space for all States. Consequently, as has been persuasively asserted by the UN Secretary-General, since 'all States share in the benefits of safer and more secure oceans, they also share in the responsibility for addressing major threats and challenges to maritime security'.[159] The shared interests and responsibilities provide a platform for different States to cooperate to ensure that appropriate measures are taken to maintain a secure maritime environment.

The spirit of cooperation is particularly relevant between the coastal State and the flag State of a vessel suspected of engaging in unlawful

156 UNCLOS Article 228(1).

157 Natalie Klein, 'Legal Limitations on Ensuring Australia's Maritime Security' (2006) 7(2) Melb J Int'l L 278, 334.

158 UNCLOS Preamble; Rainer Lagoni, 'Preamble', in Proelss (2017), 7–8.

159 UNGA A/63/63 paras 35, 40.

activities in the EEZ. Under the maritime security threats scenario, conflicting interests between the coastal State and other States are minimised. As discussed earlier, there has been an increase in State practice to provide coastal States with the ability to monitor the movement of ships in their EEZs at the expense of the flag State relinquishing relevant information. The acknowledgement of the common interest in sharing information and providing concurrent jurisdiction is a reflection of 'the collective concerns generated from the varied maritime security threats that are currently recognized'.[160]

Maritime security is characterised by its complex and cross-cutting nature, comprising multiple different but often related threats and incorporating themes of law enforcement, criminal justice, economic development and environmental protection.[161] This complexity implies that narrow or isolated responses to maritime security, such as one State addressing only one threat at a time, are unlikely to succeed and may even prove counterproductive.[162] To achieve collective maritime security means that responses often need to take place across and outside the maritime boundaries of States, with cooperation among multiple stakeholders.[163]

At the same time, maritime security concerns differ across States and regions. Some maritime security threats transcend maritime boundaries and hence are internationally shared, such as piracy and smuggling of drugs or WMD. Other issues, such as terrorist attacks or human trafficking, may be targeted to certain States or regions. Moreover, the level of priority attached to maritime security issues of the same State or region can vary widely at different times. Hence, individual States or regions may have unique and distinct security concerns that co-exist with collective maritime security, which gives them different perspectives when it comes to identifying priorities and allocating resources.[164]

In addition, States have different enforcement competences that directly affect their ability to maintain effective jurisdiction over vessels flying their flag and provide adequate surveillance over the maritime

160 Klein (2011) 255.

161 Bueger (2015) 163.

162 Christian Bueger, Timothy Edmunds and Robert McCabe, 'Maritime Security, Capacity Building, and the Western Indian Ocean', in Christian Bueger, Timothy Edmunds and Robert McCabe (eds.), *Capacity Building for Maritime Security: The Western Indian Ocean Experience* (Palgrave Macmillan 2021) 7–8.

163 Zhao (2015) 749.

164 Jon D. Peppetti, 'Building the Global Maritime Security Network: A Multinational Legal Structure to Combat Transnational Threats' (2008) 55 Naval L Rev 73, 77.

domain under their jurisdiction. The cause of the threats to maritime security, especially piracy, terrorism, human smuggling and trafficking, may be rooted in severe domestic turmoil, poverty, infectious diseases and environmental degradation.[165] Affected States frequently lack the capability and resources to maintain order at sea, let alone the ability to implement maritime security measures. This lack of security often results in the disruption of marine activities that are needed in order to improve the domestic situation.[166] These factors feed into one another creating a deadly cycle that leaves the EEZ of these coastal States even more vulnerable.

Given the complexities of maritime security, the international community should adopt a multi-level cooperative framework to respond to various threats while taking into consideration three characteristics. First, threats to maritime security are often interconnected and interdependent of one another, so the responses should involve a range of stakeholders to enhance cooperation and coordination. Second, most maritime security issues need to be addressed with measures on land, which requires support and capacity-building for the affected States. Third, the cross-jurisdictional nature of most maritime security threats requires cooperation transcending maritime boundaries at various levels of governance.[167] To this end, States are expected to cooperate at both the global and regional levels to identify a common discourse and shared view regarding common threats, in particular to remedy the inadequacy of an individual State's competence to address specific security concerns. International organisations, including the UN and IMO, and regional organisations, such as the African Union and the Association of Southeast Asian Nations (ASEAN), can play an important role in enhancing maritime security cooperation, particularly with respect to sharing information, resources and expertise needed for law enforcement activities and building capacity and mutual trust.[168]

[165] UNGA A/59/565, 2 December 2004, A More Secure World: Our Shared Responsibility, Report of the High-Level Panel on Threats, Challenges and Changes, paras 17–23, 44–58.

[166] UNGA A/63/63 para 127.

[167] Simona Piattoni, 'Multi-Level Governance: A Historical and Conceptual Analysis' (2009) 31(2) J Eur Integr 163–180; Christian Bueger and Timothy Edmunds, 'Beyond Seablindness: A New Agenda for Maritime Security Studies' (2017) 93(6) International Affairs 1293, 1302–1303; Bueger, Edmunds and McCabe (2021) 4.

[168] UNSC S/23500, 31 January 1992, Note by the President of the Security Council, paras 139, 143.

7.4.2 Operations under the Authorisation of the Security Council

Efforts to secure greater law enforcement powers for the coastal State in relation to maritime security threats beyond the territorial sea have largely been resisted because of the preference accorded to upholding exclusive flag State jurisdiction over vessels. Besides seeking flag State authorisation through international conventions and bilateral agreements, another critical source of rights for intervention to respond to certain imminent maritime security threats comes from the UNSC.[169] The role of the UNSC in the law of sea has significantly evolved since the end of the Cold War and again after the 9/11 terrorist attacks on the United States.[170] The UNSC has primary responsibility for the maintenance of international peace and security and it may authorise various enforcement actions to deal with breaches of the peace, threats to the peace or acts of aggression, with or without the use of armed force.[171] These measures include sanctions, embargoes, demonstrations, blockades and other operations by air or sea forces of Member States, which may completely or partially interrupt sea communications.[172]

Resolutions adopted by the UNSC to enforce prescribed measures are legally binding on the Member States of the UN under the collective security system.[173] Naval forces of Member States, on call from the UNSC, undertake to make available 'armed forces, assistance, and facilities, including rights of passage' to implement these peacekeeping operations at sea.[174] The relevant maritime operations carried out by Member States are primarily in relation to the enforcement of economic sanctions, arms and export embargos, preventing and combatting piracy or terrorism, and proliferation of WMD, where their warships and military aircraft are authorised to halt and inspect international shipping.[175]

For example, the potential threat of the development or proliferation of illegal nuclear weapons and ballistic missiles by the Democratic People's Republic of Korea (North Korea) has long been a serious

[169] Churchill, Lowe and Sander (2022) 283.
[170] Rothwell and Stephens (2010) 262.
[171] Charter of the United Nations (26 June 1945, in force 24 October 1945), 557UNTS 143, Articles 24(1), 39 (UN Charter).
[172] Ibid Articles 41–42.
[173] Ibid Articles 24–25; Malcolm N. Shaw, *International Law* (8th ed., Cambridge University Press 2017) 85, 946–947; Crawford (2019) 732.
[174] UN Charter Articles 43(1), 45.
[175] Rothwell and Stephens (2010) 262–263; Klein (2011) 276–285.

concern of the UNSC.[176] The UNSC has repeatedly affirmed that the proliferation of nuclear, chemical and biological weapons and their means of delivery constitute a threat to international peace and security, and that the actions taken by North Korea pose a danger to 'peace and stability in the region and beyond'.[177] Resolution 1874 (2009) called on all Member States to not only take action against their own flagged vessels, but also to 'inspect vessels, with the consent of the flag State, on the high seas, if they have information that provides reasonable grounds to believe' that the vessel was carrying prohibited cargo.[178] This effectively gives all States enforcement jurisdiction, with flag State consent, over suspected vessels engaged in illicit trafficking of nuclear, chemical and biological weapons and related materials in the EEZ. The UNSC authorisation of maritime interdiction of cargo vessels has been reinforced in subsequent resolutions and numerous Member States have submitted reports on their implementation of these measures.[179]

Protracted internal conflict and the absence of an effective government since the early 1990s led to a situation where pirates could operate without hindrance in the waters around Somalia.[180] The situation continued to decline in the early 2000s, interrupting major shipping routes in the Western Indian Ocean, the Gulf of Aden and the Red Sea.[181] The situation in and around Somalia was identified as 'a threat to international peace and security in the region' by the UNSC in Resolution 1816 (2008).[182] The UNSC subsequently issued a series of *ad hoc* resolutions encouraging a package of measures for certain prescribed times aimed at repressing Somali piracy. The intention was to fill some of the

176 UNSC Res S/RES/825 (1993), 11 May 1993, Democratic People's Republic of Korea; UNSC SC/14841, 25 March 2022, Security Council Extends Mandate of Expert Panel Overseeing Sanctions against Democratic People's Republic of Korea Until 30 April 2023 https://press.un.org/en/2022/sc14841.doc.htm.

177 UNSC Res S/RES/1718 (2006), 14 October 2006, Non-Proliferation/Democratic People's Republic of Korea, Preamble; UNSC Res S/RES/1874 (2009), 16 June 2009, Non-Proliferation/Democratic People's Republic of Korea, Preamble; UNSC Res S/RES/2375 (2017), 11 September 2017.

178 UNSC Res S/RES/1874 (2009) paras 11–12.

179 UNSC Res S/RES/2627 (2022), 25 March 2022; UNSC S/2022/132, 1 March 2022, Note by the President of the Security Council, Annex, Report by the Panel of Experts.

180 Guilfoyle (2009) 61–62.

181 Ved P. Nanda, 'Maritime Piracy: How Can International Law and Policy Address this Growing Global Menace?' (2010–2011) 39(2) Denv J Int'l L & Pol'y 177, 178–180; Doris Konig, 'Maritime Security: Cooperative Means to Address New Challenges' (2014) 57 German YB Int'l L 209, 213.

182 UNSC Res S/RES/1816 (2008), 2 June 2008, Somalia, Preamble.

gaps in the current international legal framework relating to piracy by expanding enforcement jurisdiction and encouraging cooperation among States to enhance their ability to combat Somali piracy. Naval vessels and military aircraft of Member States were encouraged to 'increase and coordinate their efforts to deter acts of piracy and armed robbery at sea in cooperation with the Transitional Federal Government (TFG)', and these vessels were authorised to 'enter the territorial waters of Somalia' for this purpose.[183]

The international community responded by undertaking naval operations to deter pirates and to ensure the safety of sea lane communications and international navigation. These operations have been coordinated by the North Atlantic Treaty Organization (NATO) Operations Allied Protector and Ocean Shield, the EU Naval Force counter-piracy mission (Operation Atalanta) and the Combined Maritime Forces' Combined Task Force 151, in addition to several countries that have deployed naval ships and military aircraft in the region to patrol and escort merchant ships.[184] As a means to tackle the enforcement challenges, all States and regional organisations fighting piracy off the coast of Somalia were invited to conclude 'shiprider' agreements with countries prepared to prosecute pirates, particularly regional States, in order to facilitate investigation and prosecution of those captured while undertaking suspected pirate attacks.[185] In addition, the UNSC resolutions repeatedly called for States to take domestic legislative measures to criminalise piracy and armed robbery at sea, and to prosecute captured or transferred suspected offenders.[186] These counter-piracy measures have been renewed on an annual basis since they were initially authorised in Resolutions 1846 (2008) and 1851

[183] Ibid paras 2, 7.

[184] UNSC S/2011/662, 25 October 2011, Report of the Secretary-General Pursuant to Security Council Resolution 1950 (2010), paras 39–50; UNSC S/2013/623, 21 October 2013, Report of the Secretary-General on the Situation with respect to Piracy and Armed Robbery at Sea off the Coast of Somalia, paras 37–41. States operating on their own include China, India, Indonesia, Islamic Republic of Iran, Japan, Malaysia, Republic of Korea, Pakistan, Russian Federation, Saudi Arabia and Yemen.

[185] UNSC Res S/RES/1851 (2008) para 3; UNSC Res S/RES/1897 (2009) para 6.

[186] UNSC Resolutions concerning the situation in Somalia S/RES/1814 (2008), S/RES/1816 (2008), S/RES/1838 (2008), S/RES/1844 (2008), S/RES/1846 (2008), S/RES/1851 (2008), S/RES/1897 (2009), S/RES/1918 (2010), S/RES/1950 (2010), S/RES/1976 (2011), S/RES/2015 (2011), S/RES/2020 (2011), S/RES/2077 (2012), S/RES/2125 (2013), S/RES/2184 (2014), S/RES/2246 (2015), S/RES/2316 (2016), S/RES/2383 (2017), S/RES/2442 (2018), S/RES/2500 (2019), S/RES/2554 (2020) and S/RES/2608 (2021).

(2008).[187] Moreover, the UNSC collaborated with the African Union and the federal government of Somalia to establish and support the work of the African Union Mission in Somalia (AMISOM), which was established in 2007. AMISOM was reconfigured into the African Union Transition Mission in Somalia (ATMIS) in 2022 and takes a comprehensive approach to addressing the domestic challenges and building long-lasting peace and stability in Somalia.[188]

Notably, although the powers endowed to the UNSC under Chapter VII of the UN Charter are 'extremely far-reaching and subject to very few express limitations',[189] its exercise of these powers in regard to both North Korea and Somalia have been rather cautious. In both cases, it was the determination that the specific situations constituted a threat to international peace and security in the region that triggered the prescription of enforcement authorisation from the UNSC.[190] When prescribing specific enforcement measures, the resolutions required the States exercising such measures to also obtain authorisation from the flag State when boarding suspected vessels or from the TFG for entering the territorial waters of Somalia. Hence, the UNSC authorisations do not alter the legal framework under UNCLOS and international law.

7.4.3 Collective Regional Approach to Maritime Security

A regional approach is a common theme in international relations that can promote beneficial cooperation under the framework of 'collective self-reliance' and provide institutional mechanisms in various fields for the development and growth of regional State entities, including for issues relating to regional security.[191] Regional cooperation is also promoted in UNCLOS, principally in regard to the conservation of living

[187] UNSC Res S/RES/2608 (2021), 3 December 2021; UNSC S/2021/920, 3 November 2021, The Situation with respect to Piracy and Armed Robbery at Sea off the Coast of Somalia, Report of the Secretary-General.

[188] African Union Mission in Somalia (AMISOM), https://amisom-au.org/; UNSC Res S/RES/1744 (2007), 20 February 2007; UNSC Res S/RES/2568 (2021), 12 March 2021; UNSC Res S/RES/2628 (2022), 31 March 2022.

[189] Bruno Simma (ed.), *The Charter of the United Nations: A Commentary*, Vol. I (2nd ed., Oxford University Press 2002) 705–707.

[190] UNSC Res S/RES/1718 (2006) Preamble; UNSC Res S/RES/1816 (2008) Preamble; Guilfoyle (2009) 65; Shaw (2017) 947–950.

[191] Bharti Chhibber, *Regional Security and Regional Cooperation: A Comparative Study of ASEAN and SAARC* (New Century Publications 2004) 2–8.

resources, the protection of the marine environment, and the development and transfer of marine scientific technology.[192] In practice, regional solutions have also been advocated as a possible solution to address threats to maritime security, in particular in relation to piracy.[193] Collective measures taken at a regional level would avoid the traditional jurisdictional competition between coastal States and other States in the EEZ and promote cooperation in sharing of information, building capacity and conducting joint enforcement activities among all participating States. Several collective regional approaches to maritime security promoted by States in Africa and Asia are examined below. The discussion focuses on the multi-level cooperative framework fostered in both regions that crosses maritime boundaries among States, as well as different threats to maritime security. The selected frameworks share the features of a formal multilateral instrument adopted by the participating States, a coordinating body and having taken practical measures to fulfil its mandates.

The first example is the collective response to piracy off Somalia. In 2009, under the auspice of IMO, twenty regional States, out of twenty-one eligible States, adopted the Djibouti Code of Conduct (Djibouti COC).[194] The purpose of the Djibouti COC is, consistent with the participating States' capacities and applicable laws, to promote regional cooperation to the fullest possible extent, thereby enhancing their effectiveness in the prevention, interdiction, prosecution and punishment of those individuals suspected of engaging in piracy and armed robbery at sea.[195] With support from IMO and the international community, the cooperative framework of the Djibouti COC consists of four

[192] UNCLOS Articles 61(2), 63, 118, 123, 197–200, 207(3)–(4), 208(4)–(5), 210(4), 211(3), 268(e), 270, 272, 276–277.

[193] Samuel Pyeatt Menefee, 'Maritime Terror in Europe and the Mediterranean' (1988) 12 Marine Policy 143, 149; Keyuan Zou, 'Enforcing the Law of Piracy in the South China Sea' (2000) 31(1) J Mar L & Com 107, 115–116; Robert C. Beckman and J. Ashley Roach, 'The Way Forward: Enhancing Legal Cooperation between ASEAN Member States', in Robert C. Beckman and J. Ashley Roach (eds.), *Piracy and International Maritime Crimes in ASEAN: Prospects for Cooperation* (Edward Elgar 2012) 234–238.

[194] Djibouti Code of Conduct, 29 January 2009 (Djibouti COC); IMO, 'The Djibouti Code of Conduct' www.imo.org/en/OurWork/Security/Pages/Content-and-Evolution-of-the-Djibouti-Code-of-Conduct.aspx. The 20 signatory States are: Djibouti, Ethiopia, Kenya, Madagascar, Maldives, Seychelles, Somalia, Tanzania and Yemen, Comoros, Egypt, Eritrea, Jordan, Mauritius, Mozambique, Oman, Saudi Arabia, South Africa, Sudan and the United Arab Emirates.

[195] IMO C.102/14, 3 April 2009, Protection of Vital Shipping Lanes, Annex, Code of Conduct Concerning the Repression of Piracy and Armed Robbery against Ships in the Western Indian Ocean and the Gulf of Aden, Article 2(1).

thematic pillars: sharing information and raising MDA; enhancing national legislation; delivering national and regional training; and building counter-piracy capacity.[196]

Following the successful repression of Somalia pirates, States in the region adopted the 2017 Jeddah Amendment to the Djibouti COC, extending its scope to cover other threats to maritime security, including trafficking in arms and drugs, illegal trade in wildlife, human trafficking and smuggling, illegal dumping of toxic waste and IUU fishing.[197] The implementation of the Jeddah Amendment is delivered under a governance framework comprised of a Steering Committee, a Working Group on Information Sharing and a Working Group on Capacity Building Coordination.[198] Two noticeable developments following adoption of the Jeddah Amendment are the commitment of participating States to establish multi-agency, multidisciplinary national maritime security and facilitation committees, and the increased cooperation with relevant States to coordinate activities to facilitate rescue, interdiction, investigation and prosecution of suspected illegal activities.[199]

In response to the increasing threats of piracy, armed robbery against ships and other illicit maritime activities in the Gulf of Guinea, the Economic Community of Central African States, the Economic Community of West African States and the Gulf of Guinea Commission, with the assistance of IMO, adopted the Yaoundé Code of Conduct (Yaoundé COC) in 2013.[200] Modelled after the Djibouti

[196] Djibouti COC Articles 4–11.

[197] Revised Code of Conduct Concerning the Repression of Piracy and Armed Robbery against Ships in the Western Indian Ocean and the Gulf of Aden, 12 January 2017, Article 1(3)–(4) https://dcoc.org/about-us/jeddah-amendment/ (The Jeddah Amendment). Sixteen of the 20 Djibouti COC signatory States have signed the Jeddah Amendment: Comoros, Djibouti, Ethiopia, Jordan, Kenya, Madagascar, Maldives, Mauritius, Mozambique, Oman, Saudi Arabia, Seychelles, Somalia, United Arab Emirates, United Republic of Tanzania and Yemen.

[198] Djibouti Code of Conduct, 'Steering Committee' https://dcoc.org/steering-committee/; UNSC S/2021/920 (2021) para 37.

[199] The Jeddah Amendment Articles 3(2), 8(2); IMO, 'Djibouti Code of Conduct' www.imo.org/en/OurWork/Security/Pages/DCoC.aspx.

[200] Code of Conduct Concerning the Repression of Piracy, Armed Robbery against Ships, and Illicit Maritime Activity in West and Central Africa, 25 June 2013 (Yaoundé COC) www.prc.cm/files/f7/26/ec/8acea8ec3a597473a76bd03c76140019.pdf; IMO, 'Maritime security in West and Central Africa' www.imo.org/en/OurWork/Security/Pages/West-and-Central-Africa.aspx. UNSC SC/11091, 14 August 2013, Security Council, in Statement, Welcomes Adoption of Code of Conduct by Regional Leaders to Prevent Piracy in Gulf of Guinea https://press.un.org/en/2013/sc11091.doc.htm. Signatory States

COC, the Yaoundé COC sets out another comprehensive regional strategy and framework concerning the prevention and repression of piracy, terrorism, illegal arms and drug trafficking, human trafficking and smuggling, marine pollution, IUU fishing and other transnational organised crime in the maritime domain of West and Central Africa.[201] Under the Yaoundé COC, signatory States set up the Interregional Coordination Centre, the Regional Centre for Maritime Security of West Africa and the Regional Centre for Maritime Security of Central Africa to facilitate information sharing and coordination.[202] The work of the three regional centres is supported by five zone-based Multinational Maritime Coordination Centres that oversee nineteen national Maritime Operations Centres.[203] Similar to the Djibouti COC, the Yaoundé COC is a non-binding instrument that relies on the goodwill of the signatory States to implement these commitments and measures to address maritime security threats.[204]

The development of both regional approaches to maritime security is aligned with the increasing emphasis on the blue economy in Africa, which recognises the financial costs of unlawful activities at sea.[205] In 2016, Member States of the African Union adopted the Charter on Maritime Security and Safety and Development in Africa (Lomé Charter) under the auspice of the 2050 Africa's Integrated Maritime Strategy.[206] The Lomé Charter covers the prevention and control of all transnational crimes at sea, all measures to prevent or minimise navigational accidents

to the Yaoundé COC include Angola, Benin, Burkina Faso, Cameroon, Cabo Verde, Chad, Congo, Democratic Republic of Congo, Côte d'Ivoire, Gabon, the Gambia, Ghana, Guinea, Guinea Bissau, Liberia, Mali, Niger, Nigeria, Sao Tome and Principe, Senegal, Sierra Leone and Togo.

201 Yaoundé COC Article 1.

202 Yaoundé COC Preamble, Article 11; European Union External Action, EU Maritime Security Factsheet: The Gulf of Guinea, 25 January 2021, www.eeas.europa.eu/eeas/eu-maritime-security-factsheet-gulf-guinea_en.

203 Yaoundé COC Preamble, Articles 7, 11–14, 17; EU Maritime Security Factsheet: The Gulf of Guinea.

204 Edwin E Egede, 'Gulf of Guinea and Maritime (In)Security: Musings on some Implications of Applicable Legal Instruments' (2022) 46(2) Brook J Int'l L 369, 391–401; UNSC S/RES/2634 (2022), 31 May 2022.

205 Curtis Bell et al., Pirates of the Gulf of Guinea: A Cost Analysis for Coastal States (Stable Seas November 2021) www.unodc.org/documents/Maritime_crime/UNODC_Pirates_GoG_A_Cost_Analysis_for_Coastal_States.pdf.

206 African Union, African Charter on Maritime Security and Safety and Development in Africa (15 October 2016, not in force) (Lomé Charter) https://au.int/en/treaties/african-charter-maritime-security-and-safety-and-development-africa-lome-charter.

and all measures for the sustainable development of natural resources.[207] By emphasising social economic measures and developing the blue economy as a means to increase State parties' capacities, the Lomé Charter attempts to reconcile the traditional approach of restrictions to counter maritime instability with human developmental aspects.[208]

The range of maritime security challenges within the Southeast Asian region includes terrorism, illicit trafficking of weapons, drug trafficking, people smuggling, piracy, environmental deterioration and IUU fishing.[209] These challenges affect some of the busiest shipping lanes in the Straits of Malacca and Singapore, through the archipelagic waters of Indonesia and the Philippines, and in and around the South China Sea.[210] Maintaining the safe passage of international commercial trade lanes through this region is essential – not just to the coastal States but also to the global economy.[211] The increasing number of incidents in this region and the transnational nature of these threats call for concerted efforts among the regional States and other States to combat these threats effectively.[212] Collective measures to promote maritime security in Asia on an organisational basis are taken under the auspices of ASEAN, which is an important diplomatic and legal forum to 'foster cooperation in the furtherance of the cause of peace, harmony, and stability in the region' and 'achieve regional prosperity and security'.[213] These measures can be

[207] Ibid Article 4.

[208] Ibid Articles 5, 19–24; Pieter Brits and Michelle Nel, 'African Maritime Security and the Lomé Charter: Reality or Dream?' (2018) 27(3-4) African Security Review 226, 230–232.

[209] UNODC, Regional Office for Southeast Asia and the Pacific, 'Transnational Organised Crime' www.unodc.org/roseap/en/what-we-do/toc/index.html; Rommel C. Banlaoi, 'Maritime Security Threats in Post-9/11 Southeast Asia: Regional Responses', in Rupert Herbert-Burns, Sam Bateman and Peter Lehr (eds.), *Lloyd's MIU Handbook of Maritime Security* (CRC Press Taylor & Francis Group 2009) 254–262; Rachel Baird, 'Transnational Security Issues in the Asian Maritime Environment: Responding to Maritime Piracy' (2012) 66 Australian J Int'l Affairs 501, 501–502.

[210] Rommel C. Banlaoi, 'Maritime Security Outlook for Southeast Asia', in Joshua Ho and Catherine Zara Raymond (eds.), *The Best of Times, the Worst of Times: Maritime Security in the Asia-Pacific* (World Scientific Publishing 2005) 65–67.

[211] Andrew S. Erickson, 'Maritime Security Cooperation in the South China Sea Region', in Shicun Wu and Keyuan Zou (eds.), *Maritime Security in the South China Sea: Regional Implications and International Cooperation* (Ashgate 2009) 51–53.

[212] Termsak Chalermpalanupap and Mayla Ibanez, 'ASEAN Measures in Combating Piracy and other Maritime Crimes', in Beckman and Roach (2012), 139.

[213] Association of Southeast Asian Nations (ASEAN), Treaty of Amity and Cooperation in Southeast Asia (24 February 1976, in force 15 July 1976) 1025 UNTS 297, Articles 9, 12. The ten Member States are: Brunei Darussalam, Cambodia, Indonesia, Lao, Malaysia, Myanmar, Philippines, Singapore, Thailand and Vietnam. ASEAN, 'ASEAN Member

viewed both from within the ASEAN framework and those developed by ASEAN as a block with external partners.

ASEAN mechanisms to address issues relating to maritime security are both comprehensive and fragmented.[214] From the institutional perspective, maritime security is mainly dealt with under one of the three ASEAN community pillars, the Political-Security Community, in accordance with the principle of comprehensive security.[215] Within the Community, various sectoral ministerial bodies have mandates to address certain issues relating to maritime security including the ASEAN Ministerial Meeting on Transnational Crime, ASEAN Defence Ministers Meeting, ASEAN Ministers/Attorneys-General Meeting of the Central Authorities on Mutual Legal Assistance in Criminal Matters and the ASEAN Ministerial Meeting on Drug Matters.[216] Each of these ministerial bodies may have under its purview the relevant senior officials and subsidiary bodies to undertake its functions. From the policy perspective, ASEAN has developed numerous non-binding declarations, statements, plan of actions and work plans, guidelines and terms of references that directly or indirectly address maritime security issues.[217] There are also a number of binding instruments, including the 2004 Treaty on Mutual Legal Assistance in Criminal Matters, the 2007 ASEAN Convention on Counter Terrorism, and the 2015 ASEAN Convention Against Trafficking in Persons, Especially Women and Children.[218]

States' https://asean.org/about-asean/member-states/. Charter of the Association of Southeast Asian Nations (20 November 2007, in force 15 December 2008) 2624 UNTS 223 Article 1 (ASEAN Charter).

214 Edwards (2022) 94–99.

215 ASEAN, 'ASEAN Political Security Community' https://asean.org/our-communities/asean-political-security-community/.

216 ASEAN Charter Annex 1: ASEAN Sectoral Ministerial Bodies; ASEAN Plan of Action in Combating Transnational Crime (2016–2025), 20 September 2017 https://asean.org/wp-content/uploads/2021/01/ASEAN-Plan-of-Action-in-Combating-TC_Adopted-by-11th-AMMTC-on-20Sept17-1.pdf.

217 ASEAN Document Series on Transnational Crime: Terrorism and Violent Extremism; Drugs; Cybercrime; and Trafficking in Persons (ASEAN Secretariat 2017) https://asean.org/wp-content/uploads/2012/05/ASEAN-Document-Series-on-Transnational-Crime-FINAL-with-link2.pdf; ASEAN Documents on Combating Transnational Crime and Terrorism (ASEAN 2012) https://asean.org/wp-content/uploads/2021/01/ASEAN-Documents-on-Combating-Transnational-Crime-and-Terrorism-3.pdf.

218 Treaty on Mutual Legal Assistance in Criminal Matters (29 November 2004, in force for each party upon ratification, last ratification on 31 January 2013); ASEAN Convention on Counter Terrorism (13 January 2007, in force 27 May 2011); ASEAN Convention Against Trafficking in Persons, Especially Women and Children (21 November 2015, in

Recognising that national and regional efforts alone will not be suffice in effectively dealing with maritime security threats, Member States of ASEAN have cooperated closely with dialogue partners and regional and international organisations.[219] In 1993, the ASEAN Regional Forum (ARF) was established as a consultative Asia-Pacific Forum for promoting open dialogue on political and security cooperation in the region.[220] In 2008, the Inter-Sessional Meeting on Maritime Security was established under the ambit of ARF as a dedicated platform to discuss maritime security.[221] Maritime security issues have also been considered under the auspices of the ASEAN Plus Three Cooperation since 1997,[222] the East Asia Summit established in 2005[223] and the Expanded ASEAN Maritime Forum established in 2012.[224]

ASEAN functions in an 'ASEAN way', upholding the practice of intense dialogues and exhaustive consultations to generate consensus among participating States on contentious issues facing the region whereby votes and binding instruments are uncommon.[225] The priority areas of cooperation on maritime security are centred on building

force 8 March 2017). All available from 'ASEAN Legal Instruments' https://agreement.asean.org/.

219 ASEAN Charter Articles 44–45; ASEAN, 'External Relations' https://asean.org/our-communities/asean-political-security-community/outward-looking-community/external-relations/.

220 'Twenty-Sixth ASEAN Ministerial Meeting, Singapore, 23–24 July 1993, Joint Communique' (1993) 10(2) ASEAN Economic Bulletin 191.

221 ASEAN, 'Maritime Security, Priority Areas of Cooperation' https://asean.org/our-communities/asean-political-security-community/peaceful-secure-and-stable-region/maritime-security/priority-areas-of-cooperation/.

222 The three countries are China, Japan and Republic of Korea. 'ASEAN Plus Three Cooperation, Overview' https://asean.org/asean-plus-three/; ASEAN Plus Three Cooperation Work Plan 2023 – 2027, 4 August 2022 https://asean.org/asean-plus-three-cooperation-work-plan-2023-2027/.

223 ASEAN, Chairman's Statement of the First East Asia Summit, Kuala Lumpur, 14 December 2005, https://asean.org/chairmans-statement-of-the-first-east-asia-summit-kuala-lumpur-14-december-2005/; ASEAN, Chairman's Statement of the 16th East Asia Summit, 28 October 2021 https://asean.org/chairmans-statement-of-the-16th-east-asia-summit/. Participating countries included ASEAN, Australia, China, India, Japan, New Zealand, Republic of Korea, Russia and the United States.

224 ASEAN, Chairman's Statement, 1st Expanded ASEAN Maritime Forum, Manila, 9 October 2012 https://asean.org/chairmans-statement-1st-expanded-asean-maritime-forum-manila/. The dialogue partners are: Australia, China, India, Japan, New Zealand, Republic of Korea, Russia and the United States.

225 S. Jayakumar, 'UNCLOS – Two Decades On' (2005) 9 Singapore YB Int'l L 1, 6–7; Banlaoi (2009) 262–263.

confidence and trust, sharing information and developing capacities through training and joint exercises. Although cooperation measures among ASEAN members and with external partners show progress in terms of practical security cooperation, they remain largely dialogue-based and are far from achieving collective regional maritime security.[226]

These regional approaches will provide a platform under which the regional States and the international community can cooperate and coordinate their efforts to prevent and suppress maritime security threats through increasing the capacity of the countries, enhancing effective border controls and promoting information sharing. The key characteristics for a functional regional governance system are the existence of political goodwill, shared concern of a common threat, the availability of rule-based regulation, the commitment of resources of cooperation and the expected gain from coordinated cooperation.[227]

Increasingly, States recognise that they have shared interests and responsibilities to ensure the security of the uses of sea areas. There is a growing willingness among States to develop bilateral and multilateral cooperative measures to combat threats to maritime security. As the above discussion illustrates, these actions remain within the legal framework of UNCLOS in exercising enforcement jurisdiction over maritime security threats in the EEZ. The most influential mechanism to promote collective maritime security is the establishment of international and regional resolutions to improve cooperation that facilitates the exchange and sharing of information, sustained capacity-building in the affected States and the commitment to take concrete operations to promote the granting of flag State authorisation.

7.5 The Way Forward

Ensuring open and protected ocean space and sea routes is critical for international trade and access to natural resources. In addition to the traditional concerns of sea power balance and the legal framework

[226] I. Gusti Bagus Dharma Agastia, 'Maritime Security Cooperation within the ASEAN Institutional Framework: A Gradual Shift towards Practical Cooperation' (2021) 9(1) Journal of ASEAN Studies 25, 28–29.

[227] Indra Alverdian, Marko Joas and Nina Tynkkynen, 'Prospects for Multi-level Governance of Maritime Security in the Sulu-Celebes Sea: Lessons from the Baltic Sea Region' (2020) 12(2) Australian Journal of Maritime & Ocean Affairs 108, 111–113.

governing the ocean, maritime security measures need to recognise the interconnectivity of multifaceted threats and different stakeholders, the novel forms of governance and order at sea and the promotion of competence and capacity-building.[228]

As a general proposition established under UNCLOS, the rights and jurisdiction of a coastal State over its maritime zones diminishes with the greater distance of the zone from its coast. In the EEZ, the coastal State's intent to extend and tighten its jurisdiction over maritime security threats once again clashes with other States' efforts to maximise the freedoms of navigation and overflight. However, there are two important features with regard to maritime security that have potential implications for the attribution of the rights to protect maritime security interests in the EEZ. First, all States share an interest in maintaining the security of navigation and other communication rights where the divergence between coastal State and other States blurs. Hence, there is a tendency to share concurrent jurisdiction over certain activities through international instruments or under the authorisation of the UNSC. Second, although interdicting suspicious vessels far from the coast may be the most effective way to protect the coastal State's maritime security, it remains a restricted approach. This is further complicated by the incapability or reluctance of some States to undertake effective measures within the vast area of the EEZ, which highlights the importance for States to cooperate and collaborate, in particular on regional basis, to this end.

UNCLOS continues to play an important role in shaping the contemporary international legal framework for ensuring maritime security.[229] Although UNCLOS does not explicitly attribute rights or jurisdiction over the protection of maritime security in the EEZ, it is fairly clear on the allocation and exercise of jurisdiction over various threats to maritime security. Current developments show an emerging willingness by States to develop new rules directed towards specific threats, including efforts to establish jurisdiction through multilateral agreements and for coastal States to obtain comprehensive information under the framework of the MDA. However, apart from some procedural steps to promptly obtain a flag State's consent to take action against a foreign vessel under certain conditions, there is no obvious deviation from the principle of

[228] Germond (2015) 74–75; Bueger and Edmunds (2017) 1294.
[229] Rothwell and Klein (2010) 22.

exclusive flag State jurisdiction in the EEZ.[230] The fact that the flag State maintains exclusive jurisdiction requires that the coastal State recognises the existence of such enforcement rights in its EEZ and does not unreasonably impede its implementation. Where the flag State is unable or unwilling to exercise such enforcement power over certain maritime security threats that are of concern to the coastal State, it should cooperate with the coastal State to effectively combat such threats.

There is also an emerging trend for States to cooperate at the international and regional levels to address maritime security threats. While *ad hoc* operations are well suited as a short-term solution for a particular threat, a comprehensive approach and multilateral cooperation are the only means to effectively address the root causes of the maritime security phenomena. This is particularly true in situations where the relevant State lacks capacity to prevent and combat certain imminent threats in areas under its jurisdiction and the situation threatens the peace and security of a region or even the international community. State practice in both Asia and Africa has shown that regional efforts improve information and resources sharing, enhance capacity-building and enforcement techniques of the coastal State and, in some situations, allow third States, with the consent of the flag State, to exercise a degree of authority over foreign vessels in the EEZ.

With regard to maritime security in the EEZ, the coastal State is gaining prescriptive jurisdiction to promote awareness and readiness in order to prevent potential threats. Although the flag State retains exclusive enforcement jurisdiction, there is an increasing tendency for them to relinquish it under treaty obligations or through authorisations under the UNSC. Finally, all States are required to cooperate to protect the interests of the international community as a whole. The rules of international law that address maritime security threats are in a state of transition, but the UNCLOS system and subsequent special international agreements and regional measures are flexible enough to face these new challenges.[231]

[230] M. D. Fink, 'Book Review on "N. Klein, Maritime Security and the Law of the Sea, Oxford 2011"' (2011) 58 Netherlands Int'l L Rev 438, 439.

[231] Rüdiger Wolfrum, 'Security At Sea', in UN Audiovisual Library of International Law, Lecture Series, https://legal.un.org/avl/ls/Wolfrum_LS.html.

Annex

Table 7A.1 *International laws relating to maritime security threats*

Maritime Security Threats	International Conventions	Other Relevant Instruments
Piracy	1958 Convention on the High Seas[a] 1982 UNCLOS 1988 Convention for the Suppression of Unlawful Acts against the Safety of Maritime Navigation (SUA Convention) and the 2005 Protocol[b]	United Nations Documents on Piracy[c] International Maritime Organization (IMO) Guidance and Documents on Piracy[d]
Terrorist Acts	1974 International Convention for the Safety of Life at Sea, as amended (SOLAS)[e] 1982 UNCLOS 1988 SUA Convention and 2005 SUA Protocol 1988 Protocol for the Suppression of Unlawful Acts against the Safety of Fixed Platforms Located on the Continental Shelf (SUA Platforms Protocol) and the 2005 Platforms Protocol[f]	Currently, there are 55 instruments pertaining to international terrorism. Of those, 19 are universal and 36 are regional[g] UN Documents and Resolutions[h] 2001 IMO Review of Measures and Procedures to Prevent Acts of Terrorism which Threaten the Security of Passengers and Crews and the Safety of Ships[i]
Illicit Trafficking of Arms and Weapons of Mass Destruction	1982 UNCLOS 1992 Convention on the Prohibition of the Development,	2001 Programme of Action to Prevent, Combat and Eradicate the Illicit Trade in Small Arms

Table 7A.1 (*cont.*)

Maritime Security Threats	International Conventions	Other Relevant Instruments
	Production, Stockpiling and Use of Chemical Weapons and on their Destruction[j] 2000 United Nations Convention against Transnational Organized Crime (UNCTOC)[k] 2001 Protocol against the Illicit Manufacturing of and Trafficking in Firearms, Their Parts and Components and Ammunition, supplementing the UNCTOC[l] 2005 SUA Protocol 2013 Arms Trade Treaty[m]	and Light Weapons in All Its Aspects (PoA)[n] 2005 International Tracing Instrument (ITI)[o] Disarmament Treaties Database[p]
Smuggling of Illicit Drugs	1961 Single Convention on Narcotic Drugs, as amended by the 1972 Protocol[q] 1971 Convention on Psychotropic Substances[r] 1982 UNCLOS; 1988 United Nations Convention against Illicit Traffic in Narcotic Drugs and Psychotropic Substances[s]	2006 IMO Revised Guidelines for the Prevention and Suppression of the Smuggling of Drugs, Psychotropic Substances and Precursor Chemicals on Ships Engaged in International Maritime Traffic[t]
Human Trafficking and Illegal Migrants	1965 Convention on Facilitation of International Maritime Traffic (FAL)[u] 1979 International Convention on	2001 IMO Review of Safety Measures and Procedures for the Treatment of Persons Rescued at Sea[y]

Table 7A.1 (*cont.*)

Maritime Security Threats	International Conventions	Other Relevant Instruments
	Maritime Search and Rescue (SAR)[v] 1982 UNCLOS 2000 Protocol against the Smuggling of Migrants by Land, Sea and Air, supplementing UNCTOC (Migrants Smuggling Protocol)[w] 2000 Protocol to Prevent, Suppress and Punish Trafficking in Persons, especially Women and Children, supplementing UNCTOC (Trafficking Protocol)[x]	2016 IMO Interim Measures for Combating Unsafe Practices Associated with the Trafficking, Smuggling or Transport of Migrants by Sea[z] 2018 Global Compact for Safe, Orderly and Regular Migration[aa]
IUU Fishing	1982 UNCLOS 1993 Agreement to Promote Compliance with International Conservation and Management Measures by Fishing Vessels on the High Seas[bb] 1995 Agreement for the Implementation of the Provisions of the UNCLOS relating to the Conservation and Management of Straddling Fish Stocks and Highly Migratory Fish Stocks (Fish Stocks Agreement)[cc] 2009 Agreement on Port State Measures to	1995 Food and Agriculture Organization of the United Nations (FAO) Code of Conduct for Responsible Fisheries[ee] 2001 FAO International Plan of Action to Prevent, Deter and Eliminate IUU Fishing (IPOA-IUU)[ff] 2015 FAO Voluntary Guidelines for Flag State Performance[gg]

Table 7A.1 (*cont.*)

Maritime Security Threats	International Conventions	Other Relevant Instruments
	Prevent, Deter and Eliminate IUU Fishing[dd]	
Environmental Security	1972 Convention on the Prevention of Marine Pollution by Dumping of Wastes and Other Matter and the 1996 Protocol (London Convention/Protocol)[hh] 1973/78 International Convention for the Prevention of Pollution from Ships, as amended (MARPOL)[ii] 1974 SOLAS[jj] 1982 UNCLOS 1989 Basel Convention on the Control of Transboundary Movements of Hazardous Wastes and their Disposal (Basel Convention)[kk]	1990 International Atomic Energy Agency (IAEA) Code of Practice on the International Transboundary Movement of Radioactive Waste[ll] 2018 IAEA Regulations for the Safe Transport of Radioactive Material[mm]

[a] 29 April 1958, in force 30 September 1962, 450 UNTS 11

[b] SUA Convention: 10 March 1988, in force 1 March 1992, 1678 UNTS 221; 2005 Protocol: 14 October 2005, in force 28 July 2010

[c] For the up-to-date document, see 'United Nations Documents on Piracy' www.un.org/depts/los/piracy/piracy_documents.htm (Updated 21 June 2024); 'UN Documents for Piracy' www.securitycouncilreport.org/un-documents/piracy/

[d] IMO, 'Piracy and Armed Robbery against Ships' www.imo.org/en/OurWork/Security/Pages/PiracyArmedRobberydefault.aspx

[e] 1 November 1974, in force 25 May 1980, 1184 UNTS 2

[f] 1988 SUA Platforms Protocol: 10 March 1988, in force 1 March 1992, 1678 UNTS 304; 2005 Platforms Protocol: 14 October 2005, in force 28 July 2010

[g] UNGA A/78/221, 24 July 2023, Measures to Eliminate International Terrorism, Report of the Secretary-General, para 41; United Nations, Office of Counter-Terrorism, 'International Legal Instruments' www.un.org/counterterrorism/international-legal-instruments

[h] United Nations, Office of Counter-Terrorism, 'UN Documents' www.un.org/counterterrorism/un-documents
[i] IMO Res A.924(22), 20 November 2001
[j] 3 September 1992, in force 29 April 1997, 1975 UNTS 45
[k] 15 November 2000, in 29 September 2003, 2225 UNTS 209
[l] 31 May 2001, in force 3 July 2005, 2326 UNTS 208
[m] 2 April 2013, in force 24 December 2014, 3013 UNTS 269
[n] *Report of the United Nations Conference on the Illicit Trade in Small Arms and Light Weapons in All Its Aspects, New York, 9-20 July 2001*, A/CONF.192/15 (United Nations 2001)
[o] UNODC, International Instrument to Enable States to Identify and Trace, in a Timely and Reliable Manner, Illicit Small Arms and Light Weapons www.unodc.org/documents/organized-crime/Firearms/ITI.pdf
[p] United Nations, Office for Disarmament Affairs, 'Disarmament Treaties Database' https://treaties.unoda.org/
[q] Convention: 30 March 1961, in force 13 December 1964, 520 UNTS 151; 1972 Protocol: 25 March 1972, in force 8 August 1975
[r] 21 February 1971, in force 16 August 1976, 1019 UNTS 175
[s] 20 December 1988, in force 11 November 1990, 1582 UNTS 164
[t] IMO Res MSC.228(82), 7 December 2006,
[u] 9 April 1965, in force 5 March 1967, 591 UNTS 265
[v] 27 April 1979, in force 22 June 1985, 1405 UNTS 118; a revised Annex to the SAR Convention was adopted in May 1998 and entered into force in January 2000
[w] 15 December 2000, in force 28 January 2008, 2241 UNTS 507
[x] 15 December 2000, in force 25 December 2003, 2237 UNTS 319
[y] IMO Res A.920(22), 29 November 2001
[z] IMO MSC.1/Circ.896/Rev.2, 26 May 2016
[aa] UNGA A/RES/73/195, 11 January 2019, Resolution adopted by the General Assembly on 19 December 2018
[bb] 24 November 1993, in force 24 April 2003, 2221 UNTS 91
[cc] 4 August 1995, in force 11 December 2001, 2167 UNTS 3
[dd] 22 November 2009, in force 5 June 2016 www.fao.org/port-state-measures/resources/detail/en/c/1111616/
[ee] 31 October 1995 https://www.fao.org/fishery/en/publication/56346?lang%C2%BCen=
[ff] 2 March 2001 www.fao.org/documents/card/en/c/71be21c9-8406-5f66-ac68-1e74604464e7
[gg] Adopted at the Thirty-First Session of FAO Committee on Fisheries, Rome, 9–13 June 2014, COFI/2014/4.2/Rev.1
[hh] Convention: 29 December 1972, in force 30 August 1975 1046 UNTS 120; 1996 Protocol: 17 November 1996, in force 24 March 2006

[ii] 1973 Convention: 2 November 1973, not in force; 1978 Protocol: 17 February 1978, in force 2 October 1983, 1340 UNTS 67 (MARPOL); 1997 Protocol (Annex VI): 26 September 1997, in force 19 May 2005
[jj] SOLAS, Chapter VII, 2001 International Code for the Safe Carriage of Packaged Irradiated Nuclear Fuel, Plutonium and High-Level Radioactive Wastes on Board Ships (INF Code); 2004 International Maritime Dangerous Goods (IMDG) Code
[kk] 22 March 1989, in force 5 May 1992, 1673 UNTS 126
[ll] IAEA INFCIRC/386, 13 November 1990 www.iaea.org/sites/default/files/infcirc386.pdf
[mm] IAEA, *Specific Safety Requirements*, No. SSR-6 (Rev. 1) www.iaea.org/publications/12288/regulations-for-the-safe-transport-of-radioactive-material

8

Underwater Archaeological and Historical Objects

8.1 Introduction

Underwater archaeological and historical objects refer to materials and remains lying on or in the seabed that have the potential to yield information and knowledge about natural and historical existence of human civilisation.[1] These include submerged sites and structures of remains of a prehistoric settlement, wreck sites and wreckage of ships, aircraft and spacecraft along with the items contained therein, and their archaeological and natural context.[2] In particular of shipwrecks, the estimation is that until the nineteenth century, almost 5 per cent of all seagoing ships were lost every year because of bad weather, incidents of navigation, maritime crimes, naval battles or other events.[3] These shipwrecks and sites are known as a 'time capsule', meaning that everything may well be as it was when it disappeared beneath the water's surface, loaded with irreplaceable information about the history of humankind.[4]

Land-based archaeology is a vintage academic science, but maritime or underwater archaeology only became an 'independent' or 'specialised'

[1] Sarah Dromgoole, *Underwater Cultural Heritage and International Law* (Cambridge University Press 2013) 1.

[2] International Council of Museums and Sites (ICOMOS), Charter on the Protection and Management of Underwater Cultural Heritage (Sofia Charter), ratified by the 11th ICOMOS General Assembly in Sofia, Bulgaria, October 1996 www.icomos.org/en/faq-doccen/179-articles-en-francais/ressources/charters-and-standards/161-charter-on-the-protection-and-management-of-underwater-cultural-heritage; Convention on the Protection of the Underwater Cultural Heritage (2 November 2001, in force 2 January 2009) 2562 UNTS 3, Article 1(1)(a) (CPUCH); Dromgoole (2013) 66.

[3] Tullio Scovazzi, 'The Relationship between Two Conventions Applicable to Underwater Cultural Heritage', in James Crawford et al. (eds.), *The International Legal Order: Current Needs and Possible Responses: Essays in Honour of Djamchid Momtaz* (Brill 2017) 504.

[4] David Nutley, 'Submerged Cultural Sites: Opening a Time Capsule' (2008) 60(4) Museum International – Underwater Cultural Heritage 7, 7–9; Patrick J. O'Keefe, 'Underwater Cultural Heritage', in Francesco Francioni and Ana Filipa Vrdoljak (eds.), *The Oxford Handbook of International Cultural Heritage Law* (Oxford University Press 2020) 295.

subject by the end of the 1960s due to the growing awareness of the significance of shipwrecks and other forms of underwater cultural heritage (UCH).[5] This was made possible through innovations in marine technology, in particular the aqualung, which permitted and generalised scuba diving, and the application of remote sensing and underwater robotics.[6] Access to underwater archaeological and historical objects had a twofold impact: scientific discovery of historical vestiges and, at the same time, information that could be used for purposes such as commercial exploitation. In addition, the growing human utilisation of the ocean and its resources increasingly threatens the existence of these objects, deliberately or otherwise.[7] Moreover, these objects are vulnerable to changes of the marine environment, such as natural disasters, global warming, acidification and water pollution.

The international law to protect underwater archaeological and historical objects, however, has remained underdeveloped to adequately regulate human activities in the interests of their preservation. The 1982 United Nations Convention on the Law of the Sea (UNLCOS) refers to these objects twice.[8] While Article 149 relates only to those archaeological and historical objects located in the Area, Article 303 lays down a general obligation for all States to protect such objects found at sea with a particular focus on the contiguous zone. However, UNCLOS does not define any specific rules relating to such objects found on the continental shelf or in the exclusive economic zone (EEZ), that is, the space located between the external limit of the contiguous zone and the limit of the Area.[9] In this regard, UNCLOS left a legal vacuum that would threaten the protection of these objects, as it emphasises the principle of flag State jurisdiction and the freedom of the high seas, which could easily lead to a first-come-first-served approach.[10]

[5] Dromgoole (2013) 28.

[6] Howard H. Shore, 'Marine Archaeology and International Law: Background and Some Suggestions' (1972) 9(3) San Diego L Rev 668, 668.

[7] Dromgoole (2013) 3–4.

[8] United Nations Convention on the Law of the Sea (10 December 1982, in force 16 November 1994) 1833 UNTS 3, Articles 149, 303 (UNCLOS).

[9] Myron H. Nordquist, Shabtai Rosenne and Louis B. Sohn (eds.), *United Nations Convention on the Law of the Sea 1982: A Commentary*, Vol. V (Martinus Nijhoff 1989) 161–162.

[10] Dromgoole (2013) 35–36; Tullio Scovazzi, 'Article 303', in Alexander Proelss (ed.), *United Nations Convention on the Law of the Sea: A Commentary* (Hart 2017) 1955.

On a positive note, the international law of the sea, including the implementation of UNCLOS, is not static, but evolves through State practice and subsequent agreements. Certain threats to the majority of underwater archaeological and historical objects have been addressed by the United Nations Organization for Education, Science and Culture (UNESCO), particularly through the 2001 Convention on the Protection of Underwater Cultural Heritage (CPUCH).[11] The CPUCH, without altering the jurisdictional framework of maritime zones established by UNCLOS, institutes an international State cooperation scheme based on information sharing and cooperative protection.[12] Of particular interest to the EEZ, the coastal State has been granted a special role as a Coordinating State for the protection of UCH found in the EEZ and on the continental shelf on behalf of State parties as a whole.[13]

This chapter analyses and discusses the jurisdiction over activities that are pertinent to the archaeological and historical objects found in the EEZ. In Section 8.2, the development of the legal framework to protect these objects under UNCLOS and the CPUCH is reviewed, together with an interpretation of how these objects are defined under each treaty. The jurisdictional arrangements over activities that may affect the protection of these objects found in the EEZ is then analysed in Section 8.3. Special attention is given to the relevant provisions of the CPUCH, which somewhat clarifies the role of the coastal State in protecting UCH in the EEZ. This is followed by a discussion in Section 8.4 of the legal procedures that could be invoked to settle disputes relating to these objects.

A central strand of the discussion in this chapter is premised on the argument that the subject of underwater archaeological and historical objects falls under the unattributed rights and jurisdiction in the EEZ.[14] With this understanding, all States have the right to undertake activities

[11] United Nations Organization for Education, Science and Culture (UNESCO), 'Underwater Heritage (Convention 2001)' www.unesco.org/en/underwater-heritage?hub=412.

[12] Sarah Dromgoole, '2001 UNESCO Convention on the Protection of the Underwater Cultural Heritage' (2003) 18(1) Int'l J Marine & Coastal L 59, 68–69.

[13] CPUCH Articles 9–10.

[14] Anastasia Strati, 'Protection of the Underwater Cultural Heritage: from Shortcomings of the UN Convention on the Law of the Sea to the Compromises of the UNESCO Convention', in Anastasia Strati, Maria Gavouneli and Nikolaos Skourtos (eds.), *Unresolved Issues and the New Challenges to the Law of the Sea: Time Before and Time After* (Brill 2006) 32; Dromgoole (2013) 259.

relating to the archaeological and historical objects found in the EEZ. In addition to the due regard obligation, the exercise of such a right must not breach the acting State's obligation to protect such objects and those obligations it undertook as a State party to the CPUCH. Given the lack of specific provisions in UNCLOS addressing the issues relating to these objects found in the EEZ, the provisions of CPUCH on the protection of UCH in the EEZ can be considered an agreement substantiating the rules codified in UNCLOS Article 59.[15]

8.2 Overview of the Legal Framework

8.2.1 Historical Development

Beginning in the 1950s, modern technological advances allowed the discovery and recovery of archaeological and historical objects from the marine environment. At the time, international law was not clear on who had the right to explore these objects or allocate their property rights.[16] States had adopted national legislation to regulate certain activities of their nationals to provide protection of these objects from intentional human interference.[17] The issue of these objects did not receive any special attention during the First and Second United Nations Conference on the Law of the Sea and was only discussed at the Third Conference towards the end of the negotiation process.[18] This resulted in only one provision, Article 303, which was incorporated in the Part XVI 'General Provisions' that applies to all maritime zones, with the intention to avoid upsetting the specific jurisdictional balance adopted in various maritime zones.[19]

[15] Alexander Proelss, 'Article 59', in Proelss (2017) 462; Robin Churchill, Vaughan Lowe and Amy Sander, *The Law of the Sea* (4th ed., Manchester University Press 2022) 293.

[16] Shore (1972) 669; Bernard H. Oxman, 'Marine Archaeology and the International Law of the Sea' (1987–1988) 12(3) Colum-VLA JL & Arts 353, 353–355.

[17] Dromgoole (2013) 68–70; Patrick J. O'Keefe and James A. R. Nafziger, 'The Draft Convention on Underwater Cultural Heritage' (1994) 25(4) Ocean Dev & Int'l L 391, 394–396; Geoffrey N. Bailey, Jan Harff and Dimitris Sakellariou, 'Archaeology and Palaeolandscapes of the Continental Shelf: An Introduction', in Geoffrey N. Bailey, Jan Harff and Dimitris Sakellariou (eds.), *Under the Sea: Archaeology and Palaeolandscapes of the Continental Shelf* (Springer 2017) 1; Craig Forrest, *Maritime Legacies and the Law: Effective Legal Governance of WWI Wrecks* (Edward Elgar 2019) 193–197.

[18] Nordquist, Rosenne and Sohn (1989) 159.

[19] Ibid 160; Scovazzi 'Article 303' (2017) 1952.

The negotiation history of Article 303 of UNCLOS has been well described in the literature and can be summarised as follows.[20] The provision originated in a proposal submitted by Greece, with revisions and support by other States, that the sovereign rights of the coastal State in respect of both the continental shelf and the EEZ be extended to include rights regarding the discovery and salvage of any 'object of purely archaeological or historical nature on the seabed and subsoil'.[21] This proposal met with strong opposition from other maritime States, namely, the United States, the United Kingdom and the Netherlands, which feared the creeping jurisdiction of the coastal State in the EEZ and on the continental shelf. Instead, the United States proposed to include a general duty of all States to protect archaeological and historical objects found in the marine environment. Ultimately, the US proposal was adopted after much debate on the basis that it was 'closer to a compromise than any of the others' presented.[22]

Article 303 has four paragraphs, with one declaring the general duties to protect and cooperate to protect objects of an archaeological and historical nature found at sea, one giving coastal States a limited jurisdictional right to control traffic in such objects up to the outer limit of their contiguous zone when declared, and two disclaimer provisions of relevant rights holder and other international agreements. Activities directed at these objects, or activities that might incidentally affect them, between the outer limit of the contiguous zone and the Area were not regulated but rather subordinated to the rights and duties related to the exploration and exploitation of the EEZ and the continental shelf.

The legal framework for protecting underwater archaeological and historical objects created under UNCLOS has been harshly criticised as

[20] Bernard H. Oxman, 'The Third United Nations Conference on the Law of the Sea: The Eighth Session (1979)' (1980) 74 Am J Int'l L 1, 23–24; L. Van Meurs, 'Legal Aspects of Marine Archaeological Research' (1986) Acta Juridica 83, 90–100; Nordquist, Rosenne and Sohn (1989) 159–161; Tullio Scovazzi, 'Article 149', in Proelss (2017) 1053–1054; Scovazzi 'Article 303' (2017) 1951–1952; Mariano J. Aznar, *Maritime Claims and Underwater Archaeology: When History Meets Politics* (Brill 2020) 8.

[21] United Nations Conference on the Law of the Sea (Third Conference), Official Records, Vol. XIII: Ninth Session, A/CONF.62/L.51, 29 March 1980, Report of the Chairman of the Second Committee, paras 12, 16, informal proposal presented by Cabo Verde, Greece, Italy, Malta, Portugal, Tunisia and Yugoslavia (C.2/Informal Meeting/43/Rev.2); Myron H. Nordquist, Satya N. Nandan, Michael W. Logde and Shabtai Rosenne (eds.), *United Nations Convention on the Law of the Sea 1982: A Commentary*, Vol. VI (Martinus Nijhoff 2002) 230.

[22] Third Conference, Official Records, Vol. XIV: Resumed Ninth Session, A/CONF.62/L.58, 22 August 1980, Report of the President on the Work of the Informal Plenary Meeting of the Conference on General Provisions, paras 13–15.

complicated and incomplete.[23] Several historical conditions contributed to this legal gap. During the 1970s, recognition of marine archaeology as an independent scientific discipline was still limited, and it was not considered marine scientific research during the Third Conference, as it does not involve the study of the natural marine environment.[24] These objects were seen by some lead negotiating States as commodities and were thus subject to appropriation, the law of finds and/or salvage, and trade with commercial values. Additionally, the risks and threats to these objects were not perceived the same in the 1970s as they are today.

Subsequent development on using legal tools to protect underwater archaeological and historical objects was mainly driven by concerned States of the Mediterranean Sea through proceedings at the European level. Notable instruments adopted by the Council of Europe include the Roper Report and Recommendation 848, a 1985 draft European Convention on the Protection of the Underwater Cultural Heritage and the 1992 revised European Convention on the Protection of the Archaeological Heritage.[25] These initiatives made vital contributions to the evolution of international law in the field. They demonstrated that there were political recognition and commitment, certainly within Europe, to develop a treaty framework to afford protection to UCH. Additionally, the debates and draft provisions showed that acceptable compromises could be reached on areas of contention such as the definition and criteria of UCH, jurisdictional attribution over certain

[23] O'Keefe and Nafziger (1994) 397–399; Tullio Scovazzi, 'A Contradictory and Counterproductive Regime', in Roberta Garabello and Tullio Scovazzi (eds.), *The Protection of the Underwater Cultural Heritage, Before and After the 2001 UNESCO Convention* (Brill 2003) 3–17; Strati (2006) 28–34; Mariano J. Aznar, 'The Legal Protection of Underwater Cultural Heritage: Concerns and Proposals,' in Carlos Espósito et al. (eds.), *Ocean Law and Policy: Twenty Years of Development under the UNCLOS Regime* (Brill 2017) 124–147.

[24] Alfred H. A. Soons, *Marine Scientific Research and the Law of the Sea* (Kluwer 1982) 275; Sarah Dromgoole, 'Revisiting the Relationship between Marine Scientific Research and the Underwater Cultural Heritage' (2010) 25 Int'l J Marine & Coastal L 33, 44–46.

[25] Parliamentary Assembly of the Council of Europe, The Underwater Cultural Heritage: Report of the Committee on Culture and Education (Rapporteur: Mr. John Roper) (Doc 4200-E, Strasbourg, 1978) https://pace.coe.int/en/files/4425; Parliamentary Assembly of the Council of Europe, Recommendation 848 (1978), Underwater Cultural Heritage, https://pace.coe.int/en/files/14882; European Convention on the Protection of the Archaeological Heritage (Revised) (16 January 1992, in force 25 May 1995) ETS No. 143 www.coe.int/en/web/conventions/full-list?module=treaty-detail&treatynum=143; Janet Blake, 'The Protection of the Underwater Cultural Heritage' (1996) 45(4) Int'l & Compar LQ 819, 820–831; Dromgoole (2013) 45–46.

activities targeted at these objects beyond the outer limit of the contiguous zone, and the scientific standards of archaeology and conservation.[26]

The protection of UCH has also been the subject of discussion and initiatives in other forums. A notable example of the legal instruments is the 1993 Draft Convention on the Protection of the Underwater Cultural Heritage produced by the International Law Association (ILA).[27] The ILA Draft Convention had been taken up by UNESCO, along with other instruments and conventions, as a basis to develop an international agreement on this subject.[28] There was considerable political commitment during the negotiation process of the CPUCH to find acceptable compromises on the core areas of contention. Mirroring the process at the Third Conference, the main tension remained between the coastal States arguing for broader jurisdiction within certain maritime zones to adequately protect the UCH and the maritime powers resisting the pressure for coastal States to be given such direct jurisdiction.[29] A consensus could not be reached on a number of key provisions, and the negotiations concluded with a majority vote to adopt the CPUCH in 2001. Several maritime powers rejected the draft convention over concerns about two particular issues. First, they regarded the regulatory framework established for the continental shelf and EEZ as prejudicial, or at least potentially, to the 'package deal' and jurisdictional balance enshrined in UNCLOS; second, they were dissatisfied with the treatment of sunken State vessels including warships.[30]

[26] Dromgoole (2013) 37–44.

[27] O'Keefe and Nafziger (1994) 404–417.

[28] UNESCO Recommendation on International Principles Applicable to Archaeological Excavations, 5 December 1956, reprinted in Convention and Recommendations of UNESCO Concerning the Protection of the Cultural Heritage (UNESCO 1985) 101–114; Convention for the Protection of the World Cultural and Natural Heritage (16 November 1972, in force 17 December 1975) 1037 UNTS 151; Ricardo J. Elia, 'ICOMOS Adopts Archaeological Heritage Charter: Text and Commentary' (1993) 20(1) J Field Archaeology 97, 97–98; United Nations General Assembly (UNGA) A/51/645, 1 November 1996, Law of the Sea Report of the Secretary-General, paras 142–144; Draft Convention on the Protection of Underwater Cultural Heritage: A Commentary, prepared for UNESCO by Anastasia Strati, 1999 https://unesdoc.unesco.org/ark:/48223/pf0000115994.

[29] UNGA A/54/429, 30 September 1999, Oceans and the Law of the Sea Report of the Secretary-General, paras 522–526; Roberta Garabello, 'The Negotiating History of the Convention on the Protection of the Underwater Cultural Heritage', in Garabello and Scovazzi (2003) 138–151.

[30] 'Statements on Vote for All the Relevant Maritime States With the Exception of Germany', reproduced in Garabello and Scovazzi (2003) 239–253; Robert C. Blumberg,

The CPUCH was negotiated for the main purpose of solving the caveats left unresolved by UNCLOS and creating a new international legal regime for the protection of UCH according to generally accepted scientific standards.[31] It focuses on how State parties can regulate human activities that could affect UCH in different maritime zones rather than on the objects themselves. Therefore, the regulatory regime established by CPUCH is heavily reliant on flag State jurisdiction and cooperation. The wide participation of and implementation by State parties are crucial for the regime to be fully functional and effective. Major historical maritime powers such as Spain, Portugal, Italy and Tunisia are parties and there are an increasing number of Latin American States (where a lot of UCH lies) have also ratified. Non-State parties including Australia, Canada, China, Germany, Greece, Russia, the Netherlands, the United Kingdom, the United States and Türkiye generally support the principles and standards of the CPUCH.[32] It is, nevertheless, the most complete and up-to-date regulation of activities directed at or incidentally affecting UCH in continental and marine waters and has seventy-seven State parties worldwide as of July 2024.[33]

The CPUCH was the culmination of an evolutionary process in the development of international law in the field of UCH protection taking place over more than four decades.[34] From the perspective of the scope of application, the CPUCH only covers certain archaeological and historical objects – the broader term used by UNCLOS – that meet its criteria and have been under water for at least 100 years.[35] From the perspective of

'International Protection of Underwater Cultural Heritage', in Myron Nordquist, John Norton Moore and Kuen-Chen Fu (eds.), *Recent Developments in the Law of the Sea and China* (Brill 2006) 493–497; J. Ashley Roach, *Excessive Maritime Claims* (4th ed., Brill 2021) 665–668.

31 CPUCH Preamble; Dromgoole (2013) 24, 281.

32 黄伟和南雁冰,'中国加入《保护水下文化遗产公约》的方案探究——以《〈条例〉修订草案》和《公约》的比较与结合为视角',2019年3月,第4卷第2期,边界与海洋研究,56–73页,第57–59页 (HUANG Wei and NAN Yanbing, 'Research on Measures of China's Accession to the Convention on the Protection of the Underwater Cultural Heritage: From the Perspective of Comparison and Combination between the Draft Revision to Regulation and the Convention' (2019) 4(2) Journal of Boundary and Ocean Studies 56, 57–59.); Aznar (2020) 11–12.

33 Guido Carducci, 'New Developments in the Law of the Sea: The UNESCO Convention on the Protection of Underwater Cultural Heritage' (2002) 96 Am J Int'l L 419, 433; UNESCO, 'Convention on the Protection of the Underwater Cultural Heritage, States Parties' www.unesco.org/en/legal-affairs/convention-protection-underwater-cultural-heritage.

34 Dromgoole (2013) 71.

35 CPUCH Article 1(1).

the hierarchy relationship between these two instruments, both UNCLOS and CPUCH provide that it is subject to the other, which is a rather paradoxical situation.[36] An attempt to resolve this deadlock could be to apply the general principles of law according to which the special rules prevail over the general rules (*lex specialis* derogates from *legi generali*), and the later treaty relating to the same subject matter suspends the earlier treaty among the same State parties.[37] In this regard, among State parties to both treaties, the interpretation and implementation of Articles 149 and 303 of UNCLOS should follow, insofar as they are compatible with the basic principles of UNCLOS, the more specific and later CPUCH regime. Article 3 of CPUCH guarantees that all the UNCLOS provisions other than those two specifically related to the UCH are unaffected.

8.2.2 *Objects of Archaeological and Historical Nature*

In the practice of heritage law, the definitions of subject matter often include two types of criteria. One is the 'definitional criteria' that sets out the type of subject matter capable of being afforded protection by the legislation, and the other is the 'selection criteria' that limits the scope of the definition by reference to some value, or is indicative of value, which determines what is to be protected in fact.[38] This approach to defining the subject matter has been employed by both UNCLOS and CPCUH.

Both Articles 149 and 303 of UNCLOS used the same phrase, 'objects of an archaeological and historical nature', to define their subject matter. The word 'objects' describes the subject matter that is capable of being covered, and the phrase 'of an archaeological and historical nature' describe the value that these objects must possess in order to be covered in fact. However, UNCLOS did not define any of the terms used. Under the general rules of treaty interpretation, each term must be interpreted in good faith in accordance with its ordinary meaning in the context in which it is found and in light of the treaty's object and purpose, taking

[36] CPUCH Article 3; UNCLOS Article 303(4).

[37] Vienna Convention on the Law of Treaties (23 May 1969, in force 27 January 1980) 1155 UNTS 331, Article 30(3); UNCLOS Article 311(3); Dromgoole (2013) 277–281; Scovazzi (2017) 517–518; Malcolm N. Shaw, *International Law* (8th ed., Cambridge University Press 2017) 48.

[38] Roger M. Thomas, 'Heritage Protection Criteria: An Analysis' (2006) J Plan & Env't L 956, 960–962.

into account any subsequent agreements, practice and other relevant rules of international law.[39]

It should be noted that the 'objects of an archaeological and historical nature' were clearly excluded from the notion of 'resources' as used in UNCLOS.[40] In its commentary on a draft article describing the coastal State's sovereign right over the continental shelf, the International Law Commission (ILC) declared that '[i]t is clearly understood that the rights in question do not cover objects such as wrecked ships and their cargoes (including bullion) lying on the seabed or covered by the sand of the subsoil'.[41] This firm statement made it clear that the ILC was of the view that shipwrecks were not included within the sovereign rights of the coastal State on the continental shelf, which was 'for the purpose of exploring and exploiting its natural resources'.[42] In light of the ILC's early pronouncement, it became generally accepted that the sovereign rights of coastal States over natural resources on the continental shelf and in the EEZ, as codified in UNCLOS, could not be interpreted as extending to shipwrecks.[43]

As to the 'definitional criteria', the ordinary meaning of the term 'object' is a material thing that can been seen and touched, and is generally associated with a thing that is movable. It may at first appear questionable whether something that was originally a fixed, immovable site or structure can qualify as an object. In light of the object and purpose of Articles 149 and 303, the context of the term as found therein, and taking into account the *travaux préparatoires*, there is no doubt that a broad interpretation was intended that would encompass sites, fixed structures and shipwrecks.[44] A distinction between the subject matter of

39 Vienna Convention on the Law of Treaties Article 31; Request for An Advisory Opinion submitted by the Commission of Small Island States on Climate Change and Internaitonal Law, Advisory Opinion of 21 May 2024, ITLOS List of cases: No. 31, para 135 (Climate Change Advisory Opinion).

40 Alleged Violations of Sovereign Rights and Maritime Spaces in the Caribbean Sea (Nicaragua v. Colombia), Judgment of 21 April 2022, ICJ Reports 2022, p. 266, para 184.

41 'Report of the International Law Commission (ILC) to the United Nations General Assembly (UNGA), A/3159, Articles Concerning the Law of the Sea with Commentaries' (1956) 2 YB ILC 298, Article 68, Commentary 5 (ILC Draft Articles).

42 Ibid Article 68.

43 UNCLOS Articles 56(1)(a), 77(1); Nordquist, Rosenne and Sohn (1989) 162; Dromgoole (2013) 29–30.

44 Moritaka Hayashi, 'Archaeological and Historical Objects under the United Nations Convention on the Law of the Sea' (1996) 20(4) Marine Policy 291, 291; 赵亚娟,'国际法视角下"水下文化遗产"的界定',2008年1月,第26卷第1期,河北法学,143–147页,第144页 (ZHAO Ya-juan, 'Evolution of the Meaning of the "Underwater Cultural

the two provisions can be observed in that Article 149 explicitly applies to 'all objects of an archaeological and historical nature', whereas Article 303 applies to such objects generally and does not refer to 'all'.

In order to fall within the scope of Articles 149 and 303, objects must be 'of an archaeological and historical nature'. This phrase represents the 'selection criteria'. Although the words 'archaeological and historical' are frequently used to describe the subject matter of protective legislation, it seems that no consideration was given to definitions at the Third Conference.[45] The adjectives 'archaeological and historical' imply objects of antiquity rather than those of more recent origin, and the value of these objects is evident by their association to humankind.[46] The key challenge and difficulty to applying the selection criterion used in Articles 149 and 303 is the question of time, that is, how to define the age of the object or a date prior to which such object be considered 'archaeological and historical'. Commentators and national legislation have adopted different thresholds for protection of these objects. It has been argued that, given the negotiation history was heavily influenced by the practice and approaches of the Mediterranean States, this phrase should be interpreted as covering only things that are 'many hundreds of years old' and was not intended to apply to 'modern objects whatever their historical interest'.[47] However, State practice and scholarly opinions have evolved to interpret 'archaeological and historical' to include objects of more recent origin, and there is no evidence that objects are limited to things that are centuries old.[48]

The CPUCH adopted the term 'UCH' to define the subject matter. It refers to 'all traces of human existence having a cultural, historical or archaeological character which have been partially or totally under water, periodically or continuously, for at least 100 years'.[49] This is followed by a list of examples and two specific exclusions from the scope of application of the CPUCH, namely pipelines and cables and other operational installations.[50] The 'definitional criteria' require that the subject matter

Heritage" in the Context of International Law' (2008) Hebei Law Science 143, 144); Dromgoole (2013) 72.

45 Oxman (1987–1988) 364; Nordquist, Rosenne and Sohn (1989) 160.

46 Dromgoole (2013) 73.

47 Oxman (1987–1988) 364; Dromgoole (2013) 74.

48 Nordquist, Nandan, Logde and Rosenne (2002) 231; Strati (2006) 32; Dromgoole (2013) 74–75.

49 CPUCH Article 1(1)(a).

50 CPUCH Article 1(1)(b)–(c).

be 'all traces of human existence', whereas the 'selection criteria' is limited to those 'having a cultural, historical or archaeological character' and having been under water for more than 100 years.[51] The fact that the subject matter must represent a trace of human existence, or form part of the context for such traces, excludes natural materials such as sediments, peat and fossilised fauna and flora dating from prehistoric times that are not directly associated with evidence of human existence.[52] Moreover, this definition gives no further indication of how significant the subject matter should be or how to assess its value. The threshold of having been under water for more than 100 years defines its value on the one hand and excludes the remains of cultural, historical and archaeological significance that fall outside its protective regime on the other hand.[53]

It is clear that UNCLOS covers a much broader scope of subject matter than the CPUCH, as the more precise definition of UCH only forms part of the archaeological and historical objects found at sea. Thus, despite the fact that the term itself is commonly used in practice, the definition of UCH under the CPUCH cannot be used to interpret the term used in Articles 149 and 303 of UNCLOS.[54] Subsequent analyses and discussions will follow the general interpretation and scope of objects of an archaeological and historical nature as defined under UNCLOS, and will highlight the additional rights attributed to State parties over UCH under the CPUCH.

8.2.3 The Duties to Protect Archaeological and Historical Objects Found at Sea

Article 303 is located in Part XVI 'General Provisions' of UNCLOS. With the exception of paragraph 2, which relates specifically to the contiguous zone, it applies generally and is not geographically restricted. The effect of this is that the duties on States in paragraph 1 apply to all maritime areas, including the EEZ, as do the provisions for the rights of identifiable

[51] Garabello (2003) 105; Yin-Cheng Hsu, 'Developments in International Cultural Heritage Law: What Hampers the Convention on the Protection of the Underwater Cultural Heritage' (2016) 3(1) Edinburgh Student L Rev 116, 117.

[52] Dromgoole (2013) 88–89. See the explanatory comments on Article 1 of the 1998 UNESCO Draft which form part of UNESCO Doc. CLT-96/Conf.202/2, April 1998 (reproduced in the appendix to Sarah Dromgoole and Nicholas Gaskell, 'Draft UNESCO Convention on the Protection of the Underwater Cultural Heritage 1998' (1999) 14(2) Int'l J Marine & Coastal L 171, 195–196).

[53] Dromgoole (2003) 63–64.

[54] Scovazzi 'Article 149' (2017) 1054–1055; Scovazzi 'Article 303' (2017) 1950–1951.

owners, the law of salvage, other international agreements and additional matters set out in paragraphs 3 and 4.

Under Article 303(1), States have two very general duties to protect and cooperate to protect all archaeological and historical objects found at sea. It does not require that the State should have an interest in or be in any way relevant to the objects of concern; the duties apply generally irrespective of the origins of the objects.[55] These duties are not without vagueness due to the lack of precision in their content.[56] States have broad discretion to decide on the means to protect these subjects, albeit such protection cannot be considered a basis for any State to claim jurisdiction over the area where these objects are found. This limitation was clear from the negotiation history such that Article 303 is a compromise resulting from major maritime powers' concern for avoiding any further erosion of the high seas freedoms.[57] Nevertheless, the duty to protect has some legal consequences. For example, States should take all necessary measures, including legislative, administrative and enforcement measures, necessary to protect these objects. More importantly, a State that knowingly allows its nationals or ships flying its flag to damage or destroy objects of archaeological and historical nature could be held responsible for an internationally wrongful act.[58]

While it is established that States have a duty to cooperate for the protection of underwater archaeological and historical objects, the extent that they are required to do so is not clear, as cooperation can mean different things in different contexts.[59] The duty to cooperate is a duty of concuct and can be seen as implying a duty to act in good faith in pursuing the protection of these objects, and in taking into account the positions of the other relevant States.[60] States are expected to implement this duty to cooperate through subsequent regional and international initiatives to effectively protect these objects.

55 Dromgoole (2013) 246.

56 Lucius Caflisch, 'Submarine Antiquities and the International Law of the Sea' (1982) 13 (3) Netherlands YBIL 3, 20; Blumberg (2006) 493.

57 Scovazzi 'Article 303' (2017) 1955.

58 Ibid 1953; International Law Commission (ILC), 'Draft Articles on Responsibility of States for Internationally Wrongful Acts, with Commentaries' (2001) 2(2) YB ILC 31, Articles 1–2.

59 Michail Risvas, 'The Duty to Cooperate and the Protection of Underwater Cultural Heritage' (2013) 2(3) Cambridge J Int'l & Comp L 562, 568–569.

60 UNCLOS Article 300; North Sea Continental Shelf Cases (Federal Republic of Germany v. Netherlands/; Federal Republic of Germany v. Denmark), Judgment of 20 February 1969, ICJ Reports 1969, p. 3, para 85; Scovazzi 'Article 303' (2017) 1953; Climate Change Advisory Opinion para 306.

As the name indicates, the objectives of the CPUCH are to 'ensure and strengthen the protection of [UCH]', and State parties assume the duty to cooperate to this end.[61] State parties are obligated, individually or jointly, to take all appropriate measures using 'the best practice means at their disposal and in accordance with their capabilities' in conformity with the CPUCH and international law to protect UCH.[62] State parties are further encouraged to develop bilateral, regional or other multilateral agreements to protect UCH.[63] The CPUCH also explicitly states that '[a]ll States Parties have a responsibility to protect [UCH]' in the EEZ and on the continental shelf.[64] The CPUCH could be considered a subsequent agreement that clarifies the general duties to protect UCH, particularly through the establishment of a cooperation mechanism among relevant States that will be discussed below.

Paragraph 2 of UNCLOS Article 303 gives the coastal State limited competence in respect of the removal of underwater archaeological and historical objects found in the contiguous zone. With respect to the rest of the EEZ, the coastal State is afforded no rights in respect of these objects, and its rights and duties over activities that might affect these objects will be governed by relevant provisions of UNCLOS and general international law. However, the precise nature of the jurisdictional competence afforded to coastal States by paragraph 2 is far from clear.[65] The exercise of this right is conditioned on the coastal State proclaiming a contiguous zone up to 24 nautical miles (NM) from the baselines.[66] The coastal State's right is based on a presumption and a legal fiction, which assumes that its customs, fiscal, immigration or sanitary laws and regulations would be infringed with the unauthorised removal of archaeological and historical objects from such zone.[67] If understood literally, the legal basis for the coastal State to take action is not the domestic legislation on the protection of these objects. Moreover, the coastal State's right is only triggered with the actual and detected removal of such objects from the contiguous zone. It is not clear whether such a

61 CPUCH Article 2(1)–(2).

62 CPUCH Article 2(4).

63 CPUCH Article 6.

64 CPUCH Article 9(1).

65 Mariano J Aznar, 'The Contiguous Zone as an Archaeological Maritime Zone' (2014) 29 Int'l J Marine & Coastal L 1, 6; Scovazzi (2017) 508–509; Scovazzi 'Article 303' (2017) 1954–1955.

66 UNCLOS Article 33.

67 UNCLOS Articles 33(1), 303(2); Dromgoole (2013) 250–252; Aznar (2014) 7, 10.

right would extend to take actions against activities that cause other damage to these objects *in situ*. The lack of clarity of this coastal State right is, in part, because of the negotiation history where some maritime powers, notably the United States, the United Kingdom and the Netherlands, wished to avoid a formal extension of coastal State jurisdiction over these objects beyond the limit of the territorial sea.[68]

In the 2022 *Nicaragua v Colombia* case, the International Court of Justice (ICJ) had the opportunity to examine the legal status and scope of Article 303(2). Colombia is not a party to UNCLOS but adopted national legislation to protect cultural heritage in the declared 24 NM 'integral contiguous zone' based on the claim that both Articles 33(1) and 303(2) reflect customary international law.[69] The ICJ, after considering State practice and other legal developments in this field, accepted Colombia's argument and declared that under customary law, Colombia is 'entitled to a contiguous zone', and 'it includes the power of control with respect to archaeological and historical objects' found therein.[70] Although provided with no further content, the statement of 'power of control' is broader than merely 'control traffic in such objects' in case of a 'removal from the seabed' from the contiguous zone. The ICJ's declaration of the customary law status of Article 303(2) and the expanded interpretation of the coastal State's right could serve as a legal basis for coastal States to control activities affecting these objects in the contiguous zone. The ICJ's interpretation reflects the development of the law by the CPUCH and State practice.

The coastal State's right relating to the UCH in the contiguous zone has been, to some extent, clarified and expanded by the CPUCH.[71] Rather than referring to the 'removal' of these objects from the seabed, State parties have been granted the right to regulate and authorise activities directed at UCH within their contiguous zones.[72] Although the wording goes quite far from Article 303(2) of UNCLOS, CPUCH

[68] Oxman (1987–1988) 363; Nordquist, Rosenne and Sohn (1989) 161; Robert C. Blumberg, 'International Protection of Underwater Cultural Heritage', paper presented at University of Virginia Center for Oceans Law and Policy Annual Conference on the Law of the Sea Issues in the East and South China Sea, Xiamen, China, 12 March 2005 https://2001-2009.state.gov/g/oes/rls/rm/51256.htm (archived content).

[69] Nicaragua v. Colombia (2022), paras 148, 157 and 169. Certain geographical extent of the 'integral contiguous zone' went beyond 24 NM that had been declared by the ICJ as not in conformity with customary international law, as reflected in Article 33, paragraph 2, of UNCLOS (para 175).

[70] Nicaragua v. Colombia (2022), paras 155, 163–164, 186.

[71] Aznar (2014) 11–12.

[72] CPUCH Article 8.

has acknowledged that this provision is 'without prejudice to' and 'in accordance' with UNCLOS.[73] This article could be understood from two perspectives. CPUCH has a relatively narrow focus on UCH, which is only part of the archaeological and historical objects covered by UNCLOS. In addition, CPUCH is a later developed and more specialised law. Therefore, it would modify the rights and obligations between States that are parties to both treaties, whereas legal matters that fall outside of these two perspectives will continue to be governed by UNCLOS.[74] It is worth noting that there is a strong trend of State practice to adopt an expanded interpretation of the coastal State right in relation to archaeological and historical objects found in the contiguous zone as recognised by the ICJ in the *Nicaragua v Colombia* case.[75] Several States – Mauritius, South Africa, and some from the Mediterranean Sea region – have established a 24 NM 'archaeological zone' or 'cultural heritage/protection zone' with the aim to protect UCH.[76]

Paragraph 3 of Article 303 protects 'the rights of identifiable owners, the law of salvage or other rules of admiralty, or laws and practices with respect to cultural exchanges'. As a non-prejudice clause, it allows the application of private law and admiralty law, including salvage law, to underwater archaeological and historical objects found at sea. This paragraph also fails to provide precise definitions of the terminology used and has the potential to further weaken the general duties to protect these objects.

The tension between ownership rights and the protection of these objects has been a constant challenge in the field of cultural heritage law.[77] Likewise for Article 303(3), neither the negotiation history nor the paragraph explains who are the 'identifiable owners', how ownership established and whether ownership could be transferred through salvage

[73] Ibid.

[74] Vienna Convention on the Law of Treaties Article 30(3)–(4).

[75] Aznar (2014) 13-30; Nicaragua v. Colombia (2022), para 185.

[76] Luigi Migliorino, 'In Situ Protection of the Underwater Cultural Heritage under International Treaties and National Legislation' (1995)10(4) Int'l J Marine & Coastal L 483, 488–493; Robyn Frost, 'Underwater Cultural Heritage Protection' (2004) 23 Aust YBIL 25, 37–39; Dromgoole (2013) 253–255; Scovazzi 'Article 303' (2017) 1955; Churchill, Lowe and Sander (2022) 297.

[77] 马明飞和任鹏举,'南海海域水下文化遗产的所有权归属：冲突与协调',2021年3月,第39卷第2期,海南大学学报人文社会科学版,27–37页,第27–32页 (MA Ming-fei and REN Peng-ju, 'On the Ownership of Underwater Cultural Heritage in the South China Sea: Conflict and Coordination' (2021) 39(2) Humanities & Social Sciences Journal of Hainan University 27, 27–32.); Dromgoole (2013) 96–97.

or through abandonment after being submerged.[78] It would be clear that the ownership referred to here is in a private law context compared with the terms of 'the preferential rights of the State or country of origin, or the State of cultural origin, or the State of historical and archaeological origin' as used in Article 149 of UNCLOS. Article 303(3) does not address the relationship between the rights of the identifiable owner and the rights that could be recognised by salvors, if any, and the preferential rights of other States.

The implications of the phrase 'the law of salvage and other rules of admiralty' differ between countries. The law of salvage is essentially a matter of private law that governs relationships between private parties. In many national laws, the law of salvage is related to the service to recover property lost at sea that has a value to be salvaged.[79] But some common law jurisdictions, such as the United States, have interpreted salvage law to cover treasure salvage, and applied admiralty law in an extra-territorial manner to grant salvors and finders rights over wrecks and properties found at sea, wherever they are located.[80] Should this approach be commonly adopted, the protection phrase in Article 303(3) could function as an active encouragement to the unregulated recovery of underwater archaeological and historical objects.[81] The International Convention on Salvage, in contrast, allows its State parties to make reservations to exclude its application 'when the property involved is maritime cultural property of prehistoric, archaeological or historic interest and is situated on the sea-bed'.[82]

It has been argued that the duty to protect underwater archaeological and historical objects could be carried out using the law of salvage,

[78] Dromgoole (2013) 114–115; Nordquist, Rosenne and Sohn (1989) 160.

[79] Dromgoole (2013) 169–171.

[80] James A. R. Nafziger, 'The Evolving Role of Admiralty Courts in Litigation Related to Historic Wreck' (2003) 44(1) Harv Int'l LJ 251, 253–256 Craig Forrest, 'Historic Wreck Salvage: An International Perspective' (2008–2009) 33(2) Tul Mar LJ 347, 359–364; Scovazzi (2017) 510–511.

[81] Scovazzi 'Article 303' (2017) 1956–1957; Garabello (2003) 125.

[82] International Convention on Salvage (28 April 1989, in force, 14 July 1996) 1954 UNTS 165, Article 30(1)(d); International Maritime Organization (IMO), 'Status of IMO Treaties: Comprehensive information on the status of multilateral Conventions and Instruments in respect of which the International Maritime Organization or its Secretary-General performs depositary or other functions, 24 July 2024' www.imo.org/en/About/Conventions/Pages/StatusOfConventions.aspx. As of 2024, this reservation has been made by twenty-five of the seventy-eight States Parties including Australia, Bulgaria, Canada, China, Croatia, Ecuador, Estonia, Finland, France, Germany, Iran, Jamaica, Mexico, the Netherlands, New Zealand, Norway, Poland, the Russian Federation, Saudi Arabia, Spain, Sweden, Tunisia, Türkiye, Ukraine and the United Kingdom.

provided that the operation is consistent with the public interest as reflected in the scientific rules of recovery and the international standards of conservation and curation.[83] As a negotiated compromise, the CPUCH did not ban the application of the law of salvage or law of finds to UCH but eliminated its undesirable effects. In addition to declaring that UCH should not be commercially exploited, the CPUCH provides that activities relating to UCH may only be subject to the law of salvage or law of finds if it is authorised by the competent authorities, in full conformity with the CPUCH, and ensures that any recovery of UCH receives maximum protection.[84]

Finally, Article 303(4) protects in another non-prejudice clause 'other international agreements and rules of international law regarding the protection of objects of an archaeological and historical nature'. The intention of this clause is not to affect, for example, existing agreements such as the 1972 Agreement between Australia and the Netherlands on Old Dutch Shipwrecks located in Australian waters, or other similar agreements to be concluded.[85] Among possible subsequent agreements, the CPUCH, which began to be negotiated at UNESCO when UNCLOS entered into force, has become the most influential multilateral agreement for the protection of UCH.

The most glaring problem with the application of the general duties to protect underwater archaeological and historic objects under UNCLOS is the geographical 'gap' in the provisions they afford. This gap relates to the EEZ and continental shelf beyond the contiguous zone to the outer limit of the juridical continental shelf that forms the boundary with the Area. As a result, activities affecting these objects, deliberately or incidentally, are governed by the general rules of UNCLOS. But archaeological research and protection do not fall directly within the purposes

[83] Ben Juvelier, '"Salvaging" History: Underwater Cultural Heritage and Commercial Salvage' (2017) 32(5) Am U Int'l L Rev 1023, 1037–1045; Ole Varmer and Caroline M. Blanco, 'The Case for Using the Law of Salvage to Preserve Underwater Cultural Heritage: The Integrated Marriage of the Law of Salvage and Historic Preservation' (2018) 49(3) J Mar L & Comm 401, 413.

[84] CPUCH Articles 2(7), 4; Scovazzi 'Article 303' (2017) 1957–1958.

[85] Agreement between Australia and the Netherlands concerning Old Dutch Shipwrecks and Arrangement (6 November 1972, in force 6 November 1972) ATS No. 18; Australia Government, 'Underwater Cultural Heritage: International Agreements' www.dcceew.gov.au/parks-heritage/heritage/underwater-heritage/international-agreements; Antony Firth, 'UK Safeguarding of Underwater Cultural Heritage: Factual Background', unpublished briefing paper for BA/HFF Steering Committee on Underwater Cultural Heritage. Fjordr Ref: 16200 (Fjordr Ltd 2014); Scovazzi 'Article 303' (2017) 1960.

for which 'sovereign rights' are granted to the coastal State as set forth in UNCLOS. In essence, subject to the undefined general duties to protect these objects, the obligations of due regard and non-abuse of rights, it is the flag State that has the competence to control these activities.[86] Presumably, in the course of time, this gap in law will be dealt with by the competent international organisation, in particular UNESCO, and by State practice.[87]

8.2.4 State Cooperation Mechanism under the Convention on the Protection of Underwater Cultural Heritage

Developed by UNESCO, the CPUCH is the international community's response to the inadequacy of the international legal protections and to concerns about the increasing incidence of commercial exploitation of shipwrecks and other UCH. It is the product of thirteen years of preparatory work at different levels at UNESCO, including four years of formal negotiations.[88] Its purpose is to afford a comprehensive legal regime for protecting UCH in all maritime zones for the benefit of the whole of humanity.[89] The CPUCH embodies a form of scientific cooperation built around three main ideas. First, the performance of any activity directed at the UCH must follow widely recognised scientific standards; second, any commercial approach to UCH must be avoided; and third, it creates a cooperation mechanism among the State parties to protect the UCH.[90] At the core of the CPUCH is a complex regime that enables State parties, individually and collectively as appropriate, to regulate activities in international waters. It develops the twofold duties to protect and to cooperate to protect underwater archaeological and historical objects mandated in Article 303(1) UNCLOS. For the purpose of this chapter, the discussion will focus on the State cooperation mechanism applicable in the EEZ, including the contiguous zone.

As discussed earlier, the CPUCH has clarified and expanded the right and jurisdiction given to coastal States with respect to the protection of UCH found in the contiguous zone. In the contiguous zone, where

[86] Dromgoole (2013) 35–36.
[87] Nordquist, Rosenne and Sohn (1989) 161–162; Scovazzi 'Article 303' (2017) 1951.
[88] Dromgoole (2013) 24.
[89] CPUCH Preamble.
[90] CPUCH Articles 2, 9–12, 19, 23–24, 33, Annex Rules Concerning Activities Directed at Underwater Cultural Heritage; Dromgoole (2013) 61; Aznar (2020) 16.

declared, State parties may 'regulate and authorize' activities directed at UCH, and in so doing require these activities to be taken in accordance with internationally accepted archaeological principles and standards of behaviour.[91] State parties also assume the obligation to implement other relevant provisions of the CPUCH. For example, when authorising and regulating such activities, there should be a presumption in favour of preservation *in situ* until such time as intervention is justified for scientific or protective purposes.[92]

At the heart of the CPUCH are the provisions with respect to the protection of UCH in the EEZ and on the continental shelf, which to some extent fills the legal gap left by UNCLOS.[93] Articles 9 and 10 of the CPUCH establish a complex cooperation mechanism that involves a reporting and notification procedure, as well as the taking of various forms of protective actions by relevant States parties, acting alone and in concert. In attempting to create a formula to accommodate the competing interests of different States, Articles 9 and 10 incorporate a number of constructive ambiguities and accord a special role to a 'Coordinating State', which may or may not be the coastal State.[94]

The State cooperation mechanism, as a compromise achieved in the CPUCH, involves the participation of all the States linked to the heritage. The mechanism is achieved through the coordination by the 'Coordinating State', normally the coastal State in whose EEZ or on whose continental shelf the UCH is located unless otherwise decided.[95] Any State party may declare, through diplomatic channels, to the State party in whose EEZ or on whose continental shelf the UCH is located 'its interest in being consulted on how to ensure the effective protection of that [UCH]' and assume the role as one of the 'interested State Parties'.[96] However, the interest must be based on 'a verifiable link, especially a cultural, historical, or archaeological link, to the [UCH] concerned' and

91 CPUCH Articles 8, 33, Annex.

92 CPUCH Article 2(5); Dromgoole (2013) 24.

93 It should be acknowledged that the CPUCH also adopted rules and obligations for State parties to protect UCH in the Area that clarified the rules stated in Article 149 of UNCLOS.

94 UNESCO, Underwater Cultural Heritage 2001 Convention, 'State Protection Mechanism: State Cooperation Mechanism' www.unesco.org/en/underwater-heritage/state-protection-mechanism?hub=412.

95 CPUCH Article 10(3).

96 CPUCH Article 9(5).

supported by relevant evidence and documentation.[97] This cooperation mechanism may entail the performance of preliminary research, the authorisation of archaeological activities to prevent undesirable activities and regulate desirable ones, and/or the adoption of urgent and preventive measures.[98] The three-step procedure – reporting, consultations and urgent measures – can be summarised as follows.

State parties to the CPUCH have the obligation to follow the reporting and notification requirements laid out in Article 9. Primarily, State parties are required to ensure their nationals or vessels flying their flags report any discoveries or intentions to engage in activities directed at UCH in their EEZs or on their continental shelves. They are further required to ensure that their nationals or vessels flying their flags report such discoveries or activities in the EEZ or on the continental shelf of another State party to them or to that State party. The relevant State party is then requested to notify the Director-General of UNESCO of such reported discoveries or activities, who then will promptly make such information available to all State parties. Upon receiving such information, any State party may declare to the State party in whose EEZ or on whose continental shelf the UCH is located its interest to be consulted.

Under Article 10 of the CPUCH, the State party in whose EEZ or on whose continental shelf the UCH is located will assume the role as 'Coordinating State' to coordinate the consultation process with all other interested State parties on how best to protect the UCH. If the coastal State does not wish to assume the role as Coordinating State, the role will be jointly appointed by other interested State parties. The Coordinating State shall implement the protective measures that have been agreed to by the consulting States, and shall issue all necessary authorisations for these measures in conformity with the rules concerning activities directed at the UCH.[99] These provisions are consistent with the general duties under UNCLOS to protect UCH and cooperate for that purpose and do not upset the delicate jurisdictional balance between different States in the EEZ.

[97] Ibid; UNESCO, Operational Guidelines for the Convention on the Protection of the Underwater Cultural Heritage, CLT/HER/CHP/OG 1/REV, August 2015, Chapter II, B Declarations of Interest; Thijs J. Maarleveld, 'The Notion of "Verifiable Links" in the 2001 UNESCO Convention on the Protection of the Underwater Cultural Heritage' (2014) 19(2) Art Antiquity and Law 101, 103–112.

[98] Aznar (2020) 18–19.

[99] CPUCH Annex.

Article 10(4) further authorises the Coordinating State to take all practical measures and/or issue any necessary authorisation to prevent any immediate danger to UCH arising from human activities or any other cause, including looting. Such urgent measures could be taken prior to the consultation process with all other interested State parties. Moreover, the Coordinating State may request assistance from other State parties in taking the urgent measures to protect the UCH. This authorisation, however, has generated debates on whether it gives the Coordinating State unchecked power to take any measures, not excluding the use of force, on the pretext of protecting the UCH in the EEZ.[100] As such, the immediate paragraph states that the Coordinating State shall act 'on behalf of the States parties as a whole and not in its own interest', and any coordinating action 'shall not in itself constitute a basis for the assertion of any preferential or jurisdictional rights not provided for in international law, including the [UNCLOS]'.[101] This statement should constitute a bar to any creeping jurisdiction temptation.

In addition to this three-step procedure to facilitate cooperation, State parties have a general duty to cooperate to protect the UCH under the CPUCH. State parties are required to cooperate and assist each other in the protection and management of UCH, including, 'where practicable, collaborating in the investigation, excavation, documentation, conservation, study and presentation of such heritage'.[102] In order to prevent secrecy and unregulated activities directed at UCH, each State party undertakes to share information with other State parties about the 'discovery of heritage, location of heritage, heritage excavated or recovered contrary to this Convention or otherwise in violation of international law, pertinent scientific methodology and technology, and legal developments relating to such heritage'.[103]

In 2021–2022, the State cooperation mechanism under the CPUCH was activated for the first time with respect to an archaeological site on the Skerki Bank, a geological featured between Sicily and Tunisia hosting numerous wrecks from Phoenician times to the Second World War, with Tunisia acting as the Coordinating State and the participation of seven

[100] UNESCO, Records of the General Conference, Proceedings of the 31st session, 2 November 2001, Vol. 2, Statement by Mr Sidorov (Russian Federation), 562 https://unesdoc.unesco.org/ark:/48223/pf0000128966.

[101] CPUCH Article 10(6).

[102] CPUCH Article 19(1).

[103] CPUCH Article 19(1)–(2).

interested State parties.[104] A Coordinating Committee, composed of the eight State parties, has been established to support the initiative with each State represented by a designated focal point. The Coordination Committee is responsible for developing strategies and action plans to achieve the objectives of the initiative. Researchers from the eight States collaborated to carry out an international underwater archaeological mission on the Skerki Bank in 2022 that led to the discovery of three new shipwrecks and the retrieval of relevant archaeological information.[105] The establishment of this cooperation mechanism represents a real opportunity for the Mediterranean States to protect an archaeological site beyond the limit of their territorial waters.

Underpinning the entire treaty framework is the principle that State parties must cooperate in the protection of UCH. The all-important cooperation mechanism the CPUCH creates for the EEZ and the continental shelf is dependent upon State parties sharing information and taking collaborative and coordinated actions. In accordance with international law and UNCLOS, regulation by maritime zone allows the CPUCH to facilitate and improve cooperation between State parties. The CPUCH establishes sufficient firewalls against any kind of creeping jurisdiction that deviates from the jurisdictional framework set up by UNCLOS. The only provision that goes beyond what was explicitly declared by UNCLOS is with respect to the contiguous zone in which State parties may regulate and authorise activities directed at UCH.[106] This provision is still in line with the objective of Article 303(2) of UNCLOS as acknowledged by the ICJ in the *Nicaragua v Colombia* case, which gives the coastal State 'the power of control with respect to archaeological and historical objects', and it was unchallenged and generally accepted by States that negotiated the CPUCH.[107] Any of the acts or activities undertaken on the basis of the CPUCH cannot be used as a

[104] UNESCO, 'Underwater Archaeological Mission for UNESCO and 8 Member States in the Mediterranean: A Multilateral Underwater Archaeological Mission under the Framework of UNESCO' www.unesco.org/en/skerki-bank-mission. International scientists from Algeria, Croatia, Egypt, France, Italy, Morocco, Spain and Tunisia participated in the mission.

[105] UNESCO, 'Fact Sheet: Multilateral underwater archaeological mission under the auspices of UNESCO on the Skerki Bank and in the Sicilian Channel' https://unesdoc.unesco.org/ark:/48223/pf0000388533.

[106] CPUCH Article 8.

[107] Aznar (2020) 22; Nicaragua v. Colombia (2022), para 186.

legal argument to expand, reinforce or dispute current jurisdictional or sovereign rights as recognised by UNCLOS.[108]

8.3 Rights and Jurisdiction over Activities Affecting Archaeological and Historical Objects

The key objective of the legal framework relating to underwater archaeological and historical objects is to provide adequate protection. Central to this framework is for States to regulate activities that affect these objects to ensure that they are not unduly interfered with or damaged. As acknowledged in the earlier discussion, such objects found in the EEZ or on the continental shelf are not natural resources but are human-made resources. Considering the sovereign rights and jurisdiction attributed to the coastal State under UNCLOS, jurisdiction relating to these objects is not automatically attributed to the coastal State. Likewise, they do not fall under the high seas freedoms that have been explicitly preserved for all States in the EEZ. Thus, when a conflict on the attribution and exercise of rights and jurisdiction over these objects arises, it must be resolved based on the principles of Article 59 of UNCLOS and other rules of international law.

The nationality principle is a well-established principle of jurisdiction under international law, and as such, its utilisation by any flag State over its own nationals and ships flying its flag to protect underwater archaeological and historical objects is not a matter of controversy.[109] When a conflict arises between a coastal State and another State with respect to activities affecting these objects in the EEZ, all the relevant factors need to be weighed on a case-by-case basis. The relevant factors would include whether these activities interfere with the exercise of the rights and fulfilment of duties of the relevant States, the duties of all States – the international community – to protect these objects, any subsequent agreement that is applicable to both States, and whether there is a verifiable link between the objects and any State.[110] The two legal doctrines that guide the attribution and exercise of rights and freedoms in the EEZ could provide some guidance.[111] Where the dispute relates to

[108] CPUCH Articles 2(11), 10(6).

[109] Shaw (2017) 455–457, 493–494; James Crawford, *Brownline's Principles of Public International Law* (9th ed., Oxford University Press 2019) 443–444.

[110] Dromgoole (2013) 259–260.

[111] See Chapter 3 in this volume.

the exploration and exploitation of natural resources, it should probably be resolved in favour of the coastal State; where it relates to the communication freedoms, then the interests of other States – or the international community as a whole – would be favoured. The exercise of such rights and jurisdiction must also follow the due regard obligation and not constitute an abuse of rights.

In order to discuss jurisdictional issues over the activities carried out by a non-national, an important distinction should be made between two forms of activities affecting these objects: those that are 'directed at' them and those 'incidentally affecting' them. This distinction is only explicitly recognised and defined by the CPUCH for the benefit of UCH.[112] UNCLOS only refers to 'traffic in such objects' once in Article 303(2), which is an activity directed at these objects. Jurisdiction over other activities that may affect these objects can only be discussed in the general jurisdictional framework under the international law and UNCLOS. The CPUCH limits both activities to those that may 'physically disturb or otherwise damage' UCH.[113] It primarily focuses on controlling activities directed at UCH to ensure that they are undertaken in accordance with the archaeological benchmark standards.

8.3.1 Activities Directed at Underwater Archaeological and Historical Objects

Broadly speaking, activities directed at underwater archaeological and historical objects can be defined to mean human activities having these objects as their primary target. It would also be reasonable to add the requirement that these activities should have the potential to, directly or incidentally, physically disturb or otherwise damage these objects. If the activities have no impact on these objects, it would not be justifiable to put a restriction on the conduct of these human activities.[114] Activities that have those objects as the main target commonly involve the search for, exploration of, recording of and extraction and removal of items of the object, such as artefacts from shipwrecks.

The coastal State, through its role as the flag State, has the right to regulate and authorise activities directed at the archaeological and historical objects found in its EEZ or on its continental shelf by its nationals

[112] Dromgoole (2013) 345.
[113] CPUCH Article 1(6)–(7).
[114] Dromgoole (2013) 65.

and vessels flying its flag. While this right is not explicitly stated in UNCLOS, it could be assumed through the nationality principle, the exclusive flag State jurisdiction over ships and the general duty to protect these objects.[115] The CPUCH also requires that State parties to 'take all practicable measures to ensure that their nationals and vessels flying their flag do not engage in any activity directed at [UCH] in a manner not in conformity with this Convention'.[116] This flag State right, in principle, will apply to activities conducted by its nationals in the EEZ of another State and other maritime zones. Therefore, it is primarily the flag State jurisdiction that is applicable to these activities conducted in the EEZ and on the continental shelf provided that the exercise of such right has due regard to the rights and duties of the coastal State and complies with the applicable laws and regulations adopted by the coastal State.[117]

States have been using the nationality principle to collectively protect archaeological and historical sites found outside of the limits of national jurisdiction. Since its discovery in 1985, the wreck of the *Titanic*, lying more than 300 miles off the coast of Newfoundland, has been the subject of numerous expeditions that have led to the recovery of thousands of artefacts.[118] Puzzled by the lack of clear international regulations and protection, and concerned about the ongoing activities at the site and its deteriorating condition, the United Kingdom and the United States, together with France and Canada, negotiated the Agreement concerning the Shipwrecked Vessel RMS *Titanic* (Titanic Agreement) in 2003 that will afford the wreck some specific legal protection.[119] The Titanic Agreement refers specifically to the relevance of Article 303 of UNCLOS and establishes a protective scheme based on the exercise by State parties of the nationality and territorial principles of jurisdiction.[120] Another example is the multilateral agreement between Finland, Estonia and Sweden regarding the protection of the passenger ferry M/S *Estonia*,

[115] UNCLOS Articles 94, 303(1).
[116] CPUCH Article 16.
[117] UNCLOS Article 58(3).
[118] Marian Leigh Miller, 'Underwater Cultural Heritage: Is the Titanic Still in Peril as Courts Battle over the Future of the Historical Vessel' (2006) 20 Emory Int'l L Rev 345, 345–346.
[119] Agreement Concerning the Shipwrecked Vessel RMS Titanic (6 November 2003, in force 18 November 2019) UKTS No 8 (2019) www.state.gov/multilateral-19-1118.
[120] Ibid Preamble, Articles 3–5; Sarah Dromgoole, 'The International Agreement for the Protection of the Titanic: Problems and Prospects' (2006) 37(1) Ocean Dev & Int'l L 1, 7.

which sank on the Finnish continental shelf in 1994.[121] State parties to this agreement assume the right to criminalise activities by their nationals that disturb the peace of the resting place of more than 800 victims of the disaster.[122]

In addition to flag State jurisdiction over activities directed at the archaeological and historical objects, the coastal State has the right to regulate the 'removal' of these objects from the contiguous zone.[123] This right has been expanded by the CPUCH to the right to regulate and authorise activities directed at UCH by State parties, and by the ICJ to include the power of control with respect to archaeological and historical objects.[124] Moreover, a number of factors could warrant concurrent jurisdiction of non-flag States in the EEZ or on the continental shelf. The first category of factors includes some of these activities, which, although directed at the underwater archaeological and historical objects, may actually affect the exercise of other rights and jurisdiction by different States. The second category comprises the rights and jurisdiction provided by subsequent agreements, primarily the CPUCH.

The discovery and exploration activities directed at archaeological and historical objects involve the use of acoustic and magnetic remote sensing devices to explore the ocean floor that are often referred to as survey operations.[125] These devices include side-scan and bathymetric sonar systems to identify seabed protrusions and indentations, sub-bottom profilers to provide cross-sectional analyses of the sub-sea strata to enable identification of material buried in sediment, and magnetometers to locate ferrous material.[126] Technology development has revolutionised the field of shipwreck search and recovery, and the mapping of the seafloor. For example, marine archaeologists have discovered thousands of wrecks, ranging from Roman and Phoenician vessels to German U-boats and modern fishing vessels, and identified and mapped the layout

[121] Agreement between the Republic of Finland, the Republic of Estonia and the Kingdom of Sweden Regarding the M/S Estonia (23 February 1995, in force 26 August 1995) 1890 UNTS 176 (M/S Estonia Agreement). The Agreement was opened for accession by other States through a Protocol adopted on 23 April 1996.

[122] M/S Estonia Agreement Article 4.

[123] UNCLOS Article 303(2).

[124] CPUCH Article 8; Nicaragua v. Colombia (2022), para 186.

[125] Tine Missiaen, Dimitris Sakellariou and Nicholas C Flemming, 'Survey Strategies and Techniques in Underwater Geoarchaeological Research: An Overview with Emphasis on Prehistoric Sites', in Bailey, Harff and Sakellariou (2017) 21.

[126] Roderick Mather, 'Technology and the Search for Shipwrecks', (1999) 30(2) J Mar L & Com 175, 177–180.

of the submerged Bronze Age city of Pavlopetri and the Ice Age Scandinavian Mesolithic dwelling remains, graves and fishing structures.[127] The devices and technology employed for surveying these objects are almost identical to those used in hydrographic survey that deals with the measurement and description of the physical features of the ocean.[128] The data collected through these operations, depending on the objectives and devices employed, could reveal important information to be used for navigation, exploration and exploitation of the seabed and its natural resources, environmental protection and management, marine science and maritime boundary delimitation.[129] The survey operations could potentially affect the sovereign rights and jurisdiction attributed to the coastal State in the EEZ and on the continental shelf. However, the question of whether or not survey operations of any kind, including those targeted at underwater archaeological and historical objects, constitute marine scientific research is itself controversial and has been subject to much debate.[130]

Activities directed at archaeological and historical objects could also involve the use of equipment constituting an 'installation' or 'structure'. Under UNCLOS, the coastal State has exclusive right to construct and to authorise and regulate the construction, operation and use of installations and structures either for economic purposes or if such structures interfere with the exercise of its rights in the EEZ or on the continental shelf.[131] Although national and international laws have repeatedly called

[127] Mather (1999) 182–183; Helena Smith, 'Lost Greek City That May Have Inspired Atlantis Myth Gives Up Secrets', The Guardian, 16 October 2009 (online); Ole Grøn and Lars Froberg Mortensen, 'Stone Age in the Danish North Sea Sector' (2011) 26 Maritime Archaeology Newsletter from Denmark 3; Jon Henderson, Chrysanthi Gallou, Nicholas Flemming and Elias Spondylis, 'The Pavlopetri Underwater Archaeology Project: Investigating an Ancient Submerged Town', in Jonathan Benjamin et al., *Submerged Prehistory* (Oxbow Books 2011) 207.

[128] Roach (2021) 490; International Hydrographic Organization (IHO), S-32 IHO – Hydrographic Dictionary, (Hydrographic Dictionary Working Group (HDWG) 2019), Eng ID 5244, https://iho.int/en/standards-and-specifications.

[129] IHO, Manual on Hydrograph, Publication C-13 (1st ed, May 2005 (corrections to February 2011)), 2–6 https://iho.int/uploads/user/pubs/cb/c-13/english/C-13_Chapter_1_and_contents.pdf.

[130] Dromgoole (2010) 49–53; Ronán Long, *Marine Resources Law* (Thomson Round Hall 2007) 695–696; Guifang (Julia) Xue, 'Marine Scientific Research and Hydrographic Survey in the EEZs: Closing up the Legal Loopholes?', in Myron H. Nordquist, Tommy T. B. Koh and John Norton Moore (eds.), *Freedom of Seas, Passage Rights and the 1982 Law of the Sea Convention* (Martinus Nijhoff 2009) 209–232; Roach (2021) 491–493. For discussion on survey for submarine cables and pipelines, see Chapter 5 in this volume; for discussion on military survey, see Chapter 6 in this volume.

[131] UNCLOS Articles 60, 80. See Chapter 4 in this volume.

for protection of these objects and tried to prevent the commercialisation of them, it is unavoidable that some of these activities would be commercially driven, such as treasure hunting and looting. It is unclear whether this type of commercial exploitation would constitute the 'economic purposes' as used in UNCLOS, particularly given that these objects are not considered natural resources. However, it would be less controversial for the coastal State to claim jurisdiction if the installation or structure is located in a fishing ground or near an offshore oil platform. In addition, if the installation or structure is located in a busy shipping lane or in other ways interferes with navigation, it may potentially affect the freedom of navigation enjoyed by all States.

Exploration and excavation activities may also involve 'drilling' on the continental shelf. UNCLOS has granted the coastal State the exclusive right to authorise and regulate drilling on the continental shelf for all purposes.[132] Although the term 'drilling' is not defined by UNCLOS, the ordinary meaning could encompass digging or blowing, the use of propwash deflectors and other similar devices, and perhaps even the use of explosives.[133] It would be plausible that the excavation and other activities directed at underwater archaeological and historical objects be subject to the coastal State's jurisdiction if they probe or otherwise disturb the seabed of the continental shelf.[134] The use of drilling is further subject to the duty of having due regard to the sovereign rights and jurisdiction of the coastal State. Moreover, the use of drilling should also have due regard to other uses of the seabed, such as the laying of submarine cables and pipelines by all States.[135]

Another potential interference of other rights by the activities directed at underwater archaeological and historical objects relates to the natural marine environment. This close relationship has been acknowledged by the CPUCH when defining UCH and referring to environmental precaution and mitigation considerations.[136] Underwater archaeology and the natural marine environment, particularly marine life, are closely related, and such objects can be of considerable ecological value.[137] For example,

[132] UNCLOS Article 81.
[133] Dromgoole (2013) 269.
[134] Blumberg (2006) 496.
[135] See Chapter 5 in this volume.
[136] CPUCH Article 1(1)(a), Annex Rules 10(l), 14, 29.
[137] Dromgoole (2013) 16; James Delgado and Ole Varmer, 'The Public Importance of World War I Shipwrecks: Why a State Should Care and the Challenges of Protection', in UNESCO, Underwater Cultural Heritage from World War I: Proceedings of the

some objects may have become an artificial reef or be embedded in a fragile marine environment. In some cases, though, the object may be a potential or actual hazard for the marine environment. For example, a large number of sunken warships during the two world wars carried bunker or cargo oils, mercury, munitions, or other poisonous or noxious cargos.[138] Therefore, any interference with or recovery of such materials from an object will almost inevitably disturb or damage the environment of both the water column and the seabed to varying degrees.[139] Even though the coastal State's jurisdiction to protect and preserve the marine environment is limited and may not directly include those activities, it could make a strong claim for their potential interference with the exercise of its sovereign rights over natural resources.[140]

It is apparent from the preceding discussion that the coastal State may find legal basis, albeit slim and indirect, to claim concurrent jurisdiction over certain activities directed at archaeological and historical objects found in its EEZ or on the continental shelf if they interfere with its sovereign rights and jurisdiction. A potential, and rather controversial, remedy to this situation would be treating certain activities as marine scientific research that is subject to coastal State jurisdiction in the EEZ and on the continental shelf. The generally accepted position is that marine archaeological activities do not qualify as marine scientific research on the basis that they are directed at the human-made objects rather than the natural environment.[141] However, it is arguable that an increasingly common precursor to direct intervention – the use of scientific methodologies – is directed at the seabed and subsoil that are components of the natural marine environment. Importantly, in some cases the data gathered could be of direct significance for the exploration and exploitation of natural resources. As such, these activities may have a significant influence on the sovereign rights and jurisdiction of the coastal State in the EEZ and on the continental shelf. Giving the coastal

Scientific Conference on the Occasion of the Centenary of World War I, Bruges, Belgium, 26 & 27 June 2014 (UNESCO 2015) 112 https://unesdoc.unesco.org/ark:/48223/pf0000233355; Wessex Archaeology, 'Wrecks on the Seabed: Ecology' www.wessexarch.co.uk/our-work/wrecks-seabed-ecology.

[138] Craig Forrest, 'Culturally and Environmentally Sensitive Sunken Warships' (2012) 26(1) Austl & NZ Mar LJ 80, 80–81.

[139] Dromgoole (2013) 267–268.

[140] Daniel P. O'Connell, *The International Law of the Sea*, Vol. II (Oxford University Press 1988) 918.

[141] Soons (1982) 6, 124; Dromgoole (2010) 43; Roach (2021) 500.

State rights over certain activities has the advantage of avoiding potential destabilisation of these objects and their natural context, and possible interference in its sovereign rights and jurisdiction.[142]

A second category of concurrent rights and jurisdiction provided by the CPUCH to its State parties is applicable to the UCH. The CPUCH focuses on addressing undesirable threats, such as treasure hunting and other unregulated activities, and regulating the authorised activities targeted at the UCH. State parties are obligated to ensure that any activity directed at UCH is undertaken in accordance with internationally accepted archaeological principles and standards of behaviour.[143] The fundamental archaeological principle requires that preservation *in situ* should be the first management option for any UCH, and that activities should be authorised only when justified for scientific or protective purposes.[144]

Under the CPUCH, the coastal State in whose EEZ or on whose continental shelf the UCH is located has been given 'the right to prohibit or authorize any activity directed at such heritage to prevent interference with its sovereign rights or jurisdiction as provided for by international law including the [UNCLOS]'.[145] In addition, the coastal State is required to take measures to prohibit the use of artificial islands, installations and structures under its jurisdiction in the EEZ or on the continental shelf in support of any activity directed at UCH that is not in conformity with the CPUCH.[146] These authorisations echo those under UNCLOS whereby the coastal State may establish jurisdiction over activities directed at UCH that have the potential to affect its sovereign rights and jurisdiction. The CPUCH provides State parties with a concrete basis for taking actions to prevent activities directed at UCH from damaging natural resources that is unlikely to be challenged by any another State.[147]

As discussed earlier, under the State cooperation mechanism, the CPUCH creates the roles of Coordinating State, generally the coastal

[142] Dromgoole (2013) 271–272.

[143] CPUCH Articles 7(2), 8, 10(5), Annex.

[144] Ibid Article 2(5); Dromgoole (2013) 24; Mariano J. Aznar, 'In Situ Preservation of Underwater Cultural Heritage as an International Legal Principle' (2018) 13 J Mari Arch 67, 68–72; UNESCO, UCH/23/9.MSP/7.INF, 9 June 2023, Convention on the Protection of the Underwater Cultural Heritage, Meeting of States Parties, Ninth Session, 13–14 June 2023, Evaluation of Examples of Best Practices, p. 33–34.

[145] CPUCH Article 10(2).

[146] Ibid Article 15.

[147] Dromgoole (2013) 290–291.

State in whose EEZ or on whose continental shelf the UCH is located, and interested State parties that collectively regulate activities directed at UCH. As such, the coastal State could assume, against another State party, the right to require a non-national or master of a foreign flagged vessel to report to it the discovery or activity directed at UCH in its EEZ or on its continental shelf.[148] Moreover, the coastal State, acting as the Coordinating State, may 'take all practicable measures' to prevent any immediate danger to UCH arising from human activities, including those undertaken by a foreign national or vessel.[149]

It should be noted that some States assert unilateral jurisdiction over certain archaeological and historical objects found in their EEZs or on their continental shelves, particularly with respect to the contiguous zone.[150] The United States has a well-established national system to afford legal protection to historical, cultural and archaeological resources at sea. The United States adopted the National Marine Sanctuaries Act in 1972, supported by other laws and regulations, that provides for the designation of areas of the marine environment as 'national marine sanctuaries' to 200 NM offshore, including heritage sites.[151] Activities in each sanctuary are governed by a tailor-made set of regulations that are designed to protect the sanctuary's particular 'historical', 'cultural' and 'archaeological' resources, and activities that involve the removal of or injury to such resources and any alteration of the seabed are prohibited.[152] As of 2024, the network includes a system of sixteen national marine sanctuaries and the Papahānaumokuākea and Rose Atoll marine national monuments.[153]

148 CPUCH Article 9(1)(b)(ii).

149 Ibid Article 10(4).

150 Barbara Kwiatkowska, 'Creeping Jurisdiction Beyond 200 Miles in the Light of the 1982 Law of the Sea Convention and State Practice' (1991) 22(2) Ocean Dev & Int'l L 153, 163–164; Dromgoole (2013) 264–266.

151 National Marine Sanctuaries Act, Title 16, Chapter 32, Sections 1431 et seq. United States Code, as amended by Public Law 106-513, November 2000, https://nmssanctuaries.blob.core.windows.net/sanctuaries-prod/media/archive/library/national/nmsa.pdf; United States National Oceanic and Atmospheric Administration (NOAA), 'National Marine Sanctuaries: Maritime Heritage' https://sanctuaries.noaa.gov/maritime/.

152 Ole Varmer, 'United States of America', in Sarah Dromgoole (ed.), *The Protection of the Underwater Cultural Heritage National Perspectives in Light of the UNESCO Convention 2001* (2nd ed., Martinus Nijhoff 2006) 359–366.

153 NOAA, 'National Marine Sanctuary System' www.sanctuaries.noaa.gov.

8.3.2 Activities Incidentally Affecting Underwater Archaeological and Historical Objects

There is no doubt that human activities may inadvertently cause serious damage and destruction to archaeological and historical objects, even when not directed at them. In particular, activities that have physical contact with the seabed, such as bottom trawling, dredging, dumping, seabed mining, the laying of submarine cables and pipelines, and the construction of wind farms, fixed offshore platforms and other installations, can all have a negative impact on these objects.

The duties to protect and cooperate to protect underwater archaeological and historical objects under UNCLOS have legal implications for all States. As such, all States, including the coastal State, are obligated to take the necessary measures to protect these objects from risks caused by activities undertaken by their own nationals and vessels. However, it is unclear whether the duties to protect these objects would automatically trump the right of other uses of the ocean in circumstances where the existing objects come into conflict with these activities. The CPUCH further strengthened this obligation by requiring all State parties to 'use the best practicable means at its disposal to prevent or mitigate any adverse effects that might arise from activities under its jurisdiction incidentally affecting [UCH]'.[154] However, it did not define what constitute 'best practicable means at its disposal' and left it to each individual State party to decide.[155] Among State parties to the CPUCH, it would be plausible to argue that the State of concern should consult the Coordinating State before conducting any activities that might incidentally affect UCH in the EEZ or on the continental shelf.[156]

Shipwrecks, by virtue of their number and physical mass, are the main constituent of underwater archaeological and historical objects, and some have the potential to pose a hazard to navigation in the EEZ.[157] The legal framework that facilitates State intervention is not straightforward when the shipwreck lays in the EEZ. UNCLOS made no reference to the safety of navigation and shipwrecks in general. The flag State, whose vessel could be affected, may not have the immediate right to remove the wreck,

[154] CPUCH Article 5.
[155] Forrest (2019) 219.
[156] CPUCH Article 7(4)–(5).
[157] Forrest (2019) 177–179; IMO, 'Nairobi International Convention on the Removal of Wrecks' www.imo.org/en/About/Conventions/Pages/Nairobi-International-Convention-on-the-Removal-of-Wrecks.aspx.

since such operations might affect the seabed. The coastal State, even if it has the knowledge of such a hazard to navigation in its EEZ, is not obligated to give appropriate publicity to such dangers, as is required in its territorial sea, let alone a duty to remove the hazard.[158] Moreover, unless the shipwreck poses a threat to cause marine pollution, the coastal State does not have a strong legal basis to take action either. Nevertheless, the coastal State may inform other mariners of such navigational hazards based on good intentions and its due regard obligation to the freedom of navigation. It is worth noting that the coastal State has been given the right to remove or have removed, at the shipowner's expense, a wreck that poses a hazard to navigation under the 2007 Wreck Removal Convention.[159] The Wreck Removal Convention imposes the primary responsibility for the removal of a hazardous wreck on the shipowner and is created to address more contemporary wrecks.[160] It makes no reference to wrecks that predate the entry into force of the Convention, and it is not entirely clear whether it applies to wrecks of archaeological and historical nature.[161]

The existence of certain archaeological and historical objects may also pose an obstacle to the development of the seabed in the EEZ. The State that undertakes such development, mainly the coastal State, would have the discretion to find a balance between its duties to protect these objects and its right to explore and exploit the natural resources, to use artificial islands, installations and structures, or to lay submarine cables and pipelines. This balance could only be assessed on a case-by-case basis. Given its sovereign rights over the exploration and exploitation of natural resources, the coastal State would be in a position to decide how these activities should be carried out.[162] Imposing any conditions deriving from the intention to protect these objects, nevertheless, must be balanced with its due regard obligation to the rights of other States. For example, the *Danton*, a battleship dating from the First World War, was discovered in 2008 by the Fugro geosciences company during a survey for the Galsi gas pipeline project between Algeria and Italy.[163] Upon confirming its identity, the flag State, France, asked for the site to be

[158] UNCLOS Article 24(2).

[159] Nairobi International Convention on the Removal of Wrecks (18 May 2007, in force 14 April 2015) 3283 UNTS I-55565 (RWC). See Chapter 4 in this volume.

[160] RWC Article 10.

[161] Forrest (2019) 191–192.

[162] Dromgoole (2013) 266–267.

[163] Franca Cibecchini and Olivia Hulot, 'The Danton and U-95: Two Symbolic Wrecks to Illustrate and Promote the Heritage of the First World War', in UNESCO (2014) 192.

protected and requested that the pipeline be redirected 100 yards.[164] A Swedish wooden warship wreck, scuttled in 1715 in the Bay of Greifswald in Germany, was excavated in 2009 to make way for the Nord Stream gas pipeline constructed between Russia and Germany.[165]

State parties to the CPUCH are obligated to report discoveries by any national or vessel undertaking activities in the EEZ and on the continental shelf, not just by those who intend to engage in activities directed at UCH.[166] Such report of a discovery will trigger the procedures set out in Articles 9 and 10 relating to notification, consultation and protection, as well as the procedures for relevant States to assume the role as Coordinating State and interested State parties.[167] There are now a number of States, including Australia, China, Greece and Norway, that require their nationals to report, and to provide subsequent treatment, of UCH discovered incidentally during any offshore operation.[168] The imposition of this reporting obligation could bring these UCH to the relevant States' attention and offer them the opportunity to provide effective means to prevent or mitigate inadvertent damage during these development activities.

The coastal State may also designate, through the International Maritime Organization (IMO), a Particular Sensitive Sea Area (PSSA) to protect the archaeological and historical objects found in its EEZ or on its continental shelf.[169] A PSSA is 'an area that needs special protection through action by IMO because of its significance for recognized ecological, socio-economic, or scientific attributes where such attributes may be vulnerable to damage by international shipping activities'.[170] The

[164] Cibecchini and Hulot (2014) 193.

[165] Nord Stream, 'Underwater Investigation of Shipwreck Parts in the Bay of Greifswald Enters Second Phase', 31 August 2008 www.nord-stream.com/press-info/press-releases/underwater-investigation-of-shipwreck-parts-in-the-bay-of-greifswald-enters-second-phase-198/; Nord Stream, 'First Shipwreck Parts Salvaged from Bay of Greifswald', 15 July 2009 www.nord-stream.com/media/news/press_releases/en/2009/07/first-shipwreck-parts-salvaged-from-bay-of-greifswald_20090715.pdf.

[166] CPUCH Article 9(1).

[167] Dromgoole (2013) 348–349.

[168] On national implementation of the CPUCH, see Sarah Dromgoole (ed.), *The Protection of the Underwater Cultural Heritage National Perspectives in Light of the UNESCO Convention 2001* (2nd ed., Martinus Nijhoff 2006).

[169] IMO, 'Particularly Sensitive Sea Areas (PSSA)' www.imo.org/en/OurWork/Environment/Pages/PSSAs.aspx. For the designation of a PSSA in the EEZ, see Chapter 4 in this volume.

[170] IMO Res A 24/Res.982, 6 February 2006, Revised Guidelines for the Identification and Designation of Particularly Sensitive Sea Areas, para 1.2.

presence of 'significant historical and archaeological sites' would qualify the social, cultural and economic criteria that is required for such designation and justify appropriate associated protective measures for the area.[171] The United States, for example, has designated the cultural heritage Papahānaumokuākea Marine National Monument (Northwestern Hawaiian Islands or NWHI) as a PSSA through IMO.[172] On justifying the social, cultural and economic criteria, it was highlighted that the NWHI is rich in historical and archaeological heritage resources that are rare, representative of broad themes of maritime history, and a testimony to the uniqueness of Pacific seafaring history.[173] It should be noted that the establishment of PSSAs for their historical and/or archaeological significance would need to be examined within the context of the general duties to protect these objects under Article 303 of UNCLOS, and the regulations under the CPUCH. And the associated protective measures are designed to prevent damage to these objects by international shipping activities.

These potentially negative impacts on the archaeological and historical objects are expected to grow with the intensive use of the EEZ and the continental shelf for human activities. The central role in avoiding and minimising these impacts rests with the relevant national and flag States. In most situations, it is the coastal State that shares such a role. Should the coastal State have relevant information and knowledge of the presence of these objects in its EEZ or on its continental shelf, it could employ holistic marine control procedures, including marine spatial planning and environmental impact assessment, to manage other potential competing activities.[174]

8.4 Settlement of Disputes

It is apparent from the preceding discussion that there are plenty of opportunities for disputes to arise between States relating to the underwater archaeological and historical objects found in the EEZ or on the continental shelf. For example, disputes could arise concerning the

[171] Ibid paras 4.4.14, 6.1–6.2.

[172] IMO MEPC 56/23, 30 July 2007, Report of the Marine Environment Protection Committee on Its Fifty-Sixth Session, paras 8.1–8.9.

[173] IMO MEPC 56/8, 5 April 2007, Designation of the Papahānaumokuākea Marine National Monument as a Particularly Sensitive Sea Area, Submitted by the United States, paras 3.13.1, 21.

[174] Dromgoole (2013) 348.

interpretation and application of whether a certain State has breached the general duties to protect and cooperate to protect these objects, whether the coastal State may exercise enforcement jurisdiction over a foreign vessel that caused pollution due to treasure salvage activities, or whether the coastal State could deny consent to the delineation of a foreign pipeline to avoid damaging a heritage shipwreck. Given the differences between UNCLOS and the CPUCH on coastal State rights in the contiguous zone, and more generally the inconsistent State practices and interpretations, there could be disputes concerning the relationship between these two treaties and whether any of their provisions are considered customary law.

As a matter of general international law, and the provisions of UNCLOS, States are obligated to settle disputes between them by peaceful means.[175] For disputes concerning the interpretation or application of UNCLOS, State parties may choose to accept the jurisdiction of the International Tribunal for the Law of the Sea (ITLOS), the International Court of Justice, an Annex VII arbitral tribunal or a special Annex VIII arbitral tribunal.[176] If a State does not make a choice of procedures, it is deemed to have accepted the Annex VII arbitration.[177] The dispute settlement system is fundamentally consensual in the sense that State parties to the dispute could choose the means and procedures by agreements.[178] Under UNCLOS, this system is reinforced by a compulsory dispute settlement procedure when the State parties to the dispute cannot reach settlement by recourse to the means of their choice.[179] In this case, any party to the dispute may submit their dispute to the same procedure as accepted by both parties, or to Annex VII arbitration.[180]

To date, there are two international cases included claims relating to underwater archaeological and historical objects. ITLOS recognised, indirectly through accepting the Respondent's action to invoke domestic law, the exclusive right of the coastal State over the UCH located in its internal waters and the territorial sea in the M/V *Louisa* case.[181] ICJ

[175] Charter of the United Nations (26 June 1945, in force 24 October 1945) 1 UNTS XVI, Article 2(3); UNCLOS Article 279.

[176] UNCLOS Article 287(1), Annex VII Arbitration, Annex VIII Sepcial Aritration.

[177] UNCLOS Article 287(3).

[178] UNCLOS Article 280.

[179] UNCLOS Articles 281, 286.

[180] UNCLOS Articles 286, 287(4)–(5).

[181] The M/V 'Louisa' Case (Saint Vincent and the Grenadines v. Kingdom of Spain), Judgment of 28 May 2013, ITLOS Reports 2013, p. 4, paras 104, 113.

declared the customary law status of Article 303(2) and expended its interpretation of coastal States' right over these objects to reflect the development by the CPUCH and State practice.[182]

CPUCH also requires State parties to settle their disputes concerning its interpretation or application through peaceful means of their own choice.[183] When a dispute arises, State parties to the dispute shall negotiate in good faith before submitting it to mediation by UNESCO by agreement, or, if it cannot be thus settled, to the provisions set out in Part XV of UNCLOS, to be applied *mutatis mutandis*, whether or not the parties to the dispute are also a party to UNCLOS.[184] A State party to CPUCH, even if it is not a party to UNCLOS, may use the same procedure established by UNCLOS to declare which court or tribunal jurisdiction it accepts.[185]

Part XV clearly stated that the UNCLOS court or tribunal shall 'have jurisdiction over any dispute concerning the interpretation or application of an international agreement related to the purposes of this Convention, which is submitted to it in accordance with the agreement'.[186] The incorporation of the dispute settlement procedures under UNCLOS into the provision made by CPUCH for dispute settlement could be controversial. It effectively obliges States that are not party to UNCLOS to be subject to its dispute settlement mechanism. States are often reluctant to accept compulsory dispute settlement mechanisms before the dispute arises. This potential implication for States that are not party to UNCLOS may affect their consideration to ratify the CPUCH. Indeed, both Türkiye and Venezuela voted against the CPUCH citing this concern.[187]

8.5 Conclusion

Underwater archaeological and historical objects were not genuinely considered when the law of the sea was negotiated and codified at the Third Conference. This was largely due to the lack of understanding of

182 Nicaragua v. Colombia (2022), paras 185–186.

183 CPUCH Article 25(1).

184 Ibid Article 25(2)–(3).

185 UNCLOS Article 287; CPUCH Article 25(4)–(5).

186 UNCLOS Artile 288(2), Annex VI Statute of the International Tribunal for the Law of the Sea, Article 21; Internatioanl Tribunal for the Law of the Sea, International Agreements Conferring Jurisdiction on the Tribunal, www.itlos.org/en/main/jurisdiction/international-agreements-conferring-jurisdiction-on-the-tribunal/.

187 Statements on Vote by Türkiye and Venezuela reproduced in Garabello and Scovazzi (2003) 432, 434.

underwater archaeology as a scientific discipline, as well as the underestimated value of and threats to these objects. The drafting history and final wording of Article 303 bears witness to the limited scope ultimately accepted. During the past few decades, the international scientific community, with the support of a number of interested States, insisted on the need to delineate a new legal canvas to adequately protect underwater cultural heritage for the benefit of all humankind. In 2001, a new legal regime was established by CPUCH, completing and resolving some of the legal gaps left by UNCLOS.

UNCLOS set out the general duties of all States to protect and cooperate to protect archaeological and historical objects found at sea, but provided no details on how States should fulfil such duties. The CPUCH provides some clarifications with respect to the rights and jurisdiction over UCH found in the EEZ or on the continental shelf. First, it explicitly stated that the coastal State may regulate and authorise activities directed at UCH in the contiguous zone, going beyond the scope recognised by UNCLOS.[188] Second, it clearly recognised that the activities directed at UCH found in the EEZ or on the continental shelf could have the potential to affect the sovereign rights and jurisdiction of the coastal State, and gave the coastal State the right to prohibit or authorise such activities.[189] Third, it created the role of the Coordinating State that gives the coastal State a potentially prominent role in respect of UCH in the EEZ or on the continental shelf, such as taking all practical measures to prevent immediate threats to UCH.[190] Nevertheless, both legal frameworks place their reliance on the nationality principle of jurisdiction, which means the support of flag States, particularly the handful that have deepwater technological capability, is absolutely crucial if the framework is to succeed in fulfilling its primary objective to protect these objects.

CPUCH shows neutrality regarding any 'creeping jurisdiction' temptation that may arise when interpreting, evoking or applying its provisions.[191] Except in regards to the contiguous zone, it is hard to argue that any provisions of the CPUCH could be used to support any excessive claim. Moreover, Article 59 of UNCLOS may help to bolster the legitimacy of the role afforded by the CPUCH to the coastal State as the Coordinating State for CUH found in the EEZ or on the continental

[188] UNCLOS Articles 33, 303(2); CPUCH Article 8.
[189] CPUCH Article 10(2).
[190] Ibid Article 10(3)–(5).
[191] Ibid Articles 2(11), 10(6).

shelf. The goal of the CPUCH is to protect underwater heritage by ensuring that all activities directed at UCH are undertaken in accordance with benchmark archaeological standards. The coastal State, when fulfilling the role of a Coordinating State, acts on behalf of the State parties as a whole and represents the collective interests of the international community.[192]

State practice during the past four decades shows that many coastal States have been expanding their rights over the contiguous zone by adding legislative powers to protect underwater heritage, a practice that generally has been accepted.[193] Nonetheless, extending this jurisdiction beyond the outer limit of the contiguous zone, as several States have done, is not yet supported by general State practice.[194] However, the coastal State, based on the connection and potential impacts on is sovereign rights and jurisdiction, as well as fulfilling its general duties to protect, may find legal basis to claim concurrent jurisdiction over certain activities that affect the archaeological and historical objects found in its EEZ or on the continental shelf.

[192] UNCLOS Article 59; Dormgoole (2013) 302–303.
[193] Aznar (2014) 38; Nicaragua v. Colombia (2022), paras 185–186.
[194] Aznar (2020) 93–95.

9

General Conclusions

The modern law of the sea, codified in the twentieth century through customary international law and State practice, has its roots deep in the past.[1] Its main objective is to establish legal order over the ocean space by setting up a framework of doctrines to determine the attribution and exercise of the rights and duties of States in respect of their uses of the ocean. Throughout its history, the law of the sea has been characterised by a tension between the concepts of *mare liberum* and *mare clausum*, and this tension has had a profound influence on its development.[2] As such, a central feature of the evolving framework responding to this tension is the division of the ocean into distinct maritime zones, each with its own specific legal regime of rights and duties of States.

The Third United Nations Conference on the Law of the Sea (Third Conference), which began in 1973 and concluded in 1982, produced a treaty that become the pre-eminent source of the law of the sea today.[3] The United Nations Convention on the Law of the Sea (UNCLOS) has been called a 'Constitution for the Oceans' because it provides a comprehensive legal and policy framework for conduct on, over and under ocean spaces which cover more than 70 per cent of the globe.[4] To understand UNCLOS in general, and particularly the *sui generis* exclusive economic

[1] Barbara Kwiatkowska, *The 200 Mile Exclusive Economic Zone in the New Law of the Sea* (Martinus Nijhoff 1989) 30–32; Robin Churchill, Vaughan Lowe and Amy Sander, *The Law of the Sea* (4th ed., Manchester University Press 2022) 10–20.

[2] Tullio Treves, 'Historical Development of the Law of the Sea', in Donald R. Rothwell, Alex G. Oude Elferink, Karen N. Scott and Tim Stephens (eds.), *The Oxford Handbook of the Law of the Sea* (Oxford University Press 2015) 3–6; James R. Crawford, *Brownlie's Principles of Public International Law* (9th ed., Oxford University Press 2019) 241–243.

[3] United Nations, 'Third United Nations Conference on the Law of the Sea (1973–1982)' https://legal.un.org/diplomaticconferences/1973_los/.

[4] United Nations Convention on the Law of the Sea (10 December 1982, in force 16 November 1994) 1833 UNTS 3 (UNCLOS); Tommy T. B. Koh, 'A Constitution for the Oceans', in Myron H. Nordquist (ed.), *United Nations Convention on the Law of the Sea 1982: A Commentary*, Vol. I (Martinus Nijhoff 1985) 14–15.

zone (EEZ) that is at the centre of the tension between *mare liberum* and *mare clausum*, it is necessary to appreciate the politically charged nature of this area of law.[5] The respective rights and duties of States over the ocean have huge cultural, economic, societal, strategic, military and security implications. Under UNCLOS, the concept of *mare liberum*, embodied in the notion of freedom of the high seas, has been subject to a certain degree of erosion, particularly by the recently developed EEZ concept. Today, in the international arena, the historical debate continues between two opposing political groups. The predominant interest of the coastal States is to preserve the integrity of their rights over their coastal waters and, at times, to extend those rights, whereas the flag States (or other States as used in the EEZ context) want to preserve their communicational freedoms so that their merchant and military fleets can move freely about the globe.

This book has examined the EEZ regime as provided by the relevant provisions of UNCLOS, from its origins to contemporary State practice. The rights and duties of the coastal State and other States are the most fundamental aspects that form the integrated legal regime and reaffirm the *sui generis* character of the EEZ. UNCLOS seeks to maintain a careful balance among these vital interests by establishing the general doctrines for the attribution and exercise of these rights and duties. The coastal State is granted sovereign rights over the natural resources and jurisdiction over specified activities, while all States enjoy the freedoms of navigation and overflight, the laying of submarine cables and pipelines, and other internationally lawful uses of the sea related to these freedoms.[6] In exercising their rights and performing their duties, both the coastal State and other States are obliged to have due regard to the rights and duties of the other party and to act in a manner compatible with other provisions of UNCLOS.[7] With respect to rights or jurisdiction that are not explicitly attributed to either the coastal State or other States, conflicts must be resolved on the basis of equity and in the light of all

[5] Philip Allott, 'Power Sharing in the Law of the Sea' (1983) 77 Am J Int'l L 1, 1–3; Alan Beesley, 'The Negotiating Strategy of UNCLOS III: Developing and Developed Countries as Partners – A Pattern for Future Multilateral International Conferences?' (1983) 46(2) Law & Contemp Probs 183, 183–184; Deborah Cass, 'The Quiet Revolution: The Development of the Exclusive Economic Zone and Implications for Foreign Fishing Access in the Pacific' (1987–1988) 16 Melb U L Rev 83, 83–84.

[6] UNCLOS Articles 56(1), 58(1).

[7] UNCLOS Articles 56(2), 58(3), 300–301.

relevant circumstances.[8] Furthermore, the above doctrines of the attribution and exercise of co-existing rights apply to residual rights and jurisdiction. This regime is safeguarded by the dispute settlement procedures established under Part XV of UNCLOS. Although a range of coastal State discretionary powers are exempted from mandatory third-party review, disputes arising from the most common conflicting uses of the EEZ are subject to compulsory procedures entailing binding decisions with optional exceptions.[9] The dispute settlement mechanisms are necessary to give greater definition to the vague provisions contained in Articles 56, 58 and 59 and reinforce the continuing balance of powers in the EEZ.

However, significant disagreement remains in the interpretation and application of the EEZ regime.[10] This is because the EEZ reduced a large area from the transnational commons and set the stage for an evolving battle between core economic interests of coastal States and communicational freedoms of all States. Additionally, there is the issue of how to identify and address a number of residual rights that are not specifically included in the regime itself and remain for further discussion. In the law of the sea, the uses of the EEZ have become one of the most difficult and complex issues to give rise to international disputes. Subsequent agreements and State practice have shown that the EEZ regime has sufficient flexibility and resilience, and a dynamic balance could be maintained on an *ad hoc* basis to accommodate the growing and changing needs of States.

With respect to navigation, by and large, this freedom has been subjected to moderate changes under the EEZ regime compared with its application on the high seas. In contrast, the freedom of overflight has been less affected by the establishment of the EEZ. On navigation, the coastal State shares limited concurrent jurisdiction over foreign vessels in

[8] UNCLOS Article 59.

[9] UNCLOS Articles 297, 298(1)(b).

[10] Ivan Shearer, 'Ocean Management Challenges for the Law of the Sea in the First Decade of the 21st Century', in Alex G. Oude Elferink and Donald R. Rothwell (eds.), *Ocean Management in the 21st Century: Institutional Frameworks and Responses* (Martinus Nijhoff 2004) 10–13; Robin R. Churchill, 'The Impact of State Practice on the Jurisdictional Framework Contained in the LOS Convention', in Alex G. Oude Elferink (ed.), *Stability and Change in the Law of the Sea: The Role of the LOS Convention* (Martinus Nijhoff 2005) 126–136; Alexandre Pereira da Silva, 'From the First Claims to the Exclusive Economic Zone: Reviewing Latin America's 200-Nautical Mile Sea Seventy Years On' (2019) 33 Ocean YB 131, 140–159; J Ashley Roach, *Excessive Maritime Claims* (4th ed., Brill 2021) 163–175, 442–482.

its EEZ. This is notable in relation to vessel-source pollution triggered by a violation of applicable international rules and standards, and fisheries and activities ancillary to fishing that violate applicable domestic laws.[11] Where the foreign vessel is subject to the concurrent jurisdiction of both the coastal State and the flag State, it is conceivable that the former could only exercise jurisdiction for explicitly assigned activities while the latter maintains primary responsibility for the conduct of the vessel within the EEZ. However, in the case of marine environmental protection from vessel-source pollution, and sometimes for the safety of navigation, the coastal State is increasingly gaining prescriptive jurisdiction through the development of generally accepted international rules and standards, which signals the expanding nature of the jurisdiction of the coastal State in the EEZ.

With regard to the freedom to lay submarine cables and pipelines in the EEZ, the coastal State is given explicit rights and jurisdiction to take reasonable measures to protect its economic interests, particularly with regard to pipelines for environmental protection purposes, provided that such measures do not impede the laying or maintenance of such cables or pipelines.[12] On the one hand, while the competition between uses continues, a review of State practice indicates that some States have made certain inconsistent and excessive claims over activities related to submarine cables and pipelines, a finding that highlights the necessity of each State obeying the due regard obligation in exercising its co-existing rights. On the other hand, with the growing awareness of the importance of submarine cables and pipelines, States are expected to enhance their efforts, individually and jointly, to protect their safety and security. The coastal State, in particular, must regulate competing uses under its jurisdiction with due diligence and ensure its nationals or vessels flying its flag do not interfere, maliciously or unreasonably, with the submarine cables and pipelines laid in its EEZ.

Driven by various motivations, States are pressing their claims in the EEZ, in particular with respect to the residual rights of security concerns, with many States adopting numerous military, diplomatic, policy and legal measures to serve their own interests. Security interests at sea originated from the inherent right of States to defend and resist any possible violation, interference, destruction and damage coming from the ocean space against their sovereignty, territorial integrity, internal affairs

[11] UNCLOS Articles 56(1)(a) and (b)(iii), 58(3), 62(4), 73(1), 211(5), 220(3) and (5)–(6).
[12] UNCLOS Articles 58(1), 79(1)–(4).

and social order, and their nationals' lives and property abroad.[13] The protection of security interests is reflected in the activities of naval and air forces, maritime enforcement and ocean management, which combine the functions of the military, police and administrative agencies of the State. The security rights enjoyed by States are manifested not only in the maritime zones under their jurisdiction but also in the jurisdictional zones of other States and on the high seas as the freedom of safe transit. Within the EEZ, both traditional military interests and non-traditional non-military interests of the coastal State co-exist with those of other States. As such, in theory, all States could assert the right to conduct military activities and address threats to maritime security in an established EEZ, provided that there is a jurisdictional basis under international law. The key to finding a dynamic balance in the EEZ is the obedience of the mutual due regard obligation and non-abuse of rights.[14] It has been observed that special consideration should be given to the coastal State to ensure their sovereign rights over natural resources and recognized jurisdiction are not unduly affected. States will continue to use the EEZ for military and security purposes despite different interpretations and practices on their legal basis. It is in the interests of all States to find a balance between maximising their individual rights and jurisdiction in adjacent maritime areas and maintaining the common interest of all States to use the multifunctional EEZ.[15] Moreover, there has been an emerging trend of treating maritime security as collective security for which multilateral cooperation and collaboration among States are needed to secure the peaceful use of the ocean. Where there is a conflict that arises between the asserted right and another use of the ocean, the dispute should be resolved on the basis of equity and take into account all relevant circumstances and interests.[16]

UNCLOS provides little guidance on the rights and jurisdiction of archaeological and historical objects found in the EEZ, except for the general duties of all States to protect and cooperate to protect them.[17]

[13] Natalie Klein, *Maritime Security and the Law of the Sea* (Oxford University Press 2011) 6–7.

[14] UNCLOS Articles 56(2), 58(3), 300.

[15] Tim Stephens and Donald R. Rothwell, 'The LOSC Framework for Maritime Jurisdiction and Enforcement 30 Years On' (2012) 27 Int'l J Marine & Coastal L 701, 705–706; Yoshifumi Tanaka, *The International Law of the Sea* (3rd ed., Cambridge University Press 2019) 471–472.

[16] UNCLOS Article 59.

[17] UNCLOS Article 303(1).

Subsequent State practice and international agreements, most importantly the 2001 Convention on the Protection of Underwater Cultural Heritage (CPUCH), have provided some clarity on this issue.[18] For the first 12 nautical miles (NM) of the EEZ, based on its rights over the contiguous zone when declared, the coastal State has the 'power of control with respect to archaeological and historical objects' found therein.[19] Compared with the right to 'control traffic' in such objects by 'their removal from the seabed' as stated in UNCLOS, this right has been further developed by CPUCH, State practice and acknowledged by the International Court of Justice.[20] For the remaining 176 NM of the EEZ, the coastal State has the right to take necessary measures over activities that affect these objects, both directly and incidentally, undertaken by its nationals or ships flying its flag. This right will be reduced to concurrent jurisdiction over activities undertaken by foreign nationals or vessels when such activities interfere with its sovereign rights or recognized jurisdiction. Among States parties to the CPUCH, the coastal State may assume the role of a Coordinating State to coordinate the consultation process and implementation of agreed measures for the protection of underwater cultural heritage found in its EEZ or on the continental shelf.[21]

Compared to when the ocean was clearly divided between the territorial sea and the high seas, under UNCLOS there has been a major change in favour of the coastal State in terms of natural resources. The establishment of the EEZ puts an end to the chaotic situation of inconsistent unilateral claims, known as creeping jurisdiction, that had prevailed from the late 1940s to the late 1970s.[22] Since then, there have been no attempts by the coastal State to extend their jurisdiction over the water column beyond the 200 NM limit.[23] There has been some inconsistent interpretation and

[18] Convention on the Protection of the Underwater Cultural Heritage (2 November 2001, in force 2 January 2009) 2562 UNTS 3 (CPUCH).

[19] Alleged Violations of Sovereign Rights and Maritime Spaces in the Caribbean Sea (Nicaragua v. Colombia), Judgment of 21 April 2022, ICJ Reports 2022, p. 266, para 186.

[20] UNCLOS Article 303(2); CPUCH Article 8; Nicaragua v. Colombia (2022) para 185; Mariano J. Aznar, 'The Contiguous Zone as an Archaeological Maritime Zone' (2014) 29 Int'l J Marine & Coastal L 1, 30–38.

[21] CPUCH Articles 9–10.

[22] Tommy Koh, *Building a New Legal Order for the Oceans* (National University of Singapore Press 2020) 25–33; Satya N. Nandan with Kristine E. Dalaker, *Reflections on the Making of the Modern Law of the Sea* (National University of Singapore Press 2021) 124–128.

[23] Gemma Andreone, 'The Exclusive Economic Zone', in Rothwell, Oude Elferink, Scott and Stephens (2015) 178–180; Churchill, Lowe and Sander (2022) 297–299.

application of certain subject matters, and some occasional conflicts between the exercise of certain rights and freedoms in the EEZ, but these are limited to a relatively small number of States. The confluence of different approaches to coordinate and harmonise State practice has and will continue to shape the development of the EEZ regime.

For any legal system to be able to respond to the evolving needs of States, it must have the capability to adapt to changing circumstances that affect the reality it purports to regulate, and the international law of the sea is no exception.[24] In the forty years since its establishment under UNCLOS, the EEZ regime still stands out as a robust legal framework, containing clearer doctrines than often thought and, notwithstanding the need to interpret its provisions in light of serious factual challenges, remains well suited for continuing to balance the different interests between coastal State and other States.[25] It is the responsibility of all State parties to ensure the continued relevance of the EEZ regime by bearing in mind the spirit and substance underlying this regime. Only when the rights and freedoms are exercised on the basis of mutual respect and due regard and in the spirit of multi-level cooperation will the national interests and communicational freedoms be safe and secure, and the EEZ enjoy peace, security and good order.

[24] Jose Luis Jesus, 'Protection of Foreign Ships against Piracy and Terrorism at Sea: Legal Aspects' (2003) 18 Int'l J Marine & Coastal L 363, 382; Malcolm D Evans, 'The Law of the Sea', in Malcolm D. Evans (ed.), *International Law* (5th ed., Oxford University Press 2018) 637–638.

[25] Shanmugam Jayakumar, 'UNCLOS – Two Decades On' (2005) 9 Singapore YB Int'l L 1, 6; Alexander Proelss, 'The Law on the Exclusive Economic Zone in Perspective: Legal Status and Resolution of User Conflicts Revisited' (2012) 26 Ocean YB 87, 87; Margaret A. Young, 'A Quiet Revolution: The Exclusivity of Exclusive Economic Zones', in Kim Rubenstein (ed.), *Traversing the Divide: Honouring Deborah Cass's Contributions to Public and International Law* (Australian National University Press 2021) 86.

SELECT BIBLIOGRAPHY

Attard, David J, *The Exclusive Economic Zone in International Law* (Clarendon Press 1987).

Aust, Anthony, *Modern Treaty Law and Practice* (Cambridge University Press 2013).

Aznar, Mariano J, *Maritime Claims and Underwater Archaeology: When History Meets Politics* (Brill 2020).

Bailey, Geoffrey N, Jan Harff and Dimitris Sakellariou (eds.), *Under the Sea: Archaeology and Palaeolandscapes of the Continental Shelf* (Springer 2017).

Banet, Catherine (ed.), *The Law of the Seabed: Access, Uses, and Protection of Seabed Resources* (Brill 2020).

Beckman, Robert C and J Ashley Roach (eds.), *Piracy and International Maritime Crimes in ASEAN: Prospects for Cooperation* (Edward Elgar 2012).

Bjorge, Eirik, *The Evolutionary Interpretation of Treaties* (Oxford University Press 2014).

Booth, Ken, *Theory of World Security* (Cambridge University Press 2007).

Boyle, Alan and David Freestone (eds.), *International Law and Sustainable Development* (Oxford University Press 1999).

Boyle, Alan and Catherine Redgwell, *Birnie, Boyle and Redgwell's International Law and the Environment* (4th ed, Oxford University Press 2021).

Breeze, Heather and Tracy Horsman (eds.), *Scotian Shelf: An Atlas of Human Activities* (Fisheries and Oceans Canada 2005).

Brown, Edward Duncan, *The International Law of the Sea Volume I: Introductory Manual* (Dartmouth 1994).

Bueger, Christian, Timothy Edmunds and Robert McCabe (eds.), *Capacity Building for Maritime Security: The Western Indian Ocean Experience* (Palgrave Macmillan 2021).

Burke, William T, *The New International Law of Fisheries: UNCLOS 1982 and Beyond* (Oxford University Press 1994).

Burnett, Douglas R, Robert C Beckman and Tara M Davenport (eds.), *Submarine Cables: The Handbook of Law and Policy* (Martinus Nijhoff 2014).

Chandrasekhara, Rao P. and Philippe Gautier, *The International Tribunal for the Law of the Sea: Law, Practice and Procedure* (Edward Elgar 2018).

Chhibber, Bharti, *Regional Security and Regional Cooperation: A Comparative Study of ASEAN and SAARC* (New Century Publications 2004).

Chircop, Aldo, Floris Goerlandt, Claudio Aporta and Ronald Pelot (eds.), *Governance of Arctic Shipping: Rethinking Risk, Human Impacts and Regulation* (Springer 2020).

Churchill, Robin and A Vaughn Lowe, *The Law of the Sea* (3rd ed., Manchester University Press 1999).

Churchill, Robin, Vaughan Lowe and Amy Sander, *The Law of the Sea* (4th ed., Manchester University Press 2022).

Crawford, James, *Brownlie's Principles of Public International Law* (9th ed., Oxford University Press 2019).

International Law as An Open System: Selected Essays (Cameron May 2002).

Crawford, James, Abdul G Koroma, Said Mahmoudi and Alain Pellet (eds.), *The International Legal Order: Current Needs and Possible Responses: Essays in Honour of Djamchid Momtaz* (Brill 2017).

Dahmani, Mohamed, *The Fisheries Regime of the Exclusive Economic Zone* (Martinus Nijhoff 1987).

Djeffal, Christian, *Static and Evolutive Treaty Interpretation: A Functional Reconstruction* (Cambridge University Press 2015).

Dromgoole, Sarah (ed.), *The Protection of the Underwater Cultural Heritage National Perspectives in Light of the UNESCO Convention 2001* (2nd ed., Martinus Nijhoff 2006).

Underwater Cultural Heritage and International Law (Cambridge University Press 2013).

Dupuy, René-Jean and Daniel Vignes, *A Handbook on the New Law of the Sea, Vol. II* (Brill | Nijhoff 1991).

Dux, Thomas, *Specially Protected Marine Areas in the Exclusive Economic Zone: The Regime for the Protection of Specific Areas of the EEZ for Environmental Reasons under International Law* (LIT Berlin 2011).

Espósito, Carlos, James Kraska, Harry N Scheiber and Moon-Sang Kwon (eds.), *Ocean Law and Policy: Twenty Years of Development under the UNCLOS Regime* (Brill 2017).

Evans, Malcolm D (ed), *International Law* (5th ed., Oxford University Press 2018).

Extavour, Winston Conrad, *The Exclusive Economic Zone: A Study of the Evolution and Progressive Development of the International Law of the Sea* (Institut universitaire de hautes études internationales 1979).

Fitzmaurice, Malgosia, Olufemi Elias and Panos Merkouris (eds.), *Treaty Interpretation and the Vienna Convention on the Law of Treaties: 30 Years* (Martinus Nijhoff 2011).

Forrest, Craig, *Maritime Legacies and the Law: Effective Legal Governance of WWI Wrecks* (Edward Elgar 2019).

Francioni, Francesco and Ana Filipa Vrdoljak (eds.), *The Oxford Handbook of International Cultural Heritage Law* (Oxford University Press 2020).

Franckx, Erik, *Vessel-Source Pollution and Coastal State Jurisdiction: The Work of the ILA Committee on Coastal State Jurisdiction Relating to Marine Pollution (1991–2000)* (Kluwer Law International 2001).

Freedman, Lawrence, *The Official History of the Falklands Campaign* (Routledge 2005).

Freestone, David (ed.), *The 1982 Law of the Sea Convention at 30: Successes, Challenges and New Agendas* (Martinus Nijhoff 2013).

Freestone, David, Richard Barnes and David M Ong (eds.), *The Law of the Sea: Progress and Prospects* (Oxford University Press 2006).

Fulton, Thomas Wemyss, *The Sovereignty of the Sea* (Blackwood 1911).

Garabello, Roberta and Tullio Scovazzi (eds.), *The Protection of the Underwater Cultural Heritage, Before and After the 2001 UNESCO Convention* (Brill 2003).

Gardiner, Richard, *Treaty Interpretation* (2nd ed., Oxford University Press 2015).

Gavouneli, Maria, *Functional Jurisdiction in the Law of the Sea* (Martinus Nijhoff 2007).

Geiss, Robin and Anna Petrig, *Piracy and Armed Robbery at Sea: The Legal Framework for Counter-Piracy Operations in Somalia and the Gulf of Aden* (Oxford University Press 2011).

Germond, Basil, *The Maritime Dimension of European Security Seapower and the European Union* (Palgrave MacMillan 2015).

Gordon, Gary A and Richard R Yong (eds.), *Intermodal Maritime Security: Supply Chain Risk Mitigation* (Elsevier 2021).

Gordon, Greg, John Paterson and Emre Üşenmez (eds.), *UK Oil and Gas Law: Current Practice and Emerging Trends: Volume I: Resource Management and Regulatory Law* (Edinburgh University Press 2018).

Gray, Christine, *International Law and the Use of Force* (4th ed., Oxford University Press 2018).

Guilfoyle, Douglas (ed.), *Modern Piracy: Legal Challenges and Responses* (Edward Elgar 2013).

Shipping Interdiction and the Law of the Sea (Cambridge University Press 2009).

Guo, Boyun, Shanhong Song, Ali Ghalambor and Tian Ran Lin, *Offshore Pipelines: Design, Installation, and Maintenance* (2nd ed., Elsevier 2014).

Harris, David and Sandesh Sivakumaran, *Cases and Materials on International Law* (8th ed., Sweet & Maxwell 2015).

Harrison, James, *Making the Law of the Sea* (Cambridge University Press 2011).

Saving the Oceans Through Law: The International Legal Framework for the Protection of the Marine Environment (Oxford University Press 2017).

Herbert-Burns, Rupert, Sam Bateman and Peter Lehr (eds.), *Lloyd's MIU Handbook of Maritime Security* (CRC Press Taylor & Francis Group 2009).

Ho, Joshua and Catherine Zara Raymond (eds.), *The Best of Times, The Worst of Times: Maritime Security in the Asia-Pacific* (World Scientific Publishing 2005).

Hollis, Duncan B (ed.), *The Oxford Guide to Treaties* (2nd ed., Oxford University Press 2020).

Hore-Lacy, Ian, *Nuclear Energy in the 21st Century* (World Nuclear University Press 2007).

Igbinovia, Patrick Edobor, *Oil Thefts and Pipeline Vandalization in Nigeria* (Safari Books Ltd 2014).

International Tribunal for the Law of the Sea (eds.), *The Contribution of the International Tribunal for the Law of the Sea to the Rule of Law: 1996–2016* (Brill 2017).

Jalloh, Charles C, Kamari M Clarke and Vincent O Nmehielle (eds.), *The African Court of Justice and Human and Peoples' Rights in Context: Development and Challenges* (Cambridge University Press 2019).

Jessup, Philip C, *The Law of Territorial Waters and Maritime Jurisdiction* (GA Jennings 1927).

Johnson, Lindy S, *Coastal State Regulation of International Shipping* (Oceana Publications 2004).

Johnston, Douglas M, *The International Law of Fisheries: A Framework for Policy-Oriented Inquires* (Yale 1965).

Kelleher, Graeme, *Guidelines for Marine Protected Areas* (IUCN 1999).

Klein, Natalie, *Dispute Settlement in the UN Convention on the Law of the Sea* (Cambridge University Press 2005).

Maritime Security and the Law of the Sea (Oxford University Press 2011).

(ed.), *Unconventional Law Making in the Law of the Sea* (Oxford University Press 2022).

Klein, Natalie, Joanna Mossop and Donald R Rothwell (eds.), *Maritime Security: International Law and Policy Perspectives from Australia and New Zealand* (Routledge 2010).

Koh, Tommy, *Building A New Legal Order for the Oceans* (NUS Press 2020).

Koutrakos, Panos and Achilles Skordas (eds.), *The Law and Practice of Piracy at Sea: European and International Perspectives* (Hart 2014).

Kraska, James, *Maritime Power and the Law of the Sea: Expeditionary Operations in World Politics* (Oxford University Press 2011).

Kraska, James and Raul Pedrozo, *Disruptive Technology and the Law of Naval Warfare* (Oxford University Press 2022).

International Maritime Security Law (Martinus Nijhoff 2013).

Kwiatkowska, Barbara, *Decisions of the World Court Relevant to the UN Convention on the Law of the Sea: A Reference Guide* (Kluwer Law International 2002).

The 200 Mile Exclusive Economic Zone in the New Law of the Sea (Martinus Nijhoff 1989).

Kyriakides, Stelios and Edmundo Corona, *Mechanics of Offshore Pipelines: Volume 1 Buckling and Collapse* (Elsevier 2007).

Lay, S Houston, Robin Churchill and Myron Nordquist (eds.), *New Directions in the Law of the Sea, Documents Volume I* (New York 1973).

Lo, Chang-Fa, *Treaty Interpretation Under the Vienna Convention on the Law of Treaties: A New Round of Codification* (Springer 2017).

Long, Ronán, *Marine Resources Law* (Thomson Round Hall 2007).

Lowe, Vaughan, *International Law* (Oxford University Press 2007).

Martínez Gutiérrez, Norman A (ed.), *Serving the Rule of International Maritime Law: Essays in Honour of Professor David Joseph Attard* (Routledge 2010).

McDougal, Myres S and William T Burke, *The Public Order of the Oceans: A Contemporary International Law of the Sea* (Yale University Press 1962).

McNicholas, Michael A (ed.), *Maritime Security: An Introduction* (Elsevier 2016).

Miyoshi, Masahiro, *Considerations of Equity in the Settlement of Territorial and Boundary Disputes* (Martinus Nijhoff 1993).

Molenaar, Erik J, *Coastal State Jurisdiction over Vessel-Source Pollution* (Kluwer Law International 1998).

de Mora, Stephen, Timothy Fileman and Thomas Vance (eds.), *Environmental Impact of Ships* (Cambridge University Press 2020).

Morell, James B, *The Law of the Sea: An Historical Analysis of the 1982 Treaty and Its Rejection by the United States* (McFarland 1992).

Mueller, TJ, JM Steele and AC Gellender, *Environmental Monitoring and Disposal of Radioactive Wastes from U.S. Naval Nuclear-Powered Ships and Their Support Facilities* (Naval Nuclear Propulsion Program, Department of the Navy, Report NT-19-1, May 2019).

Nandan, Satya N with Kristine E Dalaker, *Reflections on the Making of the Modern Law of the Sea* (National University of Singapore 2021).

Ndiaye, Tafsir M and Rüdiger Wolfrum (eds.), *Law of the Sea, Environmental Law and Settlement of Disputes* (Martinus Nijhoff 2007).

Nolte, Georg (ed.), *Treaties and Subsequent Practice* (Oxford University Press 2013).

Nordquist, Myron, John Norton Moore and Kuen-Chen Fu (eds.), *Recent Developments in the Law of the Sea and China* (Brill 2006).

Nordquist, Myron and Kenneth R Simmonds (eds.), *New Directions in the Law of the Sea, Documents Volume X* (New York 1973).

Nordquist, Myron H (ed.), *United Nations Convention on the Law of the Sea 1982: A Commentary*, Vol. I (Martinus Nijhoff 1985).

Nordquist, Myron H, Tommy Koh and John Norton Moore (eds.), *Freedom of Seas, Passage Rights and the 1982 Law of the Sea Convention* (Brill 2009).

Nordquist, Myron, Ronán Long, Tomas Heidar and John Norton Moore (eds.), *Law, Science & Ocean Management* (Brill 2007).

Nordquist, Myron H, Satya N Nandan, Michael W Logde and Shabtai Rosenne (eds.), *United Nations Convention on the Law of the Sea 1982: A Commentary*, Vol. VI (Martinus Nijhoff 2002).

Nordquist, Myron H, Satya N Nandan and Shabtai Rosenne (eds.), *United Nations Convention on the Law of the Sea 1982: A Commentary*, Vol. II (Martinus Nijhoff 1993).

(eds.), *United Nations Convention on the Law of the Sea 1982: A Commentary*, Vol. III (Martinus Nijhoff 1995).

Nordquist, Myron H, Shabtai Rosenne and Louis B Sohn (eds.), *United Nations Convention on the Law of the Sea 1982: A Commentary*, Vol. V (Martinus Nijhoff 1989).

Nordquist, Myron H, Shabtai Rosenne and Alexander Yankov (eds.), *United Nations Convention on the Law of the Sea 1982: A Commentary*, Vol. IV (Martinus Nijhoff 1991).

Nordquist, Myron H, Rüdiger Wolfrum and Ronán Long (eds.), *Legal Challenges in Maritime Security* (Brill 2008).

Nowacek, Douglas P and Brandon L Southall, *Effective Planning Strategies for Managing Environmental Risk Associated with Geophysical and other Imaging Surveys* (IUCN 2016).

O'Connell, Daniel P, *The International Law of the Sea*, Vol. I (Oxford University Press 1982).

The International Law of the Sea, Vol. II (Oxford University Press 1988).

Oda, Shigeru, *International Control of Sea Resources* (2nd ed., Martinus Nijhoff 1989).

The Law of the Sea in Our Time II: The United Nations Seabed Committee, 1968–1973 (Sijthoff Leyden 1977).

Orakhelashvili, Alexander, *The Interpretation of Acts and Rules in Public International Law* (Oxford University Press 2008).

Otto, Lisa (ed.), *Global Challenges in Maritime Security: An Introduction* (Springer 2020).

Oude Elferink, Alex G (ed.), *Stability and Change in the Law of the Sea: The Role of the LOS Convention* (Brill 2005).

Oude Elferink, Alex G and Donald R Rothwell (eds.), *Ocean Management in the 21st Century: Institutional Frameworks and Responses* (Martinus Nijhoff 2004).

Pandya, Amit A and Rupert Herbert-Burns with Junko Kobayashi, *Maritime Commerce and Security: The Indian Ocean* (Stimson Center 2011).

Papastavridis, Efthymios, *The Interception of Vessels on the High Seas: Contemporary Challenges to the Legal Order of the Oceans* (Hart 2013).

Platzöder, Renate (ed.), *Third United Nations Conference on the Law of the Sea: Documents*, Vol. I (Ocean Publications 1982).

Third United Nations Conference on the Law of the Sea: Documents, Vol. IV (Ocean Publications 1983).

Popper, Arthur N and Anthony Hawkins (eds.), *The Effects of Noise on Aquatic Life II* (Springer 2016).

Poulantzas, Nicholas M, *The Right of Hot Pursuit in International Law* (2nd ed., Martinus Nijhoff 2002).

Proelss, Alexander (ed.), *United Nations Convention on the Law of the Sea: A Commentary* (Hart 2017).

Quince, Charles, *The Exclusive Economic Zone* (Vernon Press 2019).

Ringbom, Henrik (ed.), *Jurisdiction over Ships: Post-UNCLOS Developments in the Law of the Sea* (Brill 2015).

Roach, J Ashley, *Excessive Maritime Claims* (4th ed., Brill 2021).

Rochette, Julien, Matthieu Wemaëre, Lucien Chabason and Sarah Callet, *Seeing Beyond the Horizon for Deepwater Oil and Gas: Strengthening the International Regulation of Offshore Exploration and Exploitation* (IDDRI Studies N°01/14 2014).

Rothwell, Donald R, Alex G Oude Elferink, Karen N Scott and Tim Stephens (eds.), *The Oxford Handbook of the Law of the Sea* (Oxford University Press 2015).

Rothwell, Donald R and Tim Stephens, *The International Law of the Sea* (Hart 2010).

Rubenstein, Kim (ed.), *Traversing Divides: Honouring Deborah Cas's Contribution to Public and International Law* (Australian National University Press 2021).

Ruys, Tom, *'Armed Attack' and Article 51 of the UN Charter: Evolutions in Customary Law and Practice* (Cambridge University Press 2010).

Sands, Philippe and Jacqueline Peel, with Adriana Fabra and Ruth MacKenzie, *Principles of International Environmental Law* (4th ed., Cambridge University Press 2018).

Schmitt, Michael N, *Tallinn Manual 2.0 on the International Law Applicable to Cyber Operations* (Cambridge University Press 2017).

Secretary of State for Transport, *Safer Ships, Cleaner Seas – Report of Lord Donaldson's Inquiry into the Prevention of Pollution from Merchant Shipping*, presented to Parliament by Command of Her Majesty, May 1994 (HM Stationery Office 1994).

Shaw, Malcolm N, *International Law* (8th ed., Cambridge University Press 2017).

Siebels, Dirk, *Maritime Security in East and West Africa: A Tale of Two Regions* (Palgrave Macmillan 2020).

Simma, Bruno (ed.), *The Charter of the United Nations: A Commentary*, Vol. I (2nd ed, Oxford University Press 2002).

Smith, Robert W, *Exclusive Economic Zone Claims: An Analysis and Primary Documents* (Martinus Nijhoff 1986).

Soons, Alfred HA, *Marine Scientific Research and the Law of the Sea* (TMC Hague 1982).

Stephan III, Paul B and Boris M Klimenko (eds.), *International Law and International Security: Military and Political Dimensions* (ME Sharpe 1991).

Strati, Anastasia, Maria Gavouneli and Nikolaos Skourtos (eds.), *Unresolved Issues and the New Challenges to the Law of the Sea: Time Before and Time After* (Brill 2006).

Symmons, Clive R, *Selected Contemporary Issues in the Law of the Sea* (Martinus Nijhoff 2011).

Tan, Alan Khee-Jin, *Vessel-Source Marine Pollution: The Law and Politics of International Regulation* (Cambridge University Press 2006).

Tanaka, Yoshifumi, *The International Law of the Sea* (3rd ed., Cambridge University Press 2019) 159.

Tang, Shiping, *A Theory of Security Strategy for Our Time: Defensive Realism* (Palgrave Macmillan 2010).

Thakur, Ramesh, *The United Nations, Peace and Security: From Collective Security to the Responsibility to Protect* (2nd ed., Cambridge University Press 2017).

United Nations Food and Agriculture Organization, *The Law and the Sea: Essays in Memory of Jean Carroz* (Rome 1987).

Vicuña, Francisco Orrego (ed.), *The Exclusive Economic Zone: A Latin American Perspective* (Westview 1984).

The Exclusive Economic Zone: Regime and Legal Nature under International Law (Cambridge University Press 1989).

Walker, George K (ed.), *Definitions for the Law of the Sea: Terms Not Defined by the 1982 Convention* (Martinus Nijhoff 2012).

Wang, James CF, *Handbook on Ocean Politics & Law* (Greenwood 1992).

Wu, Shicun and Keyuan Zou (eds.), *Maritime Security in the South China Sea: Regional Implications and International Cooperation* (Ashgate 2009).

INDEX

200-mile maritime zone
  early initiatives for 22–27
  post-Geneva developments 32–34

Africa
  blue economy and maritime security 309–310
  post-Geneva developments 34–35
  see also individually named countries
air defence identification zones (ADIZ) 244–245, 293–295
aircraft 79
Alaska, Bering Sea fur-seals arbitrations 15–17
Antarctic
  demilitarisation 264–265
  specially protected areas 116–117
Antarctic Treaty 264–265
arbitration tribunals 358
  see also International Tribunal for the Law of the Sea (ITLOS)
  Annex VII arbitration 358
  Annex VIII arbitration 358
archaeological objects *see* underwater archaeological and historical objects
Arctic States
  Polar Code 116–117
  specially protected areas 116–117, 121
Arctic Sunrise Arbitration 133–134
armed robbery 308–309
  see also piracy
arms *see* weapons
artefacts *see* underwater archaeological and historical objects
artificial islands, installations and structures
  enforcement jurisdiction 133–134
  general scope of coastal State rights 124–128
  safeguards 130–133
  safety zones 129–130
Association of Southeast Asian Nations (ASEAN) 302
attribution of rights 233
Australia
  maritime security 287–288, 292–293
  submarine cables and pipelines 183–184
  underwater archaeological and historical objects 339
automatic identification system (AIS) 289–290

Baltic Operations (BALTOPS) 236–238
Baltic Sea
  foreign military exercises 236–238
  submarine cables and pipelines 187–188
Bangladesh, security claims over the EEZ 225–227
Barbados v. Trinidad and Tobago 65–66
Bering Sea fur-seals arbitrations 15–17
Black Sea, foreign military exercises 236–238
blue economy 309–310
Brazil, security claims over the EEZ 225–227
Britain *see* United Kingdom
broadcasting facilities 125–126

cables *see* submarine cables and pipelines
Cambodia, security claims over the EEZ 225–227
Canada
  Arctic regulations 116, 121
  Canadian Arctic Waters Pollution Prevention Act 121
  maritime domain awareness (MDA) 287–288
Cabo Verde, security claims over the EEZ 225–227
Caribbean, Santo Domingo Declaration 34
Castañeda-Vindenes Group 42, 53–54, 209–210
Chagos Marine Protected Area 51, 135
Charter of the UN *see* UN Charter
Chicago Convention 80–81
Chile
  Declaration on the Maritime Zone (Santiago Declaration) 26–27
  security claims over the EEZ 224–230
China
  foreign intelligence 242–243
  foreign military exercises 236–238
  international efforts to reconcile conflicts over military activities 261–263
  military survey 250–251
  security claims over the EEZ 225–227
  South China Sea 90
  submarine cables and pipelines 165–166
climate
  climate change 282–283
  ice-covered areas 115–117
  intentional and unlawful damage to the marine environment 282–283
  global warming 282–283
coastal States
  artificial islands, installations and structures
    enforcement jurisdiction 133–134
    general scope of coastal State rights 124–128
    safeguards 130–133
    safety zones 129–130
  choosing not to claim EEZ 43–44
  dispute settlement 59–64
  economic zone concept 40
  EEZ as success for 9
  EEZ rights 44
  environmental jurisdiction 105
  historical context
    1930 Hague Codification Conference 17–21
    post-Geneva developments 30–35
    three-mile limit 13–14
  Law of the Sea Conferences 27–30
  maritime security 285–286
    collective security as 300–302
    law enforcement, right of hot pursuit and right of visit 295–300
    maritime domain awareness 286–288
    means to collect information 289–295
  navigational freedoms
    dispute resolution 134–139
    impact of rights on 77–78
    modified freedoms in the EEZ 139–141
    scope of 78–82
  sovereign rights 82
    enforcement jurisdiction 97–103, 119–124
    living resources 83–85
    non-living resources 94–95
    other activities for economic uses 95–96
    protection of marine species, habitats and ecosystem 85–90
    regulation of activities ancillary to fishing 90–94
  status of international rules and standards
    ships and shipping 108–111
    specially protected areas 111–117
  submarine cables and pipelines
    exploration and exploitation considerations 156–160
    freedom to lay 148–154
    reasonable measures 156

in UNCLOS 2–4
natural resources 367–368
uses of the sea 53–56
Code for Unplanned Encounters at Sea (CUES) 263
Codification of International Law 20
First Conference 20
Cold War 260–264
collective security 300–302
see also maritime security
Colombia, Nicaragua v 336
communicational interests consideration 48–50
conservation *see* protection of the marine environment; underwater archaeological and historical objects
contiguous zone
coastal State rights 43
dispute settlement 358
Geneva Conferences 28–29
sui generis functional zone 42–45
underwater archaeological and historical objects 335–336, 339
Territorial Sea and the Contiguous Zone Convention 28–29
continental shelf
enforcement jurisdiction 97–103
installations on 131–132, 256
laying submarine cables 149–150, 156–160, 166–167
living resources 83–84
scientific research 247
security claims over the EEZ 225–227
sovereign rights of coastal States 206–207
underwater archaeological and historical objects 323–324, 340–345, 349–350, 356–357
Continental Shelf Convention *see* Convention on the Continental Shelf
Continental Shelf Proclamation 22–27
Convention on the Continental Shelf (1958)
installations and other devices 131–132, 256
laying submarine cables 149–150, 166–167
scientific research 247
sovereign rights of coastal States 206–207
Convention on the High Seas
maritime security 278–279, 316–321
submarine cables and pipelines 149–150, 155, 190
Convention on the International Regulations for Preventing Collisions at Sea (COLREG) 179–181
Convention on the Protection of Underwater Cultural Heritage (CPUCH) 324–325, 329–330, 334–335, 340–345, 354, 366–367
Costa Rica, fishing vessels 88
CPUCH *see* Convention on the Protection of Underwater Cultural Heritage (CPUCH)
cultural heritage *see* underwater archaeological and historical objects
cyber operations, military activities 203

Declaration on the Maritime Zone (Santiago Declaration) 26–27
Denmark, submarine cables and pipelines 165–166, 191–193
disarmament, regional disarmament efforts 264–267
see also military activities
dispute settlement
navigational freedoms 134–139
submarine cables and pipelines 193–196
underwater archaeological and historical objects 357–359
United Nations Conferences on the Law of the Sea 4–6, 59–64
DPR of Korea
military exercises 236–238
security claims over the EEZ 225–227
threat of nuclear weapons and ballistic missiles 303–304

drug trafficking 280–281, 316–321
'due regard'
exercise of rights and freedoms 50–56
military use of the sea in peacetime 218–220
as obligation 52–53, 81
submarine cables and pipelines 172–177
in UNCLOS 2–4, 50–53
dumping 118–119

economic interests consideration 46–48
ecosystem 85–90
Ecuador
Declaration on the Maritime Zone (Santiago Declaration) 26–27
security claims over the EEZ 225–227
Egypt, security claims over the EEZ 225–227
El Salvador, security claims over the EEZ 225–227
enforcement jurisdiction
artificial islands, installations and structures 133–134
maritime security 295–300
national resources and other economic activities 97–103
protection of the marine environment 119–124
Enrica Lexie case 51
environmental impact assessment (EIA) 161–163
environmental jurisdiction 105
environmental security 316–321
equity 57–59
espionage 239–246
European Convention on the Protection of the Archaeological Heritage 327–328
Evensen Group 40–41, 209–210
exclusive economic zone (EEZ) 1–7
competing uses 8
customary law status 65–66
development and status 7–8, 11–12
disagreement in interpretation and application 364–367
dispute settlement 4–6
jurisdictional framework 45–46
attribution of rights and freedoms 46–50
exercise of rights and freedoms 50–56
resolving conflicts regarding residual rights 56–59
settlement of disputes 59–64
legal status 2–3
as a new legal regime
codification history 38–42
sui generis functional zone 42–45
origins and evolution 13–36
1930 Hague Codification Conference 17–21
development of concept 27–35
early claims to marine living resources 13–17
early initiatives for a 200-mile maritime zone 22–27
progressive development 6–7
resolving conflicts regarding unattributed rights and jurisdiction 199–200
role in resolving conflicts 8–9, 368
in State practice 75–76
status of 64–71
as success for coastal States 8–9
table of claims 67–70
exercise of rights 50–56

fisheries
coastal and floating 15–17
dispute settlement 61–62, 136–139
living resources 83–85
post-Geneva developments 30–36
Truman Proclamations 24
Fisheries Convention (1960) 28–29
Fisheries Jurisdiction 50–51
Fisheries Jurisdiction cases 31–32, 36, 50–51
Fisheries Proclamation 22–27
fishery zone 30–31, 36, 42–45
fishing
enforcement powers 97–103
illegal, unreported and unregulated (IUU) 87–88, 281–282, 316–321

industrial-scale fishing 24–27
regulation of activities ancillary to fishing 90–94
floating craft 79
see also ships and shipping
floating platforms 126
freedom of the seas
history of doctrine 1–7
peacetime military uses of the sea 202–205
state practice pre-**1930** 17–20
fur-seals arbitrations 15–17

generally accepted international rules and standards 54–55, 105–111, 129–130
Geneva Conferences 28–29
beyond the territorial sea 29–30
post-Geneva developments 30–35
Germany
military use of the sea 211
submarine cables and pipelines 187–188, 191–193
Guinea 92–94
Gulf of Guinea 308–309
Gulf of Maine Area case 65–66
gunboat diplomacy 204
see also military activities
Guyana
security claims over the EEZ 225–227
Suriname/Guyana case 216–218

habitat protection 85–90
see also protection of the marine environment
Hague Codification Conference 17–21
high seas
dichotomy with territorial sea 17
IUU fishing 281–282
law enforcement, right of hot pursuit and right of visit 295–300
laying submarine cables 154–155, 172–177, 182–185
maritime security 278–279
military use of the sea 202–205, 212–214, 260–261
natural resources 367–368
United Nations Conferences on the Law of the Sea 27–30
High Seas Convention *see* Convention on the High Seas
historical context
EEZ origins and evolution 13–36
1930 Hague Codification Conference 17–21
development of concept 27–35
early claims to marine living resources 13–17
early initiatives for a 200-mile maritime zone 22–27
military use of the sea 206–207
international efforts to reconcile conflicts over military activities 260–264
submarine cables and pipelines 148–149, 154–155, 178–181, 187, 190
underwater archaeological and historical objects 325–330
historical objects *see* underwater archaeological and historical objects
hot pursuit, right of 295–300
human trafficking 281, 316–321
humanitarian interventions 215–217
hydrographic survey 246–252, 348–352

ice-covered areas 115–117, 121
Iceland, post-Geneva developments 36
illegal, unreported and unregulated (IUU) fishing 87–88, 281–282, 316–321
India
military survey 250–251
security claims over the EEZ 225–227
Indian Ocean 265–266
Indonesia, security claims over the EEZ 225–227
Informal Composite Negotiating Text (ICNT) Part V 42
Informal Single Negotiation Text (ISNT) Part II 40–41
intelligence gathering 239–246

International Cable Protection Committee (ICPC) 175
International Convention for the Prevention of Pollution from Ships (MARPOL)
  protection of the marine environment 106–107
  special areas 111–112
International Convention for the Safety of Life at Sea (SOLAS) 289–290
International Court of Justice (ICJ) 31–32, 65–66, 336, 357–359
international customs, definition 64–65
International Law Association (ILA), underwater cultural heritage 328, 331
International Law Commission (ILC)
  enforcement powers 97–103
  submarine cables and pipelines 149–150, 154–155, 182–185
  United Nations Conferences on the Law of the Sea 27–30
International Maritime Organisation (IMO)
  as competent international organisation 105–106, 131–132
  defining 'ship' 79
  Particularly Sensitive Sea Areas (PSSAs) 356–357
  Polar Code 116–117
  regulation of ships and shipping 105–111
  ship-source pollution 54–55
  submarine cable laying 160–161
International Tribunal for the Law of the Sea (ITLOS)
  coastal State's rights 54–56, 92–94
  dispute settlement 136–139, 358
  enforcement powers 101–102
  freedom of navigation 80
  protection of the marine environment 89–90
Iran, security claims over the EEZ 225–227
Italy, military use of the sea 211
IUU *see* illegal, unreported and unregulated (IUU) fishing

jurisdiction
  maritime security 283–285
  underwater archaeological and historical objects 345–346
jurisdictional framework of the EEZ 45–46
  attribution of rights and freedoms 46–50
  exercise of rights and freedoms 50–56
  resolving conflicts regarding residual rights 56–59
  settlement of disputes 59–64

Kenya, security claims over the EEZ 225–227

Latin American States
  maritime claims 24–27
  post-Geneva developments 32–34
  see also individually named countries
Latvia, protests against foreign military exercises 236–238
law of the sea
  history of 1–7
    post-Geneva developments 30–35
    United Nations Conferences 27–30
    see also United Nations Convention on the Law of the Sea (UNCLOS)
lex specialis 298
Liberia, security claims over the EEZ 224–230
Libya
  Libya v. Malta 65–66
  security claims over the EEZ 225–227
  Tunisia v. Libya 65–66
Lima Declaration 33–35
living resources
  coastal State rights 46–48, 62–63, 84
  early claims to marine living resources 13–17
  in the EEZ 83–84
  fisheries 61, 83–85
  protection of marine species, habitats and ecosystem 85–90
  see also protection of the marine environment

London Convention 118–119
London Protocol 176–177
Long-Range Identification and Tracking (LRIT) System 290–292

M/S Estonia 347–348
M/T San Padre Pio 80
M/V Saiga 54–55
M/V Virginia G 92–94
Madagascar, national security interests 231
Malaysia, security claims over the EEZ 225–227
Maldives
  fishing vessels 88
  security claims over the EEZ 225–227
Malta, *Libya v. Malta* 65–66
Mare Liberum (De Grotius) 13–14
mare liberum/mare clausum 71–72, 362–363
marine living resources
  early claims to
    Bering Sea fur-seals arbitrations 15–17
    preferential rights to sedentary species 13–15
marine species, habitats and ecosystem 85–90
  see also protection of the marine environment
maritime domain awareness (MDA) 286–288, 314–315
maritime security 199–200, 271–272
  coastal State implementation under the current legal framework 285–286
    law enforcement, right of hot pursuit and right of visit 295–300
    maritime domain awareness 286–288
    means to collect information 289–295
  definition 272–275
  environmental security 316–321
  espionage 239–246
  international efforts to enhance
    collective regional approach to maritime security 306–313
    maritime security as collective security 300–302
    operations under the authorisation of the Security Council 303–306
  legal framework 278
    international instruments and marine security threats 278–283
    international laws 316–321
    remarks on attribution of jurisdiction 283–285
  military security in the EEZ 221
    national security interests 221–224
    protection of security interests as a residual right 230–232
    security claims 224–230
  uses of the sea in peacetime
    codification of the law 205–212
    freedom of the seas 202–205
    obligations in conducting peacetime military activities 212–221
  the way forward 313–315
Marshall Islands, submarine cables and pipelines 180
Mauritius
  dispute on jurisdiction 137–138
  security claims over the EEZ 225–227
MDA *see* maritime domain awareness (MDA)
Mediterranean Sea
  foreign military exercises 236–238
  underwater archaeological and historical objects 327–328
memoranda of understanding (MOUs) 262
Mexican Presidential Declaration 25–26
Mexico, security claims over the EEZ 225–227
migrant smuggling 281, 316–321
military activities 199–202
  conflicts regarding 233

military activities (cont.)
- espionage, intelligence gathering and surveillance 239–246
- military installations, structures and other devices 252–257
- military survey and research 246–252
- navigation, overflight and military manoeuvres 233–239
- remarks on conflicting practices 257–259

international efforts to reconcile conflicts
- agreements to prevent incidents at sea 260–264
- regional disarmament efforts 264–267

military security in the EEZ 221
- national security interests 221–224
- protection of security interests as a residual right 230–232
- security claims 224–230

uses of the sea in peacetime
- codification of the law 205–212
- freedom of the seas 202–205
- obligations in conducting peacetime military activities 212–221

the way forward 267–270

Montevideo Declaration 33

Myanmar, security claims over the EEZ 225–227

Nairobi International Convention on the Removal of Wrecks (RWC) 107–108

nationality principle 345–346

NATO, foreign military exercises 236–238

natural resources
- living resources 83–85
- sovereign rights 82

Naval presence at sea 202–205
- *see also* military activities

navigation
- military activities 233–239
- routeing systems 89

navigational freedoms
- coastal States
  - dispute resolution 134–139
  - impact of rights 77–78
  - modified freedoms in the EEZ 139–141
  - scope 78–82

navigational safety, artificial islands, installations and structures 129–130

the Netherlands
- military use of the sea 211
- underwater archaeological and historical objects 339

New Zealand, submarine cables and pipelines 183–184

Nicaragua
- *Nicaragua v. Colombia* 336
- *Nicaragua v. Honduras* 65–66
- security claims over the EEZ 224–230

Nord Stream pipelines 161–163, 191–193, 355

North Atlantic Treaty Organization (NATO) 236

North Korea, power of the United Nations Security Council (UNSC) 306; *see also* DPR of Korea

Norway, submarine cables and pipelines 165–166

nuclear weapons
- international efforts to reconcile conflicts over military activities 260–264
- nuclear weapon free zones 266–267
- peacetime prohibition on the threat or use of force 214–218
- regional disarmament efforts 264–267
- Seabed Treaty (1971) 254
- United Nations Security Council (UNSC) 303–304

oceanographic survey 246–247

Organization of African Unity (OAU Declaration) 35

Pakistan, security claims over the EEZ 225–227
Paris Convention (1884) 148–149, 154–155, 178–181, 187, 190
Particularly Sensitive Sea Areas (PSSAs) 112–113, 356–357
  see also protection of the marine environment
'patrimonial sea' 34
peacetime military uses of the sea
  codification of the law 205–212
  freedom of the seas 202–205
  obligations in conducting peacetime military activities 212–221
penalties 97–103
Peru
  Declaration on the Maritime Zone (Santiago Declaration) 26–27
  security claims over the EEZ 225–227
pipelines *see* submarine cables and pipelines
piracy
  Convention on the High Seas 278–279
  in international law 316–321
  United Nations Security Council (UNSC) 304–305
platforms
  offfshore airports 125–126
  offshore surveillance structures 125–126
  oil and gas platforms 175–176
Polar Code 116–117
pollution 118–119
  artificial islands, installations and structures 133–134
  International Convention for the Prevention of Pollution from Ships (MARPOL) 106–107
  from seabed activities and by dumping 118–119
  see also protection of the marine environment
prescriptive jurisdiction 121
preservation *see* protection of the marine environment; underwater archaeological and historical objects
Proliferation Security Initiative (PSI) 298–299
protection of the marine environment
  enforcement jurisdiction 119–124
  general obligation of environmental protection 103–104
  intentional and unlawful damage 282–283
  International Convention for the Prevention of Pollution from Ships (MARPOL) 106–107
  in international law 316–321
  marine species, habitats and ecosystem 85–90
  prescriptive jurisdiction 105
    pollution from seabed activities and by dumping 118–119
    regulation of ships and shipping 105–111
    specially protected areas 111–117
  submarine cables and pipelines 160–165
  underwater archaeological and historical objects 350–351

'reasonable regard' 50–53
reconnaissance 239–246
reporting systems for ships 88–89, 289
research *see* scientific research; surveillance
'residual rights' 56–59
Revised Single Negotiating Text (RSNT) Part II 41–42
right of hot pursuit 49, 97–99, 295–300
right of visit 47–49, 190, 280–281, 295–300
Roper Report 327–328
routeing systems
  artificial islands, installations and structures 129–130
  navigation regulations 89
  Particularly Sensitive Sea Areas (PSSAs) 112–113
  protection of the marine environment 86–87, 89
  submarine cables and pipelines 184–185

Russia
Alaska and the Bering Sea 15–17
Arctic regulations 116
artificial islands, installations and structures 130–133
foreign military exercises 236–238
military use of the sea 265–266
natural resources 85–90
protection and preservation of the marine environment 48, 103–104, 119–124
submarine cables and pipelines 191–193
US-USSR Agreement 260–261

safeguards, coastal states' enforcement powers 97–103, 119–124, 130–133
SafeSeaNet 292
safety zones
artificial islands, installations and structures 129–130
submarine cables and pipelines 182–185
Santiago Declaration 26–27
Santo Domingo Declaration 34
satellite-based reconnaissance 239–246, 289–295
remote sensing 348–352
Saudi Arabia, security claims over the EEZ 225–227
Science Monitoring And Reliable Telecommunications (SMART) 152–153
scientific research
installations 125–126
military survey and research 246–252
submarine cables and pipelines 157–158
underwater archaeological and historical objects 348–352
Sea-Bed Committee 39
Seabed Treaty (1971) 207–208, 254
security *see* maritime security; military activities
Security Council *see* United Nations Security Council (UNSC)
sedentary species 13–15
settlement of disputes *see* dispute settlement
ships and shipping
artificial islands, installations and structures 127, 129–130
definition 79
dispute settlement 63
navigational freedoms 78–82
protection of marine species, habitats and ecosystem 85–90
protection of the marine environment 105–111
regulation of 105–111
reporting systems 88–89, 289
routeing systems 89, 112–113, 292
submarine cables and pipelines
freedom to lay 159–160, 178–181
protection from intentional damage 188–193
shipwrecks 107–108, 322–325, 355
see also underwater archaeological and historical objects
Siciliy, Skerki Bank site 277.150SOLAS *see* International Convention for the Safety of Life at Sea
Somalia
collective response to piracy 306–308
security claims over the EEZ 224–230
Southeast Asian region, maritime security 310–313
see also individually named countries
sovereign rights
coastal States 82
enforcement jurisdiction 97–103
living resources 83–85
non-living resources 94–95
other activities for economic uses 95–96
protection of marine species, habitats and ecosystem 85–90
regulation of activities ancillary to fishing 90–94
maritime security 295–300

sovereignty 20
  exclusive nature of the coastal State's rights 46–48
Soviet Union *see* USSR
state cooperation mechanism, protection of underwater cultural heritage 340–345
submarine cables and pipelines 142–154
  contemporary context 196–197
  decommissioning 175–176
  dispute settlement 193–196
  freedom to lay 148–154
  limitations on the freedom to lay
    due regard obligation and other limitations 172–177
    environmental considerations 160–165
    exploration and exploitation considerations 156–160
    reasonable measures taken by the coastal state 156
    regulations of specific submarine cables and pipelines 169–172
    route planning 165–169
  protection of 177–178
    competing uses 181–188
    intentional damage 188–193
    operational activities ancillary to the laying of 178–181
  protection zones 183–184
  types of 143–148
Sudan, security claims over the EEZ 225–227
sui generis
  adoption of EEZ 2–3, 37–38, 42–45
  character of the EEZ 363–364
  military activities 268
  military security in the EEZ 221
  'residual rights' 56–59
Suriname/Guyana case 216–218
surveillance 239–246
Sweden
  protests against foreign military exercises 236–238
  submarine cables and pipelines 191–193
Syria, security claims over the EEZ 225–227
Territorial Sea and the Contiguous Zone Convention 28–29
territorial seas
  agreements to prevent incidents at sea 260–264
  development of the EEZ 11, 17
  dichotomy with high seas 17
  fisheries jurisdiction 31–32
  Geneva Conference debates on breadth of 29–31
  international agreement on 20–21
  regulations of specific submarine cables and pipelines 169–172
  maritime domain awareness (MDA) 287–288
  maritime security 298–299
  military survey and research 249–250
  security claims 224–230
  sui generis functional zone 42–45
terrorism
  in international law 316–321
  national security interests at sea 221–224, 279–280
  see also maritime security
Thailand, security claims over the EEZ 225–227
Third United Nations Conference *see under* United Nations Conferences
threat of force, prohibition on 214–218
three-mile limit
  historical context 13–14
    Bering Sea fur-seals arbitrations 15–17
    Continental Shelf Proclamation 22–23
    Hague Codification Conference 21
    laying submarine cables 148–154
    state practice pre-1930 17–20
Titanic Agreement 347–348
Titanic shipwreck 347–348
Torrey Canyon 121–122
trafficking of arms and WMD 280, 316–321
Trinidad and Tobago, Barbados v. 65–66
Truman Proclamations 22–24

Tunisia
  Skerki Bank site 343–345
  Tunisia v. Libya 65–66
twelve-mile contiguous zone
  post-Geneva developments 34–36
  separate jurisdictional zone 28–29
  using the seabed for military purposes 207–208

UN Charter
  military uses of the sea
    codification of the law 205–212
    peacetime prohibition on the threat or use of force 216–218
    reservation for peaceful purposes 212–213
UNCLOS *see* United Nations Convention on the Law of the Sea
underwater archaeological and historical objects 199–200, 322–325, 359–361, 366–367
  dispute settlement 357–359
  legal framework
    definitional criteria 330–333
    duty to protect 333–340
    historical development 325–330
    state cooperation mechanism 340–345
  rights and jurisdiction over activities affecting 345–346
    activities directed at 346–353
    activities incidentally affecting 354–357
underwater cultural heritage (UCH) 322–325
UNESCO *see* United Nations Organization for Education, Science and Culture
Union of Soviet Socialist Republics (USSR) 260–264
United Kingdom
  Cornwall Submarine Mines Act 14
  decommissioning oil and gas platforms 175–176
  dispute on jurisdiction 137–138
  foreign intelligence gathering 241–242
  military use of the sea 211, 265–266
  three-mile limit and extended zones 18–19
United Nations Conferences on the Law of the Sea
  first and second 27–30
  third
    dispute settlement 59–64
    EEZ concept accepted 37–38, 44–45
    legal status of the EEZ 1–2, 36, 362–363
United Nations Convention on the Law of the Sea (UNCLOS)
  dispute settlement 4–6, 59–64, 134–139, 193–196
  EEZ regime
    acceptance and application 37–38
    status of 64–71
  as legal framework 2–4, 64–71
  parties to 64
  progressive development 6–7
  submarine cables and pipelines
    dispute settlement 193–196
    reasonable measures 142–143
  unattributed rights and jurisdiction 199–200
  underwater archaeological and historical objects 323–324
United Nations Convention on the Law of the Sea (UNCLOS) articles
  Article 2 50–53
  Article 55 42–45
  Article 56 46–48, 50, 52–56, 95–96, 105
  Article 58 48–50, 52, 54, 78–81, 150–151, 209–210, 212–221
  Article 59 56–59, 232–233
  Article 60 125–127, 134, 171–172
  Articles 61–73 84
  Article 62 91–92
  Article 68 83–84
  Article 73 101–102
  Article 78 173
  Article 79 160–161, 163, 165–172
  Article 86 42–43
  Article 87 173
  Articles 88–115 49

Article 113 188–193
Article 114 185–186
Article 115 186–187
Article 149 330–332
Article 192 103–104
Article 220 122–123
Article 226 122–123
Article 228 123
Article 297 61–62, 134–139
Article 298 62–63, 136–139
Article 301 212–214
Article 303 325–327, 330–340
United Nations General Assembly (UNGA) 38–39
United Nations Organization for Education, Science and Culture (UNESCO) 324–325, 340–345
United Nations Security Council (UNSC) 303–306
United States
Arctic regulations 116
Bering Sea fur-seals arbitrations 15–17
Hovering Acts 18–19
liquor laws 19–20
maritime domain awareness (MDA) 286–287
military activities
definition 259–260
disarmament efforts 265–266
foreign intelligence gathering 241–242, 244
foreign military exercises 236–238
international efforts to reconcile conflicts over military activities 260–264
Military Sealift Command 240–241, 249–250
naval presence 203
satellite-based reconnaissance 239–246
survey and research 249–250
Particularly Sensitive Sea Areas 356–357
submarine cables and pipelines 180
Truman Proclamations 22–24
US–USSR Agreement 260–261
Uruguay
post-Geneva developments 32–33
security claims over the EEZ 225–227
use of force, prohibition on 214–218
USSR (Soviet Union)
Alaska and the Bering Sea 15–17
Arctic regulations 116
foreign military exercises 236–238
military use of the sea 265–266
submarine cables and pipelines 191–193
US–USSR Agreement 260–261

Venezuela, submarine cables and pipelines 167
vessel *see* ships and shipping
Vienna Convention 6
Vietnam, security claims over the EEZ 225–227
visit, right of 295–300

weapons
international efforts to reconcile conflicts over military activities 260–264
in international law 316–321
peacetime prohibition on the threat or use of force 214–218
regional disarmament efforts 264–267
trafficking of arms and WMD 280
see also military activities
weapons of mass destruction
in international law 280, 316–321
regional disarmament efforts 264–267
Seabed Treaty (1971) 254
United Nations Security Council 303–304
uses of the sea for military purposes 207–208

Yemen, security claims over the EEZ 225–227

For EU product safety concerns, contact us at Calle de José Abascal, 56–1°, 28003 Madrid, Spain or eugpsr@cambridge.org.

www.ingramcontent.com/pod-product-compliance
Lightning Source LLC
Chambersburg PA
CBHW051932060326
40768CB00021B/803
* 9 7 8 1 0 0 9 4 7 1 3 0 5 *